iOS 26 App Development Essentials

SwiftUI Edition

iOS 26 App Development Essentials - SwiftUI Edition

ISBN-13: 978-1-965764-27-5

Rev: 1.0

Payload
publishing

https://www.payloadbooks.com

Contents

Table of Contents

1. Start Here

This book teaches the skills needed to build iOS applications using SwiftUI, Xcode, and the Swift programming language.

Beginning with the basics, this book outlines the steps to set up an iOS development environment, along with an introduction to using Swift Playgrounds for learning and experimenting with the Swift programming language.

The book also includes in-depth chapters that introduce the Swift programming language, covering data types, control flow, functions, object-oriented programming, property wrappers, structured concurrency, and error handling.

This guide begins with an introduction to key concepts of SwiftUI and project architecture, followed by a detailed tour of Xcode and AI-assisted development using Coding Intelligence. The book also covers how to create custom SwiftUI views, combine them to build user interface layouts, including stacks, frames, and forms.

Other topics covered include data handling using state properties and observable, state, and environment objects, as well as key user interface design concepts such as modifiers, lists, tabbed views, context menus, user interface navigation, and outline groups.

The book also includes chapters covering graphics and Liquid Glass effects, user interface animation, view transitions, and gesture handling, as well as WidgetKit, Live Activities, document-based apps, Core Data, SwiftData, and CloudKit.

Throughout the book, each concept is reinforced with hands-on tutorials and downloadable source code. Additionally, over 50 online quizzes are available to test your knowledge and understanding.

Assuming you are ready to download Xcode and have a Mac, you are now ready to get started.

1.1 For Swift Programmers

This book has been designed to address the needs of both existing Swift programmers and those new to Swift and iOS app development. If you are familiar with the Swift programming language, you can probably skip the Swift-specific chapters. If you are not yet familiar with the SwiftUI-specific language features of Swift, however, we recommend that you at least read the sections covering implicit returns from single expressions, opaque return types, and property wrappers. These features are central to the implementation and understanding of SwiftUI.

1.2 For Non-Swift Programmers

If you are new to programming in Swift, then the entire book is appropriate for you. Just start at the beginning and keep going.

1.3 Source Code Download

The source code and Xcode project files for the examples contained in this book are available for download at:

https://www.payloadbooks.com/product/ios26code/

1.4 Download the Color eBook

Thank you for purchasing the print edition of this book. Your purchase includes a color copy of the book in PDF format.

If you would like to download the PDF version of this book, please email proof of purchase (for example, a receipt, delivery notice, or photo of the physical book) to *info@payloadbooks.com*, and we will provide you with a download link.

1.5 Feedback

We want you to be satisfied with your purchase of this book. Therefore, if you find any errors in the book or have any comments, questions, or concerns, please contact us at *info@payloadbooks.com*.

1.6 Errata

While we make every effort to ensure the accuracy of the content of this book, inevitably, a book covering a subject area of this size and complexity may include some errors and oversights. Any known issues with the book will be outlined, together with solutions, at the following URL:

https://www.payloadbooks.com/ios26errata/

In the event that you find an error not listed in the errata, please let us know by emailing our technical support team at *info@payloadbooks.com*.

1.7 Take the Knowledge Tests

Look for this section at the end of most chapters and use the link or scan the QR code to take a knowledge quiz to test and reinforce your understanding of the covered topic. Use the following link to review the full list of tests available for this book:

https://www.answertopia.com/g3um

2. Joining the Apple Developer Program

The first step in the process of learning to develop iOS 26 based applications involves gaining an understanding of the advantages of enrolling in the Apple Developer Program and deciding the point at which it makes sense to pay to join. With these goals in mind, this chapter will outline the costs and benefits of joining the developer program and, finally, walk through the steps involved in enrolling.

2.1 Downloading Xcode 26 and the iOS 26 SDK

The latest versions of both the iOS SDK and Xcode can be downloaded free of charge from the macOS App Store. Since the tools are free, this raises the question of whether to enroll in the Apple Developer Program, or to wait until it becomes necessary later in your app development learning curve.

2.2 Apple Developer Program

Membership in the Apple Developer Program currently costs $99 per year to enroll as an individual developer. Organization level membership is also available.

Much can be achieved without the need to pay to join the Apple Developer program. There are, however, areas of app development which cannot be fully tested without program membership. Of particular significance is the fact that Siri integration, iCloud access, Apple Pay, Game Center and In-App Purchasing can only be enabled and tested with Apple Developer Program membership.

Of further significance is the fact that Apple Developer Program members have access to technical support from Apple's iOS support engineers (though the annual fee initially covers the submission of only two support incident reports, more can be purchased). Membership also includes access to the Apple Developer forums; an invaluable resource both for obtaining assistance and guidance from other iOS developers, and for finding solutions to problems that others have encountered and subsequently resolved.

Program membership also provides early access to the pre-release Beta versions of Xcode, macOS and iOS.

By far the most important aspect of the Apple Developer Program is that membership is a mandatory requirement in order to publish an application for sale or download in the App Store.

Clearly, program membership is going to be required at some point before your application reaches the App Store. The only question remaining is when exactly to sign up.

2.3 When to Enroll in the Apple Developer Program?

Clearly, there are many benefits to Apple Developer Program membership and, eventually, membership will be necessary to begin selling your apps. As to whether to pay the enrollment fee now or later will depend on individual circumstances. If you are still in the early stages of learning to develop iOS apps or have yet to come up with a compelling idea for an app to develop then much of what you need is provided without program membership. As your skill level increases and your ideas for apps to develop take shape you can, after all, always enroll in the developer program later.

If, on the other hand, you are confident that you will reach the stage of having an application ready to publish, or know that you will need access to more advanced features such as Siri support, iCloud storage, In-App Purchasing and Apple Pay then it is worth joining the developer program sooner rather than later.

2.4 Enrolling in the Apple Developer Program

If your goal is to develop iOS apps for your employer, then it is first worth checking whether the company already has membership. That being the case, contact the program administrator in your company and ask them to send you an invitation from within the Apple Developer Program Member Center to join the team. Once they have done so, Apple will send you an email entitled *You Have Been Invited to Join an Apple Developer Program* containing a link to activate your membership. If you or your company is not already a program member, you can enroll online at:

https://developer.apple.com/programs/enroll/

Apple provides enrollment options for businesses and individuals. To enroll as an individual, you will need to provide credit card information in order to verify your identity. To enroll as a company, you must have legal signature authority (or access to someone who does) and be able to provide documentation such as a Dun & Bradstreet D-U-N-S number and documentation confirming legal entity status.

Acceptance into the developer program as an individual member typically takes less than 24 hours with notification arriving in the form of an activation email from Apple. Enrollment as a company can take considerably longer (sometimes weeks or even months) due to the burden of the additional verification requirements.

While awaiting activation you may log in to the Member Center with restricted access using your Apple ID and password at the following URL:

https://developer.apple.com/membercenter

Once logged in, clicking on the *Your Account* tab at the top of the page will display the prevailing status of your application to join the developer program as *Enrollment Pending*. Once the activation email has arrived, log in to the Member Center again and note that access is now available to a wide range of options and resources, as illustrated in Figure 2-1:

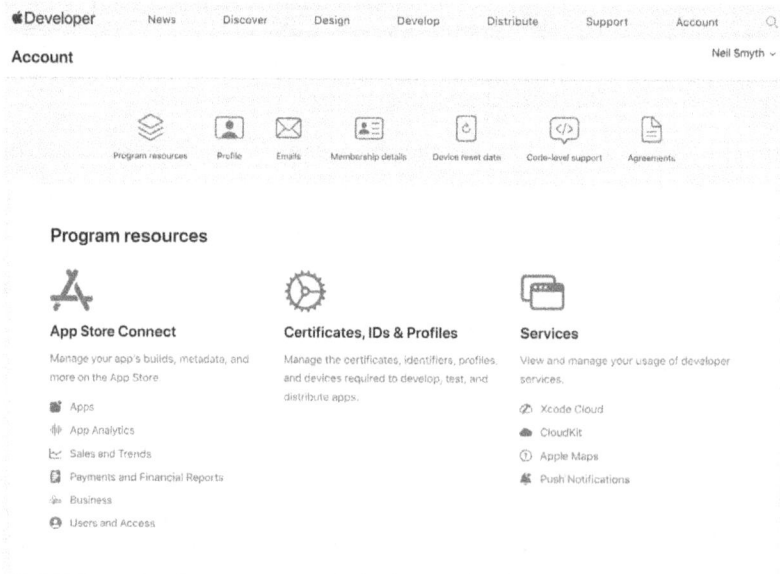

Figure 2-1

2.5 Summary

An important early step in the iOS 26 application development process involves identifying the best time to enroll in the Apple Developer Program. This chapter has outlined the benefits of joining the program, provided some guidance to keep in mind when considering developer program membership and walked briefly through the enrollment process. The next step is to download and install the iOS 26 SDK and Xcode 26 development environment.

3. Installing Xcode 26 and the iOS 26 SDK

iOS apps are developed using the iOS SDK and Apple's Xcode development environment. Xcode is an integrated development environment (IDE) within which you will code, compile, test, and debug your iOS applications.

All of the examples in this book are based on Xcode version 26 and use features unavailable in earlier Xcode versions. This chapter covers the steps involved in installing Xcode 26 and the iOS 26 SDK on macOS.

3.1 Identifying Your macOS Version

When developing with Xcode 26, a system running macOS Sequoia 15.6 or later is required. If you are unsure of the version of macOS on your Mac, you can find this information by clicking on the Apple menu in the top left corner of the screen and selecting *About This Mac* from the menu. In the resulting dialog, check the *macOS* line:

MacBook Pro

14-inch, Nov 2023

Chip	Apple M3 Pro
Memory	18 GB
Serial number	MCPXN2L2K4
macOS	Tahoe 26.0

More Info...

Regulatory Certification
™ and © 1983-2025 Apple Inc.
All Rights Reserved.

Figure 3-1

If the "About This Mac" dialog does not indicate that macOS Sequoia 15.6 or later is running, click on the *More Info...* button to open the Settings app and check for available operating system updates.

3.2 Installing Xcode 26 and the iOS 26 SDK

The best way to obtain the latest Xcode and iOS SDK versions is to download them from the Apple Mac App Store. Launch the App Store on your macOS system, enter Xcode into the search box, and click the *Get* button to initiate the installation. This will install both Xcode and the iOS SDK.

3.3 Starting Xcode

Having successfully installed the SDK and Xcode, the next step is to launch it so we are ready to start development work. To start up Xcode, open the macOS Finder and search for *Xcode*. Since you will use this tool frequently, take this opportunity to drag and drop it onto your dock for easier access in the future. Click on the Xcode icon in the dock to launch the tool. The first time Xcode runs, you may be prompted to install additional components. Follow these steps, entering your username and password when prompted.

Once Xcode has loaded, and assuming this is the first time you have used Xcode on this system, you will be presented with the *Welcome* screen from which you are ready to proceed:

Xcode
Version 26.0

No Recent Projects

⊕ Create New Project...

🖐 Clone Git Repository...

🗁 Open Existing Project...

Figure 3-2

3.4 Adding Your Apple ID to the Xcode Preferences

Whether or not you enroll in the Apple Developer Program, it is worth adding your Apple ID to Xcode now that it is installed and running. Select the *Xcode -> Settings...* menu option followed by the *Apple Accounts* entry in the navigation panel. On the Apple Accounts screen, click on the *Add Apple Account...* button highlighted in Figure 3-3, and enter your Apple ID and password to add the account:

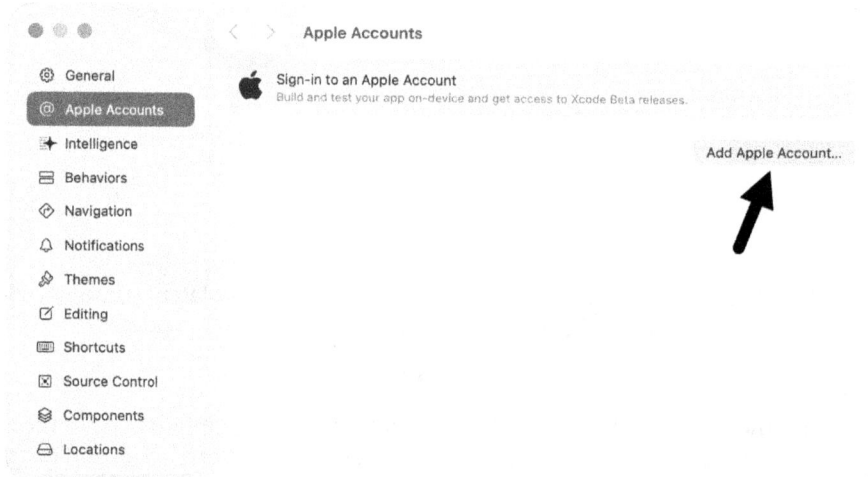

● ⊙ ●   ‹ ›   Apple Accounts

⚙ General
@ Apple Accounts   🍎 Sign-in to an Apple Account
                            Build and test your app on-device and get access to Xcode Beta releases.
✦ Intelligence
🖿 Behaviors   Add Apple Account...
◈ Navigation
🔔 Notifications
🎜 Themes
☑ Editing
⌨ Shortcuts
☒ Source Control
❀ Components
🖨 Locations

Figure 3-3

3.5 Developer and Distribution Signing Identities

Once the Apple ID has been entered, the next step is to generate signing identities. To view the current signing identities, select the newly added Apple ID in the Apple Accounts panel, followed by the team, as shown in Figure 3-4:

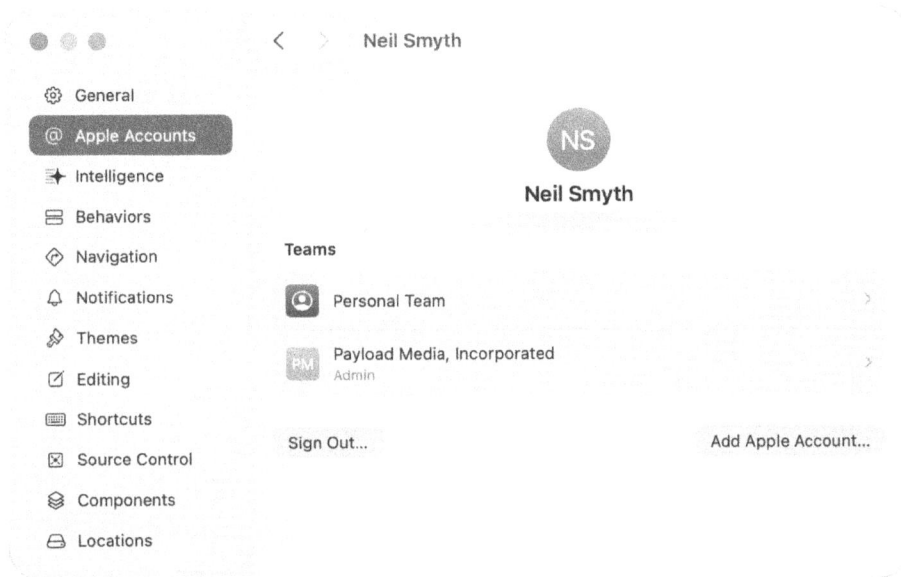

Figure 3-4

On the team panel, click the *Manage Certificates...* button to display a list of available signing identity types:

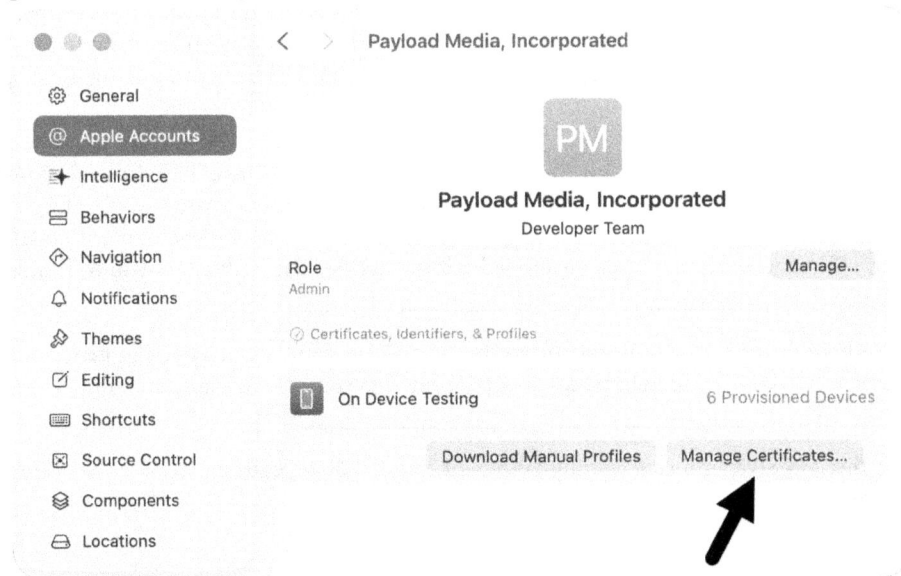

Figure 3-5

To create a signing identity, click on the + button highlighted in Figure 3-6 and make the appropriate selection from the menu:

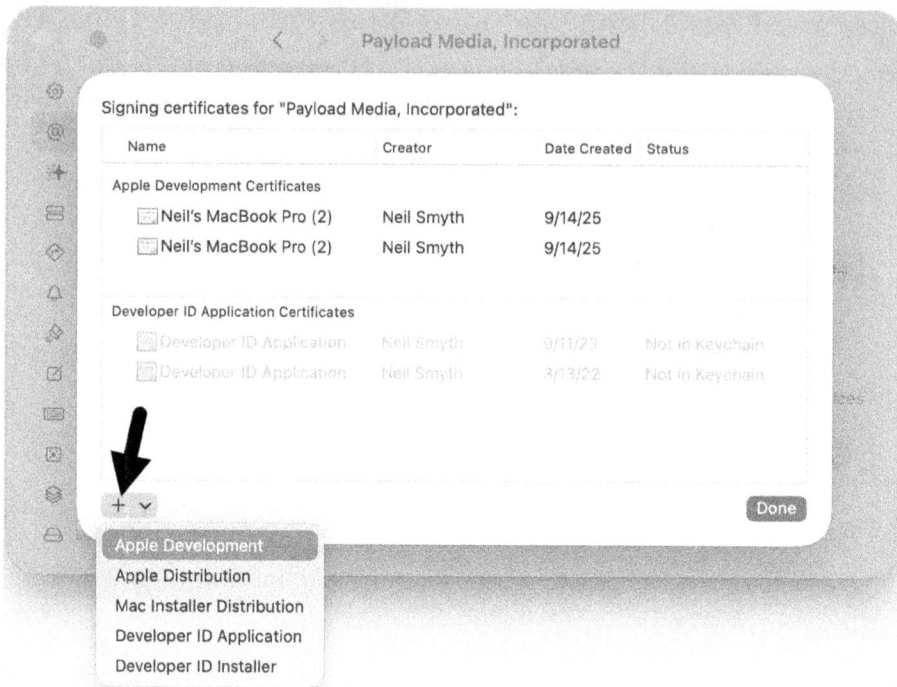

Figure 3-6

If the Apple ID has been used to enroll in the Apple Developer Program, the option to create an *Apple Distribution* certificate will appear in the menu. Clicking this option will generate the signing identity required to submit the app to the Apple App Store. You will also need to create a *Developer ID Application* certificate if you plan to integrate features such as iCloud and Siri into your app projects. If you have not yet signed up for the Apple Developer program, select the *Apple Development* option to allow apps to be tested during development.

3.6 Summary

This book was written using Xcode 26 and the iOS 26 SDK running on macOS Tahoe 26. Before beginning SwiftUI development, the first step is to install Xcode and configure it with your Apple ID via the accounts section of the Preferences screen. Once these steps have been performed, a development certificate must be generated, which will be used to sign apps developed within Xcode. This will allow you to build and test your apps on physical iOS-based devices.

When you are ready to upload your finished app to the App Store, you will also need to generate a distribution certificate. This process requires membership in the Apple Developer Program, as outlined in the previous chapter.

Having installed the iOS SDK and successfully launched Xcode 26, we can now look at Xcode in more detail, starting with Playgrounds.

4. An Introduction to Xcode 26 Playgrounds

Before introducing the Swift programming language in the following chapters, it is first worth learning about a feature of Xcode known as *Playgrounds*. This is a feature of Xcode designed to make learning Swift and experimenting with the iOS SDK much easier. The concepts covered in this chapter can be put to use when experimenting with many of the introductory Swift code examples contained in the chapters that follow.

4.1 What is a Playground?

A playground is an interactive environment where Swift code can be entered and executed with the results appearing in real-time. This makes an ideal environment in which to learn the syntax of Swift and the visual aspects of iOS app development without the need to work continuously through the edit/compile/run/debug cycle that would ordinarily accompany a standard Xcode iOS project. With support for rich text comments, playgrounds are also a good way to document code for future reference or as a training tool.

4.2 Creating a New Playground

To create a new Playground, start Xcode and select the *File -> New -> Playground...* menu option. Choose the iOS option on the resulting panel and select the Blank template.

The Blank template is useful for trying out Swift coding. The Single View template, on the other hand, provides a view controller environment for trying out code that requires a user interface layout. The game and map templates provide preconfigured playgrounds that allow you to experiment with the iOS MapKit and SpriteKit frameworks respectively.

On the next screen, name the playground *LearnSwift* and choose a suitable file system location into which the playground should be saved before clicking on the *Create* button.

Once the playground has been created, the following screen will appear ready for Swift code to be entered:

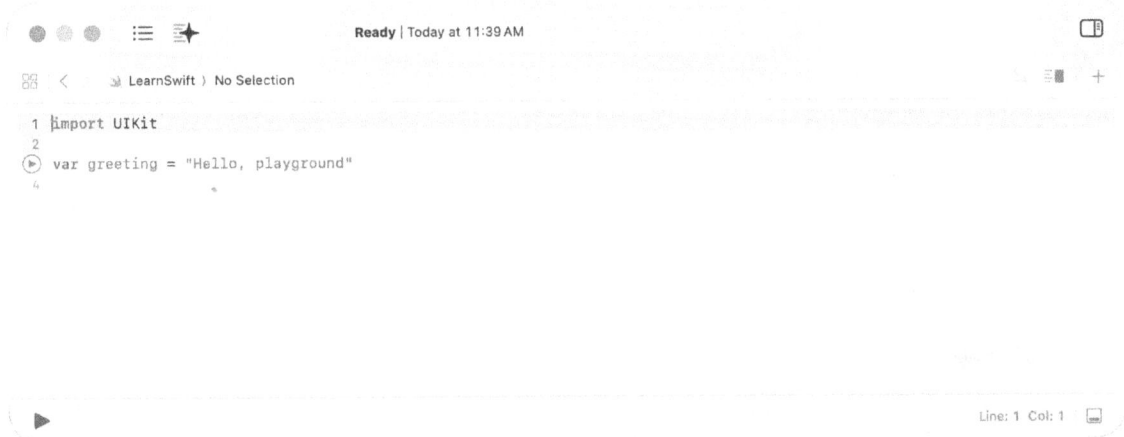

Figure 4-1

The Playground window will display various panels depending on the current state of the playground and options you select. Figure 4-2 below illustrates the appearance of the window during a typical playground session:

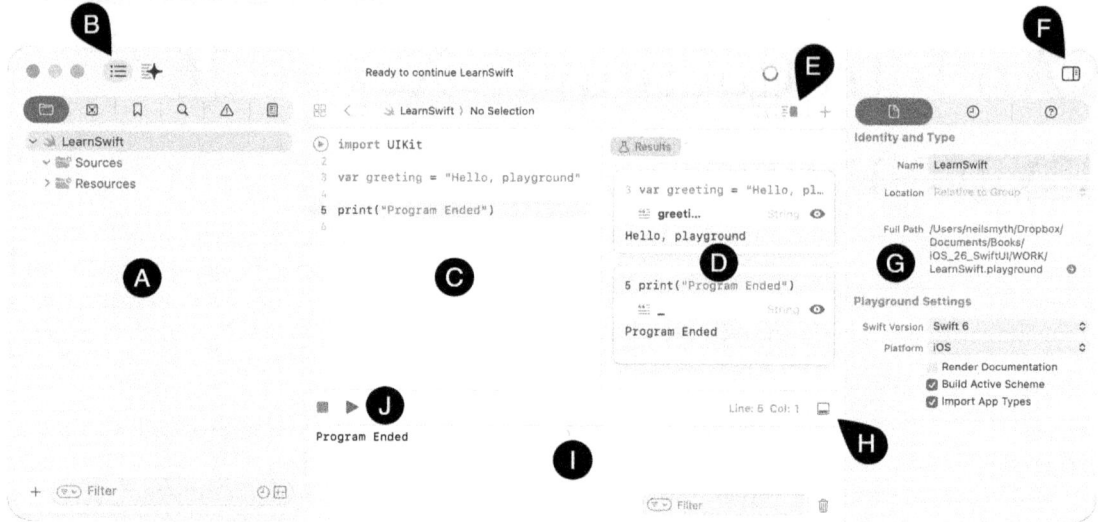

Figure 4-2

The panel on the left-hand side of the window (marked A in Figure 4-2) is the Navigators panel. The toolbar along the top of this panel provides access to the file navigator, source code control, bookmarks, search, the issues navigator for locating problems in the playground code, and the reports navigator listing activities you have performed in the playground. To hide and show this panel, click on the button marked B. The center panel (C) is the *playground editor* where the lines of Swift code are entered. The adjacent panel (D) is referred to as the *results panel* where the results appear when the playground is executing appear. The visibility of this panel is controlled using button E.

The button marked F hides and shows the Inspectors panel (marked G) where a variety of properties relating to the playground may be configured. Button H displays the Debug Area (I) where diagnostic output relating to the playground will appear when code is executed. Finally, the buttons marked J start and stop playground execution.

By far the quickest way to gain familiarity with the playground environment is to work through some simple examples.

4.3 A Swift Playground Example

Perhaps the simplest of examples in any programming language (that at least does something tangible) is to write some code to output a single line of text. Swift is no exception to this rule so, within the playground window, begin adding another line of Swift code so that it reads as follows:

```
import UIKit

var greeting = "Hello, playground"

print("Welcome to Swift")
```

All that the additional line of code does is make a call to the built-in Swift *print* function which takes as a parameter a string of characters to be displayed on the console. Those familiar with other programming languages will note the absence of a semi-colon at the end of the line of code. In Swift, semi-colons are optional and generally only used as a separator when multiple statements occupy the same line of code.

Note that although some extra code has been entered, nothing yet appears in the results panel. This is because the code has yet to be executed. One option to run the code is to click on the Execute Playground button located in the bottom left-hand corner of the main panel as indicated by the arrow in Figure 4-3:

Line: 5 Col: 26

Figure 4-3

When clicked, this button will execute all the code in the current playground page from the first line of code to the last. Another option is to execute the code in stages using the run button located in the margin of the code editor, as shown in Figure 4-4:

Figure 4-4

This button executes the line numbers with the shaded blue background including the line on which the button is currently positioned. In the above figure, for example, the button will execute lines 1 through 3 and then stop.

The position of the run button can be moved by hovering the mouse pointer over the line numbers in the editor. In Figure 4-5, for example, the run button is now positioned on line 5 and will execute lines 4 and 5 when clicked. Note that lines 1 to 3 are no longer highlighted in blue indicating that these have already been executed and are not eligible to be run this time:

Figure 4-5

This technique provides an easy way to execute the code in stages making it easier to understand how the code functions and to identify problems in code execution.

To reset the playground so that execution can be performed from the start of the code, simply click on the stop button as indicated in Figure 4-6:

Figure 4-6

Using this incremental execution technique, execute lines 1 through 3 and note that output now appears in the results panel indicating that the variable has been initialized:

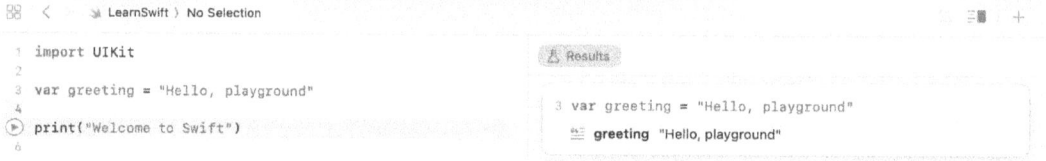

Figure 4-7

Next, execute the remaining lines up to and including line 5 at which point the "Welcome to Swift" output should appear both in the results panel and debug area:

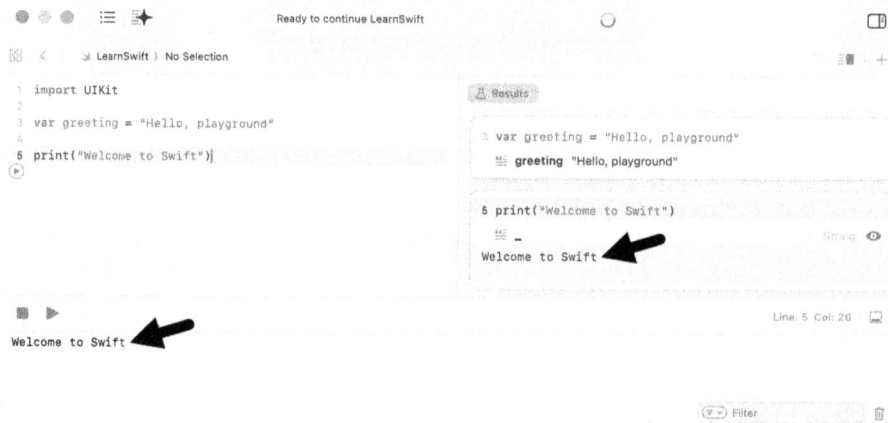

Figure 4-8

To hide individual output values in the results, toggle the quick view "eye" button highlighted in Figure 4-9:

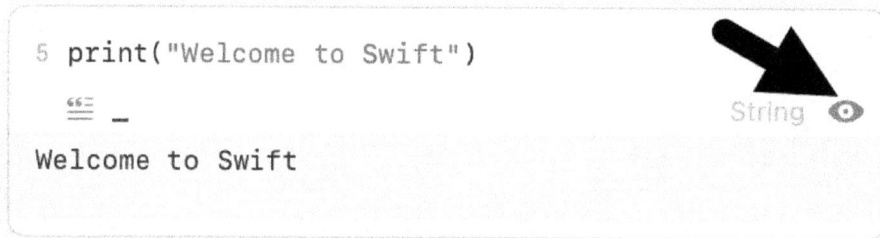

Figure 4-9

4.4 Value History

Playgrounds are particularly useful when working with Swift algorithms, especially when combined with the value history feature. Remaining within the playground editor, enter the following lines of code beneath the existing print statement:

```
var x = 10
```

```
for index in 1...20 {
    let y = index * x
    x -= 1
}
```

This expression repeats 20 times, performing arithmetic expressions on each iteration of the loop. Once the code has been entered into the editor, click on the run button to execute these new lines of code. The playground will execute the loop and display in the results panel the final value for each variable:

Figure 4-10

To view the history of changes to a value, click the button indicated in Figure 4-11 and select the Value History option:

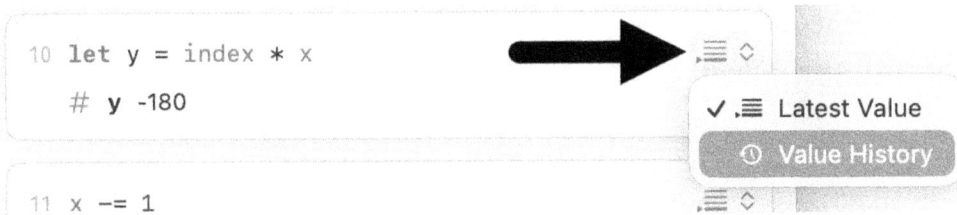

Figure 4-11

The result panel will now display the history of changes to the y value during the loop execution:

Figure 4-12

4.5 Adding Rich Text Comments

Rich text comments allow the code within a playground to be documented in a way that is easy to format and read. A single line of text can be marked as being rich text by preceding it with a //: marker. For example:

```
//: This is a single line of documentation text
```

Blocks of text can be added by wrapping the text in /*: and */ comment markers:

```
/*:
This is a block of documentation text that is intended
to span multiple lines
*/
```

The rich text uses the Markup language and allows text to be formatted using a lightweight and easy-to-use syntax. A heading, for example, can be declared by prefixing the line with a '#' character while text is displayed in italics when wrapped in '*' characters. Bold text, on the other hand, involves wrapping the text in '**' character sequences. It is also possible to configure bullet points by prefixing each line with a single '*'. Among the many other features of Markup is the ability to embed images and hyperlinks into the content of a rich text comment.

To see rich text comments in action, enter the following markup content into the playground editor immediately after the *print("Welcome to Swift")* line of code:

```
/*:
# Welcome to Playgrounds
This is your *first* playground which is intended to demonstrate:
* The use of **Quick Look**
* Placing results **in-line** with the code
*/
```

As the comment content is added it is said to be displayed in *raw markup* format. To display in *rendered markup* format, either select the *Editor -> Show Rendered Markup* menu option, or enable the *Render Documentation* option located under *Playground Settings* in the Inspector panel (marked G in Figure 4-2). If the Inspector panel is not currently visible, click the button marked F to display it. Once rendered, the above rich text should appear, as illustrated in Figure 4-13:

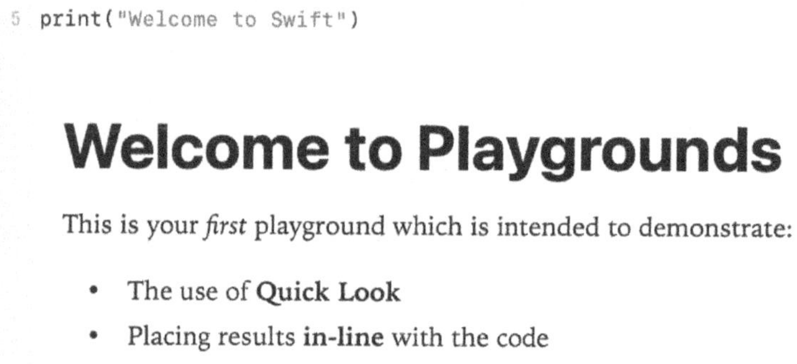

```
5  print("Welcome to Swift")
```

Welcome to Playgrounds

This is your *first* playground which is intended to demonstrate:

* The use of **Quick Look**
* Placing results **in-line** with the code

Figure 4-13

Detailed information about the Markup syntax can be found online at the following URL:

https://developer.apple.com/library/content/documentation/Xcode/Reference/xcode_markup_formatting_ref/index.html

4.6 Working with Playground Pages

A playground can consist of multiple pages, with each page containing its own code, resources and, rich text comments. So far, the playground used in this chapter contains a single page. Add a page to the playground now by selecting the LearnSwift entry at the top of the Navigator panel, right-clicking, and selecting the *New Playground Page* menu option. If the Navigator panel is not currently visible, click the button indicated by the left-most arrow in Figure 4-1 above to display it. Note that two pages are now listed in the Navigator named

"Untitled Page" and "Untitled Page 2". Select and then click a second time on the "Untitled Page 2" entry so that the name becomes editable and change the name to *SwiftUI Example* as outlined in Figure 4-14:

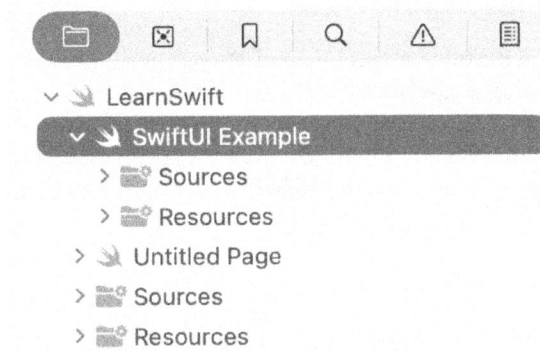

Figure 4-14

Note that the newly added page has Markup links which, when clicked, navigate to the previous or next page in the playground.

4.7 Working with SwiftUI and Live View in Playgrounds

In addition to allowing you to experiment with the Swift programming language, playgrounds may also be used to work with SwiftUI. Not only does this allow SwiftUI views to be prototyped, but when combined with the playground live view feature, it is also possible to run and interact with those views.

To try out SwiftUI and live view, begin by selecting the newly added SwiftUI Example page, deleting the current code lines, and modifying it to import both the SwiftUI and PlaygroundSupport frameworks:

```
import SwiftUI
import PlaygroundSupport
```

The PlaygroundSupport module provides several useful features for playgrounds including the ability to present a live view within the playground timeline.

Beneath the import statements, add the following code (rest assured, all of the techniques used in this example will be thoroughly explained in later chapters):

```
struct ExampleView: View {

    var body: some View {

        VStack {
            Rectangle()
                .fill(Color.blue)
                .frame(width: 200, height: 200)
            Button(action: {
                    }) {
                    Text("Rotate")
            }
        }
        .padding(10)
    }
```

```
}
```

This declaration creates a custom SwiftUI view named *ExampleView* consisting of a blue Rectangle view and a Button, both contained within a vertical stack (VStack).

The PlaygroundSupport module includes a class named PlaygroundPage which allows playground code to interact with the pages that make up a playground. This is achieved through a range of methods and properties of the class, one of which is the *current* property. This property, in turn, provides access to the current playground page. To execute the code within the playground, the *liveView* property of the current page needs to be set to our new container. To display the live content, add the code to assign the container to the live view of the current page as follows:

.

.

```
VStack {
    Rectangle()
        .fill(Color.blue)
        .frame(width: 200, height: 200)
    Button(action: {
            }) {
            Text("Rotate")
        }
    }
    .padding(10)
}
}
```

```
PlaygroundPage.current.setLiveView(ExampleView()
    .padding(100))
```

With the changes made, click on the run button and, within the results panel, select the Live View tab so that the SwiftUI layout appears as shown below:

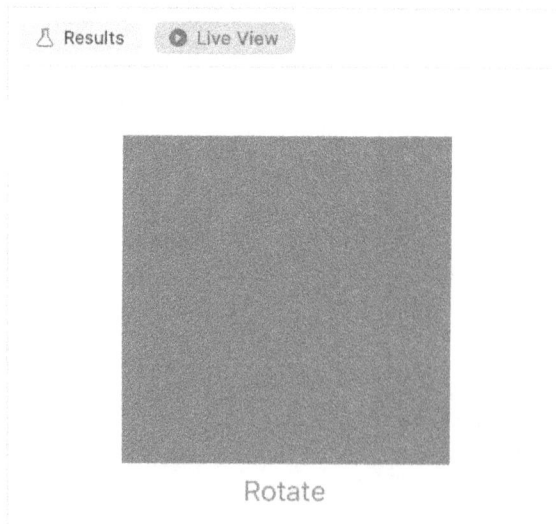

Figure 4-15

Since the button is not yet configured to do anything when clicked, it is difficult to see that the view is live. To see the live view in action, click on the stop button and modify the view declaration to rotate the blue square by 60° each time the button is clicked:

```
import SwiftUI
import PlaygroundSupport

struct ExampleView: View {

    @State private var rotation: Double = 0

    var body: some View {

        VStack {
            Rectangle()
                .fill(Color.blue)
                .frame(width: 200, height: 200)
                .rotationEffect(.degrees(rotation))
                .animation(.linear(duration: 2), value: rotation)
            Button(action: {
                rotation = (rotation < 360 ? rotation + 60 : 0)
            }) {
                Text("Rotate")
            }
        }
        .padding(10)
    }
}

PlaygroundPage.current.setLiveView(ExampleView()
    .padding(100))
```

Click the run button to launch the view in the live view and note that the square rotates each time the button is clicked:

Figure 4-16

4.8 Summary

This chapter has introduced the concept of playgrounds. Playgrounds provide an environment in which Swift code can be entered and the results of that code viewed dynamically. This provides an excellent environment both for learning the Swift programming language and for experimenting with many of the classes and APIs included in the iOS SDK without the need to create Xcode projects and repeatedly edit, compile and run code.

5. Swift Data Types, Constants, and Variables

If you are new to the Swift programming language then the next few chapters are recommended reading. Although SwiftUI makes the development of apps easier, it will still be necessary to learn Swift programming both to understand SwiftUI and develop fully functional apps.

If, on the other hand, you are familiar with the Swift programming language you can skip the Swift specific chapters that follow (though if you are not familiar with *implicit returns from single expressions*, *opaque return types* and *property wrappers* you should at least read the sections and chapters relating to these features before moving on to the SwiftUI chapters).

Prior to the introduction of iOS 8, the stipulated programming language for the development of iOS applications was Objective-C. When Apple announced iOS 8, however, the company also introduced an alternative to Objective-C in the form of the Swift programming language.

Due entirely to the popularity of iOS, Objective-C had become one of the more widely used programming languages. With origins firmly rooted in the 40-year-old C Programming Language, however, and despite recent efforts to modernize some aspects of the language syntax, Objective-C was beginning to show its age.

Swift, on the other hand, is a relatively new programming language designed specifically to make programming easier, faster and less prone to programmer error. Starting with a clean slate and no burden of legacy, Swift is a new and innovative language with which to develop applications for iOS, iPadOS, macOS, watchOS and tvOS with the advantage that much of the syntax will be familiar to those with experience of other programming languages.

The next several chapters will provide an overview and introduction to Swift programming. The intention of these chapters is to provide enough information so that you can begin to confidently program using Swift. For an exhaustive and in-depth guide to all the features, intricacies and capabilities of Swift, some time spent reading Apple's excellent book entitled "The Swift Programming Language" (available free of charge from within the Apple Books app) is strongly recommended.

5.1 Using a Swift Playground

Both this and the following few chapters are intended to introduce the basics of the Swift programming language. As outlined in the previous chapter, entitled *"An Introduction to Xcode 26 Playgrounds"* the best way to learn Swift is to experiment within a Swift playground environment. Before starting this chapter, therefore, create a new playground and use it to try out the code in both this and the other Swift introduction chapters that follow.

5.2 Swift Data Types

When we look at the different types of software that run on computer systems and mobile devices, from financial applications to graphics intensive games, it is easy to forget that computers are really just binary machines. Binary systems work in terms of 0 and 1, true or false, set and unset. All the data sitting in RAM, stored on disk drives and flowing through circuit boards and buses are nothing more than sequences of 1s and 0s. Each 1 or 0 is referred to as a *bit* and bits are grouped together in blocks of 8, each group being referred to as a *byte*. When people talk about 32-bit and 64-bit computer systems they are talking about the number of bits that can be handled simultaneously by the CPU bus. A 64-bit CPU, for example, is able to handle data in 64-bit blocks, resulting in faster performance than a 32-bit based system.

Humans, of course, don't think in binary. We work with decimal numbers, letters and words. In order for a human to easily (easily being a subjective term in this context) program a computer, some middle ground between human and computer thinking is needed. This is where programming languages such as Swift come into play. Programming languages allow humans to express instructions to a computer in terms and structures we understand, and then compile that down to a format that can be executed by a CPU.

One of the fundamentals of any program involves data, and programming languages such as Swift define a set of *data types* that allow us to work with data in a format we understand when programming. For example, if we want to store a number in a Swift program, we could do so with syntax similar to the following:

```
var mynumber = 10
```

In the above example, we have created a variable named *mynumber* and then assigned to it the value of 10. When we compile the source code down to the machine code used by the CPU, the number 10 is seen by the computer in binary as:

```
1010
```

Now that we have a basic understanding of the concept of data types and why they are necessary we can take a closer look at some of the more commonly used data types supported by Swift.

5.2.1 Integer Data Types

Swift integer data types are used to store whole numbers (in other words a number with no decimal places). Integers can be *signed* (capable of storing positive, negative and zero values) or *unsigned* (positive and zero values only).

Swift provides support for 8, 16, 32, 64, and 128-bit integers (represented by the Int8, Int16, Int32, Int64, and Int128 types respectively). The same variants are also available for unsigned integers (UInt8, UInt16, UInt32, UInt64, and UInt128).

In general, Apple recommends using the *Int* data type rather than one of the above specifically sized data types. The Int data type will use the appropriate integer size for the platform on which the code is running.

All integer data types contain bounds properties which can be accessed to identify the minimum and maximum supported values of that particular type. The following code, for example, outputs the minimum and maximum bounds for the 32-bit signed integer data type:

```
print("Int32 Min = \(Int32.min) Int32 Max = \(Int32.max)")
```

When executed, the above code will generate the following output:

```
Int32 Min = -2147483648 Int32 Max = 2147483647
```

5.2.2 Floating Point Data Types

The Swift floating point data types are able to store values containing decimal places. For example, 4353.1223 would be stored in a floating-point data type. Swift provides two floating point data types in the form of *Float* and *Double*. Which type to use depends on the size of value to be stored and the level of precision required. The Double type can be used to store up to 64-bit floating point numbers with a level of precision of 15 decimal places or greater. The Float data type, on the other hand, is limited to 32-bit floating point numbers and offers a level of precision as low as 6 decimal places depending on the native platform on which the code is running. Alternatively, the Float16 type may be used to store 16-bit floating point values. Float16 provides greater performance at the expense of lower precision.

5.2.3 Bool Data Type

Swift, like other languages, includes a data type for the purpose of handling true or false (1 or 0) conditions. Two Boolean constant values (*true* and *false*) are provided by Swift specifically for working with Boolean data types.

5.2.4 Character Data Type

The Swift Character data type is used to store a single character of rendered text such as a letter, numerical digit, punctuation mark or symbol. Internally characters in Swift are stored in the form of *grapheme clusters*. A grapheme cluster is made of two or more Unicode scalars that are combined to represent a single visible character.

The following lines assign a variety of different characters to Character type variables:

```
var myChar1 = "f"
var myChar2 = ":"
var myChar3 = "X"
```

Characters may also be referenced using Unicode code points. The following example assigns the 'X' character to a variable using Unicode:

```
var myChar4 = "\u{0058}"
```

5.2.5 String Data Type

The String data type is a sequence of characters that typically make up a word or sentence. In addition to providing a storage mechanism, the String data type also includes a range of string manipulation features allowing strings to be searched, matched, concatenated and modified. Strings in Swift are represented internally as collections of characters (where a character is, as previously discussed, comprised of one or more Unicode scalar values).

Strings can also be constructed using combinations of strings, variables, constants, expressions, and function calls using a concept referred to as *string interpolation*. For example, the following code creates a new string from a variety of different sources using string interpolation before outputting it to the console:

```
var userName = "John"
var inboxCount = 25
let maxCount = 100


var message = "\(userName) has \(inboxCount) messages. Message capacity remaining
is \(maxCount - inboxCount) messages."


print(message)
```

When executed, the code will output the following message:

```
John has 25 messages. Message capacity remaining is 75 messages.
```

A multiline string literal may be declared by encapsulating the string within triple quotes as follows:

```
var multiline = """

    The console glowed with flashing warnings.
    Clearly time was running out.

    "I thought you said you knew how to fly this!" yelled Mary.

    "It was much easier on the simulator" replied her brother,
```

23

```
        trying to keep the panic out of his voice.

"""

print(multiline)
```

The above code will generate the following output when run:

```
    The console glowed with flashing warnings.
    Clearly time was running out.

    "I thought you said you knew how to fly this!" yelled Mary.

    "It was much easier on the simulator" replied her brother,
    trying to keep the panic out of his voice.
```

The amount by which each line is indented within a multiline literal is calculated as the number of characters by which the line is indented minus the number of characters by which the closing triple quote line is indented. If, for example, the fourth line in the above example had a 10-character indentation and the closing triple quote was indented by 5 characters, the actual indentation of the fourth line within the string would be 5 characters. This allows multiline literals to be formatted tidily within Swift code while still allowing control over the indentation of individual lines.

5.2.6 Special Characters/Escape Sequences

In addition to the standard set of characters outlined above, there is also a range of *special characters* (also referred to as *escape sequences*) available for specifying items such as a new line, tab or a specific Unicode value within a string. These special characters are identified by prefixing the character with a backslash (a concept referred to as *escaping*). For example, the following assigns a new line to the variable named newline:

```
var newline = "\n"
```

In essence, any character that is preceded by a backslash is considered to be a special character and is treated accordingly. This raises the question as to what to do if you actually want a backslash character. This is achieved by *escaping* the backslash itself:

```
var backslash = "\\"
```

Commonly used special characters supported by Swift are as follows:

- **\n** - New line

- **\r** - Carriage return

- **\t** - Horizontal tab

- **** - Backslash

- **\"** - Double quote (used when placing a double quote into a string declaration)

- **\'** - Single quote (used when placing a single quote into a string declaration)

- **\u{*nn*}** – Single byte Unicode scalar where *nn* is replaced by two hexadecimal digits representing the Unicode character.

- **\u{*nnnn*}** – Double byte Unicode scalar where *nnnn* is replaced by four hexadecimal digits representing the Unicode character.

- **\u{*nnnnnnnn*}** – Four-byte Unicode scalar where *nnnnnnnn* is replaced by eight hexadecimal digits representing the Unicode character.

5.3 Swift Variables

Variables are essentially locations in computer memory reserved for storing the data used by an application. Each variable is given a name by the programmer and assigned a value. The name assigned to the variable may then be used in the Swift code to access the value assigned to that variable. This access can involve either reading the value of the variable or changing the value. It is, of course, the ability to change the value of variables, which gives them the name *variable*.

5.4 Swift Constants

A constant is like a variable in that it provides a named location in memory to store a data value. Constants differ in one significant way in that once a value has been assigned to a constant it cannot subsequently be changed.

Constants are particularly useful if a value is used repeatedly throughout the application code. Rather than use the value each time, it makes the code easier to read if the value is first assigned to a constant which is then referenced in the code. For example, it might not be clear to someone reading your Swift code why you used the value 5 in an expression. If, instead of the value 5, you use a constant named interestRate the purpose of the value becomes much clearer. Constants also have the advantage that if the programmer needs to change a widely used value, it only needs to be changed once in the constant declaration and not each time it is referenced.

As with variables, constants have a type, a name and a value. Unlike variables, however, once a value has been assigned to a constant, that value cannot subsequently be changed.

5.5 Declaring Constants and Variables

Variables are declared using the *var* keyword and may be initialized with a value at creation time. If the variable is declared without an initial value, it must be declared as being *optional* (a topic that will be covered later in this chapter). The following, for example, is a typical variable declaration:

```
var userCount = 10
```

Constants are declared using the *let* keyword.

```
let maxUserCount = 20
```

A constant can be declared without an initial value, but the declaration must specify the type and be initialized before it is used:

```
let userName: String
userName = "Juliette Nichols"

print(userName)
```

For greater code efficiency and execution performance, Apple recommends using constants rather than variables whenever possible.

5.6 Type Annotations and Type Inference

Swift is categorized as a *type safe* programming language. This essentially means that once the data type of a variable has been identified, that variable cannot subsequently be used to store data of any other type without inducing a compilation error. This contrasts to *loosely typed* programming languages where a variable, once declared, can subsequently be used to store other data types.

There are two ways in which the type of a constant or variable will be identified. One approach is to use a *type annotation* at the point the variable or constant is declared in the code. This is achieved by placing a colon after the constant or variable name followed by the type declaration. The following line of code, for example, declares a variable named userCount as being of type Int:

```
var userCount: Int = 10
```

In the absence of a type annotation in a declaration, the Swift compiler uses a technique referred to as *type inference* to identify the type of the constant or variable. When relying on type inference, the compiler looks to see what type of value is being assigned to the constant or variable at the point that it is initialized and uses that as the type. Consider, for example, the following variable and constant declarations:

```
var signalStrength = 2.231
let companyName = "My Company"
```

During compilation of the above lines of code, Swift will infer that the signalStrength variable is of type Double (type inference in Swift defaults to Double for all floating-point numbers) and that the companyName constant is of type String.

When a constant is declared without a type annotation it must be assigned a value at the point of declaration:

```
let bookTitle = "iOS 26 App Development Essentials"
```

If a type annotation is used when the constant is declared, however, the value can be assigned later in the code. For example:

```
let bookTitle: String
.
.
if iosBookType {
    bookTitle = "iOS 26 App Development Essentials"
} else {
    bookTitle = "Android Studio Development Essentials"
}
```

It is important to note that a value may only be assigned to a constant once. A second attempt to assign a value to a constant will result in a syntax error.

5.7 The Swift Tuple

Before proceeding, now is a good time to introduce the Swift tuple. The tuple is perhaps one of the simplest, yet most powerful features of the Swift programming language. A tuple is, quite simply, a way to temporarily group together multiple values into a single entity. The items stored in a tuple can be of any type and there are no restrictions requiring that those values all be of the same type. A tuple could, for example, be constructed to contain an Int value, a Double value and a String as follows:

```
let myTuple = (10, 432.433, "This is a String")
```

The elements of a tuple can be accessed using a number of different techniques. A specific tuple value can be accessed simply by referencing the index position (with the first value being at index position 0). The code below, for example, extracts the string resource (at index position 2 in the tuple) and assigns it to a new string variable:

```
let myTuple = (10, 432.433, "This is a String")
let myString = myTuple.2
print(myString)
```

Alternatively, all the values in a tuple may be extracted and assigned to variables or constants in a single statement:

```
let (myInt, myFloat, myString) = myTuple
```

This same technique can be used to extract selected values from a tuple while ignoring others by replacing the values to be ignored with an underscore character. The following code fragment extracts the integer and string values from the tuple and assigns them to variables, but ignores the floating-point value:

```
var (myInt, _, myString) = myTuple
```

When creating a tuple, it is also possible to assign a name to each value:

```
let myTuple = (count: 10, length: 432.433, message: "This is a String")
```

The names assigned to the values stored in a tuple may then be used to reference those values in code. For example, to output the *message* string value from the *myTuple* instance, the following line of code could be used:

```
print(myTuple.message)
```

Perhaps the most powerful use of tuples is, as will be seen in later chapters, the ability to return multiple values from a function.

5.8 The Swift Optional Type

The Swift optional data type is a new concept that does not exist in most other programming languages. The purpose of the optional type is to provide a safe and consistent approach to handling situations where a variable or constant may not have any value assigned to it.

Variables are declared as being optional by placing a ? character after the type declaration. The following code declares an optional Int variable named index:

```
var index: Int?
```

The variable *index* can now either have an integer value assigned to it or have nothing assigned to it. Behind the scenes, and as far as the compiler and runtime are concerned, an optional with no value assigned to it actually has a value of nil.

An optional can easily be tested (typically using an if statement) to identify whether it has a value assigned to it as follows:

```
var index: Int?

if index != nil {
    // index variable has a value assigned to it
} else {
    // index variable has no value assigned to it
}
```

If an optional has a value assigned to it, that value is said to be "wrapped" within the optional. The value wrapped in an optional may be accessed using a concept referred to as *forced unwrapping*. This simply means that the underlying value is extracted from the optional data type, a procedure that is performed by placing an exclamation mark (!) after the optional name.

To explore this concept of unwrapping optional types in more detail, consider the following code:

```
var index: Int?

index = 3

var treeArray = ["Oak", "Pine", "Yew", "Birch"]

if index != nil {
```

```
        print(treeArray[index!])
} else {
    print("index does not contain a value")
}
```

The code simply uses an optional variable to hold the index into an array of strings representing the names of tree species (Swift arrays will be covered in more detail in the chapter entitled *"Working with Array and Dictionary Collections in Swift"*). If the index optional variable has a value assigned to it, the tree name at that location in the array is printed to the console. Since the index is an optional type, the value has been unwrapped by placing an exclamation mark after the variable name:

```
print(treeArray[index!])
```

Had the index not been unwrapped (in other words the exclamation mark omitted from the above line), the compiler would have issued an error similar to the following:

```
Value of optional type 'Int?' must be unwrapped to a value of type 'Int'
```

As an alternative to forced unwrapping, the value assigned to an optional may be allocated to a temporary variable or constant using *optional binding*, the syntax for which is as follows:

```
if let constantname = optionalName {


}


if var variablename = optionalName {


}
```

The above constructs perform two tasks. In the first instance, the statement ascertains whether the designated optional contains a value. Second, in the event that the optional has a value, that value is assigned to the declared constant or variable and the code within the body of the statement is executed. The previous forced unwrapping example could, therefore, be modified as follows to use optional binding instead:

```
var index: Int?


index = 3


var treeArray = ["Oak", "Pine", "Yew", "Birch"]


if let myvalue = index {
    print(treeArray[myvalue])
} else {
    print("index does not contain a value")
}
```

In this case the value assigned to the index variable is unwrapped and assigned to a temporary (also referred to as *shadow*) constant named *myvalue* which is then used as the index reference into the array. Note that the *myvalue* constant is described as temporary since it is only available within the scope of the if statement. Once the if statement completes execution, the constant will no longer exist. For this reason, there is no conflict in using the same temporary name as that assigned to the optional. The following is, for example, valid code:

.

.

```
if let index = index {
    print(treeArray[index])
} else {
.

.
```

When considering the above example, the use of the temporary value begins to seem redundant. Fortunately, the Swift development team arrived at the same conclusion and introduced the following shorthand if-let syntax in Swift 5.7:

```
var index: Int?

index = 3

var treeArray = ["Oak", "Pine", "Yew", "Birch"]

if let index {
    print(treeArray[index])
} else {
    print("index does not contain a value")
}
```

Using this approach it is no longer necessary to assign the optional to a temporary value.

Optional binding may also be used to unwrap multiple optionals and include a Boolean test condition, the syntax for which is as follows:

```
if let constname1 = optName1, let constname2 = optName2,
    let optName3 = …, <boolean statement> {


}
```

The shorthand if-let syntax is also available when working with multiple optionals and test conditions avoiding the need to use temporary values:

```
if let constname1, let constname2,
    let optName3, ... <boolean statement> {


}
```

The following code, for example, uses shorthand optional binding to unwrap two optionals within a single statement:

```
var pet1: String?
var pet2: String?

pet1 = "cat"
pet2 = "dog"

if let pet1, let pet2 {
    print(pet1)
    print(pet2)
```

```
} else {
    print("insufficient pets")
}
```

The code fragment below, on the other hand, also makes use of the Boolean test clause condition:

```
if let pet1, let pet2, petCount > 1 {
    print(pet1)
    print(pet2)
} else {
    print("insufficient pets")
}
```

In the above example, the optional binding will not be attempted unless the value assigned to *petCount* is greater than 1.

It is also possible to declare an optional as being *implicitly unwrapped*. When an optional is declared in this way, the underlying value can be accessed without having to perform forced unwrapping or optional binding. An optional is declared as being implicitly unwrapped by replacing the question mark (?) with an exclamation mark (!) in the declaration. For example:

```
var index: Int! // Optional is now implicitly unwrapped

index = 3

var treeArray = ["Oak", "Pine", "Yew", "Birch"]

if index != nil {
    print(treeArray[index])
} else {
    print("index does not contain a value")
}
```

With the index optional variable now declared as being implicitly unwrapped, it is no longer necessary to unwrap the value when it is used as an index into the array in the above print call.

One final observation with regard to optionals in Swift is that only optional types are able to have no value or a value of nil assigned to them. In Swift it is not, therefore, possible to assign a nil value to a non-optional variable or constant. The following declarations, for instance, will all result in errors from the compiler since none of the variables are declared as optional:

```
var myInt = nil // Invalid code
var myString: String = nil // Invalid Code
let myConstant = nil // Invalid code
```

5.9 Type Casting and Type Checking

When writing Swift code, situations will occur where the compiler is unable to identify the specific type of a value. This is often the case when a value of ambiguous or unexpected type is returned from a method or function call. In this situation it may be necessary to let the compiler know the type of value that your code is expecting or requires using the *as* keyword (a concept referred to as *type casting*).

The following code, for example, lets the compiler know that the value returned from the *object(forKey:)* method needs to be treated as a String type:

```
let myValue = record.object(forKey: "comment") as! String
```

In fact, there are two types of casting which are referred to as *upcasting* and *downcasting*. Upcasting occurs when an object of a particular class is cast to one of its superclasses. Upcasting is performed using the *as* keyword and is also referred to as *guaranteed conversion* since the compiler can tell from the code that the cast will be successful. The UIButton class, for example, is a subclass of the UIControl class, as shown in the fragment of the UIKit class hierarchy shown in Figure 5-1:

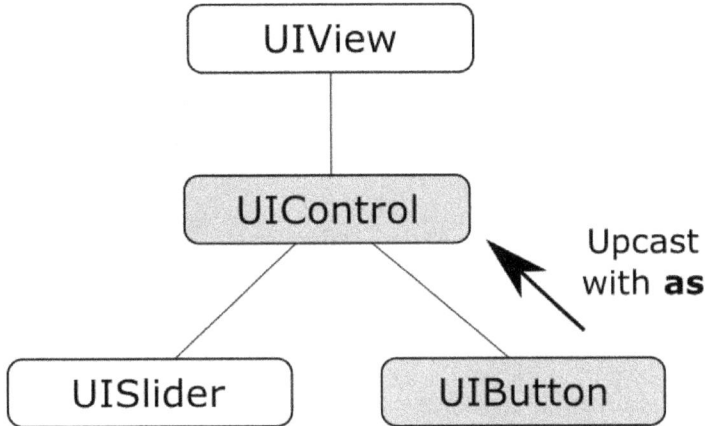

Figure 5-1

Since UIButton is a subclass of UIControl, the object can be safely upcast as follows:

```
let myButton: UIButton = UIButton()

let myControl = myButton as UIControl
```

Downcasting, on the other hand, occurs when a conversion is made from one class to another where there is no guarantee that the cast can be made safely or that an invalid casting attempt will be caught by the compiler. When an invalid cast is made in downcasting and not identified by the compiler it will most likely lead to an error at runtime.

Downcasting usually involves converting from a class to one of its subclasses. Downcasting is performed using the *as!* keyword syntax and is also referred to as *forced conversion*. Consider, for example, the UIKit UIScrollView class which has as subclasses both the UITableView and UITextView classes, as shown in Figure 5-2:

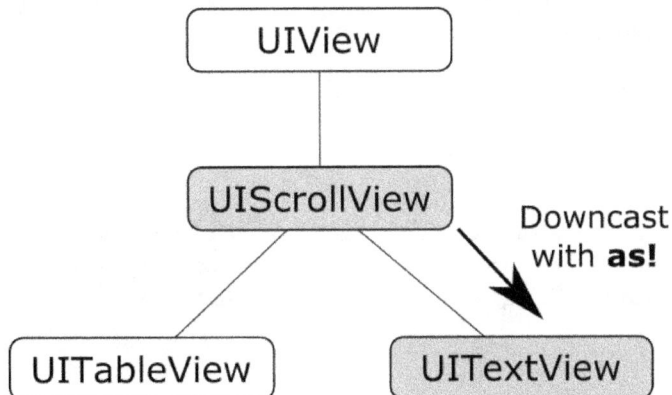

Figure 5-2

In order to convert a UIScrollView object to a UITextView class a downcast operation needs to be performed. The following code attempts to downcast a UIScrollView object to UITextView using the *guaranteed conversion* or *upcast* approach:

```
let myScrollView: UIScrollView = UIScrollView()
```

```
let myTextView = myScrollView as UITextView
```

The above code will result in the following error:

```
'UIScrollView' is not convertible to 'UITextView'
```

The compiler is indicating that a UIScrollView instance cannot be safely converted to a UITextView class instance. This does not necessarily mean that it is incorrect to do so, the compiler is simply stating that it cannot guarantee the safety of the conversion for you. The downcast conversion could instead be forced using the *as!* annotation:

```
let myTextView = myScrollView as! UITextView
```

Now the code will compile without an error. As an example of the dangers of downcasting, however, the above code will crash on execution stating that UIScrollView cannot be cast to UITextView. Forced downcasting should, therefore, be used with caution.

A safer approach to downcasting is to perform an optional binding using *as?*. If the conversion is performed successfully, an optional value of the specified type is returned, otherwise the optional value will be nil:

```
if let myTextView = myScrollView as? UITextView {
    print("Type cast to UITextView succeeded")
} else {
    print("Type cast to UITextView failed")
}
```

It is also possible to *type check* a value using the *is* keyword. The following code, for example, checks that a specific object is an instance of a class named MyClass:

```
if myobject is MyClass {
    // myobject is an instance of MyClass
}
```

5.10 Take the Knowledge Test

Click the link below or scan the QR code to test your knowledge and understanding of Swift data types:

https://www.answertopia.com/q6c8

5.11 Summary

This chapter has begun the introduction to Swift by exploring data types together with an overview of how to declare constants and variables. The chapter has also introduced concepts such as type safety, type inference and optionals, each of which is an integral part of Swift programming, and designed specifically to make code writing less prone to error.

6. Swift Operators and Expressions

So far we have looked at using variables and constants in Swift and also described the different data types. Being able to create variables, however, is only part of the story. The next step is to learn how to use these variables and constants in Swift code. The primary method for working with data is in the form of *expressions*.

6.1 Expression Syntax in Swift

The most basic Swift expression consists of an *operator*, two *operands* and an *assignment*. The following is an example of an expression:

```
var myresult = 1 + 2
```

In the above example, the (+) operator is used to add two operands (1 and 2) together. The *assignment operator* (=) subsequently assigns the result of the addition to a variable named *myresult*. The operands could just have easily been variables (or a mixture of constants and variables) instead of the actual numerical values used in the example.

In the remainder of this chapter we will look at the basic types of operators available in Swift.

6.2 The Basic Assignment Operator

We have already looked at the most basic of assignment operators, the = operator. This assignment operator simply assigns the result of an expression to a variable. In essence, the = assignment operator takes two operands. The left-hand operand is the variable or constant to which a value is to be assigned and the right-hand operand is the value to be assigned. The right-hand operand is, more often than not, an expression that performs some type of arithmetic or logical evaluation, the result of which will be assigned to the variable or constant. The following examples are all valid uses of the assignment operator:

```
var x: Int? // Declare an optional Int variable
var y = 10 // Declare and initialize a second Int variable

x = 10 // Assign a value to x
x = x! + y // Assign the result of x + y to x
x = y // Assign the value of y to x
```

6.3 Swift Arithmetic Operators

Swift provides a range of operators for the purpose of creating mathematical expressions. These operators primarily fall into the category of *binary* operators in that they take two operands. The exception is the *unary negative operator* (-) which serves to indicate that a value is negative rather than positive. This contrasts with the *subtraction operator* (-) which takes two operands (i.e. one value to be subtracted from another). For example:

```
var x = -10 // Unary - operator used to assign -10 to variable x
x = x - 5 // Subtraction operator. Subtracts 5 from x
```

The following table lists the primary Swift arithmetic operators:

Operator	Description
-(unary)	Negates the value of a variable or expression

*		Multiplication
/		Division
+		Addition
-		Subtraction
%		Remainder/Modulo

Table 6-1

Note that multiple operators may be used in a single expression.

For example:

```
x = y * 10 + z - 5 / 4
```

6.4 Compound Assignment Operators

In an earlier section we looked at the basic assignment operator (=). Swift provides a number of operators designed to combine an assignment with a mathematical or logical operation. These are primarily of use when performing an evaluation where the result is to be stored in one of the operands. For example, one might write an expression as follows:

```
x = x + y
```

The above expression adds the value contained in variable x to the value contained in variable y and stores the result in variable x. This can be simplified using the addition compound assignment operator:

```
x += y
```

The above expression performs exactly the same task as $x = x + y$ but saves the programmer some typing.

Numerous compound assignment operators are available in Swift, the most frequently used of which are outlined in the following table:

Operator	Description
x += y	Add x to y and place result in x
x -= y	Subtract y from x and place result in x
x *= y	Multiply x by y and place result in x
x /= y	Divide x by y and place result in x
x %= y	Perform Modulo on x and y and place result in x

Table 6-2

6.5 Comparison Operators

Swift also includes a set of logical operators useful for performing comparisons. These operators all return a Boolean result depending on the result of the comparison. These operators are *binary operators* in that they work with two operands.

Comparison operators are most frequently used in constructing program flow control logic. For example, an *if* statement may be constructed based on whether one value matches another:

```
if x == y {
     // Perform task
}
```

The result of a comparison may also be stored in a *Bool* variable. For example, the following code will result in a *true* value being stored in the variable result:

```
var result: Bool?
var x = 10
var y = 20


result = x < y
```

Clearly 10 is less than 20, resulting in a *true* evaluation of the *x < y* expression. The following table lists the full set of Swift comparison operators:

Operator	Description
x == y	Returns true if x is equal to y
x > y	Returns true if x is greater than y
x >= y	Returns true if x is greater than or equal to y
x < y	Returns true if x is less than y
x <= y	Returns true if x is less than or equal to y
x != y	Returns true if x is not equal to y

Table 6-3

6.6 Boolean Logical Operators

Swift also provides a set of so-called logical operators designed to return Boolean *true* or *false* values. These operators both return Boolean results and take Boolean values as operands. The key operators are NOT (!), AND (&&) and OR (||).

The NOT (!) operator simply inverts the current value of a Boolean variable, or the result of an expression. For example, if a variable named *flag* is currently true, prefixing the variable with a '!' character will invert the value to false:

```
var flag = true // variable is true
var secondFlag = !flag // secondFlag set to false
```

The OR (||) operator returns true if one of its two operands evaluates to true, otherwise it returns false. For example, the following code evaluates to true because at least one of the expressions either side of the OR operator is true:

```
if (10 < 20) || (20 < 10) {
        print("Expression is true")

}
```

The AND (&&) operator returns true only if both operands evaluate to be true. The following example will return false because only one of the two operand expressions evaluates to true:

```
if (10 < 20) && (20 < 10) {
      print("Expression is true")

}
```

6.7 Range Operators

Swift includes several useful operators that allow ranges of values to be declared. As will be seen in later chapters, these operators are invaluable when working with looping in program logic.

The syntax for the *closed range operator* is as follows:

35

x...y

This operator represents the range of numbers starting at x and ending at y where both x and y are included within the range. The range operator 5...8, for example, specifies the numbers 5, 6, 7 and 8.

The *half-open range operator*, on the other hand uses the following syntax:

x..<y

In this instance, the operator encompasses all the numbers from x up to, but not including, y. A half-closed range operator 5..<8, therefore, specifies the numbers 5, 6 and 7.

Finally, the *one-sided range* operator specifies a range that can extend as far as possible in a specified range direction until the natural beginning or end of the range is reached (or until some other condition is met). A one-sided range is declared by omitting the number from one side of the range declaration, for example:

x...

or

...y

The previous chapter, for example, explained that a String in Swift is actually a collection of individual characters. A range to specify the characters in a string starting with the character at position 2 through to the last character in the string (regardless of string length) would be declared as follows:

2...

Similarly, to specify a range that begins with the first character and ends with the character at position 6, the range would be specified as follows:

...6

6.8 The Ternary Operator

Swift supports the *ternary operator* to provide a shortcut way of making decisions within code. The syntax of the ternary operator (also known as the conditional operator) is as follows:

```
condition ? true expression : false expression
```

The way the ternary operator works is that *condition* is replaced with an expression that will return either *true* or *false*. If the result is true then the expression that replaces the *true expression* is evaluated. Conversely, if the result was *false* then the *false expression* is evaluated. Let's see this in action:

```
let x = 10
let y = 20


print("Largest number is \(x > y ? x : y)")
```

The above code example will evaluate whether x is greater than y. Clearly this will evaluate to false resulting in y being returned to the print call for display to the user:

```
Largest number is 20
```

6.9 Nil Coalescing Operator

The *nil coalescing operator* (??) allows a default value to be used in the event that an optional has a nil value. The following example will output text which reads "Welcome back, customer" because the *customerName* optional is set to nil:

```
let customerName: String? = nil
print("Welcome back, \(customerName ?? "customer")")
```

If, on the other hand, *customerName* is not nil, the optional will be unwrapped and the assigned value displayed:

```
let customerName: String? = "John"
print("Welcome back, \(customerName ?? "customer")")
```

On execution, the print statement output will now read "Welcome back, John".

6.10 Bitwise Operators

As previously discussed, computer processors work in binary. These are essentially streams of ones and zeros, each one referred to as a bit. Bits are formed into groups of 8 to form bytes. As such, it is not surprising that we, as programmers, will occasionally end up working at this level in our code. To facilitate this requirement, Swift provides a range of *bit operators*.

Those familiar with bitwise operators in other languages such as C, C++, C#, Objective-C and Java will find nothing new in this area of the Swift language syntax. For those unfamiliar with binary numbers, now may be a good time to seek out reference materials on the subject in order to understand how ones and zeros are formed into bytes to form numbers. Other authors have done a much better job of describing the subject than we can do within the scope of this book.

For the purposes of this exercise we will be working with the binary representation of two numbers (for the sake of brevity we will be using 8-bit values in the following examples). First, the decimal number 171 is represented in binary as:

```
10101011
```

Second, the number 3 is represented by the following binary sequence:

```
00000011
```

Now that we have two binary numbers with which to work, we can begin to look at the Swift bitwise operators:

6.10.1 Bitwise NOT

The Bitwise NOT is represented by the tilde (~) character and has the effect of inverting all of the bits in a number. In other words, all the zeros become ones and all the ones become zeros. Taking our example 3 number, a Bitwise NOT operation has the following result:

```
00000011 NOT
========
11111100
```

The following Swift code, therefore, results in a value of -4:

```
let y = 3
let z = ~y


print("Result is \(z)")
```

6.10.2 Bitwise AND

The Bitwise AND is represented by a single ampersand (&). It makes a bit by bit comparison of two numbers. Any corresponding position in the binary sequence of each number where both bits are 1 results in a 1 appearing in the same position of the resulting number. If either bit position contains a 0 then a zero appears in the result. Taking our two example numbers, this would appear as follows:

```
10101011 AND
```

```
00000011
========
00000011
```

As we can see, the only locations where both numbers have 1s are the last two positions. If we perform this in Swift code, therefore, we should find that the result is 3 (00000011):

```
let x = 171
let y = 3
let z = x & y

print("Result is \(z)")
```

6.10.3 Bitwise OR

The bitwise OR also performs a bit by bit comparison of two binary sequences. Unlike the AND operation, the OR places a 1 in the result if there is a 1 in the first or second operand. The operator is represented by a single vertical bar character (|). Using our example numbers, the result will be as follows:

```
10101011 OR
00000011
========
10101011
```

If we perform this operation in a Swift example the result will be 171:

```
let x = 171
let y = 3
let z = x | y

print("Result is \(z)")
```

6.10.4 Bitwise XOR

The bitwise XOR (commonly referred to as *exclusive OR* and represented by the caret '^' character) performs a similar task to the OR operation except that a 1 is placed in the result if one or other corresponding bit positions in the two numbers is 1. If both positions are a 1 or a 0 then the corresponding bit in the result is set to a 0. For example:

```
10101011 XOR
00000011
========
10101000
```

The result in this case is 10101000 which converts to 168 in decimal. To verify this we can, once again, try some Swift code:

```
let x = 171
let y = 3
let z = x ^ y

print("Result is \(z)")
```

6.10.5 Bitwise Left Shift

The bitwise left shift moves each bit in a binary number a specified number of positions to the left. Shifting an integer one position to the left has the effect of doubling the value.

As the bits are shifted to the left, zeros are placed in the vacated right most (low order) positions. Note also that once the left most (high order) bits are shifted beyond the size of the variable containing the value, those high order bits are discarded:

```
10101011 Left Shift one bit
========
101010110
```

In Swift the bitwise left shift operator is represented by the '<<' sequence, followed by the number of bit positions to be shifted. For example, to shift left by 1 bit:

```
let x = 171
let z = x << 1

print("Result is \(z)")
```

When compiled and executed, the above code will display a message stating that the result is 342 which, when converted to binary, equates to 101010110.

6.10.6 Bitwise Right Shift

A bitwise right shift is, as you might expect, the same as a left except that the shift takes place in the opposite direction. Shifting an integer one position to the right has the effect of halving the value.

Note that since we are shifting to the right there is no opportunity to retain the lower most bits regardless of the data type used to contain the result. As a result, the low order bits are discarded. Whether or not the vacated high order bit positions are replaced with zeros or ones depends on whether the *sign bit* used to indicate positive and negative numbers is set or not.

```
10101011 Right Shift one bit
========
01010101
```

The bitwise right shift is represented by the '>>' character sequence followed by the shift count:

```
let x = 171
let z = x >> 1

print("Result is \(z)")
```

When executed, the above code will report the result of the shift as being 85, which equates to binary 01010101.

6.11 Compound Bitwise Operators

As with the arithmetic operators, each bitwise operator has a corresponding compound operator that allows the operation and assignment to be performed using a single operator:

Operator	Description
x &= y	Perform a bitwise AND of x and y and assign result to x
x |= y	Perform a bitwise OR of x and y and assign result to x
x ^= y	Perform a bitwise XOR of x and y and assign result to x
x <<= n	Shift x left by n places and assign result to x
x >>= n	Shift x right by n places and assign result to x

Table 6-4

6.12 Take the Knowledge Test

Click the link below or scan the QR code to test your knowledge and understanding of Swift operators and expressions:

https://www.answertopia.com/jgce

6.13 Summary

Operators and expressions provide the underlying mechanism by which variables and constants are manipulated and evaluated within Swift code. This can take the simplest of forms whereby two numbers are added using the addition operator in an expression and the result stored in a variable using the assignment operator. Operators fall into a range of categories, details of which have been covered in this chapter.

7. Swift Control Flow

Regardless of the programming language used, application development is largely an exercise in applying logic, and much of the art of programming involves writing code that makes decisions based on one or more criteria. Such decisions define which code gets executed, how many times it is executed and, conversely, which code gets by-passed when the program is executing. This is often referred to as *control flow* since it controls the *flow* of program execution. Control flow typically falls into the categories of *looping control* (how often code is executed) and *conditional control flow* (whether code is executed). This chapter will provide an introductory overview of both types of control flow in Swift.

7.1 Looping Control Flow

This chapter will begin by looking at control flow in the form of loops. Loops are essentially sequences of Swift statements that are to be executed repeatedly until a specified condition is met. The first looping statement we will explore is the *for-in* loop.

7.2 The Swift for-in Statement

The *for-in* loop is used to iterate over a sequence of items contained in a collection or number range and provides a simple-to-use looping option.

The syntax of the for-in loop is as follows:

```
for constant name in collection or range {
    // code to be executed
}
```

In this syntax, *constant name* is the name to be used for a constant that will contain the current item from the collection or range through which the loop is iterating. The code in the body of the loop will typically use this constant name as a reference to the current item in the loop cycle. The *collection* or *range* references the item through which the loop is iterating. This could, for example, be an array of string values, a range operator or even a string of characters (the topic of collections will be covered in greater detail within the chapter entitled *"Working with Array and Dictionary Collections in Swift"*).

Consider, for example, the following for-in loop construct:

```
for index in 1...5 {
    print("Value of index is \(index)")
}
```

The loop begins by stating that the current item is to be assigned to a constant named *index*. The statement then declares a closed range operator to indicate that the for loop is to iterate through a range of numbers, starting at 1 and ending at 5. The body of the loop simply prints out a message to the console panel indicating the current value assigned to the *index* constant, resulting in the following output:

```
Value of index is 1
Value of index is 2
Value of index is 3
Value of index is 4
Value of index is 5
```

As will be demonstrated in the *"Working with Array and Dictionary Collections in Swift"* chapter of this book, the *for-in* loop is of particular benefit when working with collections such as arrays and dictionaries.

The declaration of a constant name in which to store a reference to the current item is not mandatory. In the event that a reference to the current item is not required in the body of the *for* loop, the constant name in the *for* loop declaration can be replaced by an underscore character. For example:

```
var count = 0


for _ in 1...5 {
    // No reference to the current value is required.
    count += 1
}
```

7.2.1 The while Loop

The Swift *for* loop described previously works well when it is known in advance how many times a particular task needs to be repeated in a program. There will, however, be instances where code needs to be repeated until a certain condition is met, with no way of knowing in advance how many repetitions are going to be needed to meet that criterion. To address this need, Swift provides the *while* loop.

Essentially, the *while* loop repeats a set of tasks while a specified condition is met. The *while* loop syntax is defined as follows:

```
while condition {
    // Swift statements go here
}
```

In the above syntax, *condition* is an expression that will return either *true* or *false* and the *// Swift statements go here* comment represents the code to be executed while the *condition* expression is *true*. For example:

```
var myCount = 0


while  myCount < 100 {
    myCount += 1
}
```

In the above example, the *while* expression will evaluate whether the *myCount* variable is less than 100. If it is already greater than 100, the code in the braces is skipped and the loop exits without performing any tasks.

If, on the other hand, *myCount* is not greater than 100 the code in the braces is executed and the loop returns to the *while* statement and repeats the evaluation of *myCount*. This process repeats until the value of *myCount* is greater than 100, at which point the loop exits.

7.3 The repeat ... while loop

The *repeat ... while* loop replaces the Swift 1.x *do .. while* loop. It is often helpful to think of the *repeat ... while* loop as an inverted *while* loop. The *while* loop evaluates an expression before executing the code contained in the body of the loop. If the expression evaluates to *false* on the first check then the code is not executed. The *repeat ... while* loop, on the other hand, is provided for situations where you know that the code contained in the body of the loop will *always* need to be executed at least once. For example, you may want to keep stepping through the items in an array until a specific item is found. You know that you have to at least check the first item in the array to have any hope of finding the entry you need. The syntax for the *repeat ... while* loop is as follows:

```
repeat {
    // Swift statements here
```

```
} while conditional expression
```

In the *repeat ... while* example below the loop will continue until the value of a variable named *i* equals 0:

```
var i = 10

repeat {
       i -= 1
} while (i > 0)
```

7.4 Breaking from Loops

Having created a loop, it is possible that under certain conditions you might want to break out of the loop before the completion criteria have been met (particularly if you have created an infinite loop). One such example might involve continually checking for activity on a network socket. Once activity has been detected it will most likely be necessary to break out of the monitoring loop and perform some other task.

For the purpose of breaking out of a loop, Swift provides the *break* statement which breaks out of the current loop and resumes execution at the code directly after the loop. For example:

```
var j = 10

for _ in 0 ..< 100
{
    j += j

    if j > 100 {
        break
    }

    print("j = \(j)")
}
```

In the above example the loop will continue to execute until the value of j exceeds 100 at which point the loop will exit and execution will continue with the next line of code after the loop.

7.5 The continue Statement

The *continue* statement causes all remaining code statements in a loop to be skipped, and execution to be returned to the top of the loop. In the following example, the print function is only called when the value of variable *i* is an even number:

```
var i = 1

while i < 20
{
        i += 1

        if (i % 2) != 0 {
            continue
        }

        print("i = \(i)")
```

```
}
```

The *continue* statement in the above example will cause the print call to be skipped unless the value of *i* can be divided by 2 with no remainder. If the *continue* statement is triggered, execution will skip to the top of the while loop and the statements in the body of the loop will be repeated (until the value of *i* exceeds 19).

7.6 Conditional Control Flow

In the previous chapter we looked at how to use logical expressions in Swift to determine whether something is *true* or *false*. Since programming is largely an exercise in applying logic, much of the art of programming involves writing code that makes decisions based on one or more criteria. Such decisions define which code gets executed and, conversely, which code gets by-passed when the program is executing.

7.7 Using the if Statement

The *if* statement is perhaps the most basic of control flow options available to the Swift programmer. Programmers who are familiar with C, Objective-C, C++ or Java will immediately be comfortable using Swift *if* statements.

The basic syntax of the Swift *if* statement is as follows:

```
if (boolean expression) {
    // Swift code to be performed when expression evaluates to true
}
```

Unlike some other programming languages, it is important to note that the braces ({}) are mandatory in Swift, even if only one line of code is executed after the *if* expression.

Essentially if the *Boolean expression* evaluates to *true* then the code in the body of the statement is executed. The body of the statement is enclosed in braces ({}). If, on the other hand, the expression evaluates to *false* the code in the body of the statement is skipped.

For example, if a decision needs to be made depending on whether one value is greater than another, we would write code similar to the following:

```
let x = 10

if (x > 9) {
    print("x is greater than 9!")
}
```

Clearly, x is indeed greater than 9 causing the message to appear in the console panel.

7.8 Using if ... else ... Statements

The next variation of the *if* statement allows us to also specify some code to perform if the expression in the *if* statement evaluates to *false*. The syntax for this construct is as follows:

```
if (boolean expression) {
    // Code to be executed if expression is true
} else {
    // Code to be executed if expression is false
}
```

Using the above syntax, we can now extend our previous example to display a different message if the comparison expression evaluates to be *false*:

```
let x = 10
```

```
if (x > 9) {
        print("x is greater than 9!")
} else {
        print("x is less than 10!")
}
```

In this case, the second print statement would execute if the value of x was less than or equal to 9.

7.9 Using if ... else if ... Statements

So far, we have looked at *if* statements that make decisions based on the result of a single logical expression. Sometimes it becomes necessary to make decisions based on a number of different criteria. For this purpose, we can use the *if ... else if ...* construct, an example of which is as follows:

```
let x = 9

if (x == 10) {
        print("x is 10")
} else if x == 9 {
        print("x is 9")
} else if x == 8 {
        print("x is 8")
}
```

This approach works well for a moderate number of comparisons but can become cumbersome for a larger volume of expression evaluations. For such situations, the Swift *switch* statement provides a more flexible and efficient solution. For more details on using the *switch* statement refer to the next chapter entitled "The Swift Switch Statement".

7.10 The guard Statement

The *guard* statement is a Swift language feature introduced as part of Swift 2. A guard statement contains a Boolean expression which must evaluate to true in order for the code located *after* the guard statement to be executed. The guard statement must include an *else* clause to be executed in the event that the expression evaluates to false. The code in the else clause must contain a statement to exit the current code flow (i.e., a *return*, *break*, *continue* or *throw* statement). Alternatively, the *else* block may call any other function or method that does not itself return.

The syntax for the guard statement is as follows:

```
guard <boolean expressions> else {
   // code to be executed if expression is false
   <exit statement here>
}

// code here is executed if expression is true
```

The guard statement essentially provides an "early exit" strategy from the current function or loop in the event that a specified requirement is not met.

The following code example implements a guard statement within a function:

```
func multiplyByTen(value: Int?) {
```

```
    guard let number = value, number < 10 else {
        print("Number is too high")
        return
    }


    let result = number * 10
    print(result)
}

multiplyByTen(value: 5)
multiplyByTen(value: 10)
```

The function takes as a parameter an integer value in the form of an optional. The guard statement uses optional binding to unwrap the value and verify that it is less than 10. In the event that the variable could not be unwrapped, or that its value is greater than 9, the else clause is triggered, the error message printed, and the return statement executed to exit the function.

If the optional contains a value less than 10, the code after the guard statement executes to multiply the value by 10 and print the result. A particularly important point to note about the above example is that the unwrapped *number* variable is available to the code outside of the guard statement. This would not have been the case had the variable been unwrapped using an *if* statement.

7.11 Take the Knowledge Test

Click the link below or scan the QR code to test your knowledge and understanding of Swift control flow:

https://www.answertopia.com/tb6n

7.12 Summary

The term *control flow* is used to describe the logic that dictates the execution path that is taken through the source code of an application as it runs. This chapter has looked at the two types of control flow provided by Swift (looping and conditional) and explored the various Swift constructs that are available to implement both forms of control flow logic.

Chapter 8

8. The Swift Switch Statement

In *"Swift Control Flow"* we looked at controlling program execution flow using the *if* and *else* statements. While these statement constructs work well for testing a limited number of conditions, they quickly become unwieldy when dealing with larger numbers of possible conditions. To simplify such situations, Swift has inherited the *switch* statement from the C programming language. Those familiar with the switch statement from other programming languages should be aware, however, that the Swift switch statement has some key differences from other implementations. In this chapter, we will explore the Swift implementation of the *switch* statement in detail.

8.1 Why Use a switch Statement?

For a small number of logical evaluations of a value the *if… else if…* construct is perfectly adequate. Unfortunately, any more than two or three possible scenarios can quickly make such a construct both time-consuming to write and difficult to read. For such situations, the *switch* statement provides an excellent alternative.

8.2 Using the switch Statement Syntax

The syntax for a basic Swift *switch* statement implementation can be outlined as follows:

```
switch expression
{
    case match1:
        statements

    case match2:
        statements

    case match3, match4:
        statements

    default:
        statements
}
```

In the above syntax outline, *expression* represents either a value, or an expression that returns a value. This is the value against which the *switch* operates.

For each possible match a *case* statement is provided, followed by a *match* value. Each potential match must be of the same type as the governing expression. Following on from the *case* line are the Swift statements that are to be executed in the event of the value matching the case condition.

Finally, the *default* section of the construct defines what should happen if none of the case statements present a match to the *expression*.

8.3 A Swift switch Statement Example

With the above information in mind, we may now construct a simple *switch* statement:

```
let value = 4

switch (value)
{
    case 0:
      print("zero")

    case 1:
      print("one")

    case 2:
      print("two")

    case 3:
      print("three")

    case 4:
      print("four")

    case 5:
      print("five")

    default:
      print("Integer out of range")
}
```

8.4 Combining case Statements

In the above example, each case had its own set of statements to execute. Sometimes a number of different matches may require the same code to be executed. In this case, it is possible to group case matches together with a common set of statements to be executed when a match for any of the cases is found. For example, we can modify the switch construct in our example so that the same code is executed regardless of whether the value is 0, 1 or 2:

```
let value = 1

switch (value)
{
    case 0, 1, 2:
      print("zero, one or two")

    case 3:
      print("three")

    case 4:
      print("four")

    case 5:
```

```
        print("five")

    default:
        print("Integer out of range")
}
```

8.5 Range Matching in a switch Statement

The case statements within a switch construct may also be used to implement range matching. The following switch statement, for example, checks a temperature value for matches within three number ranges:

```
let temperature = 83

switch (temperature)
{
        case 0...49:
            print("Cold")

        case 50...79:
            print("Warm")

        case 80...110:
            print("Hot")

        default:
            print("Temperature out of range")
}
```

8.6 Using the where statement

The *where* statement may be used within a switch case match to add additional criteria required for a positive match. The following switch statement, for example, checks not only for the range in which a value falls, but also whether the number is odd or even:

```
let temperature = 54

switch (temperature)
{
        case 0...49 where temperature % 2 == 0:
            print("Cold and even")

        case 50...79 where temperature % 2 == 0:
            print("Warm and even")

        case 80...110 where temperature % 2 == 0:
            print("Hot and even")

        default:
            print("Temperature out of range or odd")
}
```

8.7 Fallthrough

Those familiar with switch statements in other languages such as C and Objective-C will notice that it is no longer necessary to include a *break* statement after each case declaration. Unlike other languages, Swift automatically breaks out of the statement when a matching case condition is met. The fallthrough effect of other switch implementations (whereby the execution path continues through the remaining case statements) can be emulated using the *fallthrough* statement:

```
let temperature = 10

switch (temperature)
{
     case 0...49 where temperature % 2 == 0:
       print("Cold and even")
       fallthrough

     case 50...79 where temperature % 2 == 0:
       print("Warm and even")
       fallthrough

     case 80...110 where temperature % 2 == 0:
       print("Hot and even")
       fallthrough

     default:
       print("Temperature out of range or odd")
}
```

Although *break* is less commonly used in Swift switch statements, it is useful when no action needs to be taken for the default case. For example:

```
.
.
.
default:
     break
}
```

8.8 Take the Knowledge Test

Click the link below or scan the QR code to test your knowledge and understanding of the Swift switch statement:

https://www.answertopia.com/rr94

8.9 Summary

While the *if.. else..* construct serves as a good decision-making option for small numbers of possible outcomes, this approach can become unwieldy in more complex situations. As an alternative method for implementing flow control logic in Swift when many possible outcomes exist as the result of an evaluation, the *switch* statement invariably makes a more suitable option. As outlined in this chapter, however, developers familiar with switch implementations from other programming languages should be aware of some subtle differences in the way that the Swift switch statement works.

9. Swift Functions, Methods, and Closures

Swift functions, methods and closures are a vital part of writing well-structured and efficient code and provide a way to organize programs while avoiding code repetition. This chapter will look at how functions, methods, and closures are declared and used within Swift.

9.1 What is a Function?

A function is a named block of code that can be called upon to perform a specific task. It can be provided data on which to perform the task and is capable of returning results to the code that called it. For example, if a particular arithmetic calculation needs to be performed in a Swift program, the code to perform the arithmetic can be placed in a function. The function can be programmed to accept the values on which the arithmetic is to be performed (referred to as *parameters*) and to return the result of the calculation. At any point in the program code where the calculation is required the function is simply called, parameter values passed through as *arguments* and the result returned.

The terms *parameter* and *argument* are often used interchangeably when discussing functions. There is, however, a subtle difference. The values that a function is able to accept when it is called are referred to as *parameters*. At the point that the function is actually called and passed those values, however, they are referred to as *arguments*.

9.2 What is a Method?

A method is essentially a function that is associated with a particular class, structure, or enumeration. If, for example, you declare a function within a Swift class (a topic covered in detail in the chapter entitled ""), it is considered to be a method. Although the remainder of this chapter refers to functions, the same rules and behavior apply equally to methods unless otherwise stated.

9.3 How to Declare a Swift Function

A Swift function is declared using the following syntax:

```
func <function name> (<para name>: <para type>,
                  <para name>: <para type>, ... ) -> <return type> {
    // Function code
}
```

This combination of function name, parameters and return type are referred to as the *function signature*. Explanations of the various fields of the function declaration are as follows:

- **func** – The prefix keyword used to notify the Swift compiler that this is a function.

- **<function name>** - The name assigned to the function. This is the name by which the function will be referenced when it is called from within the application code.

- **<para name>** - The name by which the parameter is to be referenced in the function code.

- **<para type>** - The type of the corresponding parameter.

- **<return type>** - The data type of the result returned by the function. If the function does not return a result then no return type is specified.

- **Function code** - The code of the function that does the work.

As an example, the following function takes no parameters, returns no result and simply displays a message:

```
func sayHello() {
    print("Hello")
}
```

The following sample function, on the other hand, takes an integer and a string as parameters and returns a string result:

```
func buildMessageFor(name: String, count: Int) -> String {
        return("\(name), you are customer number \(count)")
}
```

9.4 Implicit Returns from Single Expressions

In the previous example, the *return* statement was used to return the string value from within the *buildMessageFor()* function. It is worth noting that if a function contains a single expression (as was the case in this example), the return statement may be omitted. The *buildMessageFor()* method could, therefore, be rewritten as follows:

```
func buildMessageFor(name: String, count: Int) -> String {
        "\(name), you are customer number \(count)"
}
```

The return statement can only be omitted if the function contains a single expression. The following code, for example, will fail to compile since the function contains two expressions requiring the use of the return statement:

```
func buildMessageFor(name: String, count: Int) -> String {
        let uppername = name.uppercased()
        "\(uppername), you are customer number \(count)" // Invalid expression
}
```

9.5 Calling a Swift Function

Once declared, functions are called using the following syntax:

```
<function name> (<arg1>, <arg2>, ... )
```

Each argument passed through to a function must match the parameters the function is configured to accept. For example, to call a function named *sayHello* that takes no parameters and returns no value, we would write the following code:

```
sayHello()
```

9.6 Handling Return Values

To call a function named *buildMessageFor* that takes two parameters and returns a result, on the other hand, we might write the following code:

```
let message = buildMessageFor(name: "John", count: 100)
```

In the above example, we have created a new variable called *message* and then used the assignment operator (=) to store the result returned by the function.

When developing in Swift, situations may arise where the result returned by a method or function call is not used. When this is the case, the return value may be discarded by assigning it to '_'. For example:

```
_ = buildMessageFor(name: "John", count: 100)
```

9.7 Local and External Parameter Names

When the preceding example functions were declared, they were configured with parameters that were assigned names which, in turn, could be referenced within the body of the function code. When declared in this way, these names are referred to as *local parameter names*.

In addition to local names, function parameters may also have *external parameter names*. These are the names by which the parameter is referenced when the function is called. By default, function parameters are assigned the same local and external parameter names. Consider, for example, the previous call to the *buildMessageFor* method:

```
let message = buildMessageFor(name: "John", count: 100)
```

As declared, the function uses "name" and "count" as both the local and external parameter names.

The default external parameter names assigned to parameters may be removed by preceding the local parameter names with an underscore (_) character as follows:

```
func buildMessageFor(_ name: String, _ count: Int) -> String {
        return("\(name), you are customer number \(count)")
}
```

With this change implemented, the function may now be called as follows:

```
let message = buildMessageFor("John", 100)
```

Alternatively, external parameter names can be added simply by declaring the external parameter name before the local parameter name within the function declaration. In the following code, for example, the external names of the first and second parameters have been set to "username" and "usercount" respectively:

```
func buildMessageFor(username name: String, usercount count: Int)
                                                -> String {
        return("\(name), you are customer number \(count)")
}
```

When declared in this way, the external parameter name must be referenced when calling the function:

```
let message = buildMessageFor(username: "John", usercount: 100)
```

Regardless of the fact that the external names are used to pass the arguments through when calling the function, the local names are still used to reference the parameters within the body of the function. It is important to also note that when calling a function using external parameter names for the arguments, those arguments must still be placed in the same order as that used when the function was declared.

9.8 Declaring Default Function Parameters

Swift provides the ability to designate a default parameter value to be used in the event that the value is not provided as an argument when the function is called. This simply involves assigning the default value to the parameter when the function is declared. Swift also provides a default external name based on the local parameter name for defaulted parameters (unless one is already provided) which must then be used when calling the function.

To see default parameters in action the *buildMessageFor* function will be modified so that the string "Customer" is used as a default in the event that a customer name is not passed through as an argument:

```
func buildMessageFor(_ name: String = "Customer", count: Int ) -> String
```

```
{
    return ("\(name), you are customer number \(count)")
}
```

The function can now be called without passing through a name argument:

```
let message = buildMessageFor(count: 100)
print(message)
```

When executed, the above function call will generate output to the console panel which reads:

```
Customer, you are customer number 100
```

9.9 Returning Multiple Results from a Function

A function can return multiple result values by wrapping those results in a tuple. The following function takes as a parameter a measurement value in inches. The function converts this value into yards, centimeters and meters, returning all three results within a single tuple instance:

```
func sizeConverter(_ length: Float) -> (yards: Float, centimeters: Float,
                                        meters: Float) {

    let yards = length * 0.0277778
    let centimeters = length * 2.54
    let meters = length * 0.0254

    return (yards, centimeters, meters)
}
```

The return type for the function indicates that the function returns a tuple containing three values named yards, centimeters and meters respectively, all of which are of type Float:

```
-> (yards: Float, centimeters: Float, meters: Float)
```

Having performed the conversion, the function simply constructs the tuple instance and returns it.

Usage of this function might read as follows:

```
let lengthTuple = sizeConverter(20)

print(lengthTuple.yards)
print(lengthTuple.centimeters)
print(lengthTuple.meters)
```

9.10 Variable Numbers of Function Parameters

It is not always possible to know in advance the number of parameters a function will need to accept when it is called within application code. Swift handles this possibility through the use of *variadic parameters*. Variadic parameters are declared using three periods (…) to indicate that the function accepts zero or more parameters of a specified data type. Within the body of the function, the parameters are made available in the form of an array object. The following function, for example, takes as parameters a variable number of String values and then outputs them to the console panel:

```
func displayStrings(_ strings: String...)
{
    for string in strings {
        print(string)
```

```
        }
}

displayStrings("one", "two", "three", "four")
```

9.11 Parameters as Variables

All parameters accepted by a function are treated as constants by default. This prevents changes being made to those parameter values within the function code. If changes to parameters need to be made within the function body, therefore, *shadow copies* of those parameters must be created. The following function, for example, is passed length and width parameters in inches, creates shadow variables of the two values and converts those parameters to centimeters before calculating and returning the area value:

```
func calcuateArea(length: Float, width: Float) -> Float {

    var length = length
    var width = width

    length = length * 2.54
    width = width * 2.54
    return length * width
}


print(calcuateArea(length: 10, width: 20))
```

9.12 Working with In-Out Parameters

When a variable is passed through as a parameter to a function, we now know that the parameter is treated as a constant within the body of that function. We also know that if we want to make changes to a parameter value we have to create a shadow copy as outlined in the above section. Since this is a copy, any changes made to the variable are not, by default, reflected in the original variable. Consider, for example, the following code:

```
var myValue = 10

func doubleValue ( _ value: Int) -> Int {
    var value = value
    value += value
    return(value)
}

print("Before function call myValue = \(myValue)")

print("doubleValue call returns \(doubleValue(myValue))")

print("After function call myValue = \(myValue)")
```

The code begins by declaring a variable named *myValue* initialized with a value of 10. A new function is then declared which accepts a single integer parameter. Within the body of the function, a shadow copy of the value is created, doubled and returned.

The remaining lines of code display the value of the *myValue* variable before and after the function call is made. When executed, the following output will appear in the console:

```
Before function call myValue = 10
doubleValue call returns 20
After function call myValue = 10
```

Clearly, the function has made no change to the original myValue variable. This is to be expected since the mathematical operation was performed on a copy of the variable, not the *myValue* variable itself.

In order to make any changes made to a parameter persist after the function has returned, the parameter must be declared as an *in-out parameter* within the function declaration. To see this in action, modify the *doubleValue* function to include the *inout* keyword, and remove the creation of the shadow copy as follows:

```
func doubleValue ( _ value: inout Int) -> Int {
    var value = value
    value += value
    return (value)
}
```

Finally, when calling the function, the inout parameter must now be prefixed with an & modifier:

```
print ("doubleValue call returned \(doubleValue(&myValue))")
```

Having made these changes, a test run of the code should now generate output clearly indicating that the function modified the value assigned to the original *myValue* variable:

```
Before function call myValue = 10
doubleValue call returns 20
After function call myValue = 20
```

9.13 Functions as Parameters

An interesting feature of functions within Swift is that they can be treated as data types. It is perfectly valid, for example, to assign a function to a constant or variable, as illustrated in the declaration below:

```
func inchesToFeet ( _ inches: Float) -> Float {
    return inches * 0.0833333
}


let toFeet = inchesToFeet
```

The above code declares a new function named *inchesToFeet* and subsequently assigns that function to a constant named *toFeet*. Having made this assignment, a call to the function may be made using the constant name instead of the original function name:

```
let result = toFeet(10)
```

On the surface this does not seem to be a particularly compelling feature. Since we could already call the function without assigning it to a constant or variable data type it does not seem that much has been gained.

The possibilities that this feature offers become more apparent when we consider that a function assigned to a constant or variable now has the capabilities of many other data types. In particular, a function can now be passed through as an argument to another function, or even returned as a result from a function.

Before we look at what is, essentially, the ability to plug one function into another, it is first necessary to explore the concept of function data types. The data type of a function is dictated by a combination of the parameters it accepts and the type of result it returns. In the above example, since the function accepts a floating-point parameter and returns a floating-point result, the function's data type conforms to the following:

```
(Float) -> Float
```

A function that accepts an Int and a Double as parameters and returns a String result, on the other hand, would have the following data type:

```
(Int, Double) -> String
```

In order to accept a function as a parameter, the receiving function simply declares the data type of the function it is able to accept.

For the purposes of an example, we will begin by declaring two unit conversion functions and assigning them to constants:

```
func inchesToFeet ( _ inches: Float) -> Float {

    return inches * 0.0833333

}

func inchesToYards ( _ inches: Float) -> Float {

    return inches * 0.0277778

}

let toFeet = inchesToFeet
let toYards = inchesToYards
```

The example now needs an additional function, the purpose of which is to perform a unit conversion and print the result in the console panel. This function needs to be as general purpose as possible, capable of performing a variety of different measurement unit conversions. In order to demonstrate functions as parameters, this new function will take as a parameter a function type that matches both the inchesToFeet and inchesToYards function data type together with a value to be converted. Since the data type of these functions is equivalent to (Float) -> Float, our general-purpose function can be written as follows:

```
func outputConversion ( _ converterFunc: (Float) -> Float, value: Float) {

    let result = converterFunc(value)

    print("Result of conversion is \(result)")

}
```

When the outputConversion function is called, it will need to be passed a function matching the declared data type. That function will be called to perform the conversion and the result displayed in the console panel. This means that the same function can be called to convert inches to both feet and yards, simply by "plugging in" the appropriate converter function as a parameter. For example:

```
outputConversion(toYards, value: 10) // Convert to Yards
outputConversion(toFeet, value: 10) // Convert to Feet
```

Functions can also be returned as a data type simply by declaring the type of the function as the return type. The following function is configured to return either our toFeet or toYards function type (in other words a function which accepts and returns a Float value) based on the value of a Boolean parameter:

```
func decideFunction ( _ feet: Bool) -> (Float) -> Float
{
    if feet {
        return toFeet
```

```
    } else {
        return toYards
    }
}
```

9.14 Closure Expressions

Having covered the basics of functions in Swift it is now time to look at the concept of *closures* and *closure expressions*. Although these terms are often used interchangeably there are some key differences.

Closure expressions are self-contained blocks of code. The following code, for example, declares a closure expression and assigns it to a constant named sayHello and then calls the function via the constant reference:

```
let sayHello = { print("Hello") }
sayHello()
```

Closure expressions may also be configured to accept parameters and return results. The syntax for this is as follows:

```
{(<para name>: <para type>, <para name> <para type>, ... ) ->
                                        <return type> in
        // Closure expression code here
}
```

The following closure expression, for example, accepts two integer parameters and returns an integer result:

```
let multiply = {(_ val1: Int, _ val2: Int) -> Int in
    return val1 * val2
}
let result = multiply(10, 20)
```

Note that the syntax is similar to that used for declaring Swift functions with the exception that the closure expression does not have a name, the parameters and return type are included in the braces and the *in* keyword is used to indicate the start of the closure expression code. Functions are, in fact, just named closure expressions.

Before the introduction of structured concurrency in Swift 5.5 (a topic covered in detail in the chapter entitled "*An Overview of Swift Structured Concurrency*"), closure expressions were often (and still are) used when declaring completion handlers for asynchronous method calls. In other words, when developing iOS applications, it will often be necessary to make calls to the operating system where the requested task is performed in the background allowing the application to continue with other tasks. Typically, in such a scenario, the system will notify the application of the completion of the task and return any results by calling the completion handler that was declared when the method was called. Frequently the code for the completion handler will be implemented in the form of a closure expression. Consider the following code example:

```
eventstore.requestAccess(to: .reminder, completion: {(granted: Bool,
                    error: Error?) -> Void in
    if !granted {
        print(error!.localizedDescription)
    }
})
```

When the tasks performed by the *requestAccess(to:)* method call are complete it will execute the closure expression declared as the *completion:* parameter. The completion handler is required by the method to accept a Boolean value and an Error object as parameters and return no results, hence the following declaration:

```
{(granted: Bool, error: Error?) -> Void in
```

In actual fact, the Swift compiler already knows about the parameter and return value requirements for the completion handler for this method call and is able to infer this information without it being declared in the closure expression. This allows a simpler version of the closure expression declaration to be written:

```
eventstore.requestAccess(to: .reminder, completion: { (granted, error) in
    if !granted {
            print(error!.localizedDescription)
    }
})
```

9.15 Shorthand Argument Names

A useful technique for simplifying closures involves using *shorthand argument names*. This allows the parameter names and "in" keyword to be omitted from the declaration and the arguments to be referenced as $0, $1, $2 etc.

Consider, for example, a closure expression designed to concatenate two strings:

```
let join = { (string1: String, string2: String) -> String in
    string1 + string2
}
```

Using shorthand argument names, this declaration can be simplified as follows:

```
let join: (String, String) -> String = {
    $0 + $1
}
```

Note that the type declaration (*(String, String) -> String*) has been moved to the left of the assignment operator since the closure expression no longer defines the argument or return types.

9.16 Closures in Swift

A *closure* in computer science terminology generally refers to the combination of a self-contained block of code (for example a function or closure expression) and one or more variables that exist in the context surrounding that code block. Consider, for example the following Swift function:

```
func functionA() -> () -> Int {

    var counter = 0

    func functionB() -> Int {
        return counter + 10
    }
    return functionB
}


let myClosure = functionA()
let result = myClosure()
```

In the above code, *functionA* returns a function named *functionB*. In actual fact functionA is returning a closure since functionB relies on the *counter* variable which is declared outside the functionB's local scope. In other words, functionB is said to have *captured* or *closed over* (hence the term closure) the counter variable and, as such, is considered a closure in the traditional computer science definition of the word.

To a large extent, and particularly as it relates to Swift, the terms *closure* and *closure expression* have started to be used interchangeably. The key point to remember, however, is that both are supported in Swift.

9.17 Take the Knowledge Test

Click the link below or scan the QR code to test your knowledge and understanding of the Swift functions, methods, and closures:

https://www.answertopia.com/uc2w

9.18 Summary

Functions, closures and closure expressions are self-contained blocks of code that can be called upon to perform a specific task, and provide a mechanism for structuring code and promoting reuse. This chapter has introduced the concepts of functions and closures in terms of declaration and implementation.

10. The Basics of Swift Object-Oriented Programming

Swift provides extensive support for developing object-oriented applications. The subject area of object-oriented programming is, however, large. It is not an exaggeration to state that entire books have been dedicated to the subject. As such, a detailed overview of object-oriented software development is beyond the scope of this book. Instead, we will introduce the basic concepts involved in object-oriented programming and then move on to explain the concept as it relates to Swift application development. Once again, while we strive to provide the basic information you need in this chapter, we recommend reading a copy of Apple's *The Swift Programming Language* book for more extensive coverage of this subject area.

10.1 What is an Instance?

Objects (also referred to as class *instances*) are self-contained modules of functionality that can be easily used and re-used as the building blocks for a software application.

Instances consist of data variables (called *properties*) and functions (called *methods*) that can be accessed and called on the instance to perform tasks and are collectively referred to as *class members*.

10.2 What is a Class?

Much as a blueprint or architect's drawing defines what an item or a building will look like once it has been constructed, a class defines what an instance will look like when it is created. It defines, for example, what the methods will do and what the properties will be.

10.3 Declaring a Swift Class

Before an instance can be created, we first need to define the class 'blueprint' for the instance. In this chapter we will create a bank account class to demonstrate the basic concepts of Swift object-oriented programming.

In declaring a new Swift class we specify an optional *parent class* from which the new class is derived and also define the properties and methods that the class will contain. The basic syntax for a new class is as follows:

```
class NewClassName: ParentClass {
    // Properties
    // Instance Methods
    // Type methods
}
```

The *Properties* section of the declaration defines the variables and constants that are to be contained within the class. These are declared in the same way that any other variable or constant would be declared in Swift.

The *Instance methods* and *Type methods* sections define the methods that are available to be called on the class and instances of the class. These are essentially functions specific to the class that perform a particular operation when called upon and will be described in greater detail later in this chapter.

To create an example outline for our BankAccount class, we would use the following:

```
class BankAccount {
```

```
}
```

Now that we have the outline syntax for our class, the next step is to add some instance properties to it.

When naming classes, note that the convention is for the first character of each word to be declared in uppercase (a concept referred to as UpperCamelCase). This contrasts with property and function names where lower case is used for the first character (referred to as lowerCamelCase).

10.4 Adding Instance Properties to a Class

A key goal of object-oriented programming is a concept referred to as *data encapsulation*. The idea behind data encapsulation is that data should be stored within classes and accessed only through methods defined in that class. Data encapsulated in a class are referred to as *properties* or *instance variables*.

Instances of our BankAccount class will be required to store some data, specifically a bank account number and the balance currently held within the account. Properties are declared like any other variables and constants are declared in Swift. We can, therefore, add these variables as follows:

```
class BankAccount {
    var accountBalance: Float = 0
    var accountNumber: Int = 0
}
```

Having defined our properties, we can now move on to defining the methods of the class that will allow us to work with our properties while staying true to the data encapsulation model.

10.5 Defining Methods

The methods of a class are essentially code routines that can be called upon to perform specific tasks within the context of that class.

Methods come in two different forms, *type methods* and *instance methods*. Type methods operate at the level of the class, such as creating a new instance of a class. Instance methods, on the other hand, operate only on the instances of a class (for example performing an arithmetic operation on two property variables and returning the result).

Instance methods are declared within the opening and closing braces of the class to which they belong and are declared using the standard Swift function declaration syntax.

Type methods are declared in the same way as instance methods with the exception that the declaration is preceded by the *class* keyword.

For example, the declaration of a method to display the account balance in our example might read as follows:

```
class BankAccount {

    var accountBalance: Float = 0
    var accountNumber: Int = 0

    func displayBalance()
    {
        print("Number \(accountNumber)")
        print("Current balance is \(accountBalance)")
    }
```

```
}
```

The method is an *instance method* so it is not preceded by the *class* keyword.

When designing the BankAccount class it might be useful to be able to call a type method on the class itself to identify the maximum allowable balance that can be stored by the class. This would enable an application to identify whether the BankAccount class is suitable for storing details of a new customer without having to go through the process of first creating a class instance. This method will be named *getMaxBalance* and is implemented as follows:

```
class BankAccount {

    var accountBalance: Float = 0
    var accountNumber: Int = 0

    func displayBalance()
    {
        print("Number \(accountNumber)")
        print("Current balance is \(accountBalance)")
    }

    class func getMaxBalance() -> Float {
        return 100000.00
    }
}
```

10.6 Declaring and Initializing a Class Instance

So far, all we have done is define the blueprint for our class. To do anything with this class, we need to create instances of it. The first step in this process is to declare a variable to store a reference to the instance when it is created. We do this as follows:

```
var account1: BankAccount = BankAccount()
```

When executed, an instance of our BankAccount class will have been created and will be accessible via the *account1* variable.

10.7 Initializing and De-initializing a Class Instance

A class will often need to perform some initialization tasks at the point of creation. These tasks can be implemented by placing an *init* method within the class. In the case of the BankAccount class, it would be useful to be able to initialize the account number and balance properties with values when a new class instance is created. To achieve this, the *init* method could be written in the class as follows:

```
class BankAccount {

    var accountBalance: Float = 0
    var accountNumber: Int = 0

    init(number: Int, balance: Float)
    {
        accountNumber = number
        accountBalance = balance
```

```
    }

    func displayBalance()
    {
        print("Number \(accountNumber)")
        print("Current balance is \(accountBalance)")
    }
}
```

When creating an instance of the class, it will now be necessary to provide initialization values for the account number and balance properties as follows:

```
var account1 = BankAccount(number: 12312312, balance: 400.54)
```

Conversely, any cleanup tasks that need to be performed before a class instance is destroyed by the Swift runtime system can be performed by implementing the de-initializer within the class definition:

```
class BankAccount {

    var accountBalance: Float = 0
    var accountNumber: Int = 0

    init(number: Int, balance: Float)
    {
        accountNumber = number
        accountBalance = balance
    }

    deinit {
        // Perform any necessary clean up here
    }

    func displayBalance()
    {
        print("Number \(accountNumber)")
        print("Current balance is \(accountBalance)")
    }
}
```

10.8 Calling Methods and Accessing Properties

Now is probably a good time to recap what we have done so far in this chapter. We have now created a new Swift class named *BankAccount*. Within this new class we declared some properties to contain the bank account number and current balance together with an initializer and a method to display the current balance information. In the preceding section we covered the steps necessary to create and initialize an instance of our new class. The next step is to learn how to call the instance methods and access the properties we built into our class. This is most easily achieved using *dot notation*.

Dot notation involves accessing an instance variable, or calling an instance method by specifying a class instance followed by a dot followed in turn by the name of the property or method:

```
classInstance.propertyName
```

```
classInstance.instanceMethod()
```

For example, to get the current value of our *accountBalance* instance variable:

```
var balance1 = account1.accountBalance
```

Dot notation can also be used to set values of instance properties:

```
account1.accountBalance = 6789.98
```

The same technique is used to call methods on a class instance. For example, to call the *displayBalance* method on an instance of the BankAccount class:

```
account1.displayBalance()
```

Type methods are also called using dot notation, though they must be called on the class type instead of a class instance:

```
ClassName.typeMethod()
```

For example, to call the previously declared *getMaxBalance* type method, the BankAccount class is referenced:

```
var maxAllowed = BankAccount.getMaxBalance()
```

10.9 Stored and Computed Properties

Class properties in Swift fall into two categories referred to as *stored properties* and *computed properties*. Stored properties are those values that are contained within a constant or variable. Both the account name and number properties in the BankAccount example are stored properties.

A computed property, on the other hand, is a value that is derived based on some form of calculation or logic at the point at which the property is set or retrieved. Computed properties are implemented by creating *getter* and optional corresponding *setter* methods containing the code to perform the computation. Consider, for example, that the BankAccount class might need an additional property to contain the current balance less any recent banking fees. Rather than use a stored property, it makes more sense to use a computed property that calculates this value on request. The modified BankAccount class might now read as follows:

```
class BankAccount {

    var accountBalance: Float = 0
    var accountNumber: Int = 0;
    let fees: Float = 25.00

    var balanceLessFees: Float {
        get {
            return accountBalance - fees
        }
    }

    init(number: Int, balance: Float)
    {
        accountNumber = number
        accountBalance = balance
    }
    .

    .
```

```
    .
}
```

The above code adds a getter that returns a computed property based on the current balance minus a fee amount. An optional setter could also be declared in much the same way to set the balance value less fees:

```
var balanceLessFees: Float {
    get {
        return accountBalance - fees
    }

    set(newBalance)
    {
        accountBalance = newBalance - fees
    }
}
```

The new setter takes as a parameter a floating-point value from which it deducts the fee value before assigning the result to the current balance property. Although these are computed properties, they are accessed in the same way as stored properties using dot-notation. The following code gets the current balance less the fees value before setting the property to a new value:

```
var balance1 = account1.balanceLessFees
account1.balanceLessFees = 12123.12
```

10.10 Lazy Stored Properties

There are several different ways in which a property can be initialized, the most basic being direct assignment as follows:

```
var myProperty = 10
```

Alternatively, a property may be assigned a value within the initializer:

```
class MyClass {
  let title: String

  init(title: String) {
    self.title = title
  }
}
```

For more complex requirements, a property may be initialized using a closure:

```
class MyClass {

    var myProperty: String = {
        var result = resourceIntensiveTask()
        result = processData(data: result)
        return result
    }()
    .
    .
}
```

Particularly in the case of a complex closure, there is the potential for the initialization to be resource intensive and time consuming. When declared in this way, the initialization will be performed every time an instance of the class is created, regardless of when (or even if) the property is actually used within the code of the app. Also, situations may arise where the value assigned to the property may not be known until a later stage in the execution process, for example after data has been retrieved from a database or user input has been obtained from the user. A far more efficient solution in such situations would be for the initialization to take place only when the property is first accessed. Fortunately, this can be achieved by declaring the property as *lazy* as follows:

```
class MyClass {

    lazy var myProperty: String = {
        var result = resourceIntensiveTask()
        result = processData(data: result)
        return result
    }()
.
.
}
```

When a property is declared as being lazy, it is only initialized when it is first accessed, allowing any resource intensive activities to be deferred until the property is needed and any initialization on which the property is dependent to be completed.

Note that lazy properties must be declared as variables (*var*).

10.11 Using self in Swift

Programmers familiar with other object-oriented programming languages may be in the habit of prefixing references to properties and methods with *self* to indicate that the method or property belongs to the current class instance. The Swift programming language also provides the *self* property type for this purpose and it is, therefore, perfectly valid to write code that reads as follows:

```
class MyClass {
    var myNumber = 1

    func addTen() {
        self.myNumber += 10
    }
}
```

In this context, the *self* prefix indicates to the compiler that the code refers to a property named *myNumber* which belongs to the MyClass class instance. When programming in Swift, however, it is no longer necessary to use self in most situations since this is now assumed to be the default for references to properties and methods. To quote Apple's Swift Programming Language guide, "in practice you don't need to write *self* in your code very often". The function from the above example, therefore, can also be written as follows with the *self* reference omitted:

```
func addTen() {
    myNumber += 10
}
```

In most cases, use of self is optional in Swift. That being said, one situation where it is still necessary to use *self* is when referencing a property or method from within a closure expression. The use of self, for example, is mandatory in the following closure expression:

```
document?.openWithCompletionHandler({ (success: Bool) -> Void in
    if success {
        self.ubiquityURL = resultURL
    }
})
```

It is also necessary to use self to resolve ambiguity such as when a function parameter has the same name as a class property. In the following code, for example, the first print statement will output the value passed through to the function via the myNumber parameter while the second print statement outputs the number assigned to the myNumber class property (in this case 10):

```
class MyClass {

    var myNumber = 10 // class property

    func addTen(myNumber: Int) {
        print(myNumber) // Output the function parameter value
        print(self.myNumber) // Output the class property value
    }

}
```

Whether or not to use self in most other situations is largely a matter of programmer preference. Those who prefer to use self when referencing properties and methods can continue to do so in Swift. Code that is written without use of the *self* property type (where doing so is not mandatory) is, however, just as valid when programming in Swift.

10.12 Understanding Swift Protocols

By default, there are no specific rules to which a Swift class must conform as long as the class is syntactically correct. In some situations, however, a class will need to meet certain criteria in order to work with other classes. This is particularly common when writing classes that need to work with the various frameworks that comprise the iOS SDK. A set of rules that define the minimum requirements which a class must meet is referred to as a *Protocol*. A protocol is declared using the *protocol* keyword and simply defines the methods and properties that a class must contain in order to be in conformance. When a class *adopts* a protocol, but does not meet all of the protocol requirements, errors will be reported stating that the class fails to conform to the protocol.

Consider the following protocol declaration. Any classes that adopt this protocol must include both a readable String value called *name* and a method named *buildMessage()* which accepts no parameters and returns a String value:

```
protocol MessageBuilder {

    var name: String { get }
    func buildMessage() -> String

}
```

Below, a class has been declared which adopts the MessageBuilder protocol:

```
class MyClass: MessageBuilder {

}
```

Unfortunately, as currently implemented, MyClass will generate a compilation error because it contains neither the *name* variable nor the *buildMessage()* method as required by the protocol it has adopted. To conform to the protocol, the class would need to meet both requirements, for example:

```
class MyClass: MessageBuilder {

    var name: String

    init(name: String) {
      self.name = name
    }

    func buildMessage() -> String {
        "Hello " + name
    }
}
```

10.13 Opaque Return Types

Now that protocols have been explained, it is a good time to introduce the concept of opaque return types. As we have seen in previous chapters, if a function returns a result, the type of that result must be included in the function declaration. The following function, for example, is configured to return an Int result:

```
func doubleFunc1 (value: Int) -> Int {
    return value * 2
}
```

Instead of specifying a specific return type (also referred to as a *concrete type*), opaque return types allow a function to return any type as long as it conforms to a specified protocol. Opaque return types are declared by preceding the protocol name with the *some* keyword. The following changes to the *doubleFunc1()* function, for example, declare that a result will be returned of any type that conforms to the Equatable protocol:

```
func doubleFunc1(value: Int) -> some Equatable {
    value * 2
}
```

To conform to the Equatable protocol, which is a standard protocol provided with Swift, a type must allow the underlying values to be compared for equality. Opaque return types can, however, be used for any protocol, including those you create yourself.

Given that both the Int and String concrete types are in conformance with the Equatable protocol, it is possible to also create a function that returns a String result:

```
func doubleFunc2(value: String) -> some Equatable {
    value + value
}
```

Although these two methods return entirely different concrete types, the only thing known about these types is that they conform to the Equatable protocol. We therefore know the capabilities of the type, but not the actual type.

In fact, we only know the concrete type returned in these examples because we have access to the source code of the functions. If these functions resided in a library or API framework for which the source is not available to us, we would not know the exact type being returned. This is intentional and designed to hide the underlying return type used within public APIs. By masking the concrete return type, programmers will not come to rely on a function returning a specific concrete type or risk accessing internal objects which were not intended to be accessed. This also has the benefit that the developer of the API can make changes to the underlying implementation (including returning a different protocol compliant type) without having to worry about breaking dependencies in any code that uses the API.

This raises the question of what happens when an incorrect assumption is made when working with the opaque return type. Consider, for example, that the assumption could be made that the results from the *doubleFunc1()* and *doubleFunc2()* functions can be compared for equality:

```
let intOne = doubleFunc1(value: 10)
let stringOne = doubleFunc2(value: "Hello")


if (intOne == stringOne) {
    print("They match")
}
```

Working on the premise that we do not have access to the source code for these two functions there is no way to know whether the above code is valid. Fortunately, although we, as programmers, have no way of knowing the concrete type returned by the functions, the Swift compiler has access to this hidden information. The above code will, therefore, generate the following syntax error long before we get to the point of trying to execute invalid code:

```
Binary operator '==' cannot be applied to operands of type 'some
 Equatable' (result of 'doubleFunc1(value:)') and 'some Equatable'
(result of 'doubleFunc2(value:)')
```

Opaque return types are a fundamental foundation of the implementation of the SwiftUI APIs and are used widely when developing apps in SwiftUI (the *some* keyword will appear frequently in SwiftUI View declarations). SwiftUI advocates the creation of apps by composing together small, reusable building blocks and refactoring large view declarations into collections of small, lightweight subviews. Each of these building blocks will typically conform to the View protocol. By declaring these building blocks as returning opaque types that conform to the View protocol, these building blocks become remarkably flexible and interchangeable, resulting in code that is cleaner and easier to reuse and maintain.

10.14 Take the Knowledge Test

Click the link below or scan the QR code to test your knowledge and understanding of the Swift object-oriented programming:

https://www.answertopia.com/x94c

10.15 Summary

Object-oriented programming languages such as Swift encourage the creation of classes to promote code reuse and the encapsulation of data within class instances. This chapter has covered the basic concepts of classes and instances within Swift together with an overview of stored and computed properties and both instance and type methods. The chapter also introduced the concept of protocols which serve as templates to which classes must conform and explained how they form the basis of opaque return types.

Chapter 11

11. An Introduction to Swift Subclassing and Extensions

In *"The Basics of Swift Object-Oriented Programming"* we covered the basic concepts of object-oriented programming and worked through an example of creating and working with a new class using Swift. In that example, our new class was not derived from any base class and, as such, did not inherit any traits from a parent or super class. In this chapter, we will introduce the concepts of subclassing, inheritance and extensions in Swift.

11.1 Inheritance, Classes, and Subclasses

The concept of inheritance brings something of a real-world view to programming. It allows a class to be defined that has a certain set of characteristics (such as methods and properties) and then other classes to be created which are derived from that class. The derived class inherits all of the features of the parent class and typically then adds some features of its own.

By deriving classes, we create what is often referred to as a *class hierarchy*. The class at the top of the hierarchy is known as the *base class* or *root class* and the derived classes as *subclasses* or *child classes*. Any number of subclasses may be derived from a class. The class from which a subclass is derived is called the *parent class* or *super class*.

Classes need not only be derived from a root class. For example, a subclass can also inherit from another subclass with the potential to create large and complex class hierarchies.

In Swift, a subclass can only be derived from a single direct parent class. This is a concept referred to as *single inheritance*.

11.2 A Swift Inheritance Example

As with most programming concepts, the subject of inheritance in Swift is perhaps best illustrated with an example. In *"The Basics of Swift Object-Oriented Programming"* we created a class named *BankAccount* designed to hold a bank account number and corresponding current balance. The BankAccount class contained both properties and instance methods. A simplified declaration for this class is reproduced below:

```
class BankAccount {

    var accountBalance: Float
    var accountNumber: Int

    init(number: Int, balance: Float)
    {
        accountNumber = number
        accountBalance = balance
    }

    func displayBalance()
    {
        print("Number \(accountNumber)")
```

```
        print("Current balance is \(accountBalance)")
    }
}
```

Though this is a somewhat rudimentary class, it does everything necessary if all you need it to do is store an account number and account balance. Suppose, however, that in addition to the BankAccount class you also needed a class to be used for savings accounts. A savings account will still need to hold an account number and a current balance and methods will still be needed to access that data. One option would be to create an entirely new class, one that duplicates all of the functionality of the BankAccount class together with the new features required by a savings account. A more efficient approach, however, would be to create a new class that is a *subclass* of the BankAccount class. The new class will then inherit all the features of the BankAccount class but can then be extended to add the additional functionality required by a savings account.

To create a subclass of BankAccount that we will call SavingsAccount, we simply declare the new class, this time specifying BankAccount as the parent class:

```
class SavingsAccount: BankAccount {


}
```

Note that although we have yet to add any instance variables or methods, the class has actually inherited all the methods and properties of the parent BankAccount class. We could, therefore, create an instance of the SavingsAccount class and set variables and call methods in exactly the same way we did with the BankAccount class in previous examples. That said, we haven't really achieved anything unless we take steps to extend the class.

11.3 Extending the Functionality of a Subclass

So far, we have created a subclass containing all the functionality of the parent class. For this exercise to make sense, however, we now need to extend the subclass so that it has the features we need to make it useful for storing savings account information. To do this, we simply add the properties and methods that provide the new functionality, just as we would for any other class we might wish to create:

```
class SavingsAccount: BankAccount {

    var interestRate: Float = 0.0

    func calculateInterest() -> Float
    {
        return interestRate * accountBalance
    }
}
```

11.4 Overriding Inherited Methods

When using inheritance, it is not unusual to find a method in the parent class that almost does what you need, but requires modification to provide the precise functionality you require. That being said, it is also possible you'll inherit a method with a name that describes exactly what you want to do, but it actually does not come close to doing what you need. One option in this scenario would be to ignore the inherited method and write a new method with an entirely new name. A better option is to *override* the inherited method and write a new version of it in the subclass.

Before proceeding with an example, there are two rules that must be obeyed when overriding a method. First, the overriding method in the subclass must take exactly the same number and type of parameters as the overridden method in the parent class. Second, the new method must have the same return type as the parent method.

In our BankAccount class we have a method named *displayBalance* that displays the bank account number and current balance held by an instance of the class. In our SavingsAccount subclass we might also want to output the current interest rate assigned to the account. To achieve this, we simply declare a new version of the *displayBalance* method in our SavingsAccount subclass, prefixed with the *override* keyword:

```
class SavingsAccount: BankAccount {

    var interestRate: Float

    func calculateInterest() -> Float
    {
        return interestRate * accountBalance
    }

    override func displayBalance()
    {
        print("Number \(accountNumber)")
        print("Current balance is \(accountBalance)")
        print("Prevailing interest rate is \(interestRate)")
    }
}
```

It is also possible to make a call to the overridden method in the super class from within a subclass. The *displayBalance* method of the super class could, for example, be called to display the account number and balance, before the interest rate is displayed, thereby eliminating further code duplication:

```
override func displayBalance()
{
    super.displayBalance()
    print("Prevailing interest rate is \(interestRate)")
}
```

11.5 Initializing the Subclass

As the SavingsAccount class currently stands, it inherits the init initializer method from the parent BankAccount class which was implemented as follows:

```
init(number: Int, balance: Float)
{
    accountNumber = number
    accountBalance = balance
}
```

Clearly this method takes the necessary steps to initialize both the account number and balance properties of the class. The SavingsAccount class, however, contains an additional property in the form of the interest rate variable. The SavingsAccount class, therefore, needs its own initializer to ensure that the interestRate property is initialized when instances of the class are created. This method can perform this task and then make a call to the *init* method of the parent class to complete the initialization of the remaining variables:

```
class SavingsAccount: BankAccount {

    var interestRate: Float
```

```
    init(number: Int, balance: Float, rate: Float)
    {
        interestRate = rate
        super.init(number: number, balance: balance)
    }
.
.
.
}
```

Note that to avoid potential initialization problems, the *init* method of the superclass must always be called *after* the initialization tasks for the subclass have been completed.

11.6 Using the SavingsAccount Class

Now that we have completed work on our SavingsAccount class, the class can be used in some example code in much the same way as the parent BankAccount class:

```
let savings1 = SavingsAccount(number: 12311, balance: 600.00,
                                      rate: 0.07)

print(savings1.calculateInterest())
savings1.displayBalance()
```

11.7 Swift Class Extensions

Another way to add new functionality to a Swift class is to use an extension. Extensions can be used to add features such as methods, initializers, computed properties and subscripts to an existing class without the need to create and reference a subclass. This is particularly powerful when using extensions to add functionality to the built-in classes of the Swift language and iOS SDK frameworks.

A class is extended using the following syntax:

```
extension ClassName {
   // new features here
}
```

As an example, assume that we need to add some additional properties to the standard Double class that will return the value raised to the power 2 and 3. This functionality can be added using the following extension declaration:

```
extension Double {

    var squared: Double {
        return self * self
    }

    var cubed: Double {
        return self * self * self
    }
}
```

Having extended the Double class with two new computed properties we can now make use of the properties as we would any other properties of the Double class:

```
let myValue: Double = 3.0
print(myValue.squared)
```

When executed, the print statement will output the value of 9.0. Note that when declaring the myValue constant we were able to declare it as being of type Double and access the extension properties without the need to use a subclass. In fact, because these properties were added as an extension, rather than using a subclass, we can now access these properties directly on Double values:

```
print(3.0.squared)
print(6.0.cubed)
```

Extensions provide a quick and convenient way to extend the functionality of a class without the need to use subclasses. Subclasses, however, still have some advantages over extensions. It is not possible, for example, to override the existing functionality of a class using an extension and extensions cannot contain stored properties.

11.8 Take the Knowledge Test

Click the link below or scan the QR code to test your knowledge and understanding of the Swift subclassing and extensions:

https://www.answertopia.com/v0hb

11.9 Summary

Inheritance extends the concept of object re-use in object-oriented programming by allowing new classes to be derived from existing classes, with those new classes subsequently extended to add new functionality. When an existing class provides some, but not all, of the functionality required by the programmer, inheritance allows that class to be used as the basis for a new subclass. The new subclass will inherit all the capabilities of the parent class, but may then be extended to add the missing functionality.

Swift extensions provide a useful alternative option to adding functionality to existing classes without the need to create a subclass.

12. An Introduction to Swift Structures and Enumerations

Having covered Swift classes in the preceding chapters, this chapter will introduce the use of structures in Swift. Although at first glance structures and classes look similar, there are some important differences that need to be understood when deciding which to use. This chapter will outline how to declare and use structures, explore the differences between structures and classes and introduce the concepts of value and reference types.

12.1 An Overview of Swift Structures

As with classes, structures form the basis of object-oriented programming and provide a way to encapsulate data and functionality into re-usable instances. Structure declarations resemble classes with the exception that the *struct* keyword is used in place of the *class* keyword. The following code, for example, declares a simple structure consisting of a String variable, initializer and method:

```
struct SampleStruct {

    var name: String

    init(name: String) {
        self.name = name
    }

    func buildHelloMsg() {
        "Hello " + name
    }
}
```

Consider the above structure declaration in comparison to the equivalent class declaration:

```
class SampleClass {

    var name: String

    init(name: String) {
        self.name = name
    }

    func buildHelloMsg() {
        "Hello " + name
    }
}
```

Other than the use of the *struct* keyword instead of *class*, the two declarations are identical. Instances of each type are also created using the same syntax:

```
let myStruct = SampleStruct(name: "Mark")
let myClass = SampleClass(name: "Mark")
```

In common with classes, structures may be extended and are also able to adopt protocols and contain initializers.

Given the commonality between classes and structures, it is important to gain an understanding of how the two differ. Before exploring the most significant difference it is first necessary to understand the concepts of *value types* and *reference types*.

12.2 Value Types vs. Reference Types

While on the surface structures and classes look alike, major differences in behavior occur when structure and class instances are copied or passed as arguments to methods or functions. This occurs because structure instances are value type while class instances are reference type.

When a structure instance is copied or passed to a method, an actual copy of the instance is created, together with any data contained within the instance. This means that the copy has its own version of the data which is unconnected with the original structure instance. In effect, this means that there can be multiple copies of a structure instance within a running app, each with its own local copy of the associated data. A change to one instance has no impact on any other instances.

In contrast, when a class instance is copied or passed as an argument, the only thing duplicated or passed is a reference to the location in memory where that class instance resides. Any changes made to the instance using those references will be performed on the same instance. In other words, there is only one class instance but multiple references pointing to it. A change to the instance data using any one of those references changes the data for all other references.

To demonstrate reference and value types in action, consider the following code:

```
struct SampleStruct {

    var name: String

    init(name: String) {
        self.name = name
    }

    func buildHelloMsg() {
        "Hello " + name
    }
}


let myStruct1 = SampleStruct(name: "Mark")
print(myStruct1.name)
```

When the code executes, the name "Mark" will be displayed. Now change the code so that a copy of the myStruct1 instance is made, the name property changed and the names from each instance displayed:

```
let myStruct1 = SampleStruct(name: "Mark")
var myStruct2 = myStruct1
myStruct2.name = "David"
```

```
print(myStruct1.name)
print(myStruct2.name)
```

When executed, the output will read as follows:

```
Mark
David
```

Clearly, the change of name only applied to myStruct2 since this is an actual copy of myStruct1 containing its own copy of the data, as shown in Figure 12-1:

Figure 12-1

Contrast this with the following class example:

```
class SampleClass {

    var name: String

    init(name: String) {
        self.name = name
    }

    func buildHelloMsg() {
        "Hello " + name
    }
}

let myClass1 = SampleClass(name: "Mark")
var myClass2 = myClass1
myClass2.name = "David"

print(myClass1.name)
print(myClass2.name)
```

When this code executes, the following output will be generated:

```
David
David
```

In this case, the name property change is reflected for both myClass1 and myClass2 because both are references pointing to the same class instance, as illustrated in Figure 12-2 below:

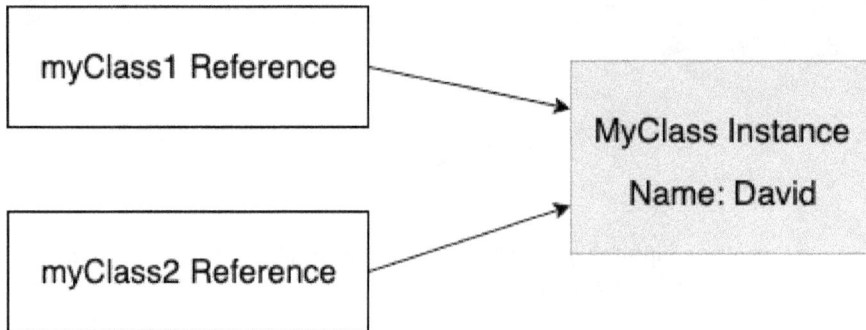

Figure 12-2

In addition to these value and reference type differences, structures do not support inheritance and sub-classing in the way that classes do. In other words, it is not possible for one structure to inherit from another structure. Unlike classes, structures also cannot contain a de-initializer (deinit) method. Finally, while it is possible to identify the type of a class instance at runtime, the same is not true of a struct.

12.3 When to Use Structures or Classes

In general, structures are recommended whenever possible because they are both more efficient than classes and safer to use in multi-threaded code. Classes should be used when inheritance is needed, only one instance of the encapsulated data is required, or extra steps need to be taken to free up resources when an instance is de-initialized.

12.4 An Overview of Enumerations

Enumerations (typically referred to as enums) are used to create custom data types consisting of pre-defined sets of values. Enums are typically used for making decisions within code such as when using switch statements. An enum might, for example be declared as follows:

```
enum Temperature {
    case hot
    case warm
    case cold
}
```

Note that in this example, none of the cases are assigned a value. An enum of this type is essentially used to reference one of a pre-defined set of states (in this case the current temperature being hot, warm or cold). Once declared, the enum may, for example, be used within a switch statement as follows:

```
func displayTempInfo(temp: Temperature) {
    switch temp {
        case .hot:
            print("It is hot.")
        case .warm:
            print("It is warm.")
        case .cold:
            print("It is cold.")
    }
}
```

It is also worth noting that because an enum has a definitive set of valid member values, the switch statement does not need to include a default case. An attempt to pass an invalid enum case through the switch will be caught by the compiler long before it has a chance to cause a runtime error.

To test out the enum, the *displayTempInfo()* function must be passed an instance of the Temperature enum with one of the following three possible states selected:

```
Temperature.hot
Temperature.warm
Temperature.cold
```

For example:

```
displayTempInfo(temp: Temperature.warm)
```

When executed, the above function call will output the following information:

```
It is warm.
```

Individual cases within an enum may also have *associated values*. Assume, for example, that the "cold" enum case needs to have associated with it a temperature value so that the app can differentiate between cold and freezing conditions. This can be defined within the enum declaration as follows:

```
enum Temperature {
    case hot
    case warm
    case cold(centigrade: Int)
}
```

This allows the switch statement to also check for the temperature for the cold case as follows:

```
func displayTempInfo(temp: Temperature) {
    switch temp {
        case .hot:
            print("It is hot")
        case .warm:
            print("It is warm")
        case.cold(let centigrade) where centigrade <= 0:
            print("Ice warning: \(centigrade) degrees.")
        case .cold:
            print("It is cold but not freezing.")
    }
}
```

When the cold enum value is passed to the function, it now does so with a temperature value included:

```
displayTempInfo(temp: Temperature.cold(centigrade: -10))
```

The output from the above function will read as follows:

```
Ice warning: -10 degrees
```

12.5 Take the Knowledge Test

Click the link below or scan the QR code to test your knowledge and understanding of the Swift structures and enumerations:

https://www.answertopia.com/h4o7

12.6 Summary

Swift structures and classes both provide a mechanism for creating instances that define properties, store values and define methods. Although the two mechanisms appear to be similar, there are significant behavioral differences when structure and class instances are either copied or passed to a method. Classes are categorized as being reference type instances while structures are value type. When a structure instance is copied or passed, an entirely new copy of the instance is created containing its own data. Class instances, on the other hand, are passed and copied by reference, with each reference pointing to the same class instance. Other features unique to classes include support for inheritance and deinitialization and the ability to identify the class type at runtime. Structures should typically be used in place of classes unless specific class features are required.

Enumerations are used to create custom types consisting of a pre-defined set of state values and are of particular use in identifying state within switch statements.

13. An Introduction to Swift Property Wrappers

Now that the topics of Swift classes and structures have been covered, this chapter will introduce a related topic in the form of property wrappers. Introduced in Swift 5.1, property wrappers provide a way to reduce the amount of duplicated code involved in writing getters, setters and computed properties in class and structure implementations.

13.1 Understanding Property Wrappers

When values are assigned or accessed via a property within a class or structure instance it is sometimes necessary to perform some form of transformation or validation on that value before it is stored or read. As outlined in the chapter entitled *"The Basics of Swift Object-Oriented Programming"*, this type of behavior can be implemented through the creation of computed properties. Frequently, patterns emerge where a computed property is common to multiple classes or structures. Prior to the introduction of Swift 5.1, the only way to share the logic of a computed property was to duplicate the code and embed it into each class or structure implementation. Not only is this inefficient, but a change in the behavior of the computation must be manually propagated across all the entities that use it.

To address this shortcoming, Swift 5.1 introduced a feature known as *property wrappers*. Property wrappers essentially allow the capabilities of computed properties to be separated from individual classes and structures and reused throughout the app code base.

13.2 A Simple Property Wrapper Example

Perhaps the best way to understand property wrappers is to study a very simple example. Imagine a structure with a String property intended to contain a city name. Such a structure might read as follows:

```
struct Address {
    var city: String
}
```

If the class was required to store the city name in uppercase, regardless of how it was entered by the user, a computed property such as the following might be added to the structure:

```
struct Address {

    private var cityname: String = ""

    var city: String {
        get { cityname }
        set { cityname = newValue.uppercased() }
    }
}
```

When a city name is assigned to the property, the setter within the computed property converts it to uppercase before storing it in the private *cityname* variable. This structure can be tested using the following code:

```
var address = Address()

address.city = "London"
print(address.city)
```

When executed, the output from the above code would read as follows:

```
LONDON
```

Clearly the computed property performs the task of converting the city name string to uppercase, but if the same behavior is needed in other structures or classes the code would need to be duplicated in those declarations. In this example this is only a small amount of code, but that won't necessarily be the case for more complex computations.

Instead of using a computed property, this logic can instead be implemented as a property wrapper. The following declaration, for example, implements a property wrapper named FixCase designed to convert a string to uppercase:

```
@propertyWrapper
struct FixCase {
    private(set) var value: String = ""

    var wrappedValue: String {
        get { value }
        set { value = newValue.uppercased() }
    }

    init(wrappedValue initialValue: String) {
        self.wrappedValue = initialValue
    }
}
```

Property wrappers are declared using the @propertyWrapper directive and are implemented in a class or structure (with structures being the preferred choice). All property wrappers must include a wrappedValue property containing the getter and setter code that changes or validates the value. An optional initializer may also be included which is passed the value being assigned. In this case, the initial value is simply assigned to the wrappedValue property where it is converted to uppercase and stored in the private variable.

Now that this property wrapper has been defined, it can be reused by applying it to other property variables wherever the same behavior is needed. To use this property wrapper, simply prefix property declarations with the @FixCase directive in any class or structure declarations where the behavior is needed, for example:

```
struct Contact {
    @FixCase var name: String
    @FixCase var city: String
    @FixCase var country: String
}

var contact = Contact(name: "John Smith", city: "London", country: "United
Kingdom")
print("\(contact.name), \(contact.city), \(contact.country)")
```

When executed, the following output will appear:

JOHN SMITH, LONDON, UNITED KINGDOM

13.3 Supporting Multiple Variables and Types

In the above example, the property wrapper accepted a single value in the form of the value to be assigned to the property being wrapped. More complex property wrappers may also be implemented that accept other values that can be used when performing the computation. These additional values are placed within parentheses after the property wrapper name. A property wrapper designed to restrict a value within a specified range might read as follows:

```
struct Demo {
    @MinMaxVal(min: 10, max: 150) var value: Int = 100
}
```

The code to implement the above MinMaxVal property wrapper could be written as follows:

```
@propertyWrapper
struct MinMaxVal {
  var value: Int
  let max: Int
  let min: Int

    init(wrappedValue: Int, min: Int, max: Int) {
    value = wrappedValue
    self.min = min
    self.max = max
  }

  var wrappedValue: Int {
    get { return value }
    set {
      if newValue > max {
       value = max
      } else if newValue < min {
       value = min
      } else {
       value = newValue
      }
    }
  }
}
```

Note that the *init()* method has been implemented to accept the min and max values in addition to the wrapped value. The wrappedValue setter checks the value and modifies it to the min or max number if it falls above or below the specified range.

The above property wrapper can be tested using the following code:

```
struct Demo {
    @MinMaxVal(min: 100, max: 200) var value: Int = 100
}
```

```
var demo = Demo()
demo.value = 150
print(demo.value)

demo.value = 250
print(demo.value)
```

When executed, the first print statement will output 150 because it falls within the acceptable range, while the second print statement will show that the wrapper restricted the value to the maximum permitted value (in this case 200).

As currently implemented, the property wrapper will only work with integer (Int) values. The wrapper would be more useful if it could be used with any variable type which can be compared with another value of the same type. Fortunately, protocol wrappers can be implemented to work with any types that conform to a specific protocol. Since the purpose of this wrapper is to perform comparisons, it makes sense to modify it to support any data types that conform to the Comparable protocol which is included with the Foundation framework. Types that conform to the Comparable protocol are able to be used in equality, greater-than and less-than comparisons. A wide range of types such as String, Int, Date, Date Interval and Character conform to this protocol.

To implement the wrapper so that it can be used with any types that conform to the Comparable protocol, the declaration needs to be modified as follows:

```
@propertyWrapper
struct MinMaxVal<V: Comparable> {
  var value: V
  let max: V
  let min: V

    init(wrappedValue: V, min: V, max: V) {
    value = wrappedValue
    self.min = min
    self.max = max
  }

  var wrappedValue: V {
    get { return value }
    set {
      if newValue > max {
        value = max
      } else if newValue < min {
        value = min
      } else {
        value = newValue
      }
    }
  }
}
```

The modified wrapper will still work with Int values as before but can now also be used with any of the other types that conform to the Comparable protocol. In the following example, a string value is evaluated to ensure that it fits alphabetically within the min and max string values:

```
struct Demo {
    @MinMaxVal(min: "Apple", max: "Orange") var value: String = ""
}

var demo = Demo()
demo.value = "Banana"
print(demo.value)
// Banana <--- Value fits within alphabetical range and is stored.

demo.value = "Pear"
print(demo.value)
// Orange <--- Value is outside of the alphabetical range so is changed to the
max value.
```

Similarly, this same wrapper will also work with Date instances, as in the following example where the value is limited to a date between the current date and one month in the future:

```
struct DateDemo {
    @MinMaxVal(min: Date(), max: Calendar.current.date(byAdding: .month,
        value: 1, to: Date())! ) var value: Date = Date()
}
```

The following code and output demonstrate the wrapper in action using Date values:

```
var dateDemo = DateDemo()

print(dateDemo.value)
// 2019-08-23 20:05:13 +0000. <--- Property set to today by default.

dateDemo.value = Calendar.current.date(byAdding: .day, value: 10, to: Date())! //
<--- Property is set to 10 days into the future.
print(dateDemo.value)
// 2019-09-02 20:05:13 +0000 <--- Property is within acceptable range and is
stored.
dateDemo.value = Calendar.current.date(byAdding: .month, value: 2, to: Date())!
// <--- Property is set to 2 months into the future.

print(dateDemo.value)
// 2019-09-23 20:08:54 +0000 <--- Property is outside range and set to max date
(i.e. 1 month into the future).
```

13.4 Take the Knowledge Test

Click the link below or scan the QR code to test your knowledge and understanding of Swift property wrappers:

https://www.answertopia.com/q523

13.5 Summary

Introduced with Swift 5.1, property wrappers allow the behavior that would normally be placed in the getters and setters of a property implementation to be extracted and reused through the codebase of an app project avoiding the duplication of code within the class and structure declarations. Property wrappers are declared in the form of structures using the @propertyWrapper directive.

Property wrappers are a powerful Swift feature and allow you to add your own custom behavior to the Swift language. In addition to creating your own property wrappers, you will also encounter them when working with the iOS SDK. In fact, pre-defined property wrappers are used extensively when working with SwiftUI as will be covered in later chapters.

14. Working with Array and Dictionary Collections in Swift

Arrays and dictionaries in Swift are objects that contain collections of other objects. This chapter will cover some of the basics of working with arrays and dictionaries in Swift.

14.1 Mutable and Immutable Collections

Collections in Swift come in mutable and immutable forms. The contents of immutable collection instances cannot be changed after the object has been initialized. To make a collection immutable, assign it to a *constant* when it is created. On the other hand, collections are mutable if assigned to a *variable*.

14.2 Swift Array Initialization

An array is a data type designed specifically to hold multiple values in a single ordered collection. An array, for example, could be created to store a list of String values. Strictly speaking, a single Swift based array is only able to store values that are of the same type. An array declared as containing String values, therefore, could not also contain an Int value. As will be demonstrated later in this chapter, however, it is also possible to create mixed type arrays. The type of an array can be specified specifically using type annotation or left to the compiler to identify using type inference.

An array may be initialized with a collection of values (referred to as an *array literal*) at creation time using the following syntax:

```
var variableName: [type] = [value 1, value2, value3, ……. ]
```

The following code creates a new array assigned to a variable (thereby making it mutable) that is initialized with three string values:

```
var treeArray = ["Pine", "Oak", "Yew"]
```

Alternatively, the same array could have been created immutably by assigning it to a constant:

```
let treeArray = ["Pine", "Oak", "Yew"]
```

In the above instance, the Swift compiler will use type inference to decide that the array contains values of String type and prevent values of other types being inserted into the array elsewhere within the application code.

Alternatively, the same array could have been declared using type annotation:

```
var treeArray: [String] = ["Pine", "Oak", "Yew"]
```

Arrays do not have to have values assigned at creation time. The following syntax can be used to create an empty array:

```
var variableName = [type]()
```

Consider, for example, the following code which creates an empty array designated to store floating point values and assigns it to a variable named priceArray:

```
var priceArray = [Float]()
```

Another useful initialization technique allows an array to be initialized to a certain size with each array element pre-set with a specified default value:

```
var nameArray = [String](repeating: "My String", count: 10)
```

When compiled and executed, the above code will create a new 10 element array with each element initialized with a string that reads "My String".

Finally, a new array may be created by adding together two existing arrays (assuming both arrays contain values of the same type). For example:

```
let firstArray = ["Red", "Green", "Blue"]
let secondArray = ["Indigo", "Violet"]

let thirdArray = firstArray + secondArray
```

14.3 Working with Arrays in Swift

Once an array exists, a wide range of methods and properties are provided for working with and manipulating the array content from within Swift code, a subset of which is as follows:

14.3.1 Array Item Count

A count of the items in an array can be obtained by accessing the array's count property:

```
var treeArray = ["Pine", "Oak", "Yew"]
var itemCount = treeArray.count

print(itemCount)
```

Whether or not an array is empty can be identified using the array's Boolean *isEmpty* property as follows:

```
var treeArray = ["Pine", "Oak", "Yew"]

if treeArray.isEmpty {
    // Array is empty
}
```

14.3.2 Accessing Array Items

A specific item in an array may be accessed or modified by referencing the item's position in the array index (where the first item in the array has index position 0) using a technique referred to as *index subscripting*. In the following code fragment, the string value contained at index position 2 in the array (in this case the string value "Yew") is output by the print call:

```
var treeArray = ["Pine", "Oak", "Yew"]

print(treeArray[2])
```

This approach can also be used to replace the value at an index location:

```
treeArray[1] = "Redwood"
```

The above code replaces the current value at index position 1 with a new String value that reads "Redwood".

14.3.3 Random Items and Shuffling

A call to the *shuffled()* method of an array object will return a new version of the array with the item ordering randomly shuffled, for example:

```
let shuffledTrees = treeArray.shuffled()
```

To access an array item at random, simply make a call to the *randomElement()* method:

```
let randomTree = treeArray.randomElement()
```

14.3.4 Appending Items to an Array

Items may be added to an array using either the *append* method or + and += operators. The following, for example, are all valid techniques for appending items to an array:

```
treeArray.append("Redwood")
treeArray += ["Redwood"]
treeArray += ["Redwood", "Maple", "Birch"]
```

14.3.5 Inserting and Deleting Array Items

New items may be inserted into an array by specifying the index location of the new item in a call to the array's *insert(at:)* method. An insertion preserves all existing elements in the array, essentially moving them to the right to accommodate the newly inserted item:

```
treeArray.insert("Maple", at: 0)
```

Similarly, an item at a specific array index position may be removed using the *remove(at:)* method call:

```
treeArray.remove(at: 2)
```

To remove the last item in an array, simply make a call to the array's *removeLast* method as follows:

```
treeArray.removeLast()
```

14.3.6 Array Iteration

The easiest way to iterate through the items in an array is to make use of the for-in looping syntax. The following code, for example, iterates through all of the items in a String array and outputs each item to the console panel:

```
let treeArray = ["Pine", "Oak", "Yew", "Maple", "Birch", "Myrtle"]

for tree in treeArray {
    print(tree)
}
```

Upon execution, the following output will appear in the console:

```
Pine
Oak
Yew
Maple
Birch
Myrtle
```

The same result can be achieved by calling the *forEach()* array method. When this method is called on an array, it will iterate through each element and execute specified code. For example:

```
treeArray.forEach { tree in
    print(tree)
}
```

Note that since the task to be performed for each array element is declared in a closure expression, the above example may be modified as follows to take advantage of shorthand argument names:

```
treeArray.forEach {
    print($0)
```

```
}
```

14.4 Creating Mixed Type Arrays

A mixed type array is an array that can contain elements of different class types. Clearly, an array that is either declared or inferred as being of type String cannot subsequently be used to contain non-String class object instances. Interesting possibilities arise, however, when taking into consideration that Swift includes the *Any* type. Any is a special type in Swift that can be used to reference an object of a non-specific class type. It follows, therefore, that an array declared as containing Any object types can be used to store elements of mixed types. The following code, for example, declares and initializes an array containing a mixture of String, Int and Double elements:

```
let mixedArray: [Any] = ["A String", 432, 34.989]
```

The use of the Any type should be used with care since the use of Any masks from Swift the true type of the elements in such an array thereby leaving code prone to potential programmer error. It will often be necessary, for example, to manually cast the elements in an Any array to the correct type before working with them in code. Performing the incorrect cast for a specific element in the array will most likely cause the code to compile without error but crash at runtime. Consider, for the sake of an example, the following mixed type array:

```
let mixedArray: [Any] = [1, 2, 45, "Hello"]
```

Assume that, having initialized the array, we now need to iterate through the integer elements in the array and multiply them by 10. The code to achieve this might read as follows:

```
for object in mixedArray {
    print(object * 10)
}
```

When entered into Xcode, however, the above code will trigger a syntax error indicating that it is not possible to multiply operands of type Any and Int. In order to remove this error it will be necessary to downcast the array element to be of type Int:

```
for object in mixedArray {
    print(object as! Int * 10)
}
```

The above code will compile without error and work as expected until the final String element in the array is reached at which point the code will crash with the following error:

```
Could not cast value of type 'Swift.String' to 'Swift.Int'
```

The code will, therefore, need to be modified to be aware of the specific type of each element in the array. Clearly, there are both benefits and risks to using Any arrays in Swift.

14.5 Swift Dictionary Collections

String dictionaries allow data to be stored and managed in the form of key-value pairs. Dictionaries fulfill a similar purpose to arrays, except each item stored in the dictionary has associated with it a unique key (to be precise, the key is unique to the particular dictionary object) which can be used to reference and access the corresponding value. Currently only String, Int, Double and Bool data types are suitable for use as keys within a Swift dictionary.

14.6 Swift Dictionary Initialization

A dictionary is a data type designed specifically to hold multiple values in a single unordered collection. Each item in a dictionary consists of a key and an associated value. The data types of the key and value elements type may be specified specifically using type annotation, or left to the compiler to identify using type inference.

A new dictionary may be initialized with a collection of values (referred to as a *dictionary literal*) at creation time using the following syntax:

```
var variableName: [key type: value type] = [key 1: value 1, key 2: value2 …. ]
```

The following code creates a new dictionary assigned to a variable (thereby making it mutable) that is initialized with four key-value pairs in the form of ISBN numbers acting as keys for corresponding book titles:

```
var bookDict = ["100-432112" : "Wind in the Willows",
                "200-532874" : "Tale of Two Cities",
                "202-546549" : "Sense and Sensibility",
                "104-109834" : "Shutter Island"]
```

In the above instance, the Swift compiler will use type inference to decide that both the key and value elements of the dictionary are of String type and prevent values or keys of other types being inserted into the dictionary.

Alternatively, the same dictionary could have been declared using type annotation:

```
var bookDict: [String: String] =
                ["100-432112" : "Wind in the Willows",
                "200-532874" : "Tale of Two Cities",
                "202-546549" : "Sense and Sensibility",
                "104-109834" : "Shutter Island"]
```

As with arrays, it is also possible to create an empty dictionary, the syntax for which reads as follows:

```
var variableName = [key type: value type]()
```

The following code creates an empty dictionary designated to store integer keys and string values:

```
var myDictionary = [Int: String]()
```

14.7 Sequence-based Dictionary Initialization

Dictionaries may also be initialized using sequences to represent the keys and values. This is achieved using the Swift *zip()* function, passing through the keys and corresponding values. In the following example, a dictionary is created using two arrays:

```
let keys = ["100-432112", "200-532874", "202-546549", "104-109834"]
let values = ["Wind in the Willows", "Tale of Two Cities",
                "Sense and Sensibility", "Shutter Island"]


let bookDict = Dictionary(uniqueKeysWithValues: zip(keys, values))
```

This approach allows keys and values to be generated programmatically. In the following example, a number range starting at 1 is being specified for the keys instead of using an array of predefined keys:

```
let values = ["Wind in the Willows", "Tale of Two Cities",
                "Sense and Sensibility", "Shutter Island"]


var bookDict = Dictionary(uniqueKeysWithValues: zip(1..., values))
```

The above code is a much cleaner equivalent to the following dictionary declaration:

```
var bookDict = [1 : "Wind in the Willows",
                2 : "Tale of Two Cities",
                3 : "Sense and Sensibility",
                4 : "Shutter Island"]
```

14.8 Dictionary Item Count

A count of the items in a dictionary can be obtained by accessing the dictionary's count property:

```
print(bookDict.count)
```

14.9 Accessing and Updating Dictionary Items

A specific value may be accessed or modified using key subscript syntax to reference the corresponding value. The following code references a key known to be in the bookDict dictionary and outputs the associated value (in this case the book entitled "A Tale of Two Cities"):

```
print(bookDict["200-532874"])
```

When accessing dictionary entries in this way, it is also possible to declare a default value to be used in the event that the specified key does not return a value:

```
print(bookDict["999-546547", default: "Book not found"])
```

Since the dictionary does not contain an entry for the specified key, the above code will output text which reads "Book not found".

Indexing by key may also be used when updating the value associated with a specified key, for example, to change the title of the same book from "A Tale of Two Cities" to "Sense and Sensibility"):

```
bookDict["200-532874"] = "Sense and Sensibility"
```

The same result is also possible by making a call to the *updateValue(forKey:)* method, passing through the key corresponding to the value to be changed:

```
bookDict.updateValue("The Ruins", forKey: "200-532874")
```

14.10 Adding and Removing Dictionary Entries

Items may be added to a dictionary using the following key subscripting syntax:

dictionaryVariable[key] = value

For example, to add a new key-value pair entry to the books dictionary:

```
bookDict["300-898871"] = "The Overlook"
```

Removal of a key-value pair from a dictionary may be achieved either by assigning a *nil* value to the entry, or via a call to the *removeValueForKey* method of the dictionary instance. Both code lines below achieve the same result of removing the specified entry from the books dictionary:

```
bookDict["300-898871"] = nil
bookDict.removeValue(forKey: "300-898871")
```

14.11 Dictionary Iteration

As with arrays, it is possible to iterate through dictionary entries by making use of the for-in looping syntax. The following code, for example, iterates through all of the entries in the books dictionary, outputting both the key and value for each entry:

```
for (bookid, title) in bookDict {
  print("Book ID: \(bookid) Title: \(title)")
}
```

Upon execution, the following output will appear in the console:

```
Book ID: 100-432112 Title: Wind in the Willows
Book ID: 200-532874 Title: The Ruins
```

```
Book ID: 104-109834 Title: Shutter Island
Book ID: 202-546549 Title: Sense and Sensibility
```

14.12 Take the Knowledge Test

Click the link below or scan the QR code to test your knowledge and understanding of the Swift arrays and dictionaries:

https://www.answertopia.com/pzwe

14.13 Summary

Collections in Swift take the form of either dictionaries or arrays. Both provide a way to collect together multiple items within a single object. Arrays provide a way to store an ordered collection of items where those items are accessed by an index value corresponding to the item position in the array. Dictionaries provide a platform for storing key-value pairs, where the key is used to gain access to the stored value. Iteration through the elements of Swift collections can be achieved using the for-in loop construct.

15. Understanding Error Handling in Swift 5

In a perfect world, a running iOS app would never encounter an error. The reality, however, is that it is impossible to guarantee that an error of some form or another will not occur at some point during the execution of the app. It is essential, therefore, to ensure that the code of an app is implemented such that it gracefully handles any errors that may occur. Since the introduction of Swift 2, the task of handling errors has become much easier for the iOS app developer.

This chapter will cover the handling of errors using Swift and introduce topics such as *error types*, *throwing methods and functions*, the *guard* and *defer* statements and *do-catch* statements.

15.1 Understanding Error Handling

No matter how carefully Swift code is designed and implemented, there will invariably be situations that are beyond the control of the app. An app that relies on an active internet connection cannot, for example, control the loss of signal on an iPhone device, or prevent the user from enabling "airplane mode". What the app can do, however, is to implement robust handling of the error (for example displaying a message indicating to the user that the app requires an active internet connection to proceed).

There are two sides to handling errors within Swift. The first involves triggering (or *throwing*) an error when the desired results are not achieved within the method of an iOS app. The second involves catching and handling the error after it is thrown by a method.

When an error is thrown, the error will be of a particular error type which can be used to identify the specific nature of the error and to decide on the most appropriate course of action to be taken. The error type value can be any value that conforms to the Error protocol.

In addition to implementing methods in an app to throw errors when necessary, it is important to be aware that a number of API methods in the iOS SDK (particularly those relating to file handling) will throw errors which will need to be handled within the code of the app.

15.2 Declaring Error Types

As an example, consider a method that is required to transfer a file to a remote server. Such a method might fail to transfer the file for a variety of reasons such as there being no network connection, the connection being too slow or the failure to find the file to be transferred. All these possible errors could be represented within an enumeration that conforms to the Error protocol as follows:

```
enum FileTransferError: Error {
    case noConnection
    case lowBandwidth
    case fileNotFound
}
```

Once an error type has been declared, it can be used within a method when throwing errors.

15.3 Throwing an Error

A method or function declares that it can throw an error using the *throws* keyword. For example:

```
func transferFile() throws {

}
```

In the event that the function or method returns a result, the *throws* keyword is placed before the return type as follows:

```
func transferFile() throws -> Bool {

}
```

Once a method has been declared as being able to throw errors, code can then be added to throw the errors when they are encountered. This is achieved using the *throw* statement in conjunction with the *guard* statement. The following code declares some constants to serve as status values and then implements the guard and throw behavior for the method:

```
let connectionOK = true
let connectionSpeed = 30.00
let fileFound = false


enum FileTransferError: Error {
    case noConnection
    case lowBandwidth
    case fileNotFound
}


func fileTransfer() throws {

    guard connectionOK else {
        throw FileTransferError.noConnection
    }

    guard connectionSpeed > 30 else {
        throw FileTransferError.lowBandwidth
    }

    guard fileFound else {
        throw FileTransferError.fileNotFound
    }
}
```

Within the body of the method, each guard statement checks a condition for a true or false result. In the event of a false result, the code contained within the *else* body is executed. In the case of a false result, the throw statement is used to throw one of the error values contained in the FileTransferError enumeration.

15.4 Calling Throwing Methods and Functions

Once a method or function is declared as throwing errors, it can no longer be called in the usual manner. Calls to such methods must now be prefixed by the *try* statement as follows:

```
try fileTransfer()
```

In addition to using the try statement, the call must also be made from within a *do-catch* statement to catch and handle any errors that may be thrown. Consider, for example, that the *fileTransfer* method needs to be called from within a method named *sendFile*. The code within this method might be implemented as follows:

```
func sendFile() -> String {

    do {
        try fileTransfer()
    } catch FileTransferError.noConnection {
        return("No Network Connection")
    } catch FileTransferError.lowBandwidth {
        return("File Transfer Speed too Low")
    } catch FileTransferError.fileNotFound {
        return("File not Found")
    } catch {
        return("Unknown error")
    }


    return("Successful transfer")
}
```

The method calls the *fileTransfer* method from within a *do-catch* statement which, in turn, includes catch conditions for each of the three possible error conditions. In each case, the method simply returns a string value containing a description of the error. In the event that no error was thrown, a string value is returned indicating a successful file transfer. Note that a fourth catch condition is included with no pattern matching. This is a "catch all" statement that ensures that any errors not matched by the preceding catch statements are also handled. This is required because do-catch statements must be exhaustive (in other words constructed so as to catch all possible error conditions).

Swift also allows multiple matches to be declared within a single catch statement, with the list of matches separated by commas. For example, a single catch declaration could be used to handle both the noConnection and lowBandwidth errors as follows:

```
func sendFile() -> String {

    do {
        try fileTransfer()
    } catch FileTransferError.noConnection, FileTransferError.lowBandwidth {
        return("Connection problem")
    } catch FileTransferError.fileNotFound {
        return("File not Found")
    } catch {
        return("Unknown error")
    }


    return("Successful transfer")
}
```

15.5 Accessing the Error Object

When a method call fails, it will invariably return an Error object identifying the nature of the failure. A common requirement within the catch statement is to gain access to this object so that appropriate corrective action can be taken within the app code. The following code demonstrates how such an error object is accessed from within a catch statement when attempting to create a new file system directory:

```
do {
    try filemgr.createDirectory(atPath: newDir,
                        withIntermediateDirectories: true,
                        attributes: nil)
    } catch let error {
            print("Error: \(error.localizedDescription)")
}
```

15.6 Disabling Error Catching

A throwing method may be forced to run without the need to enclose the call within a do-catch statement by using the *try!* statement as follows:

```
try! fileTransfer()
```

In using this approach we are informing the compiler that we know with absolute certainty that the method call will not result in an error being thrown. In the event that an error is thrown when using this technique, the code will fail with a runtime error. As such, this approach should be used sparingly.

15.7 Using the defer Statement

The previously implemented *sendFile* method demonstrated a common scenario when handling errors. Each of the catch clauses in the do-catch statement contained a return statement that returned control to the calling method. In such a situation, however, it might be useful to be able to perform some other task before control is returned and regardless of the type of error that was encountered. The *sendFile* method might, for example, need to remove temporary files before returning. This behavior can be achieved using the *defer* statement.

The defer statement allows a sequence of code statements to be declared as needing to be run as soon as the method returns. In the following code, the *sendFile* method has been modified to include a defer statement:

```
func sendFile() -> String {

    defer {
        removeTmpFiles()
        closeConnection()
    }

    do {
        try fileTransfer()
    } catch FileTransferError.noConnection {
        return("No Network Connection")
    } catch FileTransferError.lowBandwidth {
        return("File Transfer Speed too Low")
    } catch FileTransferError.fileNotFound {
        return("File not Found")
    } catch {
```

```
        return("Unknown error")
    }


    return("Successful transfer")
}
```

With the defer statement now added, the calls to the *removeTmpFiles* and *closeConnection* methods will always be made before the method returns, regardless of which return call gets triggered.

15.8 Take the Knowledge Test

Click the link below or scan the QR code to test your knowledge and understanding of the Swift error handling:

https://www.answertopia.com/h02s

15.9 Summary

Error handling is an essential part of creating robust and reliable iOS apps. Since the introduction of Swift 2 it is now much easier to both trigger and handle errors. Error types are created using values that conform to the Error protocol and are most commonly implemented as enumerations. Methods and functions that throw errors are declared as such using the *throws* keyword. The *guard* and *throw* statements are used within the body of these methods or functions to throw errors based on the error type.

A throwable method or function is called using the *try* statement which must be encapsulated within a do-catch statement. A do-catch statement consists of an exhaustive list of catch pattern constructs, each of which contains the code to be executed in the event of a particular error being thrown. Cleanup tasks can be defined to be executed when a method returns through the use of the *defer* statement.

16. An Overview of SwiftUI

Now that Xcode has been installed and the basics of the Swift programming language are covered, it is time to start introducing SwiftUI.

First announced at Apple's Worldwide Developer Conference in 2019, SwiftUI is an entirely new approach to developing apps for all Apple operating system platforms. The primary goals of SwiftUI are to make app development easier, faster, and less prone to the types of bugs that typically appear when developing software projects. These elements have been combined with SwiftUI-specific additions to Xcode that allow SwiftUI projects to be tested in near real-time using a live app preview during the development process.

Many of the advantages of SwiftUI originate from the fact that it is both *declarative* and *data-driven*, topics which will be explained in this chapter.

The discussion in this chapter is intended as a high-level overview of SwiftUI and does not cover the practical aspects of implementation within a project. Implementation and practical examples will be covered in detail in the remainder of the book.

16.1 UIKit and Interface Builder

To understand the meaning and advantages of SwiftUI's declarative syntax, it helps to understand how user interface layouts were designed before the introduction of SwiftUI. Until the introduction of SwiftUI, iOS apps were built entirely using UIKit, together with a collection of associated frameworks that make up the iOS Software Development Kit (SDK).

To aid in the design of the user interface layouts that make up the screens of an app, Xcode includes a tool called Interface Builder. Interface Builder is a powerful tool that allows storyboards to be created that contain the individual scenes that make up an app (with a scene typically representing a single app screen).

The user interface layout of a scene is designed within Interface Builder by dragging components (such as buttons, labels, text fields and sliders) from a library panel to the desired location on the scene canvas. Selecting a component in a scene provides access to a range of inspector panels where the attributes of the components can be changed.

The layout behavior of the scene (in other words, how it reacts to different device screen sizes and changes to device orientation between portrait and landscape) is defined by configuring a range of constraints that dictate how each component is positioned and sized in relation to both the containing window and the other components in the layout.

Finally, any components that need to respond to user events (such as a button tap or slider motion) are connected to methods in the app source code where the event is handled.

At various points during this development process, it is necessary to compile and run the app on a simulator or device to test that everything is working as expected.

16.2 SwiftUI Declarative Syntax

SwiftUI introduces a declarative syntax that provides an entirely different way of implementing user interface layouts and behavior from the UIKit and Interface Builder approach. Instead of manually designing the intricate details of the layout and appearance of components that make up a scene, SwiftUI allows the scenes to be described using a simple and intuitive syntax. In other words, SwiftUI allows layouts to be created by declaring how the user interface should appear without worrying about the complexity of how the layout is built.

This essentially involves declaring the components to be included in the layout, stating the kind of layout manager in which they are to be contained (vertical stack, horizontal stack, form, list, etc.), and using modifiers to set attributes such as the text on a button, the foreground color of a label, or the method to be called in the event of a tap gesture. Having made these declarations, all the intricate and complicated details of how to position, constrain, and render the layout are handled automatically by SwiftUI.

SwiftUI declarations are structured hierarchically, making it easy to create complex views by composing small, reusable custom subviews.

While the view layout is being declared and tested, Xcode provides a preview canvas that changes in real-time to reflect the appearance of the layout. Xcode also includes a *live preview* mode, which allows the app to be launched within the preview canvas and fully tested without the need to build and run on a simulator or device.

The SwiftUI declaration syntax's coverage begins with the chapter *"Creating Custom Views with SwiftUI"*.

16.3 SwiftUI is Data Driven

When we say that SwiftUI is data-driven, this is not to say that it is no longer necessary to handle user-generated events (in other words, the interaction between the user and the app user interface). It is still necessary, for example, to know when the user taps a button and to react in some app-specific way. Being data-driven relates more to the relationship between the underlying app data and the user interface and logic of the app.

Before the introduction of SwiftUI, an iOS app would contain code responsible for checking the current data values within the app. If data is likely to change over time, code has to be written to ensure that the user interface always reflects the latest state of the data (perhaps by writing code to frequently check for changes to the data or by providing a refresh option for the user to request a data update). Similar problems arise when keeping the user interface state consistent and ensuring issues like toggle button settings are stored appropriately. Requirements such as these can become increasingly complex when multiple areas of an app depend on the same data sources.

SwiftUI addresses this complexity by providing several ways to *bind* an app's data model to the user interface components and logic that provide the app functionality.

When implemented, the data model *publishes* data variables to which other parts of the app can then *subscribe*. This approach automatically reports changes to the published data to all subscribers. If the binding is made from a user interface component, any data changes will automatically be reflected within the user interface by SwiftUI without the need to write any additional code.

16.4 SwiftUI vs. UIKit

With the choice of using UIKit and SwiftUI now available, the obvious question arises as to which is the best option. When making this decision, it is important to understand that SwiftUI and UIKit are not mutually exclusive. In fact, several integration solutions are available.

SwiftUI provides a faster, more efficient app development environment and makes it easier to make the same app available on multiple Apple platforms (iOS, iPadOS, macOS, watchOS, and tvOS) without making significant code changes.

If you have an existing app developed using UIKit, there is no easy migration path to convert that code to SwiftUI, so it probably makes sense to keep using UIKit for that part of the project. UIKit will continue to be a valuable part of the app development toolset and will be extended, supported and enhanced by Apple for the foreseeable future. When adding new features to an existing project, however, consider doing so using SwiftUI and integrating it into the existing UIKit codebase.

When adopting SwiftUI for new projects, it will probably not be possible to avoid using UIKit entirely. Although SwiftUI comes with a wide array of user interface components, it will still be necessary to use UIKit for certain functionality not yet available in SwiftUI.

In addition, for highly complex user interface layout designs, it may also be necessary to use Interface Builder when layout needs cannot be satisfied using the SwiftUI layout container views.

16.5 Take the Knowledge Test

Click the link below or scan the QR code to test your knowledge and understanding of the fundamentals of SwiftUI:

https://www.answertopia.com/h00h

16.6 Summary

SwiftUI introduces a different approach to app development than that offered by UIKit and Interface Builder. Rather than directly implementing how a user interface is rendered, SwiftUI allows the user interface to be declared in descriptive terms and then decides the best way to perform the rendering when the app runs.

SwiftUI is also data-driven in that data changes drive the behavior and appearance of the app. This is achieved through a publisher and subscriber model.

This chapter has provided a very high-level view of SwiftUI. The remainder of this book will explore SwiftUI in greater depth.

17. Using Xcode in SwiftUI Mode

When creating a new project, Xcode now provides a choice of creating either a Storyboard or SwiftUI-based user interface for the project. When creating a SwiftUI project, Xcode appears and behaves significantly differently when designing an app project's user interface than the UIKit Storyboard mode.

When working in SwiftUI mode, most of your time as an app developer will be spent in the code editor and preview canvas, which will be explored in detail in this chapter.

17.1 Starting Xcode 26

As with all the examples in this book, the development of our example will take place within the Xcode 26 development environment. If you have not already installed this tool together with the latest iOS SDK, refer first to the *"Installing Xcode 26 and the iOS 26 SDK"* chapter of this book. Assuming the installation is complete, launch Xcode either by clicking on the icon on the dock (assuming you created one) or using the macOS Finder to locate Xcode in the Applications folder of your system.

When launched for the first time, and until you turn off the *Show this window when Xcode launches* toggle, the screen illustrated in Figure 17-1 will appear by default:

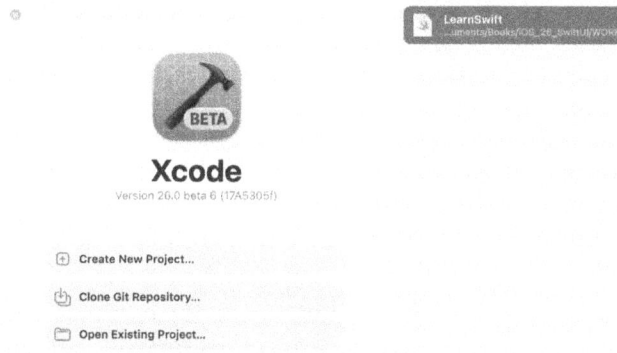

Figure 17-1

If you do not see this window, select the *Window -> Welcome to Xcode* menu option to display it. From within this window, click *Create New Project*.

17.2 Creating a SwiftUI Project

When creating a new project, the project template screen includes options to select how the app project is to be implemented. Options are available to design an app for a specific Apple platform (such as iOS, watchOS, macOS, DriveKit, or tvOS) or to create a *multiplatform* project. Selecting a platform-specific option will also provide the choice of creating either a Storyboard (UIKit) or a SwiftUI-based project.

A multiplatform project allows an app to be designed for multiple Apple platforms with a minimum of platform-specific code. Even if you plan to initially only target iOS, the multiplatform option is still recommended since it provides the flexibility to make the app available on other platforms in the future without having to restructure the project.

Templates are also available for creating a basic app, a document-based app, or a game project. For this chapter, use the multiplatform app option:

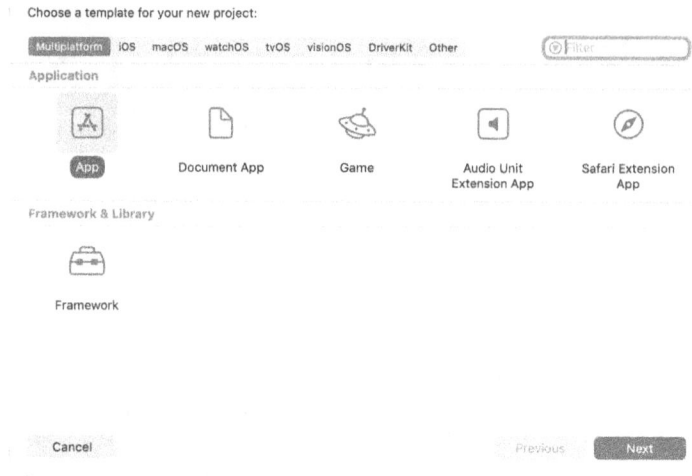

Figure 17-2

Clicking *Next* will display the project options screen where the project name needs to be entered (in this case, name the project *DemoProject*).

The Organization Identifier is typically the reversed URL of your company's website, for example, "com. mycompany". This will be used when creating provisioning profiles and certificates to enable the testing of advanced features of iOS on physical devices. It also serves to uniquely identify the app within the Apple App Store when the app is published:

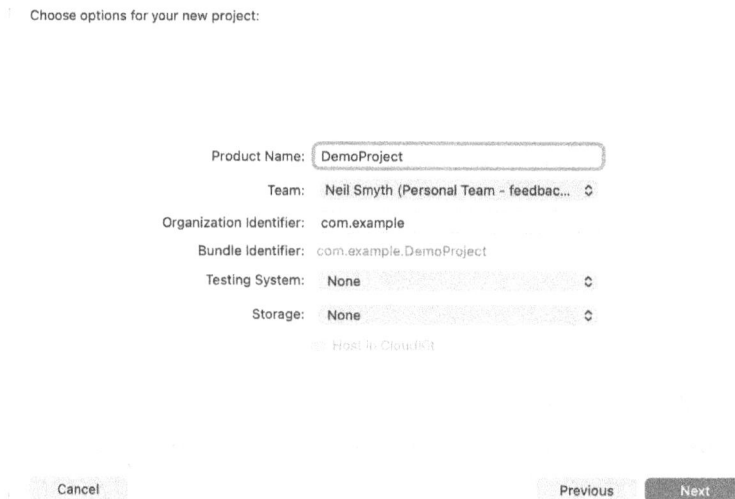

Figure 17-3

Click *Next* again and choose a location on your filesystem to place the project before clicking the *Create* button.

Once a new project has been created, the main Xcode panel will appear with the default layout for SwiftUI development displayed.

17.3 Xcode in SwiftUI Mode

Before beginning work on a SwiftUI user interface, it is worth taking some time to gain familiarity with how Xcode works in SwiftUI mode. A newly created multiplatform "app" project includes two SwiftUI View files named *<app name>App.swift* (in this case *DemoProjectApp.swift*) and *ContentView.swift*, which, when selected from the project navigation panel, will appear within Xcode, as shown in Figure 17-4 below:

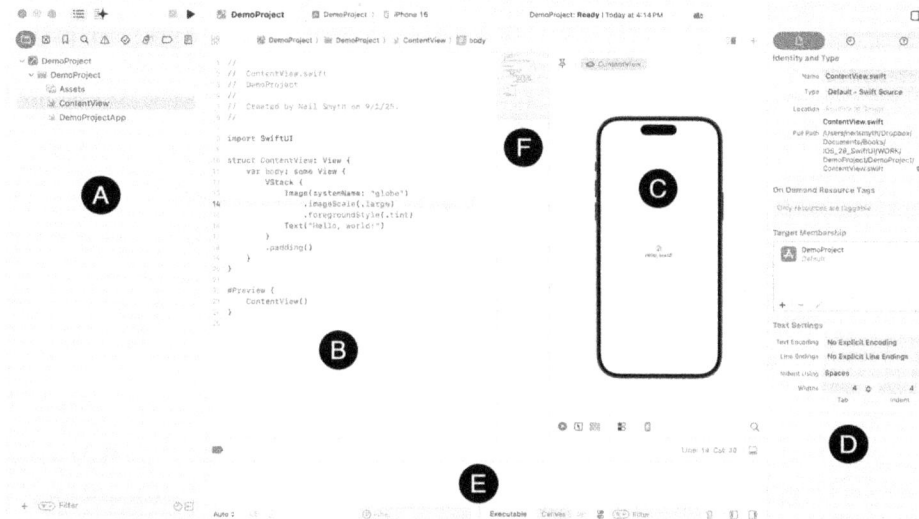

Figure 17-4

When the project loads for the first time, Xcode may default to macOS as the destination platform for building and testing your app. Before continuing, use the run destination chooser to select an iPhone device, as illustrated in Figure 17-5 below:

Figure 17-5

Located to the right of the project navigator (A) is the code editor (B). To the right is the preview canvas (C), where any changes made to the SwiftUI layout declaration will appear in real-time.

Selecting a view in the canvas will automatically select and highlight the corresponding entry in the code editor and vice versa. Attributes for the currently selected item will appear in the attributes inspector panel (D).

During debugging, the debug panel (E) will appear, containing debug output from both the iOS frameworks and any diagnostic print statements you have included in your code. If the console is not currently visible, display it by clicking on the button indicated by the arrow in Figure 17-6:

Figure 17-6

The debug panel can be configured to show a Variables view or a Console view. The variables view displays variables within the app at the point that the app crashes or reaches a debugging breakpoint. The console view, on the other hand, displays print output and messages from the running app. Figure 17-7 shows the variables view with an arrow indicating the buttons used to switch views:

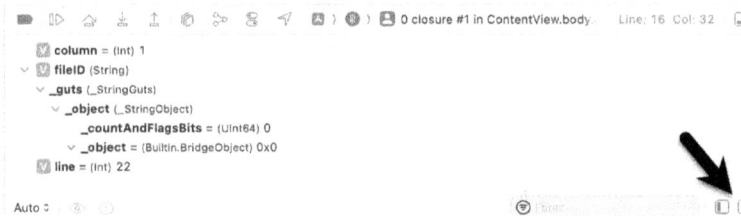

Figure 17-7

The Console can be set up to show output generated from the preview canvas or from the running app when it is launched on a device or simulator within Xcode. To toggle between these output sources, use the buttons indicated in Figure 17-8:

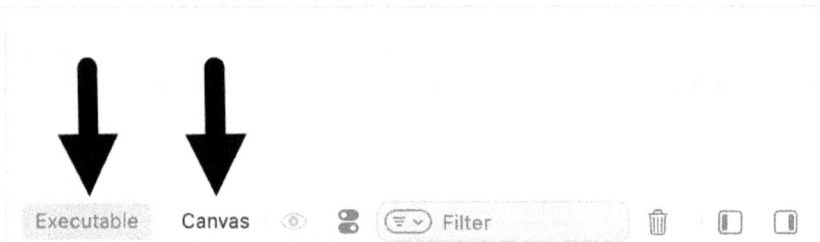

Figure 17-8

The button indicated in Figure 17-6 above may be used to hide the debug panel (E), while the two buttons highlighted in Figure 17-9 below hide and show the project navigator and inspector panels:

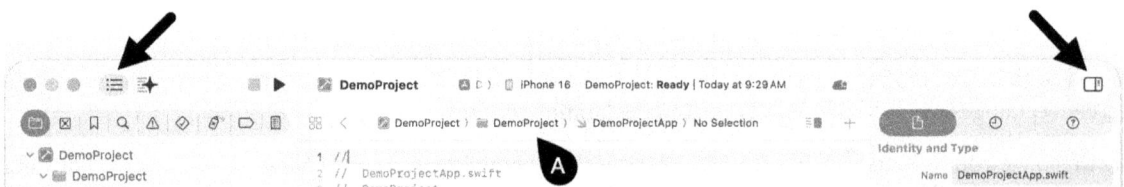

Figure 17-9

The bar (marked A above) provides quick access to specific points within the project structure, including folders, files, and code positions. For example, consider the following bar settings:

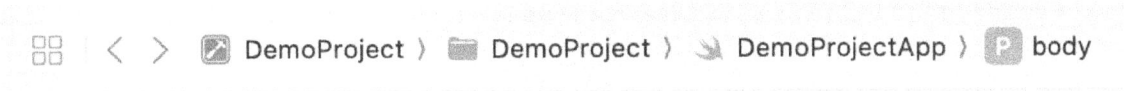

Figure 17-10

We can infer from the above configuration that we are working in the DemoProject project, editing a Swift file named *DemoProjectApp.swift* located in the *DemoProject* folder, and the editor cursor is currently positioned in a code structure named *body*.

To jump to another location, click on a path section and make a selection from the resulting menu. For example, clicking on the DemoProjectApp element will provide the option to switch the ContentView or Assets files:

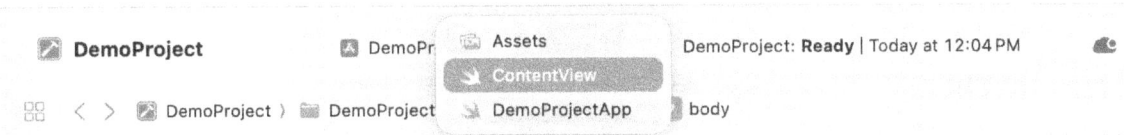

Figure 17-11

HAfter switching to the ContentView file, the file location section allows us to jump within the file to the *ContentView* or *body* code structures:

Figure 17-12

17.4 Tab Bar Navigation

The tab bar is not visible by default, but when used, it provides quick navigation when working with multiple open files. Figure 17-13, for example, shows a tab bar containing several files:

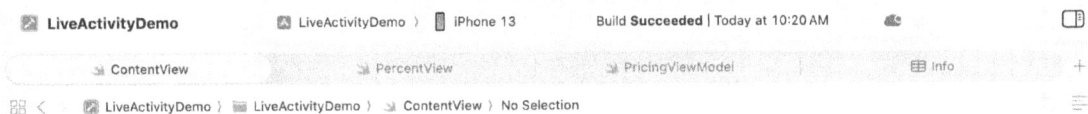

Figure 17-13

To add a file to the tab bar, use the Cmd-T keyboard accelerator or click the button marked below and select the Tab menu option:

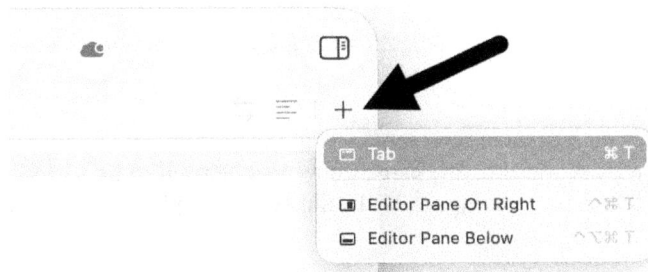

Figure 17-14

If a file is already open, it will be added to the tab bar, and a new tab will be opened. Within the selection panel, begin typing the filename in the Open Quickly text field or make a selection from the Recent Files list:

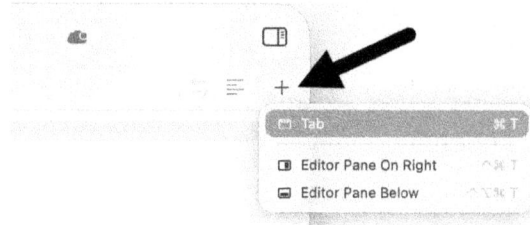

Figure 17-15

Repeat the above steps to open other files and click the corresponding tabs to switch between them.

17.5 Minimap

The area marked F in Figure 17-4 is called the *Minimap*. This map provides a miniaturized outline of the source code in the editor. Particularly useful when working with large source files, the Minimap panel provides a quick way to move to different areas of the code. Hovering the mouse pointer of a line in the Minimap will display a label indicating the class, property, or function at that location, as illustrated in Figure 17-16:

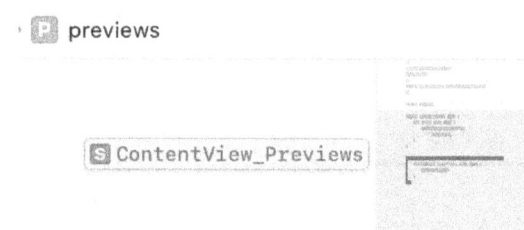

Figure 17-16

The Minimap visibility is controlled using the *Editor -> Minimap* menu option. Clicking on the label or within the map will take you to that line in the code editor. Holding down the Command key while hovering will display all of the elements contained within the source file, as shown in Figure 17-17:

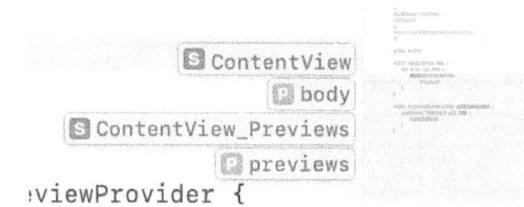

Figure 17-17

The Minimap can be displayed and hidden by toggling the *Editor -> Minimap* menu option.

17.6 The Preview Canvas

The preview canvas provides both a visual representation of the user interface design and a tool for adding and modifying views within the layout design. The canvas may also be used to perform live testing of the running app without launching an iOS simulator. Figure 17-18 illustrates a typical preview canvas for a newly created project:

Figure 17-18

If the canvas is not visible, it can be displayed using the Xcode *Editor -> Canvas* menu option.

The main canvas area (A) represents the current view as it will appear when running on a physical device (also referred to as the *canvas device*). When changes are made to the code in the editor, those changes are reflected within the preview canvas. To avoid continually updating the canvas, and depending on the nature of the changes being made, the preview will occasionally pause live updates. When this happens, the Resume button will appear, which, when clicked, will once again begin updating the preview:

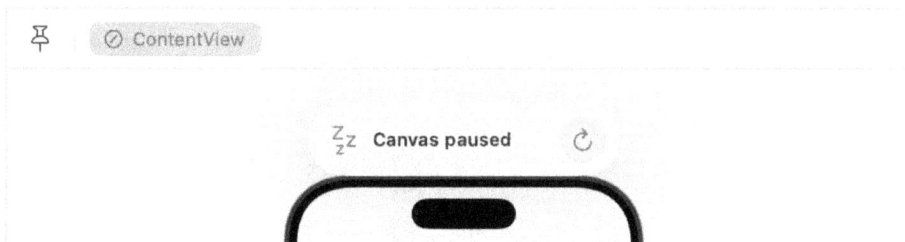

Figure 17-19

17.7 Preview Pinning

Building an app in Xcode will likely consist of several SwiftUI View files in addition to the default *ContentView. swift* file. When a SwiftUI View file is selected from the project navigator, both the code editor and preview canvas will change to reflect the currently selected file. Sometimes, you may want the user interface layout for one SwiftUI file to appear in the preview canvas while editing the code in a different file. This can be particularly useful if the layout from one file is dependent on or embedded in another view. The pin button (labeled C in

Figure 17-18 above) pins the current preview to the canvas so that it remains accessible on the canvas after navigating to a different view. Switch between pinned views by clicking on the view buttons along the top of the preview panel. In Figure 17-20, for example, buttons are provided to switch between two views:

Figure 17-20

The #Preview macro can be used to apply more meaningful names to the views as follows:

```
#Preview("Content View") {
    ContentView()
}

#Preview("Sales View") {
    SalesView()
}
```

When the above changes are applied to the *ContentView.swift* and *SalesView.swift* files, the view buttons in the preview canvas will appear, as illustrated below:

Figure 17-21

17.8 The Preview Toolbar

The preview toolbar (marked B in Figure 17-18 above and shown below) provides several options for changing the preview panel:

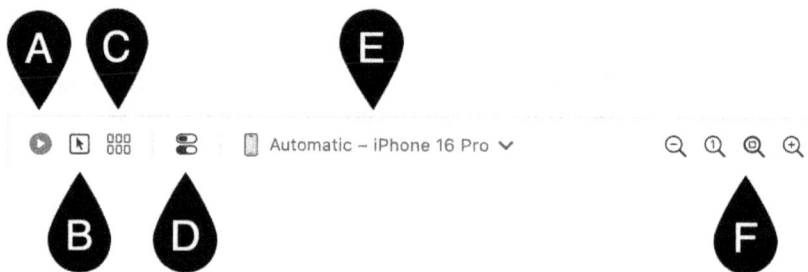

Figure 17-22

The preview panel can display the current view in either *live* or *selectable* mode. In live mode, the app runs interactively within the canvas and allows you to interact with it as if running on a device or simulator. Selectable mode allows you to select items in the canvas view to edit attributes and also to add and remove components. To switch between modes, use the buttons marked A (for live mode) and B (for selectable mode) as marked in the above figure.

The current version of the app may also be previewed on different device models by clicking on the Preview Device menu (E). If you have a physical device connected to Xcode, selecting it from the menu will launch the app on that device. As with the preview canvas, the running app on the device will update dynamically as changes are made to the code in the editor.

The Variants button (C) allows the view to be previewed in a variety of dynamic text sizes, color schemes, and device orientations:

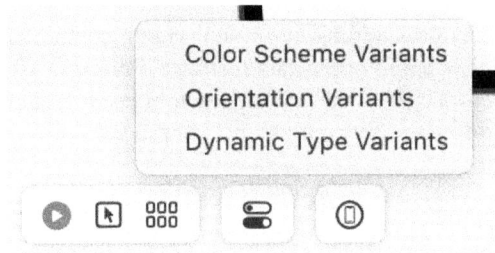

Figure 17-23

Figure 17-24, for example, shows the result of selecting the orientation variations option:

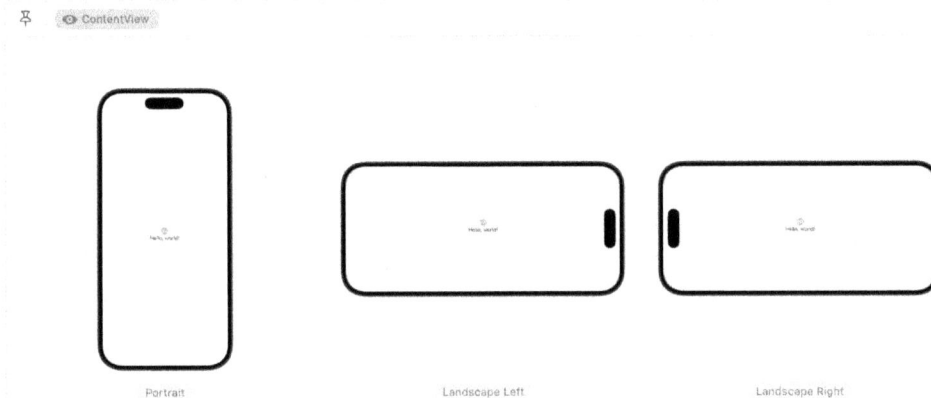

Figure 17-24

The Device Settings button (D) controls the color scheme (light or dark), orientation (portrait or landscape), and dynamic font size of the canvas device:

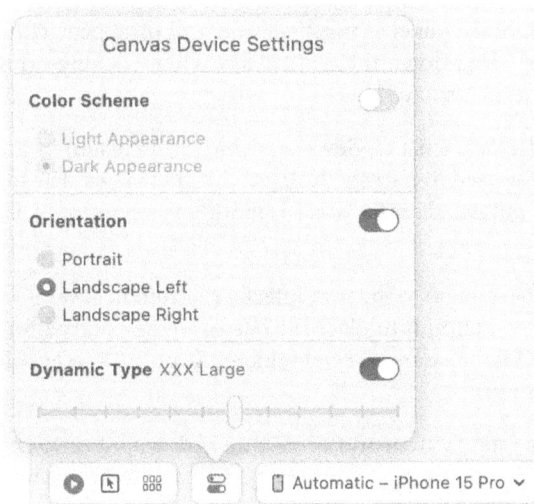

Figure 17-25

The size buttons (F) will zoom in and out of the canvas, zoom to 100%, and fit the available space.

17.9 Modifying the Design

Working with SwiftUI primarily involves adding additional views, customizing those views using modifiers, adding logic, and interacting with state and other data instance bindings. All of these tasks can be performed exclusively by modifying the structure in the code editor. The font used to display the "Hello, world!" Text view, for example, can be changed by adding the appropriate modifier in the editor:

```
Text("Hello, world!")
    .font(.largeTitle)
```

An alternative to this is to change the SwiftUI views by dragging and dropping items from the Library panel. The Library panel is displayed using the Cmd-Shift-L keyboard accelerator or selecting the *View -> Show Library* menu option. When displayed, the Library panel will appear, as shown in Figure 17-26:

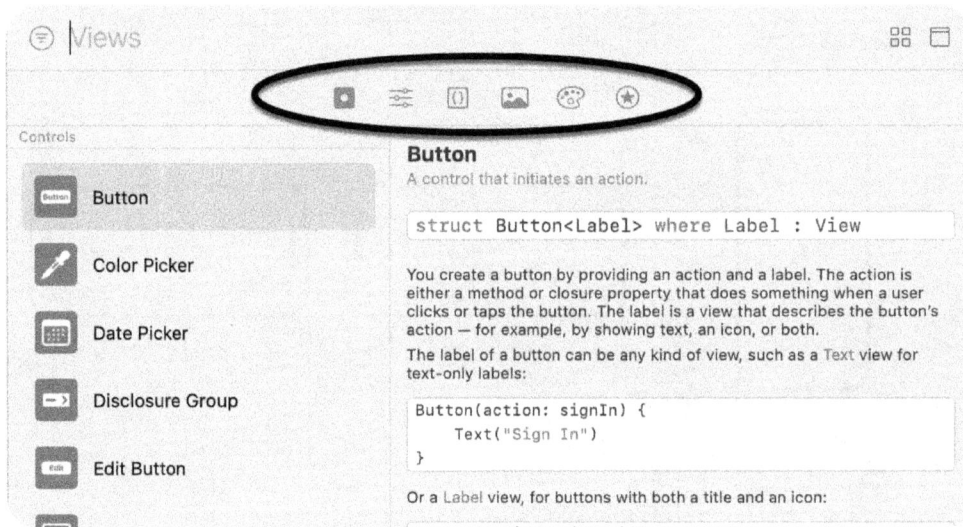

Figure 17-26

When launched this way, the Library panel is transient and will disappear either after a selection or a click is performed outside of the panel. Hold down the Option key when clicking on the View menu option or press Cmd-Opt-Shift-L to keep the panel displayed.

When first opened, the panel displays a list of views available for inclusion in the user interface design. The list can be browsed, or the search bar used to narrow the list to specific views. The toolbar (highlighted in the above figure) can be used to switch to other categories, such as modifiers, commonly used code snippets, images, color resources, and symbols.

An item within the library can be applied to the user interface design in several ways. To apply a font modifier to the "Hello, world!" Text view, one option is to place the cursor in the code editor where the code is to be added, locate the font modifier in the Library panel, and double-click on it. Xcode will then automatically insert the font modifier at the cursor position.

Another option is to locate the Library item and then drag and drop it onto the desired location either in the code editor or the preview canvas. In Figure 17-27 below, for example, the font modifier is being dragged to the Text view within the canvas:

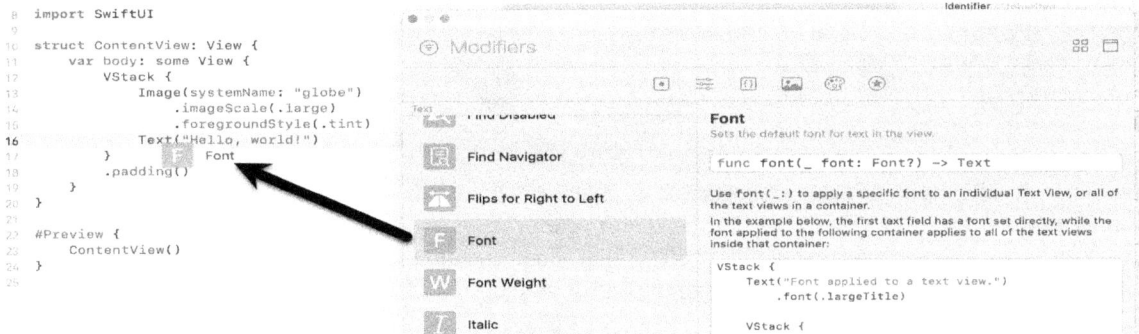

```
8  import SwiftUI
9
10  struct ContentView: View {
11      var body: some View {
12          VStack {
13              Image(systemName: "globe")
14                  .imageScale(.large)
15                  .foregroundStyle(.tint)
16              Text("Hello, world!")
17          }        Font
18          .padding()
19      }
20  }
21
22  #Preview {
23      ContentView()
24  }
25
```

Figure 17-27

Once a view or modifier has been added to the SwiftUI view file, customization steps, such as specifying the color for a foreground modifier, can be made within the editor. For example:

```
Text("Hello, world!")
    .font(.largeTitle)
    .foregroundColor(.red)
```

17.10 Editor Context Menu

Right-clicking on an item in the code editor will display the menu shown in Figure 17-28:

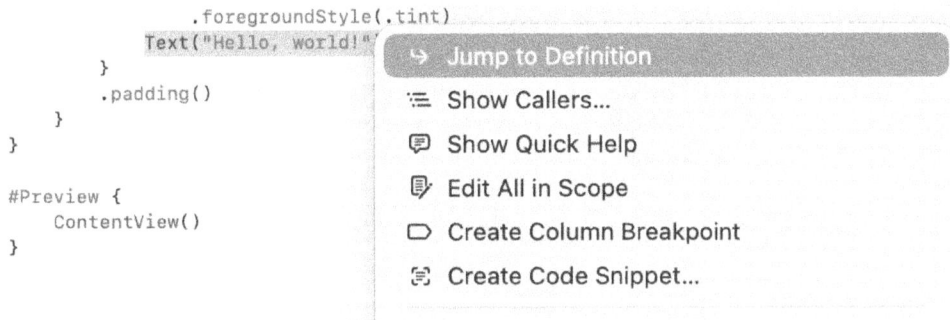

Figure 17-28

This menu provides a list of options that will vary depending on the type of item selected. Options typically include a shortcut to a popup version of the Attributes inspector for the current view, together with options to embed the current view in a stack or list container. This menu is also useful for extracting part of a view into its own self-contained subview. Creating subviews is strongly encouraged to promote reuse, improve performance, and unclutter complex design structures.

17.11 Running the App on a Simulator

Although much can be achieved using the preview canvas, there is no substitute for running the app on physical devices and simulators during testing.

Within the main Xcode project window, the menu marked C in Figure 17-29 is used to choose a target simulator. This menu will include simulators that have been configured and any physical devices connected to the development system:

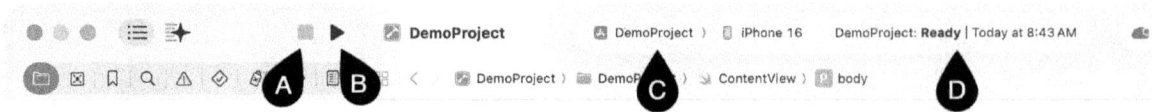

Figure 17-29

Clicking on the *Run* toolbar button (marked B in Figure 17-29 above) will compile the code and run the app on the selected target. The small panel in the center of the Xcode toolbar (D) will report the progress of the build process together with any problems or errors that cause the build process to fail. Once the app is built, the simulator will start and the app will run. Clicking on the stop button (A) will terminate the running app.

The simulator includes several options not available in the Live Preview for testing different aspects of the app. The Hardware and Debug menus, for example, include options for testing Face ID authentication and simulating geographical location changes for navigation and map-based apps.

17.12 Running the App on a Physical iOS Device

Although the Simulator environment provides a useful way to test an app on various iOS device models, it is important to also test on a physical iOS device.

If you have entered your Apple ID in the Xcode preferences screen as outlined in the *"Joining the Apple Developer Program"* chapter and selected a development team for the project, it is possible to run the app on a physical device simply by connecting it to the development Mac system with a USB cable and selecting it as the run target within Xcode.

With a device connected to the development system, and an application ready for testing, refer to the device menu located in the Xcode toolbar. There is a reasonable chance that this will have defaulted to one of the iOS Simulator configurations. Switch to the physical device by selecting this menu and changing it to the device name listed under the iOS Devices section, as shown in Figure 17-30:

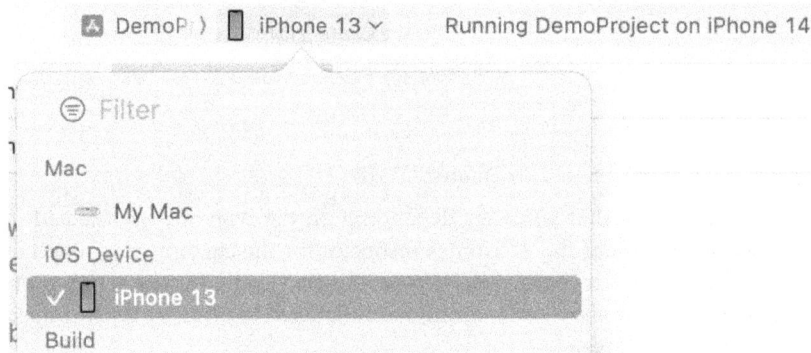

Figure 17-30

If the menu indicates that developer mode is disabled on the device, navigate to the Privacy & Security screen in the device's Settings app, locate the Developer Mode setting, and enable it. You will then need to restart the device. After the device restarts, a dialog will appear in which you will need to turn on developer mode. After entering your security code, the device will be ready for use with Xcode.

With the target device selected, make sure the device is unlocked and click on the run button at which point Xcode will install and launch the app on the device.

As will be discussed later in this chapter, a physical device may also be configured for network testing, whereby apps are installed and tested on the device via a network connection without needing a USB cable.

17.13 Managing Devices and Simulators

Currently connected iOS devices and the simulators configured for use with Xcode can be viewed and managed using the Xcode Devices window which is accessed via the *Window -> Devices and Simulators* menu option. Figure 17-31, for example, shows a typical Device screen on a system where an iPhone has been detected:

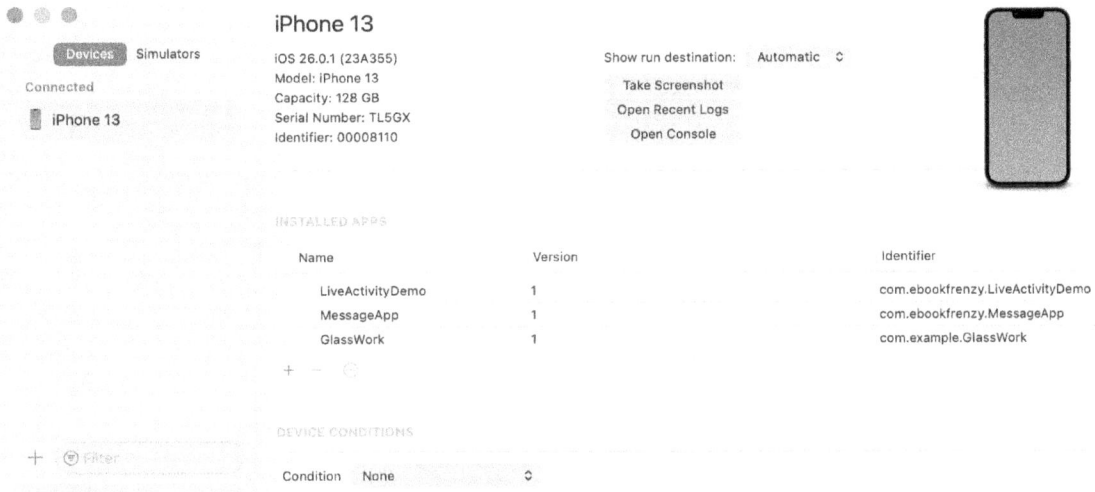

Figure 17-31

A wide range of simulator configurations are set up within Xcode by default and can be viewed by selecting the *Simulators* button at the top of the left-hand panel. Other simulator configurations can be added by clicking on the + button located in the bottom left-hand corner of the window. Once selected, a dialog will appear allowing the simulator to be configured in terms of the device model, iOS version, and name. The OS Version menu allows you download and select different iOS simulator runtime versions:

Figure 17-32

To view and manage the simulator runtimes installed on your system, select the *Xcode -> Settings...* menu option followed by the Component entry in the navigation panel of the resulting dialog:

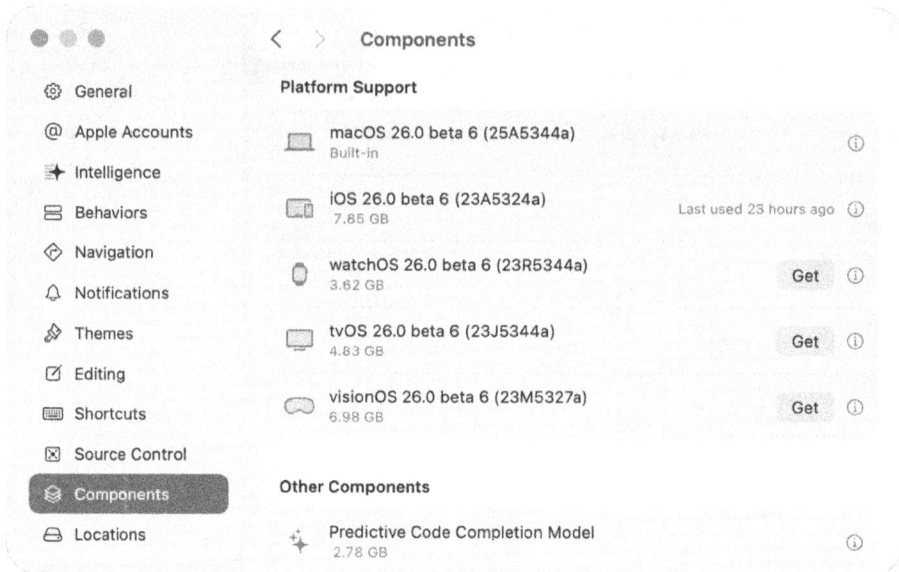

Figure 17-33

17.14 Dealing with Build Errors

If, for any reason, a build fails, the status window in the Xcode toolbar will report that an error has been detected by displaying "Build" together with the number of errors detected and any warnings. In addition, the left-hand panel of the Xcode window will update with a list of the errors. Selecting an error from this list will take you to the location in the code where corrective action needs to be taken.

17.15 Monitoring Application Performance

Another helpful feature of Xcode is the ability to monitor the performance of an application while it is running, either on a device or simulator or within the Live Preview canvas. This information is accessed by displaying the *Debug Navigator*.

When Xcode is launched, the project navigator is displayed in the left-hand panel by default. Along the top of this panel is a bar with various other options. The seventh option from the left displays the debug navigator when selected, as illustrated in Figure 17-34. When displayed, this panel shows real-time statistics relating to the performance of the currently running application such as memory, CPU usage, disk access, energy efficiency, network activity, and iCloud storage access.

Figure 17-34

When one of these categories is selected, the main panel (Figure 17-35) updates to provide additional information about that particular aspect of the application's performance:

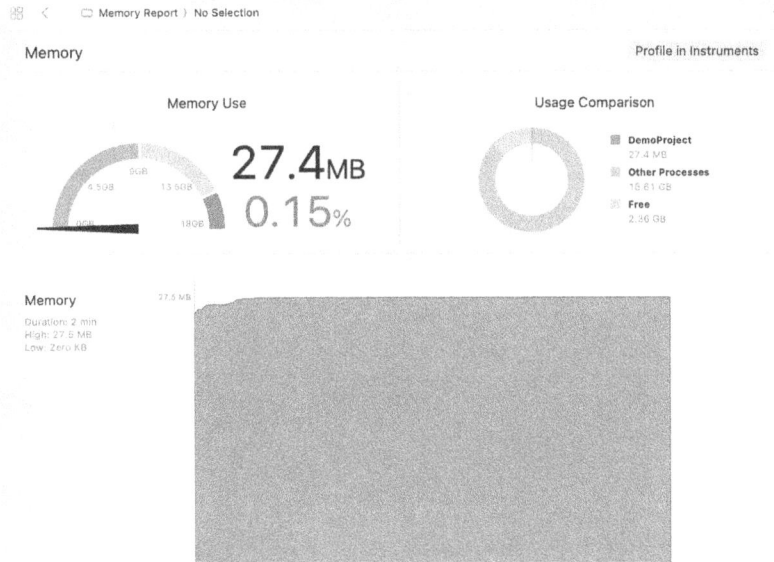

Figure 17-35

Yet more information can be obtained by clicking on the *Profile in Instruments* button in the top right-hand corner of the panel:

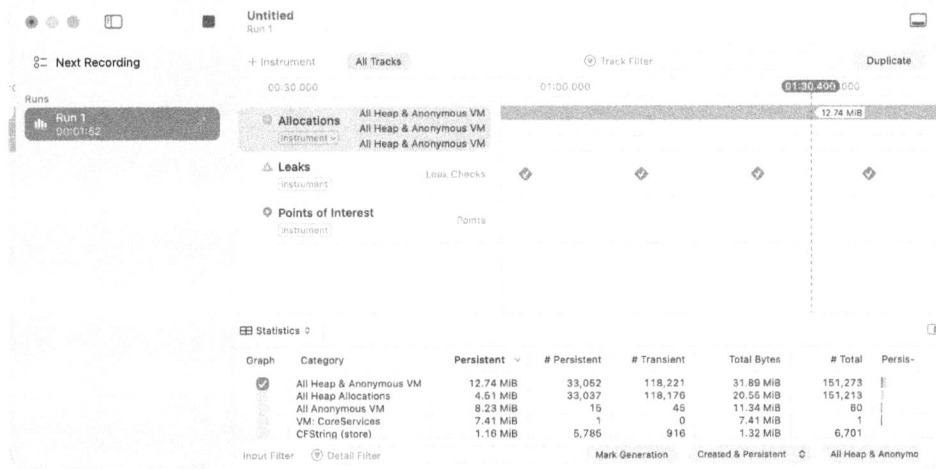

Figure 17-36

17.16 Exploring the User Interface Layout Hierarchy

Xcode also provides an option to render the user interface layout into a rotatable 3D view that shows how the view hierarchy for a user interface is constructed. This can be particularly useful for identifying situations where one view instance is obscured by another appearing on top of it or a layout is not appearing as intended. This is also useful for learning how SwiftUI works behind the scenes to construct a SwiftUI layout if only to appreciate how much work SwiftUI is saving us from having to do.

To access the view hierarchy in this mode, the app must be running on a device or simulator. Once the app is running, click on the *Debug View Hierarchy* button indicated in Figure 17-37:

Figure 17-37

Once activated, a 3D "exploded" view of the layout will appear. Clicking and dragging within the view will rotate the hierarchy allowing the layers of views that make up the user interface to be inspected:

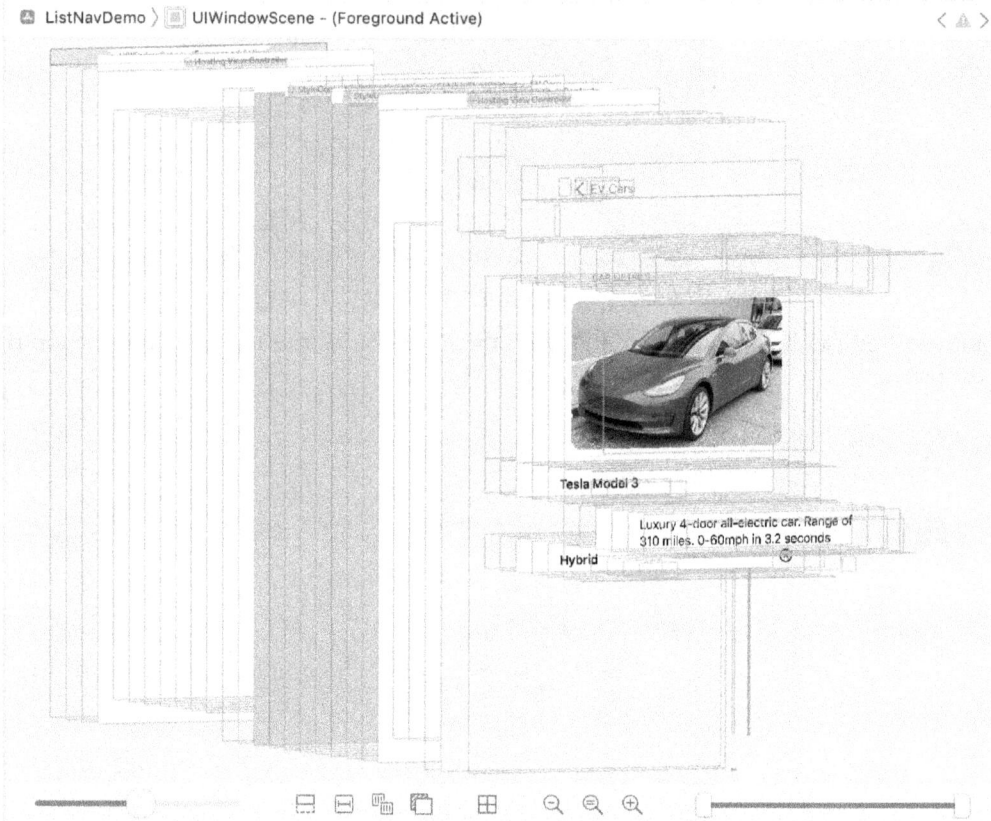

Figure 17-38

Moving the slider in the bottom left-hand corner of the panel will adjust the spacing between the different views in the hierarchy. The two markers in the right-hand slider (Figure 17-39) may also be used to narrow the range of views visible in the rendering. This can be useful, for example, to focus on a subset of views located in the middle of the hierarchy tree:

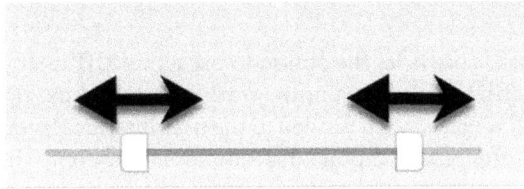

Figure 17-39

While the hierarchy is being debugged, the left-hand panel will display the entire view hierarchy tree for the layout, as shown in Figure 17-40 below:

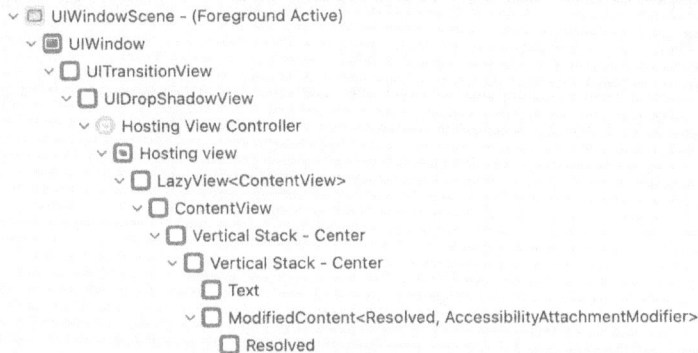

Figure 17-40

Selecting an object in the hierarchy tree will highlight the corresponding item in the 3D rendering and vice versa. The far right-hand panel will also display the attributes of the selected object. Figure 17-41, for example, shows the inspector panel while a Text view is selected within the view hierarchy.

Figure 17-41

17.17 Take the Knowledge Test

 Click the link below or scan the QR code to test your knowledge and understanding of using Xcode to develop SwiftUI projects:

https://www.answertopia.com/zyis

17.18 Summary

When creating a new project, Xcode provides the option to use either UIKit Storyboards or SwiftUI as the basis of the app's user interface. In SwiftUI mode, most of the work involved in developing an app occurs in the code editor and the preview canvas. New views can be added to the user interface layout and configured by typing into the code editor or dragging and dropping components from the Library onto the editor or the preview canvas.

The preview canvas will usually update in real-time to reflect code changes as they are typed into the code editor. However, it will occasionally pause updates in response to more significant changes. When in the paused state, clicking the Resume button will restart updates. The Attribute inspector allows the properties of a selected view to be changed and new modifiers added. Holding down the Command key while clicking on a view in the editor or canvas displays the context menu containing a range of options, such as embedding the view in a container or extracting the selection to a subview.

The preview structure at the end of the SwiftUI View file allows previewing on multiple device models simultaneously and with different environment settings.

18. Coding Intelligence in Xcode

Coding Intelligence was introduced with Xcode 26 and uses AI to generate code, resolve problems, and answer questions as you develop iOS projects. This chapter will explain how to activate, configure, and use Coding Intelligence and predictive code completion in Xcode.

18.1 About Coding Intelligence

Like many modern software development environments, Xcode uses AI language models to assist you during project development. Unlike Google's Gemini, Apple does not have its own AI model; instead, it allows integration with third-party model providers. Currently, Xcode offers the option to integrate with OpenAI's ChatGPT and Anthropic's Claude models through a simple setting.

You can also establish other integrations by entering the URL of the model provider's API, along with an API key and your account information.

While some model providers offer free AI chat capabilities, the number of responses may be subject to a daily limit unless you upgrade to the model provider's premium plan and enter your account credentials in Xcode.

18.2 Enabling Coding Intelligence

To enable Coding Intelligence, use the *Xcode -> Settings...* menu option and select the Intelligence option in the left-hand navigation panel, as shown in Figure 18-1 below:

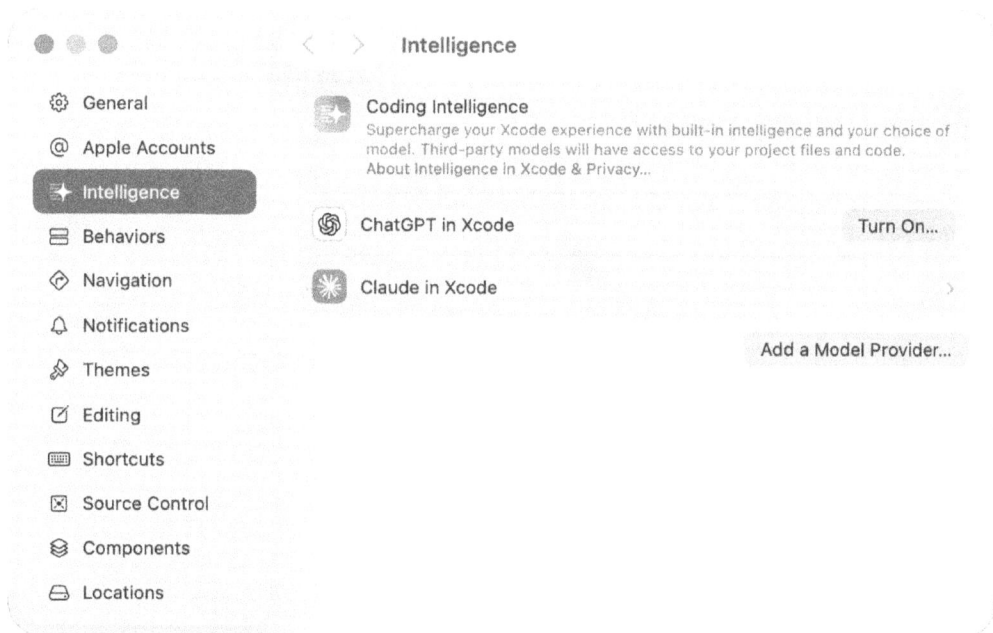

Figure 18-1

To use Claude in Xcode, you must have an existing Anthropic account. The ChatGPT option does not require an account, but you will need to create one and upgrade to a paid plan to eliminate the daily request limit.

To enable ChatGPT integration, click the *Turn On...* button and follow the informational prompts until you reach the final screen:

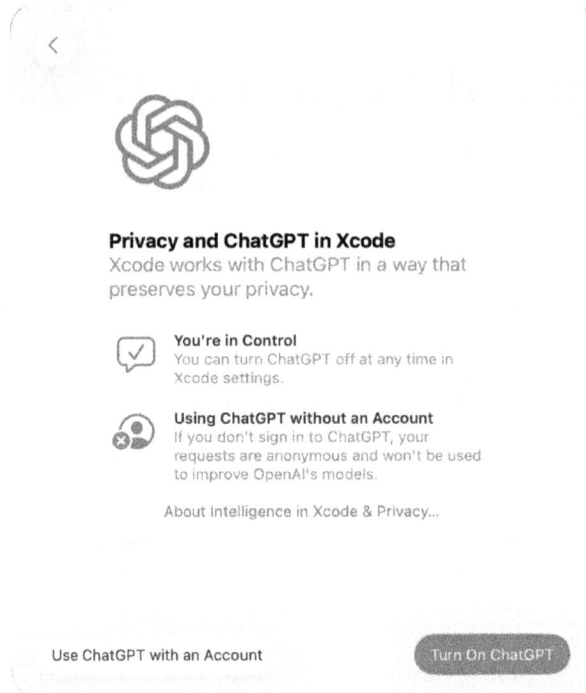

Figure 18-2

If you have a ChatGPT account and want to sign in while using Coding Intelligence, select the *Use ChatGPT with an Account* button. If not, click the *Turn On ChatGPT* button to continue anonymously.

18.3 Using the Coding Assistant

Most of your interaction with Coding Intelligence in Xcode will take place in the Coding Assistant panel, which is displayed by clicking the toolbar button indicated in Figure 18-3:

Figure 18-3

Figure 18-4, for example, illustrates the Coding Assistant during a typical chat session:

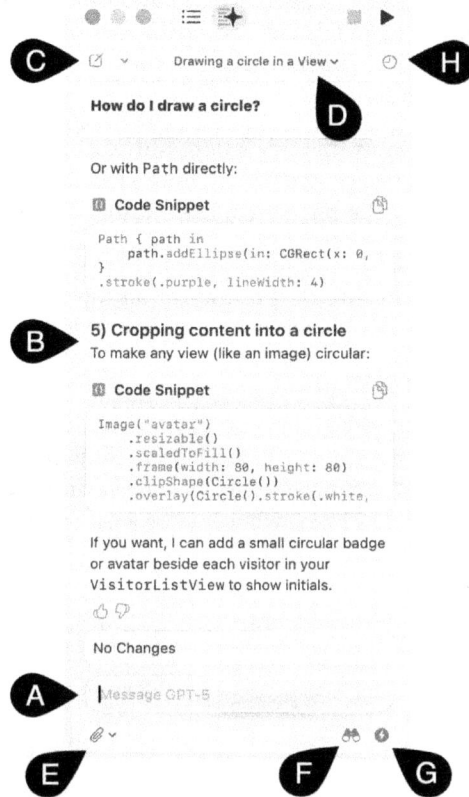

Figure 18-4

Interact with your chosen intelligence model by typing messages into the text field marked A above. The current conversation transcript appears in the area marked B. Use button C to start a new conversation, and the disclosure arrow to the right of the new conversation button to switch to a different model, as shown below:

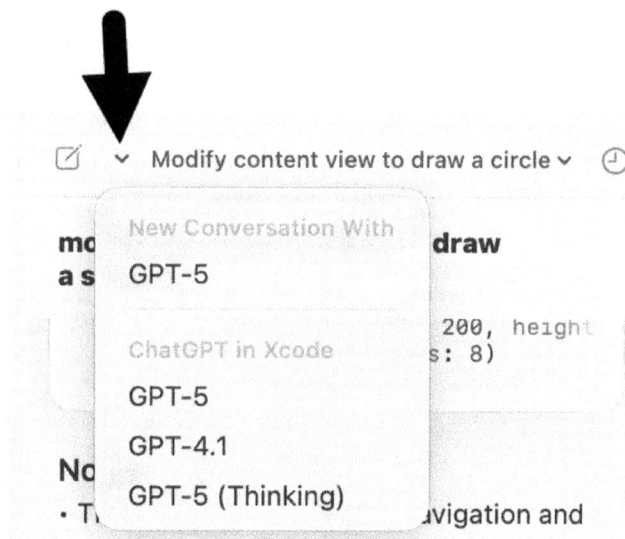

Figure 18-5

Use the conversation menu (D) to access recent conversations and the button marked E to upload attachments for analysis by the model. When interacting with the Coding Assistant, you can allow the model to access your Xcode project files to provide context and to generate responses specific to your code and requirements. Use the Project Context setting (F) to turn off code access.

Coding Intelligence will often provide you with code snippets that can be applied to your code to achieve an objective or resolve a problem. Use the setting marked G to control whether these code changes are automatically applied to your code. Keep in mind that the project context setting (F) must be enabled if changes are to be applied automatically.

The modification history button (H) contains a repository of all the code changes made to your project by Coding Intelligence, allowing you to revert to previous points in the code history.

18.4 Providing Context in Prompts

When project context is enabled, you can refer to elements of your code structure in your message prompts using the @ prefix. Suppose, for example, that the *ContentView.swift* file contains a view named ContainerDemoView and we need Coding Intelligence to make changes to the view declaration. When entering the prompt, typing @ followed by the first few letters of the view name will generate a list of possible matches in the current source file. For example:

Figure 18-6

After selecting the correct view, the prompt can be completed and submitted to the AI model:

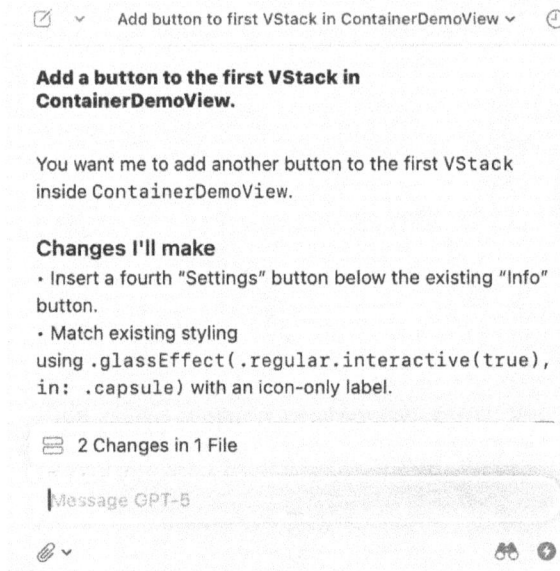

Figure 18-7

18.5 Using Coding Intelligence

Coding intelligence is available via conversations in the Code Assistant panel or within the code editor when code is highlighted or a syntax warning or error notification is visible. To experiment with Coding Intelligence, create a new Xcode multiplatform project called *IntelligenceDemo*.

With the project created, select the *Xcode -> Settings...* menu option followed by the Intelligence option as shown in Figure 18-1 above. Click the button to enable ChatGPT, follow the steps to complete the activation, and ensure that the *ContentView.swift* file is open in the code editor.

Display the Code Assistant and verify that the Project Context setting is enabled, and that the option to apply code changes automatically is turned on before entering the following request into the message text field:

Draw a magenta square that rotates in response to the motion of a slider.

In response to the prompt text, the Coding Assistant will generate the code to implement the requested behavior with accompanying explanations and integrate it into the *ContentView.swift* file:

Fix error in ContentView.swift on line 16

You're seeing this error because SwiftUI's `Color` doesn't include a built-in `.magenta`. I'll add a small `Color` extension defining `magenta` so your existing usage `.fill(Color.magenta)` compiles and renders the expected color.

Changes I'll make
· Add a `Color` extension in **ContentView.swift** ⊙ defining `static let magenta = Color(red: 1, green: 0, blue: 1, opacity: 1)`

Changes made:
· Inserted a `Color` extension right after `import SwiftUI`:

🔲 **Code Snippet**   📋

```
// Add a magenta convenience color to match UIKit
extension Color {
    static let magenta = Color(red: 1, green: 0, b
}
```

Now `.fill(Color.magenta)` compiles and displays the

🗄 2 Changes in 1 File

Figure 18-8

Coding Intelligence is also available when resolving problems in the code editor. For example, while writing this chapter, ChatGPT was unaware that the SwiftUI Color type does not include a magenta value, resulting in the following syntax error:

```
var body: some View {
    VStack(spacing: 24) {
        Rectangle()
            .fill(Color.magenta)
            .frame(width: 150, heig⌐
            .rotationEffect(.degree ⊗   Type 'Color' has no member 'magenta'
            .animation(.easeInOut(d ⊟  Generate Fix for Issue        Generate

    VStack {
```

Figure 18-9

In addition to explaining the problem, the notification includes a button to fix the issue using Coding Intelligence. Clicking the Generate button resolved the problem by adding an extension to the Color type to include a member named magenta with appropriate RGB color values:

```
// Add a magenta convenience color to match UIKit's .magenta
extension Color {
    static let magenta = Color(red: 1, green: 0, blue: 1, opacity: 1)
}
```

With the changes complete, the example should appear in the preview canvas, as shown in Figure 18-10:

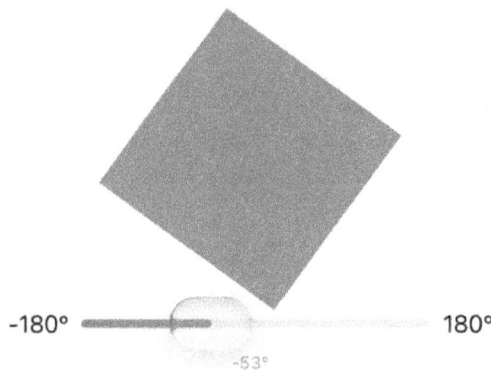

Figure 18-10

When a section of code in the editor is selected, the Coding Intelligence button highlighted in Figure 18-11 appears in the editor margin:

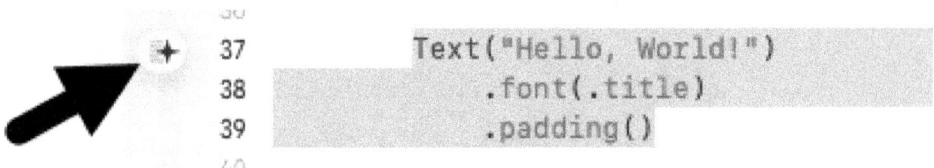

```
37          Text("Hello, World!")
38              .font(.title)
39              .padding()
```

Figure 18-11

Clicking the button will present options to ask a question related to the code, generate comments documenting the purpose of the code, or request an explanation of how the selected code works:

Figure 18-12

18.6 Creating a Git Repository

To use the modification history, you first need to create a Git repository for your project. Git is a popular source code control system that records and tracks changes in your code, enabling you to restore projects to previous points in the change history. When Git is enabled for an Xcode project, all modifications will be stored in the repository. When committed, these modifications can be shared with others working on the same project, stored remotely, and applied to the code on other Macs and code branches. However, in this chapter, we will focus primarily on source code control within the context of Coding Intelligence, which provides a quick way to roll back changes made by the AI model. In other words, the modification history does not commit the changes to the repository in a way that synchronizes them with other developers on your team or leverages the advanced features offered by Git. To commit these changes, you will need to do so manually.

A repository can be added to a project when it is created by enabling the checkbox highlighted in Figure 18-13 before clicking the Create button:

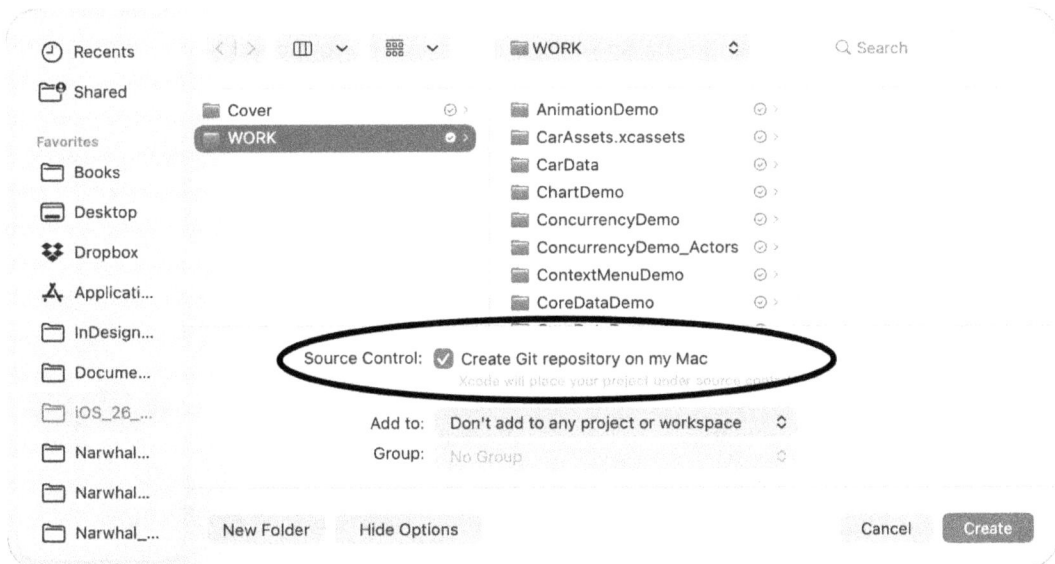

Figure 18-13

To check if a project already has a repository, select the Navigators toolbar button (marked A in Figure 18-14), followed by the Source Control navigator tab (B):

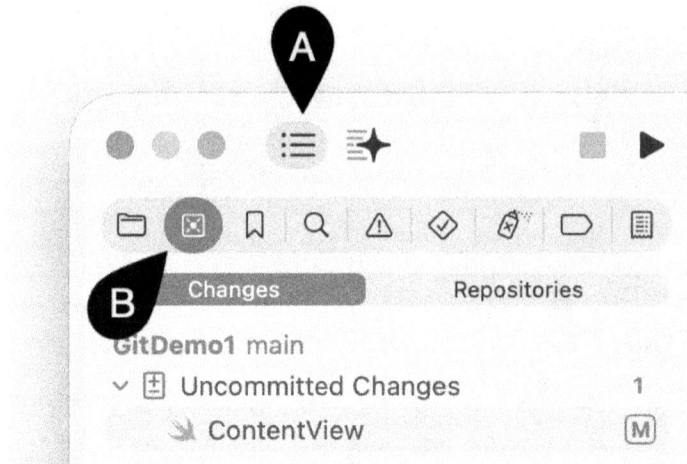

Figure 18-14

If the Source Control navigator indicates there are no repositories, one must be created to activate the Coding Assistant's modification history feature. If your IntelligenceDemo project does not include a repository, select the Xcode *Integrate -> New Git Repository...* menu option and enable the current project in the repository creation dialog:

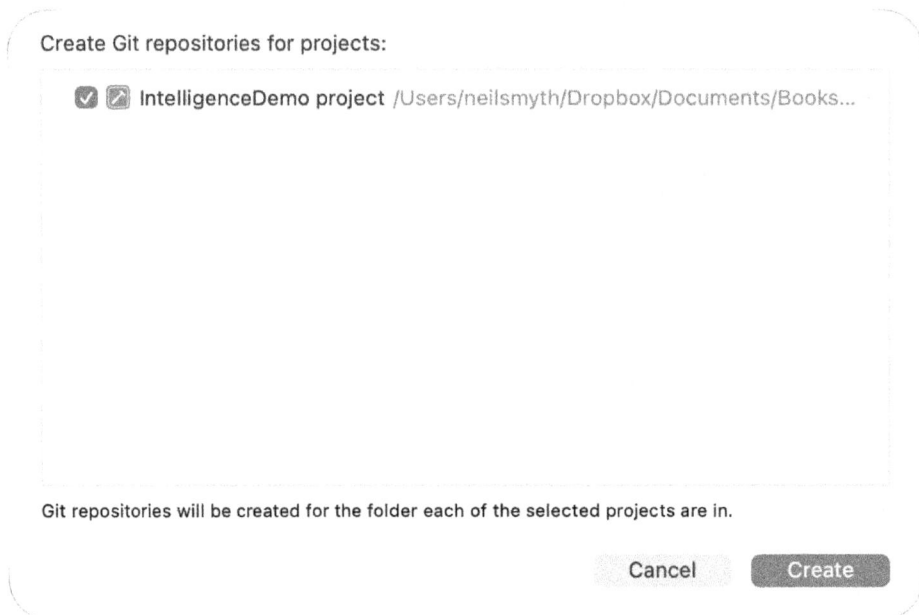

Figure 18-15

Click the Create button and enter your name and email address when prompted before clicking the Save button.

18.7 Using the Modification History

With the Git repository created, we can explore the modification history capabilities of the Coding Assistant. To do so, we need the assistant to make more changes to the ContentView declaration. Begin by asking Coding Intelligence to change the square to a star shape:

```
Change the square to a star shape.
```

After a short delay, the ContentView will be modified to replace the square with code to draw a magenta star.

With the change made, click the modification history button (marked H in Figure 18-4), where the change will be listed (A in Figure 18-16 below):

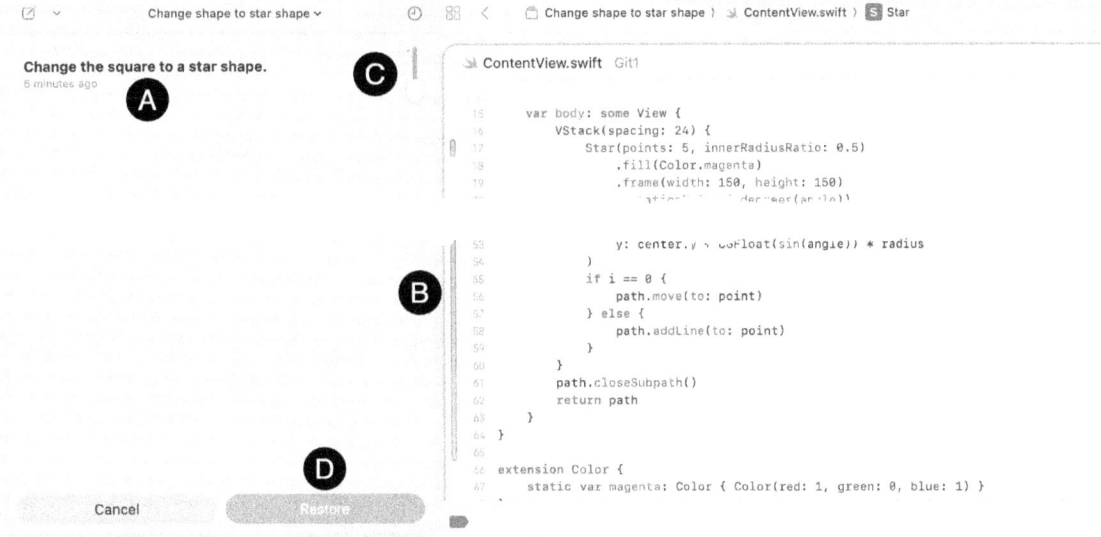

Figure 18-16

In the main panel, a colored bar appears in the margin (B) indicating where the changes occurred in the code file. To restore the code to its original state before the shape change was applied, move the slider (C) to the point before the change and click the Restore button (D). Then, click the Restore All Changes button in the confirmation dialog.

Review the code and preview canvas to verify that the square has returned, then return to the conversation where the Coding Assistant will provide the option to reapply the shape change:

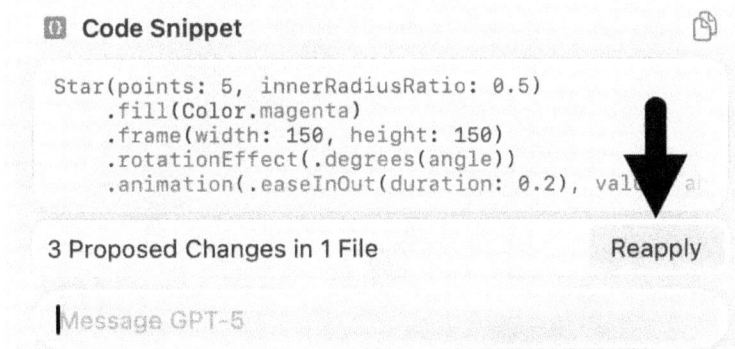

Figure 18-17

Click the modification history button to review the changes, noting that the reversion is now included in the list of changes:

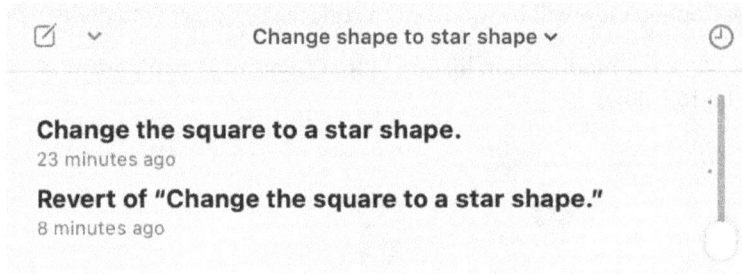

Figure 18-18

Use the Coding Assistant to make more changes to the project and experiment with the modification history to restore the project to previous states.

18.8 Conversations and Modification Histories

Xcode maintains a separate modification history for each Coding Assistant conversation. To access the modification history for a specific conversation, select it from the recent conversations menu (marked D in Figure 18-4 above) and click the Modification History button (H).

18.9 Committing Changes

As previously discussed, the modification history does not automatically commit Coding Intelligence changes to the Git repository. To commit the changes, display the Source Code navigator as outlined in Figure 18-14 above and select the uncommitted changes entry in the branch hierarchy:

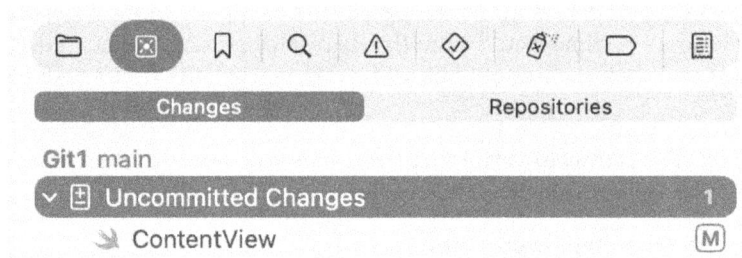

Figure 18-19

In the main panel, select the Unstaged tab and review the code changes before clicking the Stage All button, as indicated in Figure 18-20:

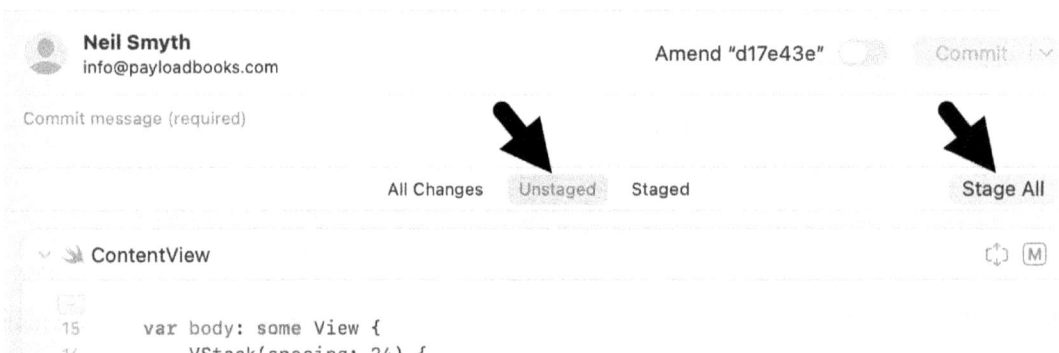

Figure 18-20

Finally, once the changes have been staged, type a description of the changes and click the Commit button:

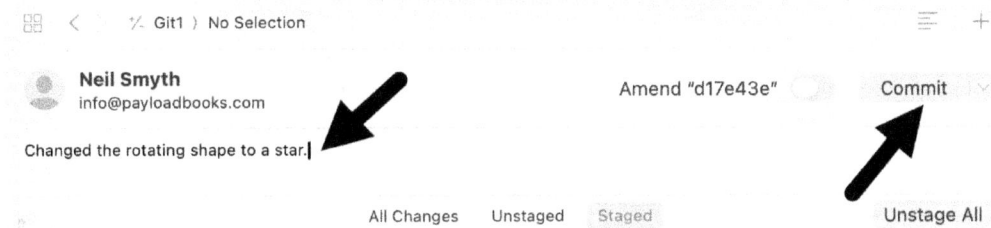

Figure 18-21

18.10 Working with Code Completion

In addition to the Coding Intelligence features covered so far, Xcode will also make code completion suggestions as you type into the code editor. It does this based on the code you are typing and an analysis of the rest of the code, including elements such as variable and structure names, as well as comments. Xcode's ability to infer your intentions is so good that it can initially feel uncanny.

In the remainder of this chapter, we will experiment with predictive code completion. Before doing so, however, it is essential to note that the code completion model is constantly learning and evolving, so you may see different coding suggestions than those outlined below.

We demonstrated Swift object-oriented programming in a previous chapter by creating a bank account class. Suppose we are writing a similar class, but this time with predictive code completion enabled. Press Cmd+N and create a new Swift File named *BankAccount.swift*. With the new file open in the editor, begin declaring the class as follows:

```
import Foundation


class BankAccount {


}
```

Within the class body, start declaring a variable. As you type the letters "var" Xcode may suggest a variable named *balance*, as illustrated below:

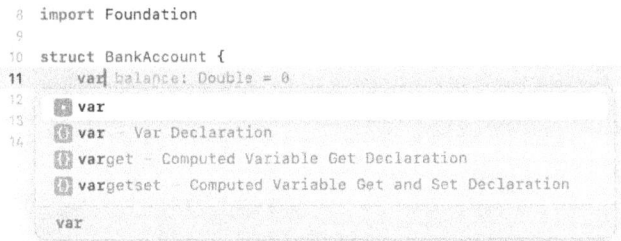

Figure 18-22

Press the Tab key to accept the code suggestion. Press enter, and Xcode may suggest the addition of a *deposit()* method as follows:

```
 8  import Foundation
 9
10  class BankAccount {
11
12      var balance: Double = 0
13
14      func deposit(amount: Double) { ••• }
15
16
17  }
```

Figure 18-23

The ellipsis highlighted by the arrow in the above figure indicates that Xcode has more code to suggest than is currently visible on the screen. Use the Tab key to accept the code suggestions or the Esc key to reject them. Press the enter key and start typing a new func declaration, at which point Xcode might suggest the following *withdraw()* method:

```
func withdraw(_ amount: Double) -> Bool {
    if amount > balance {
        return false
    } else {
        balance -= amount
        return true
    }
}
```

Return to the top of the class and begin declaring a second variable. Xcode may offer to complete the declaration as a Double value named *interestRate*. Type "func" beneath the *withdrawal()* method, and Xcode may suggest an interest calculation method.

Although your results may differ, the following class body was generated entirely using predictive code completion:

```
class BankAccount {

    var balance: Double = 0.0
    var interestRate: Double = 0.0
    var name: String = ""


    func deposit(_ amount: Double) {
        balance += amount
    }

    func withdraw(_ amount: Double) -> Bool {
        if amount > balance {
            return false
        } else {
            balance -= amount
            return true
        }
    }
}
```

```
func calculateInterest() {
    balance += balance * interestRate
}

func getBalance() -> Double {
    return balance
}

func setName(_ name: String) {
    self.name = name
}

func getName() -> String {
    "\(self.name)"
}
}
```

18.11 Take the Knowledge Test

Click the link below or scan the QR code to test your knowledge and understanding of Coding Intelligence in Xcode:

https://www.answertopia.com/35jc

18.12 Summary

Coding Intelligence was introduced with Xcode 26 and can generate code, fix errors, and answer questions during development. It allows integration with third-party AI models, such as ChatGPT and Claude, with options to restrict or allow code access and automatic code application. The Coding Assistant panel facilitates interaction with the AI model, providing code snippets, explanations, and a repository-based modification history for reverting changes.

Xcode's predictive code completion feature provides inline code suggestions as you type within the code editor based on the context of your existing code.

19. SwiftUI Architecture

A completed SwiftUI app is constructed from multiple components that are assembled hierarchically. Before embarking on creating even the most basic SwiftUI projects, it is helpful to understand how SwiftUI apps are structured. With this goal in mind, this chapter will introduce the key elements of SwiftUI app architecture, emphasizing App, Scene, and View elements.

19.1 SwiftUI App Hierarchy

When considering the structure of a SwiftUI application, it helps to view a typical hierarchy visually. Figure 19-1, for example, illustrates the hierarchy of a simple SwiftUI app:

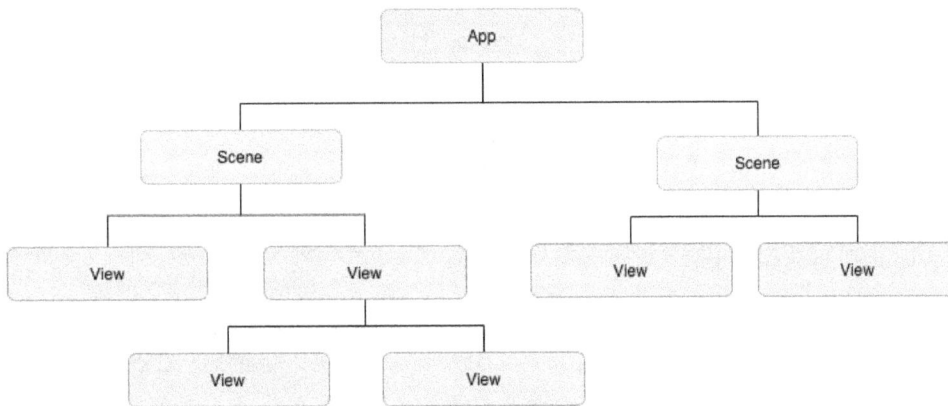

Figure 19-1

Before continuing, it is essential to distinguish the difference between the term "app" and the "App" element outlined in the above figure. The software applications that we install and run on our mobile devices have come to be referred to as "apps". In this chapter, reference will be made both to these apps and the App element in the above figure. To avoid confusion, we will use "application" to refer to the completed, installed, and running app while referring to the App element as "App". The remainder of the book will revert to using the more common "app" when discussing applications.

19.2 App

The App object is the top-level element within the structure of a SwiftUI application and is responsible for handling the launching and lifecycle of each running instance of the application.

The App element is also responsible for managing the various Scenes that make up the application's user interface. An application will include only one App instance.

19.3 Scenes

Each SwiftUI application will contain one or more scenes. A scene represents a section or region of the application's user interface. On iOS and watchOS, a scene will typically take the form of a window that takes up the entire device screen. On the other hand, SwiftUI applications running on macOS and iPadOS will likely be comprised of multiple scenes. Different scenes might, for example, contain context-specific layouts to be displayed when the user selects tabs within a dialog or to design applications that consist of multiple windows.

SwiftUI includes some pre-built primitive scene types that can be used when designing applications, the most common being WindowGroup and DocumentGroup. It is also possible to group scenes together to create your own custom scenes.

19.4 Views

Views are the basic building blocks that make up the visual elements of the user interface, such as buttons, labels, and text fields. Each scene will contain a hierarchy of the views that make up a section of the application's user interface. Views can either be individual visual elements, such as text views or buttons or take the form of containers that manage other views. The Vertical Stack view, for example, is designed to display child views in a vertical layout. In addition to the Views provided with SwiftUI, you will also create custom views when developing SwiftUI applications. These custom views will comprise groups of other views together with customizations to the appearance and behavior of those views to meet the requirements of the application's user interface.

Figure 19-2, for example, illustrates a scene containing a simple view hierarchy consisting of a Vertical Stack containing a Button and TextView combination:

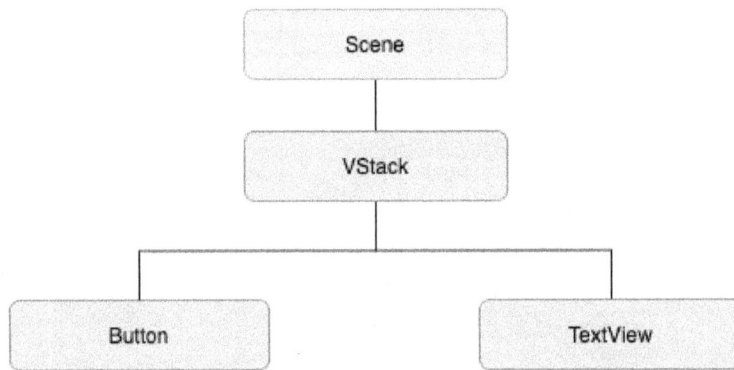

Figure 19-2

19.5 Take the Knowledge Test

Click the link below or scan the QR code to test your knowledge and understanding of SwiftUI's architecture:

https://www.answertopia.com/z871

19.6 Summary

SwiftUI applications are constructed hierarchically. At the top of the hierarchy is the App instance, which is responsible for the launching and lifecycle of the application. One or more child Scene instances contain hierarchies of the View instances that make up the application's user interface. These scenes can either be derived from one of the SwiftUI primitive Scene types, such as WindowGroup, or custom-built.

On iOS or watchOS, an application typically contains a single scene, which takes the form of a window occupying the entire display. However, on a macOS or iPadOS system, an application may comprise multiple scene instances, often represented by separate windows that can be displayed simultaneously or grouped together in a tabbed interface.

20. The Anatomy of a Basic SwiftUI Project

When a new SwiftUI project is created in Xcode using the Multiplatform App template, Xcode generates a collection of files and folders that form the basis of the project and on which the finished app will eventually be built.

Although it is not necessary to know in detail about the purpose of each of these files when beginning with SwiftUI development, each of them will become useful as you develop more complex applications.

This chapter will briefly overview each basic Xcode SwiftUI project structure element.

20.1 Creating an Example Project

If you have not already done so, creating a sample project to review may be helpful while working through this chapter. To do so, launch Xcode and, on the welcome screen, select the option to create a new project. On the resulting template selection panel, select the Multiplatform tab followed by the App option before proceeding to the next screen:

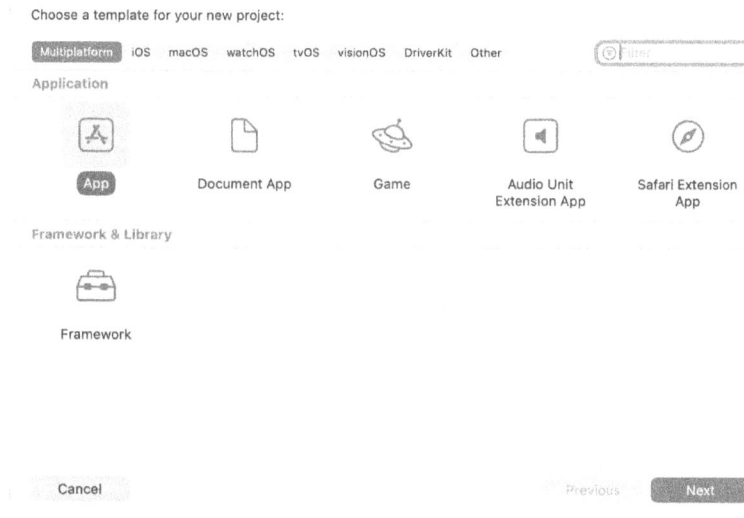

Figure 20-1

On the project options screen, name the project *DemoProject* and set the Testing System menu to "None". Click Next to proceed to the final screen, choose a suitable filesystem location for the project, and click the Create button.

20.2 The DemoProjectApp.swift File

The *DemoProjectApp.swift* file contains the declaration for the App object as described in the chapter entitled *"SwiftUI Architecture"* and will read as follows:

```
import SwiftUI

@main
struct DemoProjectApp: App {
    var body: some Scene {
        WindowGroup {
            ContentView()
        }
    }
}
```

As implemented, the declaration returns a Scene consisting of a WindowGroup containing the View defined in the *ContentView.swift* file. Note that the declaration is prefixed with *@main*. This indicates to SwiftUI that this is the entry point for the app when it is launched on a device.

20.3 The ContentView.swift File

This is a SwiftUI View file that, by default, contains the content of the first screen to appear when the app starts. This file and others like it are where most of the work is performed when developing apps in SwiftUI. By default, it contains an Image view and a Text view displaying the words "Hello, world!" arranged within a vertical stack container:

```
import SwiftUI

struct ContentView: View {
    var body: some View {
        VStack {
            Image(systemName: "globe")
                .imageScale(.large)
                .foregroundStyle(.tint)
            Text("Hello, world!")
        }
        .padding()
    }
}

#Preview {
    ContentView()
}
```

20.4 Assets.xcassets

The *Assets.xcassets* folder contains the asset catalog that stores resources used by the app, such as images, icons, and colors.

20.5 DemoProject.entitlements

The entitlements file is used to enable support for specific iOS features within the app. For example, if your app needs access to iCloud storage or the device microphone, or if you plan to integrate voice control via Siri, these entitlements must be enabled within this file.

20.6 Preview Content

The preview assets folder contains any assets and data needed when previewing the app during development but not required in the completed app. When you are ready to package your app for submission to the app store, Xcode will remove these assets from the delivery archive so they do not take up unnecessary space.

20.7 Take the Knowledge Test

Click the link below or scan the QR code to test your knowledge and understanding of Xcode SwiftUI project files:

https://www.answertopia.com/614z

20.8 Summary

When a new SwiftUI project is created in Xcode using the Multiplatform App template, Xcode automatically generates the minimal files required for the app to function. All of these files and folders can be modified to add functionality to the app, both in terms of adding resource assets, performing initialization and de-initialization tasks, and building the user interface and logic of the app.

21. Creating Custom Views with SwiftUI

A key step in learning to develop apps using SwiftUI is learning how to declare user interface layouts by using the built-in SwiftUI views and building your own custom views. This chapter will introduce the basic concepts of SwiftUI views and outline the syntax used to declare user interface layouts and modify view appearance and behavior.

21.1 SwiftUI Views

User interface layouts are composed in SwiftUI by using, creating, and combining views. An essential first step is to understand what the term "view" means. Views in SwiftUI are declared as structures that conform to the View protocol. To conform with the View protocol, a structure is required to contain a body property, and it is within this body property that the view is declared.

SwiftUI includes many built-in views that can be used when constructing a user interface, including text label, button, text field, menu, toggle, and layout manager views. Each of these is a self-contained instance that complies with the View protocol. When building an app with SwiftUI, you will use these views to create custom views of your own, which, when combined, constitute the appearance and behavior of your user interface.

These custom views will range from subviews that encapsulate a reusable subset of view components (perhaps a secure text field and a button for logging into screens within your app) to views that encapsulate the user interface for an entire screen. Regardless of the size and complexity of a custom view or the number of child views encapsulated within, a view is still just an instance that defines some user interface appearance and behavior.

21.2 Creating a Basic View

In Xcode, custom views are contained within SwiftUI View files. When a new SwiftUI project is created, Xcode will create a single SwiftUI View file containing a single custom view consisting of a single Text view and an image. Additional view files can be added to the project by selecting the *File -> New -> File...* menu option and choosing the SwiftUI View file entry from the template screen.

The default SwiftUI View file is named *ContentView.swift* and reads as follows:

```
import SwiftUI

struct ContentView: View {
    var body: some View {
        VStack {
            Image(systemName: "globe")
                .imageScale(.large)
                .foregroundStyle(.tint)
            Text("Hello, world!")
        }
        .padding()
    }
```

```
}

#Preview {
    ContentView()
}
```

The view is named ContentView and is declared as conforming to the View protocol. It also includes the mandatory body property, which, in turn, contains a vertical stack layout container containing an Image component configured to display a globe graphic and an instance of the built-in Text view component displaying text that reads "Hello, World!".

The second structure in the file creates an instance of ContentView so that it appears in the preview canvas, a topic that will be covered in detail in later chapters.

21.3 Adding Views

Additional views can be added to a parent view by placing them in the body declaration. The following is a simple example containing a single Text view:

```
struct ContentView: View {
    var body: some View {
        Text("Hello, world!")
    }
}
```

The body property is designed to return a single view, which is a Text view in the above example. Following this logic, adding a second view as follows should cause a syntax error:

```
struct ContentView: View {
    var body: some View {
        Text("Hello, world!")
        Text("Goodbye, world!")
    }
}
```

In practice, however, the above code is valid, and when the layout is previewed, the two text views will appear, as shown in Figure 21-1:

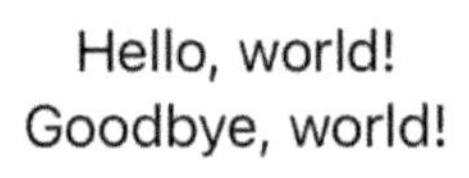

Hello, world!
Goodbye, world!

Figure 21-1

The above example contradicts the limitation that only a single view can be returned from the body. Behind the scenes, however, SwiftUI is avoiding this problem by embedding the Text views inside a TupleView. TupleView is used to create a single view containing multiple other views, but because it provides few options for changing how the layout appears, you will rarely use it when designing SwiftUI layouts.

Adding views in this way works but doesn't take advantage of the hierarchical approach to SwiftUI development, and we lose the ability to treat the child views as a group in terms of appearance and layout.

Assuming that the goal is to stack the views vertically with equal spacing, it makes more sense to place the new views within the scope of the VStack view, which, as the name suggests, positions views vertically within the containing view:

```
struct ContentView: View {
    var body: some View {
        VStack {
            Text("Hello, world!")
            Text("Goodbye, world!")
            Text("We'll miss you.")
        }
    }
}
```

21.4 SwiftUI Hierarchies

SwiftUI views are hierarchical by nature, starting with parent and child views. This allows views to be nested to multiple levels to create user interfaces of any complexity. Consider, for example, the following view hierarchy diagram:

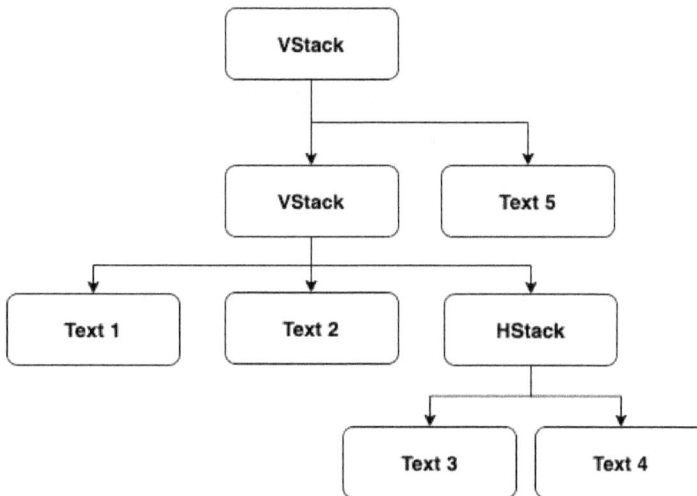

Figure 21-2

The equivalent view declaration for the above view would read as follows:

```
struct ContentView: View {
    var body: some View {
        VStack {
            VStack {
                Text("Text 1")
                Text("Text 2")
                HStack {
                    Text("Text 3")
                    Text("Text 4")
                }
            }
            Text("Text 5")
```

```
        }
    }
}
```

The above layout will appear, as shown below, when previewed:

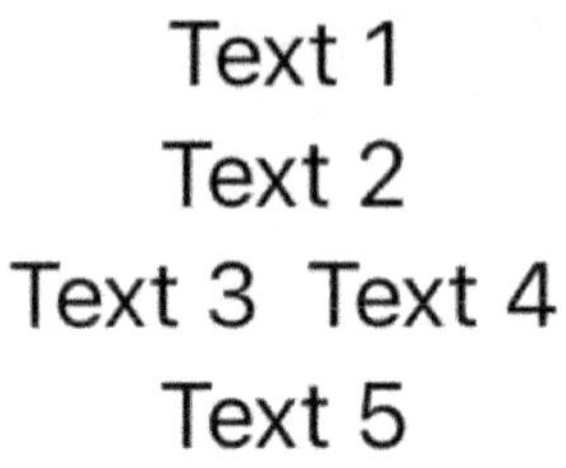

Text 1

Text 2

Text 3 Text 4

Text 5

Figure 21-3

21.5 Working with Subviews

Apple recommends that views be kept as small and lightweight as possible. This promotes the creation of reusable components, makes view declarations easier to maintain, and results in more efficient layout rendering.

If you find that a custom view declaration has become large and complex, identify areas of the view that can be extracted into a subview. As a very simplistic example, the HStack view in the above example could be extracted as a subview named "MyHStackView" as follows:

```
struct ContentView: View {
    var body: some View {
        VStack {
            VStack {
                Text("Text 1")
                Text("Text 2")
                MyHStackView()
            }
            Text("Text 5")
        }
    }
}


struct MyHStackView: View {
    var body: some View {
        HStack {
            Text("Text 3")
            Text("Text 4")
        }
    }
}
```

21.6 Views as Properties

In addition to creating subviews, views may also be assigned to properties as a way to organize complex view hierarchies. Consider the following example view declaration:

```
struct ContentView: View {

    var body: some View {

        VStack {
            Text("Main Title")
                .font(.largeTitle)
            HStack {
                Text("Car Image")
                Image(systemName: "car.fill")
            }
        }
    }
}
```

Any part of the above declaration can be moved to a property value and then referenced by name. In the following declaration, the HStack has been assigned to a property named carStack, which is then referenced within the VStack layout:

```
struct ContentView: View {

    let carStack = HStack {
        Text("Car Image")
        Image(systemName: "car.fill")
    }

    var body: some View {
        VStack {
            Text("Main Title")
                .font(.largeTitle)
            carStack
        }
    }
}
```

21.7 Modifying Views

It is unlikely that any of the views provided with SwiftUI will appear and behave exactly as required without some form of customization. These changes are made by applying *modifiers* to the views.

All SwiftUI views have sets of modifiers that can be applied to make appearance and behavior changes. These modifiers take the form of methods called on the instance of the view and wrap the original view inside another view, which applies the necessary changes. This means modifiers can be chained together to apply multiple modifications to the same view. The following, for example, changes the font and foreground color of a Text view:

```
Text("Text 1")
    .font(.headline)
    .foregroundColor(.red)
```

Similarly, the following example uses modifiers to configure an Image view to be resizable with the aspect ratio set to fit proportionally within the available space:

```
Image(systemName: "car.fill")
    .resizable()
    .aspectRatio(contentMode: .fit)
```

Modifiers may also be applied to custom subviews. In the following example, the font for both Text views in the previously declared MyHStackView custom view will be changed to use the large title font style:

```
MyHStackView()
    .font(.largeTitle)
```

21.8 Working with Text Styles

In the above example, the font used to display text on a view was declared using a built-in text style (in this case, the large title style).

iOS allows the user to select a preferred text size that applications are expected to adopt when displaying text. The current text size can be configured on a device via the *Settings -> Display & Brightness -> Text Size* screen, which provides a slider to adjust the font size, as shown below:

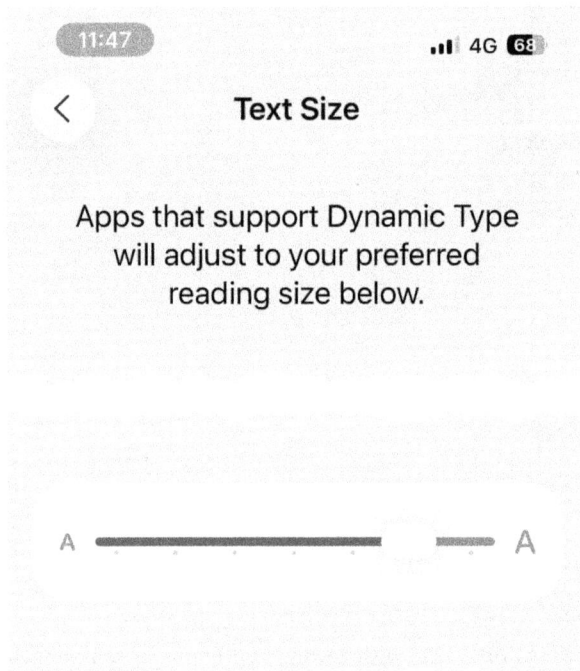

Figure 21-4

If a font has been declared on a view using a text style, the text size will dynamically adapt to the user's preferred font size. Almost without exception, the built-in iOS apps adopt the preferred size setting selected by the user when displaying text, and Apple recommends that third-party apps also conform to the user's chosen text size. The following text style options are currently available:

- Large Title

- Title, Title2, Title 3

- Headline

- Subheadline

- Body

- Callout

- Footnote

- Caption, Caption2

If none of the text styles meet your requirements, it is also possible to apply custom fonts by declaring the font family and size. Although the font size is specified in the custom font, the text will still automatically resize based on the user's preferred dynamic type text size selection:

```
Text("Sample Text")
    .font(.custom("Copperplate", size: 70))
```

The above custom font selection will render the Text view as follows:

SAMPLE TEXT

Figure 21-5

21.9 Modifier Ordering

When chaining modifiers, it is important to be aware that the order in which they are applied can be significant. Both border and padding modifiers have been applied to the following Text view.

```
Text("Sample Text")
    .border(Color.black)
    .padding()
```

The border modifier draws a black border around the view, and the padding modifier adds space around the view. When the above view is rendered, it will appear as shown in Figure 21-6:

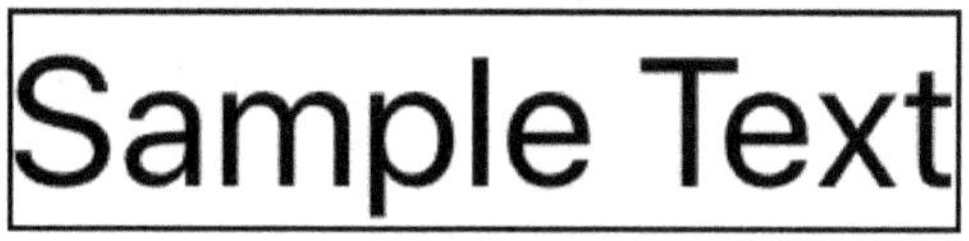

Sample Text

Figure 21-6

Given that padding has been applied to the text, it might be reasonable to expect a gap between the text and the border. In fact, the border was only applied to the original Text view. Padding was then applied to the modified view returned by the border modifier. The padding is still applied to the view but outside of the border. For the border to encompass the padding, the order of the modifiers needs to be changed so that the border is drawn on the view returned by the padding modifier:

```
Text("Sample Text")
    .padding()
    .border(Color.black)
```

With the modifier order switched, the view will now be rendered as follows:

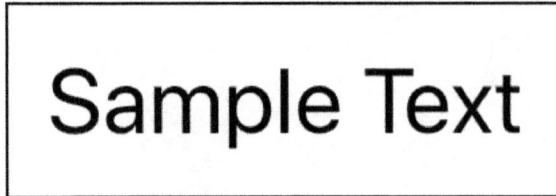

Figure 21-7

If you don't see the expected effects when working with chained modifiers, remember that this may be because of the order in which they are being applied to the view.

21.10 Custom Modifiers

SwiftUI also allows you to create your own custom modifiers. This can be particularly useful if you have a standard set of modifiers that are frequently applied to views. Suppose that the following modifiers are a common requirement within your view declarations:

```
Text("Text 1")
    .font(.largeTitle)
    .background(Color.white)
    .border(Color.gray, width: 0.2)
    .shadow(color: Color.black, radius: 5, x: 0, y: 5)
```

Instead of applying these four modifiers each time text with this appearance is required, a better solution is to group them into a custom modifier and then reference it each time the modification is needed. Custom modifiers are declared as structs that conform to the ViewModifier protocol and, in this instance, might be implemented as follows:

```
struct StandardTitle: ViewModifier {
    func body(content: Content) -> some View {
        content
            .font(.largeTitle)
            .background(Color.white)
            .border(Color.gray, width: 0.2)
            .shadow(color: Color.black, radius: 5, x: 0, y: 5)
    }
}
```

The custom modifier is then applied when needed by passing it through to the *modifier()* method:

```
Text("Text 1")
    .modifier(StandardTitle())
Text("Text 2")
    .modifier(StandardTitle())
```

With the custom modifier implemented, changes can be made to the StandardTitle implementation, and those changes will automatically propagate through to all views that use the modifier. This avoids the need to change the modifiers on multiple views manually.

21.11 Basic Event Handling

Although SwiftUI is described as being data-driven, it is still necessary to handle the events generated when a user interacts with the views in the user interface. Some views, such as the Button view, are provided solely to solicit user interaction. In fact, the Button view can be used to turn various views into a "clickable" button. A Button view needs to be declared with the action method to be called when a click is detected together with the view to act as the button content. It is possible, for example, to designate an entire stack of views as a single button. In most cases, however, a Text view will typically be used as the Button content. In the following implementation, a Button view is used to wrap a Text view, which, when clicked, will call a method named *buttonPressed()*:

```
struct ContentView: View {
    var body: some View {
        Button(action: buttonPressed) {
            Text("Click Me")
        }
    }

    func buttonPressed() {
        // Code to perform action here
    }
}
```

Instead of specifying an action function, the code to be executed when the button is clicked may also be specified as a closure in line with the declaration:

```
Button(action: {
    // Code to perform action here
}) {
    Text("Click Me")
}
```

Another common requirement is to turn an Image view into a button, for example:

```
Button(action: {
    print("Button clicked")
}) {
    Image(systemName: "square.and.arrow.down")
}
```

21.12 Building Custom Container Views

As outlined earlier in this chapter, subviews provide a valuable way to divide a view declaration into small, lightweight, and reusable blocks. One limitation of subviews, however, is that the content of the container view is static. In other words, it is not possible to dynamically specify the views to be included at the point that a subview is included in a layout. The only children included in the subview are those that are specified in the original declaration.

Consider the following subview, which consists of three TextViews contained within a VStack and modified with custom spacing and font settings.

```
struct MyVStack: View {
    var body: some View {
        VStack(spacing: 10) {
```

```
            Text("Text Item 1")
            Text("Text Item 2")
            Text("Text Item 3")
        }
        .font(.largeTitle)
    }
}
```

To include an instance of MyVStack in a declaration, it would be referenced as follows:

```
MyVStack()
```

Suppose, however, that a VStack with a spacing of 10 and a large font modifier is something that is needed frequently within a project, but in each case, different child views are required to be contained within the stack. While this flexibility isn't possible using subviews, it can be achieved using the SwiftUI ViewBuilder closure attribute when constructing custom container views.

A ViewBuilder takes the form of a Swift closure which can be used to create a custom view comprised of multiple child views, the content of which does not need to be declared until the view is used within a layout declaration. The ViewBuilder closure takes the content views and returns them as a single view, which is, in effect, a dynamically built subview.

The following is an example of using the ViewBuilder attribute to implement our custom MyVStack view:

```
struct MyVStack<Content: View>: View {
  let content: () -> Content
  init(@ViewBuilder content: @escaping () -> Content) {
    self.content = content
  }

  var body: some View {
    VStack(spacing: 10) {
      content()
    }
    .font(.largeTitle)
  }
}
```

Note that this declaration still returns an instance that complies with the View protocol and that the body contains the VStack declaration from the previous subview. Instead of including static views to be included in the stack, however, the child views of the stack will be passed to the initializer, handled by ViewBuilder, and embedded into the VStack as child views. The custom MyVStack view can now be initialized with different child views wherever it is used in a layout, for example:

```
MyVStack {
    Text("Text 1")
    Text("Text 2")
    HStack {
        Image(systemName: "star.fill")
        Image(systemName: "star.fill")
        Image(systemName: "star")
    }
```

}

21.13 Working with the Label View

The Label view is different from most other SwiftUI views in that it comprises two elements in the form of an icon and text positioned side-by-side. The image can take the form of any image asset, a SwiftUI Shape rendering, or an SF Symbol.

SF Symbols is a collection of thousands of scalable vector drawings for use when developing apps for Apple platforms and designed to complement Apple's San Francisco system font.

The full set of symbols can be browsed and selected via the Symbols screen of the Library panel, as illustrated in Figure 21-8:

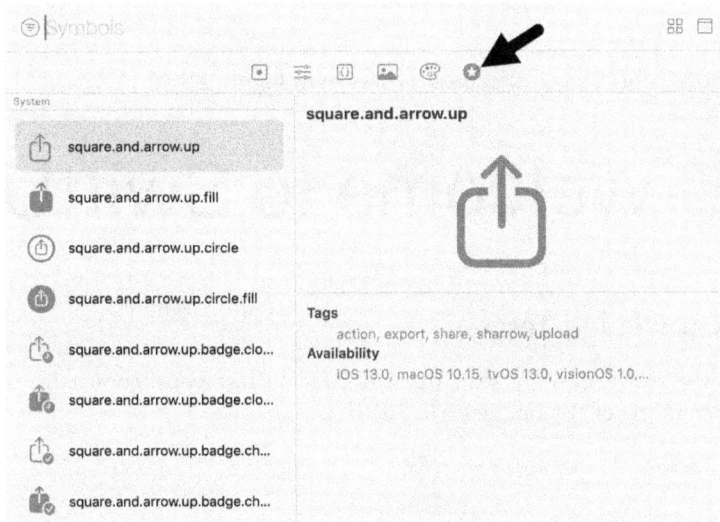

Figure 21-8

The following is an example of the Label view using an SF Symbol together with a *font()* modifier to increase the size of the icon and text:

```
Label("Welcome to SwiftUI", systemImage: "person.circle.fill")
    .font(.largeTitle)
```

The above view will be rendered as shown in Figure 21-9 below:

Figure 21-9

By referencing *systemImage:* in the Label view declaration, we indicate that the icon is to be taken from the built-in SF Symbol collection. To display an image from the app's asset catalog, the following syntax would be used instead:

```
Label("Welcome to SwiftUI", image: "myimage")
```

Instead of specifying a text string and an image, the Label may also be declared using separate views for the title

157

and icon. The following Label view declaration, for example, uses a Text view for the title and a Circle drawing for the icon:

```
Label(
    title: {
        Text("Welcome to SwiftUI")
        .font(.largeTitle)
    },
    icon: { Circle()
        .fill(Color.blue)
        .frame(width: 25, height: 25)
    }
)
```

When rendered, the above Label view will appear, as shown in Figure 21-10:

Figure 21-10

21.14 Take the Knowledge Test

Click the link below or scan the QR code to test your knowledge and understanding of custom views in SwiftUI:

https://www.answertopia.com/5089

21.15 Summary

SwiftUI user interfaces are declared in SwiftUI View files and composed of components conforming to the View protocol. To conform with the View protocol, a structure must contain a property named body, itself a View.

SwiftUI provides a library of built-in components for designing user interface layouts. The appearance and behavior of a view can be configured by applying modifiers, and views can be modified and grouped to create custom views and subviews. Similarly, custom container views can be created using the ViewBuilder closure property.

When a modifier is applied to a view, a new modified view is returned, and subsequent modifiers are then applied to this modified view. This can have significant implications for the order in which modifiers are applied to a view

22. SwiftUI Stacks and Frames

User interface design is primarily a matter of selecting the appropriate interface components, deciding how those views will be positioned on the screen, and then implementing navigation between the different screens and views of the app.

As is to be expected, SwiftUI includes a wide range of user interface components for developing an app such as button, label, slider and toggle views. SwiftUI also provides a set of layout views to define how the user interface is organized and how the layout responds to changes in screen orientation and size.

This chapter will introduce the Stack container views included with SwiftUI and explain how they can be used to create user interface designs with relative ease.

Once stack views have been explained, this chapter will cover the concept of flexible frames and explain how they can be used to control the sizing behavior of views in a layout.

22.1 SwiftUI Stacks

SwiftUI includes three stack layout views in the form of VStack (vertical), HStack (horizontal), and ZStack (views are layered on top of each other).

A stack is declared by embedding child views into a stack view within the SwiftUI View file. In the following view, for example, three Image views have been embedded within an HStack:

```
struct ContentView: View {
    var body: some View {
        HStack {
            Image(systemName: "goforward.10")
            Image(systemName: "goforward.15")
            Image(systemName: "goforward.30")
        }
    }
}
```

Within the preview canvas, the above layout will appear, as illustrated in Figure 22-1:

Figure 22-1

A similarly configured example using a VStack would accomplish the same results with the images stacked vertically:

```
VStack {
    Image(systemName: "goforward.10")
    Image(systemName: "goforward.15")
```

```
    Image(systemName: "goforward.30")
}
```

To embed an existing component into a stack, either wrap it manually within a stack declaration or right-click on the component in the editor and, from the resulting menu (Figure 22-2), select the *Embed...* option:

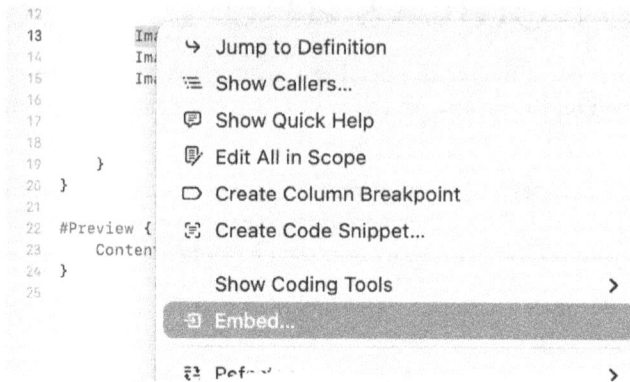

Figure 22-2

The embed option will place the component in braces and provide a *Container* placeholder into which the required stack component type can be typed (HStack, VStack or ZStack):

```
Container {
    Image(systemName: "goforward.10")
}
```

Figure 22-3

Layouts of considerable complexity can be designed simply by embedding stacks within other stacks, for example:

```
VStack {
    Text("Financial Results")
        .font(.title)

    HStack {
        Text("Q1 Sales")
            .font(.headline)

        VStack {
            Text("January")
            Text("February")
            Text("March")
        }

        VStack {
            Text("$1000")
            Text("$200")
            Text("$3000")
```

```
      }
   }
}
```

The above layout will appear, as shown in Figure 22-4:

Financial Results

	January	$1000
Q1 Sales	February	$200
	March	$3000

Figure 22-4

As currently configured, the layout needs some additional work, particularly in terms of alignment and spacing. The layout can be improved in this regard using a combination of alignment settings, the Spacer component, and the padding modifier.

22.2 Spacers, Alignment and Padding

To add space between views, SwiftUI includes the Spacer component. When used in a stack layout, the spacer will flexibly expand and contract along the axis of the containing stack (in other words, either horizontally or vertically) to provide a gap between views positioned on either side, for example:

```
HStack(alignment: .top) {
    Text("Q1 Sales")
        .font(.headline)
    Spacer()
    VStack(alignment: .leading) {
        Text("January")
        Text("February")
        Text("March")
    }
    Spacer()
.
.
```

In terms of aligning the content of a stack, this can be achieved by specifying an alignment value when the stack is declared, for example:

```
VStack(alignment: .center) {
        Text("Financial Results")
            .font(.title)
```

Alignments may also be specified with a corresponding spacing value:

```
VStack(alignment: .center, spacing: 15) {
        Text("Financial Results")
            .font(.title)
```

Spacing around the sides of any view may also be implemented using the *padding()* modifier. When called

SwiftUI Stacks and Frames

without a parameter, SwiftUI will automatically use the best padding for the layout, content, and screen size (referred to as *adaptable padding*). The following example sets adaptable padding on all four sides of a Text view:

```
Text("Hello, world!")
    .padding()
```

Alternatively, a specific amount of padding may be passed as a parameter to the modifier as follows:

```
Text("Hello, world!")
    .padding(15)
```

Padding may also be applied to a specific side of a view with or without a specific value. In the following example, a specific padding size is applied to the top edge of a Text view:

```
Text("Hello, world!")
    .padding(.top, 10)
```

Making use of these options, the example layout created earlier in the chapter can be modified as follows:

```
VStack(alignment: .center, spacing: 15) {
    Text("Financial Results")
        .font(.title)

    HStack(alignment: .top) {
        Text("Q1 Sales")
            .font(.headline)
        Spacer()
        VStack(alignment: .leading) {
            Text("January")
            Text("February")
            Text("March")
        }
        Spacer()
        VStack(alignment: .leading) {
            Text("$1000")
            Text("$200")
            Text("$3000")
        }
        .padding(5)
    }
    .padding(5)
}
.padding(5)
```

With the alignments, spacers, and padding modifiers added, the layout should now resemble the following figure:

Financial Results

Q1 Sales	January	$1000
	February	$200
	March	$3000

Figure 22-5

A later chapter entitled *"SwiftUI Stack Alignment and Alignment Guides"* will cover more advanced stack alignment topics.

22.3 Grouping Views

The Group component groups together multiple views and is useful when performing an operation on multiple views (for example, a set of related views can all be hidden in a single operation by embedding them in a Group and hiding that view):

```
Group {
    Text("$1000")
    Text("$200")
    Text("$3000")
}
```

22.4 Dynamic HStack and VStack Conversion

The choice between an HStack and a VStack during the design phase does not need to be final. SwiftUI allows the type of stack used in a layout to be changed dynamically from within the app code. We achieve this by creating an AnyLayout instance and assigning it either an HStackLayout or VStackLayout container. In the example below, we have assigned an AnyLayout instance to a state variable and configured it to stack children using the HStackLayout container. We then use this layout to arrange two Image views. Finally, we add two Button views to switch between horizontal and vertical orientation by changing the container type assigned to myLayout:

```
@State var myLayout: AnyLayout = AnyLayout(VStackLayout())


var body: some View {


    VStack {
        myLayout {
            Image(systemName: "goforward.10")
                .resizable()
                .aspectRatio(contentMode: .fit)
            Image(systemName: "goforward.15")
                .resizable()
                .aspectRatio(contentMode: .fit)
        }

        HStack {
            Button(action: {
                myLayout = AnyLayout(HStackLayout()) }){
```

```
            Text("HStack")
        }
        Button(action: {
            myLayout = AnyLayout(VStackLayout()) }) {
            Text("VStack")
        }
    }
  }
}
```

22.5 Text Line Limits and Layout Priority

By default, an HStack will attempt to display the text within its Text view children on a single line. Take, for example, the following HStack declaration containing an Image view and two Text views:

```
HStack {
    Image(systemName: "airplane")
    Text("Flight times:")
    Text("London")
}
.font(.largeTitle)
```

If the stack has enough room, the above layout will appear as follows:

Figure 22-6

If a stack has insufficient room (for example if it is constrained by a frame or is competing for space with sibling views) the text will automatically wrap onto multiple lines when necessary:

Figure 22-7

While this may work for some situations, it may become an issue if the user interface is required to display this text in a single line. The number of lines over which text can flow can be restricted using the *lineCount()* modifier. The example HStack could, therefore, be limited to 1 line of text with the following change:

```
HStack {
    Image(systemName: "airplane")
    Text("Flight times:")
    Text("London")
}
```

```
.font(.largeTitle)
.lineLimit(1)
```

A line limit restriction can also be specified as a range that provides the maximum and minimum number of lines over which text can be displayed:

```
.lineLimit(1...4)
```

When an HStack has insufficient space to display the full text and is not permitted to wrap the text over enough lines, the view will resort to truncating the text, as is the case in Figure 22-8:

Figure 22-8

Without any priority guidance, the stack view will decide how to truncate the Text views based on the available space and the length of the views. Obviously, the stack can only know whether the text in one view is more important than the text in another if the text view declarations include some priority information. This is achieved by making use of the *layoutPriority()* modifier. This modifier can be added to the views in the stack and passed values indicating the priority level for the corresponding view. The higher the number, the greater the layout priority, and the less the view will be truncated.

Assuming the flight destination city name is more important than the "Flight times:" text, the example stack could be modified as follows:

```
HStack {
    Image(systemName: "airplane")
    Text("Flight times:")
    Text("London")
        .layoutPriority(1)
}
.font(.largeTitle)
.lineLimit(1)
```

With a higher priority assigned to the city Text view (in the absence of a layout priority, the other text view defaults to a priority of 0), the layout will now appear, as illustrated in Figure 22-9:

Figure 22-9

22.6 Traditional vs. Lazy Stacks

So far in this chapter, we have only covered the HStack, VStack, and ZStack views. Although the stack examples shown so far contain relatively few child views, it is possible for a stack to contain large quantities of views. This is particularly common when a stack is embedded in a ScrollView. ScrollView is a view that allows the user to scroll through content that extends beyond the visible area of either the containing view or the device screen.

When using the traditional HStack and VStack views, the system will create all child views at initialization, regardless of whether those views are currently visible to the user. While this may not be an issue for most requirements, this can lead to performance degradation when a stack has thousands of child views.

SwiftUI also provides "lazy" vertical and horizontal stack views to address this issue. These views (named LazyVStack and LazyHStack) use the same declaration syntax as the traditional stack views but are designed only to create child views as needed. For example, as the user scrolls through a stack, views that are currently off-screen will only be created once they approach the point of becoming visible to the user. Once those views pass out of the viewing area, SwiftUI releases them so they no longer take up system resources.

When deciding whether to use traditional or lazy stacks, start using the traditional stacks and switch to lazy stacks if you encounter performance issues relating to a high number of child views.

22.7 SwiftUI Frames

By default, a view will be sized automatically based on its content and the requirements of any layout in which it may be embedded. Although much can be achieved using the stack layouts to control the size and positioning of a view, sometimes a view is required to be a specific size or to fit within a range of size dimensions. To address this need, SwiftUI includes the flexible frame modifier.

Consider the following Text view, which has been modified to display a border:

```
Text("Hello World")
    .font(.largeTitle)
    .border(Color.black)
```

Within the preview canvas, the above text view will appear as follows:

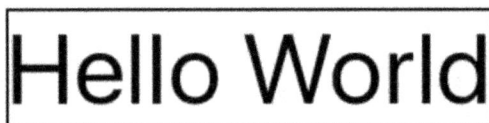

Figure 22-10

Without a frame, the text view has been sized to accommodate its content. If the Text view was required to have height and width dimensions of 100, however, a frame could be applied as follows:

```
Text("Hello World")
    .font(.largeTitle)
    .border(Color.black)
    .frame(width: 100, height: 100, alignment: .center)
```

Now that the Text view is constrained within a frame, the view will appear as follows:

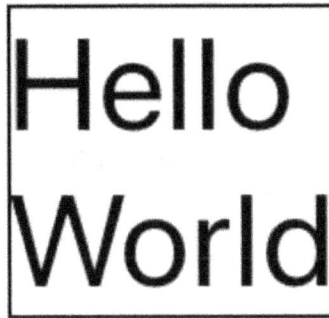

Figure 22-11

In many cases, fixed dimensions will provide the required behavior. In other cases, such as when the content of a view changes dynamically, this can cause problems. Increasing the length of the text, for example, might cause the content to be truncated:

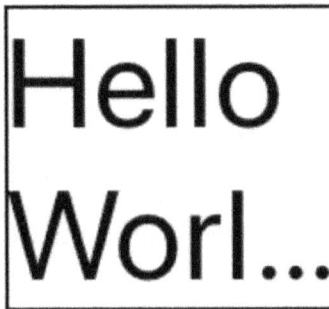

Figure 22-12

This can be resolved by creating a frame with minimum and maximum dimensions:

```
Text("Hello World, how are you?")
        .font(.largeTitle)
        .border(Color.black)
        .frame(minWidth: 100, maxWidth: 300, minHeight: 100,
               maxHeight: 100, alignment: .center)
```

Now that the frame has some flexibility, the view will be sized to accommodate the content within the defined minimum and maximum limits. When the text is short enough, the view will appear, as shown in Figure 22-11 above. Longer text, however, will be displayed as follows:

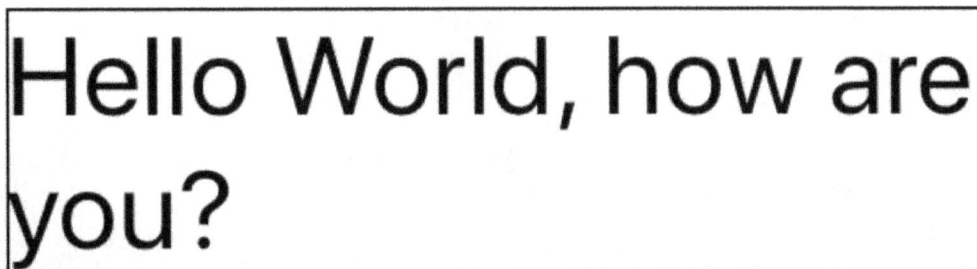

Figure 22-13

Frames may also be configured to take up all the available space by setting the minimum and maximum values to 0 and infinity respectively:

```
.frame(minWidth: 0, maxWidth: .infinity, minHeight: 0,
          maxHeight: .infinity)
```

Remember that the order in which modifiers are chained often impacts the appearance of a view. In this case, if the border is to be drawn at the edges of the available space it will need to be applied to the frame:

```
Text("Hello World, how are you?")
    .font(.largeTitle)
    .frame(minWidth: 0, maxWidth: .infinity, minHeight: 0,
          maxHeight: .infinity)
    .border(Color.black, width: 5)
```

By default, the frame will honor the safe areas on the screen when filling the display. Areas considered outside the safe area include the camera notch on some device models and the bar across the top of the screen displaying the time and WiFi and cellular signal strength icons. To configure the frame to extend beyond the safe area, simply use the *edgesIgnoringSafeArea()* modifier, specifying the safe area edges to ignore:

```
.edgesIgnoringSafeArea(.all)
```

22.8 Frames and the Geometry Reader

Frames can also be implemented so that they are sized relative to the size of the container within which the corresponding view is embedded. This is achieved by wrapping the view in a GeometryReader and using the reader to identify the container dimensions. These dimensions can then be used to calculate the frame size. The following example uses a frame to set the dimensions of two Text views relative to the size of the containing VStack:

```
GeometryReader { geometry in
    VStack {
        Text("Hello World, how are you?")
            .font(.largeTitle)
            .frame(width: geometry.size.width / 2,
                height: (geometry.size.height / 4) * 3)
        Text("Goodbye World")
            .font(.largeTitle)
            .frame(width: geometry.size.width / 3,
                height: geometry.size.height / 4)
    }
}
```

The topmost Text view is configured to occupy half the width and three-quarters of the height of the VStack, while the lower Text view occupies one third of the width and one-quarter of the height.

22.9 Take the Knowledge Test

Click the link below or scan the QR code to test your knowledge and understanding of SwiftUI stacks and frames:

https://www.answertopia.com/mbqk

22.10 Summary

User interface design mainly involves gathering components and laying them out on the screen in a way that provides a pleasant and intuitive user experience. User interface layouts must also be responsive so that they appear correctly on any device regardless of screen size and, ideally, device orientation. To ease the process of user interface layout design, SwiftUI provides several layout views and components. In this chapter we have looked at layout stack views and the flexible frame.

By default, a view will be sized according to its content and the restrictions imposed on it by any view in which it may be contained. When insufficient space is available, a view may be restricted in size, resulting in truncated content. Priority settings can be used to control how much views are reduced in size relative to container sibling views.

For greater control of the space allocated to a view, a flexible frame can be applied to the view. The frame can be fixed in size, constrained within a range of minimum and maximum values, or, using a Geometry Reader, sized relative to the containing view.

23. SwiftUI State Properties, Observation, and Environment Objects

Earlier chapters have described how SwiftUI emphasizes a data-driven approach to app development whereby the views in the user interface are updated in response to changes in the underlying data without the need to write handling code. This approach is achieved by establishing a publisher and subscriber relationship between the data and the views in the user interface.

SwiftUI offers four options for implementing this behavior in the form of *state properties*, *observation*, and *environment objects*, all of which provide the *state* that drives the way the user interface appears and behaves. In SwiftUI, the views that make up a user interface layout are never updated directly within code. Instead, the views are updated automatically based on the state objects to which they have been bound as they change over time.

This chapter will describe these four options and outline when they should be used. Later chapters, *"A SwiftUI Example Tutorial"* and *"SwiftUI Observable and Environment Objects – A Tutorial"*) will provide practical examples demonstrating their use.

23.1 State Properties

The most basic form of state is the state property. State properties are used exclusively to store state that is local to a view layout, such as whether a toggle button is enabled, the text being entered into a text field, or the current selection in a Picker view. State properties are used for storing simple data types such as a String or an Int value and are declared using the *@State* property wrapper, for example:

```
struct ContentView: View {

    @State private var wifiEnabled = true
    @State private var userName = ""

    var body: some View {
.
.
```

Since state values are local to the enclosing view, they should be declared as private properties.

Every change to a state property value signals to SwiftUI that the view hierarchy within which the property is declared needs to be re-rendered. This involves rapidly recreating and displaying all of the views in the hierarchy, which, in turn, ensures that any views that rely on the property in some way are updated to reflect the latest value.

Once declared, bindings can be established between state properties and the views contained in the layout. Changes within views referencing the binding are then automatically reflected in the corresponding state property. A binding could, for example, be established between a Toggle view and the Boolean wifiEnabled property declared above. SwiftUI automatically updates the state property to match the new toggle setting whenever the user switches the toggle.

A binding to a state property is implemented by prefixing the property name with a '$' sign. In the following example, a TextField view establishes a binding to the userName state property to use as the storage for text entered by the user:

```
struct ContentView: View {

    @State private var wifiEnabled = true
    @State private var userName = ""

    var body: some View {
        VStack {
            TextField("Enter user name", text: $userName)
        }
    }
}
```

With each keystroke performed as the user types into the TextField, the binding will store the current text into the userName property. Each change to the state property will, in turn, cause the view hierarchy to be re-rendered by SwiftUI.

Of course, storing something in a state property is only one side of the process. As previously discussed, a state change usually results in a change to other views in the layout. In this case, a Text view might need to be updated to reflect the user's name as it is typed. This can be achieved by declaring the userName state property value as the content for a Text view:

```
var body: some View {
    VStack {
        TextField("Enter user name", text: $userName)
        Text(userName)
    }
}
```

The Text view will automatically update as the user types to reflect the user's input. The userName property is declared without the '$' prefix in this case. This is because we are now referencing the value assigned to the state property (i.e., the String value being typed by the user) instead of a binding to the property.

Similarly, the hypothetical binding between a Toggle view and the wifiEnabled state property described above could be implemented as follows:

```
var body: some View {

    VStack {
        Toggle(isOn: $wifiEnabled) {
            Text("Enable Wi-Fi")
        }
        TextField("Enter user name", text: $userName)
        Text(userName)
        Image(systemName: wifiEnabled ? "wifi" : "wifi.slash")
    }
```

```
}
```

The above declaration establishes a binding between the Toggle view and the state property. The value assigned to the property is then used to decide which image will be displayed on an Image view.

23.2 State Binding

A state property is local to the view it is declared in and any child views. Situations may occur, however, where a view contains one or more subviews that may also need access to the same state properties. Consider, for example, a situation whereby the WiFi Image view in the above example has been extracted into a subview:

```
.

.

    VStack {
        Toggle(isOn: $wifiEnabled) {
            Text("Enable WiFi")
        }
        TextField("Enter user name", text: $userName)
        Text(userName)
        WifiImageView()
    }
}


struct WifiImageView: View {

    var body: some View {
        Image(systemName: wifiEnabled ? "wifi" : "wifi.slash")
    }
}
```

Clearly, the WifiImageView subview still needs access to the wifiEnabled state property. As an element of a separate subview, however, the Image view is now out of the scope of the main view. Within the scope of WifiImageView, the wifiEnabled property is an undefined variable.

This problem can be resolved by declaring the property using the *@Binding* property wrapper as follows:

```
struct WifiImageView: View {

    @Binding var wifiEnabled : Bool

    var body: some View {
        Image(systemName: wifiEnabled ? "wifi" : "wifi.slash")
    }
}
```

Now, when the subview is called, it simply needs to be passed a binding to the state property:

```
WifiImageView(wifiEnabled: $wifiEnabled)
```

23.3 Observable Objects

State properties provide a way to store the state of a view locally, are available only to the local view, and, as such, cannot be accessed by other views unless they are subviews and state binding is implemented. State properties are also transient in that when the parent view goes away, the state is also lost. On the other hand, Observable objects represent persistent data that is both external and accessible to multiple views.

An Observable object takes the form of a class that conforms to the ObservableObject protocol. Though the implementation of an observable object will be application-specific depending on the nature and source of the data, it will typically be responsible for gathering and managing one or more data values known to change over time. Observable objects can also handle events such as timers and notifications.

The observable object *publishes* the data values it is responsible for as published properties. Observer objects then *subscribe* to the publisher and receive updates whenever published properties change. As with the state properties outlined above, by binding to these published properties, SwiftUI views will automatically update to reflect changes in the data stored in the observable object.

Before the introduction of iOS 18, observable objects were managed using the Combine framework, which was introduced to make it easier to establish relationships between publishers and subscribers. While this option is still available, a simpler alternative is now available following the introduction of the *Observation framework* (typically referred to as just "Observation").

However, before we look at how to use Observation, we will cover the old Combine framework approach. We are doing this for two reasons. First, learning about the old way will help you to understand how the new Observation works behind the scenes. Second, you will encounter many code examples online that use the Combine framework. Understanding how to migrate to Observation will help you re-purpose those examples for your needs.

23.4 Observation using Combine

The Combine framework provides a platform for building custom publishers for performing various tasks, from merging multiple publishers into a single stream to transforming published data to match subscriber requirements. This allows for complex, enterprise-level data processing chains to be implemented between the original publisher and the resulting subscriber. That being said, one of the built-in publisher types will typically be all that is needed for most requirements. The easiest way to implement a published property within an observable object is to use the *@Published* property wrapper when declaring a property. This wrapper sends updates to all subscribers each time the wrapped property value changes.

The following class shows a simple observable object declaration with two published properties:

```
import Foundation
import Combine


class DemoData : ObservableObject {

    @Published var playerName = ""
    @Published var score = 0

    init(player: String) {
        // Code here to initialize data
        playerName = player
        updateData()
    }

    func updateData() {
        // Code here to update the data
```

```
        score += 1
    }
}
```

A subscriber uses either the *@ObservedObject* or *@StateObject* property wrapper to subscribe to the observable object. Once subscribed, that view and any of its child views access the published properties using the same techniques used with state properties earlier in the chapter. A sample SwiftUI view designed to subscribe to an instance of the above DemoData class might read as follows:

```
import SwiftUI

struct ContentView: View {

    @ObservedObject var demoData : DemoData = DemoData(player: "John")

    var body: some View {
        VStack {
            Text("\(demoData.playerName)'s Score = \(demoData.score)")
            Button(action: {
                demoData.updateData()
            }, label: {
                Text("Update")
            })
            .padding()
        }
    }
}
```

When the update button is clicked, the published score variable will change, and SwiftUI will automatically re-render the view layout to reflect the new state.

23.5 Combine State Objects

The State Object property wrapper (@StateObject) was introduced in iOS 14 as an alternative to the @ObservedObject wrapper. The key difference between a state object and an observed object is that an observed object reference is not owned by the view in which it is declared and, as such, is at risk of being destroyed or recreated by the SwiftUI system while still in use (for example as the result of the view being re-rendered).

Using @StateObject instead of @ObservedObject ensures that the reference is owned by the view in which it is declared and, therefore, will not be destroyed by SwiftUI while it is still needed, either by the local view in which it is declared or any child views. For example:

```
import SwiftUI

struct ContentView: View {

    @StateObject var demoData : DemoData = DemoData(player: "John")

    var body: some View {
.
.
```

```
}
```

23.6 Using the Observation Framework

Using Observation instead of the Combine framework will provide us with the same behavior outlined above but with simpler code. To switch the DemoData class to use Observation, we need to make the following changes:

```
import Foundation

@Observable class DemoData : ObservableObject {

    @Published var playerName = ""
    @Published var score = 0

    init(player: String) {
        // Code here to initialize data
        playerName = player
        updateData()
    }

    func update() {
        score += 1
    }
}
```

Instead of declaring the DemoData as a subclass of ObservableObject, we now prefix the declaration with the @ Observable macro. We also no longer need to use the @Published property wrappers because the macro handles this automatically.

The code in the ContentView is also simplified by removing the @ObservedObject directive:

```
struct ContentView: View {

    @ObservedObject var demoData : DemoData = DemoData(player: "John")

    .

    .

```

Where the @StateObject property wrapper was used, this can be replaced with @State as follows:

```
import SwiftUI

struct ContentView: View {

    @State var demoData : DemoData = DemoData(player: "John")

    var body: some View {

    .

    .

}
```

23.7 Observation and @Bindable

Earlier in the chapter, we introduced state binding and explained how it is used to pass state properties from one view to another. Suppose that our example layout uses a separate view named ScoreView to display the score as follows:

```
struct ContentView: View {

    var demoData : DemoData = DemoData(player: "John")

    var body: some View {
        VStack {
            ScoreView(score: $demoData.score) // Syntax error
            Text("\(demoData.playerName)'s Score")
            Button(action: {
                demoData.updateData()
            }, label: {
                Text("Update")
            })
            .padding()
        }
    }
}


struct ScoreView: View {

    @Binding var score: Int

    var body: some View {
        Text("\(score)")
            .font(.system(size: 150))
    }
}
```

The above code will report an error indicating that $demoData.score cannot be found. To correct this, we need to apply the @Bindable property wrapper to the demoData declaration. This property wrapper is used when we need to create bindings from the properties of observable objects. To resolve the problem with the above example, we need to make the following change:

```
@Bindable var demoData : DemoData = DemoData(player: "John")
```

23.8 Environment Objects

Observed objects are best used when a particular state needs to be used by a few SwiftUI views within an app. When one view navigates to another view that needs access to the same observed or state object, the originating view will need to pass a reference to the observed object to the destination view during the navigation (navigation will be covered in the chapter entitled *"SwiftUI Lists and Navigation"*). Consider, for example, the following code:

.

.

```
var demoData : DemoData = DemoData(player: "John")
```

.

.

```
NavigationLink(destination: SecondView(demoData)) {
    Text("Next Screen")
}
```

In the above declaration, a navigation link is used to navigate to another view named SecondView, passing through a reference to the demoData observed object.

While this technique is acceptable for many situations, it can become complex when many views within an app need access to the same observed object. In this situation, using an environment object may make more sense.

An environment object is declared in the same way as an observable object. The key difference, however, is that the object is stored in the environment of the view in which it is declared and, as such, can be accessed by all child views without needing to be passed from view to view.

Consider the following example observable declaration:

```
@Observable class SpeedSetting {
    var speed = 0.0
}
```

Views needing to subscribe to an environment object reference the object using the @Environment property wrapper. For example, the following view uses @Environment to access the SpeedSetting data:

```
struct SpeedDisplayView: View {
    @Environment(SpeedSetting.self) var speedsetting: SpeedSetting

    var body: some View {
        Text("Speed = \(speedsetting.speed)")
    }
}
```

Suppose that a second view also needs access to the speed data but needs to create a binding to the *speed* property. In this case, we need to use the @Bindable property wrapper as follows:

```
struct SpeedControlView: View {
    @Environment(SpeedSetting.self) var speedsetting: SpeedSetting

    var body: some View {
        @Bindable var speedsetting = speedsetting
        Slider(value: $speedsetting.speed, in: 0...100)
    }
}
```

At this point, we have an observable object named SpeedSetting and two views that reference an environment object of that type. Still, we have not yet initialized an instance of the observable object. The logical place to perform this task is the parent view of the above sub-views. In the following example, both views are sub-views of the main ContentView:

```
struct ContentView: View {
    let speedsetting = SpeedSetting()

    var body: some View {
```

```
        VStack {
            SpeedControlView()
            SpeedDisplayView()
        }
    }
}
```

If the app were to run at this point, however, it would crash shortly after launching with the following diagnostics:

```
Thread 1: Fatal error: No ObservableObject of type SpeedSetting found. A View.
environmentObject(_:) for SpeedSetting may be missing as an ancestor of this
view.
```

The problem is that while we have created an instance of the observable object within ContentView, we still need to insert it into the view hierarchy environment. This is achieved using the *environment()* modifier, passing through the observable object instance as follows:

```
struct ContentView: View {
    let speedsetting = SpeedSetting()

    var body: some View {
        VStack {
            SpeedControlView()
            SpeedDisplayView()
        }
        .environment(speedsetting)
    }
}
```

Once these steps have been taken, the object will behave the same way as an observed object, except that it will be accessible to all child views of the content view without being passed down through the view hierarchy. When the slider in SpeedControlView is moved, the Text view in SpeedDisplayView will update to reflect the current speed setting, thereby demonstrating that both views are accessing the same environment object:

Speed = 42.508417

Figure 23-1

23.9 Take the Knowledge Test

Click the link below or scan the QR code to test your knowledge and understanding of SwiftUI state properties, observables, and environment objects:

https://www.answertopia.com/r8e3

23.10 Summary

SwiftUI provides three ways to bind data to an app's user interface and logic. State properties store the views' state in a user interface layout and are local to the current content view. These transient values are lost when the view goes away.

SwiftUI State Properties, Observation, and Environment Objects

The Observation framework can be used for data that is external to the user interface and is required only by a subset of the SwiftUI view structures in an app. Using this approach, the @Observable macro must be applied to the class that represents the data. To bind to an observable object property in a view declaration, the property must use the @Bindable property wrapper.

The environment object provides the best solution for data external to the user interface, but for which access is required for many views. Although declared the same way as observable objects, environment object bindings are declared in SwiftUI View files using the @Environment property wrapper. Before becoming accessible to child views, the environment object must also be initialized before being inserted into the view hierarchy using the *environment()* modifier.

24. A SwiftUI Example Tutorial

Now that some of the fundamentals of SwiftUI development have been covered, this chapter will begin to put this theory into practice by building an example SwiftUI-based project.

This chapter aims to demonstrate using Xcode to design a simple interactive user interface using views, modifiers, state variables, and some basic animation effects. This tutorial will use various techniques to add and modify views. While this may appear inconsistent, the objective is to gain familiarity with the options available.

24.1 Creating the Example Project

Start Xcode and select the option to create a new project. Then, on the template selection screen, make sure Multiplatform is selected and choose the App option, as shown in Figure 24-1, before proceeding to the next screen:

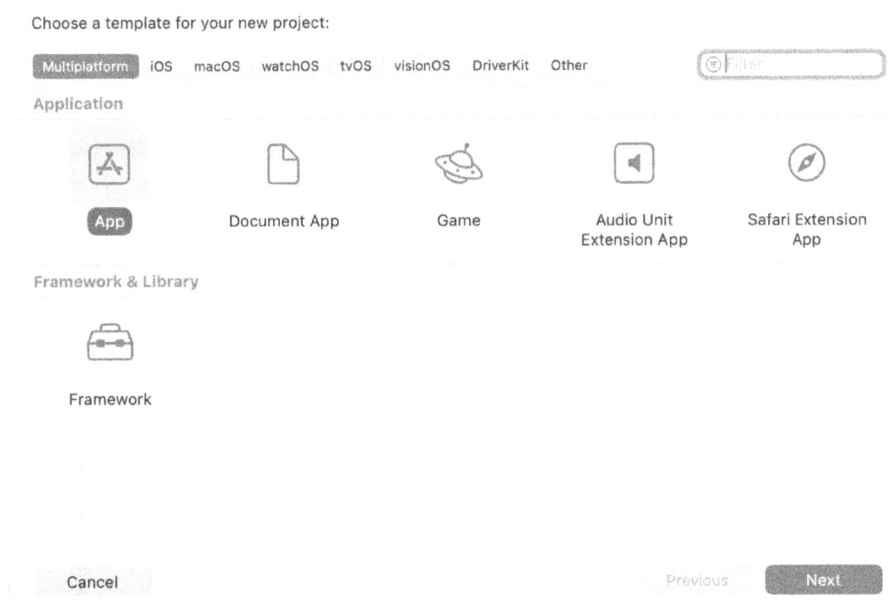

Figure 24-1

On the project options screen, name the project *SwiftUIDemo* and set the Testing System menu to "None" before clicking Next to proceed to the final screen. Choose a suitable filesystem location for the project and click the Create button.

24.2 Reviewing the Project

Once the project has been created, it will contain the *SwiftUIDemoApp.swift* file along with a SwiftUI View file named *ContentView.swift*, which should have loaded into the editor and preview canvas ready for modification (if it has not loaded, select it in the project navigator panel). Next, from the target device menu (Figure 24-2), select an iPhone 15 simulator:

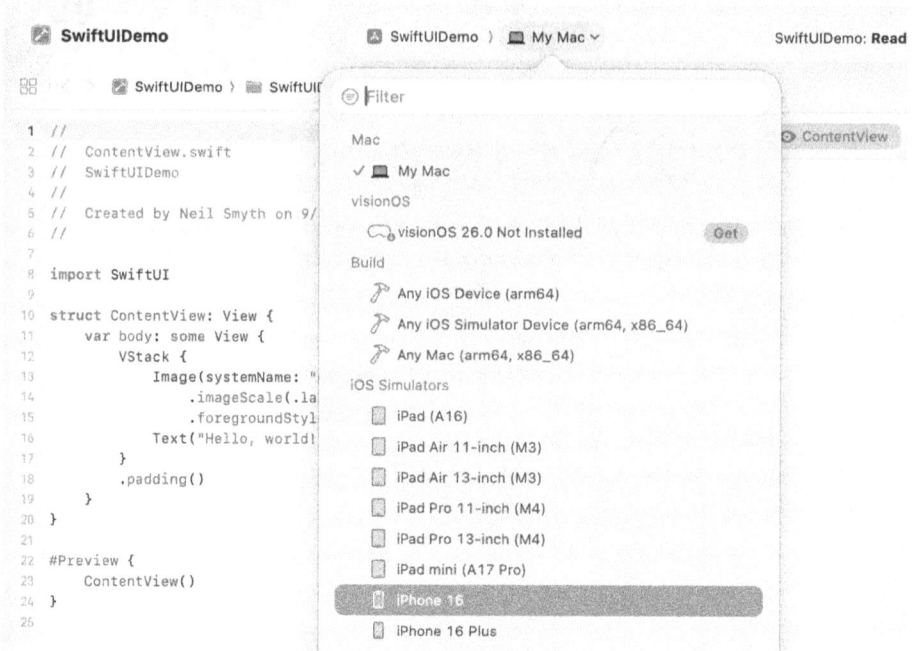

Figure 24-2

If the preview canvas is in the paused state, click on the Resume button to build the project and display the preview:

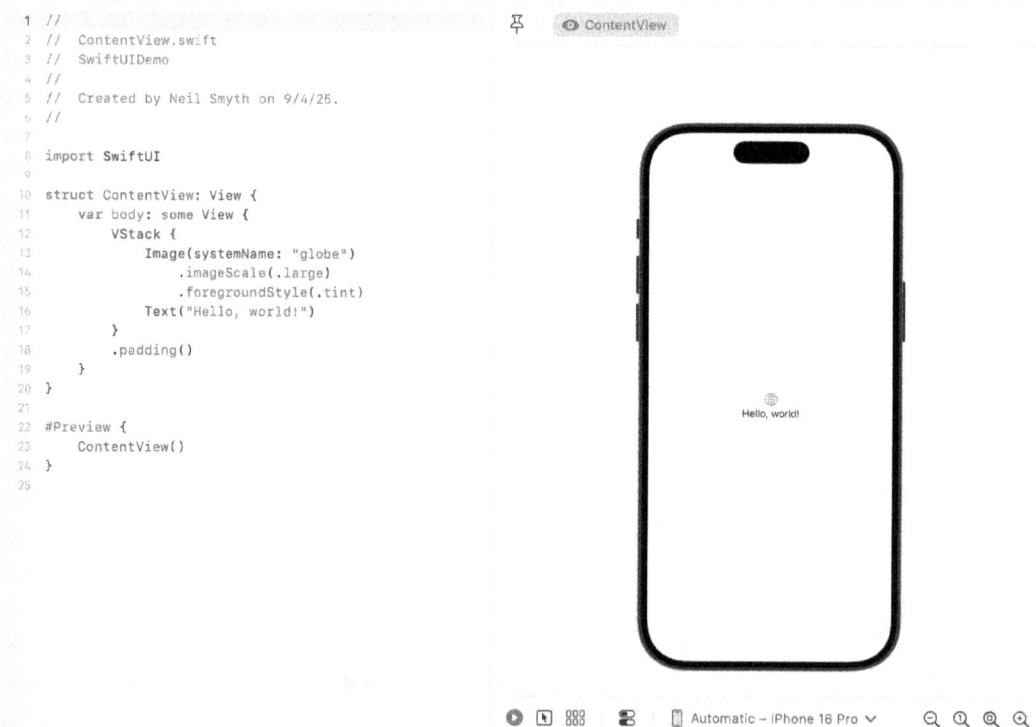

Figure 24-3

24.3 Modifying the Layout

The view body currently consists of a vertical stack layout (VStack) containing an Image and a Text view. Although we could reuse some of the existing layout for our example, we will learn more by deleting the current views and starting over. Within the Code Editor, delete the existing views from the ContentView body:

```
import SwiftUI

struct ContentView: View {
    var body: some View {
        VStack {
            Image(systemName: "globe")
                .imageScale(.large)
                .foregroundColor(.accentColor)
            Text("Hello, world!")
        }
        .padding()
    }
}
```

Next, add a VStack and Text view to the layout as follows:

```
struct ContentView: View {
    var body: some View {
        VStack {
            Text("Hello, world!")
        }
    }
}
```

24.4 Adding a Slider View to the Stack

The next item to be added to the layout is a Slider view. Display the Library panel by pressing Cmd-Shift-L, locating the Slider in the View list, and dragging it into position beneath the Text view in the editor. Ensure that the Slider view will be inserted into the existing stack before dropping the view into place:

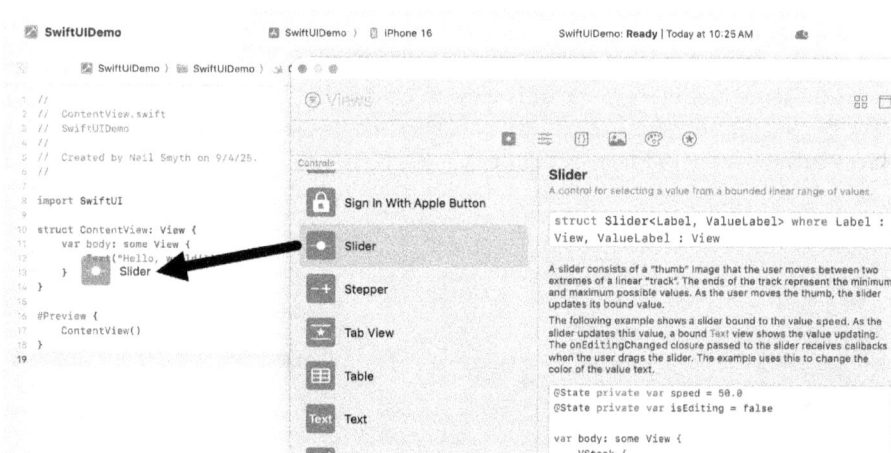

Figure 24-4

Once the slider has been dropped into place, the view implementation should read as follows:

```
struct ContentView: View {
    var body: some View {
        VStack {
            VStack {
                Text("Hello, world!")
                Slider(value: Value)
            }
        }
    }
}
```

24.5 Adding a State Property

The Slider will control the degree to which the Text view will be rotated. As such, a binding must be established between the Slider view and a state property into which the current rotation angle will be stored. Within the code editor, declare this property and configure the Slider to use a range between 0 and 360 in increments of 0.1:

```
struct ContentView: View {

    @State private var rotation: Double = 0

    var body: some View {
        VStack {
            VStack {
                Text("Hello, world!")
                Slider(value: $rotation, in: 0 ... 360, step: 0.1)
            }
        }
    }
}
```

Note that since we declare a binding between the Slider view and the rotation state property, it is prefixed by a '$' character.

24.6 Adding Modifiers to the Text View

The next step is to add some modifiers to the Text view to change the font and adopt the rotation value stored by the Slider view. Begin by displaying the Library panel, switch to the modifier list, and drag and drop a font modifier onto the Text view entry in the code editor:

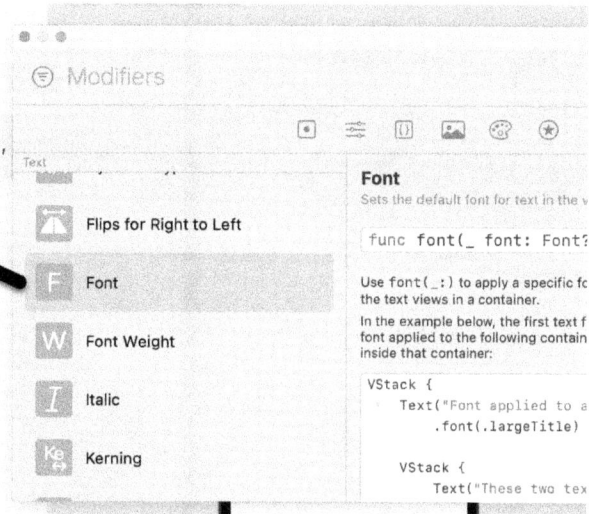

Figure 24-5

Repeat the above step to add a Font Weight modifier to the Text component, then edit the values as follows:

```
Text("Hello, world!")
    .font(.largeTitle)
    .fontWeight(.heavy)
```

On completion of these steps, the View body should read as follows:

```
var body: some View {
    VStack {
        VStack {
            Text("Hello, world!")
                .font(.largeTitle)
                .fontWeight(.heavy)
                Slider(value: $rotation, in: 0 ... 360, step: 0.1)
        }
    }
}
```

24.7 Adding Rotation and Animation

The next step is to add the rotation and animation effects to the Text view using the value stored by the Slider (animation is covered in greater detail in the *"SwiftUI Animation and Transitions"* chapter). This can be implemented using a modifier as follows:

```
Text("Hello, world!")
    .font(.largeTitle)
    .fontWeight(.heavy)
    .rotationEffect(.degrees(rotation))
```

Note that since we are simply reading the value assigned to the rotation state property, instead of establishing a binding, the property name is not prefixed with the '$' sign notation.

Click on the Live button (indicated by the arrow in Figure 24-6), wait for the code to compile, then use the slider to rotate the Text view:

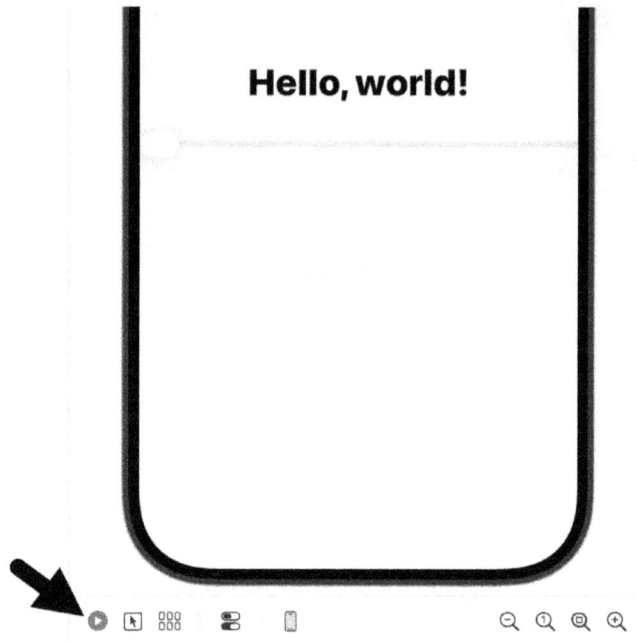

Figure 24-6

Next, add an animation modifier to the Text view to animate the rotation over 5 seconds using the Ease In Out effect:

```
Text("Hello, world!")
    .font(.largeTitle)
    .fontWeight(.heavy)
    .rotationEffect(.degrees(rotation))
    .animation(.easeInOut(duration: 5), value: rotation)
```

Use the slider once again to rotate the text, and note that rotation is now smoothly animated.

24.8 Adding a TextField to the Stack

In addition to supporting text rotation, the app will allow custom text to be entered and displayed on the Text view. This will require the addition of a TextField view to the project. To achieve this, either directly edit the View structure or use the Library panel to add a TextField so that the structure reads as follows (also note the addition of a state property in which to store the custom text string and the change to the Text view to use this property):

```
struct ContentView: View {

    @State private var rotation: Double = 0
    @State private var text: String = "Welcome to SwiftUI"

    var body: some View {
        VStack {
            VStack {
                Text(text)
                    .font(.largeTitle)
```

```
        .fontWeight(.heavy)
        .rotationEffect(.degrees(rotation))
        .animation(.easeInOut(duration: 5))

    Slider(value: $rotation, in: 0 ... 360, step: 0.1)

    TextField("Enter text here", text: $text)
        .textFieldStyle(RoundedBorderTextFieldStyle())
    }
  }
 }
}
```

When the user enters text into the TextField view, that text will be stored in the *text* state property and will automatically appear on the Text view via the binding.

Return to the preview canvas and ensure that the changes work as expected.

24.9 Adding a Color Picker

A Picker view is the final view to be added to the stack before we tidy up the layout. This view will allow the user to choose the foreground color of the Text view from a range of color options. Begin by adding some arrays of color names and Color objects, together with a state property to hold the current array index value as follows:

```
import SwiftUI

struct ContentView: View {

    var colors: [Color] = [.black, .red, .green, .blue]
    var colornames = ["Black", "Red", "Green", "Blue"]

    @State private var colorIndex = 0
    @State private var rotation: Double = 0
    @State private var text: String = "Welcome to SwiftUI"
```

With these variables configured, display the Library panel, locate the Picker in the Views screen, and drag and drop it beneath the TextField view in the code editor to embed it in the existing VStack layout. Once added, the view entry will read as follows:

```
Picker(selection: .constant(1), label: Text("Picker") {
    Text("1").tag(1)
    Text("2").tag(2)
}
```

The Picker view needs to be configured to store the current selection in the *colorIndex* state property and to display an option for each color name in the *colorNames* array. In addition, to make the Picker more visually appealing, we will change the background color for each Text view to the corresponding color in the *colors* array.

To iterate through the colorNames array, the code will use the SwiftUI *ForEach* structure. At first glance, ForEach looks like just another Swift programming language control flow statement. In fact, *ForEach* differs greatly from the Swift *forEach()* array method outlined earlier in the book.

ForEach is a SwiftUI view structure designed to generate multiple views by looping through a data set such as an array or range. We may also configure the Picker view to display the color choices in various ways. For this project, we must select the WheelPickerStyle (.*wheel*) style via the *pickerStyle()* modifier. Within the editor, modify the Picker view declaration so that it reads as follows:

```
Picker(selection: $colorIndex, label: Text("Color")) {
    ForEach (0 ..< colornames.count, id:\.self)  { color in
        Text(colornames[color])
            .foregroundColor(colors[color])
    }
}
.pickerStyle(.wheel)
```

In the above implementation, ForEach is used to loop through the elements of the colornames array, generating a Text view for each color and setting the displayed text and background color on each view accordingly.

The ForEach loop in the above example is contained within a closure expression. As outlined in the *"Swift Functions, Methods, and Closures"* chapter, this expression can be simplified using *shorthand argument names*. Using this technique, modify the Picker declaration so that it reads as follows:

```
Picker(selection: $colorIndex, label: Text("Color")) {
    ForEach (0 ..< colornames.count, id:\.self) { color in
        Text(colornames[$0])
            .foregroundColor(colors[$0])
    }
}
.pickerStyle(.wheel)
```

Remaining in the code editor, locate the Text view and add a foreground color modifier to set the foreground color based on the current Picker selection value:

```
Text(text)
    .font(.largeTitle)
    .fontWeight(.heavy)
    .rotationEffect(.degrees(rotation))
    .animation(.easeInOut(duration: 5), value: rotation)
    .foregroundColor(colors[colorIndex])
```

Test the app in the preview canvas and confirm that the Picker view appears with all of the color names using the corresponding foreground color and that color selections are reflected in the Text view.

24.10 Tidying the Layout

Until this point, the focus of this tutorial has been on the appearance and functionality of the individual views. Aside from making sure the views are stacked vertically, however, no attention has been paid to the overall appearance of the layout. At this point, the layout should resemble that shown in Figure 24-7:

Figure 24-7

The first improvement needed is to add some space around the Slider, TextField, and Picker views so that they are not so close to the edge of the device display. To implement this, we will add some padding modifiers to the views:

```
Slider(value: $rotation, in: 0 ... 360, step: 0.1)
    .padding()


TextField("Enter text here", text: $text)
    .textFieldStyle(RoundedBorderTextFieldStyle())
    .padding()


Picker(selection: $colorIndex, label: Text("Color")) {
    ForEach (0 ..< colornames.count, id:\.self) {
        Text(colornames[$0])
            .foregroundColor(colors[$0])
    }
}
```

```
.pickerStyle(.wheel)
.padding()
```

Next, the layout would look better if the Views were evenly spaced. One way to implement this is to add some Spacer views before and after the Text view:

```
.
.
VStack {
    Spacer()
    Text(text)
        .font(.largeTitle)
        .fontWeight(.heavy)
        .rotationEffect(.degrees(rotation))
        .animation(.easeInOut(duration: 5), value: rotation)
        .foregroundColor(colors[colorIndex])
    Spacer()
    Slider(value: $rotation, in: 0 ... 360, step: 0.1)
            .padding()
.
.
```

The Spacer view provides a flexible space between views that will expand and contract based on the requirements of the layout. If a Spacer is contained in a stack, it will resize along the stack axis. A Spacer view can resize horizontally and vertically when used outside a stack container.

To make the separation between the Text view and the Slider more obvious, also add a Divider view to the layout:

```
.
.
VStack {
    Spacer()
    Text(text)
        .font(.largeTitle).
        .fontWeight(.heavy)
        .rotationEffect(.degrees(rotation))
        .animation(.easeInOut(duration: 5), value: rotation)
        .foregroundColor(colors[colorIndex])
    Spacer()
    Divider()
.
.
```

The Divider view draws a line to indicate the separation between two views in a stack container.

With these changes made, the layout should now appear in the preview canvas, as shown in Figure 24-8:

Figure 24-8

24.11 Take the Knowledge Test

Click the link below or scan the QR code to test your knowledge and understanding so far of SwiftUI:

https://www.answertopia.com/ukob

24.12 Summary

The goal of this chapter has been to put into practice some of the theory covered in the previous chapters through the creation of an example app project. In particular, the tutorial used various techniques for adding views to a layout and using modifiers and state property bindings. The chapter also introduced the Spacer and Divider views and used the ForEach structure to generate views from a data array dynamically.

25. SwiftUI Stack Alignment and Alignment Guides

The chapter entitled *"SwiftUI Stacks and Frames"* touched on the basics of alignment in the context of stack container views. Inevitably, when it comes to designing complex user interface layouts, it will be necessary to move beyond the standard alignment options provided with SwiftUI stack views. With this in mind, this chapter will introduce more advanced stack alignment techniques including container alignment, alignment guides, custom alignments, and the implementation of alignments between different stacks.

25.1 Container Alignment

The most basic of alignment options when working with SwiftUI stacks is container alignment. These settings define how the child views contained within a stack are aligned in relation to each other and the containing stack. This alignment value applies to all the contained child views unless different alignment guides have been applied to individual views. Views that do not have their own alignment guide are said to be *implicitly aligned*.

When working with alignments it is important to remember that horizontal stacks (HStack) align child views vertically, while vertical stacks (VStack) align their children horizontally. In the case of the ZStack, both horizontal and vertical alignment values are used.

The following VStack declaration consists of a simple VStack configuration containing three child views:

```
VStack {
    Text("This is some text")
    Text("This is some longer text")
    Text("This is short")
}
```

In the absence of a specific container alignment value, the VStack will default to aligning the centers (.center) of the contained views, as shown in Figure 25-1:

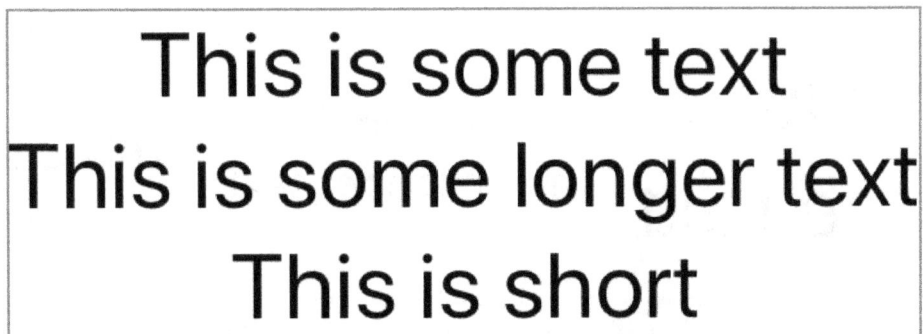

Figure 25-1

In addition to the default center alignment, a VStack can be configured using *.leading* or *.trailing* alignment, for example:

```
VStack(alignment: .trailing) {
    Text("This is some text")
    Text("This is some longer text")
    Text("This is short")
}
```

When rendered, the above VStack layout will appear with the child views aligned along the trailing edges of the views and the container:

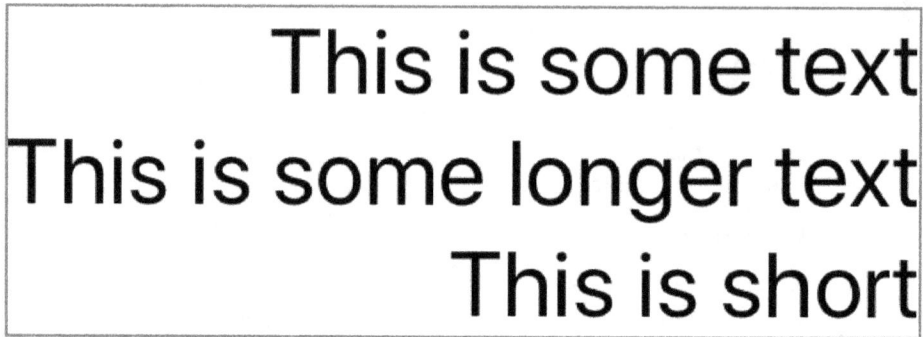

> This is some text
> This is some longer text
> This is short

Figure 25-2

Horizontal stacks also default to center alignment in the absence of a specific setting, but also provide top and bottom alignment options in addition to values for aligning text baselines. It is also possible to include spacing values when specifying an alignment. The following HStack uses the default center alignment with spacing and contains three Text view child views, each using a different font size.

```
HStack(spacing: 20) {
    Text("This is some text")
        .font(.largeTitle)
    Text("This is some much longer text")
        .font(.body)
    Text("This is short")
        .font(.headline)
}
```

The above stack will appear as follows when previewed:

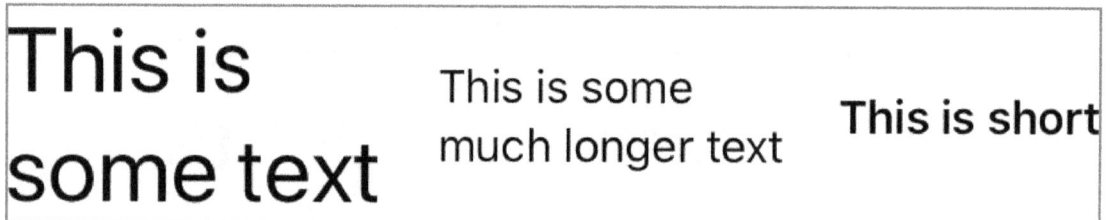

> This is some text   This is some much longer text   This is short

Figure 25-3

Text baseline alignment can be applied based on the baseline of either the first (.firstTextBaseline) or last (.lastTextBaseline) text-based view, for example:

```
HStack(alignment: .lastTextBaseline, spacing: 20) {
    Text("This is some text")
        .font(.largeTitle)
```

```
Text("This is some much longer text")
    .font(.body)
Text("This is short")
    .font(.headline)
}
```

Now the three Text views will align with the baseline of the last view:

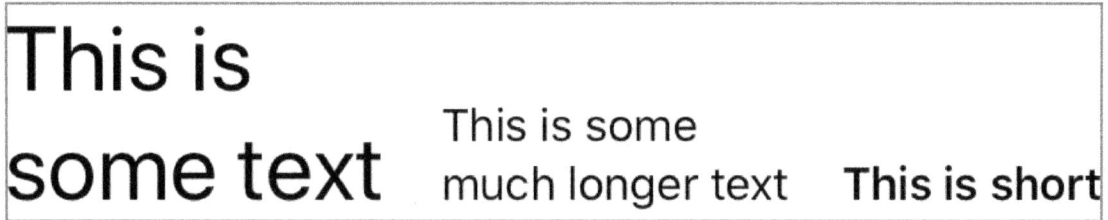

Figure 25-4

25.2 Alignment Guides

An alignment guide is used to define a custom position within a view that is to be used when that view is aligned with other views contained in a stack. This allows more complex alignments to be implemented than those offered by the standard alignment types such as center, leading, and top, though these standard types may still be used when defining an alignment guide. An alignment guide could, for example, be used to align a view based on a position two-thirds along its length or 20 points from the top edge.

Alignment guides are applied to views using the *alignmentGuide()* modifier which takes as arguments a standard alignment type and a closure that must calculate and return a value indicating the point within the view on which the alignment is to be based. To assist in calculating the alignment position within the view, the closure is passed a ViewDimensions object which can be used to obtain the width and height of the view and also the view's standard alignment positions (.top, .bottom, .leading, and so on).

Consider the following VStack containing three rectangles of differing lengths and colors, aligned on their leading edges:

```
VStack(alignment: .leading) {
    Rectangle()
        .foregroundColor(Color.green)
        .frame(width: 120, height: 50)
    Rectangle()
        .foregroundColor(Color.red)
        .frame(width: 200, height: 50)
    Rectangle()
        .foregroundColor(Color.blue)
        .frame(width: 180, height: 50)
}
```

The above layout will be rendered, as shown in Figure 25-5:

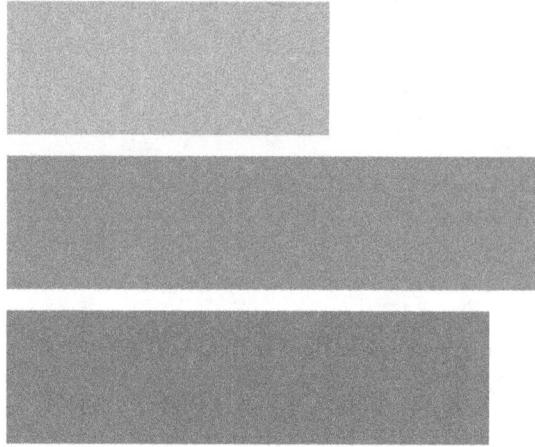

Figure 25-5

Now, suppose that instead of being aligned on the leading edge, the second view needs to be aligned 120 points inside the leading edge. This can be implemented using an alignment guide as follows:

```
VStack(alignment: .leading) {
    Rectangle()
        .foregroundColor(Color.green)
        .frame(width: 120, height: 50)
    Rectangle()
        .foregroundColor(Color.red)
        .alignmentGuide(.leading, computeValue: { d in 120.0 })
        .frame(width: 200, height: 50)
    Rectangle()
        .foregroundColor(Color.blue)
        .frame(width: 180, height: 50)
}
```

While the first and third rectangles continue to be aligned on their leading edges, the second rectangle is aligned at the specified alignment guide position:

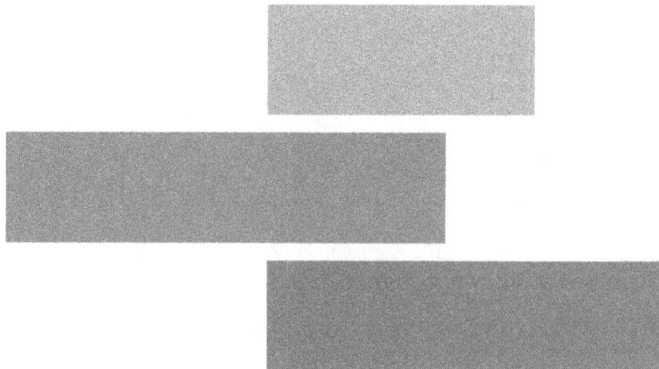

Figure 25-6

When working with alignment guides, the alignment type specified in the *alignmentGuide()* modifier must match the alignment type applied to the parent stack, as shown in Figure 25-7. If these do not match, the alignment guide will be ignored by SwiftUI when the layout is rendered.

```
VStack(alignment: .leading) {
    Rectangle()
        .foregroundColor(Color.green)
        .frame(width: 120, height: 50)
    Rectangle()
        .foregroundColor(Color.red)
        .alignmentGuide(.leading, computeValue: { d in 120.0 })
        .frame(width: 200, height: 50)
    Rectangle()
        .foregroundColor(Color.blue)
        .frame(width: 180, height: 50)
}
```

Must Match

Figure 25-7

Instead of hard-coding an offset, the properties of the ViewDimensions object passed to the closure can be used in calculating the alignment guide position. Using the width property, for example, the alignment guide could be positioned one-third of the way along the view from the leading edge:

```
VStack(alignment: .leading) {
    Rectangle()
        .foregroundColor(Color.green)
        .frame(width: 120, height: 50)
    Rectangle()
        .foregroundColor(Color.red)
        .alignmentGuide(.leading,
                    computeValue: { d in d.width / 3 })
        .frame(width: 200, height: 50)
    Rectangle()
        .foregroundColor(Color.blue)
        .frame(width: 180, height: 50)
}
```

Now when the layout is rendered it will appear, as shown in Figure 25-8:

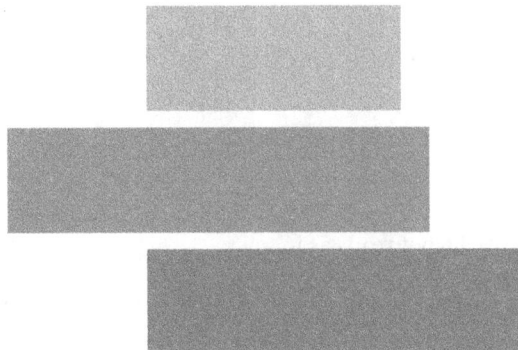

Figure 25-8

The ViewDimensions object also provides access to the HorizontalAlignment and VerticalAlignment properties of the view. In the following example, the trailing edge of the view is identified with an additional 20 points added:

```
.alignmentGuide(.leading, computeValue: {
                 d in d[HorizontalAlignment.trailing] + 20
})
```

This will cause the trailing edge of the view to be aligned 20 points from the leading edges of the other views:

Figure 25-9

25.3 Custom Alignment Types

In the previous examples, changes have been made to view alignments based on the standard alignment types. SwiftUI provides a way for the set of standard types to be extended by declaring custom alignment types. A custom alignment type named *oneThird* could, for example, be created which would make the point of alignment one-third of the distance from a specified edge of a view.

Take, for example, the following HStack configuration consisting of four rectangles centered vertically:

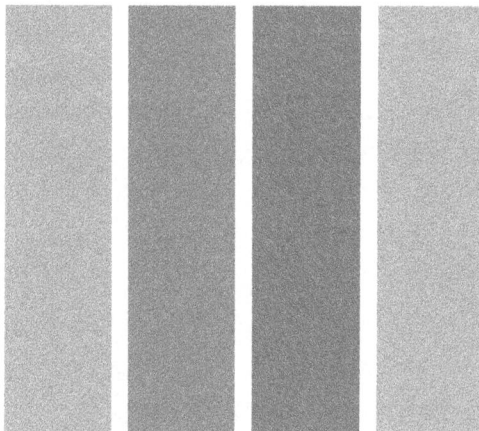

Figure 25-10

The declaration to display the above layout reads as follows:

```
HStack(alignment: .center) {
     Rectangle()
          .foregroundColor(Color.green)
          .frame(width: 50, height: 200)
```

```
    Rectangle()
        .foregroundColor(Color.red)
        .frame(width: 50, height: 200)
    Rectangle()
        .foregroundColor(Color.blue)
        .frame(width: 50, height: 200)
    Rectangle()
        .foregroundColor(Color.orange)
        .frame(width: 50, height: 200)
}
```

To change the alignment of one or more of these rectangles, alignment guides could be applied containing the calculations for a computed value. An alternative approach is to create a custom alignment that can be applied to multiple views. This is achieved by extending either VerticalAlignment or HorizontalAlignment to add a new alignment type that returns a calculated value. The following example creates a new vertical alignment type:

```
extension VerticalAlignment {
    private enum OneThird : AlignmentID {
        static func defaultValue(in d: ViewDimensions) -> CGFloat {
            return d.height / 3
        }
    }
    static let oneThird = VerticalAlignment(OneThird.self)
}
```

The extension must contain an enum that conforms to the AlignmentID protocol which, in turn, dictates that a function named *defaultValue()* is implemented. This function must accept a ViewDimensions object for a view and return a CGFloat computed value indicating the alignment guide position. In the above example, a position one-third of the height of the view is returned.

Once implemented, the custom alignment can be used, as shown in the following HStack declaration:

```
HStack(alignment: .oneThird) {
    Rectangle()
        .foregroundColor(Color.green)
        .frame(width: 50, height: 200)
    Rectangle()
        .foregroundColor(Color.red)
        .alignmentGuide(.oneThird,
            computeValue: { d in d[VerticalAlignment.top] })
        .frame(width: 50, height: 200)

    Rectangle()
        .foregroundColor(Color.blue)
        .frame(width: 50, height: 200)
    Rectangle()
        .foregroundColor(Color.orange)
        .alignmentGuide(.oneThird,
            computeValue: { d in d[VerticalAlignment.top] })
```

```
            .frame(width: 50, height: 200)
}
```

In the above example, the new *oneThird* custom alignment has been applied to two of the rectangle views, resulting in the following layout:

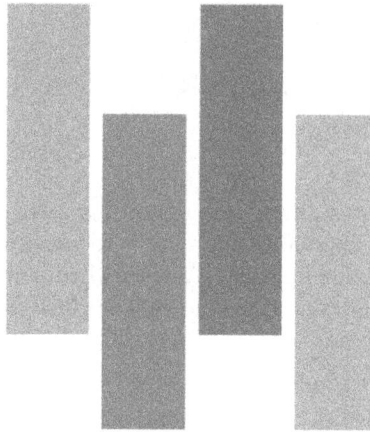

Figure 25-11

In both cases, the alignment was calculated relative to the top of the view with no additional modifications. In fact, the custom alignment can be used in the same way as a standard alignment type. For example, the following changes align the red rectangle relative to the bottom edge of the view:

```
.alignmentGuide(.oneThird,
            computeValue: { d in d[VerticalAlignment.bottom] })
```

Now when the view is rendered, the alignment guide is set to a position one-third of the view height below the bottom edge of the view:

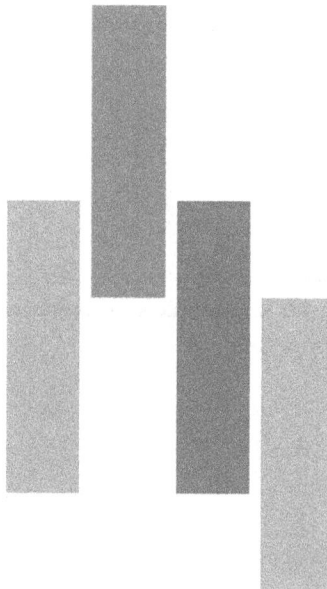

Figure 25-12

25.4 Cross Stack Alignment

A typical user interface layout will be created by nesting stacks to multiple levels. A key shortcoming of the standard alignment types is that they do not provide a way for a view in one stack to be aligned with a view in another stack. Consider the following stack configuration consisting of a VStack embedded inside an HStack. In addition to the embedded VStack, the HStack also contains a single additional view:

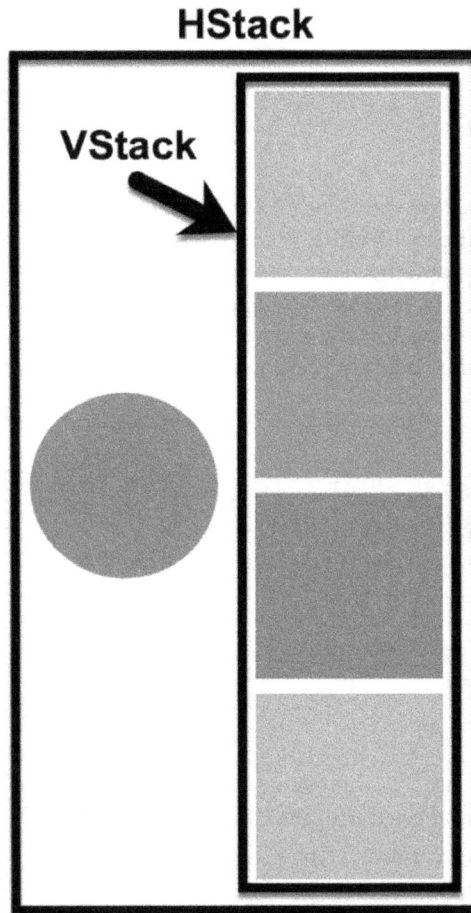

Figure 25-13

The corresponding declaration for the above nested layout reads as follows:

```
HStack(alignment: .center, spacing: 20) {

    Circle()
        .foregroundColor(Color.purple)
        .frame(width: 100, height: 100)

    VStack(alignment: .center) {
        Rectangle()
            .foregroundColor(Color.green)
            .frame(width: 100, height: 100)
```

```
            Rectangle()
                .foregroundColor(Color.red)
                .frame(width: 100, height: 100)
            Rectangle()
                .foregroundColor(Color.blue)
                .frame(width: 100, height: 100)
            Rectangle()
                .foregroundColor(Color.orange)
                .frame(width: 100, height: 100)
        }
    }
```

Currently, both the view represented by the circle and the VStack are centered in the vertical plane within the HStack. If we wanted the circle to align with either the top or bottom squares in the VStack we could change the HStack alignment to .top or .bottom and the view would align with the top or bottom squares respectively. If, on the other hand, the purple circle view needed to be aligned with either the second or third square there would be no way of doing so using the standard alignment types. Fortunately, this can be achieved by creating a custom alignment and applying it to both the circle and the square within the VStack with which it is to be aligned.

A simple custom alignment that returns an alignment value relative to the bottom edge of a view can be implemented as follows:

```
extension VerticalAlignment {
    private enum CrossAlignment : AlignmentID {
        static func defaultValue(in d: ViewDimensions) -> CGFloat {
            return d[.bottom]
        }
    }
    static let crossAlignment = VerticalAlignment(CrossAlignment.self)
}
```

This custom alignment can now be used to align views embedded in different stacks. In the following example, the bottom edge of the circle view is aligned with the third square embedded in the VStack:

```
HStack(alignment: .crossAlignment, spacing: 20) {

    Circle()
        .foregroundColor(Color.purple)
        .alignmentGuide(.crossAlignment,
            computeValue: { d in d[VerticalAlignment.center] })
        .frame(width: 100, height: 100)

    VStack(alignment: .center) {
        Rectangle()
            .foregroundColor(Color.green)
            .frame(width: 100, height: 100)
        Rectangle()
            .foregroundColor(Color.red)
            .frame(width: 100, height: 100)
```

```
Rectangle()
    .foregroundColor(Color.blue)
    .alignmentGuide(.crossAlignment, computeValue:
                    { d in d[VerticalAlignment.center] })
    .frame(width: 100, height: 100)
Rectangle()
    .foregroundColor(Color.orange)
    .frame(width: 100, height: 100)
    }
}
```

Note that the alignment of the containing HStack also needs to use the crossAlignment type for the custom alignment to take effect. When rendered, the layout now will appear, as illustrated in Figure 25-14 below:

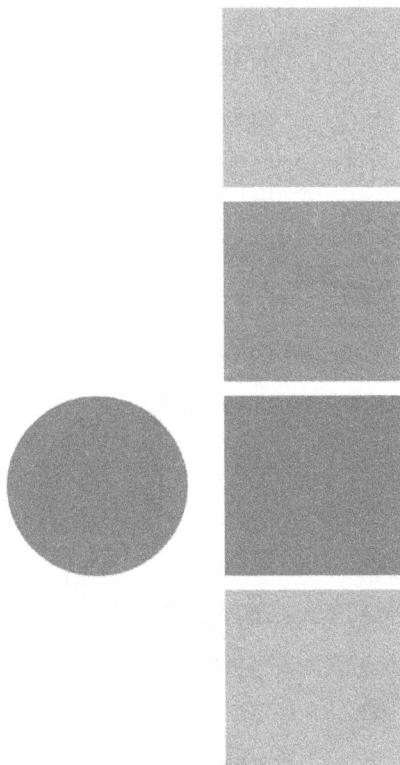

Figure 25-14

25.5 ZStack Custom Alignment

By default, the child views of a ZStack are overlaid on top of each other and center-aligned. The following figure shows three shape views (circle, square, and capsule) stacked on top of each other in a ZStack and center aligned:

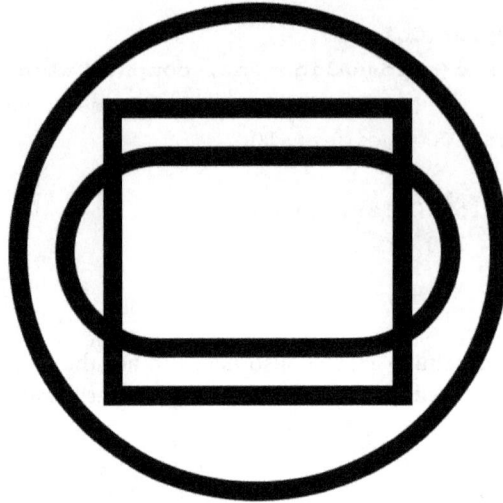

Figure 25-15

Using the standard alignment types, the alignment of all the embedded views can be changed. In Figure 25-16 for example, the ZStack has .leading alignment configured:

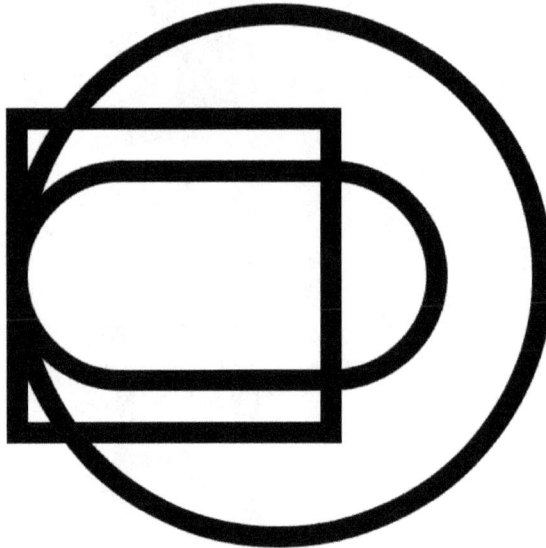

Figure 25-16

To perform more advanced alignment layouts, where each view within the stack has its own alignment, both horizontal and vertical custom alignments must be combined into a single custom alignment, for example:

```
extension HorizontalAlignment {
    enum MyHorizontal: AlignmentID {
        static func defaultValue(in d: ViewDimensions) -> CGFloat
                { d[HorizontalAlignment.center] }
    }
    static let myAlignment =
```

```
                        HorizontalAlignment(MyHorizontal.self)
}

extension VerticalAlignment {
    enum MyVertical: AlignmentID {
        static func defaultValue(in d: ViewDimensions) -> CGFloat
                { d[VerticalAlignment.center] }
    }
    static let myAlignment = VerticalAlignment(MyVertical.self)
}

extension Alignment {
    static let myAlignment = Alignment(horizontal: .myAlignment,
                            vertical: .myAlignment)
}
```

Once implemented, the custom alignments can be used to position ZStack child views on both the horizontal and vertical axes:

```
ZStack(alignment: .myAlignment) {
    Rectangle()
        .foregroundColor(Color.green)
        .alignmentGuide(HorizontalAlignment.myAlignment)
                        { d in d[.trailing]}
        .alignmentGuide(VerticalAlignment.myAlignment)
                        { d in d[VerticalAlignment.bottom] }
        .frame(width: 100, height: 100)

    Rectangle()
        .foregroundColor(Color.red)
        .alignmentGuide(VerticalAlignment.myAlignment)
                        { d in d[VerticalAlignment.top] }
        .alignmentGuide(HorizontalAlignment.myAlignment)
                        { d in d[HorizontalAlignment.center] }
        .frame(width: 100, height: 100)

    Circle()
        .foregroundColor(Color.orange)
        .alignmentGuide(HorizontalAlignment.myAlignment)
                        { d in d[.leading] }
        .alignmentGuide(VerticalAlignment.myAlignment)
                        { d in d[.bottom] }
        .frame(width: 100, height: 100)
}
```

The above ZStack will appear, as shown in Figure 25-17 when rendered:

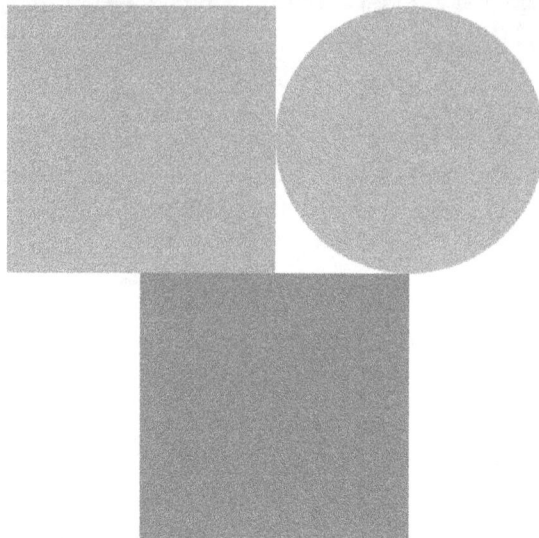

Figure 25-17

Take some time to experiment with the alignment settings on each view to gain an understanding of how ZStack custom alignment works. Begin, for example, with the following changes:

```
ZStack(alignment: .myAlignment) {
    Rectangle()
        .foregroundColor(Color.green)
        .alignmentGuide(HorizontalAlignment.myAlignment)
                        { d in d[.leading]}
        .alignmentGuide(VerticalAlignment.myAlignment)
                        { d in d[VerticalAlignment.bottom] }
        .frame(width: 100, height: 100)

    Rectangle()
        .foregroundColor(Color.red)
        .alignmentGuide(VerticalAlignment.myAlignment)
                        { d in d[VerticalAlignment.center] }
        .alignmentGuide(HorizontalAlignment.myAlignment)
                        { d in d[HorizontalAlignment.trailing] }
        .frame(width: 100, height: 100)

    Circle()
        .foregroundColor(Color.orange)
        .alignmentGuide(HorizontalAlignment.myAlignment)
                        { d in d[.leading] }
        .alignmentGuide(VerticalAlignment.myAlignment)
                        { d in d[.top] }
        .frame(width: 100, height: 100)
}
```

With these changes made, check the preview canvas and verify that the layout now matches Figure 25-18:

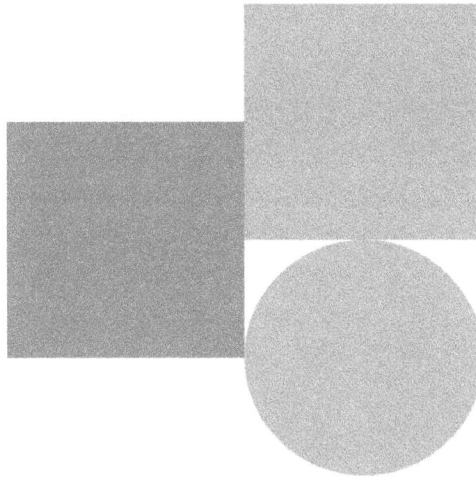

Figure 25-18

25.6 Take the Knowledge Test

Click the link below or scan the QR code to test your knowledge and understanding of SwiftUI stack alignment:

https://www.answertopia.com/6qjf

25.7 Summary

The SwiftUI stack container views can be configured using basic alignment settings that control the positioning of all child views relative to the container. The alignment of individual views within a stack may be configured using alignment guides. An alignment guide includes a closure that is passed a ViewDimensions object that can be used to compute the alignment position for the view based on the view's height and width. These alignment guides can be implemented as custom alignments which can be reused in the same way as standard alignments when declaring a stack view layout. Custom alignments are also a useful tool when views contained in different stacks need to be aligned with each other. Custom alignment of ZStack child views requires both horizontal and vertical alignment guides.

26. An Overview of Swift Structured Concurrency

Concurrency can be defined as the ability of software to perform multiple tasks in parallel. Many app development projects will need to make use of concurrent processing at some point and concurrency is essential for providing a good user experience. Concurrency, for example, is what allows the user interface of an app to remain responsive while performing background tasks such as downloading images or processing data.

In this chapter, we will explore the *structured concurrency* features of the Swift programming language and explain how these can be used to add multi-tasking support to your app projects.

26.1 An Overview of Threads

Threads are a feature of modern CPUs and provide the foundation of concurrency in any multitasking operating system. Although modern CPUs can run large numbers of threads, the actual number of threads that can be run in parallel at any one time is limited by the number of CPU cores (depending on the CPU model, this will typically be between 4 and 16 cores). When more threads are required than there are CPU cores, the operating system performs thread scheduling to decide how the execution of these threads is to be shared between the available cores.

Threads can be thought of as mini-processes running within a main process, the purpose of which is to enable at least the appearance of parallel execution paths within application code. The good news is that although structured concurrency uses threads behind the scenes, it handles all of the complexity for you and you should never need to interact with them directly.

26.2 The Application Main Thread

When an app is first started, the runtime system will typically create a single thread in which the app will run by default. This thread is generally referred to as the *main thread*. The primary role of the main thread is to handle the user interface in terms of UI layout rendering, event handling, and user interaction with views in the user interface.

Any additional code within an app that performs a time-consuming task using the main thread will cause the entire application to appear to lock up until the task is completed. This can be avoided by launching the tasks to be performed in separate threads, allowing the main thread to continue unhindered with other tasks.

26.3 Completion Handlers

As outlined in the chapter entitled *"Swift Functions, Methods, and Closures"*, Swift previously used completion handlers to implement asynchronous code execution. In this scenario, an asynchronous task would be started and a completion handler assigned to be called when the task finishes. In the meantime, the main app code would continue to run while the asynchronous task is performed in the background. On completion of the asynchronous task, the completion handler would be called and passed any results. The body of the completion handler would then execute and process those results.

Unfortunately, completion handlers tend to result in complex and error-prone code constructs that are difficult to write and understand. Completion handlers are also unsuited to handling errors thrown by the asynchronous tasks and generally result in large and confusing nested code structures.

26.4 Structured Concurrency

Structured concurrency was introduced into the Swift language with Swift version 5.5 to make it easier for app developers to implement concurrent execution safely, and in a way that is logical and easy to both write and understand. In other words, structured concurrency code can be read from top to bottom without having to jump back to completion handler code to understand the logic flow. Structured concurrency also makes it easier to handle errors thrown by asynchronous functions.

Swift provides several options for implementing structured concurrency, each of which will be introduced in this chapter.

26.5 Preparing the Project

Launch Xcode and select the option to create a new Multiplatform App project named ConcurrencyDemo. Once created, edit the *ContentView.swift* file so that it reads as follows:

```
import SwiftUI

struct ContentView: View {
    var body: some View {
        Button(action: {
            doSomething()
        }) {
            Text("Do Something")
        }
    }

    func doSomething() {
    }

    func takesTooLong() {
    }
}

#Preview {
    ContentView()
}
```

The above changes create a Button view configured to call the *doSomething()* function when clicked. In the remainder of this chapter, we will make changes to this template code to demonstrate structured concurrency in Swift.

26.6 Non-Concurrent Code

Before exploring concurrency, we will first look at an example of non-concurrent code (also referred to as *synchronous code*) execution. Begin by adding the following code to the two stub functions. The changes to the *doSomething()* function print out the current date and time before calling the *takesTooLong()* function. Finally, the date and time are output once again before the *doSomething()* function exits.

The *takesTooLong()* function uses the system *sleep()* method to simulate the effect of performing a time-consuming task that blocks the main thread until it is complete before printing out another timestamp:

```
func doSomething() {
    print("Start \(Date())")
    takesTooLong()
    print("End \(Date())")
}


func takesTooLong() {
    sleep(5)
    print("Async task completed at \(Date())")
}
```

Open the console panel and switch to Canvas mode using the button indicated below:

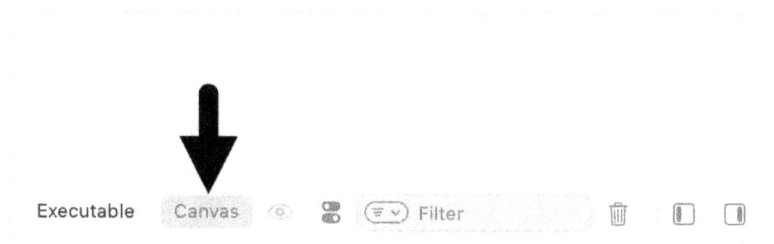

Figure 26-1

Check that the canvas is in Live mode, then click on the "Do Something" button. Output similar to the following should appear in the Xcode console panel:

```
Start 2025-09-06 14:52:03 +0000
Async task completed at 2025-09-06 14:52:08 +0000
End 2025-09-06 14:52:08 +0000
```

The key point to note in the above timestamps is that the end time is 5 seconds after the start time. This tells us not only that the call to *takesTooLong()* lasted 5 seconds as expected, but that any code after the call was made within the *doSomething()* function was not able to execute until after the call returned. During those 5 seconds, the app would appear to the user to be frozen.

The answer to this problem is to implement a Swift *async/await* concurrency structure.

26.7 Introducing async/await Concurrency

The foundation of structured concurrency is the *async/await* pair. The *async* keyword is used when declaring a function to indicate that it is to be executed asynchronously relative to the thread from which it was called. We need, therefore, to declare both of our example functions as follows (any errors that appear will be addressed later):

```
func doSomething() async {
    print("Start \(Date())")
    takesTooLong()
    print("End \(Date())")
}


func takesTooLong() async {
    try? await Task.sleep(nanoseconds: 5_000_000_000)
```

```
        print("Async task completed at \(Date())")
}
```

Note that because are now working with asynchronous functions, we have switched from *sleep()* to *Task.sleep()* in the *takesTooLong()* function to simulate the delay. Marking a function as async achieves several objectives. First, it indicates that the code in the function needs to be executed on a different thread to the one from which it was called. It also notifies the system that the function itself can be suspended during execution to allow the system to run other tasks. As we will see later, these *suspend points* within an async function are specified using the *await* keyword.

Another point to note about async functions is that they can generally only be called from within the scope of other async functions though, as we will see later in the chapter, the Task object can be used to provide a bridge between synchronous and asynchronous code. Finally, if an async function calls other async functions, the parent function cannot exit until all child tasks have also completed.

Most importantly, once a function has been declared as being asynchronous, it can only be called using the *await* keyword. Before looking at the await keyword, we need to understand how to call async functions from synchronous code.

26.8 Asynchronous Calls from Synchronous Functions

The rules of structured concurrency state that an async function can only be called from within an asynchronous context. If the entry point into your program is a synchronous function, this raises the question of how any async functions can ever get called. The answer is to use the Task object from within the synchronous function to launch the async function. Suppose we have a synchronous function named *main()* from which we need to call one of our async functions and attempt to do so as follows:

```
func main() {
    doSomething()
}
```

The above code will result in the following error notification in the code editor:

```
'async' call in a function that does not support concurrency
```

The only options we have are to make *main()* an async function or to launch the function in an unstructured task. Assuming that declaring *main()* as an async function is not a viable option, in this case, the code will need to be changed as follows:

```
func main() {
    Task {
        await doSomething()
    }
}
```

26.9 The await Keyword

As we have previously discussed, the await keyword is required when making a call to an async function and can only usually be used within the scope of another async function. Attempting to call an async function without the await keyword will result in the following syntax error:

```
Expression is 'async' but is not marked with 'await'
```

To call the *takesTooLong()* function, therefore, we need to make the following change to the *doSomething()* function:

```
func doSomething() async {
```

```
    print("Start \(Date())")
    await takesTooLong()
    print("End \(Date())")
}
```

One more change is now required because we are attempting to call the async *doSomething()* function from a synchronous context (in this case the action closure of the Button view). To resolve this, we need to use the Task object to launch the *doSomething()* function:

```
var body: some View {
    Button(action: {
        Task {
            await doSomething()
        }
    }) {
        Text("Do Something")
    }
}
```

When tested now, the console output should be similar to the following:

```
Start 2025-09-06 14:55:21 +0000
Async task completed at 2025-09-06 14:55:26 +0000
End 2025-09-06 14:55:26 +0000
```

This is where the await keyword can be a little confusing. As you have probably noticed, the *doSomething()* function still had to wait for the *takesTooLong()* function to return before continuing, giving the impression that the task was still blocking the thread from which it was called. In fact, the task was performed on a different thread, but the await keyword told the system to wait until it completed. The reason for this is that, as previously mentioned, a parent async function cannot complete until all of its sub-functions have also completed. This means that the call has no choice but to wait for the async *takesTooLong()* function to return before executing the next line of code. In the next section, we will explain how to defer the wait until later in the parent function using the *async-let* binding expression. Before doing that, however, we need to look at another effect of using the await keyword in this context.

In addition to allowing us to make the async call, the await keyword has also defined a *suspend point* within the *doSomething()* function. When this point is reached during execution, it tells the system that the *doSomething()* function can be temporarily suspended and the thread on which it is running used for other purposes. This allows the system to allocate resources to any higher priority tasks and will eventually return control to the *doSomething()* function so that execution can continue. By marking suspend points, the *doSomething()* function is essentially being forced to be a good citizen by allowing the system to briefly allocate processing resources to other tasks. Given the speed of the system, it is unlikely that a suspension will last more than fractions of a second and will not be noticeable to the user while benefiting the overall performance of the app.

26.10 Using async-let Bindings

In our example code, we have identified that the default behavior of the await keyword is to wait for the called function to return before resuming execution. A more common requirement, however, is to continue executing code within the calling function while the async function is executing in the background. This can be achieved by deferring the wait until later in the code using an async-let binding. To demonstrate this, we first need to modify our *takesTooLong()* function to return a result (in this case our task completion timestamp):

```
func takesTooLong() async -> Date {
```

213

An Overview of Swift Structured Concurrency

```
    try? await Task.sleep(nanoseconds: 5_000_000_000)
    return Date()
}
```

Next, we need to change the call within *doSomething()* to assign the returned result to a variable using a *let* expression but also marked with the *async* keyword:

```
func doSomething() async {
    print("Start \(Date())")
    async let result = takesTooLong()
    print("End \(Date())")
}
```

Now, all we need to do is specify where within the *doSomething()* function we want to wait for the result value to be returned. We do this by accessing the result variable using the await keyword. For example:

```
func doSomething() async {
    print("Start \(Date())")
    async let result = takesTooLong()
    print("After async-let \(Date())")
    // Additional code to run concurrently with async function goes here
    print ("result = \(await result)")
    print("End \(Date())")
}
```

When printing the result value, we are using await to let the system know that execution cannot continue until the async *takesTooLong()* function returns with the result value. At this point, execution will stop until the result is available. Any code between the async-let and the await, however, will execute concurrently with the *takesTooLong()* function.

Execution of the above code will generate output similar to the following:

```
Start 2025-09-07 10:30:40 +0000
After async-let 2025-09-07 10:30:40 +0000
result = 2025-09-07 10:30:45 +0000
End 2025-09-07 10:30:45 +0000
```

Note that the "After async-let" message has a timestamp that is 5 seconds earlier than the "result =" call return stamp confirming that the code was executed while *takesTooLong()* was also running.

26.11 Handling Errors

Error handling in structured concurrency makes use of the throw/do/try/catch mechanism previously covered in the chapter entitled *"Understanding Error Handling in Swift 5"*. The following example modifies our original async *takesTooLong()* function to accept a sleep duration parameter and to throw an error if the delay is outside of a specific range:

```
enum DurationError: Error {
    case tooLong
    case tooShort
}
.
.
func takesTooLong(delay: UInt32) async throws {
```

214

```
    if delay < 5 {
        throw DurationError.tooShort
    } else if delay > 20 {
        throw DurationError.tooLong
    }

    sleep(delay)
    print("Async task completed at \(Date())")
}
```

Now, when the function is called, we can use a do/try/catch construct to handle any errors that get thrown:

```
func doSomething() async {
    print("Start \(Date())")
    do {
        try await takesTooLong(delay: 25)
    } catch DurationError.tooShort {
        print("Error: Duration too short")
    } catch DurationError.tooLong {
        print("Error: Duration too long")
    } catch {
        print("Unknown error")
    }
    print("End \(Date())")
}
```

When executed, the resulting output will resemble the following:

```
Start 2025-09-07 10:41:29 +0000
Error: Duration too long
End 2025-09-07 10:41:29 +0000
```

26.12 Understanding Tasks

Any work that executes asynchronously is running within an instance of the Swift *Task* class. An app can run multiple tasks simultaneously and structures these tasks hierarchically. When launched, the async version of our *doSomething()* function will run within a Task instance. When the *takesTooLong()* function is called, the system creates a *sub-task* within which the function code will execute. In terms of the task hierarchy tree, this sub-task is a child of the *doSomething()* parent task. Any calls to async functions from within the sub-task will become children of that task, and so on.

This task hierarchy forms the basis on which structured concurrency is built. For example, child tasks inherit attributes such as priority from their parents, and the hierarchy ensures that a parent task does not exit until all descendant tasks have been completed.

As we will see later in the chapter, tasks can be grouped to enable the dynamic launching of multiple asynchronous tasks.

26.13 Unstructured Concurrency

Individual tasks can be created manually using the Task object, a concept referred to as unstructured concurrency. As we have already seen, a common use for unstructured tasks is to call async functions from within synchronous functions.

Unstructured tasks also provide more flexibility because they can be externally canceled at any time during execution. This is particularly useful if you need to provide the user with a way to cancel a background activity, such as tapping on a button to stop a background download task. This flexibility comes with some extra cost in terms of having to do a little more work to create and manage tasks.

Unstructured tasks are created and launched by making a call to the Task initializer and providing a closure containing the code to be performed. For example:

```
Task {
    await doSomething()
}
```

These tasks also inherit the configuration of the parent from which they are called, such as the actor context (a topic we will explore in the chapter entitled *"An Introduction to Swift Actors"*), priority, and task local variables. Tasks can also be assigned a new priority when they are created, for example:

```
Task(priority: .high) {
    await doSomething()
}
```

This provides a hint to the system about how the task should be scheduled relative to other tasks. Available priorities ranked from highest to lowest are as follows:

- .high / .userInitiated

- .medium

- .low / .utility

- .background

When a task is manually created, it returns a reference to the Task instance. This can be used to cancel the task, or to check whether the task has already been canceled from outside the task scope:

```
let task = Task(priority: .high) {
    await doSomething()
}
.
.
if (!task.isCancelled) {
    task.cancel()
}
```

26.14 Detached Tasks

Detached tasks are another form of unstructured concurrency, but differ in that they do not inherit any properties from the calling parent. Detached tasks are created by calling the *Task.detached()* method as follows:

```
Task.detached {
    await doSomething()
}
```

Detached tasks may also be passed a priority value, and checked for cancellation using the same techniques as outlined above:

```
let detachedTask = Task.detached(priority: .medium) {
    await doSomething()
}
.

.
if (!detachedTask.isCancelled) {
    detachedTask.cancel()
}
```

26.15 Task Management

Regardless of whether you are using structured or unstructured tasks, the Task class provides a set of static methods and properties that can be used to manage the task from within the task scope.

A task may, for example, use the *currentPriority* property to identify the priority assigned when it was created:

```
Task {
    let priority = Task.currentPriority
    await doSomething()
}
```

Unfortunately, this is a read-only property so cannot be used to change the priority of the running task.

It is also possible for a task to check if it has been canceled by accessing the *isCancelled* property:

```
if Task.isCancelled {
    // perform task cleanup
}
```

Another option for detecting cancellation is to call the *checkCancellation()* method which will throw a CancellationError error if the task has been canceled:

```
do {
    try Task.checkCancellation()
} catch {
    // Perform task cleanup
}
```

A task may cancel itself at any time by calling the *cancel()* Task method:

```
Task.cancel()
```

Finally, if there are locations within the task code where execution could safely be suspended, these can be declared to the system via the *yield()* method:

```
Task.yield()
```

26.16 Working with Task Groups

So far in this chapter, all of our examples have involved creating one or two tasks (a parent and a child). In each case, we knew in advance of writing the code how many tasks were required. Situations often arise, however, where several tasks need to be created and run concurrently based on dynamic criteria. We might, for example, need to launch a separate task for each item in an array, or within the body of a *for* loop. Swift addresses this by providing *task groups*.

Task groups allow a dynamic number of tasks to be created and are implemented using either the *withThrowingTaskGroup()* or *withTaskGroup()* functions (depending on whether or not the async functions in the group throw errors). The looping construct to create the tasks is then defined within the corresponding closure, calling the group *addTask()* function to add each new task.

Modify the two functions as follows to create a task group consisting of five tasks, each running an instance of the *takesTooLong()* function:

```
func doSomething() async {
    await withTaskGroup(of: Void.self) { group in
        for i in 1...5 {
            group.addTask {
                let result = await takesTooLong()
                print("Completed Task \(i) = \(result)")
            }
        }
    }
}


func takesTooLong() async -> Date {
    try? await Task.sleep(nanoseconds: 5_000_000_000)
    return Date()
}
```

When executed, there will be a 5-second delay while the tasks run before output similar to the following appears:

```
Completed Task 3 = 2025-09-07 10:45:57 +0000
Completed Task 1 = 2025-09-07 10:45:57 +0000
Completed Task 2 = 2025-09-07 10:45:57 +0000
Completed Task 4 = 2025-09-07 10:45:57 +0000
Completed Task 5 = 2025-09-07 10:45:57 +0000
```

Note that the tasks all show the same completion timestamp indicating that they were executed concurrently. It is also interesting to notice that the tasks did not complete in the order in which they were launched. When working with concurrency, it is important to keep in mind that there is no guarantee that tasks will complete in the order that they were created.

In addition to the *addTask()* function, several other methods and properties are accessible from within the task group including the following:

- **cancelAll()** - Method call to cancel all tasks in the group

- **isCancelled** - Boolean property indicating whether the task group has already been canceled.

- **isEmpty** - Boolean property indicating whether any tasks remain within the task group.

26.17 Avoiding Data Races

In the above task group example, the group did not store the results of the tasks. In other words, the results did not leave the scope of the task group and were not retained when the tasks ended. As an example, let's assume that we want to store the task number and result timestamp for each task within a Swift dictionary object (with the task number as the key and the timestamp as the value). When working with synchronous code, we might consider a solution that reads as follows:

```
func doSomething() async {
```

```
var timeStamps: [Int: Date] = [:]


await withTaskGroup(of: Void.self) { group in
    for i in 1...5 {
        group.addTask {
            timeStamps[i] = await takesTooLong()
        }
    }
}
```

Unfortunately, when we run the app and click the "Do Something" button, the app will crash. The problem here is that we have multiple tasks accessing the data concurrently and risk encountering a data race condition. A data race occurs when multiple tasks attempt to access the same data concurrently, and one or more of these tasks is performing a write operation. This generally results in data corruption problems that can be hard to diagnose.

One option is to create an *actor* in which to store the data. Actors, and how they might be used to solve this particular problem, will be covered in the chapter entitled *"An Introduction to Swift Actors"*.

Another solution is to adapt our task group to return the task results sequentially and add them to the dictionary. We originally declared the task group as returning no results by passing Void.self as the return type to the *withTaskGroup()* function as follows:

```
await withTaskGroup(of: Void.self) { group in
.
.
.
```

The first step is to design the task group so that each task returns a tuple containing the task number (Int) and timestamp (Date) as follows. We also need a dictionary in which to store the results:

```
func doSomething() async {

    var timeStamps: [Int: Date] = [:]

    await withTaskGroup(of: (Int, Date).self) { group in
        for i in 1...5 {
            group.addTask {
                return(i, await takesTooLong())
            }
        }
    }
}
```

Next, we need to declare a second loop to handle the results as they are returned from the group. Because the results are being returned individually from async functions, we cannot simply write a loop to process them all at once. Instead, we need to wait until each result is returned. For this situation, Swift provides the *for-await* loop.

26.18 The for-await Loop

The *for-await* expression allows us to step through sequences of values that are being returned asynchronously and *await* the receipt of values as they are returned by concurrent tasks. The only requirement for using for-

An Overview of Swift Structured Concurrency

await is that the sequential data conforms to the AsyncSequence protocol (which should always be the case when working with task groups).

In our example, we need to add a for-await loop within the task group scope, but after the addTask loop as follows:

```
func doSomething() async {

    var timeStamps: [Int: Date] = [:]

    await withTaskGroup(of: (Int, Date).self) { group in

        for i in 1...5 {
            group.addTask {
                return (i, await takesTooLong())
            }
        }

        for await (task, date) in group {
            timeStamps[task] = date
        }
    }
}
```

As each task returns, the for-await loop will receive the resulting tuple and store it in the timeStamps dictionary. To verify this, we can add some code to print the dictionary entries after the task group exits:

```
func doSomething() async {

.

.

        for await (task, date) in group {
            timeStamps[task] = date
        }
    }

    for (task, date) in timeStamps {
        print("Task = \(task), Date = \(date)")
    }
}
```

When executed, the output from the completed example should be similar to the following:

```
Task = 3, Date = 2025-09-07 10:54:35 +0000
Task = 2, Date = 2025-09-07 10:54:35 +0000
Task = 4, Date = 2025-09-07 10:54:35 +0000
Task = 1, Date = 2025-09-07 10:54:35 +0000
Task = 5, Date = 2025-09-07 10:54:35 +0000
```

26.19 Asynchronous Properties

In addition to async functions, Swift also supports async properties within class and struct types. Asynchronous properties are created by explicitly declaring a getter and marking it as async as demonstrated in the following example. Currently, only read-only properties can be asynchronous.

```swift
struct MyStruct {
    var myResult: Date {
        get async {
            return await self.getTime()
        }
    }
    func getTime() async -> Date {
        sleep(5)
        return Date()
    }
}
.
.
.
func doSomething() async {

    let myStruct = MyStruct()

    Task {
        let date = await myStruct.myResult
        print(date)
    }
}
```

26.20 Take the Knowledge Test

Click the link below or scan the QR code to test your knowledge and understanding of Swift concurrency:

https://www.answertopia.com/rcds

26.21 Summary

Modern CPUs and operating systems are designed to execute code concurrently allowing multiple tasks to be performed at the same time. This is achieved by running tasks on different *threads* with the *main thread* being primarily responsible for rendering the user interface and responding to user events. By default, most code in an app is also executed on the main thread unless specifically configured to run on a different thread. If that code performs tasks that occupy the main thread for too long the app will appear to freeze until the task completes. To avoid this, Swift provides the structured concurrency API. When using structured concurrency, code that would block the main thread is instead placed in an asynchronous function (async properties are also supported) so that it is performed on a separate thread. The calling code can be configured to wait for the async code to complete before continuing using the *await* keyword, or to continue executing until the result is needed using *async-let*.

Tasks can be run individually or as groups of multiple tasks. The for-await loop provides a useful way to asynchronously process the results of asynchronous task groups. When working with concurrency, it is important to avoid data races, a problem that can usually be resolved using Swift Actors, a topic we will cover in the next chapter entitled *"An Introduction to Swift Actors"*.

Chapter 27

27. An Introduction to Swift Actors

Structured concurrency in Swift provides a powerful platform for performing multiple tasks simultaneously, greatly increasing app performance and responsiveness. One of the downsides of concurrency is that it can lead to problems when multiple tasks access the same data concurrently, and that access includes a mix of reading and writing operations. This type of problem is referred to as a *data race* and can lead to intermittent crashes and unpredictable app behavior.

In the previous chapter, we looked at a solution to this problem that involved sequentially processing the results from multiple concurrent tasks. Unfortunately, that solution only really works when the tasks involved all belong to the same task group. A more flexible solution and one that works regardless of where the concurrent tasks are launched involves the use of Swift actors.

27.1 An Overview of Actors

Actors are a Swift type that controls asynchronous access to internal mutable state so that only one task at a time can access data. Actors are much like classes in that they are a reference type and contain properties, initializers, and methods. Like classes, actors can also conform to protocols and be enhanced using extensions. The primary difference when declaring an actor is that the word "actor" is used in place of "class".

27.2 Declaring an Actor

A simple Swift class that contains a property and a method might be declared as follows:

```
class BuildMessage {

    var message: String = ""
    let greeting = "Hello"

    func setName(name: String) {
        self.message = "\(greeting) \(name)"
    }
}
```

To make the class into an actor we just need to change the type declaration from "class" to "actor":

```
actor BuildMessage {

    var message: String = ""
    let greeting = "Hello"

    func setName(name: String) {
        self.message = "\(greeting) \(name)"
    }
}
```

Once declared, actor instances are created in the same way as classes, for example:

```
let hello = BuildMessage()
```

A key difference between classes and actors, however, is that actors can only be created and accessed from within an asynchronous context, such as within an async function or Task closure. Also, when calling an actor method or accessing a property, the *await* keyword must be used, for example:

```
func someFunction() async {
    let builder = BuildMessage()
    await builder.setName(name: "Jane Smith")
    let message = await builder.message
    print(message)

}
```

27.3 Understanding Data Isolation

The data contained in an actor instance is said to be isolated from the rest of the code in the app. This isolation is imposed in part by ensuring that when a method that changes the instance data (in this case, changing the *name* variable) is called, the method is executed to completion before the method can be called from anywhere else in the code. This prevents multiple tasks from concurrently attempting to change the data. This, of course, means that method calls and property accesses may have to wait until a previous task has been handled, hence the need for the await statement. Behind the scenes, Swift achieves this by restricting isolated methods to running on the execution thread belonging to the containing actor. Any attempt to call the method from another actor, including the Main actor, will result in a syntax error.

Isolation also prevents code from directly changing the mutable internal properties of an actor. Consider, for example, the following code to directly assign a new value to the message property of our BuildMessage instance.

```
builder.message = "hello"
```

Though valid when working with class instances, the above code will generate the following error when attempted on an actor instance:

```
Actor-isolated property 'message' can not be mutated from the main actor
```

By default, all methods and mutable properties within an actor are isolated and, as such, can only be called using the await keyword. Actor methods that do not access mutable properties may be excluded from isolation using the *nonisolated* keyword. Once declared in this way, the method can be called without the await keyword, and also called from synchronous code. We can, for example, add a nonisolated method to our BuildMessage actor that returns the greeting string:

```
actor BuildMessage {

    var message: String = ""
    let greeting = "Hello"

    func setName(name: String) {
        self.message = "\(greeting) \(name)"
    }

    nonisolated func getGreeting() -> String {
        return greeting
    }

}
```

This new method can be called without the await keyword from both synchronous and asynchronous contexts:

```
var builder = BuildMessage()

func asyncFunction() async {
    let greeting = builder.getGreeting()
    print(greeting)
}

func syncFunction() {
    let greeting = builder.getGreeting()
    print(greeting)
}
```

It is possible to declare *getGreeting()* as nonisolated because the method only accesses the immutable greeting property. If the method attempted to access the mutable message property, the following error would be reported:

```
Actor-isolated property 'message' can not be mutated from a nonisolated context
```

Note that although immutable properties are excluded from isolation by default, the *nonisolated* keyword may still be declared for clarity:

```
nonisolated let greeting = "Hello"
```

27.4 A Swift Actor Example

In the previous chapter, we looked at data races and demonstrated how they can cause crashes during execution. We encountered this error when attempting to write entries to a dictionary object using the following asynchronous code:

```
func doSomething() async {

    var timeStamps: [Int: Date] = [:]

    await withTaskGroup(of: Void.self) { group in
        for i in 1...5 {
            group.addTask {
                timeStamps[i] = await takesTooLong()
            }
        }
    }
}
```

One option to avoid this problem, and the one implemented in the previous chapter, was to process the results from the asynchronous tasks sequentially using a for-await loop. As we have seen in this chapter, however, the problem could also be resolved using an actor.

With the ConcurrencyDemo project loaded into Xcode, edit the *ContentView.swift* file to add the following actor declaration to encapsulate the timeStamps dictionary and to provide a method via which data can be added:

```
import SwiftUI

actor TimeStore {

    var timeStamps: [Int: Date] = [:]
```

```
    func addStamp(task: Int, date: Date) {
        timeStamps[task] = date
    }
}
.
.
```

Having declared the actor, we can now modify the *doSomething()* method to add new timestamps via the *addStamp()* method:

```
func doSomething() async {

    let store = TimeStore()

    await withTaskGroup(of: Void.self) { group in
        for i in 1...5 {
            group.addTask {
                await store.addStamp(task: i, date: await takesTooLong())
            }
        }
    }

    for (task, date) in await store.timeStamps {
        print("Task = \(task), Date = \(date)")
    }
}


func takesTooLong() async -> Date {
    try? await Task.sleep(nanoseconds: 5_000_000_000)
    return Date()
}
```

With these changes, the code should now compile and run without error.

27.5 Introducing the MainActor

In the chapter entitled *"An Overview of Swift Structured Concurrency,"* we talked about the main thread (or main queue) and explained how it is responsible both for handling the rendering of the UI and also responding to user events. We also demonstrated the risks of performing thread-blocking tasks on the main thread and how doing so can cause the running program to freeze. As we have also seen, Swift provides a simple and powerful mechanism for running tasks on separate threads from the main thread. What we have not mentioned yet is that it is also essential that updates to the UI are *only* performed on the main thread. Performing UI updates on any separate thread other than the main thread is likely to cause instability and unpredictable app behavior that can be difficult to debug.

Within Swift, the main thread is represented by the *main actor*. This is referred to as a *global actor* because it is accessible throughout your program code when you need code to execute on the main thread.

When developing your app, situations may arise where you have code that you want to run on the main actor, particularly if that code updates the UI in some way. In this situation, the code can be marked using the @

226

MainActor attribute. This attribute may be used on types, methods, instances, functions, and closures to indicate that the associated operation must be performed on the main actor. We could, for example, configure a class so that it operates only on the main thread:

```
@MainActor
class TimeStore {

    var timeStamps: [Int: Date] = [:]

    func addStamp(task: Int, date: Date) {
        timeStamps[task] = date
    }
}
```

Alternatively, a single value or property can be marked as being main thread dependent:

```
class TimeStore {

    @MainActor var timeStamps: [Int: Date] = [:]

    func addStamp(task: Int, date: Date) {
        timeStamps[task] = date
    }
}
```

Of course, now that the timeStamps dictionary is assigned to the main actor, it cannot be accessed on any other thread. The attempt to add a new date to the dictionary in the above *addStamp()* method will generate the following error:

```
Property 'timeStamps' isolated to global actor 'MainActor' can not be mutated
from this context
```

To resolve this issue, the *addStamp()* method must also be marked using the @MainActor attribute:

```
@MainActor func addStamp(task: Int, date: Date) {
    timeStamps[task] = date
}
```

The run method of the MainActor can also be called directly from within asynchronous code to perform tasks on the main thread as follows:

```
func runExample() async {

    await MainActor.run {
        // Perform tasks on the main thread
    }
}
```

27.6 Changing Isolation Defaults

Isolation can be explicit (for example, by using @MainActor or nonisolated) or inferred (members of an actor are isolated by default). Also, when applying @MainActor at the type level, such as a class, isolation propagates to members of the type unless overridden.

With the introduction of Swift 6.2 and Xcode 26, the default isolation behavior is configurable. In the current

Xcode release, this setting is accessed in the project build settings. To view or change this option, select the ConcurrencyDemo target at the top of the Project Navigator panel (marked A in Figure 27-1), followed by the ConcurrencyDemo project entry (B) and then the Build Settings tab (C):

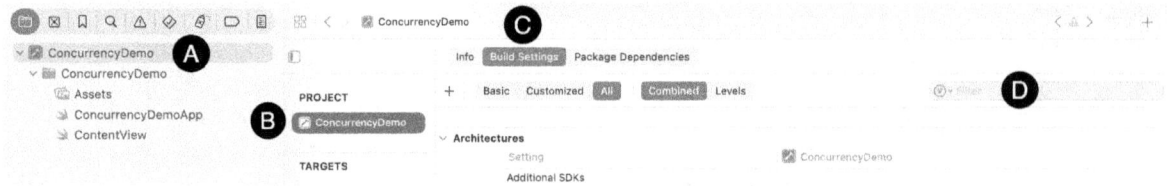

Figure 27-1

Within the Build Settings panel, enter *nonisolated* into the search field (D) and locate the *nonisolated(nonsending) By Default* option:

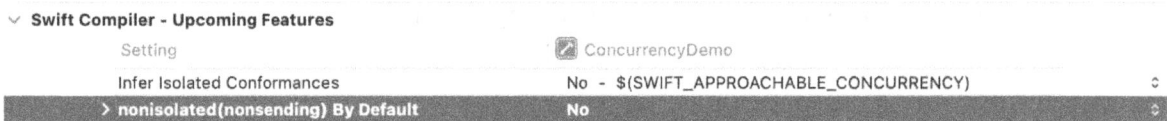

Figure 27-2

When this feature is enabled, nonisolated async closures run on the caller's actor by default. Likewise, nonisolated async functions invoked from an actor-isolated context will run on that caller's actor unless you opt into concurrent behavior. In a SwiftUI view context, that caller is typically the main actor. Until you become familiar with this concept, set the feature to *Migrate* to receive notifications in the code editor when the default behavior is applied.

Return to the *ContentView.swift* file where the *doSomething()* function reads as follows:

```
await withTaskGroup(of: Void.self) { group in
    for i in 1...5 {
        group.addTask {
            await store.addStamp(task: i, date: await takesTooLong())
        }
    }
}
```

The following warning should appear in the *doSomething()* method:

```
Feature 'NonisolatedNonsendingByDefault' will cause nonisolated async closure to
run on the caller's actor; use '@concurrent' to preserve behavior
```

This message warns that the task closure will run on the caller's actor (in this case, the main actor), potentially causing the *addStamp()* calls to serialize on the main actor. While this may be the desired behavior in this case, situations may arise where the calls could safely be executed concurrently. To achieve this, use the *@concurrent* annotation, as follows:

```
await withTaskGroup(of: Void.self) { group in
    for i in 1...5 {
        group.addTask { @concurrent in
            await store.addStamp(task: i, date: await takesTooLong())
        }
    }
}
```

}

After the change, the calls to *addStamp()* will be able to execute concurrently. In the above example, the @ *concurrent* annotation was applied to a closure. The annotation can also be applied to entire async functions, for example:

```
@concurrent
func someFunction() async {
 .
 .
 .
}
```

When you use *@concurrent*, you are telling the compiler that multiple independent invocations of an async function or closure can safely run concurrently. The compiler will take you at your word and will not perform any additional checks. It is, therefore, your responsibility to ensure that the code can run concurrently without introducing data races.

27.7 Take the Knowledge Test

Click the link below or scan the QR code to test your knowledge and understanding of the Swift actors:

https://www.answertopia.com/9kd9

27.8 Summary

A key part of writing asynchronous code is avoiding data races. A data race occurs when two or more tasks access the same data and at least one of those tasks performs a write operation. This can cause data inconsistencies where the concurrent tasks see and act on different versions of the same data.

A useful tool for avoiding data races is the Swift Actor type. Actors are syntactically and behaviorally similar to Swift classes but differ in that the data they encapsulate is said to be isolated from the rest of the code in the app. If a method within an actor that changes instance data is called, that method is executed to completion before the method can be called from anywhere else in the code. This prevents multiple tasks from concurrently attempting to change the data. Actor method calls and property accesses must be called using the await keyword.

The main actor is a special actor that provides access to the main thread from within asynchronous code. The @ MainActor attribute can be used to mark types, methods, instances, functions, and closures to indicate that the associated task must be performed on the main thread.

28. SwiftUI Concurrency and Lifecycle Event Modifiers

One of the key strengths of SwiftUI is that, through the use of features such as views, state properties, and observable objects, much of the work required in making sure an app handles lifecycle changes correctly is performed automatically.

It is still often necessary, however, to perform additional actions when certain lifecycle events occur. An app might, for example, need to perform a sequence of actions at the point that a view appears or disappears within a layout. Similarly, an app may need to execute some code each time a value changes or to detect when a view becomes active or inactive. It will also be a common requirement to launch one or more asynchronous tasks at the beginning of a view lifecycle.

All of these requirements and more can be met by making use of a set of event modifiers provided by SwiftUI.

Since event modifiers are best understood when seen in action, this chapter will create a project that uses the four most commonly used modifiers.

28.1 Creating the LifecycleDemo Project

Launch Xcode and select the option to create a new Multiplatform App project named LifecycleDemo.

28.2 Designing the App

Begin by editing the *ContentView.swift* file and modifying the body declaration so that it reads as follows:

```
import SwiftUI

struct ContentView: View {
    var body: some View {
        TabView {
            FirstTabView()
                .tabItem {
                    Image(systemName: "01.circle")
                    Text("First")
                }

            SecondTabView()
                .tabItem {
                    Image(systemName: "02.circle")
                    Text("Second")
                }
        }
    }
}
```

Press Cmd-N, and in the resulting template panel, select the iOS tab followed by the SwiftUI View option from the User Interface section, as shown in Figure 28-1 below:

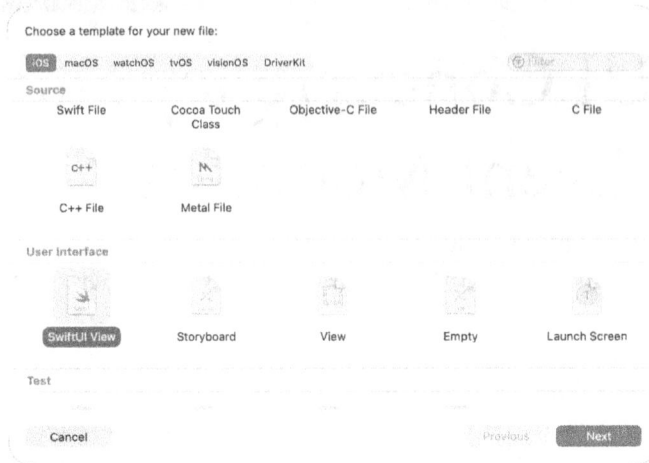

Figure 28-1

Click the Next button and name the file *FirstTabView.swift* before clicking on the Create button. With the new file loaded into the editor, change the Text view to read "View One".

Repeat the above steps to create a second SwiftUI view file named *SecondTabView.swift* with the Text view set to "View Two"

28.3 The onAppear and onDisappear Modifiers

The most basic and frequently used modifiers are *onAppear()* and *onDisappear()*. When applied to a view, these modifiers allow actions to be performed at the point that the view appears or disappears.

Within the *FirstTabView.swift* file, add both modifiers to the Text view as follows:

```
import SwiftUI

struct FirstTabView: View {

    var body: some View {

        Text("View One")
            .onAppear(perform: {
                print("onAppear triggered")
            })
            .onDisappear(perform: {
                print("onDisappeared triggered")
            })
    }
}
```

After making the changes, return to the *ContentView.swift* file. With the preview in Live mode, display the Console panel and switch to Canvas mode, where the onAppear message should appear. Click on the second tab to display SecondTabView, at which point the onDisappear modifier will be triggered. Display the first tab once again and verify that the onAppear diagnostic is output to the console.

28.4 The onChange Modifier

In basic terms, the *onChange()* modifier should be used when an action needs to be performed each time a state changes within an app. This, for example, allows actions to be triggered each time the value of a state property changes. As we will explore later in the chapter, this modifier is also particularly useful when used in conjunction with the ScenePhase environment property.

To experience the *onChange()* modifier in action, begin by editing the *SecondTabView.swift* file so that it reads as follows:

```
import SwiftUI

struct SecondTabView: View {

    @State private var text: String = ""

    var body: some View {
        TextEditor(text: $text)
            .padding()
            .onChange(of: text) {
                print("onChange triggered")
            }
    }
}


#Preview {
    SecondTabView()
}
```

Preview the app again and note that the event is triggered for each keystroke within the TextEditor view.

28.5 ScenePhase and the onChange Modifier

ScenePhase is an @Environment property that is used by SwiftUI to store the state of the current scene. When changes to ScenePhase are monitored by the *onChange()* modifier, an app can take action, for example, when the scene moves between the foreground and background or when it becomes active or inactive. This technique can be used on any view or scene but is also useful when applied to the App declaration. For example, edit the *LifecycleDemoApp.swift* file and modify it so that it reads as follows:

```
import SwiftUI

@main
struct LifecycleDemoApp: App {

    @Environment(\.scenePhase) private var scenePhase

    var body: some Scene {
        WindowGroup {
            ContentView()
```

```
        }
      .onChange(of: scenePhase) {
            switch scenePhase {
                case .active:
                    print("Active")
                case .inactive:
                    print("Inactive")
                case .background:
                    print("Background")
                default:
                    print("Unknown scenephase")
            }
        }
    }
}
```

When applied to the window group in this way, the scene phase will be based on the state of all scenes within the app. In other words, the phase will be set to active if any scene is currently active and will only be set to inactive when all scenes are inactive.

When applied to an individual view, on the other hand, the phase state will reflect only that of the scene in which the view is located. The modifier could, for example, have been applied to the content view instead of the window group as follows:

```
.
.
var body: some Scene {
    WindowGroup {
        ContentView()
            .onChange(of: scenePhase) {
.
.


    }
.
.

```

Run the app on a device or simulator, place the app in the background, and, if necessary, switch the console to Executable mode. The console output should show that the scene phase changed to the inactive state, followed by the background phase. On returning the app to the foreground, the active phase will be entered. The three scene phases can be summarized as follows:

- **active** – The scene is in the foreground, visible, and responsive to user interaction.

- **inactive** –The scene is in the foreground and visible to the user but not interactive.

- **background** – The scene is not visible to the user.

28.6 Launching Concurrent Tasks

The chapter entitled *"An Overview of Swift Structured Concurrency"* covered the topic of structured concurrency in Swift but did not explain how asynchronous tasks can be launched in the context of a SwiftUI view. In practice, all of the techniques described in that earlier chapter still apply when working with SwiftUI. All that is required is a call to the *task()* modifier on a view together with a closure containing the code to be executed. This code will be executed within a new concurrent task at the point that the view is created. We can, for example, modify the FirstTabView to display a different string on the Text view using an asynchronous task:

```
import SwiftUI

struct FirstTabView: View {

    @State var title = "View One"

    var body: some View {
        Text(title)
            .onAppear(perform: {
                print("onAppear triggered")
            })
            .onDisappear(perform: {
                print("onDisappeared triggered")
            })
            .task(priority: .background) {
                title = await changeTitle()
            }
    }

    func changeTitle() async -> String {
        try? await Task.sleep(nanoseconds: 5_000_000_000)
        return "Async task complete"
    }
}

#Preview {
    FirstTabView()
}
```

When the view is created, a task is launched with an optional priority setting. The task calls a function named *changeTitle()* and then waits for the code to execute asynchronously.

The *changeTitle()* function puts the thread to sleep for 5 seconds to simulate a long-running task before returning a new title string. This string is then assigned to the title state variable where it will appear on Text view.

Build and run the app and verify that the tabs remain responsive during the 5-second delay and that the new title appears on the first tab.

28.7 Take the Knowledge Test

Click the link below or scan the QR code to test your knowledge and understanding of SwiftUI concurrency and lifecycle event management:

https://www.answertopia.com/xcvu

28.8 Summary

SwiftUI provides a collection of modifiers designed to allow actions to be taken in the event of lifecycle changes occurring in a running app. The *onAppear()* and *onDisappear()* modifiers can be used to perform actions when a view appears or disappears from view within a user interface layout. The *onChange()* modifier, on the other hand, is useful for performing tasks each time the value assigned to a property changes.

The ScenePhase environment property, when used with the *onChange()* modifier, allows an app to identify when the state of a scene changes. This is particularly useful when an app needs to know when it moves between foreground and background modes. Asynchronous tasks can be launched when a view is created using the *task()* modifier.

29. SwiftUI Observable and Environment Objects – A Tutorial

The chapter entitled *"SwiftUI State Properties, Observation, and Environment Objects"* introduced the concept of observable and environment objects and explained how these are used to implement a data-driven approach to app development in SwiftUI.

This chapter will build on the knowledge from the earlier chapter by creating a simple example project that uses both observation and environment objects.

29.1 About the ObservableDemo Project

Observable objects are particularly powerful when used to wrap dynamic data (in other words, data values that change repeatedly). To simulate data of this type, an observable data object will be created, which uses the Foundation framework Timer object configured to update a counter once every second. This counter will be published so that it can be observed by views within the app project.

Initially, the data will be treated as an observable object and passed from one view to another. Later in the chapter, the data will be converted to an environment object so that it can be accessed by multiple views without being passed between views.

29.2 Creating the Project

Launch Xcode and select the option to create a new Multiplatform App project named ObservableDemo.

29.3 Adding the Observable Object

The first step after creating the new project is to add an observable data class. Press Cmd-N, and in the resulting template dialog, select the iOS tab, followed by the *Swift File* option. Click the Next button and name the file *TimerData* before clicking the Create button.

With the *TimerData.swift* file loaded into the code editor, implement the TimerData class as follows:

```
import Foundation


@Observable class TimerData {

    var timeCount = 0
    var timer : Timer?

    init() {
        timer = Timer.scheduledTimer(
                withTimeInterval: 1.0, repeats: true) {_ in
            self.update()
        }
    }
```

```
    func update() {
        timeCount += 1
    }


    func resetCount() {
        timeCount = 0
    }
}
```

The class is declared as implementing the Observation and contains an initializer that configures a Timer instance to call a function named *update()* once every second, which, in turn, increments the value assigned to the timeCount variable. The class also includes a method named *resetCount()* to reset the counter to zero.

29.4 Designing the ContentView Layout

The user interface for the app will consist of two screens, the first of which will be represented by the *ContentView. swift* file. Select this file to load it into the code editor and modify it so that it reads as follows:

```
import SwiftUI

struct ContentView: View {

    var timerData: TimerData = TimerData()

    var body: some View {

        NavigationView {
            VStack {
                Text("Timer count = \(timerData.timeCount)")
                    .font(.largeTitle)
                    .fontWeight(.bold)
                    .padding()

                Button(action: resetCount) {
                    Text("Reset Counter")
                }
            }
        }
    }

    func resetCount() {
        timerData.resetCount()
    }
}


#Preview {
    ContentView()
```

```
}
```

With the changes made, use Live Preview to test the view. Once the Live Preview starts, the counter should begin incrementing:

Figure 29-1

Next, click on the Reset Counter button and verify that the counter restarts counting from zero. Now that the initial implementation is working, the next step is to add a second view which will also need access to the same observable object.

29.5 Adding the Second View

Press Cmd-N, this time choosing the *SwiftUI View* option and naming the view SecondView. Edit the *SecondView. swift* file so that it reads as follows:

```
import SwiftUI

struct SecondView: View {

    var timerData: TimerData

    var body: some View {

        VStack {
            Text("Second View")
                .font(.largeTitle)
            Text("Timer Count = \(timerData.timeCount)")
```

239

```
                    .font(.headline)
        }
        .padding()
    }
}


#Preview {
    SecondView(timerData: TimerData())
}
```

Use Live Preview to test that the layout matches Figure 29-2 and that the timer begins counting.

In the Live Preview, the view has its own instance of TimerData, which was configured in the SecondView_Previews declaration. To make sure that both ContentView and SecondView are using the same TimerData instance, the observed object needs to be passed to the SecondView when the user navigates to the second screen.

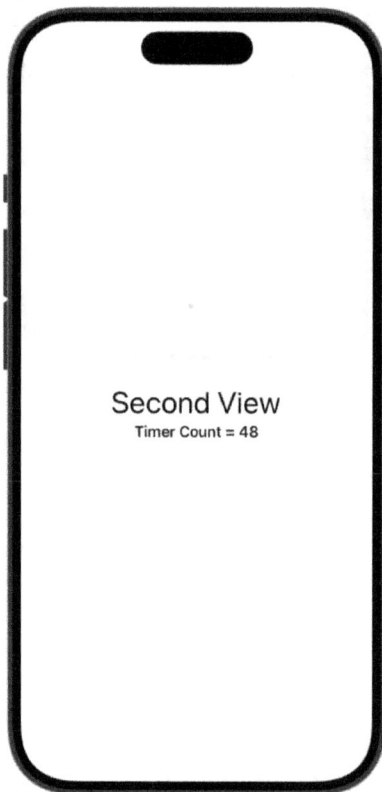

Figure 29-2

29.6 Adding Navigation

A navigation link now needs to be added to ContentView and configured to navigate to the second view. Open the *ContentView.swift* file in the code editor and add this link as follows:

```
var body: some View {

    NavigationView {
```

```
    VStack {
        Text("Timer count = \(timerData.timeCount)")

            .font(.largeTitle)
            .fontWeight(.bold)
            .padding()

        Button(action: resetCount) {
            Text("Reset Counter")
        }

        NavigationLink(destination:
                SecondView(timerData: timerData)) {
            Text("Next Screen")
        }
        .padding()
    }
  }
}
```

Once again, using Live Preview, test the ContentView and check that the counter increments. Taking note of the current counter value, click on the Next Screen link to display the second view and verify that counting continues from the same number. This confirms that both views are subscribed to the same observable object instance.

29.7 Using an Environment Object

The final step in this tutorial is to convert the observable object to an environment object. This will allow both views to access the same TimerData object without needing a reference to be passed from one view to the other.

This change does not require any modifications to the *TimerData.swift* class declaration and only minor changes are needed within the two SwiftUI view files. Starting with the *ContentView.swift* file, modify the navigation link destination so that timerData is no longer passed through to SecondView. Also add a call to the *environment()* modifier to insert the timerData instance into the view hierarchy environment:

```
import SwiftUI

struct ContentView: View {

    var timerData: TimerData = TimerData()

    var body: some View {

        NavigationView {
.
.
            NavigationLink(destination: SecondView(timerData: timerData)) {
                Text("Next Screen")
            }
```

```
                    .padding()
            }
        }
        .environment(timerData)
    }
}
.
.
#Preview {
    ContentView()
}
```

Next, modify the *SecondView.swift* file so that it reads as follows:

```
import SwiftUI

struct SecondView: View {

    @Environment(TimerData.self) var timerData: TimerData

    var body: some View {
        VStack {
            Text("Second View")
                .font(.largeTitle)
            Text("Timer Count = \(timerData.timeCount)")
                .font(.headline)
        }.padding()
    }
}

#Preview {
    SecondView().environment(TimerData())
}
```

Return to the *ContentView.swift* file and use Live Preview to check that both screens access the same counter data via the environment.

29.8 Take the Knowledge Test

Click the link below or scan the QR code to test your knowledge and understanding of observable and environment objects in SwiftUI:

https://www.answertopia.com/qkxc

29.9 Summary

This chapter has worked through a tutorial demonstrating the use of observed and environment objects to bind dynamic data to the views in a user interface, including implementing an observable object, publishing a property, subscribing to an observable object, and using environment objects.

Chapter 30

30. SwiftUI Data Persistence using AppStorage and SceneStorage

It is a common requirement for an app to need to store small amounts of data that will persist through app restarts. This is particularly useful for storing user preference settings, or when restoring a scene to the exact state it was in the last time it was accessed by the user. SwiftUI provides two property wrappers (@AppStorage and @SceneStorage) for the specific purpose of persistently storing small amounts of app data, details of which will be covered in this chapter.

30.1 The @SceneStorage Property Wrapper

The @SceneStorage property wrapper is used to store small amounts of data within the scope of individual app scene instances and is ideal for saving and restoring the state of a screen between app launches. Consider a situation where a user, partway through entering information into a form within an app, is interrupted by a phone call or text message and places the app in the background. The user subsequently forgets to return to the app, complete the form and save the entered information. If the background app were to exit (either because of a device restart, the user terminating the app, or the system killing the app to free up resources) the partial information entered into the form would be lost. Situations such as this can be avoided, however, by using scene storage to retain and restore the data.

Scene storage is declared using the @SceneStorage property wrapper together with a key string value which is used internally to store the associated value. The following code, for example, declares a scene storage property designed to store a String value using a key name set to "city" with an initial default value set to an empty string:

```
@SceneStorage("city") var city: String = ""
```

Once declared, the stored property could, for example, be used in conjunction with a TextEditor as follows:

```
var body: some View {
    TextEditor(text: $city)
        .padding()
}
```

When implemented in an app, this will ensure that any text entered into the text field is retained within the scene through app restarts. If multiple instances of the scene are launched by the user on multi-windowing platforms such as iPadOS or macOS, each scene will have its own distinct copy of the saved value.

30.2 The @AppStorage Property Wrapper

The @SceneStorage property wrapper allows each individual scene within an app to have its own copy of stored data. In other words, the data stored by one scene is not accessible to any other scenes in the app (even other instances of the same scene). The @AppStorage property wrapper, on the other hand, is used to store data that is universally available throughout the entire app.

App Storage is built on top of UserDefaults, a feature that has been available in iOS for many years. Primarily provided as a way for apps to access and store default user preferences (such as language preferences or color choices), UserDefaults can also be used to store small amounts of data needed by the app in the form of key-value pairs.

As with scene storage, the @AppStorage property wrapper requires a string value to serve as a key and may be declared as follows:

```
@AppStorage("mystore") var mytext: String = ""
```

By default, data will be stored in the *standard* UserDefaults storage. It is also possible, however, to specify a custom App Group in which to store the data. App Groups allow apps to share data with other apps and targets within the same group. App Groups are assigned a name (typically similar to *group.com.mydomain.myappname*) and are enabled and configured within the Xcode project *Signing & Capabilities* screen. Figure 30-1, for example, shows a project target with App Groups enabled and a name set to *group.com.payloadbooks.userdefaults*:

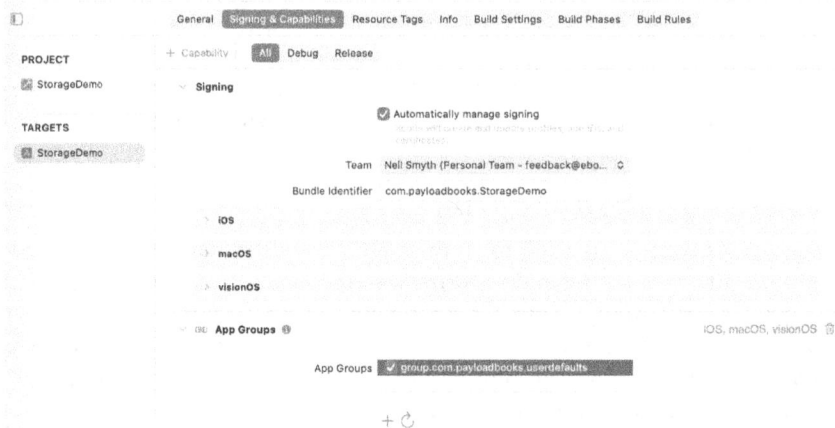

Figure 30-1

The following @AppStorage declaration references an app group to use for storing data:

```
@AppStorage("mystore",
  store: UserDefaults(
        suiteName: "group.com.payloadbooks.userdefaults"))
            var mytext: String = ""
```

As with the @State property wrapper, changes to the stored value will cause the user interface to refresh to reflect the new data.

With the basics of app and scene storage covered, the remainder of this chapter will demonstrate these property wrappers in action.

30.3 Creating and Preparing the StorageDemo Project

Begin this tutorial by launching Xcode and selecting the options to create a new Multiplatform App project named *StorageDemo*.

Next, select the *ContentView.swift* file and change the view body so that it contains a TabView, as outlined below:

```
import SwiftUI

struct ContentView: View {

    var body: some View {

        TabView {
```

```
            SceneStorageView()
                .tabItem {
                    Image(systemName: "circle.fill")
                    Text("SceneStorage")
                }


            AppStorageView()
                .tabItem {
                    Image(systemName: "square.fill")
                    Text("AppStorage")
                }
        }
    }
}
.
.
.
```

Next, use the Cmd-N keyboard shortcut to add two new *SwiftUI View* files named SceneStorageView and AppStorageView, respectively.

30.4 Using Scene Storage

Edit the *SceneStorageView.swift* file and modify it so that it reads as follows:

```
import SwiftUI

struct SceneStorageView: View {

    @State private var editorText: String = ""

    var body: some View {
        TextEditor(text: $editorText)
            .padding(30)
            .font(.largeTitle)
    }
}
```

This declaration makes use of the TextEditor view. This is a view designed to allow multiline text to be displayed and edited within a SwiftUI app and includes scrolling when the displayed text extends beyond the viewable area. The TextEditor view is passed a binding to a state property into which any typed text will be stored (note that we aren't yet using scene storage).

With the changes made, build and run the app on a device or simulator and, once launched, enter some text into the TextEditor view. Place the app in the background so that the device home screen appears, then terminate the app using the stop button located in the Xcode toolbar.

Run the app a second time and verify that the previously entered text has not been restored into the TextEditor view. Clearly, this app would benefit from the use of scene storage.

Return to the *SceneStorageView.swift* file and convert the @State property to an @SceneStorage property as follows:

```
struct SceneStorageView: View {

    @SceneStorage("mytext") private var editorText = ""
.

.
```

Run the app again, enter some text, place it in the background, and terminate it. This time, when the app is relaunched, the text will be restored into the TextEditor view.

When working with scene storage it is important to keep in mind that each instance of a scene has its own storage which is entirely separate from any other scenes. To experience this in action, run the StorageDemo app on an iPad device or simulator running iPadOS 26 in landscape orientation. Once the app is running, drag the resize handle in the bottom left corner to reduce the window size:

Figure 30-2

With the window resized, perform a long press on the app icon in the Dock and select the New Window menu option:

Figure 30-3

Reposition both windows so that they appear side-by-side as shown in Figure 30-4, then enter different text into each scene, as shown in Figure 30-4 below:

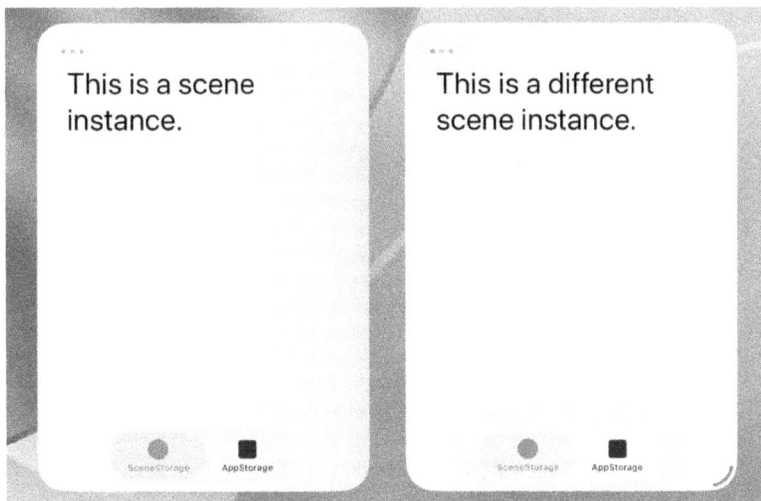

Figure 30-4

Click the home button twice to place the app into the background, terminate the app, and then re-launch it. On restarting, display both scenes which will appear just as they were before the app was placed in the background, thereby demonstrating that each scene has a copy of its own stored data.

30.5 Using App Storage

The final task in this tutorial is to demonstrate the use of app storage. Within Xcode, edit the *AppStorageView. swift* file and modify it so that it reads as follows:

```
import SwiftUI

struct AppStorageView: View {

    @AppStorage("mytext") var editorText: String = "Sample Text"

    var body: some View {
        TextEditor(text: $editorText)
            .padding(30)
            .font(.largeTitle)
    }
}
.
.
.
```

With the changes made, run the app on the iPad once again and repeat the steps to display two scene instances side-by-side. Select the App Storage tab within both scenes and note that the scene instances are displaying the default sample text. Tap in one of the scenes and add some additional text. As text is added in one scene, the changes are reflected in the second scene as each character is typed:

Figure 30-5

Terminate the app while it is in the foreground (unlike scene storage, app storage data is stored in real-time, not just when the app is placed in the background) and relaunch it to confirm that the text changes were saved and restored.

30.6 Storing Custom Types

The @AppStorage and @SceneStorage property wrappers only allow values of certain types to be stored. Specifically Bool, Int, Double, String, URL, and Data types. This means that any other type that needs to be stored must first be encoded as a Swift Data object in order to be stored and subsequently decoded when retrieved.

Consider, for example, the following struct declaration and initialization:

```
struct UserName {
    var firstName: String
    var secondName: String
}


var username = UserName(firstName: "Mark", secondName: "Wilson")
```

Because UserName is not a supported type, it is not possible to store our username instance directly into app or scene-based storage. Instead, the instance needs to be encoded and encapsulated into a Data instance before it can be saved. The exact steps to perform the encoding and decoding will depend on the type of data being stored. The key requirement, however, is that the type conforms to the Encodable and Decodable protocols. For example:

```
struct UserName: Encodable, Decodable {
    var firstName: String
    var secondName: String
}
```

The following example uses a JSON encoder to encode our username instance and store it using the @AppStorage property wrapper:

```
@AppStorage("username") var namestore: Data = Data()

.

.
```

```
let encoder = JSONEncoder()

if let data = try? encoder.encode(username) {
    namestore = data
}
```

When the time comes to retrieve the data from storage, the process is reversed using the JSON decoder:

```
let decoder = JSONDecoder()

if let name = try? decoder.decode(UserName.self, from: namestore) {
    username = name
}
```

Using this technique, it is even possible to store an image using either of the storage property wrappers, for example:

```
@AppStorage("myimage") var imagestore: Data = Data()

var image = UIImage(named: "profilephoto")

// Encode and store image

if let data = image!.pngData() {
    imagestore = data
}

// Retrieve and decode image

if let decodedImage: UIImage = UIImage(data: imagestore) {
    image = decodedImage
}
```

30.7 Take the Knowledge Test

Click the link below or scan the QR code to test your knowledge and understanding of SwiftUI data persistence and app storage:

https://www.answertopia.com/1geh

30.8 Summary

The @SceneStorage and @AppStorage property wrappers provide two ways to persistently store small amounts of data within a SwiftUI app. Scene storage is intended primarily for saving and restoring the state of a scene when an app is terminated while in the background. Each scene within an app has its own local scene storage which is not directly accessible to other areas of the app. App storage uses the UserDefaults system and is used for storing data that is to be accessible from anywhere within an app. Through the use of App Groups, app storage may also be shared between different targets within the samwe app project, or even entirely different apps. Changes to app storage are immediate regardless of whether the app is currently in the foreground or background.

SwiftUI Data Persistence using AppStorage and SceneStorage

Both the @AppStorage and @SceneStorage property wrappers support storing Bool, Int, Double, String, URL, and Data types. Other types need to be encoded and encapsulated in Data objects before being placed into storage.

31. SwiftUI Lists and Navigation

The SwiftUI List view provides a way to present information to the user as a vertical list of rows. Often the items within a list will navigate to another area of the app when tapped by the user. Behavior of this type is implemented in SwiftUI using the NavigationStack and NavigationLink components.

The List view can present both static and dynamic data and may also be extended to allow for the addition, removal, and reordering of row entries.

This chapter will provide an overview of the List View used in conjunction with NavigationStack and NavigationLink in preparation for the tutorial in the next chapter entitled *"A SwiftUI List and NavigationStack Tutorial"*.

31.1 SwiftUI Lists

The SwiftUI List control provides similar functionality to the UIKit TableView class in that it presents information in a vertical list of rows with each row containing one or more views contained within a cell. Consider, for example, the following List implementation:

```
struct ContentView: View {
    var body: some View {

        List {
            Text("Wash the car")
            Text("Vacuum house")
            Text("Pick up kids from school bus @ 3pm")
            Text("Auction the kids on eBay")
            Text("Order Pizza for dinner")
        }
    }
}
```

When displayed in the preview, the above list will appear, as shown in Figure 31-1:

Figure 31-1

A list cell is not restricted to containing a single component. In fact, any combination of components can be displayed in a list cell. Each row of the list in the following example consists of an image and text component within an HStack:

```
List {
    HStack {
        Image(systemName: "trash.circle.fill")
        Text("Take out the trash")
    }
    HStack {
        Image(systemName: "person.2.fill")
        Text("Pick up the kids") }
    HStack {
        Image(systemName: "car.fill")
        Text("Wash the car")
    }
}
```

The preview canvas for the above view structure will appear, as shown in Figure 31-2 below:

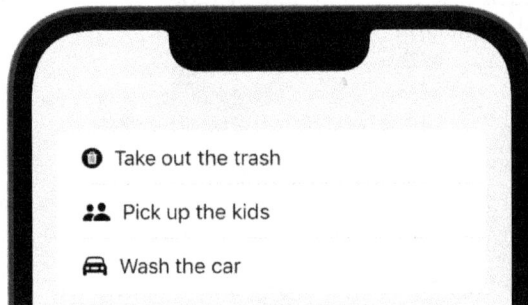

Figure 31-2

31.2 Modifying List Separators and Rows

The lines used by the List view to separate rows can be hidden by applying the *listRowSeparator()* modifier to the cell content views. The *listRowSeparatorTint()* modifier, on the other hand, can be used to change the color of the lines. It is even possible to assign a view to appear as the background of a row using the *listRowBackground()* modifier. The following code, for example, hides the first separator, changes the tint of the next two separators, and displays a background image on the final row:

```
List {
    Text("Wash the car")
        .listRowSeparator(.hidden)
    Text("Pick up kids from school bus @ 3pm")
        .listRowSeparatorTint(.green)
    Text("Auction the kids on eBay")
        .listRowSeparatorTint(.red)
    Text("Order Pizza for dinner")
        .listRowBackground(Image("MyBackgroundImage"))
}
```

The above examples demonstrate the use of a List to display static information. To display a dynamic list of items a few additional steps are required.

31.3 SwiftUI Dynamic Lists

A list is considered to be dynamic when it contains a set of items that can change over time. In other words, items can be added, edited, and deleted and the list updates dynamically to reflect those changes.

To support a list of this type, each data element to be displayed must be contained within a class or structure that conforms to the Identifiable protocol. The Identifiable protocol requires that the instance contain a property named *id* which can be used to uniquely identify each item in the list. The id property can be any Swift or custom type that conforms to the Hashable protocol which includes the String, Int, and UUID types in addition to several hundred other standard Swift types. If you opt to use UUID as the type for the property, the *UUID()* method can be used to automatically generate a unique ID for each list item.

The following code implements a simple structure for the To Do list example that conforms to the Identifiable protocol. In this case, the id is generated automatically via a call to *UUID()*:

```
struct ToDoItem : Identifiable {
    var id = UUID()
    var task: String
    var imageName: String
}
```

For example, an array of ToDoItem objects can be used to simulate the supply of data to the list which can now be implemented as follows:

```
struct ContentView: View {

    @State var listData: [ToDoItem] = [
       ToDoItem(task: "Take out trash", imageName: "trash.circle.fill"),
       ToDoItem(task: "Pick up the kids", imageName: "person.2.fill"),
       ToDoItem(task: "Wash the car", imageName: "car.fill")
       ]

    var body: some View {

       List(listData) { item in
           HStack {
               Image(systemName: item.imageName)
               Text(item.task)
           }
       }
    }
}
.
.
.
```

Now the list no longer needs a view for each cell. Instead, the list iterates through the data array and reuses the same HStack declaration, simply plugging in the appropriate data for each array element.

In situations where dynamic and static content needs to be displayed together within a list, the ForEach statement can be used within the body of the list to iterate through the dynamic data while also declaring static entries. The following example includes a static toggle button together with a ForEach loop for the dynamic content:

```
struct ContentView: View {

    @State private var toggleStatus = true
    .
    .
    var body: some View {

        List {
            Toggle(isOn: $toggleStatus) {
                Text("Allow Notifications")
            }

            ForEach (listData) { item in
                HStack {
                    Image(systemName: item.imageName)
                    Text(item.task)
                }
            }
        }
    }
}
```

Note the appearance of the toggle button and the dynamic list items in Figure 31-3:

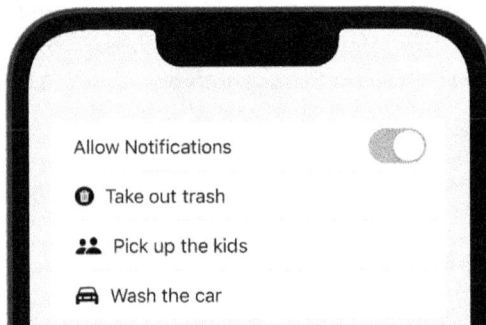

Figure 31-3

A SwiftUI List implementation may also be divided into sections using the Section view, including headers and footers if required. Figure 31-4 shows the list divided into two sections, each with a header:

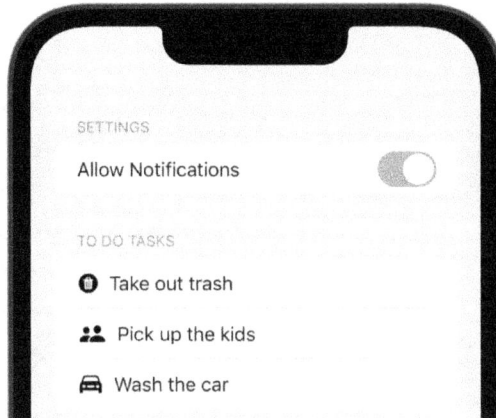

Figure 31-4

The changes to the view declaration to implement these sections are as follows:

```
List {
    Section(header: Text("Settings")) {
        Toggle(isOn: $toggleStatus) {
            Text("Allow Notifications")
        }
    }

    Section(header: Text("To Do Tasks")) {
        ForEach (listData) { item in
            HStack {
                Image(systemName: item.imageName)
                Text(item.task)
            }
        }
    }
}
```

Often the items within a list will navigate to another area of the app when tapped by the user. Behavior of this type is implemented in SwiftUI using the NavigationStack and NavigationLink views.

31.4 Adding a Section Index

If you have used the iOS Contacts app, you will be familiar with the section index that provides a quick way to jump to specific alphabetic sections of the contact list. The same effect can be added to any list using the Section view's *sectionIndexLabel()* modifier, passing it the text to be used as the index entry. For example:

```
let indexLetters = ["A", "B", "C", "D", "E", "F", "G", "H", "I", "J",
                    "K", "L", "M", "N", "O", "P", "Q", "R", "S", "T",
                    "U", "V", "W", "X", "Y", "Z"]


var body: some View {

    List(indexLetters, id: \.self) { letter in
```

```
        Section(letter) {
            ForEach(1..<6) { number in
                Text("List Item \(number)")
            }
        }
        .sectionIndexLabel(letter)
    }
```

The example uses an array of letters to represent the section header and index label, and will appear as follows:

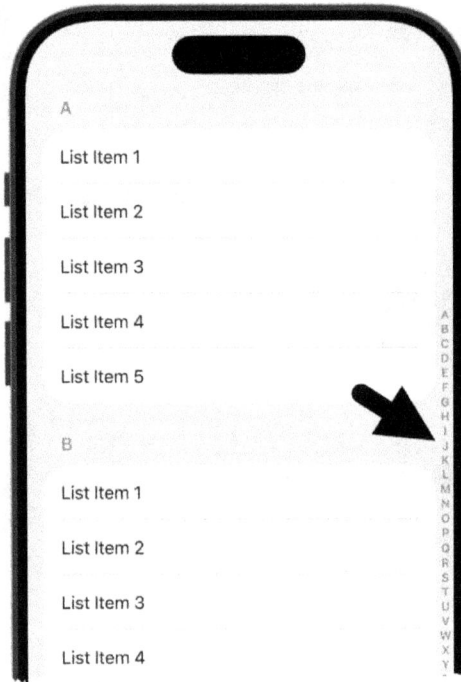

Figure 31-5

When working with index labels, the labels can contain any text and do not need to match the corresponding section header. The *listSectionIndexVisibility()* modifier can be applied to the parent List to hide and show the index. For example:

```
List(indexLetters, id: \.self) { letter in
    Section("section \(letter)") {

    .

    .

    }
    .sectionIndexLabel(letter)
}
.listSectionIndexVisibility(.hidden)
```

31.5 Creating a Refreshable List

The data displayed on a screen is often derived from a dynamic source which is subject to change over time. The standard paradigm within iOS apps is for the user to perform a downward swipe to refresh the displayed data. During the refresh process, the app will typically display a spinning progress indicator after which the latest data is displayed. To make it easy to add this type of refresh behavior to your apps, SwiftUI provides the *refreshable()* modifier. When applied to a view, a downward swipe gesture on that view will display the progress indicator and execute the code in the modifier closure. For example, we can add refresh support to our list as follows:

```
List {
    Section(header: Text("Settings")) {
        Toggle(isOn: $toggleStatus) {
            Text("Allow Notifications")
        }
    }

    Section(header: Text("To Do Tasks")) {
        ForEach (listData) { item in
            HStack {
                Image(systemName: item.imageName)
                Text(item.task)
            }
        }
    }
}
.refreshable {
    listData = [
        ToDoItem(task: "Order dinner", imageName: "dollarsign.circle.fill"),
        ToDoItem(task: "Call financial advisor", imageName: "phone.fill"),
        ToDoItem(task: "Sell the kids", imageName: "person.2.fill")
    ]
}
```

Figure 31-6 demonstrates the effect of performing a downward swipe gesture within the List view after adding the above modifier. Note both the progress indicator at the top of the list and the appearance of the updated to-do list items:

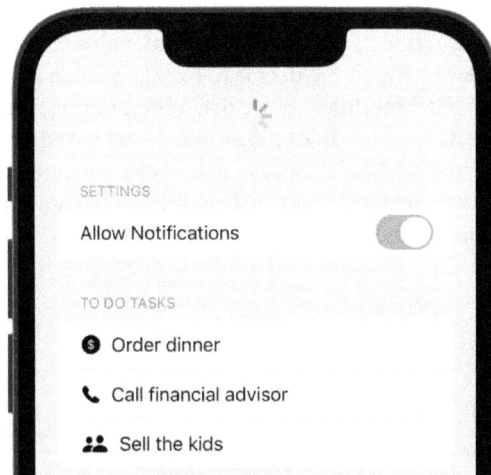

Figure 31-6

When using the *refreshable()* modifier, be sure to perform any time-consuming activities as an asynchronous task using structured concurrency (covered previously in the chapter entitled *"An Overview of Swift Structured Concurrency"*). This will ensure that the app remains responsive during the refresh.

31.6 SwiftUI NavigationStack and NavigationLink

To make items in a list navigable, the first step is to embed the entire list within a NavigationStack. Once the list is embedded, the individual rows must be wrapped in a NavigationLink control which is, in turn, passed a value that uniquely identifies each navigation link within the context of the NavigationStack.

The following changes to our example code embed the List view in a NavigationStack and wrap the row content in a NavigationLink:

```
NavigationStack {
    List {
        Section(header: Text("Settings")) {
            Toggle(isOn: $toggleStatus) {
                Text("Allow Notifications")
            }
        }

        Section(header: Text("To Do Tasks")) {
            ForEach (listData) { item in
                NavigationLink(value: item.task) {
                    HStack {
                        Image(systemName: item.imageName)
                        Text(item.task)
                    }
                }
            }
        }
    }
}
```

Note that we have used the item task string as the NavigationLink value to uniquely identify each row. The next step is to specify the destination view to which the user is to be taken when the row is tapped. We achieve this by applying the *navigationDestination(for:)* modifier to the list. When adding this modifier, we need to pass it the value type for which it is to provide navigation. In our example we are using the task string, so we need to specify *String.self* as the value type. Within the trailing closure of the *navigationDestination(for:)* call we need to call the view that is to be displayed when the row is selected. This closure is passed the value from the NavigationLink, allowing us to display the appropriate view:

```
NavigationStack {
    List {
.

.

        Section(header: Text("To Do Tasks")) {
            ForEach (listData) { item in
                NavigationLink(value: item.task) {
                    HStack {
```

```
                    Image(systemName: item.imageName)
                    Text(item.task)
                }
            }
        }
    }
}
.navigationDestination(for: String.self) { task in
    Text("Selected task = \(task)")
}
}
```

In this example, the navigation link will simply display a new screen containing the destination Text view displaying the *item.task* string value. The finished list will appear, as shown in Figure 31-7 with the title and chevrons on the far right of each row now visible indicating that navigation is available. Tapping the links will navigate to and display the destination Text view.

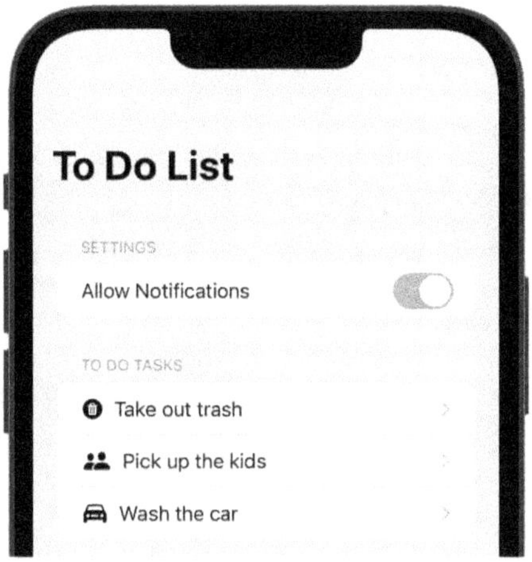

Figure 31-7

31.7 Navigation by Value Type

The *navigationDestination()* modifier is particularly useful for adding navigation support to lists containing values of different types, with each type requiring navigation to a specific view. Suppose, for example, that in addition to the string-based task navigation link, we also have a NavigationLink which is passed an integer value indicating the number of tasks in the list. This could be implemented in our example as follows:

```
NavigationStack {

    List {

        Section(header: Text("Settings")) {
            Toggle(isOn: $toggleStatus) {
                Text("Allow Notifications")
            }
        }

        NavigationLink(value: listData.count) {
```

```
                    Text("View Task Count")
            }
        }
```

.

.

When this link is selected, we need the app to navigate to a Text view that displays the current task count. All this requires is a second *navigationDestination()* modifier, this time configured to handle Int instead of String values:

.

.

```
}

    .navigationDestination(for: String.self) { task in
        Text("Selected task = \(task)")
    }
    .navigationDestination(for: Int.self) { count in
        Text("Number of tasks = \(count)")
    }
```

.

.

This technique allows us to configure multiple navigation destinations within a single navigation stack based solely on the value type passed to each navigation link.

31.8 Working with Navigation Paths

As the name suggests, NavigationStack provides a stack on which navigation targets are stored as the user navigates through the screens of an app. When a user navigates from one view to another, a reference to the originating view is *pushed* onto the stack. If the user then navigates to another view, the current view will also be placed onto the stack. At any point, the user can tap the back arrow displayed in the navigation bar to move back to the previous view. As the user navigates back through the views, each one is *popped* off the stack until the view from which navigation began is reached.

The views through which a user navigates are called the *navigation path*. SwiftUI allows us to provide our own path by passing an instance of NavigationPath to the NavigationStack instance as follows:

```
struct ContentView: View {

    @State private var stackPath = NavigationPath()

    var body: some View {

        NavigationStack(path: $stackPath) {
```

.

.

With NavigationStack using our path, we can perform tasks such as manually popping targets off the stack to jump back multiple navigation levels instead of making the user navigate through the targets individually. We could, for example, configure a button on a view deep within the stack to take the user directly back to the home screen. We can do this by identifying how many navigation targets are in the stack and then removing them via a call to the *removeLast()* method of the path instance, for example:

```
var stackCount = stackPath.count
```

```
stackPath.removeLast(stackCount)
```

We can also programmatically navigate to specific destination views by calling the navigation path's *append()* method and passing through the navigation value associated with the destination:

```
stackPath.append(value)
```

31.9 Navigation Bar Customization

The NavigationStack title bar may also be customized using modifiers on the List component to set the title and add buttons to perform additional tasks. The following example calls the *navigationTitle()* modifier to set the title to "To Do List." The code also adds a button labeled "Add" to the toolbar. This button is applied to the layout as the child of a ToolbarItem instance using the *toolbar()* modifier and configured to call a hypothetical method named *addTask()*:

```
NavigationStack {
    List {
.

.

    }
    .navigationTitle(Text("To Do List"))
    .toolbar {
        ToolbarItem(placement: .navigationBarLeading) {
            Button(action: addTask) {
                Text("Add")
            }
        }
    }
.

.

}
```

31.10 Making the List Editable

It is common for an app to allow the user to delete items from a list and, in some cases, even move an item from one position to another. Deletion can be enabled by adding an *onDelete()* modifier to each list cell, specifying a method to be called which will delete the item from the data source. When this method is called it will be passed an IndexSet object containing the offsets of the rows being deleted and it is the responsibility of this method to remove the selected data from the data source. Once implemented, the user will be able to swipe left on rows in the list to reveal the Delete button, as shown in Figure 31-8:

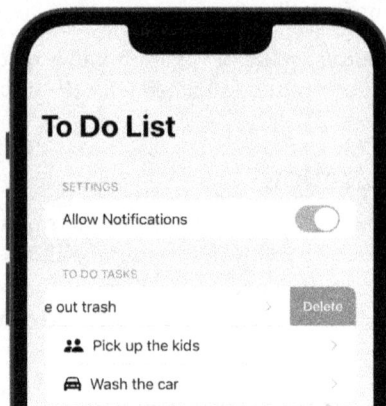

Figure 31-8

The changes to the example List to implement this behavior might read as follows:

```
.
.
List {
    Section(header: Text("Settings")) {
        Toggle(isOn: $toggleStatus) {
            Text("Allow Notifications")
        }
    }

    Section(header: Text("To Do Tasks")) {
        ForEach (listData) { item in
            NavigationLink(value: item.task) {
                HStack {
                    Image(systemName: item.imageName)
                    Text(item.task)
                }
            }
        }
        .onDelete(perform: deleteItem)
    }
}
.
.

func deleteItem(at offsets: IndexSet) {
    // Delete items from the data source here
}
```

To allow the user to move items up and down in the list the *onMove()* modifier must be applied to the cell, once again specifying a method to be called to modify the ordering of the source data. In this case, the method will be passed an IndexSet object containing the positions of the rows being moved and an integer indicating the destination position.

In addition to adding the *onMove()* modifier, an EditButton instance needs to be added to the List. When tapped, this button automatically switches the list into editable mode and allows items to be moved and deleted by the user. The List declaration can be modified as follows to add this functionality:

```
List {
    Section(header: Text("Settings")) {
        Toggle(isOn: $toggleStatus) {
            Text("Allow Notifications")
        }
    }

    Section(header: Text("To Do Tasks")) {
        ForEach (listData) { item in
            NavigationLink(value: item.task) {
                HStack {
                    Image(systemName: item.imageName)
                    Text(item.task)
                }
            }
        }
        .onDelete(perform: deleteItem)
        .onMove(perform: moveItem)
    }

}
.navigationTitle(Text("To Do List"))
.toolbar {
    ToolbarItem(placement: .navigationBarLeading) {
        NavigationLink(value: "Add Car") { Text("Add") }
    }
    ToolbarItem(placement: .navigationBarTrailing) {
        EditButton()
    }
}
.
.
.
func moveItem(from source: IndexSet, to destination: Int) {
    // Reorder items in source data here
}
```

Viewed within the preview canvas, the list will appear, as shown in Figure 31-9 when the Edit button is tapped. Clicking and dragging the three lines on the right side of each row allows the row to be moved to a different list position (in the figure below the "Pick up the kids" entry is in the process of being moved):

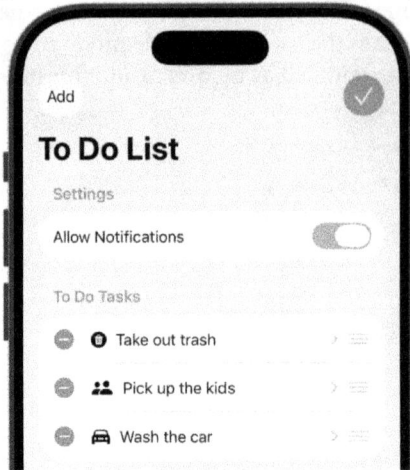

Figure 31-9

31.11 Hierarchical Lists

SwiftUI also includes support for organizing hierarchical data for display in list format, as shown in Figure 31-10 below:

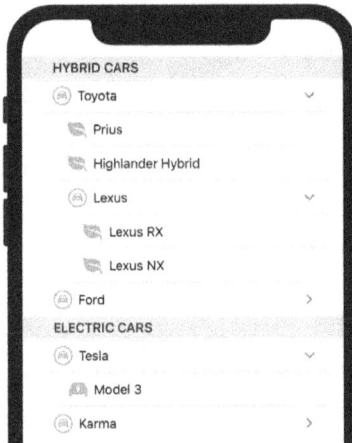

Figure 31-10

This behavior is achieved using features of the List view together with the OutlineGroup and DisclosureGroup views which automatically analyze the parent-child relationships within a data structure to create a browsable list containing controls to expand and collapse branches of data. This topic is covered in detail beginning with the chapter titled *"An Overview of List, OutlineGroup and DisclosureGroup"*.

31.12 Multicolumn Navigation

NavigationStack provides navigation between views where each destination occupies the entire device screen. SwiftUI also supports multicolumn navigation where the destinations appear together on the screen with each appearing in a separate column. Multicolumn navigation is provided by the NavigationSplitView component and will be covered beginning with the chapter titled *"An Overview of Split View Navigation"*.

31.13 Take the Knowledge Test

Click the link below or scan the QR code to test your knowledge and understanding of SwiftUI list navigation:

https://www.answertopia.com/utji

31.14 Summary

The SwiftUI List view provides a way to order items in a single column of rows, each containing a cell. Each cell, in turn, can contain multiple views when those views are encapsulated in a container view such as a stack layout. The List view provides support for displaying both static and dynamic items or a combination of both. Lists may also be used to group, organize and display hierarchical data.

List views are used to allow the user to navigate to other screens. This navigation is implemented by wrapping the List declaration in a NavigationStack and each row in a NavigationLink, using the *navigationDestination()* modifier to define the navigation target view.

Lists can be divided into titled sections and assigned a navigation bar containing a title and buttons. Lists may also be configured to allow rows to be added, deleted, and moved.

32. A SwiftUI List and NavigationStack Tutorial

The previous chapter introduced the List, NavigationStack, and NavigationLink views and explained how these can be used to present a navigable and editable list of items to the user. This chapter will create a project that provides a practical example of these concepts.

32.1 About the ListNavDemo Project

When completed, the project will consist of a List view in which each row contains a cell displaying image and text information. Selecting a row within the list will navigate to a details screen containing more information about the selected item. In addition, the List view will include options to add and remove entries and to change the ordering of rows in the list.

The project extensively uses state properties and observable objects to synchronize the user interface with the data model.

32.2 Creating the ListNavDemo Project

Launch Xcode and select the option to create a new Multiplatform App named *ListNavDemo*.

32.3 Preparing the Project

Before beginning the development of the app project, some preparatory work needs to be performed involving the addition of image and data assets which will be needed later in the chapter.

The assets to be used in the project are included in the source code sample download provided with the book available from the following URL:

https://www.payloadbooks.com/product/ios26code/

Once the code samples have been downloaded and unpacked, open a Finder window, and locate the *CarAssets. xcassets* folder, and drag and drop it onto the project navigator panel, as illustrated in Figure 32-1:

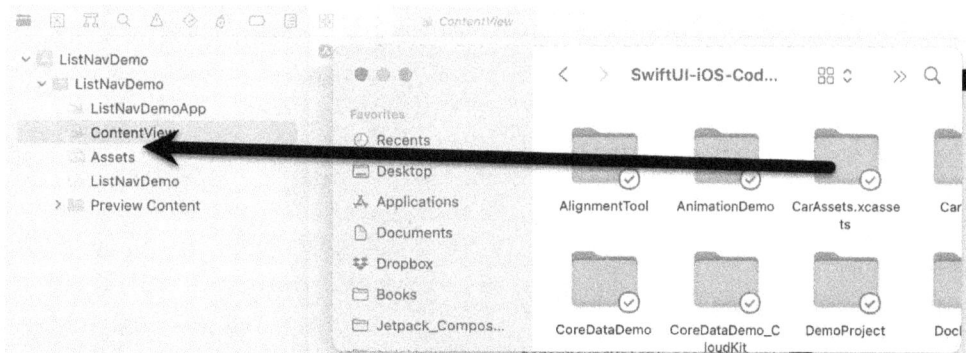

Figure 32-1

When the options dialog appears, ensure the *Copy files to destination* option is selected so that the assets are included within the project folder before clicking on the Finish button.

32.4 Adding the Car Structure

A structure needs to be declared to represent each car model. Add a new Swift file to the project by pressing Cmd-N, selecting Swift File, and clicking on the Next button. Name the file *Car.swift* on the subsequent screen before clicking on the Create button.

Once created, the new file will load into the code editor, where it needs to be modified so that it reads as follows:

```
import SwiftUI

struct Car : Hashable, Codable, Identifiable {
    var id: UUID = UUID()
    var name: String

    var desc: String
    var isHybrid: Bool

    var imageName: String
}
```

As we can see, the structure is declared as conforming to the Identifiable protocol and includes a unique identifier property so that each instance can be uniquely identified within the List view.

32.5 Adding the Data Store

When the user interface has been designed, the List view will rely on observation to ensure that the latest data is always displayed to the user. The last step in getting the data ready for use in the app is to add a data store structure. This structure will contain an array of Car objects that will be observed by the user interface to keep the List view current. Add another Swift file to the project, this time named *CarStore.swift*, and implement the class as follows:

```
import SwiftUI

@Observable class CarStore: Identifiable {

    var cars: [Car] = [Car(name: "Tesla Model 3", desc: "Luxury 4-door.",
                            isHybrid: false, imageName: "tesla_model_3"),
                Car(name: "Tesla Model S", desc: "5-door liftback.",
                            isHybrid: false, imageName: "tesla_model_s"),
                Car(name: "Toyota Prius", desc: "5-door liftback",
                            isHybrid: false, imageName: "toyota_prius"),
                Car(name: "Nissan Leaf", desc: "Compact five-door.",
                            isHybrid: false, imageName: "nissan_leaf"),
                Car(name: "Chevrolet Volt", desc: "5-door hatchback.",
                            isHybrid: false, imageName: "chevrolet_volt")]
}
```

With the data side of the project complete, it is now time to begin designing the user interface.

32.6 Designing the Content View

Edit the *ContentView.swift* file, add a state object, and initialize it with an instance of CarStore class:

```
import SwiftUI

struct ContentView: View {

    @State var carStore: CarStore = CarStore()
.

.
```

The content view will require a List view to display information about each car. Now that we have access to the array of cars via the carStore property, we can use a ForEach loop to display a row for each car model. The cell for each row will be implemented as an HStack containing an Image and a Text view, the content of which will be extracted from the carData array elements. Remaining in the *ContentView.swift* file, add a view named ListCell:

```
struct ListCell: View {

    var car: Car

    var body: some View {
        HStack {
            Image(car.imageName)
                .resizable()
                .aspectRatio(contentMode: .fit)
                .frame(width: 100, height: 60)
            Text(car.name)
        }
    }
}
```

Next, modify the ContentView body so that it reads as follows:

```
.

.

    var body: some View {

        List {
            ForEach($carStore.cars, id: \.self) { $car in
                ListCell(car: car)
            }
        }
    }
}
.

.
```

With the change made to the view, use the preview canvas to verify that the list populates with content, as shown in Figure 32-2:

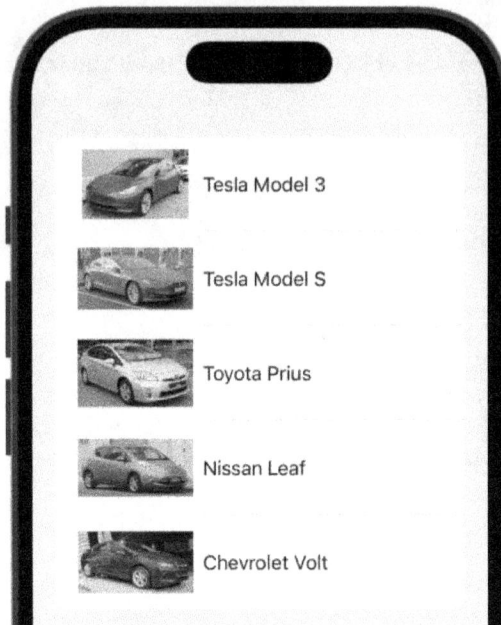

Figure 32-2

32.7 Designing the Detail View

When a user taps a row in the list, a detail screen will appear showing additional information about the selected car. The layout for this screen will be declared in a separate SwiftUI View file which now needs to be added to the project. Use the Cmd-N keyboard shortcut once again, this time selecting the SwiftUI View template option and naming the file CarDetailView.

When the user navigates to this view from within the List, it must be passed the Car instance for the selected car so that the correct details are displayed. Begin by adding a property to the structure and configuring the preview provider to display the details of the first car in the carData array within the preview canvas as follows:

```
import SwiftUI

struct CarDetailView: View {

    let selectedCar: Car

    var body: some View {
.

.

#Preview {
    CarDetailView(selectedCar: CarStore().cars.first!)
}
```

For this layout, a Form container will be used to organize the views. This is a container view that allows views to be grouped and divided into different sections. The Form also places a line divider between each child view. Within the body of the *CarDetailView.swift* file, implement the layout as follows:

```
var body: some View {
    Form {
```

```
Section(header: Text("Car Details")) {
    Image(selectedCar.imageName)
        .resizable()
        .cornerRadius(12.0)
        .aspectRatio(contentMode: .fit)
        .padding()

    Text(selectedCar.name)
        .font(.headline)

    Text(selectedCar.desc)
        .font(.body)

    HStack {
        Text("Hybrid").font(.headline)
        Spacer()
        Image(systemName: selectedCar.isHybrid ?
                "checkmark.circle" : "xmark.circle" )
    }
  }
 }
}
}
```

Note that the Image view is configured to be resizable and scaled to fit the available space while retaining the aspect ratio. Rounded corners are also applied to make the image more visually appealing and either a circle or checkmark image is displayed in the HStack based on the setting of the isHybrid Boolean setting of the selected car.

When previewed, the screen should match that shown in Figure 32-3:

Figure 32-3

32.8 Adding Navigation to the List

The next step in this tutorial is to return to the List view in the *ContentView.swift* file and implement navigation so that selecting a row displays the detail screen populated with the corresponding car details.

With the *ContentView.swift* file loaded into the code editor, locate the call to the ListCell subview declaration and embed it within a NavigationLink using the current ForEach counter as the link value:

```
var body: some View {
    List {
        ForEach($carStore.cars, id: \.self) { $car in
            NavigationLink(value: car) {
                ListCell(car: car)
            }
        }

    }
}
```

For this navigation link to function, the List view must also be embedded in a NavigationStack as follows:

```
var body: some View {
    NavigationStack {
        List {
            ForEach($carStore.cars, id: \.self) { $car in
                NavigationLink(value: car) {
                    ListCell(car: car)
                }
            }
        }
    }
}
```

Next, we need to add the navigation destination modifier to the list so that tapping an item navigates to the CarDetailView view containing details of the selected car:

```
NavigationStack {
    List {
        ForEach($carStore.cars, id: \.self) { $car in
            NavigationLink(value: car) {
                ListCell(car: car)
            }
        }
    }
    .navigationDestination(for: Car.self) { car in
        CarDetailView(selectedCar: car)
    }
}
```

Test that the navigation works using the preview canvas in Live mode and selecting different rows, confirming each time that the detail view appears containing information matching the selected car model.

32.9 Designing the Add Car View

The final view to be added to the project is the screen to be displayed when the user is adding a new car to the list. Add a new SwiftUI View file to the project named *AddNewCarView.swift* including some state properties and a declaration for storing a reference to the carStore binding (this reference will be passed to the view from the ContentView when the user taps an Add button). Also, modify the preview provider to pass the carData array into the view for testing purposes:

```
import SwiftUI

struct AddNewCarView: View {

    @State var carStore : CarStore
    @State private var isHybrid = false
    @State private var name: String = ""
    @State private var description: String = ""

.

.

#Preview {
    AddNewCarView(carStore: CarStore())
}
```

Next, add a new subview to the declaration that can be used to display a Text and TextField view pair into which the user will enter details of the new car. This subview will be passed a String value for the text to appear on the Text view and a state property binding into which the user's input is to be stored. As outlined in the chapter entitled *"SwiftUI State Properties, Observation, and Environment Objects"*, a property must be declared using the @Binding property wrapper if the view is being passed a state property. Remaining in the *AddNewCarView.swift* file, implement this subview as follows:

```
struct DataInput: View {

    var title: String
    @Binding var userInput: String

    var body: some View {
        VStack(alignment: HorizontalAlignment.leading) {
            Text(title)
                .font(.headline)
            TextField("Enter \(title)", text: $userInput)
                    .textFieldStyle(RoundedBorderTextFieldStyle())
        }
        .padding()
    }
}
```

With the subview added, declare the user interface layout for the main view as follows:

```
var body: some View {

    Form {
```

A SwiftUI List and NavigationStack Tutorial

```
        Section(header: Text("Car Details")) {
            Image(systemName: "car.fill")
                .resizable()
                .aspectRatio(contentMode: .fit)
                .padding()

            DataInput(title: "Model", userInput: $name)
            DataInput(title: "Description", userInput: $description)

            Toggle(isOn: $isHybrid) {
                Text("Hybrid").font(.headline)
            }.padding()
        }

        Button(action: addNewCar) {
                Text("Add Car")
            }
        }
    }
}
```

Note that two instances of the DataInput subview are included in the layout with an Image view, a Toggle, and a Button. The Button view is configured to call an action method named addNewCar when clicked. Within the body of the ContentView declaration, add this function now so that it reads as follows:

```
.
.
        Button(action: addNewCar) {
            Text("Add Car")
            }
        }
    }

    func addNewCar() {
        let newCar = Car(id: UUID(),
                    name: name, desc: description,
                    isHybrid: isHybrid, imageName: "tesla_model_3" )

        carStore.cars.append(newCar)
    }
}
```

The new car function creates a new Car instance using the Swift *UUID()* method to generate a unique identifier for the entry and the content entered by the user. For simplicity, rather than add code to select a photo from the photo library, the function reuses the tesla_model_3 image for new car entries. Finally, the new Car instance is appended to the carStore car array.

When rendered in the preview canvas, the AddNewCarView view should match Figure 32-4 below:

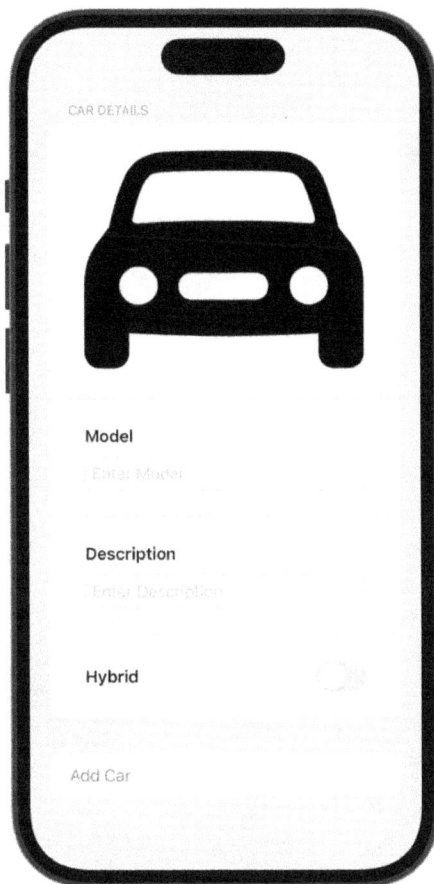

Figure 32-4

With this view completed, the next step is to modify the ContentView layout to include Add and Edit buttons.

32.10 Implementing Add and Edit Buttons

The Add and Edit buttons will be added to a navigation bar applied to the List view in the ContentView layout. The Navigation bar will also be used to display a title at the top of the list. These changes require the use of the *navigationTitle()* and *toolbar()* modifiers as follows:

```
var body: some View {

    NavigationStack {
        List {

            ForEach($carStore.cars, id: \.self) { $car in
                NavigationLink(value: car) {
                    ListCell(car: car)
                }
            }
            .onDelete(perform: deleteItems)
            .onMove(perform: moveItems)
```

```
        }
        .navigationDestination(for: Car.self) { car in
            CarDetailView(selectedCar: car)
        }
        .navigationTitle(Text("EV Cars"))
        .toolbar {
                ToolbarItem(placement: .navigationBarLeading) {
                    NavigationLink(value: "Add Car") { Text("Add") }
                }
                ToolbarItem(placement: .navigationBarTrailing) {
                    EditButton()
                }
            }
        }
}
```

The Add button is configured to appear at the leading edge of the navigation bar and is implemented as a NavigationLink using a string value that reads "Add Car". We now need to add a second navigation destination modifier for this string-based link that displays the AddNewCarView view:

```
NavigationStack {
    List {
        ForEach($carStore.cars, id: \.self) { $car in
            NavigationLink(value: car) {
                ListCell(car: car)
            }
        }
    }
    .navigationDestination(for: Car.self) { car in
        CarDetailView(selectedCar: car)
    }
    .navigationDestination(for: String.self) { _ in
        AddNewCarView(carStore: carStore)
    }
    .navigationTitle(Text("EV Cars"))
    .toolbar {
        ToolbarItem(placement: .navigationBarLeading) {
            NavigationLink(value: "Add Car") { Text("Add") }
        }
    .
    .
```

The Edit button, on the other hand, is positioned on the trailing edge of the navigation bar and is configured to display the built-in EditButton view. A preview of the modified layout at this point should match the following figure:

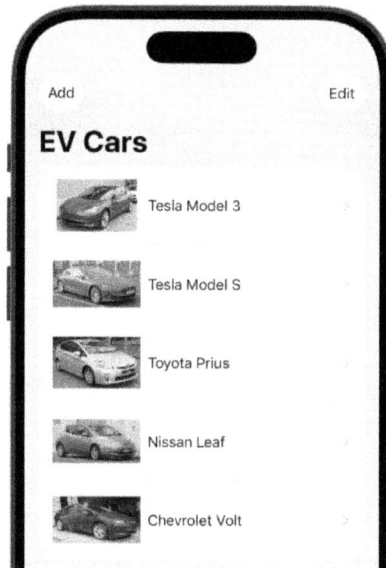

Figure 32-5

Using Live Preview mode, test that the Add button displays the new car screen and that entering new car details and clicking the Add Car button causes the new entry to appear in the list after tapping the back button to return to the content view screen. Ideally, the Add Car button should automatically return us to the content view without using the back button. To implement this, we will need to use a navigation path.

32.11 Adding a Navigation Path

Begin by editing the *ContentView.swift* file, adding a NavigationPath declaration, and passing it through to the NavigationStack:

```
struct ContentView: View {

    @State var carStore: CarStore = CarStore()
    @State private var stackPath = NavigationPath()

    var body: some View {
        NavigationStack(path: $stackPath) {
.
.
```

Having created a navigation path, we need to pass it to the AddNewCarView view so that it can be used to return to the content view within the *addNewCar()* function. Edit the string-based *navigationDestination()* modifier to pass the path binding to the view:

```
.navigationDestination(for: String.self) { _ in
    AddNewCarView(carStore: carStore: carStore, path: $stackPath)
}
```

Edit the *AddNewCarView.swift* file to add the path binding parameter as follows:

```
struct AddNewCarView: View {

    @State var carStore : CarStore
```

277

```
@Binding var path: NavigationPath
```

.

.

We also need to comment out the preview provider since the view is now expecting to be passed a navigation view to which we do not have access within the live preview:

```
/*
#Preview {
    AddNewCarView(carStore: CarStore())
}
*/
```

The last task in this phase of the tutorial is to call *removeLast()* on the navigation path to pop the current view off the navigation stack and return to the content view:

```
func addNewCar() {
    let newCar = Car(id: UUID(),
                    name: name, desc: description,
                    isHybrid: isHybrid, imageName: "tesla_model_3" )

    carStore.cars.append(newCar)
    path.removeLast()
}
```

Select the *ContentView.swift* file and use the preview panel to test that the Add Car button on the AddNewCarView screen returns to the content view when clicked.

32.12 Adding the Edit Button Methods

The final task in this tutorial is to add some action methods to be used by the EditButton view added to the navigation bar in the previous section. Because these actions are to be available for every row in the list, the actions must be applied to the list cells in the *ContentView.swift* file as follows:

```
var body: some View {

    NavigationStack(path: $stackPath) {
        List {

            ForEach($carStore.cars, id: \.self) { $car in
                NavigationLink(value: car) {
                    ListCell(car: car)
                }
            }
            .onDelete(perform: deleteItems)
            .onMove(perform: moveItems)
        }
        .navigationDestination(for: Car.self) { car in
            CarDetailView(selectedCar: car)
```

.

.

Next, add the *deleteItems()* and *moveItems()* functions within the scope of the body declaration:

```
          .navigationTitle(Text("EV Cars"))
```



```
        }
    }

    func deleteItems(at offsets: IndexSet) {
        carStore.cars.remove(atOffsets: offsets)
    }

    func moveItems(from source: IndexSet, to destination: Int) {
        carStore.cars.move(fromOffsets: source, toOffset: destination)
    }
}
```

In the case of the *deleteItems()* function, the offsets of the selected rows are provided and used to remove the corresponding elements from the car store array. The *moveItems()* function, on the other hand, is called when the user moves rows to a different location within the list. This function is passed source and destination values which are used to match the row position in the array.

Run the app on a device or simulator, click the Edit button, and verify that it is possible to delete rows by tapping the red delete icon next to a row and to move rows by clicking and dragging on the three horizontal lines at the far-right edge of a row. In each case, the list contents should update to reflect the changes:

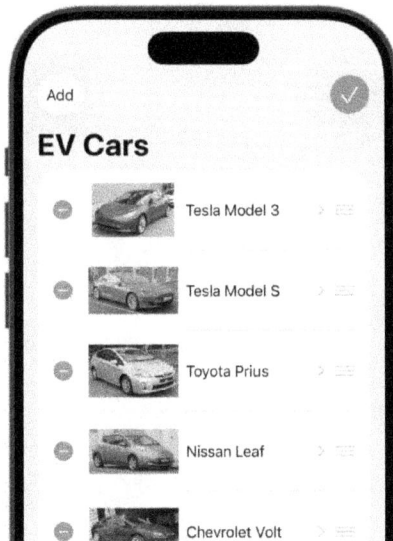

Figure 32-6

32.13 Summary

The main objective of this chapter has been to provide a practical example of using lists, navigation views, and navigation links within a SwiftUI project. This included the implementation of dynamic lists and list editing features. The chapter also reinforced topics covered in previous chapters, including using observable objects, state properties, and property bindings. The chapter also introduced additional SwiftUI features, including the Form container view, navigation bar items, and the TextField view.

Chapter 33

33. An Overview of Split View Navigation

The NavigationStack and NavigationLink views outlined in the previous chapters are ideal for adding navigation when each destination view needs to fill the entire device screen. While this is generally the preferred navigation paradigm when working on most iOS devices, it doesn't take advantage of larger display configurations available on the iPad or the iPhone Pro Max in landscape orientation. To take advantage of wider displays, SwiftUI includes the NavigationSplitView component which is designed to provide multicolumn-based navigation.

In this chapter, we will explain how to use NavigationSplitView in preparation for the next chapter titled *"A NavigationSplitView Tutorial"*.

33.1 Introducing NavigationSplitView

The purpose of NavigationSplitView is to provide multicolumn-based navigation on wide displays. It supports a maximum of three columns consisting of the sidebar (marked A in Figure 33-1), content (B), and detail (C) columns. A selection in one column controls the content displayed in the next column. The screen in Figure 33-1 shows the example app we will create in the next chapter. In this case, the app is running on an iPad in landscape orientation:

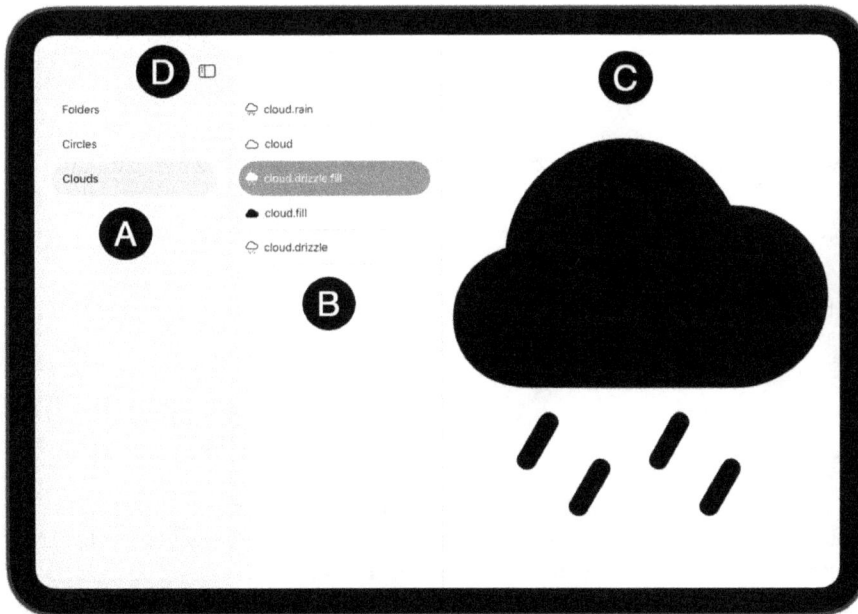

Figure 33-1

When sufficient screen space is available, the view will display all three columns. If screen space is limited, such as an iPhone Pro Max in landscape orientation, the sidebar will appear as a popover panel when the button (D) is selected as shown below:

Figure 33-2

Tap the button or anywhere outside the overlay panel to hide the sidebar.

When running on narrower displays such as an iPhone in portrait orientation, NavigationSplitView behaves similarly to the NavigationStack where each destination view fully occupies the screen.

33.2 Using NavigationSplitView

NavigationSplitView uses a simple syntax that differs depending on whether you need two or three-column navigation. The following syntax is for two-column navigation, which consists of the sidebar and detail columns:

```
NavigationSplitView {
    // Sidebar List here
}  detail: {
    // Detail view here
}
```

Three-column navigation consists of sidebar, content, and detail columns declared using the following syntax:

```
NavigationSplitView {
    // Sidebar List here
} content: {
    // Content List here
} detail: {
    // Detail view here
}
```

33.3 Handling List Selection

Both the sidebar and content columns will typically contain a List view from which the user will choose the content to be displayed in the next column. Selections made in a column are tracked by declaring a state variable and passing it to the List view via the *selection* parameter, for example:

```
@State private var colors = ["Red", "Green", "Blue"]
@State private var selectedColor: String?


var body: some View {
    NavigationSplitView {
        List(colors, id: \.self, selection: $selectedColor) { color in
```

```
        Text(color).tag(color)
    }
} detail: {
    Text( selectedColor ?? "No color selected")
}
}
```

In the code above, for example, the selection made within the List of color names controls the content displayed by the detail column via the *selectedColor* state variable. Note that the *tag()* modifier has been applied to the Text list item. This is used by SwiftUI to differentiate between selectable items in views such as List, Picker, and TabView.

33.4 NavigationSplitView Configuration

Several options are available to customize the appearance of a NavigationSplitView. For example, the width of an individual column can be controlled using the *navigationSplitViewColumnWidth()* modifier. In the following code the sidebar column has been assigned a fixed width of 100 points:

```
NavigationSplitView {
    List(colors, id: \.self, selection: $selectedColor) { color in
        Text(color).tag(color)
    }
    .navigationSplitViewColumnWidth(100)
} detail: {
    Text( selectedColor ?? "No color selected")
}
```

Style options can also be configured by applying the *navigationSplitViewStyle()* modifier to the NavigationSplitView parent declaration as follows:

```
NavigationSplitView {
    List(colors, id: \.self, selection: $selectedColor) { color in
        Text(color).tag(color)
    }
} detail: {
    Text( selectedColor ?? "No color selected")
}
.navigationSplitViewStyle(.automatic)
```

NavigationSplitView supports the following style options:

- **automatic** - This style allows the navigation view to decide how to present columns based on factors such as current content, screen size, and column selections.

- **balanced** - The balanced style reduces the width of the detail column when necessary to provide space for the sidebar and content columns.

- **prominentDetail** - This style prevents the size of the detail column from changing when the sidebar and content columns are added and removed from view. This style usually results in the sidebar and content columns overlapping the detail column.

33.5 Controlling Column Visibility

Column visibility can be controlled programmatically by passing an appropriately configured state value to NavigationSplitView via its columnVisibility initialization parameter. Changes to the state value will dynamically update the column visibility. Visibility options are provided by the NavigationSplitViewVisibility structure which includes the following options:

- **automatic** - Allows the navigation view to decide which columns should be visible based on the available screen space.

- **all** - Displays the sidebar, content, and detail columns.

- **doubleColumn** - In a two-column configuration, this setting displays the sidebar and detail columns. In a three-column configuration, only the content and detail columns will be visible.

- **detailOnly** - Only the detail column is visible.

The following code provides an example of setting column visibility based on a state variable set to *detailOnly*:

```
.
.
@State private var colors = ["Red", "Green", "Blue"]
@State private var selectedColor: String?
@State private var columnVisibility = NavigationSplitViewVisibility.detailOnly

var body: some View {
    NavigationSplitView(columnVisibility: $columnVisibility) {
        List(colors, id: \.self, selection: $selectedColor) { color in
            Text(color).tag(color)
        }
    } detail: {
        Text( selectedColor ?? "No color selected")
    }
    .navigationSplitViewStyle(.automatic)
}
```

33.6 Take the Knowledge Test

Click the link below or scan the QR code to test your knowledge and understanding of SwiftUI Split View Navigation:

https://www.answertopia.com/dhan

33.7 Summary

The NavigationSplitView component allows you to build multicolumn-based navigation into your SwiftUI apps. When enough screen width is available, NavigationSplitView will display up to three columns consisting of sidebar, content, and detail columns. The sidebar and content panels contain List view items that, when selected, control the content in the next column. Selection handling is implemented by passing a state variable to the *selection* parameter of the column's List view. The column widths and style of a split navigation user interface can be configured using the *navigationSplitViewColumnWidth()* and *navigationSplitViewStyle()* modifiers.

Several combinations of column visibility may be configured programmatically using the NavigationSplitView *columnVisibility* initialization parameter.

34. A NavigationSplitView Tutorial

The previous chapter introduced us to the SwiftUI NavigationSplitView component and described how multicolumn navigation is implemented and configured. This chapter will take what we have learned about NavigationSplitView and use it to create an example iOS app project.

34.1 About the Project

This tutorial will create the three-column split navigation app illustrated in Figure 33-1 in the previous chapter. The sidebar column will list categories which, when selected, will update the content column to list icons belonging to the chosen category. The detail column will, in turn, display the currently selected icon from the content list.

34.2 Creating the NavSplitDemo Project

Launch Xcode and select the option to create a new Multiplatform App project named *NavSplitDemo*.

34.3 Adding the Project Data

Our first requirement is a class declaration we can use to store category names and corresponding icons. Press Cmd-N and create a new Swift file named *IconCategory.swift*. With the file added to the project, modify it to declare a structure for storing each icon category:

```
import Foundation


struct IconCategory: Identifiable, Hashable {
    let id = UUID()
    var categoryName: String
    var images: [String]
}
```

Next, edit the *ContentView.swift* file and add a state array variable populated with categories and icon names:

```
import SwiftUI


struct ContentView: View {


    @State private var categories = [
        IconCategory(categoryName: "Folders", images: ["questionmark.folder.ar",
                                         "questionmark.folder",
                                         "questionmark.folder.fill.ar",
                                         "folder.fill.badge.gear",
                                         "questionmark.folder.fill"]),
        IconCategory(categoryName: "Circles", images: ["book.circle",
                                               "books.vertical.circle",
                                               "books.vertical.circle.fill",
                                               "book.circle.fill",
                                               "book.closed.circle"]),
```

```
                IconCategory(categoryName: "Clouds", images: ["cloud.rain",
                                                    "cloud",
                                                    "cloud.drizzle.fill",
                                                    "cloud.fill",
                                                    "cloud.drizzle"])
    ]
    .
    .
```

34.4 Creating the Navigation View

The next step is to replace the default view within the ContentView with a NavigationSplitView as outlined below. As the project requires three columns, we need to include the sidebar, content, and detail declarations:

```
    .
    .
var body: some View {
    NavigationSplitView {

    } content: {

    } detail: {

    }
}
    .
    .
```

34.5 Building the Sidebar Column

Now that we have added the NavigationSplitView we are ready to add the list of categories in the sidebar column. While doing this, we also need to add a state variable to store the currently selected item in the list. Remaining in the *ContentView.swift* file, make these changes as follows:

```
    .
    .
@State private var selectedCategory: IconCategory?

var body: some View {
    NavigationSplitView(columnVisibility: $columnVisibility) {
        List(categories, selection: $selectedCategory) { category in
            Text(category.categoryName).tag(category)
        }
    } content: {
    .
    .
```

The code we have added displays a List view where each item is a Text view displaying a category name from the categories array. The List is passed a reference to our *selectedCategory* state variable for storing the most recent item selection.

Check the Preview panel and verify that the sidebar appears, as shown in Figure 34-1 below:

Folders

Circles

Clouds

Figure 34-1

34.6 Adding the Content Column List

With the sidebar completed, we are ready to add a list within the content column. Since we also need to keep track of the currently selected icon name we will need another state variable. To avoid showing a blank column, we also need to add some code to display a message if the user has not yet made a category selection. We can do this by using an *if-let* statement to evaluate the *selectedCategory* state variable:

```
.
.
.
@State private var selectedCategory: IconCategory?
@State private var selectedImage: String?

var body: some View {
    NavigationSplitView {
        List(categories, selection: $selectedCategory) { category in
            Text(category.categoryName).tag(category)
        }
    } content: {
        if let selectedCategory {
            List(selectedCategory.images, id: \.self,
                        selection: $selectedImage) { image in
                HStack {
                    Image(systemName: image)
                    Text(image)
                }.tag(image)
            }
        } else {
            Text("Select a category")
        }
    } detail: {

    }
}
```

For each item in the list, we are using a horizontal stack containing the icon and name text. At the bottom of the preview panel, use the menu marked E in Figure 17-22 to select an iPad model, then the settings menu (D) to change the device orientation to landscape. If the app is functioning as expected, selecting items from the sidebar should cause the content column to list the corresponding icon options, as shown in Figure 34-2:

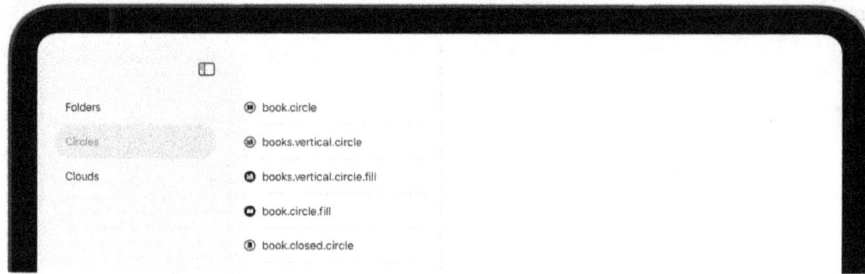

Figure 34-2

34.7 Adding the Detail Column

The detail column will display the selected icon in response to selections made within the content list. Locate the detail section within the NavigationSplitView declaration and modify it as follows, once again adding code to let the user know an icon needs to be selected:

```
NavigationSplitView {

.

.
} detail: {
    if let selectedImage {
        Image(systemName: selectedImage)
            .resizable()
            .aspectRatio(contentMode: .fit)
            .padding()
    } else {
        Text("Select an image")
    }
}
```

All three panels should be visible when selections are made from the sidebar and content columns:

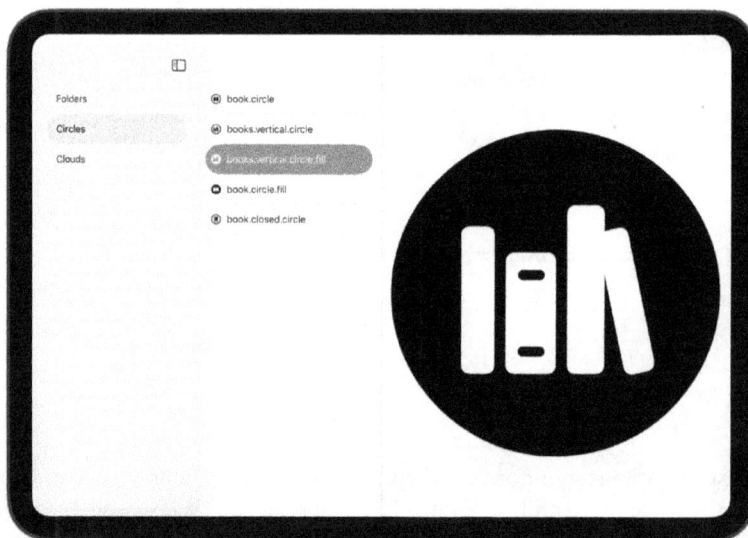

Figure 34-3

Clicking on the button marked by the arrow in the above figure will display the content column. Unfortunately, since we haven't yet made a category selection, this column only shows the "Select a category" message. Clicking the Back button will finally give us access to the sidebar column where we can begin to make selections. Once a category and icon have been selected we can see that the detail column is obscured by the sidebar and content panels. To view the entire icon image we have to click on the detail column to hide the other two columns. While this may be the desired behavior in some situations, this is the opposite of the experience we are looking for in our app so some additional configuration is required.

34.8 Summary

In this chapter, we created a SwiftUI-based app project that implements three-column navigation using the NavigationSplitView component. We also changed the default navigation behavior to match the requirements of our app.

35. An Overview of List, OutlineGroup and DisclosureGroup

The preceding chapters explored the use of the SwiftUI List view to display information to users in an ordered manner. Lists provide a way to present large amounts of information to the user in a navigable and scrollable format.

The features of the List covered so far, however, have not introduced any way to display hierarchical information within a list other than displaying an entirely new screen to the user in response to list item selections. A standard list also has the potential to overwhelm the user with options through which to scroll, with no way to hide sub-groups of items to ease navigation.

In this chapter, we will explore some features that address these issues, together with the OutlineGroup and DisclosureGroup views. Once these topics have been covered, the next chapter entitled *"A SwiftUI List, OutlineGroup and DisclosureGroup Tutorial"* will demonstrate the practical use of these views.

35.1 Hierarchical Data and Disclosures

In keeping with the automotive theme adopted in the previous chapter, consider an app required to present the user with the hierarchical data illustrated in Figure 35-1:

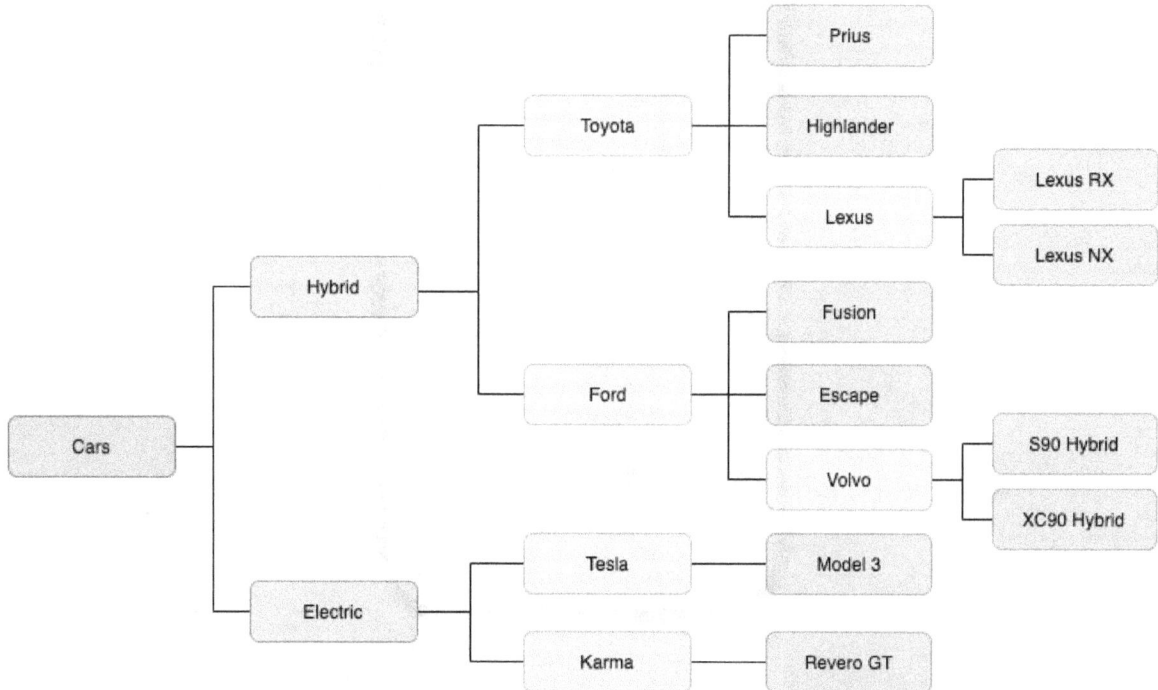

Figure 35-1

When designing such an app, one option would be to begin with a List containing only the two categories of cars

(Hybrid and Electric), presenting each subsequent layer of data on separate screens. A typical path through such a user interface might involve selecting the Hybrid category to navigate to a list containing the two hybrid car manufacturers, within which selecting Toyota would display a third screen containing the two hybrid models together with a selectable entry to display the hybrid models manufactured by Toyota's Lexus sub-brand. Having viewed the Lexus hybrid models, the user would then need to navigate back through multiple list levels to be able to navigate to view Tesla electric vehicles.

Clearly, a better option would be to display the information hierarchically within a single list, allowing the user to hide and show different sections of the hierarchy. Fortunately, this can be achieved using the List and OutlineGroup SwiftUI components.

35.2 Hierarchies and Disclosure in SwiftUI Lists

The previous chapter demonstrated the use of the List component to display so-called "flat", non-hierarchical data to the user. In fact, the List component can also present hierarchically structured data. It does this by traversing the data to identify the child elements in a data structure, and then presenting the resulting hierarchy visually. Figure 35-2 for example, shows the hierarchical data illustrated in Figure 35-1 above presented within a List view:

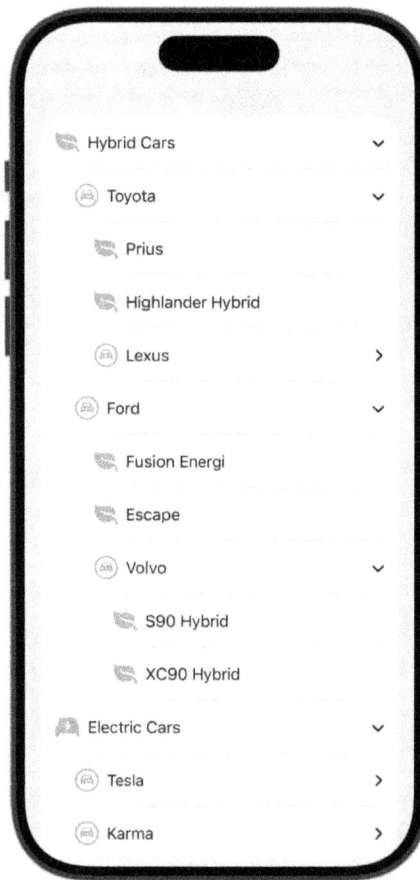

Figure 35-2

Clearly, this provides a better way to present the data to the user without having to traverse multiple depths of list navigation. Note also that disclosure controls are provided in the list to hide and show individual branches of data. Figure 35-3, for example, shows how the disclosure controls (highlighted) have been used to collapse the

Toyota, Volvo, and electric car data branches:

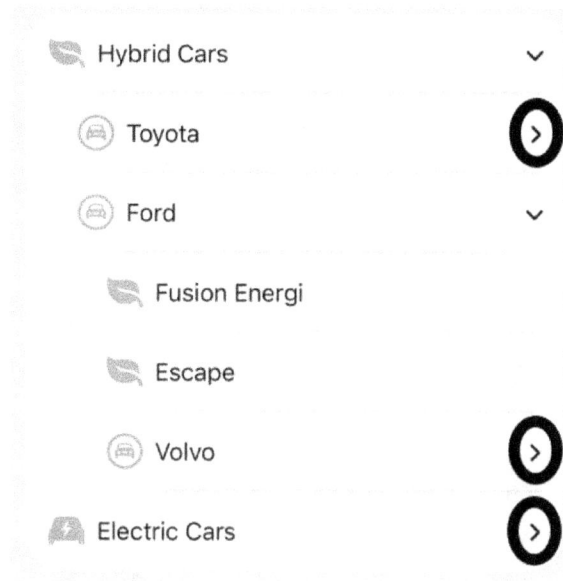

Figure 35-3

Clicking on a collapsed disclosure control will expand the corresponding section of the tree so that it is once again visible.

Assuming that the data to be displayed is correctly structured (an example data structure will be used in the chapter entitled *"A SwiftUI List, OutlineGroup and DisclosureGroup Tutorial"*), the above example was rendered with the following simple SwiftUI declaration:

```
struct ContentView: View {
    var body: some View {
        List(carItems, children: \.children) { item in
            HStack {
                Image(systemName: item.image)
                    .resizable()
                    .scaledToFit()
                    .frame(width: 25, height: 25)
                    .foregroundColor(.green)

                Text(item.name)
                    .font(.system(.title3, design: .rounded))
                    .bold()
            }
        }
    }
}
```

All that was required to enable this behavior was to pass through the data structure (carItems in the above example) to the List view together with a keypath to the children and then iterate through each item.

35.3 Using OutlineGroup

Behind the scenes of the above example, the List view is making use of the OutlineGroup view. When used directly, OutlineGroup provides the same basic functionality such as automatically traversing the data tree structure and providing disclosure controls, but with greater control in terms of customizing the display of the data, particularly in terms of organizing data into groups.

Figure 35-4, for example, shows the same car data displayed using OutlineGroup within a List to categorize the data into sections titled Hybrid Cars and Electric cars:

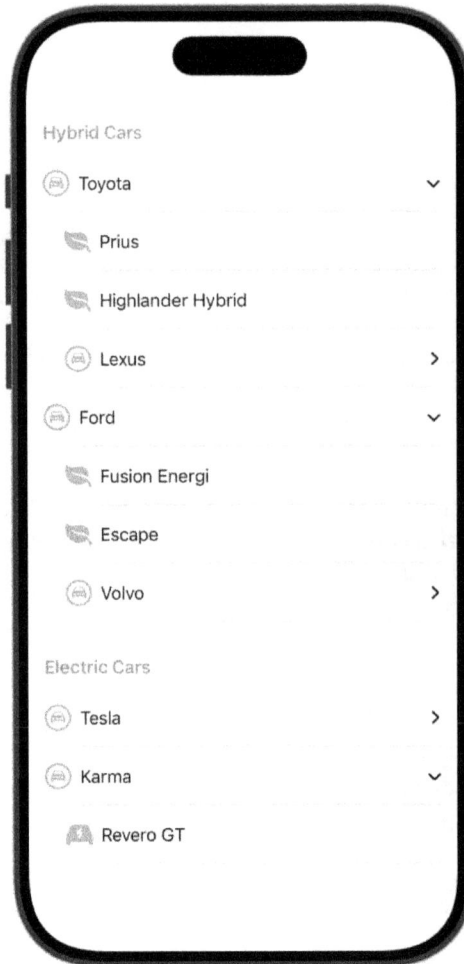

Figure 35-4

The SwiftUI declaration to create and implement the above display using the same car data reads as follows:

```
struct ContentView: View {
    var body: some View {
        List {
            ForEach(carItems) { carItem in
                Section(header: Text(carItem.name)) {
                    OutlineGroup(carItem.children ?? [Car](),
                                 children: \.children) { child in
```

```
                            HStack {
                                Image(systemName: child.image)
                                    .resizable()
                                    .scaledToFit()
                                    .frame(width: 30, height: 30)
                                    .foregroundColor(.green)
                                Text(child.name)
                            }
                        }
                    }
                }
            }
        }
    }
}
```

In the above example, the OutlineGroup is embedded within a List view. This is not a requirement for using OutlineGroup but results in a more visually pleasing result when the view is rendered.

35.4 Using DisclosureGroup

The disclosure behavior outlined in the previous sections is implemented in the background using the DisclosureGroup view which is also available for use directly in SwiftUI-based apps to allow the user to hide and show non-structured items in a layout. The DisclosureGroup view is particularly useful when used in conjunction with the Form view.

Consider, for example, the following Form based layout:

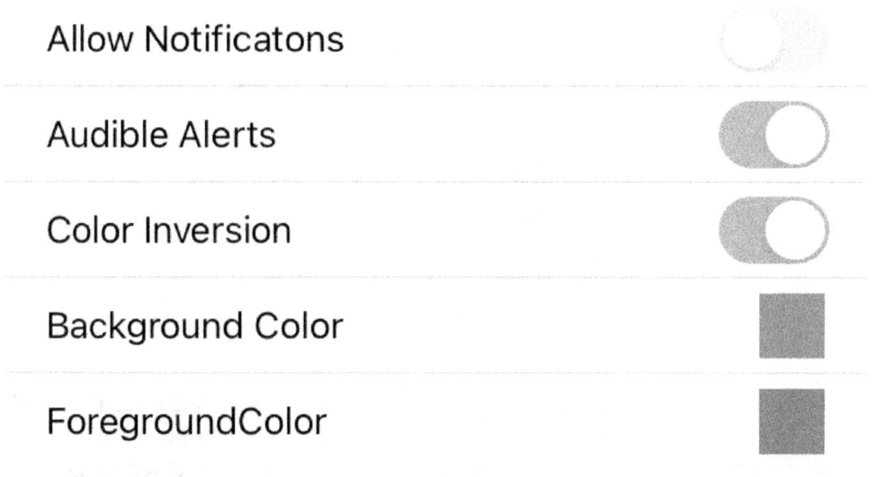

Figure 35-5

The above screen shows part of the settings screen for an app, the SwiftUI declaration for which reads as follows:

```
Form {
    Toggle("Allow Notifications", isOn: $stateOne)
        .padding(.leading)
        Toggle("Audible Alerts", isOn: $stateTwo)
```

```
        .padding(.leading)
    Toggle("Color Inversion", isOn: $stateThree)
        .padding(.leading)
    ColorControl(color: .red, label: "Background Color")
    ColorControl(color: .blue, label: "ForegroundColor")
}
```

The form has been implemented without consideration for grouping items into categories and, while this may be manageable with just five entries, this screen could become difficult to navigate with larger numbers of items.

Using DisclosureGroups, the form might be better organized, as shown in Figure 35-6:

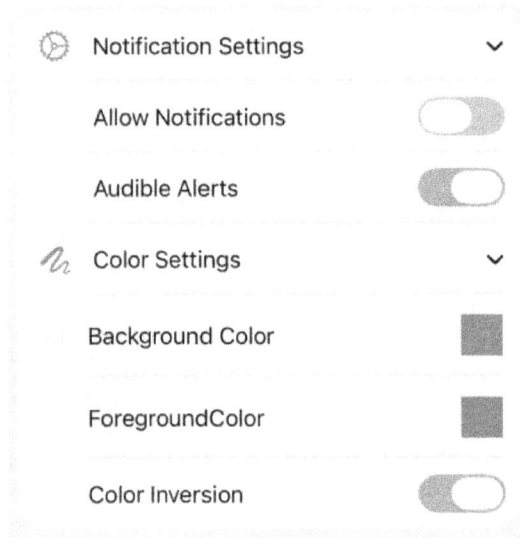

Figure 35-6

In this scenario, the form is divided into groups which can be expanded and collapsed using the embedded disclosure controls.

DisclosureGroups are declared using the following syntax:

```
DisclosureGroup(isExpanded: $controlsVisible) {
        // Content Views go here
        } label: {
            Label("Some Text", systemImage: "gear")
        }
```

Note that the DisclosureGroup accepts an optional trailing closure for declaring the label to appear above the content views. The above example uses a Label view, though this could be any combination of views. The Boolean isExpanded argument is also optional and can be used to control whether the group is expanded when first displayed.

The declaration for the form shown in Figure 35-5 above, might read as follows:

```
Form {
    DisclosureGroup {
        Toggle("Allow Notifications", isOn: $stateOne)
            .padding(.leading)
```

```
          Toggle("Audible Alerts", isOn: $stateTwo)
              .padding(.leading)
    } label: {
        Label("Notification Settings", systemImage: "gear")
    }

        DisclosureGroup {
            Toggle("Color Inversion", isOn: $stateThree)
                .padding(.leading)
            ColorControl(color: .red, label: "Background Color")
            ColorControl(color: .blue, label: "ForegroundColor")
        } label: {
            Label("Color Settings", systemImage: "scribble")
        }
}
```

35.5 Take the Knowledge Test

Click the link below or scan the QR code to test your knowledge and understanding of the SwiftUI OutlineGroup and DisclosureGroup views:

https://www.answertopia.com/8rgp

35.6 Summary

This chapter has introduced the hierarchical data support and disclosure features of the List, OutlineGroup, and DisclosureGroup views included with SwiftUI. The List and OutlineGroup views allow hierarchical data to be displayed to the user with just a few lines of code with disclosure controls provided to allow the user to expand and collapse sections of the hierarchy. These disclosure controls are provided by the DisclosureGroup view which may also be used directly within your own SwiftUI view layouts.

36. A SwiftUI List, OutlineGroup, and DisclosureGroup Tutorial

The previous chapter covered the List, OutlineGroup, and DisclosureGroup views and explored how these can be used to visually present hierarchical information within an app while allowing the user to selectively hide and display sections of that information.

This chapter will serve as a practical demonstration of these features in action through the creation of an example project.

36.1 About the Example Project

The project created in this chapter will recreate the user interface shown in Figure 35-4 in the previous chapter using the data represented in Figure 35-1. Initially, the project will use a List view to traverse and display the information in the car data structure. Next, the project will be modified to use the OutlineGroup within the List to display the information in groups using section headers. Finally, the project will be extended to use the DisclosureGroup view.

36.2 Creating the OutlineGroupDemo Project

Launch Xcode and select the option to create a new Multiplatform App project named *OutlineGroupDemo*.

36.3 Adding the Data Structure

The first step before a list can be displayed is to add the data structure that will form the basis of the user interface. Each row within the list will be represented by an instance of a structure named CarInfo designed to store the following information:

- **id** – A UUID to uniquely identify each CarInfo instance.

- **name** – A string value containing the name of the car type, manufacturer, or car model.

- **image** – A string referencing the SF Symbol image to be displayed.

- **children** – An array of CarInfo objects representing the children of the current CarInfo instance.

Within the project navigator panel, select the *ContentView.swift* file and modify it to add the CarInfo structure declaration as follows:

```
import SwiftUI


struct CarInfo: Identifiable {
    var id = UUID()
    var name: String
    var image: String
    var children: [CarInfo]?
}
```

```
struct ContentView: View {
    var body: some View {
.

.
```

Now that a structure has been defined, some data needs to be added to populate the CarInfo instances. As mentioned previously, this data structure is represented in Figure 35-1 in the previous chapter. Staying within the *ContentView.swift* file, add the data as a variable declaration as follows (to avoid typing in the structure, it can be cut and pasted from the *CarInfoData.swift* file located in the CarData directory of the code samples download):

```
.

.

struct CarInfo: Identifiable {
    var id = UUID()
    var name: String
    var image: String
    var children: [CarInfo]?
}


let carItems: [CarInfo] = [

    CarInfo(name: "Hybrid Cars", image: "leaf.fill", children: [
        CarInfo(name: "Toyota", image: "car.circle", children : [
            CarInfo(name: "Prius", image: "leaf.fill"),
            CarInfo(name: "Highlander Hybrid", image: "leaf.fill"),
            CarInfo(name: "Lexus", image: "car.circle", children: [
                CarInfo(name: "Lexus RX", image: "leaf.fill"),
                CarInfo(name: "Lexus NX", image: "leaf.fill")])
        ]),
        CarInfo(name: "Ford", image: "car.circle", children : [
            CarInfo(name: "Fusion Energi", image: "leaf.fill"),
            CarInfo(name: "Escape", image: "leaf.fill"),
            CarInfo(name: "Volvo", image: "car.circle", children: [
                CarInfo(name: "S90 Hybrid", image: "leaf.fill"),
                CarInfo(name: "XC90 Hybrid", image: "leaf.fill")])
        ]),
    ]),

    CarInfo(name: "Electric Cars", image: "bolt.car.fill", children: [
        CarInfo(name: "Tesla", image: "car.circle", children : [
            CarInfo(name: "Model 3", image: "bolt.car.fill")
        ]),
        CarInfo(name: "Karma", image: "car.circle", children : [
            CarInfo(name: "Revero GT", image: "bolt.car.fill")
        ])
    ])
```

```
]

struct ContentView: View {
    var body: some View {
        VStack {
.

.

        }
    }
}
.

.
```

36.4 Adding the List View

With the data structure added to the project, the next step is to modify the content view so that it uses a List configured to extract the structured data from the *carItems* array. Before doing that, however, we first need to design a custom view to be presented within each list cell. Add this view to the *ContentView.swift* file as follows:

```
struct CellView: View {

    var item: CarInfo

    var body: some View {
        HStack {
            Image(systemName: item.image)
                .resizable()
                .scaledToFit()
                .frame(width: 25, height: 25)
                .foregroundColor(.green)
            Text(item.name)
        }
    }
}
```

The above view expects to be passed a CarInfo instance before constructing a horizontal stack displaying the image and a Text view containing the name of the current item. In the case of the image, it is scaled and the foreground is changed to green.

Next, edit the ContentView structure and replace the default "Hello, world!" Text view so that the declaration reads as follows:

```
.

.

struct ContentView: View {
    var body: some View {
        List(carItems, children: \.children) { item in
            CellView(item: item)
        }
    }
```

```
}
.
.
```

36.5 Testing the Project

Test the progress so far by referring to the preview canvas and switching into Live Preview mode. On launching, the two top-level categories will be listed with disclosure controls available:

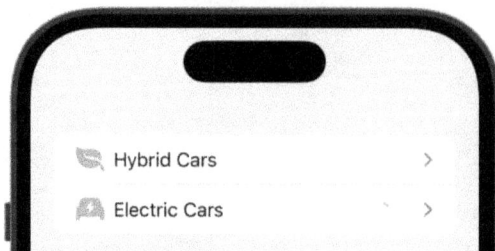

Figure 36-1

Using the disclosure controls, navigate through the levels to make sure that the view is working as expected:

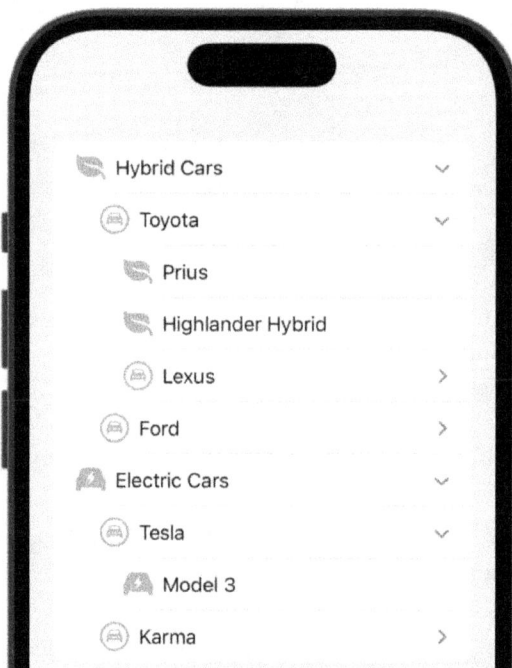

Figure 36-2

36.6 Using OutlineGroup

Now that we've seen the use of the List view to display hierarchical data, the project will be modified to make use of the OutlineGroup view within a list to divide the list into groups, each with a section header.

Once again working within the *ContentView.swift* file, modify the ContentView declaration so that it reads as follows:

```
struct ContentView: View {
    var body: some View {
```

```
List {

    ForEach(carItems) { carItem in

        Section(header: Text(carItem.name)) {

            OutlineGroup(carItem.children ?? [CarInfo](),
                            children: \.children) { child in

                CellView(item: child)
            }

        }
    }
}
.listStyle(InsetListStyle())
}
}
```

The above declaration takes the first entry in the data structure (in this case "Hybrid Cars") and assigns it as the title of a Section view. The OutlineGroup then iterates through all of the children of the Hybrid Cars entry. Once all of the children have been processed, the "Electric Cars" item is used as the title for another Section before iterating through all the electric car children.

When reviewed using Live Preview, the app should behave as before, with the exception that the information is now grouped into headed sections, as shown in Figure 36-3, noting that this time the List is configured with the InsetListStyle modifier:

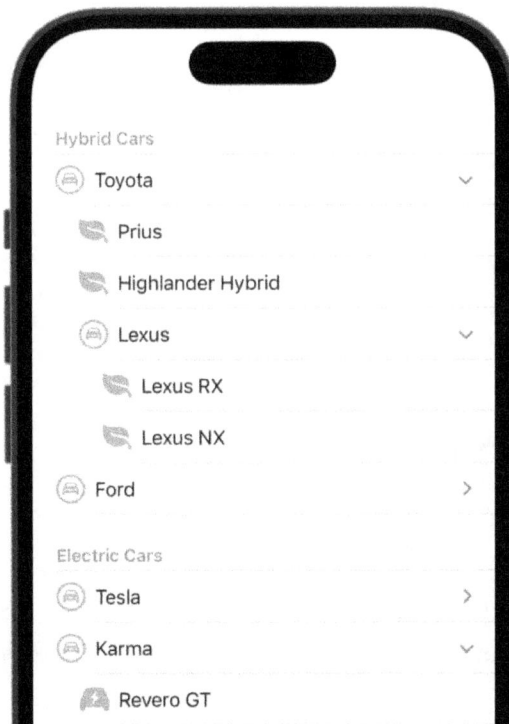

Figure 36-3

36.7 Working with DisclosureGroups

The DisclosureGroup view will be demonstrated within a new SwiftUI View file. To add this view, press Cmd-N, select the SwiftUI View file option in the new file template dialog, click Next, and name the file *SettingsView* before clicking on the Create button.

With the *SettingsView.swift* file loaded into the editor, make the following additions to add some custom views and state properties that will be used to simulate settings controls:

```
import SwiftUI

struct SettingsView: View {

    @State private var hybridState: Bool = false
    @State private var electricState: Bool = true
    @State private var fuelCellState: Bool = false
    @State private var inversionState: Bool = true
.
.
struct ColorControl: View {

    var color: Color
    var label: String

    var body: some View {
        HStack {
            Text(label)
            Spacer()
            Rectangle()
                .fill(color)
                .frame(width: 30, height: 30)
        }
        .padding(.leading)
        .scaledToFill()
    }
}

struct ToggleControl: View {
    var title: String
    @State var state: Bool

    var body: some View {
        Toggle(title, isOn: $state)
            .padding(.leading)
    }
}
```

Next, modify the body of the SettingsView structure to add a Form view containing the settings controls:

```
struct SettingsView: View {

    @State private var hybridState: Bool = false
    @State private var electricState: Bool = true
    @State private var fuelCellState: Bool = false
    @State private var inversionState: Bool = true

    var body: some View {

        Form {
            ToggleControl(title: " Hybrid Cars", state: hybridState)
            ToggleControl(title: " Electric Cars", state: electricState)
            ToggleControl(title: " Fuel Cell Cars", state: fuelCellState)

            ColorControl(color: .red, label: "Background Color")
            ColorControl(color: .blue, label: "ForegroundColor")
            ToggleControl(title: "Color Inversion",
                                    state: inversionState)
        }
    }
}
```

When reviewed in the preview canvas, the user interface layout should appear, as shown in Figure 36-4:

Figure 36-4

With the initial steps of the settings form designed, the next step is to organize the form into groups with titles and disclosure controls. To achieve this, modify the Form view declaration as follows:

```
var body: some View {

    Form {
        DisclosureGroup {
            ToggleControl(title: "Hybrid Cars", state: hybridState)
            ToggleControl(title: "Electric Cars", state: electricState)
            ToggleControl(title: "Fuel Cell Cars", state: fuelCellState)
```

```
    } label : {
        Label("Categories Filters", systemImage: "car.2.fill")
    }


    DisclosureGroup {
        ColorControl(color: .red, label: "Background Color")
        ColorControl(color: .blue, label: "ForegroundColor")
        ToggleControl(title: "Color Inversion",
                                    state: inversionState)
    } label : {
        Label("Color Settings", systemImage: "scribble.variable")
    }
    }
}
```

With the form separated into disclosure groups, the view should appear in the preview canvas as follows:

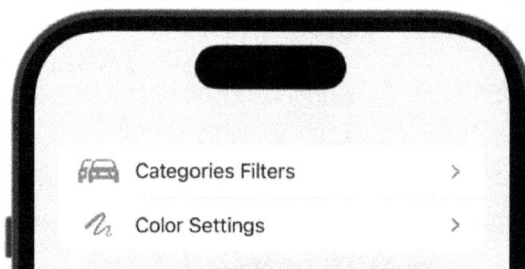

Figure 36-5

Switch into Live Preview mode and verify that the disclosure controls can be used to expand and collapse the two groups of settings:

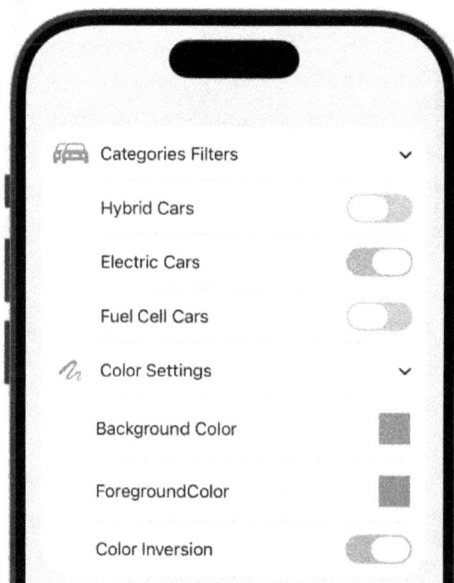

Figure 36-6

By default, disclosure groups are initially collapsed when displayed. To configure a group to appear in expanded mode, simply pass through a Boolean value to the DisclosureGroup declaration. The following code changes, for example, will cause the Category Filters section of the settings form to expand on initialization:

```
    .
    .
@State private var filtersExpanded: Bool = true

var body: some View {

    Form {
        DisclosureGroup(isExpanded: $filtersExpanded) {
            ToggleControl(title: "Hybrid Cars", state: hybridState)
            ToggleControl(title: "Electric Cars", state: electricState)
            ToggleControl(title: "Fuel Cell Cars", state: fuelCellState)
        } label : {
            Label("Categories Filters", systemImage: "car.2.fill")
        }
    .
    .
```

Using Live Preview once again, make sure that the category filters group is expanded when the user interface first appears.

36.8 Summary

The List and OutlineGroup views provide an easy way to group and display hierarchical information to users with minimal coding. The DisclosureGroup view is used by these views to allow users to expand and collapse sections of information, and may also be used directly in your own SwiftUI declarations. This chapter has demonstrated these views in action within an example project.

37. Building SwiftUI Grids with LazyVGrid and LazyHGrid

In previous chapters, we used stacks, lists, and outline groups to present information to the user. None of these solutions, however, are particularly useful for displaying content in a grid format. SwiftUI also includes three views to display multi-column grids within a user interface layout in the form of LazyVGrid, LazyHGrid, and GridItem.

This chapter will introduce these views and demonstrate how, when combined with the ScrollView, they can be used to build scrolling horizontal and vertical grid layouts.

37.1 SwiftUI Grids

SwiftUI grids provide a way to display information in a multicolumn layout oriented either horizontally or vertically. When embedded in a ScrollView instance, the user will be able to scroll through the grid if it extends beyond the visible screen area of the device in which the app is running.

As the names suggest, the LazyVGrid and LazyHGrid views only create items to be displayed within the grid when they are about to become visible to the user and then discard those items from memory as they scroll out of view (a concept covered previously in the chapter entitled *"SwiftUI Stacks and Frames"*). This allows scrollable grids of potentially infinite numbers of items to be constructed without adversely impacting app performance.

The syntax for declaring a vertical grid is as follows:

```
LazyVGrid(columns: [GridItem], alignment: <horizontal alignment>,
                    spacing: CGFloat?, pinnedViews: <views>) {
    // Content Views
}
```

In the above syntax, only the *columns* argument is mandatory and takes the form of an array of GridItem instances.

Similarly, a horizontal grid would be declared as follows where, once again, all arguments are optional except for the *rows* argument:

```
LazyHGrid(rows: [GridItem], alignment: <vertical alignment>,
                    spacing: CGFloat?, pinnedViews: <views>) {
    // Content Views
}
```

In the above syntax, the pinnedViews argument is used to specify views that should remain fixed in place while other content scrolls.

37.2 GridItems

Each row or column in a grid layout is represented by an instance of the GridItem view. In other words, a GridItem instance represents each row in a LazyHGrid layout and each column when using the LazyVGrid view. The GridItem view defines the properties of the row or column in terms of sizing behavior, spacing, and

311

alignment. The GridItem view also provides control over the number of rows or columns displayed within a grid and the minimum size to which an item may be reduced to meet those constraints.

GridItems are declared using the following syntax:

```
GridItem(sizing, spacing: CGFloat?, alignment: <alignment>)
```

The sizing argument is of type GridItemSize and must be declared as one of the following:

- **flexible()** – The number of rows or columns in the grid will be dictated by the number of GridItem instances in the array passed to LazyVGrid or LazyHGrid view.

- **adaptive(minimum: CGFloat)** – The size of the row or column is adjusted to fit as many items as possible into the available space. The minimum size to which the item may be reduced can be specified using the optional minimum argument.

- **fixed(size: CGFloat)** – Specifies a fixed size for the item.

Note that the GridItems in an array can use a mixture of the above settings, for example, to make the first column a fixed width with the remaining items configured to fit as many columns as possible into the remaining available space.

Since grids in SwiftUI are best explored visually, the remainder of this chapter will create a project demonstrating many of the features of LazyVGrid, LazyHGrid, and GridItem.

37.3 Creating the GridDemo Project

Launch Xcode and select the option to create a new Multiplatform App project named *GridDemo*. Once the project has been created, edit the *ContentView.swift* file to add a custom view to act as grid cell content together with an array of colors to make the grid more visually appealing:

```
import SwiftUI

struct ContentView: View {

    private var colors: [Color] = [.blue, .yellow, .green]
.

.

    struct CellContent: View {
        var index: Int
        var color: Color

        var body: some View {
            Text("\(index)")
                .frame(minWidth: 50, maxWidth: .infinity, minHeight: 100)
                .background(color)
                .cornerRadius(8)
                .font(.system(.largeTitle))
        }
    }
.

.
```

37.4 Working with Flexible GridItems

As previously discussed, if all of the GridItems contained in the array passed to a LazyVGrid view are declared as flexible, the number of GridItems in the array will dictate the number of columns included in the grid.

To see this in action, begin by editing the *ContentView.swift* file once again and declaring an array of three GridItems as follows:

```
struct ContentView: View {

    private var colors: [Color] = [.blue, .yellow, .green]
    private var gridItems = [GridItem(.flexible()),
                             GridItem(.flexible()),
                             GridItem(.flexible())]
.
.
```

Next, edit the body declaration to declare a vertical grid containing 9 instances of the custom CellContent custom view (numbered from 0 to 8), as follows:

```
var body: some View {
    LazyVGrid(columns: gridItems, spacing: 5) {
            ForEach((0...8), id: \.self) { index in
                CellContent(index: index,
                        color: colors[index % colors.count])

            }
        }
        .padding(5)
    }
}
```

With the changes made, refer to the preview canvas where the grid should appear, as shown in Figure 37-1 below:

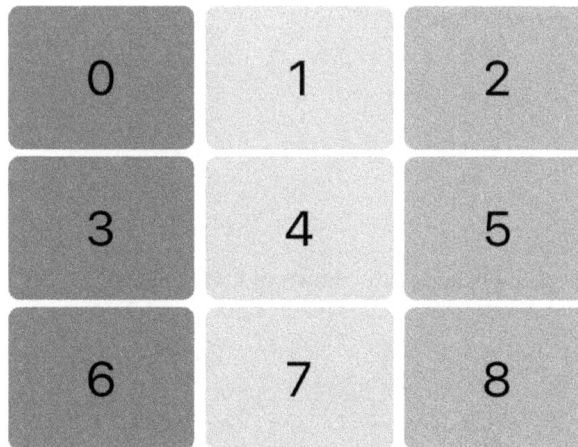

Figure 37-1

Clearly, the grid has been populated with three columns as expected. To add a column, simply place another

313

GridItem into the array. It is worth noting at this point that flexible mode is the default setting for the GridItem view, so the flexible declaration can be omitted if desired:

```
private var gridItems = [GridItem(), GridItem(), GridItem(), GridItem()]
```

When previewed, the grid will appear with four columns, as shown in Figure 37-2:

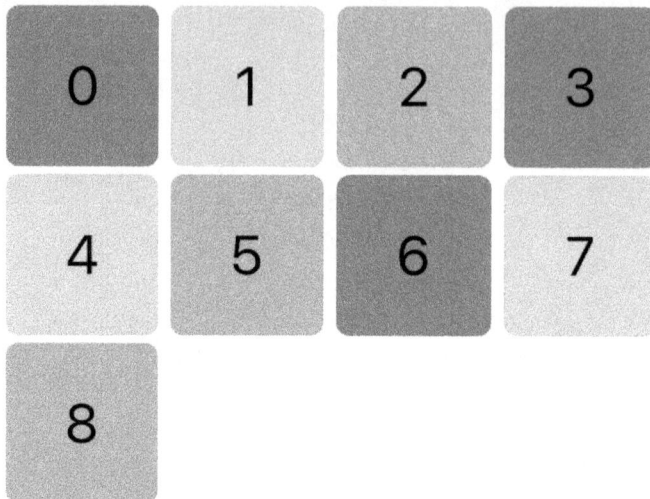

Figure 37-2

37.5 Adding Scrolling Support to a Grid

The above example grids contained a small number of items that could fit entirely within the viewing area of the device. A greater number of items will invariably cause the grid to extend beyond the available screen area. Try, for example, increasing the number of items in the ForEach loop of the body view declaration from 8 to 99 as follows:

```
var body: some View {

    LazyVGrid(columns: gridItems, spacing: 5) {
            ForEach((0...99), id: \.self) { index in
                CellContent(index: index,
                    color: colors[index % colors.count])
            }
        }
        .padding(5)
    }
}
```

When the grid is now previewed, it will appear, as shown in Figure 37-3:

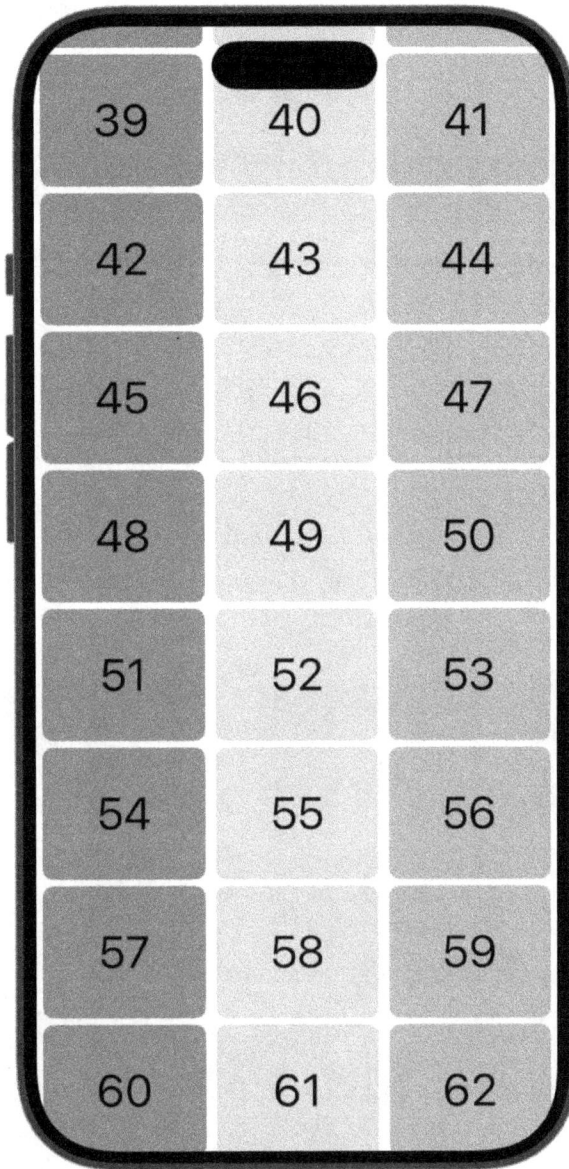

Figure 37-3

It is clear from the preview that the grid is now too tall to fit entirely on the screen. The screen also has the grid centered vertically so that the cells from the middle of the grid are visible instead of starting at the first row. It is also not possible to scroll up and down to view the rest of the grid. All of these issues can be addressed simply by embedding the LazyVGrid in a ScrollView as follows:

```
var body: some View {

    ScrollView {
        LazyVGrid(columns: gridItems, spacing: 5) {
            ForEach((0...99), id: \.self) { index in
                CellContent(index: index,
```

```
                                    color: colors[index % colors.count])
                }
            }
        .padding(5)
        }
    }
}
```

The top of the grid will now be visible within the preview and, if Live Preview is selected, it will be possible to scroll vertically through the grid.

37.6 Working with Adaptive GridItems

So far, we have seen how the flexible GridItem size setting allows us to define how many columns or rows appear in a grid. The adaptive setting, however, configures the grid view to automatically display as many rows or columns as it can fit into the space occupied by the view. To use adaptive sizing, modify the *gridItems* array to contain a single adaptive item as follows:

```
private var gridItems = [GridItem(.adaptive(minimum: 50))]
```

This change will result in the grid displaying as many columns as possible with the restriction that the column width cannot be less than 50dp. The following figure demonstrates a partial example of this change as it appears on an iPhone 11 in portrait orientation:

Figure 37-4

Figure 37-5, on the other hand, shows the same grid in landscape orientation. Note that the grid has automatically adapted the number of columns to occupy the wider viewing area:

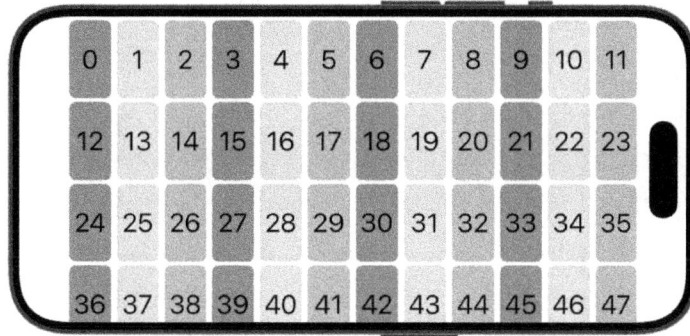

Figure 37-5

37.7 Working with Fixed GridItems

The GridItem fixed size setting allows rows or columns to be set at a specific size. When using only fixed GridItems in the array passed to the grid view, the number of GridItems will dictate the number of rows or columns. For example, the following array, when passed to a LazyVGrid view, will display a grid containing a single column with a width of 100dp.

```
private var gridItems = [GridItem(.fixed(100))]
```

The following array, on the other hand, will display a three-column grid with the columns sized at 75dp, 125dp, and 175dp respectively:

```
private var gridItems = [GridItem(.fixed(75)), GridItem(.fixed(125)),
                         GridItem(.fixed(175))]
```

When rendered, the grid will appear, as shown in Figure 37-6:

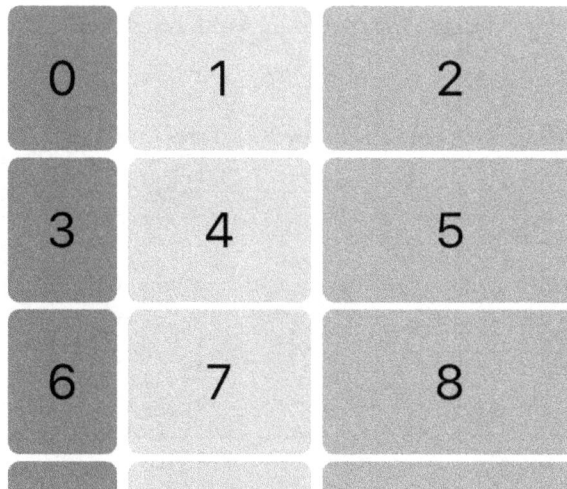

Figure 37-6

When working with grids it is also possible to combine GridItem sizing configurations. The following array, for example, will display the first column of each row with a fixed width with the second and third columns sized equally to occupy the remaining space:

```
private var gridItems = [GridItem(.fixed(85)), GridItem(),
                         GridItem()]
```

When rendered, the grid will appear, as illustrated in Figure 37-7 below:

Figure 37-7

Similarly, the following array uses a combination of fixed and adaptive sizing:

```
private var gridItems = [GridItem(.fixed(100)),
                 GridItem(.adaptive(minimum: 50))]
```

This will result in the first column of each row appearing with a fixed size, with the remainder of the row filled with as many columns as possible subject to the minimum width restriction:

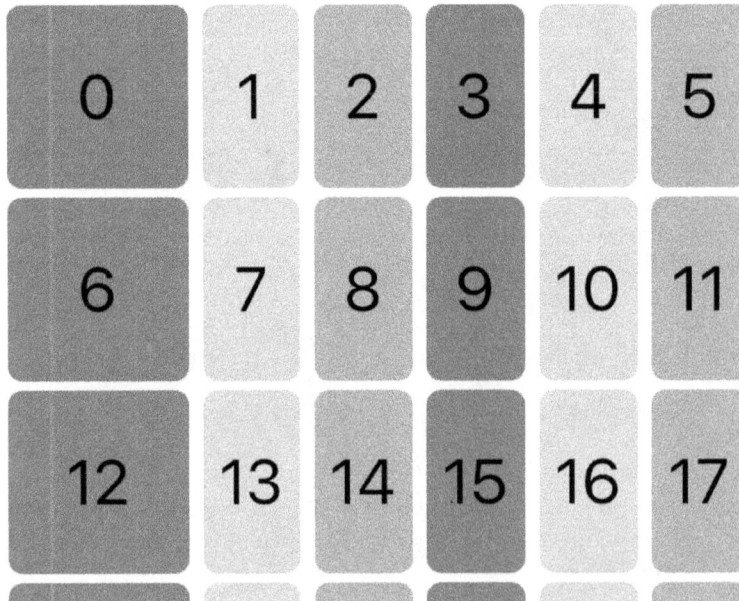

Figure 37-8

37.8 Using the LazyHGrid View

Horizontal grids work in much the same way as vertically oriented grids with the exception that the configuration is based on rows instead of columns, and that the fixed, minimum, and maximum values relate to row height instead of column width. Also, when scrolling is required the grid should be embedded in a horizontal ScrollView instance. The following declaration, for example, places a LazyHGrid within a horizontal ScrollView using adaptive sizing on all rows:

```
struct ContentView: View {

    private var colors: [Color] = [.blue, .yellow, .green]
    private var gridItems = [GridItem(.adaptive(minimum: 50))]

    var body: some View {

        ScrollView(.horizontal) {
            LazyHGrid(rows: gridItems, spacing: 5) {
                ForEach((0...99), id: \.self) { index in
                    CellContent(index: index,
                                color: colors[index % colors.count])
                }
            }
            .padding(5)
        }
    }
}

struct CellContent: View {
    var index: Int
    var color: Color

    var body: some View {
        Text("\(index)")
            .frame(minWidth: 75, minHeight: 50, maxHeight: .infinity)
            .background(color)
            .cornerRadius(8)
            .font(.system(.largeTitle))
    }
}
```

When previewed, the above declaration will display the grid shown in Figure 37-9 including the ability to scroll horizontally:

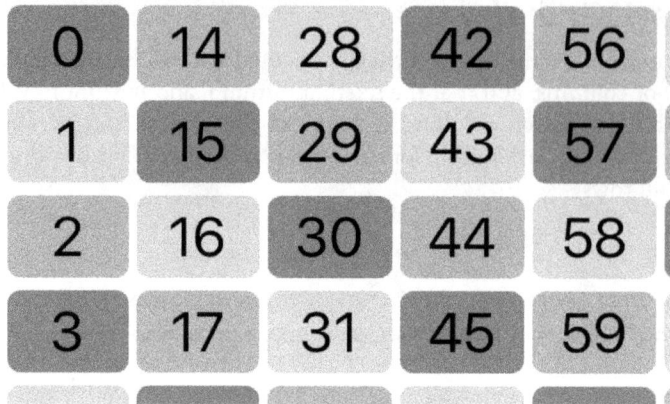

Figure 37-9

The following GridItem array, on the other hand, mixes fixed height with adaptive sizing to increase the height of the first and last grid rows:

```
private var gridItems = [GridItem(.fixed(150)),
    GridItem(.adaptive(minimum: 50)), GridItem(.fixed(150))]
```

When tested, the grid will appear, as shown in Figure 37-10 below:

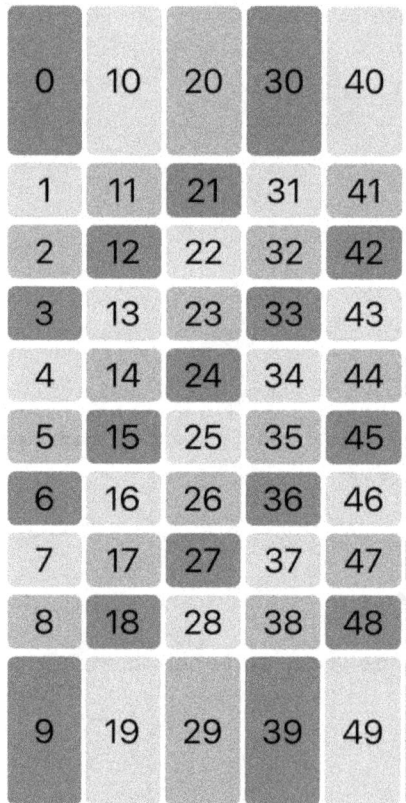

Figure 37-10

As a final example, consider the following GridItem array:

```
private var gridItems = [GridItem(.fixed(150)),
            GridItem(.flexible(minimum: 50)), GridItem(.fixed(150))]
```

When executed, the grid consists of fixed height first and last rows, while the middle row will size to fill the available remaining height:

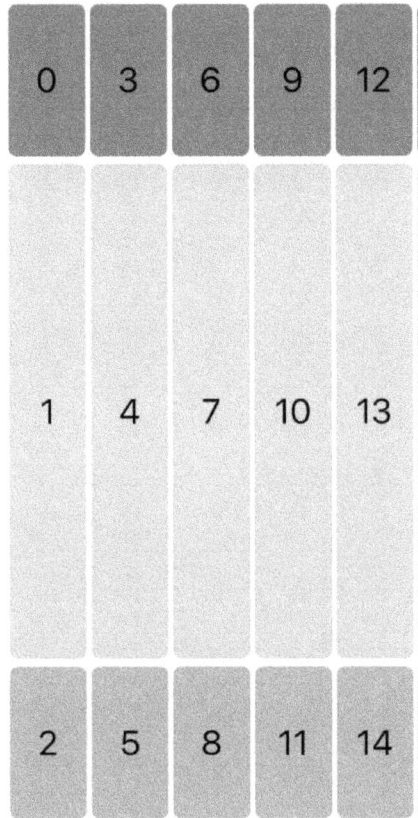

Figure 37-11

37.9 Take the Knowledge Test

Click the link below or scan the QR code to test your knowledge and understanding of the SwiftUI grid layout views:

https://www.answertopia.com/2urc

37.10 Summary

Grid-style layouts in SwiftUI are implemented using the LazyHGrid and LazyVGrid views which are designed to organize instances of the GridItem view. The LazyHGrid and LazyVGrid views are passed an array of GridItem views configured to define how the rows and columns of the grid are to be sized together with the content views to be displayed in the grid cells. Wrapping a grid in a ScrollView instance will add scrolling behavior to grids that extend beyond the visible area of the parent view.

38. Building SwiftUI Grids with Grid and GridRow

The previous chapter introduced the LazyHGrid, LazyVGrid, and GridItem views and explored how they can be used to create scrollable multicolumn layouts. While these views can handle large numbers of rows, they lack flexibility, particularly in terms of grid cell arrangement and positioning.

In this chapter, we will work with two grid layout views (Grid and GridRow) that were introduced in iOS 17. While lacking support for large grid layouts, these two views provide several features that are not available when using the lazy grid views including column spanning cells, empty cells, and a range of alignment and spacing options.

38.1 Grid and GridRow Views

A grid layout is defined using the Grid view with each row represented by a GridRow child, and direct child views of a GridRow instance represent the column cells in that row.

The syntax for declaring a grid using Grid and GridRow is as follows:

```
Grid {

    GridRow {
        // Cell views here
    }

    GridRow {
        // Cell views here
    }
    .
    .
    .
}
```

38.2 Creating the GridRowDemo Project

Launch Xcode and select the option to create a new Multiplatform App project named *GridRowDemo*. Once the project is ready, edit the *ContentView.swift* file to add a custom view to be used as the content for the grid cells in later examples:

```
struct CellContent: View {

    var index: Int
    var color: Color

    var body: some View {
        Text("\(index)")
```

```
            .frame(minWidth: 50, maxWidth: .infinity, minHeight: 100)
            .background(color)
            .cornerRadius(8)
            .font(.system(.largeTitle))
    }
}
```

38.3 A Simple Grid Layout

As a first step, we will create a simple grid 5 x 3 grid by modifying the body of the ContentView structure in the *ContentView.swift* file as follows:

```
struct ContentView: View {
    var body: some View {

        Grid {
            GridRow {
                ForEach(1...5, id: \.self) { index in
                    CellContent(index: index, color: .red)
                }
            }

            GridRow {
                ForEach(6...10, id: \.self) { index in
                    CellContent(index: index, color: .blue)
                }
            }

            GridRow {
                ForEach(11...15, id: \.self) { index in
                    CellContent(index: index, color: .green)
                }
            }
        }
        .padding()
    }
}
```

The above example consists of a Grid view parent containing three GridRow children. Each GridRow contains a ForEach loop that generates three CellContent views. After making these changes, the layout should appear within the Preview panel, as shown in Figure 38-1:

Figure 38-1

38.4 Non-GridRow Children

So far in this chapter, we have implied that the direct children of a Grid view must be GridRows. While this is the most common use of the Grid view, it is also possible to include children outside the scope of a GridRow. Grid children not contained within a GridRow will expand to occupy an entire row within the grid layout.

The following changes, for example, add a fourth row to the grid containing a single CellContent view that fills the row:

```
struct ContentView: View {
    var body: some View {
        Grid {
            GridRow {
                ForEach(1...5, id: \.self) { index in
                    CellContent(index: index, color: .red)
                }
            }

            GridRow {
                ForEach(6...10, id: \.self) { index in
                    CellContent(index: index, color: .blue)
                }
            }

            GridRow {
                ForEach(11...15, id: \.self) { index in
                    CellContent(index: index, color: .green)
                }
            }

            CellContent(index: 16, color: .blue)
        }
        .padding()
    }
}
```

Within the Preview panel, the grid should appear, as shown in Figure 38-2 below:

Figure 38-2

38.5 Automatic Empty Grid Cells

When creating grids, we generally assume that each row must contain the same number of columns. This is not, however, a requirement when using the Grid and GridRow views. When the Grid view is required to display rows containing different cell counts, it will automatically add empty cells to shorter rows so that they match the longest row. To experience this in our example, change the ForEach loop ranges as follows:

```
.
.
GridRow {
    ForEach(1...5, id: \.self) { index in
        CellContent(index: index, color: .red)
    }
}

GridRow {
    ForEach(6...8, id: \.self) { index in
        CellContent(index: index, color: .blue)
    }
}

GridRow {
    ForEach(11...12, id: \.self) { index in
        CellContent(index: index, color: .green)
    }
}
.
.
```

When the grid is rendered, it will place empty cells within the rows containing fewer cells, as shown in Figure 38-3:

Figure 38-3

38.6 Adding Empty Cells

In addition to allowing GridRow to add empty cells, you can also insert empty cells into fixed positions in a grid layout. Empty cells are represented by a Color view configured with the "clear" color value. Applying the *gridCellUnsizedAxes()* modifier to the Color view ensures that the empty cell matches the default height and width of the occupied cells. Modify the first grid row in our example so that even-numbered columns contain empty cells:

```
GridRow {
    ForEach(1...5, id: \.self) { index in
        if (index % 2 == 1) {
            CellContent(index: index, color: .red)
        } else {
            Color.clear
                .gridCellUnsizedAxes([.horizontal, .vertical])
        }
    }
}
```

Refer to the Live Preview to verify that the empty cells appear in the first row of the grid, as illustrated in Figure 38-4:

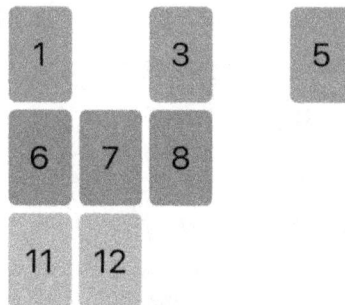

Figure 38-4

38.7 Column Spanning

A key feature of Grid and GridRow is the ability for a single cell to span a specified number of columns. We can achieve this by applying the *gridCellColumns()* modifier to individual content cell views within GridRow declarations. Add another row to the grid containing two cells configured to span two and three columns respectively:

.

.

```
CellContent(index: 16, color: .blue)

GridRow {
    CellContent(index: 17, color: .orange)
        .gridCellColumns(2)
    CellContent(index: 18, color: .indigo)
        .gridCellColumns(3)
}
```

.

.

The layout will now appear, as shown below:

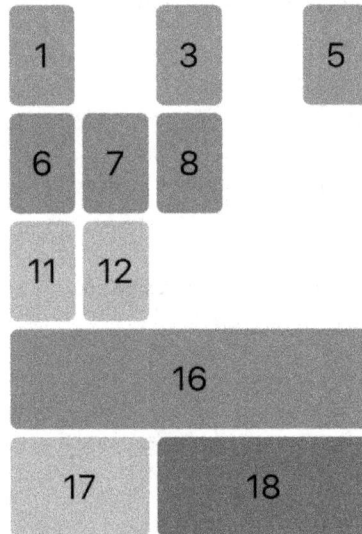

Figure 38-5

38.8 Grid Alignment and Spacing

Spacing between rows and columns can be applied using the Grid view's verticalSpacing and horizontalSpacing parameters, for example:

```
Grid(horizontalSpacing: 30, verticalSpacing: 0) {
    GridRow {
        ForEach(1...5, id: \.self) { index in
```

.

.

The above changes increase the spacing between columns while removing the spacing between rows so that the grid appears, as shown in the figure below:

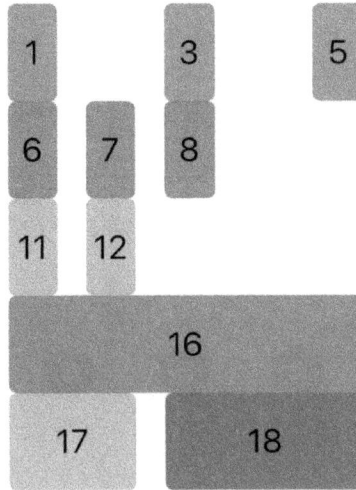

Figure 38-6

We designed the CellContent view used throughout this chapter to fill the available space within a grid cell. As this makes it impossible to see changes in alignment, we need to add cells containing content that will demonstrate alignment settings. Begin by inserting two new rows at the top of the grid as outlined below. Also, remove the code that placed empty cells in the row containing cells 1 through 5 so that all cells are displayed:

```
struct ContentView: View {
    var body: some View {
        Grid {

            GridRow {
                CellContent(index: 0, color: .orange)
                Image(systemName: "record.circle.fill")
                Image(systemName: "record.circle.fill")
                Image(systemName: "record.circle.fill")
                CellContent(index: 0, color: .yellow)

            }
            .font(.largeTitle)

            GridRow {
                CellContent(index: 0, color: .orange)
                Image(systemName: "record.circle.fill")
                Image(systemName: "record.circle.fill")
                Image(systemName: "record.circle.fill")
                CellContent(index: 0, color: .yellow)

            }
            .font(.largeTitle)
```

```
GridRow {
    ForEach(1...5, id: \.self) { index in
            CellContent(index: index, color: .red)
    }
}
.
.
```

After making these changes, refer to the preview and verify that the top three rows of the grid match that shown in Figure 38-7:

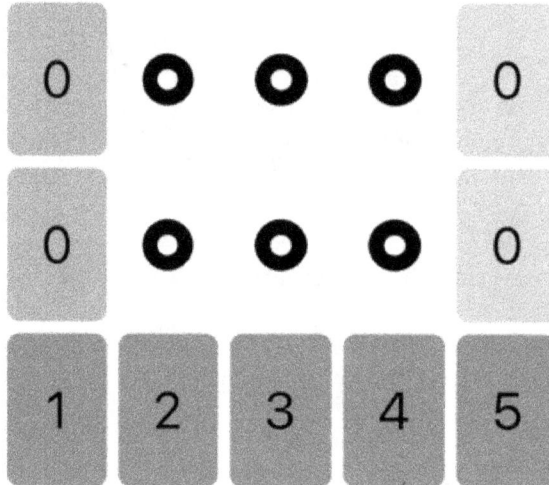

Figure 38-7

We can see from the positioning of the circle symbols that the Grid and GridRow views default to centering content within grid cells. The default alignment for all cells within a grid can be changed by assigning one of the following values to the alignment parameter of the Grid view:

- .trailing

- .leading

- .top

- .bottom

- .topLeading

- .topTrailing

- .bottomLeading

- .bottomTrailing

- .center

Cell content can also be aligned with the baselines of text contained in adjoining cells using the following alignment values:

- .centerFirstTextBaseline

- .centerLastTextBaseline

- .leadingFirstTextBaseline

- .leadingLastTextBaseline

- .trailingFirstTextBaseline

- .trailingLastTextBaseline

Modify the Grid declaration in the example code so that all content is aligned at the leading top of the containing cell:

```
struct ContentView: View {
    var body: some View {
        Grid(alignment: .topLeading) {
.
.
```

Review the preview panel and confirm that the positioning of the circle symbols matches the layout shown in Figure 38-8:

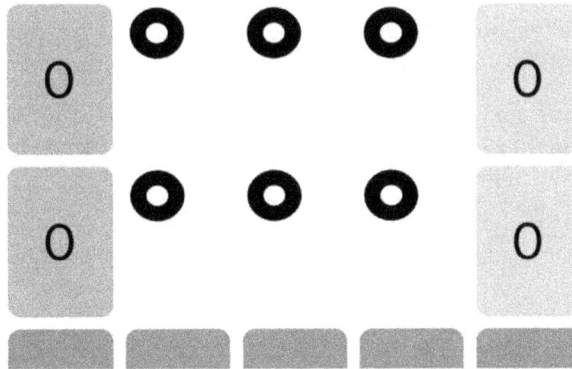

Figure 38-8

It is also possible to override the default vertical alignment setting on individual rows using the alignment property of the GridRow view. The following code modifications, for example, change the second row of symbols to use bottom alignment:

```
struct ContentView: View {
    var body: some View {
        Grid(alignment: .topLeading) {

        GridRow(alignment: .bottom) {
            CellContent(index: 0, color: .orange)
            Image(systemName: "record.circle.fill")
            Image(systemName: "record.circle.fill")
            Image(systemName: "record.circle.fill")
            CellContent(index: 0, color: .yellow)
```

```
    }
    .font(.largeTitle)
```

.

.

The circles in the first row are now positioned along the bottom of the row while the second row continues to adopt the default alignment specified by the parent grid view:

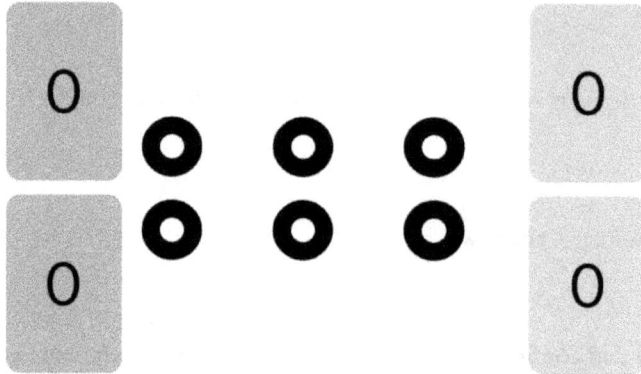

Figure 38-9

Note that GridRow alignment will only adjust the vertical positioning of cell content. As illustrated above, the first row of circles has continued to use the leading alignment applied to the parent Grid view.

Horizontal content alignment for the cells in individual columns can be changed by applying the *gridColumnAlignment()* modifier to any cell within the corresponding column. The following code change, for example, applies trailing alignment to the second grid column:

```
struct ContentView: View {
    var body: some View {
        Grid(alignment: .topLeading) {

        GridRow(alignment: .bottom) {
            CellContent(index: 0, color: .orange)
            Image(systemName: "record.circle.fill")
                .gridColumnAlignment(.trailing)
            Image(systemName: "record.circle.fill")
            Image(systemName: "record.circle.fill")
            CellContent(index: 0, color: .yellow)


        }
        .font(.largeTitle)
```

.

.

When previewed, the first grid rows will appear, as illustrated in Figure 38-10:

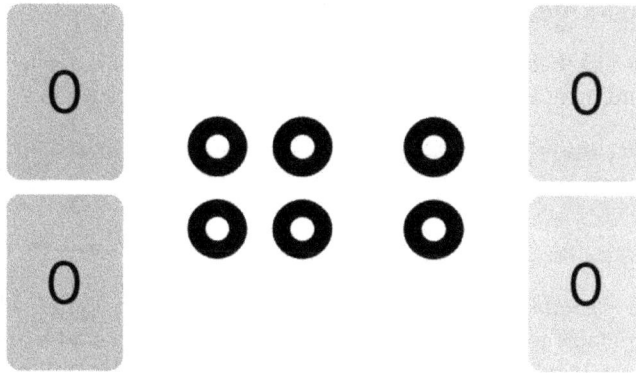

Figure 38-10

Finally, you can override content alignment in an individual cell using the *gridCellAnchor()* modifier as follows:

```
Grid(alignment: .topLeading) {

GridRow(alignment: .bottom) {
    CellContent(index: 0, color: .orange)
    Image(systemName: "record.circle.fill")
        .gridColumnAlignment(.trailing)
    Image(systemName: "record.circle.fill")
        .gridCellAnchor(.center)
    Image(systemName: "record.circle.fill")
        .gridCellAnchor(.top)
    CellContent(index: 0, color: .yellow)
}
.font(.largeTitle)
```

Once the preview updates to reflect the above changes, the circle symbol rows should appear, as shown below:

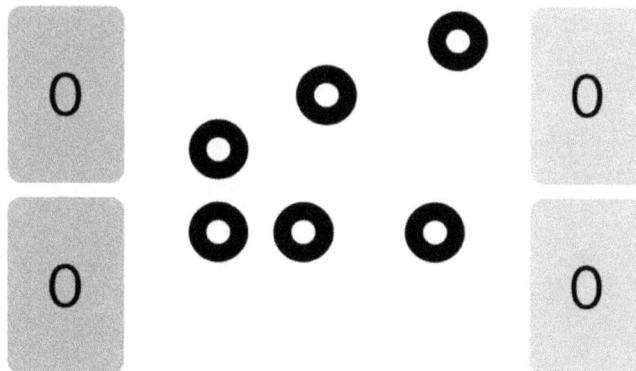

Figure 38-11

38.9 Take the Knowledge Test

Click the link below or scan the QR code to test your knowledge and understanding of the SwiftUI Grid and GridRow layout views:

https://www.answertopia.com/9wzd

38.10 Summary

The Grid and GridRow views combine to provide highly flexible grid layout options when working with SwiftUI. While these views are unsuitable for displaying scrolling grids containing a large number of views, they have several advantages over the LazyVGrid and LazyHGrid views covered in the previous chapter. Particular strengths include the ability for a single cell to span multiple columns, support for empty cells, automatic addition of empty cells to maintain matching column counts, and the ability to adjust content alignment at the grid, row, and individual cell levels.

39. Building Custom Containers

Container views are the foundation on which all SwiftUI view hierarchies are built. They allow us to group views and control and define how they are positioned on the screen. We've already worked with many of the container views provided with SwiftUI, such as lists, stacks, and grids. Although these built-in containers provide extensive flexibility in arranging and positioning child views, there will be situations where the layout needs of your app cannot be met using an existing container. In this chapter, we will learn how to overcome these challenges by building custom containers.

39.1 Introducing custom containers

SwiftUI allows you to create custom containers that offer all of the advantages of the built-in containers. These include adding child views statically (where each child is hard-coded within the body of the view declaration) or dynamically using ForEach loops. What your container does with those children in terms of layout and interactive behavior is limited only by your imagination. For example, if you want each child view to be tilted at a random angle or positioned to match the stars in a given constellation, you can probably achieve it by creating a custom container.

Before we create an example custom container, we need to understand how custom containers are constructed.

39.2 Working with ViewBuilder Closures

From previous chapters, we know that we can pass parameters to a SwiftUI View function. However, a typical SwiftUI view or group of views cannot be passed on to another view. Suppose we are building a custom container named DemoContainer. When we use this container in our code, it needs to support both hard-coded and dynamic subviews. We might, for example, use our container as follows to display Text subviews:

```
let tasklist = [
    "Don't just do something, sit there",
    "Get promoted through guile and deception",
    ...
]
.
.
DemoContainer {
  Text("Vacuum the ceiling")
  Text("Dance like everyone's watching")
  Text("Run the MacBook through the car wash")
  Text("Get promoted through guile and deception")

  ForEach(tasklist, id: \.self) { task in
    Text(task)
  }
}
```

Behind the scenes, the Text subviews are passed to DemoContainer wrapped in a ViewBuilder closure. When we declare the DemoContainer view, therefore, we need to configure it to expect this ViewBuilder closure parameter, which we do using the @ViewBuilder parameter attribute:

```
struct DemoContainer<Content: View>: View {
    @ViewBuilder var content: Content

    var body: some View {
.

.

    }
}
```

When our custom container is called, the *content* parameter contains all the views that DemoContainer needs to display, so we need a way to iterate through those subviews. We can perform this iteration using the *ForEach(subview:)* initializer. For example:

```
struct DemoContainer<Content: View>: View {
    @ViewBuilder var content: Content

    var body: some View {
        ForEach(subviews: content) { subview in
            // Code to display subview
        }
    }
}
```

From this point on, we have the full power of SwiftUI to control how we present, position, and configure the subviews in our container.

39.3 Supporting Section Headers

Many built-in container views we covered in earlier chapters allow subviews to be grouped into sections with optional header titles. For example, when listing car models, we might create sections that allow us to group cars by manufacturer. SwiftUI's customer container API allows us to implement similar behavior in our own container designs.

As with built-in List containers, we create sections by embedding subviews within Section views:

```
DemoContainer {

    Section("Realistic tasks") {
        Text("Vacuum the ceiling")
        Text("Dance like everyone's watching")
        Text("Run the MacBook through the car wash")
        Text("Get promoted through guile and deception")
    }

    Section("Unrealistic Tasks") {
        ForEach(tasklist, id: \.self) { task in
            Text(task)
        }
    }
```

}

When the customer container is called, the ViewBuilder content now contains one or more sections, each containing a group of subviews. We must now iterate through each section and its corresponding subviews within the custom container. To add section support, we use the *ForEach(section:)* initializer, using *ForEach(subviews:)* to access the subviews in each section:

```
struct DemoContainer<Content: View>: View {
    @ViewBuilder var content: Content

    var body: some View {
        ForEach(sections: content) { section in

            ForEach(subviews: content) { subview in
                // Code to display subview
            }
        }
    }
}
```

For each section, we need to identify if a header has been declared and, if so, display it. Each section contains a header property that we can check for the presence of a header string and then extract that string to display in a custom header view, for example:

```
struct DemoContainer<Content: View>: View {
    @ViewBuilder var content: Content

    var body: some View {
        ForEach(sections: content) { section in
            if !section.header.isEmpty {
                MyCustomHeader {
                    section.header
                }
            }

            ForEach(subviews: content) { subview in
                // Code to display subview
            }
        }
    }
}
```

39.4 Take the Knowledge Test

Click the link below or scan the QR code to test your knowledge and understanding of SwiftUI custom containers:

https://www.answertopia.com/ls00

39.5 Summary

SwiftUI containers allow us to group and arrange views to create user interface layouts. SwiftUI includes built-in containers, such as the List, Grid, and Stack views, which can be used individually or combined to meet most layout needs. When the built-in layouts do not suffice, we can design custom containers. This chapter explored how ViewBuilder closures and ForEach loops are used to create custom container views.

40. A SwiftUI Custom Container Tutorial

The previous chapter explained how to create a custom container in SwiftUI. This chapter will build on this knowledge to create an app that presents a checklist interface using a custom container view.

40.1 About the Custom Container Project

The project we will create in this chapter is a checklist app that uses a custom container view. The container will support Text subviews and allow those items to be selected and deselected when tapped. Before completing the project, we will also add support for section headers. The completed app will appear as illustrated in Figure 40-1:

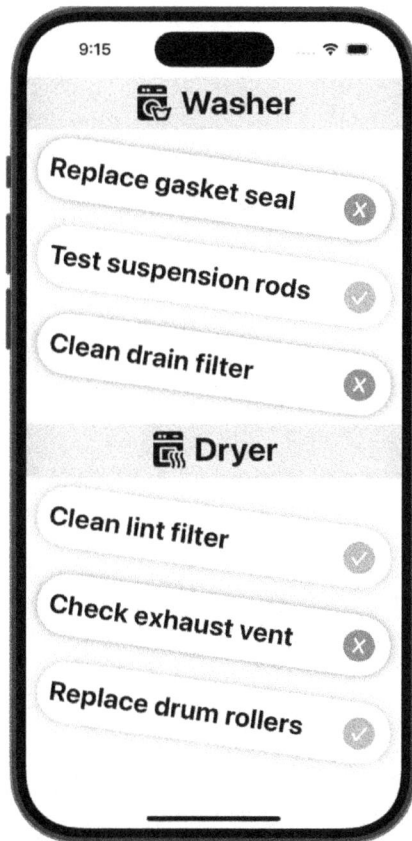

Figure 40-1

40.2 Creating the CustomContainerDemo Project

Launch Xcode and select the option to create a new Multiplatform App project named *CustomContainerDemo*.

40.3 Adding the Sample Data

Our example app simulates an appliance repair checklist consisting of a scrollable list of checkable items. The first step in the design process is adding arrays containing checklist items. Edit the *ContentView.swift* file to declare these arrays as follows:

```
import SwiftUI

let washerlist = [
    "Replace gasket seal",
    "Test suspension rods",
    "Clean drain filter"
]

let dryerlist = [
    "Clean lint filter",
    "Check exhaust vent",
    "Replace drum rollers"
]
.
.
```

40.4 Declaring the Item View

Each checklist item will be displayed using a custom view. When this item view is called, it is passed a ViewBuilder closure containing the subview to be displayed. We will enhance the item view later in the chapter, but for now, declare the basic view outline as follows:

```
struct CheckItemView<Content: View>: View {

    @ViewBuilder let content: Content

    var body: some View {
        ZStack {
            RoundedRectangle(cornerRadius: 50)
                .fill(.white)
                .padding(5)

            HStack {
                content
                    .font(.title)
                    .fontWeight(.bold)
            }
            .padding(18)
        }
        .padding(5)
        .frame(width: .infinity)
    }
}
```

40.5 Designing the Container

With an initial version of the item view added, we can start work on the custom container view. Once again, the view will be passed a ViewBuilder closure containing the subviews. Using the *ForEach(subviews:)* initializer, we can loop through the subviews, passing each to CheckItemView for rendering:

```
struct CheckList<Content: View>: View {
    @ViewBuilder var content: Content

    var body: some View {

        ScrollView(.vertical) {
            VStack(spacing: 20) {
                ForEach(subviews: content) { subview in
                    CheckItemView {
                        subview
                    }
                }
            }
        }
    }
}
```

40.6 Using the Custom Container

Though more work will be necessary before the app resembles Figure 40-1, we have completed enough that the checklist should at least appear in the preview panel. To test our progress so far, modify the ContentView declaration to pass the checklist items to the container view:

```
struct ContentView: View {
    var body: some View {
        CheckList {
            ForEach(washerlist, id: \.self) { item in
                Text(item)
            }

            ForEach(dryerlist, id: \.self) { item in
                Text(item)
            }
        }
    }
}
```

When the view is rendered in the preview panel, it should appear as shown in Figure 40-2:

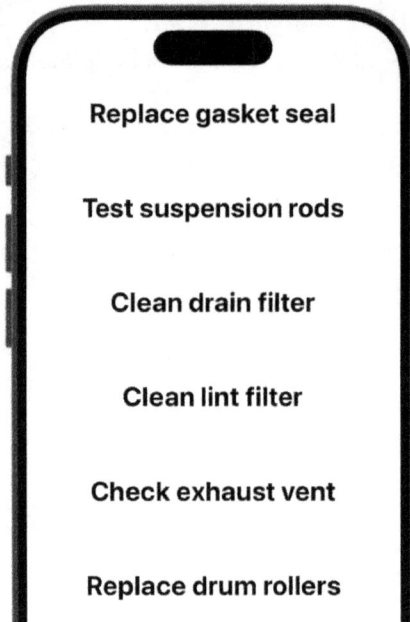

Figure 40-2

40.7 Completing the Item View

The next step is to complete the CheckItemView implementation to enhance the appearance with colors, shading, and checkmark images and to add tap gesture recognition. We will begin by adding some state properties to store the current item state (whether the item is selected or not) and configure the corresponding color:

```
struct CheckItemView<Content: View>: View {
    @ViewBuilder let content: Content

    @State private var color = Color.green
    @State private var isEnabled:Bool = false

    var body: some View {

        let color = (self.isEnabled ? Color.green : Color.purple)

        ZStack {

.

.

```

We also need to apply a tap gesture modifier to the RoundedRectangle view to toggle the *isEnabled* state and apply the *color* state value using the *.shadow()* modifier:

```
.

.

ZStack {
    RoundedRectangle(cornerRadius: 50)
        .fill(.white)
        .shadow(color: color, radius: 5)
```

```
        .onTapGesture {
            isEnabled.toggle()
        }
        .padding(5)
.
.
```

Use the Preview panel to verify that the checklist items toggle between green and purple shadowing when tapped.

The last changes to CheckItemView involve adding checkmark images and a rotation angle. We will use images from the built-in SF Symbols library for the checkmarks and apply visual effects when the app launches and an item is tapped. Locate the HStack in the CheckItemView declaration and make the following additions:

```
.
.
HStack {
    content
        .font(.title)
        .fontWeight(.bold)
    Spacer()
    Image(systemName: (isEnabled ? "checkmark.circle.fill" : "x.circle.fill"))
        .foregroundColor(color)
        .font(.largeTitle)
        .symbolEffect(.rotate, options: .nonRepeating)
        .contentTransition(.symbolEffect(.replace))
}
.padding(18)
.
.
```

Finally, apply the *.rotationModifier()* to the ZStack container as follows to tilt each item by 8 degrees:

```
.
.
ZStack {
    RoundedRectangle(cornerRadius: 50)
.
.
            .contentTransition(.symbolEffect(.replace))
    }
    .padding(18)
}
.padding(5)
.frame(width: .infinity)
.rotationEffect(Angle(degrees: 8))
.
.
```

Refresh the Preview and test that the checkmarks perform a single rotation when the view appears and that tapping gestures toggle between checked and unchecked images. With these changes completed, the checklist view will resemble the following figure:

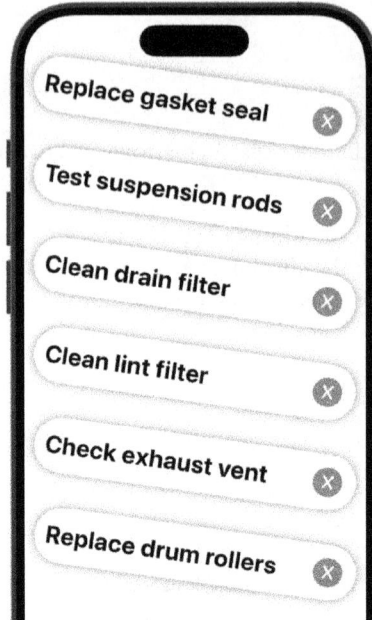

Figure 40-3

40.8 Adding Section Headers

The sole remaining task is to add section support to the container. We will begin by adding a section header view as follows:

```
struct ChecklistSectionHeader<Content: View>: View {

    @ViewBuilder var content: Content

    var body: some View {
        HStack {
            content
                .font(.largeTitle)
                .fontWeight(.bold)
        }
        .padding(5)
        .frame(maxWidth: .infinity)
        .background(Color.purple.opacity(0.2))
    }
}
```

This header view will be called from within the CheckList container view using a *ForEach(sections:)* loop as follows:

```
struct CheckList<Content: View>: View {
    @ViewBuilder var content: Content
```

```
var body: some View {

    ScrollView(.vertical) {
        VStack(spacing: 20) {

            ForEach(sections: content) { section in

                if !section.header.isEmpty {
                    ChecklistSectionHeader {
                        section.header
                    }
                }

                ForEach(subviews: section.content) { subview in
                    CheckItemView {
                        subview
                    }
                }
            }
        }
    }
}
```

As the loop executes, each section will have an optional header and a group of subviews belonging to that section. When calling CheckItemView, therefore, we have modified the *ForEach(subviews:)* construct to access each section's *content* property:

```
ForEach(subviews: section.content) { subview in
```

Modify ContentView as follows to add sections, and check the preview to confirm that the app appears as illustrated in Figure 40-1 above:

```
struct ContentView: View {
    var body: some View {
        CheckList {
            Section("\(Image(systemName: "washer.fill")) Washer") {
                ForEach(washerlist, id: \.self) { item in
                    Text(item)
                }
            }

            Section("\(Image(systemName: "dryer.fill")) Dryer") {
                ForEach(dryerlist, id: \.self) { item in
                    Text(item)
                }
            }
        }
    }
}
```

}

40.9 Summary

This chapter demonstrated creating and using a SwiftUI custom container view, including ViewBuilder closures, ForEach loops, and sections and headers.

41. Building Tabbed and Paged Views in SwiftUI

The SwiftUI TabView component allows the user to navigate between different child views either by selecting tab items located in a tab bar or, when using the page view tab style, by making swiping motions. This chapter will demonstrate how to implement a TabView-based interface in a SwiftUI app.

41.1 An Overview of SwiftUI TabView

Tabbed views are created in SwiftUI using the TabView container view and consist of a range of child views which represent the screens through which the user will navigate.

By default, the TabView presents a tab bar at the bottom of the layout containing the tab items used to navigate between the child views. A tab item is applied to each content view using a modifier and can be customized to contain Text and Image views (other view types are not supported in tab items).

The currently selected tab may also be controlled programmatically by adding tags to the tab items.

Figure 41-1 shows an example TabView layout:

First Content View

Figure 41-1

41.2 Creating the TabViewDemo App

Launch Xcode and select the option to create a new Multiplatform App project named *TabViewDemo*.

41.3 Adding the TabView Container

With the *ContentView.swift* file loaded into the code editor, delete the default body content and add a TabView as follows:

```
import SwiftUI

struct ContentView: View {
    var body: some View {
        TabView {


        }
    }
}
```

41.4 Adding the Content Views

Next, add three content views to the layout. For the purposes of this example, Text views will be used, but in practice, these are likely to be more complex views consisting of stack layouts (note the addition of a font modifier to increase the size of the content text):

```
var body: some View {
    TabView {
        Text("First Content View")
        Text("Second Content View")
        Text("Third Content View")
    }
    .font(.largeTitle)
}
```

41.5 Adding View Paging

If the app were to be previewed at this point, the first view would appear but there would be no way to navigate to the other views. One way to implement navigation is to apply PageTabViewStyle to the TabView. This will allow the user to move between the three views by making left and right swiping motions on the screen. To apply this style, add the *tabViewStyle()* modifier to the TabView as follows:

```
var body: some View {
    TabView {
        Text("First Content View")
        Text("Second Content View")
        Text("Third Content View")
    }
    .font(.largeTitle)
    .tabViewStyle(PageTabViewStyle())
}
```

With the changes made, use Live Preview to test the view and verify that swiping left and right moves between the views.

41.6 Adding the Tab Items

As currently implemented, there is no visual indication to the user that more views are available other than the first view. An alternative to the page view style is to implement the TabView with a tab bar located along the bottom edge of the screen. Since no tab items have been added, the tab bar is currently empty. Clearly, the next step is to apply a tab item to each content view using the *tabItem()* modifier. In this example, each tab item will contain a Text and an Image view:

```
var body: some View {
    TabView {
        Text("First Content View")
            .tabItem {
                Image(systemName: "1.circle")
                Text("Screen One")
            }
        Text("Second Content View")
            .tabItem {
                Image(systemName: "2.circle")
                Text("Screen Two")
            }
        Text("Third Content View")
            .tabItem {
                Image(systemName: "3.circle")
                Text("Screen Three")
            }
    }
    .font(.largeTitle)
    .tabViewStyle(PageTabViewStyle())
}
```

Note also that the PageTabViewStyle modifier must be removed when using the tab bar, otherwise the tab bar will not appear.

With the changes made, verify that the tab items now appear in the tab bar before using Live Preview to test that clicking on a tab item displays the corresponding content view. The completed app should resemble that illustrated in Figure 41-1 above.

41.7 Adding Tab Item Tags

To control the currently selected tab in code, a tag needs to be added to each tab item and a state property declared to store the current selection as follows:

```
struct ContentView: View {

    @State private var selection = 1

    var body: some View {
        TabView() {
            Text("First Content View")
                .tabItem {
                    Image(systemName: "1.circle")
```

```
                    Text ("Screen One")
              }.tag(1)
         Text ("Second Content View")
              .tabItem {
                   Image (systemName: "2.circle")
                   Text ("Screen Two")
              }.tag(2)
         Text ("Third Content View")
              .tabItem {
                   Image (systemName: "3.circle")
                   Text ("Screen Three")
              }.tag(3)
     }
     .font (.largeTitle)
}
}
```

Next, bind the current selection value of the TabView to the selection state property:

```
var body: some View {
    TabView(selection: $selection) {
        Text ("First Content View")
             .tabItem {
.

.
```

Any changes to the selection state property to a different value within the tag range (in this case a value between 1 and 3) elsewhere in the view will now cause the tabbed view to switch to the corresponding content view.

Test this behavior by changing the value assigned to the selection state property while the app is running in Live Preview mode.

41.8 Adding Minimizing Behavior

The final step in this chapter is to configure the tab bar to minimize when the user scrolls down in the content area. Before enabling this behavior, we need to add a longer content view to at least one of the tabs. Begin by adding the following custom view to the *ContentView.swift* file to display a list of items:

```
struct LongListView: View {
    var body: some View {
        List {
            ForEach(1..<25) { number in
                Text ("List Item \(number)")
            }
        }
    }
}
```

Next, modify the first tab to call the new custom view instead of the Text view:

```
var body: some View {
    TabView(selection: $selection) {
```

350

```
LongListView()
    .tabItem {
        Image(systemName: "1.circle")
        Text("Screen One")
    }.tag(1)
Text("Second Content View")
```

.

.

.

Use the live preview to test that the list appears and is scrollable, and that the tab bar remains unchanged as the list scrolls.

Minimizing behavior is applied to a tab bar using the *tabBarMinimizeBehavior()* modifier, passing as an argument one of the following values:

- **automatic** - Minimizing behavior is determined by the system.

- **onScrollDown** - The tab bar minimizes when the content scrolls downward.

- **onScrollUp** - The tab bar minimizes when the content scrolls upward.

- **never** - The tab bar is not minimized during scrolling.

Try out minimizing behavior for downward scrolling by applying the *tabBarMinimizeBehavior()* modifier to the TabBar view as follows:

```
TabView(selection: $selection) {
    LongListView()
        .tabItem {
            Image(systemName: "1.circle")
            Text("Screen One")
        }.tag(1)

.

.

.

}
.tabBarMinimizeBehavior(.onScrollDown)
.font(.largeTitle)
```

With the first tab selected, gradually scroll down the list and note that the tab bar shrinks slightly, then minimizes to show only the icon for the currently selected tab, as illustrated in, as illustrated in Figure 41-2:

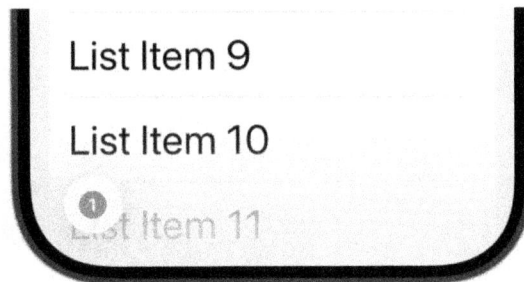

Figure 41-2

The tab bar will reappear either when you attempt to scroll beyond the bottom of the list or return to the top.

41.9 Take the Knowledge Test

Click the link below or scan the QR code to test your knowledge and understanding of SwiftUI tabbed and paged views:

https://www.answertopia.com/vabe

41.10 Summary

The SwiftUI TabView container provides a mechanism via which the user can navigate between content views by selecting tabs in a tab bar or, when using the page view style, making swiping motions. When using the tab bar, the TabView is implemented by declaring child content views and assigning a tab item to each view. The tab items appear in the tab bar and can be constructed from a Text view, an Image view, or a combination of Text and Image views.

To control the current selection of a TabView programmatically, each tab item must be assigned a tag containing a unique value, binding the TabView current selection value to a state property.

42. Building Context Menus in SwiftUI

A context menu in SwiftUI is a menu of options that appears when the user performs a long press over a view on which a menu has been configured. Each menu item will typically contain a Button view configured to perform an action when selected, together with a Text view and an optional Image view.

This chapter will work through the creation of an example app that makes use of a context menu to perform color changes on a view.

42.1 Creating the ContextMenuDemo Project

Launch Xcode and select the option to create a new Multiplatform App project named *ContextMenuDemo*.

42.2 Preparing the Content View

A context menu may be added to any view within a layout, but for the purposes of this example, a Text view will be used. Within Xcode, load the *ContentView.swift* file into the editor, add some state properties to store the foreground and background color values, and use these to control the color settings of a Text view. Also, use the *font()* modifier to increase the text font size:

```
import SwiftUI

struct ContentView: View {

    @State private var foregroundColor: Color = Color.black
    @State private var backgroundColor: Color = Color.white

    var body: some View {

        Text("Hello, world!")
            .padding()
            .font(.largeTitle)
            .foregroundColor(foregroundColor)
            .background(backgroundColor)
    }
```

.
.

42.3 Adding the Context Menu

Context menus are added to views in SwiftUI using the *contextMenu()* modifier and declaring the views that are to serve as menu items. Add menu items to the context menu by making the following changes to the body view of the *ContentView.swift* file:

```
var body: some View {
```

```
Text("Hello, world!")
    .font(.largeTitle)
    .padding()
    .foregroundColor(foregroundColor)
    .background(backgroundColor)
    .contextMenu {
        Button(action: {

        }) {
            Text("Normal Colors")
            Image(systemName: "paintbrush")
        }

        Button(action: {

        }) {
            Text("Inverted Colors")
            Image(systemName: "paintbrush.fill")
        }
    }
}
```

Finally, add code to the two button actions to change the values assigned to the foreground and background state properties:

```
var body: some View {

    Text("Hello, world!")
        .font(.largeTitle)
        .padding()
        .foregroundColor(foregroundColor)
        .background(backgroundColor)

        .contextMenu {
            Button(action: {
                self.foregroundColor = .black
                self.backgroundColor = .white
            }) {
                Text("Normal Colors")
                Image(systemName: "paintbrush")
            }

            Button(action: {
                self.foregroundColor = .white
                self.backgroundColor = .black
            }) {
```

```
            Text("Inverted Colors")
            Image(systemName: "paintbrush.fill")
        }
    }
}
```

42.4 Testing the Context Menu

Use Live Preview mode to test the view and perform a long press on the Text view. After a short delay the context menu should appear resembling Figure 42-1 below:

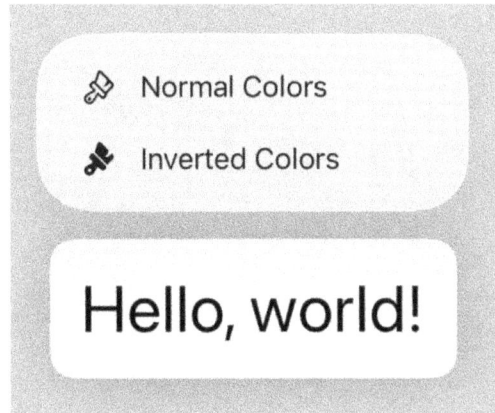

Figure 42-1

Select the Inverted Colors option to dismiss the menu and invert the colors on the Text view:

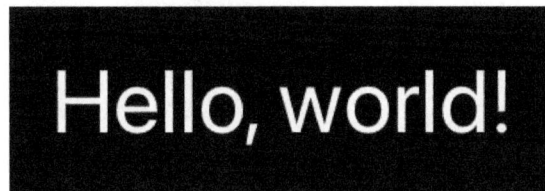

Figure 42-2

42.5 Take the Knowledge Test

Click the link below or scan the QR code to test your knowledge and understanding of context menus in SwiftUI:

https://www.answertopia.com/98zu

42.6 Summary

Context menus appear when a long press gesture is performed over a view in a layout. A context menu can be added to any view type and is implemented using the *contextMenu()* modifier. The menu is comprised of menu items which usually take the form of Button views configured with an action together with a Text view and an optional Image view.

43. Basic SwiftUI Graphics Drawing

The goal of this chapter is to introduce SwiftUI 2D drawing techniques. In addition to a group of built-in shape and gradient drawing options, SwiftUI also allows custom drawing to be performed by creating entirely new views that conform to the Shape and Path protocols.

43.1 Creating the DrawDemo Project

Launch Xcode and select the option to create a new Multiplatform App named *DrawDemo*.

43.2 SwiftUI Shapes

SwiftUI includes a set of five pre-defined shapes that conform to the Shape protocol which can be used to draw circles, rectangles, rounded rectangles, and ellipses. Within the DrawDemo project, open the *ContentView.swift* file and add a single rectangle:

```
struct ContentView: View {
    var body: some View {
        Rectangle()
}
```

By default, a shape will occupy all the space available to it within the containing view and will be filled with the foreground color of the parent view (by default this will be black). Within the preview canvas, a black rectangle will fill the entire safe area of the screen.

The color and size of the shape may be adjusted using the *fill()* modifier and by wrapping it in a frame. Delete the Rectangle view and replace it with the declaration which draws a red-filled 200x200 circle:

```
Circle()
    .fill(.red)
    .frame(width: 200, height: 200)
```

When previewed, the above circle will appear, as illustrated in Figure 43-1:

Figure 43-1

Basic SwiftUI Graphics Drawing

To draw an unfilled shape with a stroked outline, the *stroke()* modifier can be applied, passing through an optional line width value. By default, a stroked shape will be drawn using the default foreground color which may be altered using the *foregroundColor()* modifier. Remaining in the *ContentView.swift* file, replace the circle with the following:

```
Capsule()
    .stroke(lineWidth: 10)
    .foregroundColor(.blue)
    .frame(width: 200, height: 100)
```

Note that the frame for the above Capsule shape is rectangular. A Capsule contained in a square frame simply draws a circle. The above capsule declaration appears as follows when rendered:

Figure 43-2

The stroke modifier also supports different style types using a StrokeStyle instance. The following declaration, for example, draws a rounded rectangle using a dashed line:

```
RoundedRectangle(cornerRadius: CGFloat(20))
    .stroke(style: StrokeStyle(lineWidth: 8, dash: [CGFloat(10)]))
    .foregroundColor(.blue)
    .frame(width: 200, height: 100)
```

The above shape will be rendered as follows:

Figure 43-3

By providing additional dash values to a *StrokeStyle()* instance and adding a dash phase value, a range of different dash effects can be achieved, for example:

```
Ellipse()
    .stroke(style: StrokeStyle(lineWidth: 20,
```

```
        dash: [CGFloat(10), CGFloat(5), CGFloat(2)],
        dashPhase: CGFloat(10)))
.foregroundColor(.blue)
.frame(width: 250, height: 150)
```

When run or previewed, the above declaration will draw the following ellipse:

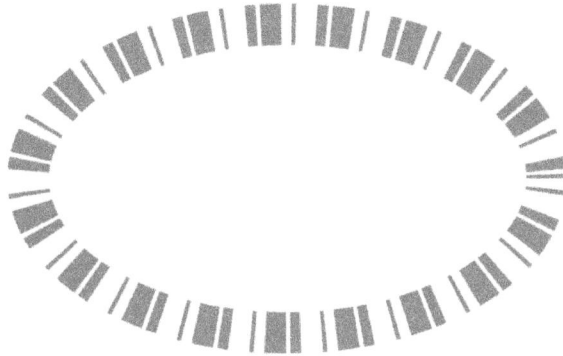

Figure 43-4

43.3 Using Overlays

When drawing a shape, it is not possible to combine the fill and stroke modifiers to render a filled shape with a stroked outline. This effect can, however, be achieved by overlaying a stroked view on top of the filled shape, for example:

```
Ellipse()
    .fill(.red)
    .overlay(Ellipse()
        .stroke(.blue, lineWidth: 10))
    .frame(width: 250, height: 150)
```

The above example draws a red-filled ellipse with a blue stroked outline, as illustrated in Figure 43-5:

Figure 43-5

43.4 Drawing Custom Paths and Shapes

The shapes used so far in this chapter are essentially structure objects that conform to the Shape protocol. To conform with the shape protocol, a structure must implement a function named *path()* which accepts a rectangle in the form of a CGRect value and returns a Path object that defines what is to be drawn in that rectangle.

A Path instance provides the outline of a 2D shape by specifying coordinate points and defining the lines drawn between those points. Lines between points in a path can be drawn using straight lines, cubic and quadratic Bézier curves, arcs, ellipses, and rectangles.

In addition to being used in a custom shape implementation, paths may also be drawn directly within a view. Try modifying the *ContentView.swift* file so that it reads as follows:

```
struct ContentView: View {
    var body: some View {
        Path { path in
            path.move(to: CGPoint(x: 10, y: 0))
            path.addLine(to: CGPoint(x: 10, y: 350))
            path.addLine(to: CGPoint(x: 300, y: 300))
            path.closeSubpath()
        }
    }
}
```

A path begins with the coordinates of the start point using the *move()* method. Methods are then called to add additional lines between coordinates. In this case, the *addLine()* method is used to add straight lines. Lines may be drawn in a path using the following methods. In each case, the drawing starts at the current point in the path and ends at the specified endpoint:

- **addArc** – Adds an arc based on radius and angle values.

- **addCurve** – Adds a cubic Bézier curve using the provided end and control points.

- **addLine** – Adds a straight line ending at the specified point.

- **addLines** – Adds straight lines between the provided array of endpoints.

- **addQuadCurve** – Adds a quadratic Bézier curve using the specified control and endpoints.

- **closeSubPath** – Closes the path by connecting the endpoint to the start point.

A full listing of the line drawing methods and supported arguments can be found online at:

https://developer.apple.com/documentation/swiftui/path

When rendered in the preview canvas, the above path will appear, as shown in Figure 43-6:

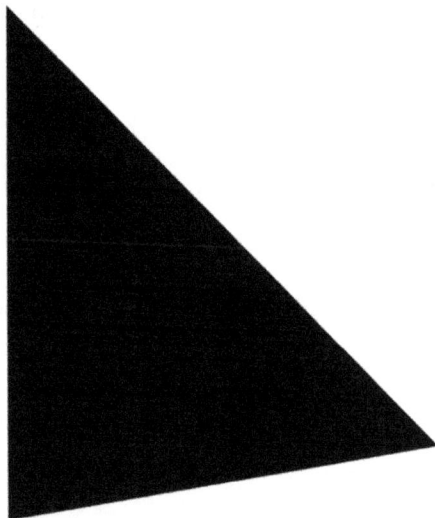

Figure 43-6

The custom drawing may also be adapted by applying modifiers, for example with a green fill color:

```
Path { path in
    path.move(to: CGPoint(x: 10, y: 0))
    path.addLine(to: CGPoint(x: 10, y: 350))
    path.addLine(to: CGPoint(x: 300, y: 300))
    path.closeSubpath()
}
.fill(.green)
```

Although it is possible to draw directly within a view, it generally makes more sense to implement custom shapes as reusable components. Within the *ContentView.swift* file, implement a custom shape as follows:

```
struct MyShape: Shape {
    func path(in rect: CGRect) -> Path {
        var path = Path()

        path.move(to: CGPoint(x: rect.minX, y: rect.minY))
        path.addQuadCurve(to: CGPoint(x: rect.minX, y: rect.maxY),
            control: CGPoint(x: rect.midX, y: rect.midY))
        path.addLine(to: CGPoint(x: rect.minX, y: rect.maxY))
        path.addLine(to: CGPoint(x: rect.maxX, y: rect.maxY))
        path.closeSubpath()
        return path
    }
}
```

The custom shape structure conforms to the Shape protocol by implementing the required *path()* function. The CGRect value passed to the function is used to define the boundaries into which a triangle shape is drawn, with one of the sides drawn using a quadratic curve.

Now that the custom shape has been declared, it can be used in the same way as the built-in SwiftUI shapes, including the use of modifiers. To see this in action, change the body of the main view to read as follows:

```
struct ContentView: View {
    var body: some View {
        MyShape()
            .fill(.red)
            .frame(width: 360, height: 350)
    }
}
```

When rendered, the custom shape will appear in the designated frame, as illustrated in Figure 43-7 below:

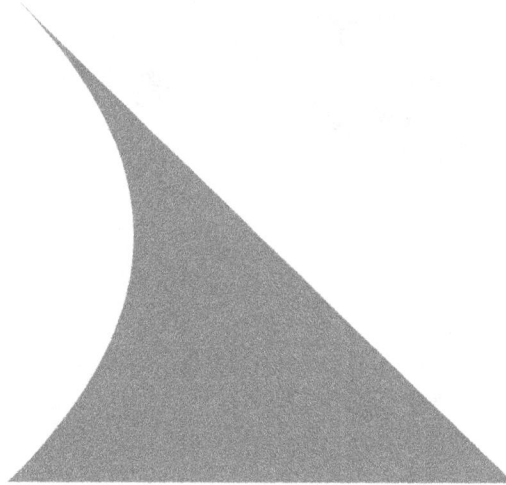

Figure 43-7

43.5 Color Mixing

The examples used so far in this chapter have used single-color values. Different colors can be created by combining existing colors using the *.mix()* modifier, providing the color to be mixed and the mixing percentage (expressed as a value between 0 and 1).

The following example mixes red with 50% blue:

```
Circle()
    .fill(.red.mix(with: .blue, by: 0.5))
    .frame(width: 200, height: 200)
```

For more complex color results, *.mix()* modifier calls can be chained, as follows:

```
.red.mix(with: .blue, by: 1).mix(with: .green, by: 0.7)
```

Mixed colors may be rendered using the perceptual or device color space. The perceptual color space is the default setting and should provide more consistent color rendering between devices. It is also considered to be attuned to human color perceptions. The following example switches a color mix to the device color space:

```
Circle()
    .fill(.red.mix(with: .blue, by: 0.5, in: .device))
    .frame(width: 200, height: 200)
}
```

The perceptual and device color spaces can result in significant color differences, so experiment to arrive at your preferred results.

43.6 Color Gradients and Shadows

A standard gradient effect can be added to any color choice by applying *.gradient* to the color declaration, for example:

```
Circle()
    .fill(.blue.gradient)
    .frame(width: 200, height: 200)
```

Similarly, shadow effects can be applied to color renderings using the *shadow()*, *drop()*, and *inner()* modifiers. The following example applies a drop shadow effect to a blue circle using black as the shadow color and a radius of 10 points:

```
Circle()
    .fill(.blue.shadow(.drop(color: .black, radius: 10)))
    .frame(width: 200, height: 200)
```

The following example, on the other hand, draws a white inner shadow on a black circle using a 15-point radius:

```
Circle()
    .fill(.blue.shadow(.inner(color: .white, radius: 15)))
    .frame(width: 200, height: 200)
```

Figure 43-8 illustrates how these effects appear when rendered on the screen:

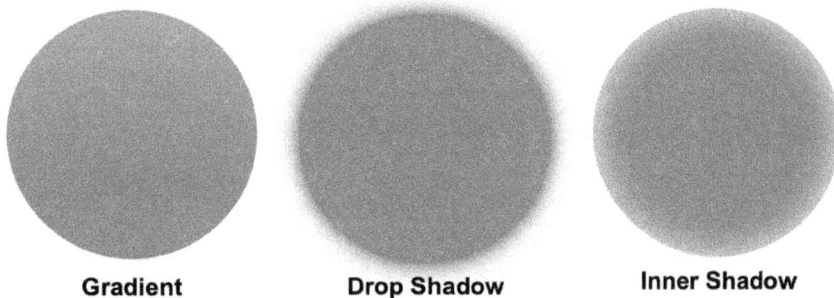

Gradient   **Drop Shadow**   **Inner Shadow**

Figure 43-8

43.7 Drawing Gradients

For more advanced requirements, SwiftUI provides support for drawing gradients including linear, angular (conic), and radial gradients. In each case, the gradient is provided with a Gradient object initialized with an array of colors to be included in the gradient and values that control how the gradient is rendered.

The following declaration, for example, generates a radial gradient consisting of five colors applied as the fill pattern for a Circle:

```
struct ContentView: View {

    let colors = Gradient(colors: [Color.red, Color.yellow, Color.green,
                        Color.blue, Color.purple, Color.orange, Color.pink])

    var body: some View {
```

```
    Circle()
        .fill(RadialGradient(gradient: colors,
              center: .center,
              startRadius: CGFloat(0),
              endRadius: CGFloat(300)))
    }
}
```

When rendered the above gradient will appear as follows:

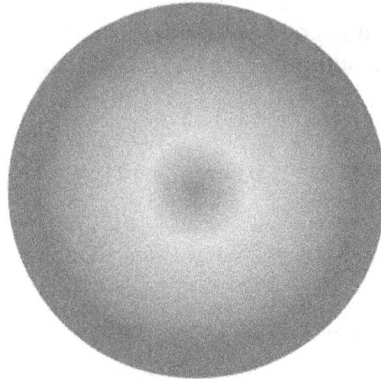

Figure 43-9

The following declaration, on the other hand, generates an angular gradient with the same color range:

```
Circle()
    .fill(AngularGradient(gradient: colors, center: .center))
```

The angular gradient will appear, as illustrated in the following figure:

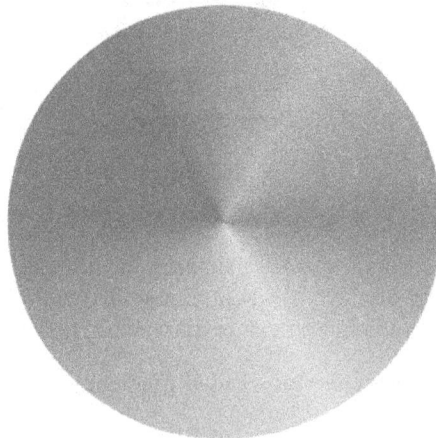

Figure 43-10

Similarly, a LinearGradient running diagonally would be implemented as follows:

```
Rectangle()
    .fill(LinearGradient(gradient: colors,
              startPoint: .topLeading,
```

```
                       endPoint: .bottomTrailing))
    .frame(width: 360, height: 350)
```

The above linear gradient will be rendered as follows:

Figure 43-11

We can also apply gradients for the fill and background modifiers for our MyShape instance as follows:

```
MyShape()
    .fill(RadialGradient(gradient: colors,
                      center: .center,
                 startRadius: CGFloat(0),
                   endRadius: CGFloat(300)))
    .background(LinearGradient(gradient: Gradient(colors:
                         [Color.black, Color.white]),
                 startPoint: .topLeading,
                   endPoint: .bottomTrailing))
    .frame(width: 360, height: 350)
```

With the gradients added, the MyShape rendering should match the figure below:

Figure 43-12

43.8 Mesh Gradients

The MeshGradient view divides an area into a grid and renders color gradients relative to each grid cell based on the position of control points. The control points can be specified as x and y coordinates or as Floating-point SIMD2 vectors. SIMD2 vectors define positions along the x and y axes as percentages expressed as values between 0 and 1. For example, the top-left corner of a grid cell is [0, 0], the bottom-right is [1,1], and the center is [0.5, 0.5].

Behind the scenes, MeshGradient performs complex calculations using Bezier and cubic curves, vertices, and tiling to render the gradients. The following code renders a 3 x 3 grid using the MeshGradient view:

```
MeshGradient(
    width: 3,
    height: 3,
    points: [
        [0, 0], [0.5 ,0], [1, 0],
        [0, 0.5], [0.5, 0.5], [1, 0.5],
        [0, 1], [0.5, 1], [1, 1]
    ],
    colors: [
        .red, .green, .pink,
        .orange, .cyan, .purple,
        .yellow, .green, .mint
    ]
)
```

The above gradient will appear as illustrated in Figure 43-13 below:

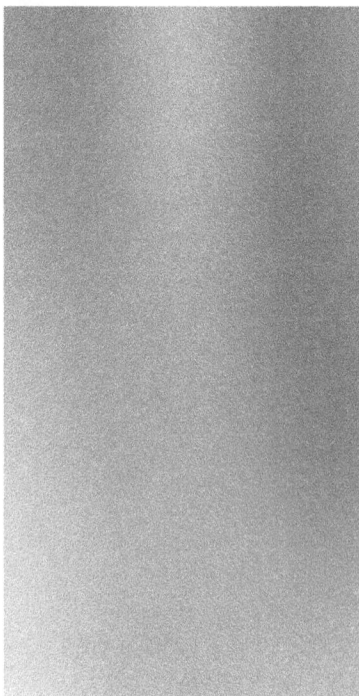

Figure 43-13

In addition to static gradients like the one above, animated mesh gradients can be created by changing the control points and colors. The following changes to our example mesh gradient add a Slider control that adjusts several of the control points and animates the resulting gradient changes:

```
@State private var x: Float = 0

.

.

    VStack {
        MeshGradient(
            width: 3,
            height: 3,
            points: [
                [0, 0], [0.5 + (x / 2) ,0], [1, 0],
                [0, 0.5], [x + 1 / 2, 0.5 - (x / 2)], [1, 0.5],
                [0, 1], [0.5, 1], [1, 1]
            ],
            colors: [
                .red, .green, .pink,
                .orange, .cyan, .purple,
                .yellow, .green, .mint
            ]
        )

        Slider(value: $x.animation(.linear(duration: 5)),
                            in: -0.2...0.3)
    }

.

.
```

43.9 Take the Knowledge Test

Click the link below or scan the QR code to test your knowledge and understanding of SwiftUI graphics drawing:

https://www.answertopia.com/9oe5

43.10 Summary

SwiftUI includes a built-in set of views that conform to the Shape protocol for drawing standard shapes such as rectangles, circles, and ellipses. Modifiers can be applied to these views to control stroke, fill, and color properties.

Custom shapes are created by specifying paths that consist of sets of points joined by straight or curved lines. SwiftUI also supports drawing radial, linear, and angular gradient patterns and advanced dynamic mesh-based gradients.

44. SwiftUI Animation and Transitions

This chapter will provide an overview and examples of animating views and implementing transitions within a SwiftUI app. Animation can take various forms, including the rotation, scaling, and motion of a view on the screen.

Transitions, on the other hand, define how a view will appear as it is added to or removed from a layout, for example, whether a view slides into place when it is added, or shrinks from view when it is removed.

44.1 Creating the AnimationDemo Example Project

To try out the examples in this chapter, create a new Multiplatform App Xcode project named *AnimationDemo*.

44.2 Implicit Animation

Many of the built-in view types included with SwiftUI contain properties that control the appearance of the view such as scale, opacity, color, and rotation angle. Properties of this type are *animatable*, in that the change from one property state to another can be animated instead of occurring instantly. One way to animate these changes to a view is to use the *animation()* modifier (a concept referred to as *implicit animation* because the animation is implied for any modifiers applied to the view that precede the animation modifier).

To experience basic animation using this technique, modify the *ContentView.swift* file in the AnimationDemo project so that it contains a Button view configured to rotate in 60-degree increments each time it is tapped:

```
struct ContentView : View {

    @State private var rotation: Double = 0

    var body: some View {
        Button(action: {
            self.rotation =
                (self.rotation < 360 ? self.rotation + 60 : 0)
        }) {
        Text("Click to animate")
            .rotationEffect(.degrees(rotation))
        }
    }
}
```

When tested using Live Preview, each click causes the Button view to rotate as expected, but the rotation is immediate. Similarly, when the rotation reaches a full 360 degrees, the view rotates counter-clockwise 360 degrees, but so quickly the effect is not visible. These effects can be slowed down and smoothed out by adding the *animation()* modifier with an optional animation curve to control the timing of the animation:

```
var body: some View {
```

```
    Button(action: {
        self.rotation =
                (self.rotation < 360 ? self.rotation + 60 : 0)
    }) {
        Text("Click to Animate")
            .rotationEffect(.degrees(rotation))
            .animation(.linear, value: rotation)
    }
}
```

The optional animation curve defines the linearity of the animation timeline. This setting controls whether the animation is performed at a constant speed or whether it starts slow and speeds up. SwiftUI provides the following basic animation curves:

- **linear** – The animation is performed at a constant speed for the specified duration and is the option declared in the above code example.

- **easeOut** – The animation starts fast and slows as the end of the sequence approaches.

- **easeIn** – The animation sequence starts slow and speeds up as the end approaches.

- **easeInOut** – The animation starts slow, speeds up, and then slows down again.

The value parameter tells the animation function which value is being used to control the animation which, in this case, is our *rotation* variable.

Preview the animation once again and note that the rotation now animates smoothly. When defining an animation, the duration may also be specified. Change the animation modifier so that it reads as follows:

```
.animation(.linear(duration: 1), value: rotation)
```

Now the animation will be performed more slowly each time the Button is clicked.

As previously mentioned, an animation can apply to more than one modifier. The following changes, for example, animate both rotation and scaling effects:

```
.
.
@State private var scale: CGFloat = 1

var body: some View {
    Button(action: {
        self.rotation =
                (self.rotation < 360 ? self.rotation + 60 : 0)
        self.scale = (self.scale < 2.8 ? self.scale + 0.3 : 1)
    }) {
        Text("Click to Animate")
            .scaleEffect(scale)
            .rotationEffect(.degrees(rotation))
            .animation(.linear(duration: 1), value: rotation)
    }
}
```

These changes will cause the button to increase in size with each rotation, then scale back to its original size during the return rotation.

Figure 44-1

A variety of spring effects may also be added to the animation using the *spring()* modifier, for example:

```
Text("Click to Animate")
    .scaleEffect(scale)
    .rotationEffect(.degrees(rotation))
    .animation(.spring(response: 1, dampingFraction: 0.2, blendDuration: 0),
                    value: rotation)
```

This will cause the rotation and scale effects to go slightly beyond the designated setting, then bounce back and forth before coming to rest at the target angle and scale.

When working with the *animation()* modifier, it is important to be aware that the animation is only implicit for modifiers that are applied before the animation modifier itself. In the following implementation, for example, only the rotation effect is animated since the scale effect is applied after the animation modifier:

```
Text("Click to Animate")
    .rotationEffect(.degrees(rotation))
    .scaleEffect(scale)
    .animation(.spring(response: 1, dampingFraction: 0.2, blendDuration: 0),
                    value: rotation)
    .scaleEffect(scale)
```

44.3 Repeating an Animation

By default, an animation will be performed once each time it is initiated. An animation may, however, be configured to repeat one or more times. In the following example, the animation is configured to repeat a specific number of times:

```
.animation(Animation.linear(duration: 1).repeatCount(10), value: rotation)
```

Each time an animation repeats, it will perform the animation in reverse as the view returns to its original state. If the view is required to instantly revert to its original appearance before repeating the animation, the autoreverses parameter must be set to false:

```
.animation(Animation.linear(duration: 1).repeatCount(10,
        autoreverses: false), value: rotation)
```

An animation may also be configured to repeat indefinitely using the *repeatForever()* modifier as follows:

```
.repeatForever(autoreverses: true))
```

44.4 Explicit Animation

As previously discussed, implicit animation using the *animation()* modifier implements animation on any of the animatable properties on a view that appear before the animation modifier. SwiftUI provides an alternative approach referred to as *explicit animation* which is implemented using the *withAnimation()* closure. When using explicit animation, only the property changes that take place within the *withAnimation()* closure will be animated. To experience this in action, modify the example so that the rotation effect is performed within a *withAnimation()* closure and remove the *animation()* modifier:

```
var body: some View {
    Button(action: { withAnimation(.linear (duration: 2)) {
            self.rotation =
                (self.rotation < 360 ? self.rotation + 60 : 0)
        }
        self.scale = (self.scale < 2.8 ? self.scale + 0.3 : 1)
    }) {

    Text("Click to Animate")
        .rotationEffect(.degrees(rotation))
        .scaleEffect(scale)
        .animation(.linear(duration: 1), value: rotation)
    }
}
```

With the changes made, preview the layout and note that only the rotation is now animated and that the changes to the scale of the text occur instantly. By using explicit animation, animation can be limited to specific properties of a view without having to worry about the ordering of modifiers.

Explicit animation is also useful for quickly adding basic animation effects to changes in state. Simple animation effects are easily added to an app with just a call to *withAnimation()*. The following changes to the *ContentView.swift* file, for example, animate the foreground color change of a circle each time it is tapped:

```
struct ContentView: View {
    .
    .
    @State private var redCircle = false

    var body: some View {
        Circle()
            .fill(redCircle ? .red : .blue)
            .frame(width: 200, height: 200)
                .onTapGesture {
                    withAnimation {
                        redCircle.toggle()
                    }
                }
    }
}
```

44.5 Animation and State Bindings

Animations may also be applied to state property bindings such that any view changes that occur as a result of that state value changing will be animated. If the state of a Toggle view causes one or more other views to become visible to the user, for example, applying an animation to the binding will cause the appearance and disappearance of all those views to be animated.

Within the *ContentView.swift* file, implement the following layout which consists of a VStack, Toggle view, and two Text views. The Toggle view is bound to a state property named *visible*, the value of which is used to control which of the two Text views is visible at one time:

```
.
.
@State private var visibility = false

var body: some View {
    VStack {
        Toggle(isOn: $visibility) {
            Text("Toggle Text Views")
        }
        .padding()

        if visibility {
            Text("Hello World")
                .font(.largeTitle)
        }

        if !visibility {
            Text("Goodbye World")
                .font(.largeTitle)
        }
    }
}
.
.
```

When previewed, switching the toggle on and off will cause one or other of the Text views to appear instantly. To add an animation to this change, simply apply a modifier to the state binding as follows:

```
.
.
var body: some View {
    VStack {
        Toggle(isOn: $visibility.animation(.linear(duration: 5))) {
            Text("Toggle Text Views")
        }
        .padding()
.
.
```

Now when the toggle is switched, one Text view will gradually fade from view as the other gradually fades in. The same animation will also be applied to any other views in the layout where the appearance changes as a result of the current state of the *visibility* property.

44.6 Automatically Starting an Animation

So far in this chapter, all the animations have been triggered by an event such as a button click. Often an animation will need to start without user interaction, for example when a view is first displayed to the user. Since an animation is triggered each time an animatable property of a view changes, this can be used to automatically start an animation when a view appears.

To see this technique in action, modify the example *ContentView.swift* file as follows:

```
struct ContentView : View {

    @State private var rotation: Double = 0

    var body: some View {

        ZStack {
            Circle()
                .stroke(lineWidth: 2)
                .foregroundColor(Color.blue)
                .frame(width: 360, height: 360)

            Image(systemName: "forward.fill")
                .font(.largeTitle)
                .offset(y: -180)
        }
    }
}
```

The content view uses a ZStack to overlay an Image view over a circle drawing where the offset of the Image view has been adjusted to position the image on the circumference of the circle. When previewed, the view should match that shown in Figure 44-2:

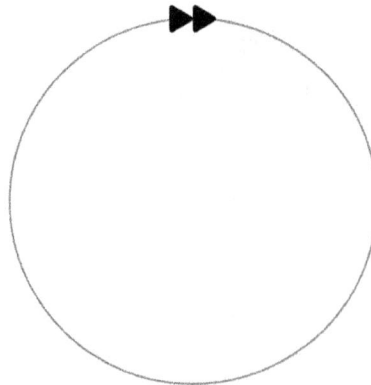

Figure 44-2

Adding a rotation effect to the Image view will give the appearance that the arrows are following the circle. Add this effect and an animation to the Image view as follows:

```
Image(systemName: "forward.fill")
    .font(.largeTitle)
    .offset(y: -180)
    .rotationEffect(.degrees(rotation))
    .animation(Animation.linear(duration: 5)
                .repeatForever(autoreverses: false), value: rotation)
```

As currently implemented the animation will not trigger when the view is tested in a Live Preview. This is because no action is taking place to change an animatable property, thereby initiating the animation.

This can be solved by making the angle of rotation subject to a Boolean state property, and then toggling that property when the ZStack first appears via the *onAppear()* modifier. In terms of implementing this behavior for our circle example, the content view declarations need to read as follows:

```
import SwiftUI

struct ContentView : View {

    @State private var rotation: Double = 0
    @State private var isSpinning: Bool = true

    var body: some View {

        ZStack {
            Circle()
                .stroke(lineWidth: 2)
                .foregroundColor(Color.blue)
                .frame(width: 360, height: 360)

            Image(systemName: "forward.fill")
                .font(.largeTitle)
                .offset(y: -180)
                .rotationEffect(.degrees(rotation))
                .animation(Animation.linear(duration: 5)
                            .repeatForever(autoreverses: false),
                                value: rotation)
        }
        .onAppear() {
            self.isSpinning.toggle()
            rotation = isSpinning ? 0 : 360
        }
    }
}
```

When SwiftUI initializes the content view, but before it appears on the screen, the isSpinning state property will be set to false and, based on the ternary operator, the rotation angle set to zero. After the view has appeared, however, the *onAppear()* modifier will toggle the isSpinning state property to true which will, in turn, cause the ternary operator to change the rotation angle to 360 degrees. As this is an animatable property, the animation modifier will activate and animate the rotation of the Image view through 360 degrees. Since this animation has been configured to repeat indefinitely, the image will continue to move around the circle.

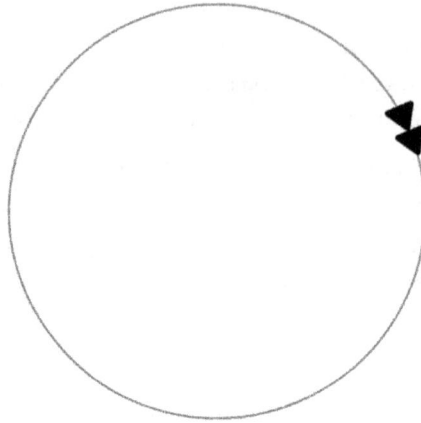

Figure 44-3

44.7 SwiftUI Transitions

A transition occurs in SwiftUI whenever a view is made visible or invisible to the user. To make this process more visually appealing than having the view instantly appear and disappear, SwiftUI allows these transitions to be animated in several ways using either individual effects or by combining multiple effects.

Begin by implementing a simple layout consisting of a Toggle button and a Text view. The toggle is bound to a state property which is then used to control whether the text view is visible. To make the transition more noticeable, animation has been applied to the state property binding:

```
struct ContentView : View {

    @State private var isButtonVisible: Bool = true

    var body: some View {
        VStack {
            Toggle(isOn: $isButtonVisible.animation(
                                    .linear(duration: 2))) {
                Text("Show/Hide Button")
            }
            .padding()

            if isButtonVisible {
                Button(action: {}) {
                    Text("Example Button")
                }
                .font(.largeTitle)
            }
        }
    }
}
```

After making the changes, use the Live Preview or a device or simulator to switch the toggle button state and note that the Text view fades in and out of view as the state changes (keeping in mind that some effects may not work in the Live Preview). This fading effect is the default transition used by SwiftUI. This default can be changed by passing a different transition to the *transition()* modifier, for which the following options are available:

- **scale** – The view increases in size as it is made visible and shrinks as it disappears.

- **slide** – The view slides in and out of view.

- **move(edge: edge)** – As the view is added or removed it does so by moving either from or toward the specified edge.

- **opacity** – The view retains its size and position while fading from view (the default transition behavior).

To configure the Text view to slide into view, change the example as follows:

```
if isButtonVisible {
    Button(action: {}) {
        Text("Example Button")
    }
    .font(.largeTitle)
    .transition(.slide)
}
```

Alternatively, the view can be made to shrink from view and then grow in size when inserted and removed:

```
.transition(.scale)
```

The *move()* transition can be used as follows to move the view toward a specified edge of the containing view. In the following example, the view moves from bottom to top when disappearing and from top to bottom when appearing:

```
.transition(.move(edge: .top))
```

When previewing the above move transition, you may have noticed that after completing the move, the Button disappears instantly. This somewhat jarring effect can be improved by combining the move with another transition.

44.8 Combining Transitions

SwiftUI transitions are combined using an instance of AnyTransition together with the *combined(with:)* method. To combine, for example, movement with opacity, a transition could be configured as follows:

```
.transition(AnyTransition.opacity.combined(with: .move(edge: .top)))
```

When the above example is implemented, the Text view will include a fading effect while moving.

To remove clutter from layout bodies and to promote re-usability, transitions can be implemented as extensions to the AnyTransition class. The above combined transition, for example, can be implemented as follows:

```
extension AnyTransition {
    static var fadeAndMove: AnyTransition {
        AnyTransition.opacity.combined(with: .move(edge: .top))
    }
}
```

When implemented as an extension, the transition can simply be passed as an argument to the *transition()* modifier, for example:

```
.transition(.fadeAndMove)
```

44.9 Asymmetrical Transitions

By default, SwiftUI will simply reverse the specified insertion transition when removing a view. To specify a different transition for adding and removing views, the transition can be declared as being asymmetric. The following transition, for example, uses the scale transition for view insertion and sliding for removal:

```
.transition(.asymmetric(insertion: .scale, removal: .slide))
```

44.10 Take the Knowledge Test

Click the link below or scan the QR code to test your knowledge and understanding of SwiftUI animation and transitions:

https://www.answertopia.com/926n

44.11 Summary

This chapter has explored the implementation of animation when changes are made to the appearance of a view. In the case of implicit animation, changes to a view caused by modifiers can be animated through the application of the *animated()* modifier. Explicit animation allows only specified properties of a view to be animated in response to appearance changes. Animation may also be applied to state property bindings such that any view changes that occur as a result of that state value changing will be animated.

A transition occurs when a view is inserted into, or removed from, a layout. SwiftUI provides several options for animating these transitions including fading, scaling, and sliding. SwiftUI also provides the ability to both combine transitions and define asymmetric transitions where different animation effects are used for insertion and removal of a view.

45. Working with Gesture Recognizers in SwiftUI

The term *gesture* is used to describe an interaction between the touch screen and the user which can be detected and used to trigger an event in the app. Drags, taps, double taps, pinching, rotation motions, and long presses are all considered to be gestures in SwiftUI.

This chapter will explore the use of SwiftUI gesture recognizers within a SwiftUI-based app.

45.1 Creating the GestureDemo Example Project

To try out the examples in this chapter, create a new Multiplatform App Xcode project named *GestureDemo*.

45.2 Basic Gestures

Gestures performed within the bounds of a view can be detected by adding a gesture recognizer to that view. SwiftUI provides recognizers for tap, long press, rotation, magnification (pinch), and drag gestures.

A gesture recognizer is added to a view using the *gesture()* modifier, passing through the gesture recognizer to be added.

In the simplest form, a recognizer will include one or more action callbacks containing the code to be executed when a matching gesture is detected on the view. The following example adds a tap gesture detector to an Image view and implements the *onEnded* callback containing the code to be performed when the gesture is completed successfully:

```
struct ContentView: View {
    var body: some View {
        Image(systemName: "hand.point.right.fill")
            .font(.largeTitle)
            .gesture(
                TapGesture()
                    .onEnded { _ in
                        print("Tapped")
                    }
            )
    }
}
```

Use Live Preview to test the above view declaration, noting the appearance of the "Tapped" message in the debug console panel in Canvas mode when the image is clicked.

When working with gesture recognizers, it is usually preferable to assign the recognizer to a variable and then reference that variable in the modifier. This makes for tidier view body declarations and encourages reuse:

```
var body: some View {
```

```
let tap = TapGesture()
            .onEnded { _ in
                print("Tapped")
            }


Image(systemName: "hand.point.right.fill")
    .font(.largeTitle)
    .gesture(tap)
}
```

When using the tap gesture recognizer, the number of taps required to complete the gesture may also be specified. The following, for example, will only detect double taps:

```
let tap = TapGesture(count: 2)
            .onEnded { _ in
                print("Double Tapped")
            }
```

The long press gesture recognizer is used in a similar way and is designed to detect when a view is touched for an extended length of time. The following declaration detects when a long press is performed on an Image view using the default time duration:

```
var body: some View {

    let longPress = LongPressGesture()
        .onEnded { _ in
            print("Long Press")
        }


    Image(systemName: "hand.point.right.fill")
        .font(.largeTitle)
        .gesture(longPress)
}
```

To adjust the duration necessary to qualify as a long press, simply pass through a minimum duration value (in seconds) to the *LongPressGesture()* call. It is also possible to specify a maximum distance from the view from which the point of contact with the screen can move outside of the view during the long press. If the touch moves beyond the specified distance, the gesture will cancel and the onEnded action will not be called:

```
let longPress = LongPressGesture(minimumDuration: 10,
                                 maximumDistance: 25)
    .onEnded { _ in
        print("Long Press")
    }
```

A gesture recognizer can be removed from a view by passing a nil value to the *gesture()* modifier:

```
.gesture(nil)
```

45.3 The onChange Action Callback

In the previous examples, the onEnded action closure was used to detect when a gesture completes. Many of the gesture recognizers (except for TapGesture) also allow the addition of an onChange action callback. The onChange callback will be called when the gesture is first recognized, and each time the underlying values of the gesture change, up until the point that the gesture ends.

The onChange action callback is particularly useful when used with gestures involving motion across the device display (as opposed to taps and long presses). The magnification gesture, for example, can be used to detect the movement of touches on the screen.

```
struct ContentView: View {

    var body: some View {

        let magnificationGesture =
                    MagnificationGesture(minimumScaleDelta: 0)
            .onEnded { _ in
                print("Gesture Ended")
            }


        Image(systemName: "hand.point.right.fill")
            .resizable()
            .font(.largeTitle)
            .gesture(magnificationGesture)
            .frame(width: 100, height: 90)
    }
}
```

The above implementation will detect a pinching motion performed over the Image view but will only report the detection after the gesture ends. Although pinch gestures can be simulated in the Live Preview by holding down the keyboard Option key while clicking in the Image view and dragging, this example works best when running on a device or simulator.

To receive notifications for the duration of the gesture, the onChanged callback action can be added:

```
let magnificationGesture =
                    MagnificationGesture(minimumScaleDelta: 0)
    .onChanged( { _ in
        print("Magnifying")
    })
    .onEnded { _ in
        print("Gesture Ended")
    }
```

Now when the gesture is detected, the onChanged action will be called each time the values associated with the pinch operation change. Each time the onChanged action is called, it will be passed a MagnificationGesture. Value instance which contains a CGFloat value representing the current scale of the magnification.

With access to this information about the magnification gesture scale, interesting effects can be implemented such as configuring the Image view to resize in response to the gesture:

```
struct ContentView: View {

    @State private var magnification: CGFloat = 1.0
```

```
    var body: some View {

        let magnificationGesture =
                MagnificationGesture(minimumScaleDelta: 0)
            .onChanged({ value in
                self.magnification = value
            })
            .onEnded({ _ in
                print("Gesture Ended")
            })

        Image(systemName: "hand.point.right.fill")
            .resizable()
            .font(.largeTitle)
            .scaleEffect(magnification)
            .gesture(magnificationGesture)
            .frame(width: 100, height: 90)
    }
}
```

45.4 The updating Callback Action

The *updating* callback action is like *onChanged* with the exception that it works with a special property wrapper named @GestureState. GestureState is like the standard @State property wrapper but is designed exclusively for use with gestures. The key difference, however, is that @GestureState properties automatically reset to the original state when the gesture ends. As such, the updating callback is ideal for storing transient state that is only needed while a gesture is being performed.

Each time an updating action is called, it is passed the following three arguments:

- DragGesture.Value instance containing information about the gesture.

- A reference to the @GestureState property to which the gesture has been bound.

- A Transaction object containing the current state of the animation corresponding to the gesture.

The DragGesture.Value instance is particularly useful and contains the following properties:

- **location (CGPoint)** - The current location of the drag gesture.

- **predictedEndLocation (CGPoint)** – Predicted final location, based on the velocity of the drag if dragging stops.

- **predictedEndTranslation (CGSize)** - A prediction of what the final translation would be if dragging stopped now based on the current drag velocity.

- **startLocation (CGPoint)** - The location at which the drag gesture started.

- **time (Date)** – The time stamp of the current drag event.

- **translation (CGSize)** - The total translation from the start of the drag gesture to the current event (essentially the offset from the start position to the current drag location).

Typically, a drag gesture updating callback will extract the translation value from the DragGesture.Value object and assign it to a @GestureState property and will typically resemble the following:

```
let drag = DragGesture()
    .updating($offset) { dragValue, state, transaction in
        state = dragValue.translation
    }
```

The following example adds a drag gesture to an Image view and then uses the updating callback to keep a @GestureState property updated with the current translation value. An *offset()* modifier is applied to the Image view using the @GestureState offset property. This has the effect of making the Image view follow the drag gesture as it moves across the screen.

```
struct ContentView: View {

    @GestureState private var offset: CGSize = .zero

    var body: some View {

        let drag = DragGesture()
            .updating($offset) { dragValue, state, transaction in
                state = dragValue.translation
            }

        Image(systemName: "hand.point.right.fill")
            .font(.largeTitle)
            .offset(offset)
            .gesture(drag)
    }
}
```

Note that once the drag gesture ends, the Image view returns to the original location. This is because the offset gesture property was automatically reverted to its original state when the drag ended.

45.5 Composing Gestures

So far in this chapter, we have looked at adding a single gesture recognizer to a view in SwiftUI. Though a less common requirement, it is also possible to combine multiple gestures and apply them to a view. Gestures can be combined so that they are detected simultaneously, in sequence, or exclusively. When gestures are composed simultaneously, both gestures must be detected at the same time for the corresponding action to be performed. In this case, if sequential gestures, the first gesture must be completed before the second gesture will be detected. For exclusive gestures, the detection of one gesture will be treated as all gestures being detected.

Gestures are composed using the *simultaneously()*, *sequenced()* and *exclusively()* modifiers. The following view declaration, for example, composes a simultaneous gesture consisting of a long press and a drag:

```
struct ContentView: View {

    @GestureState private var offset: CGSize = .zero
    @GestureState private var longPress: Bool = false

    var body: some View {
```

```
        let longPressAndDrag = LongPressGesture(minimumDuration: 1.0)
            .updating($longPress) { value, state, transition in
                state = value
            }
            .simultaneously(with: DragGesture())
            .updating($offset) { value, state, transaction in
                state = value.second?.translation ?? .zero
             }


        Image(systemName: "hand.point.right.fill")
            .foregroundColor(longPress ? Color.red : Color.blue)
            .font(.largeTitle)
            .offset(offset)
            .gesture(longPressAndDrag)
    }
}
```

In the case of the following view declaration, a sequential gesture is configured which requires the long press gesture to be completed before the drag operation can begin. When executed, the user will perform a long press on the image until it turns green, at which point the drag gesture can be used to move the image around the screen.

```
struct ContentView: View {

    @GestureState private var offset: CGSize = .zero
    @State private var dragEnabled: Bool = false

    var body: some View {

        let longPressBeforeDrag = LongPressGesture(minimumDuration: 2.0)
            .onEnded( { _ in
                self.dragEnabled = true
            })
            .sequenced(before: DragGesture())
            .updating($offset) { value, state, transaction in

                switch value {

                    case .first(true):
                        print("Long press in progress")

                    case .second(true, let drag):
                        state = drag?.translation ?? .zero

                    default: break
                }
```

```
    }
    .onEnded { value in
        self.dragEnabled = false
    }


    Image(systemName: "hand.point.right.fill")
        .foregroundColor(dragEnabled ? Color.green : Color.blue)
        .font(.largeTitle)
        .offset(offset)
        .gesture(longPressBeforeDrag)
    }
}
```

45.6 Take the Knowledge Test

Click the link below or scan the QR code to test your knowledge and understanding of SwiftUI gesture detection:

https://www.answertopia.com/2xh1

45.7 Summary

Gesture detection can be added to SwiftUI views using gesture recognizers. SwiftUI includes recognizers for drag, pinch, rotate, long press, and tap gestures. Gesture detection notification can be received from the recognizers by implementing onEnded, updated and onChange callback methods. The updating callback works with a special property wrapper named @GestureState. A GestureState property is like the standard state property wrapper but is designed exclusively for use with gestures and automatically resets to its original state when the gesture ends. Gesture recognizers may be combined so that they are recognized simultaneously, sequentially or exclusively.

46. Working with Liquid Glass

In 2025, Apple introduced a new graphical user interface theme called Liquid Glass that changes the "look and feel" of all Apple operating systems and the apps that run on them. In this chapter, we will explore some of the key Liquid Glass features and demonstrate how to apply this new design theme when working with SwiftUI.

46.1 An Overview of Liquid Glass

Liquid Glass represents the first major iOS UI design theme overhaul since the introduction of the "flat design" in 2013, and only the third since the introduction of iOS. The design goal of Liquid Glass is to present the user with a translucent, glass-like look, combined with a liquid-like fluidity in the way views morph and blend. If you have reached this chapter, then you are already familiar with the look and feel of Liquid Glass on macOS and iOS. You will also have noticed that many of the standard SwiftUI views automatically adopt the new theme without additional code changes. This chapter explores how to apply Liquid Glass effects to custom views and demonstrates features such as morphing and animated transitions.

46.2 Creating the GlassDemo Project

Start by launching Xcode and selecting the options to create a new Multiplatform App project named *GlassDemo*.

46.3 The Liquid Glass Modifier

Liquid Glass effects can be applied to custom views using the *glassEffect(_:in:)* modifier. When applied to a view, Liquid Glass draws a translucent *backdrop layer* behind the view filled with a glass-like "material" that defines characteristics such as transparency and tint. The backdrop's shape is defined by a *shape mask* provided to the *glassEffect()* modifier.

The basic outline of a *glassEffect()* modifier call is as follows:

```
.glassEffect(<Glass configuration>, in: <Shape>)
```

The first parameter in the above outline defines the appearance of the backdrop material using one of the following options from the SwiftUI Glass structure:

- **.clear** - The backdrop is rendered in its most transparent form, increasing the visibility of content behind the view.

- **.identity** - The view is rendered with no backdrop and without Liquid Glass effects.

- **.regular** - The backdrop is rendered with a more opaque, frosted appearance than the clear option.

When the glass effect is enabled, a custom view can be made interactive, allowing Liquid Glass to display additional glass effects in response to user interaction, for example:

```
.glassEffect(.interactive(true))
```

When the view is clicked or pressed, Liquid Glass provides visual feedback that includes subtle, animated changes to the size and opacity of the view and backdrop.

By default, Liquid Glass renders the view content over a *regular* backdrop. Alternatively, the color of the shape can be modified by providing a tint value to the *glassEffect()* modifier:

```
.glassEffect(.regular.tint(.red))
```

Configuration properties can be combined to apply multiple changes to the glass effects. For example:

```
.glassEffect(.regular.tint(.red).interactive())
```

The second *glassEffect()* modifier parameter defines the shape of the backdrop mask and can be any shape that conforms to the SwiftUI Shape protocol. In the following example, the shape mask is rendered as a circle:

```
.glassEffect(in: Circle())
```

Alternatively, the shape can be declared using the SwiftUI shape shorthand values:

```
.glassEffect(in: .circle)
```

In addition to the circle, SwiftUI includes shorthand values for *ellipse*, *rect*, and *capsule* backdrop shapes. In the absence of a shape parameter, the backdrop will be rendered as a capsule.

46.4 Liquid Glass Examples

Now that we have a basic understanding of Liquid Glass in the context of custom views, we can try out some examples. With the GlassDemo project open in Xcode, edit the *ContentView.swift* file and make the following changes:

```
import SwiftUI

struct ContentView: View {
    var body: some View {
        SimpleGlassView()
    }
}


struct SimpleGlassView: View {
    var body: some View {
        Label(
            title: {
                Text("Welcome to SwiftUI")
                    .font(.largeTitle)
            },
            icon: {
                Circle()
                    .fill(Color.blue)
                    .frame(width: 25, height: 25)
            }
        )
        .padding()
    }
}


#Preview {
    ContentView()
}
```

Refer to the live preview where the custom view will appear without glass effects, as shown in Figure 46-1:

● Welcome to SwiftUI

Figure 46-1

To enable glass effects using the default settings, apply the *glassEffects()* modifier to the Label view without parameters:

```
Label(
    title: {
.

.

    }
)
.padding()
.glassEffect()
```

When rendered, the view will appear as illustrated in the figure below:

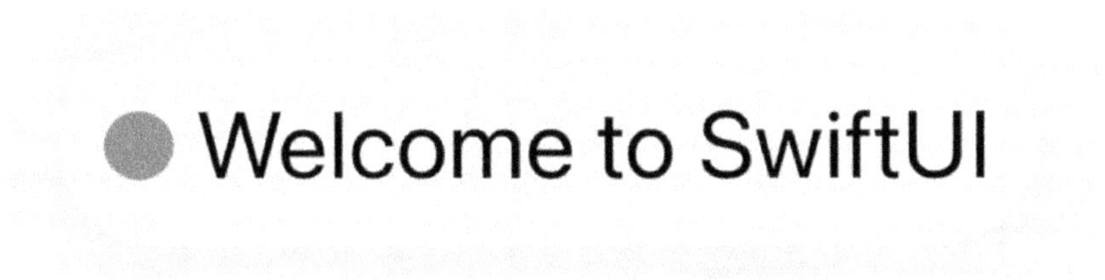

● Welcome to SwiftUI

Figure 46-2

The translucent nature of Liquid Glass becomes more apparent when the view is layered onto a colorful background. To demonstrate this, modify the ContentView declaration to embed SimpleGlassView into a ZStack and layer it over a LinearGradient background:

```
struct ContentView: View {
    var body: some View {

        ZStack {
            LinearGradient(
                colors: [.red, .orange, .yellow, .green, .mint, .blue, .purple],
                startPoint: .leading,
                endPoint: .trailing
            )
            .ignoresSafeArea()

            SimpleGlassView()
        }
    }
}
```

The view will now appear as follows:

Figure 46-3

To enhance transparency, apply the *clear* option to the modifier:

```
.glassEffect(.clear)
```

When rendered, the view will appear as shown in Figure 46-4 below, allowing more of the background color to show through the backdrop:

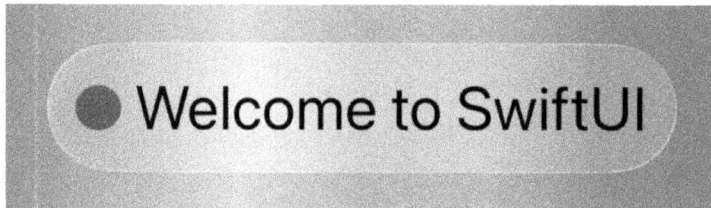

Figure 46-4

So far, the Label view backdrop has defaulted to the capsule shape. The following modifier call declares an ellipse as the backdrop shape mask:

```
.glassEffect(.clear, in: .ellipse)
```

The resulting view will appear as shown in Figure 46-5 below:

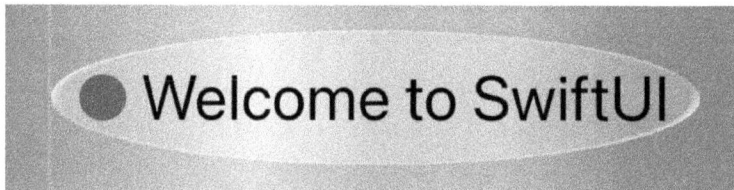

Figure 46-5

The following modifier call configures the view content to appear over a rectangular backdrop with a custom corner radius and regular material transparency:

```
.glassEffect(.regular, in: .rect(cornerRadius: 5))
```

The above change will appear as shown below:

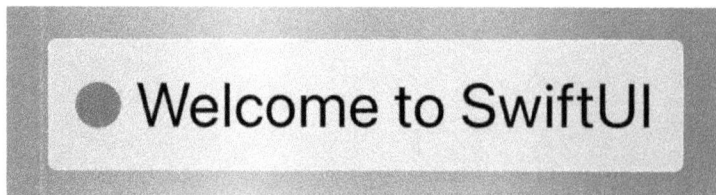

Figure 46-6

Alternatively, the color of the backdrop can be modified by passing a tint value to the *glassEffect()* modifier:

```
.glassEffect(.regular.tint(.mint))
```

When rendered, the glass material will appear with a mint colored tint:

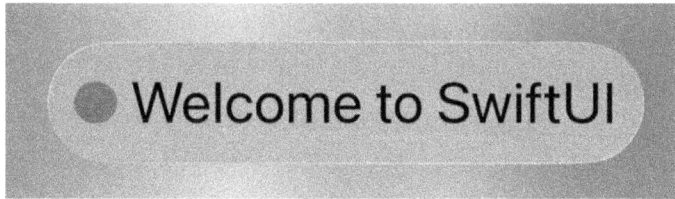

Figure 46-7

Finally, the following change adds interactive effects to the Label view using the clear material appearance:

```
.glassEffect(.clear.interactive(true))
```

Try out the interactive glass effects by clicking on the Label view in the preview canvas. This behavior is provided automatically for the Button view, but can be useful for making other view types respond to interactions.

46.5 Using the GlassEffectContainer

The GlassEffectContainer is used to group and apply glass effects to multiple views while providing additional effects such as animation and morphing views into a single backdrop shape. To experience some of GlassEffectContainer's features, edit the *ContentView.swift* file, add a view called ContainerDemoView, and call it from within the ContentView, as outlined below:

```
import SwiftUI

struct ContentView: View {
    var body: some View {

        ZStack {
            LinearGradient(
                colors: [.red, .orange, .yellow, .green, .mint, .blue, .purple],
                startPoint: .leading,
                endPoint: .trailing
            )
            .ignoresSafeArea()
            SimpleGlassView()
            ContainerDemoView()
        }
    }
}

struct ContainerDemoView: View {

    var body: some View {
        VStack(spacing: 30.0) {
            Button {
```

```
        } label: {
            Label("On", systemImage: "bolt.circle.fill")
                .labelStyle(.iconOnly)
                .font(.system(size: 34, weight: .bold))
                .padding()
        }
        .glassEffect()

        Button {

        } label: {
            Label("Off", systemImage: "bolt.slash.circle.fill")
                .labelStyle(.iconOnly)
                .font(.system(size: 34, weight: .bold))
                .padding()
        }
        .glassEffect()
        }
    }
}
```

In the above code, ContainerDemoView consists of a VStack containing two Button views configured to display icons and glass effects enabled by applying the *glassEffect()* modifier. Glass effects can also be applied to Button views using the *buttonStyle()* modifier, which can be combined with the *buttonBorderShape()* modifier to change the glass effect shape:

```
.buttonStyle(.glass)
.buttonBorderShape(.roundedRectangle(radius: 15))
```

At this point, the button views should resemble those illustrated in Figure 46-8:

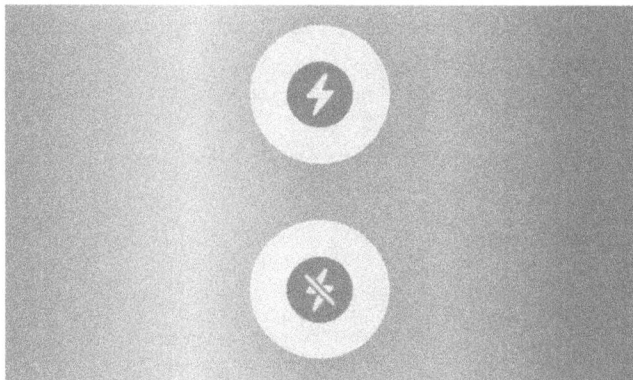

Figure 46-8

To showcase the shape blending capabilities of Liquid Glass, we will add a slider that adjusts the vertical position of the second button. The slider will be bound to a state property that, in turn, will adjust the offset of the second button along the Y-axis. Remaining in the ContainerDemoView declaration, make the following changes:

```
struct ContainerDemoView: View {
```

```
@State private var offsetY: CGFloat = 0.0

var body: some View {
    VStack(spacing: 30.0) {

        Slider(value: $offsetY, in: -100...0) {
            Text("Offset")
        }
        .padding()

        Text("Current Offset: \(offsetY, specifier: "%.0f")")
            .font(Font.largeTitle)
            .padding()
            .glassEffect(.clear)

        .
        .

        Button {

        }
        .
        .

        }
        .buttonStyle(.glass)
        .offset(x: 0.0, y: offsetY)
    }
}
}
```

Use the preview canvas to test that the slider adjusts the position of the second button, and note that the buttons overlap instead of merging as shown in Figure 46-9:

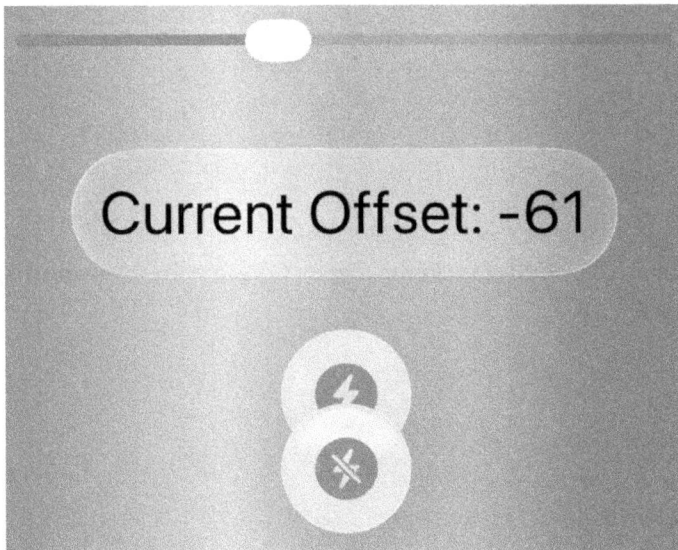

Figure 46-9

Working with Liquid Glass

To create the shape blending effect of Liquid Glass, we need to embed the VStack containing the buttons within a GlassEffectContainer as shown below:

```
struct ContainerDemoView: View {

.

.

    var body: some View {

        GlassEffectContainer(spacing: 30.0) {
            VStack(spacing: 30.0) {

.

.

                .buttonStyle(.glass)
                .offset(x: 0.0, y: offsetY)
            }
        }
    }
}
```

Figure 46-10 shows how the backdrops blend into a single shape as the proximity of the views increases:

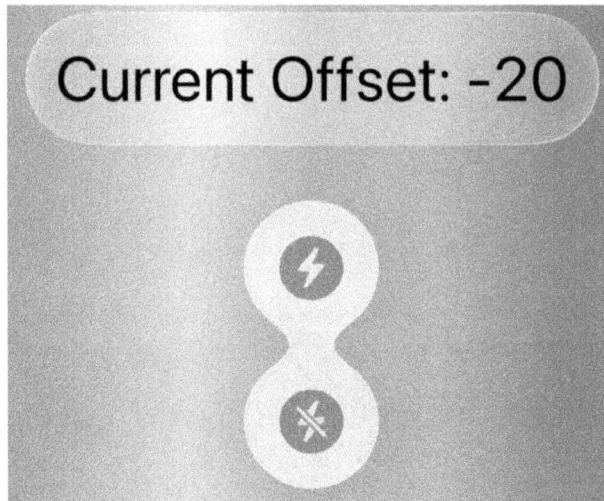

Figure 46-10

Liquid Glass can blend any combination of backdrop shapes. Consider the following shape change of the second button to a rounded rectangle:

```
Button {

} label: {
    Label("Off", systemImage: "bolt.slash.circle.fill")
        .labelStyle(.iconOnly)
        .font(.system(size: 34, weight: .bold))
        .padding()
}
```

```
.glassEffect(in: .rect(cornerRadius: 8))
.offset(x: 0.0, y: offsetY)
```

After making the change, the shapes will blend as shown below:

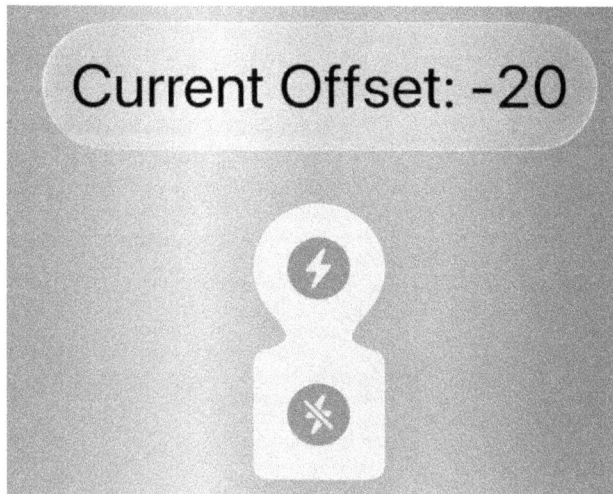

Figure 46-11

The spacing value applied to the GlassEffectContainer controls the distance between views at which the blending effect begins. The higher the spacing value, the greater the distance at which the backdrops begin morphing into a single shape. Try this effect by increasing the VStack spacing and changing the GlassEffectContainer spacing value to 100:

```
GlassEffectContainer(spacing: 100.0) {
    VStack(spacing: 50.0) {
```

Adjust the slider and note that the shapes immediately begin to blend:

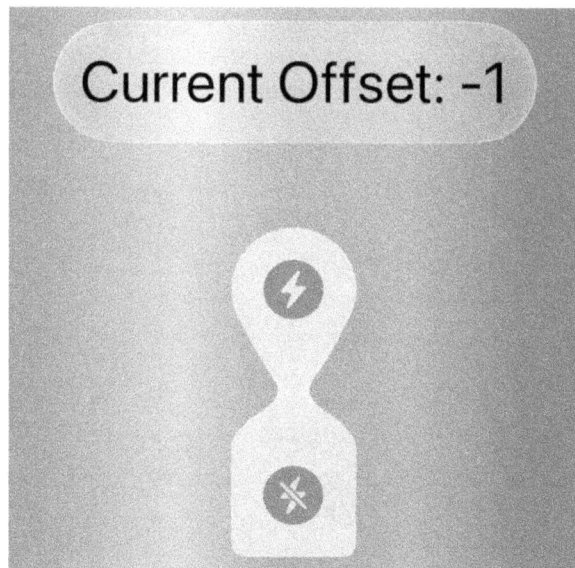

Figure 46-12

46.6 Working with Glass Effect Unions

The previous examples gradually blended backdrops based on the proximity of the views. Given enough distance, the views were represented as two separate shapes. To blend views so that they merge into a single, continuous shape, regardless of the separation distance, we must establish a seamless union between those views.

Glass effect unions are established by placing the views in a GlassEffectsContainer and applying the *glassEffectUnion()* modifier. To participate in a union, the views must be assigned matching IDs from the same namespace. Namespaces are declared using the @Namespace property wrapper and provide a way for views to share the same identity across different parts of a view hierarchy. This sharing of identity, for example, allows us to establish a union between sibling views located in separate VStack or HStack containers.

Edit the ContainerDemoView structure and make the modifications outlined below to establish a union between the two Button views:

```
struct ContainerDemoView: View {

    @State private var offsetY: CGFloat = 0.0
    @Namespace var unionNamespace

    var body: some View {
.
.
        Button {

        } label: {
            Label("On", systemImage: "bolt.circle.fill")
                .labelStyle(.iconOnly)
                .font(.system(size: 34, weight: .bold))
                .padding()
        }
        .glassEffect()
        .glassEffectUnion(id: "demoButtons", namespace: unionNamespace)

        Button {

        } label: {
            Label("Off", systemImage: "bolt.slash.circle.fill")
                .labelStyle(.iconOnly)
                .font(.system(size: 34, weight: .bold))
                .padding()
        }
        .glassEffect(in: .rect(cornerRadius: 8))
        .glassEffectUnion(id: "demoButtons", namespace: unionNamespace)
        .offset(x: 0.0, y: offsetY)
.
.
```

When previewed, the union should appear as shown in Figure 46-13 and remain a single cohesive shape regardless of the distance between the views:

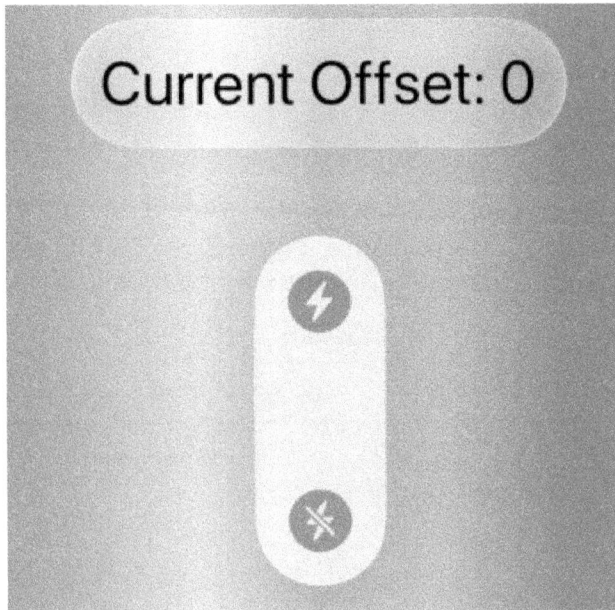

Figure 46-13

46.7 Animating Transitions

The final topic in this chapter is view transition animation in a GlassEffectContainer. As a demonstration of glass effect animation, we will add an action to the first button that toggles the visibility of the second button. To better demonstrate the animation effects, we will also remove the union modifiers and reduce the spacing properties of the GlassEffectContainer and VStack:

```
struct ContainerDemoView: View {

    @State private var offsetY: CGFloat = 0.0
    @State private var isPresented: Bool = false
    @Namespace var unionNamespace

    var body: some View {

        GlassEffectContainer(spacing: 30.0) {
            VStack(spacing: 30.0) {

.
.

                Button {
                    isPresented.toggle()
                } label: {
                    Label("On", systemImage: "bolt.circle.fill")
                        .labelStyle(.iconOnly)
                        .font(.system(size: 34, weight: .bold))
                        .padding()
                }
```

```
                .glassEffect()
                .glassEffectUnion(id: "demoButtons", namespace: unionNamespace)

        if isPresented {
            Button {

            } label: {
                Label("Off", systemImage: "bolt.slash.circle.fill")
                    .labelStyle(.iconOnly)
                    .font(.system(size: 34, weight: .bold))
                    .padding()
            }
            .glassEffect(in: .rect(cornerRadius: 8))
            .glassEffectUnion(id: "demoButtons", namespace:
                                    unionNamespace)
            .offset(x: 0.0, y: offsetY)
        }
        }
        }
    }
}
```

Preview the changes and verify that clicking the first button toggles the visibility of the second button. Next, use the *withAnimation()* function to animate the toggle action as follows:

```
Button {
    withAnimation {
        isPresented.toggle()
    }
} label: {
```

The toggle transition will now animate using the default Liquid Glass animation effects. Pass animation values to the *withAnimation()* function to apply custom effects, for example:

```
Button {
    withAnimation(.spring(response: 1, dampingFraction: 0.1, blendDuration: 0)) {
        isPresented.toggle()
    }
} label: {
```

When previewed, the second button bounces during the hide and display transitions. This effect is particularly impressive because the buttons blend together and then separate during the initial bounces, showcasing the fluidity that the designers of Liquid Glass aimed to achieve.

46.8 Take the Knowledge Test

Click the link below or scan the QR code to test your knowledge and understanding of in SwiftUI:

https://www.answertopia.com/cwca

46.9 Summary

The Liquid Glass theme, introduced in 2025, offers a translucent glass-like appearance and fluid animations. This chapter explored the application of Liquid Glass effects to custom SwiftUI views using the *glassEffect(_:in:)* modifier, allowing for various configurations such as transparency, tint, and interactivity. The GlassEffectContainer was also introduced, enabling grouping and additional effects, such as animation and morphing.

The Liquid Glass effect in SwiftUI enables the blending and merging of view backdrops based on proximity. This effect can be achieved by embedding views in a GlassEffectContainer and using the *glassEffect()* or *glassEffectUnion()* modifiers. Additionally, view transition animations within a GlassEffectContainer can be animated using the *withAnimation()* function.

47. Creating a Customized SwiftUI ProgressView

The SwiftUI ProgressView, as the name suggests, provides a way to visually indicate the progress of a task within an app. An app might, for example, need to display a progress bar while downloading a large file. This chapter will work through an example project demonstrating how to implement a ProgressView-based interface in a SwiftUI app including linear, circular, and indeterminate styles in addition to creating your own custom progress views.

47.1 ProgressView Styles

The ProgressView can be displayed in three different styles. The linear style displays progress in the form of a horizontal line, as shown in Figure 47-1 below:

Task Progress

Figure 47-1

Alternatively, progress may be displayed using the circular style, as shown in Figure 47-2:

Task Progress

Figure 47-2

Finally, for indeterminate progress, the spinning animation shown in Figure 47-3 below is used. This style is useful for indicating to the user that progress is being made on a task when the percentage of work completed is unknown.

Task Progress

Figure 47-3

As we will see later in the chapter, it is also possible to design a custom style by creating declarations conforming

Creating a Customized SwiftUI ProgressView

to the ProgressViewStyle protocol.

47.2 Creating the ProgressViewDemo Project

Launch Xcode and create a new project named *ProgressViewDemo* using the Multiplatform App template.

47.3 Adding a ProgressView

The content view for this example app will consist of a ProgressView and a Slider. The Slider view will serve as a way to change the value of a State property variable, such that changes to the slider position will be reflected by the ProgressView.

Edit the *ContentView.swift* file and modify the view as follows:

```
struct ContentView: View {

    @State private var progress: Double = 1.0

    var body: some View {

        VStack {
            ProgressView("Task Progress", value: progress, total: 100)
                .progressViewStyle(LinearProgressViewStyle())
            Slider(value: $progress, in: 1...100, step: 0.1)
        }
        .padding()
    }
}
```

Note that the ProgressView is passed a string to display as the title, a value indicating the current progress, and a total used to define when the task is complete. Similarly, the Slider is configured to adjust the *progress* state property between 1 and 100 in increments of 0.1.

Use Live Preview to test the view and verify that the progress bar moves in unison with the slider:

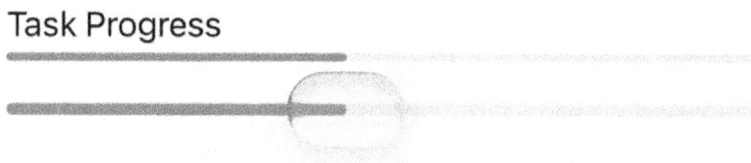

Figure 47-4

The color of the progress line may be changed using the tint argument as follows:

```
ProgressView("Task Progress", value: progress, total: 100)
    .progressViewStyle(LinearProgressViewStyle(tint: Color.red))
```

47.4 Using the Circular ProgressView Style

To display a circular ProgressView, the *progressViewStyle()* modifier needs to be called and passed an instance of CircularProgressViewStyle as follows:

```
struct ContentView: View {
```

402

```
    @State private var progress: Double = 1.0

    var body: some View {

        VStack {
            ProgressView("Task Progress", value: progress, total: 100)
                .progressViewStyle(CircularProgressViewStyle())
            Slider(value: $progress, in: 1...100, step: 0.1)
        }
        .padding()
    }
}
```

When the app is now previewed, the progress will be shown using the circular style. Note that a bug in all versions of iOS up to and including iOS 26 causes the circular style to appear using the intermediate style. This bug has been reported to Apple and will hopefully be resolved in a future release. In the meantime, the behavior can be tested by targeting macOS instead of iOS when running the app.

Although the *progressViewStyle()* modifier was applied directly to the ProgressView in the above example, it may also be applied to a container view such as VStack. When used in this way, the style will be applied to all child ProgressView instances. In the following example, therefore, all three ProgressView instances will be displayed using the circular style:

```
VStack {
    ProgressView("Task 1 Progress", value: progress, total: 100)
    ProgressView("Task 2 Progress", value: progress, total: 100)
    ProgressView("Task 3 Progress", value: progress, total: 100)
}
.progressViewStyle(CircularProgressViewStyle())
```

47.5 Declaring an Indeterminate ProgressView

The indeterminate ProgressView displays the spinning indicator shown previously in Figure 47-3 and is declared using the ProgressView without including a value binding to indicate progress:

```
ProgressView()
```

If required, text may be assigned to appear alongside the view:

```
ProgressView("Working...")
```

47.6 ProgressView Customization

The appearance of a ProgressView may be changed by declaring a structure conforming to the ProgressViewStyle protocol and passing an instance through to the *progressViewStyle()* modifier.

To conform with the ProgressViewStyle protocol, the style declaration must be structured as follows:

```
struct MyCustomProgressViewStyle: ProgressViewStyle {
    func makeBody(configuration: Configuration) -> some View {
        ProgressView(configuration)
            // Modifiers here to customize the view
    }
}
```

Creating a Customized SwiftUI ProgressView

The structure contains a *makeBody()* method which is passed the configuration information for the ProgressView on which the custom style is being applied. One option is to simply return a modified ProgressView instance. The following style, for example, applies accent color and shadow effects to the ProgressView:

```
import SwiftUI

struct ContentView: View {

    @State private var progress: Double = 1.0

    var body: some View {

        VStack {
            ProgressView("Task Progress", value: progress, total: 100)
                .progressViewStyle(ShadowProgressViewStyle())

            Slider(value: $progress, in: 1...100, step: 0.1)
        }
        .padding()
    }
}


struct ShadowProgressViewStyle: ProgressViewStyle {
    func makeBody(configuration: Configuration) -> some View {
        ProgressView(configuration)
            .accentColor(.red)
            .shadow(color: Color(red: 0, green: 0.7, blue: 0),
                    radius: 5.0, x: 2.0, y: 2.0)
            .progressViewStyle(LinearProgressViewStyle())
    }
}
.
.
```

The ProgressView will now appear with a green shadow with the progress line appearing in red. A closer inspection of the *makeBody()* method will reveal that it can return a View instance of any type, meaning that the method is not limited to returning a ProgressView instance. We could, for example, return a Text view, as shown below. The Configuration instance passed to the *makeBody()* method contains a property named fractionComplete, we can use this to display the progress percentage in the Text view:

```
.
.

        VStack {
            ProgressView("Task Progress", value: progress, total: 100)
                .progressViewStyle(MyCustomProgressViewStyle())
.
.
    }
```

```
}

struct MyCustomProgressViewStyle: ProgressViewStyle {
    func makeBody(configuration: Configuration) -> some View {
        let percent = Int(configuration.fractionCompleted! * 100)
        return  Text("Task \(percent)% Complete")
    }
}
```

When previewed, the custom style will appear, as shown in Figure 47-5:

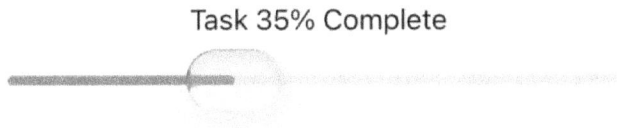

Figure 47-5

In fact, custom progress views of any level of complexity may be designed using this technique. Consider, for example, the following custom progress view implementation:

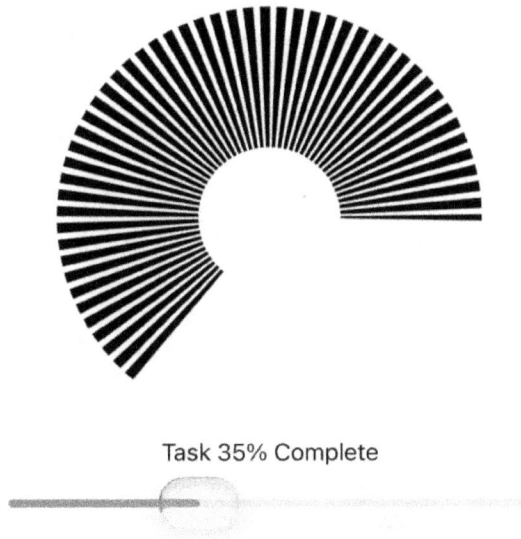

Figure 47-6

The above example was created using a Shape declaration to draw a dashed circular path based on the fractionComplete property:

```
struct MyCustomProgressViewStyle: ProgressViewStyle {
    func makeBody(configuration: Configuration) -> some View {

        let degrees = configuration.fractionCompleted! * 360
```

```
        let percent = Int(configuration.fractionCompleted! * 100)


        return VStack {

            MyCircle(startAngle: .degrees(1), endAngle: .degrees(degrees))
                .frame(width: 200, height: 200)
                .padding(50)
            Text("Task \(percent)% Complete")
        }
    }
}


struct MyCircle: Shape {
    var startAngle: Angle
    var endAngle: Angle

    func path(in rect: CGRect) -> Path {
        var path = Path()
        path.addArc(center: CGPoint(x: rect.midX, y: rect.midY),
                radius: rect.width / 2, startAngle: startAngle,
                            endAngle: endAngle, clockwise: true)

        return path.strokedPath(.init(lineWidth: 100, dash: [5, 3],
                dashPhase: 10))
    }
}
```

47.7 Take the Knowledge Test

Click the link below or scan the QR code to test your knowledge and understanding of the SwiftUI ProgresssView:

https://www.answertopia.com/15dk

47.8 Summary

The SwiftUI ProgressView provides a way for apps to visually convey to the user the progress of a long-running task such as a large download transaction. ProgressView instances may be configured to display progress either as a straight bar or using a circular style, while the indeterminate style displays a spinning icon that indicates the task is running but without providing progress information. The prevailing style is assigned using the *progressViewStyle()* modifier which may be applied either to individual ProgressView instances or all of the instances within a container view such as a VStack.

By adopting the ProgressViewStyle protocol, custom progress view designs of almost any level of complexity can be created.

48. An Overview of SwiftUI DocumentGroup Scenes

The chapter entitled *"SwiftUI Architecture"* introduced the concept of SwiftUI scenes and explained that the SwiftUI framework, in addition to allowing you to build your own scenes, also includes two pre-built scene types in the form of WindowGroup and DocumentGroup. So far, the examples in this book have made exclusive use of the WindowGroup scene. This chapter will introduce the DocumentGroup scene and explain how it can be used to build document-based apps in SwiftUI.

48.1 Documents in Apps

If you have used iOS for an appreciable amount of time, the chances are good that you will have encountered the built-in *Files* app. The Files app provides a way to browse, select and manage the Documents stored both on the local device file system and iCloud storage in addition to third-party providers such as Google Drive. Documents in this context can include just about any file type, including plain text, image, data, and binary files. Figure 48-1 shows a typical browsing session within the iOS Files app:

Figure 48-1

The purpose of the DocumentGroup scene is to allow the same capabilities provided by the Files app to be built into SwiftUI apps, in addition to the ability to create new files.

Document support can be built into an app with relatively little work. Xcode includes a project template specifically for this task which performs much of the setup work for you. Before attempting to work with DocumentGroups, however, some basic concepts first need to be covered. A good way to traverse this learning curve is to review the Document App project template generated by Xcode.

48.2 Creating the DocDemo App

Begin by launching Xcode and creating a new project using the Multiplatform Document App template option, as shown in Figure 48-2 below:

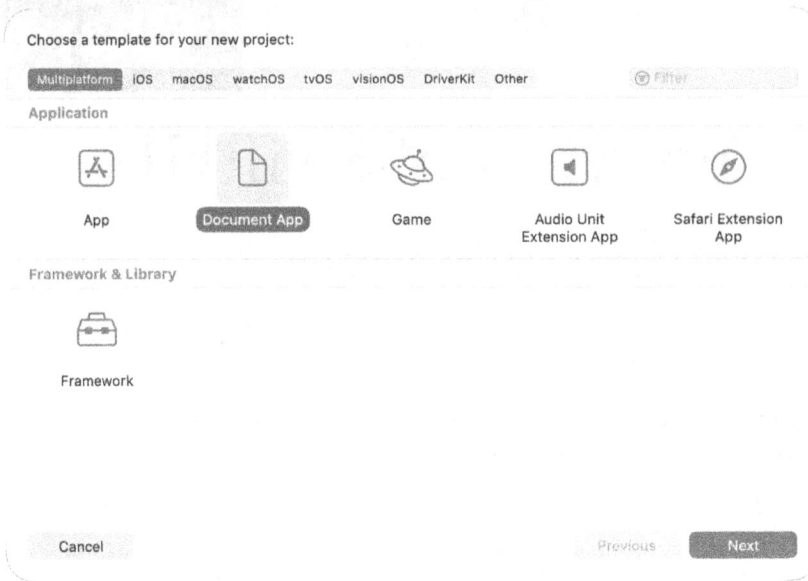

Figure 48-2

Click the Next button, name the project *DocDemo*, and save the project to a suitable location.

48.3 The DocumentGroup Scene

The DocumentGroup scene contains most of the infrastructure necessary to provide app users with the ability to create, delete, move, rename, and select files and folders from within an app. An initial document group scene is declared by Xcode within the *DocDemoApp.swift* file as follows:

```
import SwiftUI

@main
struct DocDemoApp: App {
    var body: some Scene {
        DocumentGroup(newDocument: DocDemoDocument()) { file in
            ContentView(document: file.$document)
        }
    }
}
```

As currently implemented, the first scene presented to the user when the app starts will be the DocumentGroup user interface which will resemble Figure 48-1 above. Passed through to the DocumentGroup is a DocDemoDocument instance which, along with some additional configuration settings, contains the code to create, read, and write files. When a user either selects an existing file or creates a new one, the content view is displayed and passed the DocDemoDocument instance for the selected file from which the content may be extracted and presented to the user:

```
ContentView(document: file.$document)
```

The *DocDemoDocument.swift* file generated by Xcode is designed to support plain text files and may be used as the basis for supporting other file types. Before exploring this file in detail, we first need to understand file types.

48.4 Declaring File Type Support

A key step in implementing document support is declaring the file types that the app supports. The DocumentGroup user interface uses this information to ensure that only files of supported types are selectable when browsing. A user browsing documents in an app that only supports image files, for example, would see documents of other types (such as plain text) grayed out and unselectable within the document list. This can be separated into the following components:

48.4.1 Document Content Type Identifier

Defining the types of files supported by an app begins by declaring a *document content type identifier*. This is declared using *Uniform Type Identifier* (UTI) syntax, which typically takes the form of a reverse domain name combined with a *common type identifier*. A document identifier for an app that supports plain text files, for example, might be declared as follows:

```
com.ebookfrenzy.plain-text
```

48.4.2 Handler Rank

The document content type may also declare a *handler rank* value. This value declares to the system how the app relates to the file type. If the app uses its own custom file type, this should be set to *Owner*. If the app is to be opened as the default app for files of this type, the value should be set to *Default*. If, on the other hand, the app can handle files of this type but is not intended to be the default handler, a value of *Alternate* should be used. Finally, *None* should be used if the app is not to be associated with the file type.

48.4.3 Type Identifiers

Having declared a document content type identifier, this identifier must have associated with it a list of specific data types to which it conforms. This is achieved using *type identifiers*. These type identifiers can be chosen from an extensive list of built-in types provided by Apple and are generally prefixed with "public.". For example, the UTI for a plain text document is *public.plain-text*, while that for any type of image file is *public.image*. Similarly, if an app only supports JPEG image files, the *public.jpeg* UTI would be used.

Each of the built-in UTI types has associated with it a UTType equivalent which can be used when working with types programmatically. The *public.plain-text* UTI, for example, has a UTType instance named *plainText* while the UTType instance for *public.mpeg4move* is named *mpeg4Movie*. A full list of supported UTType declarations can be found at the following URL:

https://developer.apple.com/documentation/uniformtypeidentifiers/system-declared_uniform_type_identifiers

48.4.4 Filename Extensions

In addition to declaring the type identifiers, filename extensions for which support is provided may also be specified (for example *.txt, .png, .doc, .mydata* etc.). Note that many of the built-in type identifiers are already configured to support associated file types. The *public.png* type, for example, is pre-configured to recognize *.png* filename extensions.

The extension declared here will also be appended to the filename of any new documents created by the app.

48.4.5 Custom Type Document Content Identifiers

When working with proprietary data formats (perhaps your app has its own database format), it is also possible to declare your own document content identifier without using one of the common identifiers. A document type identifier for a custom type might, therefore, be declared as follows:

```
com.ebookfrenzy.mydata
```

48.4.6 Exported vs. Imported Type Identifiers

When a built-in type is used (such as *plain.image*), it is said to be an *imported type identifier* (since it is imported into the app from the range of identifiers already known to the system). A custom type identifier, on the other hand, is described as an *exported type identifier* because it originates from within the app and is exported to the system so that the browser can recognize files of that type as being associated with the app.

48.5 Configuring File Type Support in Xcode

All of the above settings are configured within the project's *Info.plist* file. Although these changes can be made with the Xcode property list editor, a better option is to access the settings via the Xcode *Info* screen of the app target. To review the settings for the example project using this approach, select the DocDemo entry at the top of the project navigator window (marked A in Figure 48-3), followed by the DocDemo target (B) and the Info option of the menu marked C:

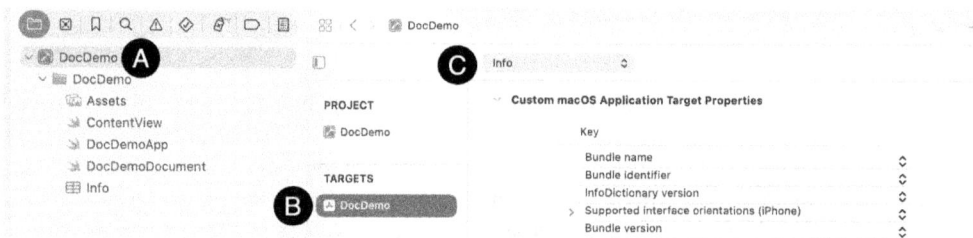

Figure 48-3

Scroll down to the *Document Types* section within the Info screen and note that Xcode has created a single document content type identifier set to *com.example.plain-text* with the handler rank set to *Default*:

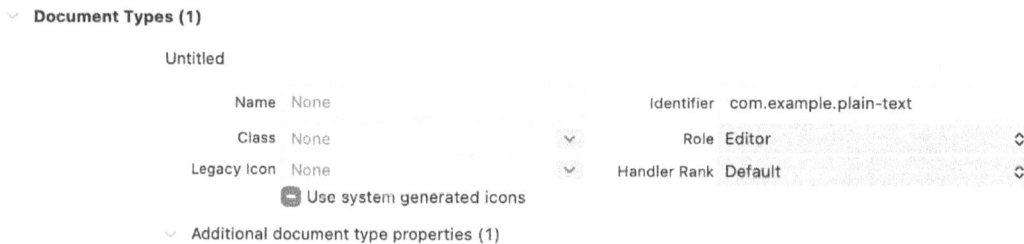

Figure 48-4

Next, scroll down to the *Imported Type Identifiers* section, where we can see that our document content type identifier (*com.example.plain-text*) has been declared as conforming to the *public.plain-text* type with a single filename extension of *exampletext*:

Figure 48-5

410

Type identifiers for custom types are declared in the *Exported Type Identifiers* section of the Info screen. For example, a binary custom file might be declared as conforming to *public.data* while the file names for this type might have a *mydata* filename extension:

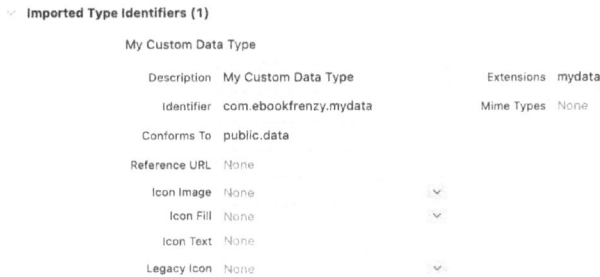

Figure 48-6

Note that in both cases, icons may be added to represent the files within the document browser user interface.

48.6 The Document Structure

When the example project was created, Xcode generated a file named *DocDemoDocument.swift*, an instance of which is passed to ContentView within the App declaration. As generated, this file reads as follows:

```
import SwiftUI
import UniformTypeIdentifiers


nonisolated struct DocDemoDocument: FileDocument {
    var text: String

    init(text: String = "Hello, world!") {
        self.text = text
    }

    static let readableContentTypes = [
        UTType(importedAs: "com.example.plain-text")
    ]


    init(configuration: ReadConfiguration) throws {
        guard let data = configuration.file.regularFileContents,
              let string = String(data: data, encoding: .utf8)
        else {
            throw CocoaError(.fileReadCorruptFile)
        }
        text = string
    }


    func fileWrapper(configuration: WriteConfiguration) throws -> FileWrapper {
        let data = text.data(using: .utf8)!
        return .init(regularFileWithContents: data)
    }
```

```
}
```

The structure is based on the FileDocument class and begins by declaring a new UTType which imports our *com.example.plain-text* identifier. This is then placed in an array called readableContentTypes to indicate which types of files can be opened by the app:

```
static let readableContentTypes = [
    UTType(importedAs: "com.example.plain-text")
]
```

The structure also includes two initializers, the first of which will be called when the creation of a new document is requested by the user and simply configures a sample text string as the initial data:

```
init(text: String = "Hello, world!") {
    self.text = text
}
```

The second initializer, on the other hand, is called when the user opens an existing document and is passed a ReadConfiguration instance:

```
init(configuration: ReadConfiguration) throws {
    guard let data = configuration.file.regularFileContents,
          let string = String(data: data, encoding: .utf8)
    else {
        throw CocoaError(.fileReadCorruptFile)
    }
    text = string
}
```

The ReadConfiguration instance holds the content of the file in Data format, which may be accessed via the regularFileContents property. Steps are then taken to decode this data and convert it to a String so that it can be displayed to the user. The exact steps to decode the data will depend on how the data was originally encoded within the *fileWrapper()* method. In this case, the method is designed to work with String data:

```
func fileWrapper(configuration: WriteConfiguration) throws -> FileWrapper {
    let data = text.data(using: .utf8)!
    return .init(regularFileWithContents: data)
}
```

The fileWrapper() method is passed a WriteConfiguration instance for the selected file and is expected to return a FileWrapper instance initialized with the data to be written. For the content to be written to the file it must first be converted to data and stored in a Data object. In this case, the text String value is simply encoded into data. The steps involved to achieve this in your own apps will depend on the type of content being stored in the document.

48.7 The Content View

As we have seen early in the chapter, the ContentView is passed an instance of the DocDemoDocument structure from within the App declaration:

```
ContentView(document: file.$document)
```

In the case of the DocDemo example, the ContentView binds to this property and references it as the content for a TextEditor view:

```
struct ContentView: View {
    @Binding var document: DocDemoDocument
```

```
var body: some View {
    TextEditor(text: $document.text)
}
```
}

When the view appears, it will display the current string assigned to the text property of the document instance, and as the user edits the text, the changes will be stored. When the user navigates back to the document browser, a call to the *fileWrapper()* method will be triggered automatically and the changes saved to the document.

48.8 Adding Navigation

Behind the scenes, the DocumentGroup uses a NavigationStack to navigate between the browser and the content views. If we were to run the DocDemo app now, we could create and edit a document, but there would be no way to return to the document browser. We can resolve this by adding a navigation title to the TextEditor view as follows:

```
import SwiftUI

struct ContentView: View {
    @Binding var document: DocDemoDocument

    var body: some View {
        TextEditor(text: $document.text)
            .navigationTitle("Edit Document")
    }
}
```

In addition to providing a back arrow to return to the browser, the navigation title includes a drop-down menu allowing the document to be renamed:

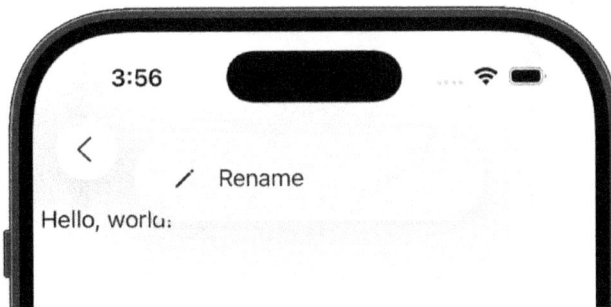

Figure 48-7

48.9 Running the Example App

Having explored the internals of the example DocDemo app, the final step is to experience the app in action. With this in mind, compile and run the app on a device or simulator and, once running, select the Browse tab located at the bottom of the screen:

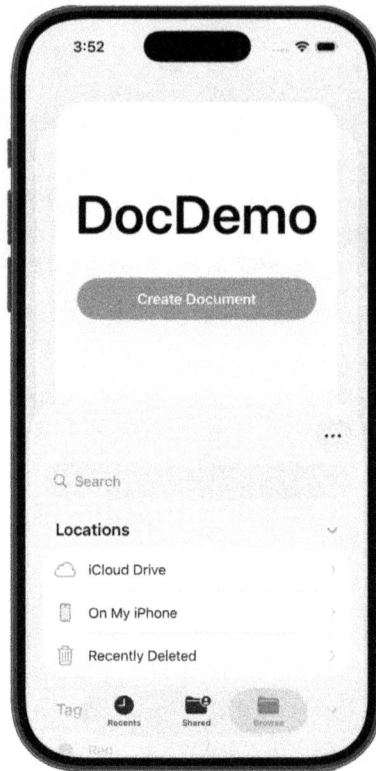

Figure 48-8

Navigate to a suitable location either on the device or within your iCloud storage and click on either the Create Document button or the Create Document entry highlighted in Figure 48-9:

Figure 48-9

The new file will be created, and the content loaded into the ContentView. Edit the sample text and return to the document browser, where the document (named *untitled*) will now be listed. Open the document once again so that it loads into the ContentView and verify that the changes were saved.

48.10 Customizing the Launch Screen

When a document-based app launches, the screen shown in Figure 48-8 appears. The screen's top section contains the app name and a button to create a new document positioned above the document browser. Extensive changes can be made to the top section of the launch screen using an instance of DocumentGroupLaunchScene, the syntax for which is as follows:

```
DocumentGroupLaunchScene("Title") {
    // Actions
} background: {

} backgroundAccessoryView: { geometry in

} overlayAccessoryView: { geometry in

}
```

The string parameter passed to DocumentGroupLaunchScene replaces the app name in the title field. To change the button text and add other buttons, insert NewDocumentButton instances into the actions closure. For example:

```
DocumentGroupLaunchScene("My Image App") {
    NewDocumentButton("Create Image")
} background: {
    .
    .
```

The background parameter is used to display an image or other view as the launcher background:

```
DocumentGroupLaunchScene("My Image App") {
    NewDocumentButton("Create Image")
} background: {
    Image(.cascadefalls)
        .resizable()
        .aspectRatio(contentMode: .fill)
}
```

The *backgroundAccessoryView* and *overlayAccessoryView* parameters allow additional views to be displayed on the launcher at positions relative to the enclosing frame or title frame (the area containing the title and button). The area of background accessory views that overlap with the title frame will be obscured, while overlay accessories will appear on top of the title frame.

The accessory view closures are passed a geometry instance from which we can obtain coordinates relative to the frame and title frame via the *.frame* and *.titleViewFrame* properties. For example, the following geometry values represent the top left-hand corner of the frame:

```
x: geometry.frame.minX,
y: geometry.frame.minY
```

Similarly, the top-right position within the title frame is referenced as follows:

```
x: geometry.titleViewFrame.maxX,
y: geometry.titleViewFrame.minY
```

The following example displays a rainbow background accessory view and two overlay views:

```
@main
struct DocDemoApp: App {
    var body: some Scene {
        DocumentGroup(newDocument: DocDemoDocument()) { file in
            ContentView(document: file.$document)
        }


        DocumentGroupLaunchScene("Image App") {
            NewDocumentButton("Create Image")
        } background: {

        } backgroundAccessoryView: { geometry in
            Image(systemName: "rainbow")
                .renderingMode(.original)
                .resizable()
                .aspectRatio(contentMode: .fit)
                .position(
                    x: geometry.titleViewFrame.midX,
                    y: geometry.titleViewFrame.minY
                )
        } overlayAccessoryView: { geometry in
            ZStack {
                Image(systemName: "paintbrush.fill")
                    .resizable()
                    .frame(width: 80, height: 80)
                    .position(
                        x: geometry.titleViewFrame.midX,
                        y: geometry.titleViewFrame.minY
                    )


                Image(systemName: "pencil.and.scribble")
                    .resizable()
                    .frame(width: 80, height: 80)
                    .position(
                        x: geometry.titleViewFrame.midX,
                        y: geometry.titleViewFrame.midY + 60
                    )

            }
        }
    }
}
```

When the app runs, the document launcher screen will resemble Figure 48-10 below:

Figure 48-10

48.11 Take the Knowledge Test

Click the link below or scan the QR code to test your knowledge and understanding of SwiftUI document-based app development:

https://www.answertopia.com/lgft

48.12 Summary

The SwiftUI DocumentGroup scene allows the document browsing and management capabilities available within the built-in Files app to be integrated into apps with relatively little effort. The core element of DocumentGroup implementation is the document declaration which acts as the interface between the document browser and views that make up the app and is responsible for encoding and decoding document content. In addition, the *Info.plist* file for the app must include information about the types of files the app can support.

49. A SwiftUI DocumentGroup Tutorial

The previous chapter introduced the DocumentGroup scene type provided with SwiftUI and explored the architecture that allows adding document browsing and management to apps.

This chapter will demonstrate how to take the standard Xcode Multiplatform Document App template and modify it to work with image files instead of plain text documents. Upon completion of the tutorial, the app will allow image files to be opened, modified using a sepia filter, and then saved back to the original file.

49.1 Creating the ImageDocDemo Project

Begin by launching Xcode and create a new project named *ImageDocDemo* using the Multiplatform Document App template.

49.2 Modifying the Info.plist File

Since the app will work with image files instead of plain text, some changes must be made to the type identifiers declared in the *Info.plist* file. To make these changes, select the ImageDocDemo entry at the top of the project navigator window (marked A in Figure 49-1), followed by the ImageDocDemo target (B), before clicking on the Info tab (C).

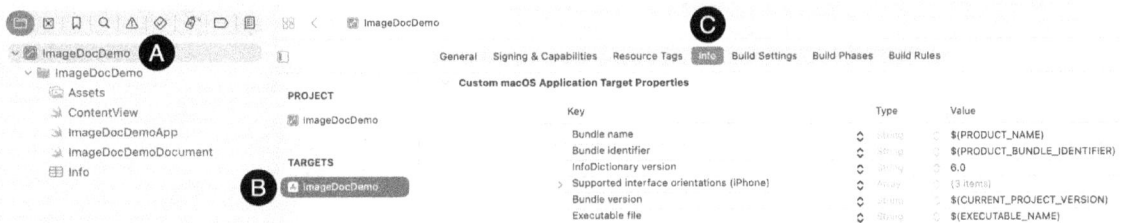

Figure 49-1

Scroll down to the *Document Types* section within the Info screen and change the *Identifier* field from com.example.plain-text to *com.payloadbooks.image*:

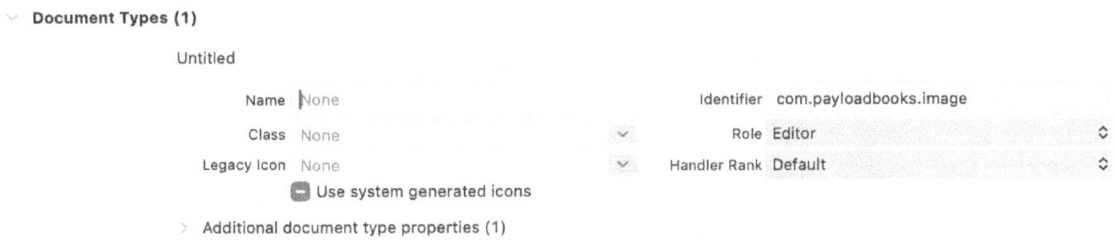

Figure 49-2

Next, locate the *Imported Type Identifiers* section and make the following changes:

- **Description** – Example Image

A SwiftUI DocumentGroup Tutorial

- **Identifier** - com.payloadbooks.image

- **Conforms To** – public.image

- **Extensions** - png

Once these changes have been made, the settings should match those shown in Figure 49-3:

Figure 49-3

49.3 Adding an Image Asset

If the user decides to create a new document instead of opening an existing one, a sample image will be displayed from the project asset catalog. For this purpose, the *cascadefalls.png* file located in the *project_images* folder of the sample code archive will be added to the asset catalog. If you do not already have the source code downloaded, it can be downloaded from the following URL:

https://www.payloadbooks.com/product/ios26code/

Once the image file has been located in a Finder window, select the *Assets* entry in the Xcode project navigator and drag and drop the image, as shown in Figure 49-4:

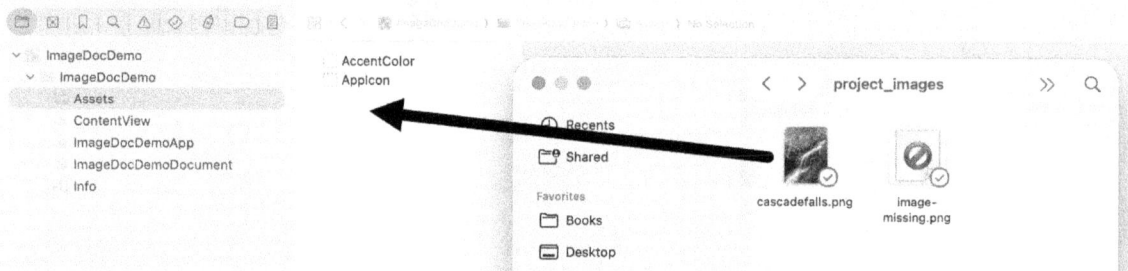

Figure 49-4

49.4 Modifying the ImageDocDemoDocument.swift File

Although we have changed the type identifiers to support images instead of plain text, the document declaration is still implemented for handling text-based content. Select the *ImageDocDemoDocument.swift* file to load it into the editor and begin by modifying the content UTType so that it reads as follows:

```
static let readableContentTypes = [
    UTType(importedAs: "com.payloadbooks.image")
]
```

The next step is to modify the structure to work with images instead of string data. Remaining in the *ImageDocDemoDocument.swift* file, change the *text* variable from a string to an image and modify the first initializer to use the *cascadefalls* image:

```
struct ImageDocDemoDocument: FileDocument {

    var text: String
    var image: UIImage = UIImage()

    init(text: String = "Hello, world!") {
        if let image = UIImage(named: "cascadefalls") {
            self.image = image
        }
    }
    .
    .
    .
```

Moving on to the second *init()* method, make the following modifications to decode image instead of string data:

```
init(configuration: ReadConfiguration) throws {
    guard let data = configuration.file.regularFileContents,
        let string = String(data: data, encoding: .utf8)
        let decodedImage: UIImage = UIImage(data: data)
    else {
        throw CocoaError(.fileReadCorruptFile)
    }
    text = string
    image = decodedImage
}
```

Finally, modify the *write()* method to encode the image to Data format so that it can be saved to the document:

```
func fileWrapper(configuration: WriteConfiguration) throws -> FileWrapper {
    let data = image.pngData()!
    return .init(regularFileWithContents: data)
}
```

49.5 Designing the Content View

Before performing some initial tests on the project so far, the content view needs to be modified to display an image instead of text content. We will also take this opportunity to add a Button view to the layout to apply the sepia filter to the image. Edit the *ContentView.swift* file and modify it so that it reads as follows:

```
import SwiftUI

struct ContentView: View {

    @Binding var document: ImageDocDemoDocument

    var body: some View {
        VStack {
            Image(uiImage: document.image)
                .resizable()
                .aspectRatio(contentMode: .fit)
```

```
                .padding()
            Button(action: {


            }, label: {
                Text("Filter Image")
            })
            .padding()
        }
        .navigationTitle("Image Editor")
    }
}
```

With the changes made, run the app on a device or simulator, use the browser to navigate to a suitable location, and then click on the Create Document button. The app will create a new image document containing the sample image from the asset catalog and then display it in the content view:

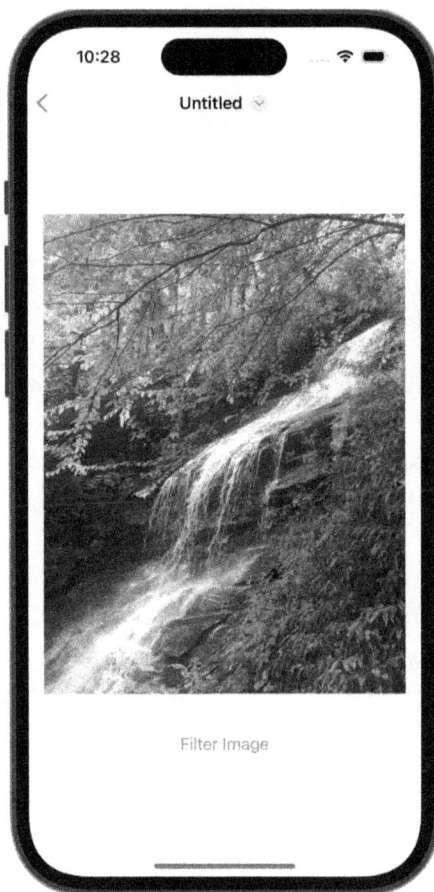

Figure 49-5

Tap the back arrow in the top left-hand corner to return to the browser, where the new document should be listed with an icon containing a thumbnail image:

Figure 49-6

49.6 Filtering the Image

The final step in this tutorial is to apply the sepia filter to the image when the Button in the content view is tapped. This will use the CoreImage Framework and involves converting the UIImage to a CIImage and applying the sepia tone filter before being converted back to a UIImage. Edit the *ContentView.swift* file and make the following changes:

```
import SwiftUI
import CoreImage
import CoreImage.CIFilterBuiltins

struct ContentView: View {

    @Binding var document: ImageDocDemoDocument
    @State private var ciFilter = CIFilter.sepiaTone()

    let context = CIContext()

    var body: some View {
        VStack {
            Image(uiImage: document.image)
                .resizable()
                .aspectRatio(contentMode: .fit)
                .padding()
            Button(action: {
                filterImage()
            }, label: {
                Text("Filter Image")
            })
            .padding()
        }
    }
```

```
func filterImage() {
    ciFilter.intensity = Float(1.0)

    let ciImage = CIImage(image: document.image)

    ciFilter.setValue(ciImage, forKey: kCIInputImageKey)

    guard let outputImage = ciFilter.outputImage else { return }

    if let cgImage = context.createCGImage(outputImage,
                                    from: outputImage.extent) {
        document.image = UIImage(cgImage: cgImage)
    }
}
}
```

49.7 Testing the App

Run the app once again and either create a new image document or select the existing image to display the content view. Within the content view, tap the Filter Image button and wait while the sepia filter is applied to the image. Tap the back arrow to return to the browser where the thumbnail image will now appear in sepia tones. Select the image to load it into the content view and verify that the sepia changes were saved to the document.

49.8 Summary

This chapter has demonstrated how to modify the Xcode Document App template to work with different content types. This involved changing the type identifiers, modifying the document declaration, and adapting the content view to handle image content.

50. An Introduction to Core Data and SwiftUI

A common requirement when developing iOS apps is to store data in some form of structured database. One option is to directly manage data using an embedded database system such as SQLite. While this is a perfectly good approach for working with SQLite in many cases, it does require knowledge of SQL and can lead to some complexity in terms of writing code and maintaining the database structure. This complexity is further compounded by the non-object-oriented nature of the SQLite API functions. In recognition of these shortcomings, Apple introduced the Core Data Framework. Core Data is essentially a framework that places a wrapper around the SQLite database (and other storage environments), enabling the developer to work with data in terms of Swift objects without requiring any knowledge of the underlying database technology.

We will begin this chapter by defining some of the concepts that comprise the Core Data model before providing an overview of the steps involved in working with this framework. Once these topics have been covered, the next chapter will work through a SwiftUI Core Data tutorial.

50.1 The Core Data Stack

Core Data consists of several framework objects that integrate to provide the data storage functionality. This stack can be visually represented, as illustrated in Figure 50-1:

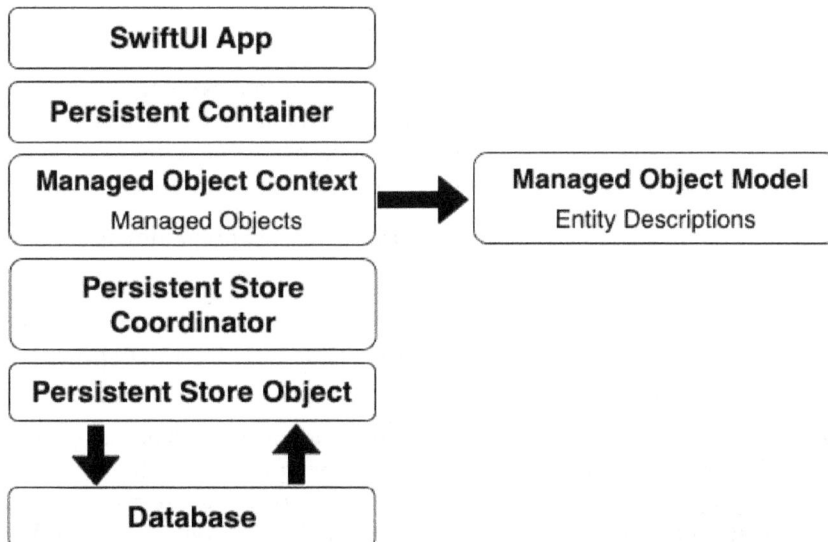

Figure 50-1

As we can see from Figure 50-1, the app sits on top of the stack and interacts with the managed data objects handled by the managed object context. Of particular significance in this diagram is the fact that although the lower levels in the stack perform a considerable amount of the work involved in providing Core Data functionality, the application code does not interact with them directly.

Before moving on to the more practical areas of working with Core Data it is important to spend some time explaining the elements that comprise the Core Data stack in a little more detail.

50.2 Persistent Container

The persistent container handles the creation of the Core Data stack and is designed to be easily subclassed to add additional application-specific methods to the base Core Data functionality. Once initialized, the persistent container instance provides access to the managed object context.

50.3 Managed Objects

Managed objects are the objects that are created by your application code to store data. A managed object may be thought of as a row or a record in a relational database table. For each new record to be added, a new managed object must be created to store the data. Similarly, retrieved data will be returned in the form of managed objects, one for each record matching the defined retrieval criteria. Managed objects are instances of the NSManagedObject class or a subclass thereof. These objects are contained and maintained by the managed object context.

50.4 Managed Object Context

Core Data-based applications never interact directly with the persistent store. Instead, the application code interacts with the managed objects contained in the managed object context layer of the Core Data stack. The context maintains the status of the objects in relation to the underlying data store and manages the relationships between managed objects defined by the managed object model. All interactions with the underlying database are held temporarily within the context until the context is instructed to save the changes, at which point the changes are passed down through the Core Data stack and written to the persistent store.

50.5 Managed Object Model

So far, we have focused on the management of data objects but have not yet looked at how the data models are defined. This is the task of the Managed Object Model, which defines a concept referred to as entities.

Much as a class description defines a blueprint for an object instance, entities define the data model for managed objects. In essence, an entity is analogous to the schema that defines a table in a relational database. As such, each entity has a set of attributes associated with it that define the data to be stored in managed objects derived from that entity. For example, a Contacts entity might contain name, address, and phone number attributes.

In addition to attributes, entities can also contain relationships, fetched properties, persistent stores, and fetch requests:

- **Relationships** – In the context of Core Data, relationships are the same as those in other relational database systems in that they refer to how one data object relates to another. Core Data relationships can be one-to-one, one-to-many, or many-to-many.

- **Fetched property** – This provides an alternative to defining relationships. Fetched properties allow properties of one data object to be accessed from another data object as though a relationship had been defined between those entities. Fetched properties lack the flexibility of relationships and are referred to by Apple's Core Data documentation as "weak, one-way relationships" best suited to "loosely coupled relationships".

- **Fetch request** – A predefined query that can be referenced to retrieve data objects based on defined predicates. For example, a fetch request can be configured into an entity to retrieve all contact objects where the name field matches "John Smith".

50.6 Persistent Store Coordinator

The persistent store coordinator is responsible for coordinating access to multiple persistent object stores. As an iOS developer, you will never directly interact with the persistent store coordinator and will very rarely need to develop an application that requires more than one persistent object store. When multiple stores are required, the coordinator presents these stores to the upper layers of the Core Data stack as a single store.

50.7 Persistent Object Store

The term persistent object store refers to the underlying storage environment in which data are stored when using Core Data. Core Data supports three disk-based and one memory-based persistent store. Disk-based options consist of SQLite, XML, and binary. By default, iOS will use SQLite as the persistent store. In practice, the type of store being used is transparent to you as the developer. Regardless of your choice of persistent store, your code will make the same calls to the same Core Data APIs to manage the data objects required by your application.

50.8 Defining an Entity Description

Entity descriptions may be defined from within the Xcode environment. When a new project is created with the option to include Core Data, a template file will be created named *<entityname>.xcdatamodeld*. Xcode also provides a way to manually add entity description files to existing projects. Selecting this file in the Xcode project navigator panel will load the model into the entity editing environment, as illustrated in Figure 50-2:

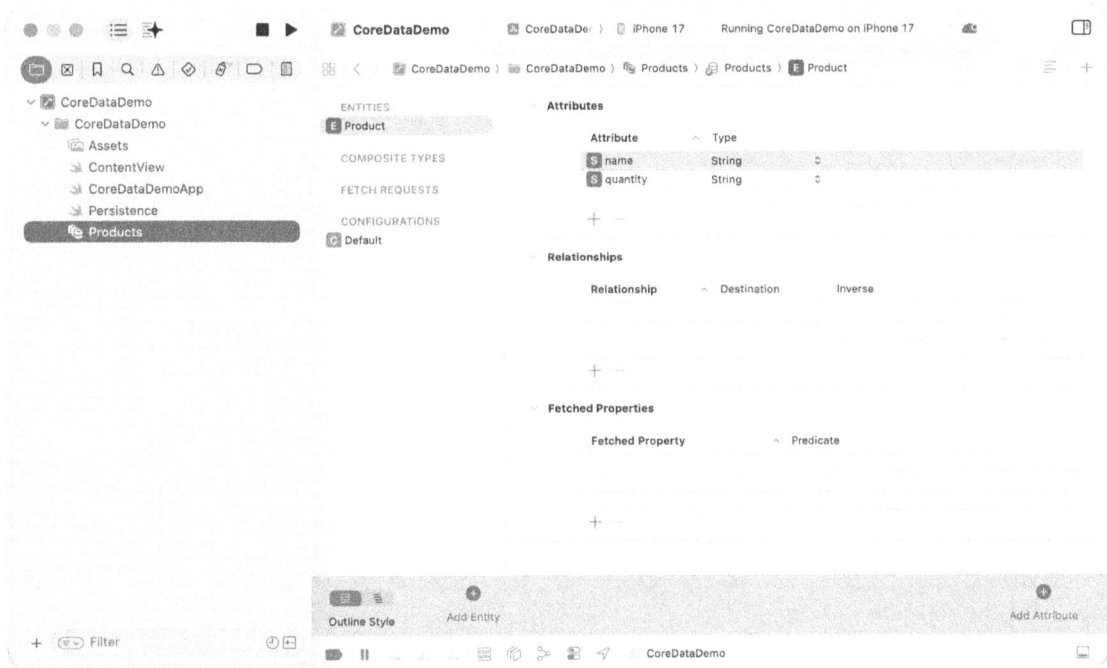

Figure 50-2

Create a new entity by clicking on the Add Entity button located in the bottom panel. The new entity will appear as a text box in the Entities list. By default, this will be named Entity. Double-click on this name to change it.

To add attributes to the entity, click on the Add Attribute button located in the bottom panel or use the + button located beneath the Attributes section. In the Attributes panel, name the attribute and specify the type and any other options that are required.

Repeat the above steps to add more attributes and additional entities.

The Xcode entity editor also allows relationships to be established between entities. Assume, for example, two entities named Contacts and Sales. To establish a relationship between the two tables, select the Contacts entity and click on the + button beneath the Relationships panel. In the detail panel, name the relationship, specify the destination as the Sales entity, and any other options that are required for the relationship:

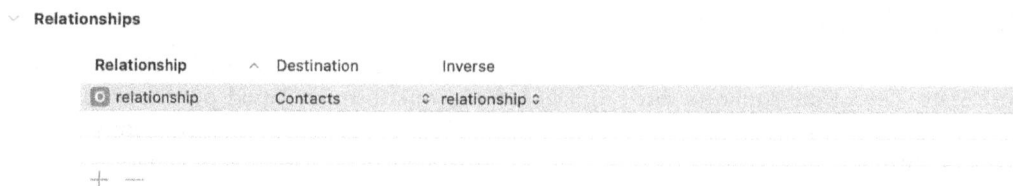

Figure 50-3

50.9 Initializing the Persistent Container

The persistent container is initialized by creating a new NSPersistentContainer instance, passing through the name of the model to be used, and then making a call to the *loadPersistentStores* method of that object as follows:

```
let persistentContainer: NSPersistentContainer

persistentContainer = NSPersistentContainer(name: "DemoData")
persistentContainer.loadPersistentStores { (storeDescription, error) in
    if let error = error as NSError? {
        fatalError("Container load failed: \(error)")
    }
}
```

50.10 Obtaining the Managed Object Context

Since many Core Data methods require the managed object context as an argument, the next step after defining entity descriptions often involves obtaining a reference to the context. This can be achieved by accessing the viewContext property of the persistent container instance:

```
let managedObjectContext = persistentContainer.viewContext
```

50.11 Setting the Attributes of a Managed Object

As previously discussed, entities and the managed objects from which they are instantiated contain data in the form of attributes. Once a managed object instance has been created, as outlined above, those attribute values can be used to store the data before the object is saved. Assuming a managed object named *contact* with attributes named *name*, *address* and *phone*, respectively, the values of these attributes may be set as follows before saving the object to storage:

```
contact.name = "John Smith"
contact.address = "1 Infinite Loop"
contact.phone = "555-564-0980"
```

50.12 Saving a Managed Object

Once a managed object instance has been created and configured with the data to be stored, it can be saved to storage using the *save()* method of the managed object context as follows:

```
do {
    try viewContext.save()
```

```
} catch {
   let error = error as NSError
   fatalError("An error occured: \(error)")
}
```

50.13 Fetching Managed Objects

Once managed objects are saved into the persistent object store, those objects and the data they contain will likely need to be retrieved. One way to fetch data from Core Data storage is to use the @FetchRequest property wrapper when declaring a variable in which to store the data. The following code, for example, declares a variable named *customers* which will be automatically updated as data is added to or removed from the database:

```
@FetchRequest(entity: Customer.entity(), sortDescriptors: [])
private var customers: FetchedResults<Customer>
```

The @FetchRequest property wrapper may also be configured to sort the fetched results. In the following example, the customer data stored in the *customers* variable will be sorted alphabetically in ascending order based on the *name* entity attribute:

```
@FetchRequest(entity: Customer.entity(),
        sortDescriptors: [NSSortDescriptor(key: "name", ascending: true)])
private var customers: FetchedResults<Customer>
```

50.14 Retrieving Managed Objects based on Criteria

The preceding example retrieved all of the managed objects from the persistent object store. More often than not only managed objects that match specified criteria are required during a retrieval operation. This is performed by defining a predicate that dictates criteria that a managed object must meet to be eligible for retrieval. For example, the following code configures a @FetchRequest property wrapper declaration with a predicate to extract only those managed objects where the name attribute matches "John Smith":

```
@FetchRequest(
   entity: Customer.entity(),
   sortDescriptors: [],
   predicate: NSPredicate(format: "name LIKE %@", "John Smith")
)
private var customers: FetchedResults<Customer>
```

The above example will maintain the *customers* variable so that it always contains the entries that match the specified predicate criteria. It is also possible to perform one-time fetch operations by creating NSFetchRequest instances, configuring them with the entity and predicate settings, and then passing them to the *fetch()* method of the managed object context. For example:

```
@State var matches: [Customer]?
let fetchRequest: NSFetchRequest<Product> = Product.fetchRequest()

fetchRequest.entity = Customer.entity()
fetchRequest.predicate = NSPredicate(
    format: "name LIKE %@", "John Smith"
)

matches = try? viewContext.fetch(fetchRequest)
```

50.15 Take the Knowledge Test

Click the link below or scan the QR code to test your knowledge and understanding of Core Data in SwiftUI:

https://www.answertopia.com/j9xl

50.16 Summary

The Core Data Framework stack provides a flexible alternative to directly managing data using SQLite or other data storage mechanisms. By providing an object-oriented abstraction layer on top of the data, the task of managing data storage is made significantly easier for the SwiftUI application developer. Now that the basics of Core Data have been covered, the next chapter, entitled *"A SwiftUI Core Data Tutorial"* will work through the creation of an example application.

51. A SwiftUI Core Data Tutorial

Now that we have explored the concepts of Core Data, it is time to put that knowledge to use by creating an example app project. In this project tutorial, we will create a simple inventory app that uses Core Data to persistently store the names and quantities of products. This will include the ability to add, delete, and search for database entries.

51.1 Creating the CoreDataDemo Project

Launch Xcode, select the option to create a new project and choose the Multiplatform App template before clicking the Next button. On the project options screen, name the project CoreDataDemo and choose an organization identifier that will uniquely identify your app (this will be important when we add CloudKit support to the project in a later chapter).

Note that the options screen includes a *Storage* menu, as Figure 51-1 highlights. Xcode will configure the project for Core Data support and generate code to implement a simple app demonstrating Core Data in action when the Core Data option is selected from this menu. Instead of using this template, this tutorial will take you through the steps of manually adding Core Data support to a project so that you have a better understanding of how Core Data works. For this reason, make sure the Storage option is set to *None* before clicking the Next button:

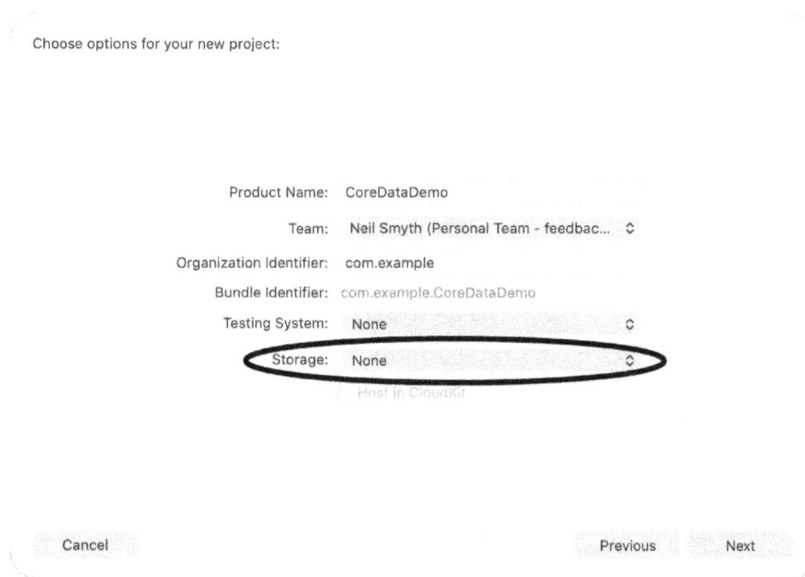

Figure 51-1

Select a suitable location to save the project before clicking the Finish button.

51.2 Defining the Entity Description

For this example, the entity takes the form of a data model designed to hold the names and quantities that will make up the product inventory. Press Cmd-N and, within the template dialog, select the Data Model entry located in the Core Data section, as shown in Figure 51-2, then click the Next button:

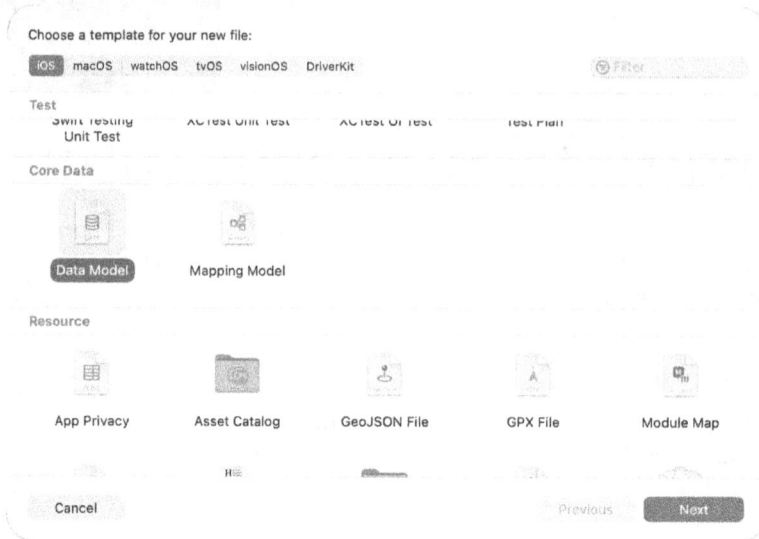

Figure 51-2

Name the file *Products.xcdatamodeld* and click on the Create button to generate the file. Once the file has been created, it will appear within the entity editor, as shown below:

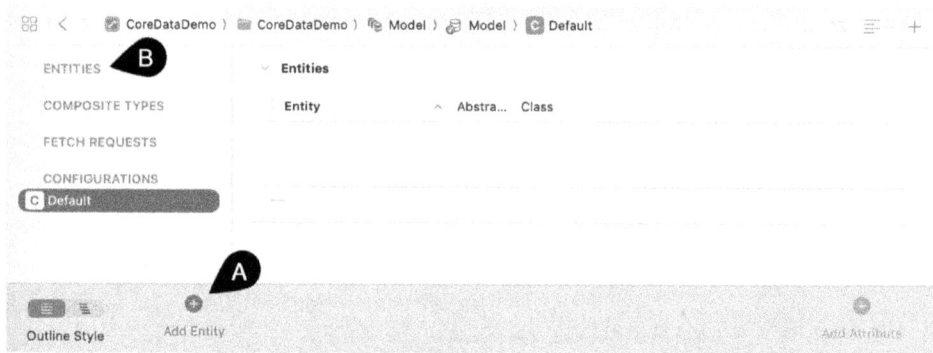

Figure 51-3

To add a new entity to the model, click on the Add Entity button marked A in Figure 51-3 above. Xcode will add a new entity (named Entity) to the model and list it beneath the Entities heading (B). Click on the new entity and change the name to Product:

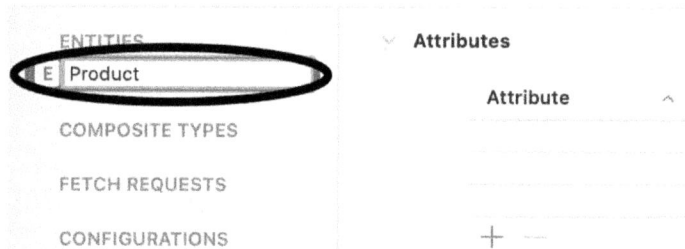

Figure 51-4

Now that the entity has been created, the next step is to add the name and quantity attributes. To add the first attribute, click on the + button located beneath the Attributes section of the main panel. Name the new attribute *name* and change the Type to String, as shown in Figure 51-5:

Figure 51-5

Repeat these steps to add a second attribute of type String named *quantity*. Upon completion of these steps, the attributes panel should match Figure 51-6:

Figure 51-6

51.3 Creating the Persistence Controller

The next requirement for our project is a persistence controller class in which to create and initialize an NSPersistentContainer instance. Press Cmd-N and, within the template dialog, select the Swift File template option and save it as *Persistence.swift*. With the new file loaded into the code editor, modify it so that it reads as follows:

```
import CoreData

struct PersistenceController {
    static let shared = PersistenceController()

    let container: NSPersistentContainer

    init() {
        container = NSPersistentContainer(name: "Products")

        container.loadPersistentStores { (storeDescription, error) in
            if let error = error as NSError? {
                fatalError("Container load failed: \(error)")
            }
        }
    }
}
```

51.4 Setting up the View Context

Now that we have created a persistent controller, we can use it to obtain a reference to the view context. An ideal place to perform this task is within the *CoreDataDemoApp.swift* file. To make the context accessible to the views that will make up the app, we will insert it into the view hierarchy as an environment object as follows:

```
import SwiftUI
```

```
import CoreData

@main
struct CoreDataDemoApp: App {

    let persistenceController = PersistenceController.shared

    var body: some Scene {
        WindowGroup {
            ContentView()
                .environment(\.managedObjectContext,
                            persistenceController.container.viewContext)
        }
    }
}
```

51.5 Preparing the ContentView for Core Data

Before we start adding views to design the app user interface, the following initial changes are required within the *ContentView.swift* file:

```
import SwiftUI
import CoreData

struct ContentView: View {

    @State var name: String = ""
    @State var quantity: String = ""

    @Environment(\.managedObjectContext) private var viewContext

    @FetchRequest(entity: Product.entity(), sortDescriptors: [])
    private var products: FetchedResults<Product>

    var body: some View {
.
.
```

In addition to importing the CoreData library, we have also declared two state objects into which the product name and quantity will be stored as the user enters them. We have also accessed the view context environment object created in the *CoreDataDemoApp.swift* file.

The @FetchRequest property wrapper is also used to declare a variable named *products* into which Core Data will store the latest product data stored in the database.

51.6 Designing the User Interface

With most of the preparatory work complete, we can now begin designing the layout of the main content view. Remaining in the *ContentView.swift* file, modify the body of the ContentView structure so that it reads as follows:

.

```
var body: some View {
    NavigationStack {
        VStack {
            TextField("Product name", text: $name)
            TextField("Product quantity", text: $quantity)

            HStack {
                Spacer()
                Button("Add") {

                }
                Spacer()
                Button("Clear") {
                    name = ""
                    quantity = ""
                }
                Spacer()
            }
            .padding()
            .frame(maxWidth: .infinity)

            List {
                ForEach(products) { product in
                    HStack {
                        Text(product.name ?? "Not found")
                        Spacer()
                        Text(product.quantity ?? "Not found")
                    }
                }
            }
            .navigationTitle("Product Database")
        }
        .padding()
        .textFieldStyle(RoundedBorderTextFieldStyle())
    }
}
```

The layout initially consists of two TextField views, two Buttons, and a List, which should render within the preview canvas as follows:

Figure 51-7

51.7 Saving Products

More code changes are now required so that data entered into the product name and quantity text fields is saved by Core Data into persistent storage when the Add button is clicked. Edit the *ContentView.swift* file once again to add this functionality:

```
.
.
var body: some View {
    NavigationStack {
        VStack {
            TextField("Product name", text: $name)
            TextField("Product quantity", text: $quantity)

            HStack {
                Spacer()
                Button("Add") {
                    addProduct()
                }
                Spacer()
                Button("Clear") {
                    name = ""
                    quantity = ""
                }
.
.
            .padding()
            .textFieldStyle(RoundedBorderTextFieldStyle())
        }
    }
}

private func addProduct() {
    withAnimation {
        let product = Product(context: viewContext)
```

```
            product.name = name
            product.quantity = quantity

            saveContext()
        }
    }

    private func saveContext() {
        do {
            try viewContext.save()
        } catch {
            let error = error as NSError
            fatalError("An error occurred: \(error)")
        }
    }
}
.
.
```

The first change configured the Add button to call a function named *addProduct()*, which was declared as follows:

```
private func addProduct() {
    withAnimation {
        let product = Product(context: viewContext)
        product.name = name
        product.quantity = quantity

        saveContext()
    }
}
```

The *addProduct()* function creates a new Product entity instance and assigns the current content of the product name and quantity state properties to the corresponding entity attributes. A call is then made to the following *saveContext()* function:

```
private func saveContext() {
    do {
        try viewContext.save()
    } catch {
        let error = error as NSError
        fatalError("An error occurred: \(error)")
    }
}
```

The *saveContext()* function uses a "do.. try .. catch" construct to save the current viewContext to persistent storage. For testing purposes, a fatal error is triggered to terminate the app if the save action fails. More comprehensive error handling would typically be required for a production-quality app.

Saving the data will cause the latest data to be fetched and assigned to the *products* data variable. This, in turn, will cause the List view to update with the latest products. To make this update visually appealing, the code in the *addProduct()* function is placed in a *withAnimation* call.

51.8 Testing the addProduct() Function

Compile and run the app on a device or simulator, enter a few product and quantity entries, and verify that those entries appear in the List view as they are added. After entering information into the text fields, check that clicking on the Clear button clears the current entries.

At this point in the tutorial, the running app should resemble that shown in Figure 51-8 after some products have been added:

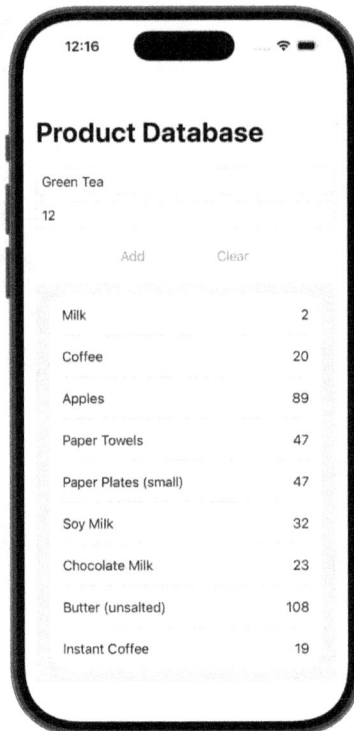

Figure 51-8

To make the list more organized, the product items need to be sorted in ascending alphabetical order based on the *name* attribute. To implement this, add a sort descriptor to the @FetchRequest definition as outlined below. This requires the creation of an NSSortDescriptor instance configured with the *name* attribute declared as the key and the ascending property set to true:

```
@FetchRequest(entity: Product.entity(),
            sortDescriptors: [NSSortDescriptor(key: "name", ascending: true)])
private var products: FetchedResults<Product>
```

When the app is run, the product list will be sorted in ascending alphabetic order.

51.9 Deleting Products

Now that the app has a mechanism for adding product entries to the database, we need a way to delete entries that are no longer needed. For this project, we will use the same steps demonstrated in the chapter entitled *"SwiftUI Lists and Navigation"*. This will allow the user to delete entries by swiping on the list item and tapping the delete button. Beneath the existing *addProduct()* function, add a new function named *deleteProduct()* that reads as follows:

```
private func deleteProducts(offsets: IndexSet) {
    withAnimation {
        offsets.map { products[$0] }.forEach(viewContext.delete)
            saveContext()
    }
}
```

When the method is called, it is passed a set of offsets within the List entries representing the positions of the items selected by the user for deletion. The above code loops through these entries calling the viewContext *delete()* function for each deleted item. Once the deletions are complete, the changes are saved to the database via a call to our *saveContext()* function.

Now that we have added the *deleteProduct()* function, the List view can be modified to call it via the *onDelete()* modifier:

```
.
.

    List {
        ForEach(products) { product in
            HStack {
                Text(product.name ?? "Not found")
                Spacer()
                Text(product.quantity ?? "Not found")
            }
        }
        .onDelete(perform: deleteProducts)
    }
    .navigationTitle("Product Database")

.
.
```

Run the app and verify both that performing a leftward swipe on a list item reveals the delete option and that clicking it removes the item from the list.

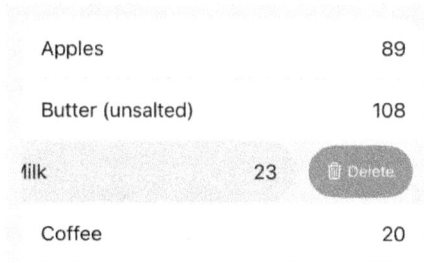

Apples	89
Butter (unsalted)	108
Milk 23	🗑 Delete
Coffee	20

Figure 51-9

51.10 Adding the Search Function

The final feature to be added to the project will allow us to search the database for products that match the text entered into the name text field. The results will appear in a list contained within a second view named ResultsView. When it is called from ContentView, ResultsView will be passed the current value of the *name* state

A SwiftUI Core Data Tutorial

property and a reference to the viewContext object.

Begin by adding the ResultsView structure to the *ContentView.swift* file as follows:

```
struct ResultsView: View {

    var name: String
    var viewContext: NSManagedObjectContext
    @State var matches: [Product]?

    var body: some View {

        return VStack {
            List {
                ForEach(matches ?? []) { match in
                    HStack {
                        Text(match.name ?? "Not found")
                        Spacer()
                        Text(match.quantity ?? "Not found")
                    }
                }
            }
            .navigationTitle("Results")
        }
    }
}
```

In addition to the name and viewContext parameters, the declaration also includes a state property named *matches* into which will be placed the matching product search results, which, in turn, will be displayed within the List view.

We now need to add some code to perform the search and will do so by applying a *task()* modifier to the VStack container view. This will ensure that searches are performed asynchronously and that all of the view's properties have been initialized before the search is executed:

```
.
.

    return VStack {
        List {

            ForEach(myMatches ?? []) { match in
                HStack {
                    Text(match.name ?? "Not found")
                    Spacer()
                    Text(match.quantity ?? "Not found")
                }
            }
        }
        .navigationTitle("Results")
```

440

```
    }
    .task {
        let fetchRequest: NSFetchRequest<Product> = Product.fetchRequest()

        fetchRequest.entity = Product.entity()
        fetchRequest.predicate = NSPredicate(
            format: "name CONTAINS %@", name
        )
        matches = try? viewContext.fetch(fetchRequest)
    }
```

So that the search finds all products that contain the specified text, the predicate is configured using the CONTAINS keyword. This provides more flexibility than performing exact match searches using the LIKE keyword by finding partial matches.

The code in the closure of the *task()* modifier obtains an NSFetchRequest instance from the Product entity and assigns it an NSPredicate instance configured to find matches between the *name* variable and the *name* product entity attribute. The fetch request is then passed to the *fetch()* method of the view context, and the results are assigned to the *matches* state object. This, in turn, will cause the List to be re-rendered with the matching products.

The last task before testing the search feature is to add a navigation link to ResultsView, keeping in mind that ResultsView expects to be passed the *name* state object and a reference to *viewContext*. This needs to be positioned between the Add and Clear buttons as follows:

```
HStack {
    Spacer()
    Button("Add") {
        addProduct()
    }
    Spacer()
    NavigationLink(destination: ResultsView(name: name,
                     viewContext: viewContext)) {
        Text("Find")
    }
    Spacer()
    Button("Clear") {
        name = ""
        quantity = ""
    }
    Spacer()
}
```

Check the preview canvas to confirm that the navigation link appears, as shown in Figure 51-10:

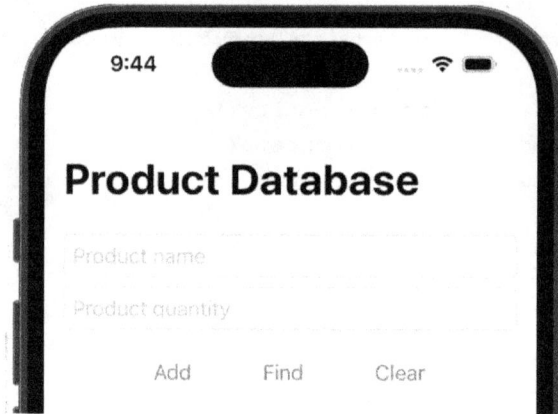

Figure 51-10

51.11 Testing the Completed App

Rerun the app and add some products, preferably with some containing the same word. Enter the common word into the name text field and click on the Find link. The ResultsView screen should appear with a list of matching items. Figure 51-11, for example, illustrates a search performed on the word "Milk":

Figure 51-11

51.12 Summary

In this chapter, we have used Core Data to provide persistent database storage within an app project. Topics covered include the creation of a Core Data entity model and the configuration of entity attributes. Steps were also taken to initialize a persistent container from which we obtained the view context. The project also used the @FetchRequest property wrapper configured to store entries alphabetically and used the view context to add, delete, and search for database entries. In implementing the search behavior, we used an NSFetchRequest instance configured with an NSPredicate object and passed that to the *fetch()* method of the view context to find matching results.

52. An Overview of SwiftUI Core Data and CloudKit Storage

CloudKit provides a way for apps to store cloud-based databases using iCloud storage so that it is accessible across multiple devices, users, and apps.

Although initially provided with a dedicated framework that allows code to be written to directly create, manage and access iCloud-based databases, the recommended approach is now to use CloudKit in conjunction with Core Data.

This chapter will provide a high-level introduction to the various elements that make up CloudKit, and explain how those correspond to Core Data.

52.1 An Overview of CloudKit

The CloudKit Framework provides applications with access to the iCloud servers hosted by Apple and provides an easy-to-use way to store, manage and retrieve data and other asset types (such as large binary files, videos, and images) in a structured way. This provides a platform for users to store private data and access it from multiple devices, and also for the developer to provide data that is publicly available to all the users of an application.

The first step in learning to use CloudKit is to gain an understanding of the key components that constitute the CloudKit framework. Keep in mind that we won't be directly working with these components when using Core Data with CloudKit. We will, instead, continue to work with the Core Data elements covered in the previous chapters using a CloudKit enabled version of the Persistent Container. This container will handle all of the work of mapping these Core Data components to their equivalents within the CloudKit ecosystem.

While it is theoretically possible to implement CloudKit-based Core Data storage without this knowledge, this information will be useful when using the CloudKit Console. Basic knowledge of how CloudKit works will also be invaluable if you decide to explore more advanced topics in the future such as CloudKit sharing and subscriptions.

52.2 CloudKit Containers

Each CloudKit enabled application has at least one container on iCloud. The container for an application is represented in CloudKit by the CKContainer class and it is within these containers that the databases reside. Containers may also be shared between multiple applications. When working with Core Data, the container can be thought of as the equivalent of the Managed Object Model.

52.3 CloudKit Public Database

Each cloud container contains a single public database. This is the database into which is stored data that is needed by all users of an application. A map application, for example, might have a set of data about locations and routes that apply to all users of the application. This data would be stored within the public database of the application's cloud container.

52.4 CloudKit Private Databases

Private cloud databases are used to store data that is private to each specific user. Each cloud container, therefore, will contain one private database for each user of the application.

52.5 Data Storage Quotas

Data and assets stored in the public cloud database of an app count against the storage quota of the app. Anything stored in a private database, on the other hand, is counted against the iCloud quota of the corresponding user. Applications should, therefore, try to minimize the amount of data stored in private databases to avoid users having to unnecessarily purchase additional iCloud storage space.

At the time of writing, each application is provided with 1PB of free iCloud storage for public data for all of its users.

Apple also imposes limits on the volume of data transfers and the number of queries per second that are included in the free tier. While official documentation on these quotas and corresponding pricing is hard to find, it is unlikely that the average project will encounter these restrictions.

52.6 CloudKit Records

Data is stored in both the public and private databases in the form of records. Records are represented by the CKRecord class and are essentially dictionaries of key-value pairs where keys are used to reference the data values stored in the record. When stored is data via CloudKit using Core Data, these records are represented by Core Data Managed Objects.

The overall concept of an application cloud container, private and public databases, zones, and records can be visualized, as illustrated in Figure 52-1:

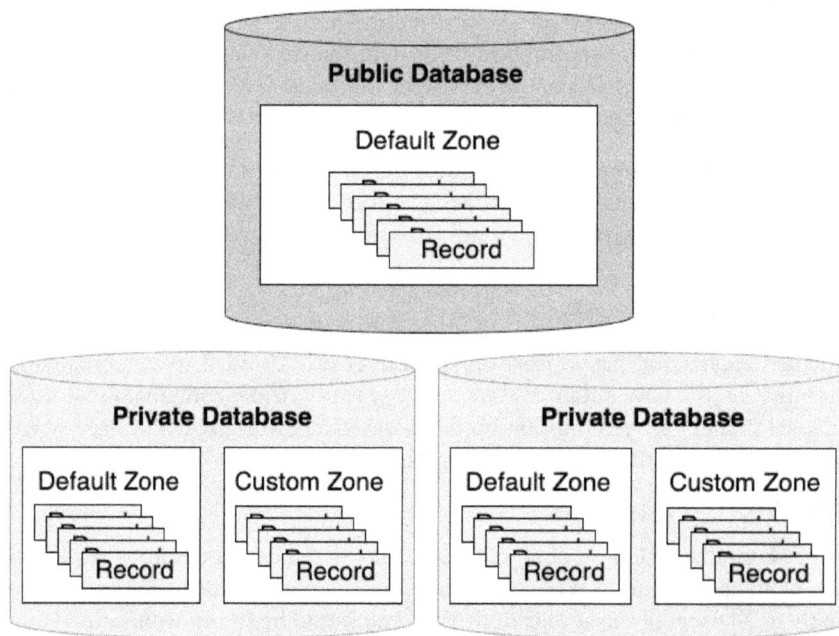

Figure 52-1

52.7 CloudKit Record IDs

Each CloudKit record has associated with it a unique record ID represented by the CKRecordID class. If a record ID is not specified when a record is first created, one is provided for it automatically by the CloudKit framework.

52.8 CloudKit References

CloudKit references are implemented using the CKReference class and provide a way to establish relationships between different records in a database. A reference is established by creating a CKReference instance for an originating record and assigning to it the record to which the relationship is to be targeted. The CKReference object is then stored in the originating record as a key-value pair field. A single record can contain multiple references to other records.

Once a record is configured with a reference pointing to a target record, that record is said to be owned by the target record. When the owner record is deleted, all records that refer to it are also deleted and so on down the chain of references (a concept referred to as cascading deletes).

52.9 Record Zones

CloudKit record zones (CKRecordZone) provide a mechanism for relating groups of records within a private database. Unless a record zone is specified when a record is saved to the cloud it is placed in the default zone of the target database. Custom zones can be added to private databases and used to organize related records and perform tasks such as writing to multiple records simultaneously in a single transaction. Each record zone has associated with it a unique record zone ID (CKRecordZoneID) which must be referenced when adding new records to a zone. All of the records within a public database are considered to be in the public default zone.

The CloudKit record zone translates to the Core Data persistent container. When working with Core Data in the previous chapter, persistent containers were created as instances of the NSPersistentContainer class. When integrating Core Data with CloudKit, however, we will be using the NSPersistentCloudKitContainer class instead. In terms of modifying code to use Core Data with CloudKit, this usually simply involves substituting NSPersistentCloudKitContainer for NSPersistentContainer.

52.10 CloudKit Console

The CloudKit Console is a web-based portal that provides an interface for managing the CloudKit options and storage for applications. The console can be accessed via the following URL:

https://icloud.developer.apple.com/dashboard/

Alternatively, the CloudKit Console can be accessed via the button located in the iCloud section of the Xcode *Signing & Capabilities* panel for a project, as shown in Figure 52-2:

Figure 52-2

Access to the dashboard requires a valid Apple developer login and password and, once loaded into a browser window, will appear providing access to the CloudKit containers associated with your team account.

Once one or more containers have been created, the console provides the ability to view data, add, update, query, and delete records, modify the database schema, view subscriptions and configure new security roles. It also provides an interface for migrating data from a development environment over to a production environment in preparation for an application to go live in the App Store

The Logs and Telemetry options provide an overview of CloudKit usage by the currently selected container, including operations performed per second, average data request size and error frequency, and log details of each transaction.

In the case of data access through the CloudKit Console, it is important to be aware that private user data cannot be accessed using the dashboard interface. Only data stored in the public database and the private databases belonging to the developer account used to log in to the console can be viewed and modified.

52.11 CloudKit Sharing

Clearly, a CloudKit record contained within the public database of an app is accessible to all users of that app. Situations might arise, however, where a user wants to share with others specific records contained within a private database. This was made possible with the introduction of CloudKit sharing.

52.12 CloudKit Subscriptions

CloudKit subscriptions allow users to be notified when a change occurs within the cloud databases belonging to an installed app. Subscriptions use the standard iOS push notifications infrastructure and can be triggered based on a variety of criteria such as when records are added, updated, or deleted. Notifications can also be further refined using predicates so that notifications are based on data in a record matching certain criteria. When a notification arrives, it is presented to the user in the same way as other notifications through an alert or a notification entry on the lock screen.

52.13 Take the Knowledge Test

Click the link below or scan the QR code to test your knowledge and understanding of CloudKit and Core Data in SwiftUI:

https://www.answertopia.com/8w9n

52.14 Summary

This chapter has covered a number of the key classes and elements that make up the data storage features of the CloudKit framework. Each application has its own cloud container which, in turn, contains a single public cloud database in addition to one private database for each application user. Data is stored in databases in the form of records using key-value pair fields. Larger data such as videos and photos are stored as assets which, in turn, are stored as fields in records. Records stored in private databases can be grouped into record zones and records may be associated with each other through the creation of relationships. Each application user has an iCloud user id and a corresponding user record both of which can be obtained using the CloudKit framework. In addition, CloudKit user discovery can be used to obtain, subject to permission having been given, a list of IDs for those users in the current user's address book who have also installed and run the app.

Finally, the CloudKit Dashboard is a web-based portal that provides an interface for managing the CloudKit options and storage for applications.

53. A SwiftUI Core Data and CloudKit Tutorial

Using the CoreDataDemo project created in the chapter entitled *"A SwiftUI Core Data Tutorial"*, this chapter will demonstrate how to add CloudKit support to an Xcode project and migrate from Core Data to CloudKit-based storage. This chapter assumes that you have read the chapter entitled *"An Introduction to Core Data and SwiftUI"*.

53.1 Enabling CloudKit Support

Begin by launching Xcode and opening the CoreDataDemo project. Once the project has loaded into Xcode, the first step is to add the iCloud capability to the app. Select the *CoreDataDemo* target located at the top of the Project Navigator panel (marked A in Figure 53-1) so that the main panel displays the project settings. From within this panel, select the *Signing & Capabilities* tab (B) followed by the CoreDataDemo target entry (C):

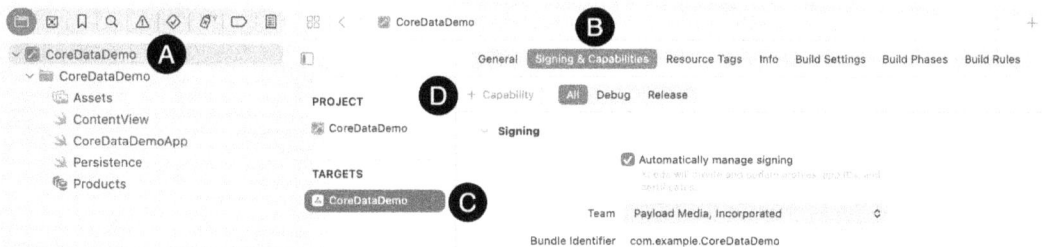

Figure 53-1

Click on the "+ Capability" button (D) to display the dialog shown in Figure 53-2. Enter *iCloud* into the filter bar, select the result and press the keyboard enter key to add the capability to the project:

Figure 53-2

If iCloud is not listed as an option, you will need to pay to join the Apple Developer program as outlined in the chapter entitled *"Joining the Apple Developer Program"*. If you are already a member, use the steps outlined in the chapter entitled *"Installing Xcode 26 and the iOS 26 SDK"* to ensure you have created a *Developer ID Application* certificate.

Within the iCloud entitlement settings, make sure that the CloudKit service is enabled before clicking on the "+" button indicated by the arrow in Figure 53-3 below to add an iCloud container for the project:

Figure 53-3

After clicking the "+" button, the dialog shown in Figure 53-4 will appear containing a text field into which you will need to enter the container identifier. This entry should uniquely identify the container within the CloudKit ecosystem, generally includes your organization identifier (as defined when the project was created), and should be set to something similar to *iCloud.com.yourcompany.CoreDataDemo*.

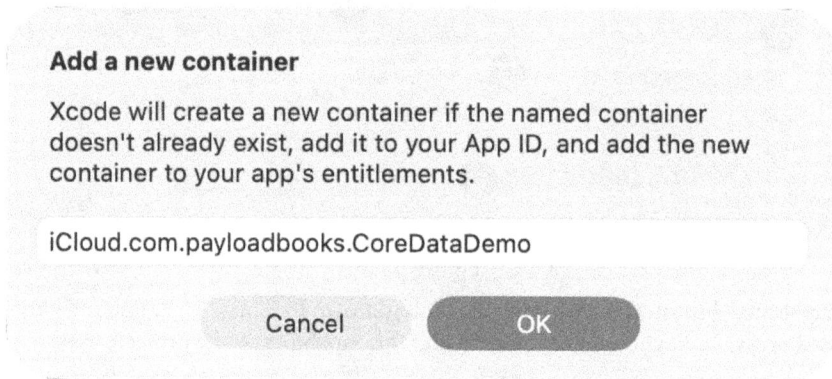

Figure 53-4

Once you have entered the container name, click the OK button to add it to the app entitlements. Returning to the *Signing & Capabilities* screen, make sure that the new container is selected:

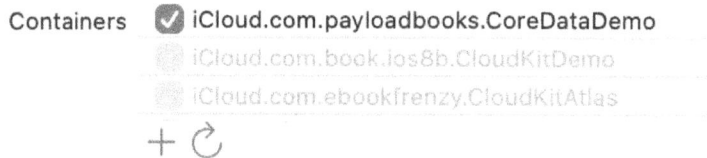

Figure 53-5

53.2 Enabling Background Notifications Support

When the app is running on multiple devices and a data change is made in one instance of the app, CloudKit will use remote notifications to notify other instances of the app to update to the latest data. To enable background notifications, repeat the above steps, this time adding the *Background Modes* capability. Once the capability has been added, review the settings and make sure that *Remote notifications* mode is enabled as highlighted in

Figure 53-6:

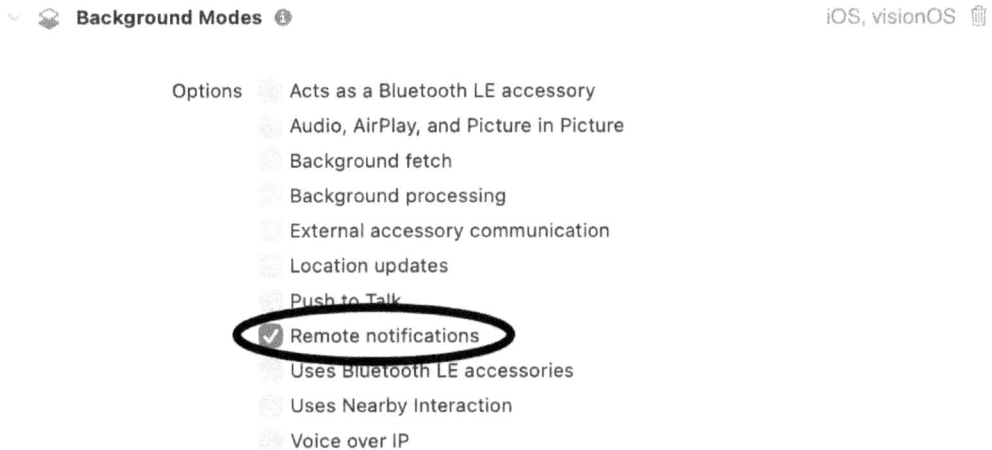

Figure 53-6

Now that the necessary entitlements have been enabled for the app, all that remains is to make some minor code changes to the project.

53.3 Switching to the CloudKit Persistent Container

Locate the *Persistence.swift* file in the project navigator panel and select it so that it loads into the code editor. Within the *init()* function, change the container creation call from NSPersistentContainer to NSPersistentCloudKitContainer as follows:

```
.
.
let container: NSPersistentCloudKitContainer
.
.
init() {
    container = NSPersistentCloudKitContainer(name: "Products")

    container.loadPersistentStores { (storeDescription, error) in
        if let error = error as NSError? {
            fatalError("Container load failed: \(error)")
        }
    }
}
```

Since multiple instances of the app could potentially change the same data at the same time, we also need to define a merge policy to make sure that conflicting changes are handled:

```
.
.
init() {
    container = NSPersistentCloudKitContainer(name: "Products")
```

```
container.loadPersistentStores { (storeDescription, error) in
    if let error = error as NSError? {
        fatalError("Container load failed: \(error)")
    }
}
container.viewContext.automaticallyMergesChangesFromParent = true
}
.
.
.
```

53.4 Testing the App

CloudKit storage can be tested on either physical devices, simulators, or a mixture of both. All test devices and simulators must be signed in to iCloud using your Apple developer account and have the iCloud Drive option enabled. Once these requirements have been met, run the CoreDataDemo app and add some product entries. Next, run the app on another device or simulator and check that the newly added products appear. This confirms that the data is being stored and retrieved from iCloud.

With both app instances running, enter a new product in one instance and check that it appears in the other. Note that a bug in the simulator means that you may need to place the app in the background and then restore it before the new data will appear.

53.5 Reviewing the Saved Data in the CloudKit Console

Once some product entries have been added to the database, return to the *Signing & Capabilities* screen for the project (Figure 53-1) and click on the CloudKit Console button. This will launch the default web browser on your system and load the CloudKit Dashboard portal. Enter your Apple developer login and password and, once the dashboard has loaded, the home screen will provide the range of options illustrated in Figure 53-7:

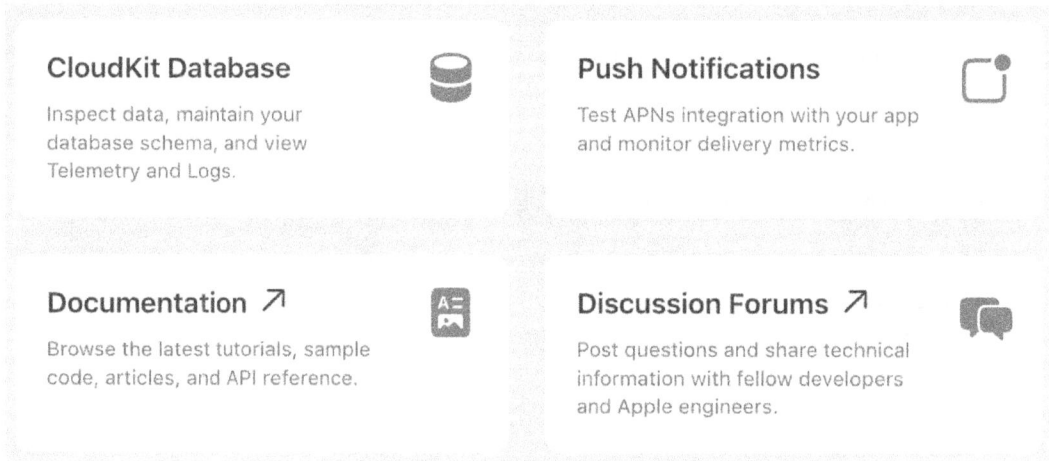

CloudKit Database

Inspect data, maintain your database schema, and view Telemetry and Logs.

Push Notifications

Test APNs integration with your app and monitor delivery metrics.

Documentation ↗

Browse the latest tutorials, sample code, articles, and API reference.

Discussion Forums ↗

Post questions and share technical information with fellow developers and Apple engineers.

Figure 53-7

Select the CloudKit Database option and, on the resulting web page, select the container for your app from the drop-down menu (marked A in Figure 53-8 below). Since the app is still in development and has not been published to the App Store, make sure that menu B is set to Development and not Production:

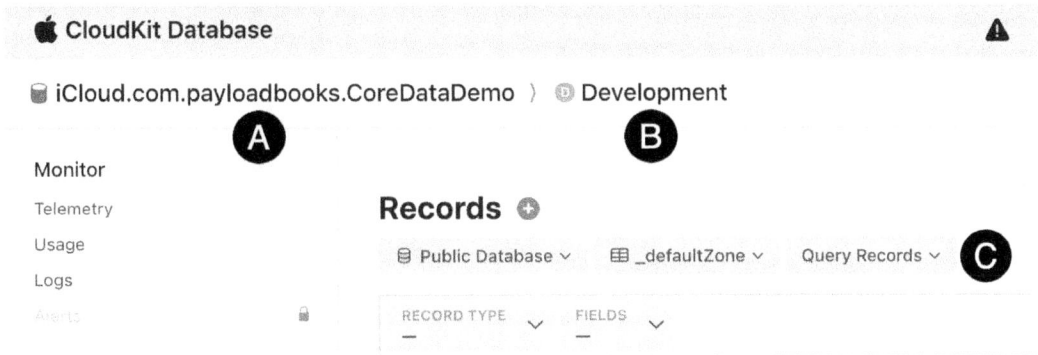

Figure 53-8

Next, we can query the records stored in the app container's private database. Set the row of menus (C) to *Private Database*, *com.apple.coredata.cloudkit.zone*, and *Query Records* respectively. Finally, set the Record Type menu to *CD_Product* and the *Fields* menu to All:

Figure 53-9

Clicking on the Query Records button should display a list of all the product items saved in the database, as illustrated in Figure 53-10:

NAME	TYPE	CD_ENTITYNAME	CD_NAME	CD_QUANTITY	CH. TAG	CREATED	MODIFIED
144AC333-6CB3-...	CD_Product	Product	Shampoo	12	5d	9/20/2023, 2:31:47 P...	9/20/2023, :
231D07BB-C44F-4...	CD_Product	Product	Cat food	10	4p	3/24/2022, 5:34:49 ...	3/24/2022, !
C4DA5BA5-63AA-...	CD_Product	Product	Coffee	2	5b	7/29/2022, 6:44:11 P...	7/29/2022, (
D32C4BDC-2E7A-...	CD_Product	Product	Batteries	5	s	3/23/2022, 7:36:08 P...	3/23/2022, :
F6D0182B-47EA-4...	CD_Product	Product	Soap	12	5e	9/20/2023, 2:33:22 P...	9/20/2023, :
FB7E28BDF-7853-4...	CD_Product	Product	Book	1	5c	9/12/2022, 7:59:58 P...	9/12/2022, 7

Figure 53-10

53.6 Filtering and Sorting Queries

The queries we have been running so far are returning all of the records in the database. Queries may also be performed based on sorting and filtering criteria by clicking in the "Add filter or sort to query" field. Clicking in this field will display a menu system that will guide you through setting up the criteria. In Figure 53-11, for example, the menu system is being used to set up a filtered query based on the *CD_name* field:

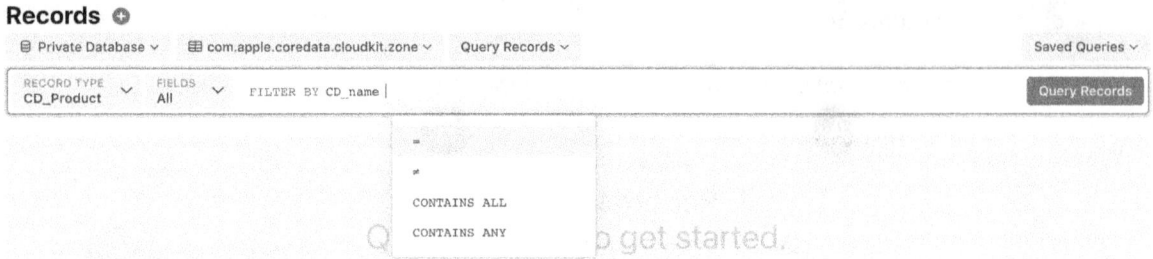

Records ⊕

Figure 53-11

Similarly, Figure 53-12 shows the completed filter and query results:

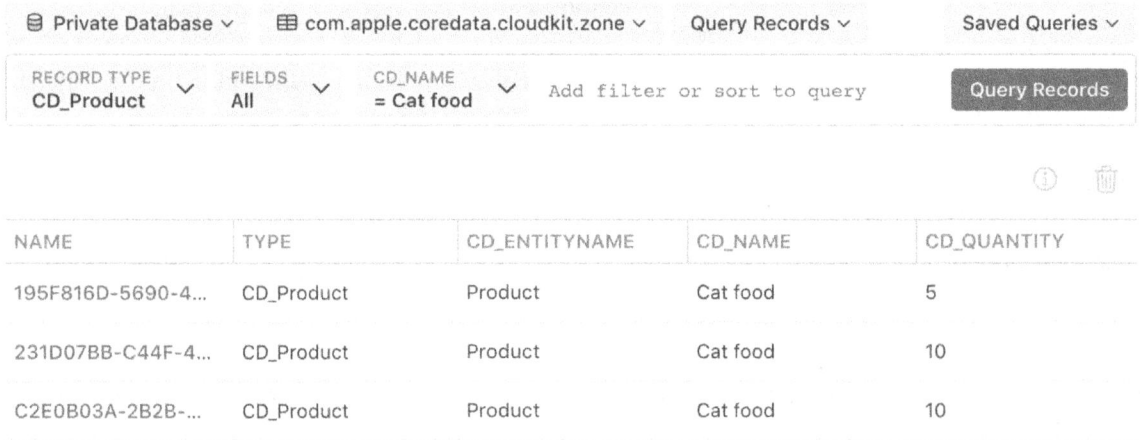

NAME	TYPE	CD_ENTITYNAME	CD_NAME	CD_QUANTITY
195F816D-5690-4...	CD_Product	Product	Cat food	5
231D07BB-C44F-4...	CD_Product	Product	Cat food	10
C2E0B03A-2B2B-...	CD_Product	Product	Cat food	10

Figure 53-12

The same technique can be used to sort the results in ascending or descending order. You can also combine multiple criteria in a single query. To edit or remove a query criterion, left-click on it and select the appropriate menu option.

53.7 Editing and Deleting Records

In addition to querying the records in the database, the CloudKit Console also allows records to be edited and deleted. To edit or delete a record, locate it in the query list and click on the entry in the name column as highlighted below:

NAME	TYPE	CD_ENTITYNAME	CD_NAME	CD_QUANTITY
144AC333-6CB3-44AF-81FE-B574576AB15D	CD_Product	Product	Shampoo	12
231D07BB-C44F-44D7-AAC9-4ABA8258F135	CD_Product	Product	Cat food	10

Figure 53-13

Once the record has been selected, the Record Details panel shown in Figure 53-14 will appear. In addition to displaying detailed information about the record, this panel also allows the record to be modified or deleted.

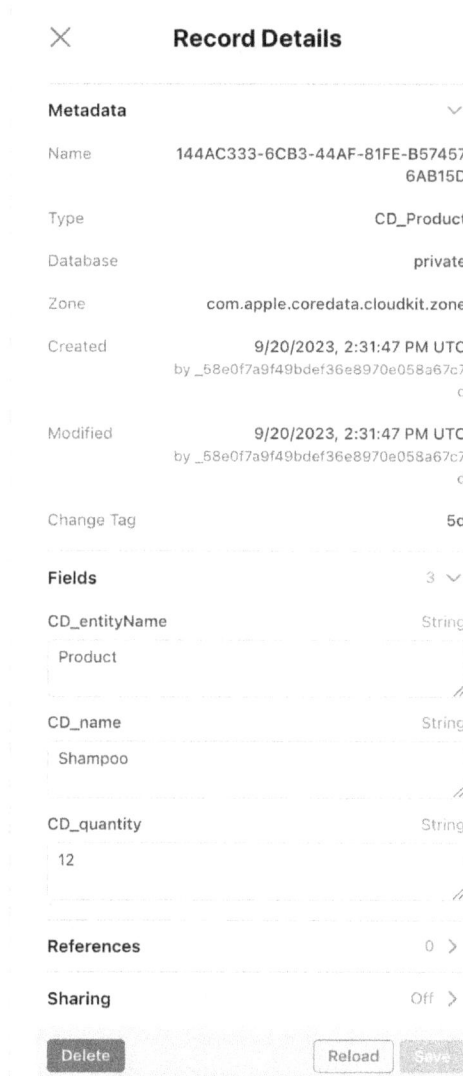

✕   **Record Details**

Metadata   ⌄

Name   144AC333-6CB3-44AF-81FE-B57457
                               6AB15D

Type   CD_Product

Database   private

Zone   com.apple.coredata.cloudkit.zone

Created   9/20/2023, 2:31:47 PM UTC
                by _58e0f7a9f49bdef36e8970e058a67c7
                                        d

Modified   9/20/2023, 2:31:47 PM UTC
                by _58e0f7a9f49bdef36e8970e058a67c7
                                        d

Change Tag   5d

Fields   3 ⌄

CD_entityName   String

  Product

CD_name   String

  Shampoo

CD_quantity   String

  12

References   0 >

Sharing   Off >

[Delete]   [Reload] [Save]

Figure 53-14

53.8 Adding New Records

To add a new record to a database, click on the "+" located at the top of the query results list and select the Create New Record option:

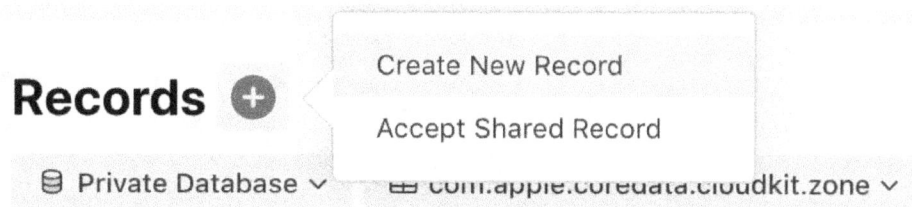

Records +   Create New Record

                 Accept Shared Record

🗄 Private Database ⌄   🗄 com.apple.coredata.cloudkit.zone ⌄

Figure 53-15

When the New Record panel appears (Figure 53-16) enter the new data before clicking the Save button:

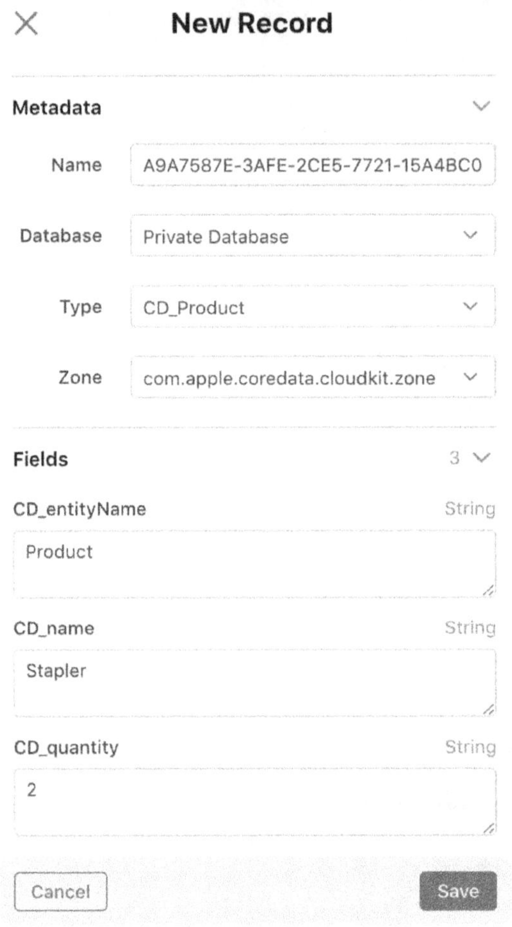

✕ **New Record**

Metadata ⌄

Name A9A7587E-3AFE-2CE5-7721-15A4BC0

Database Private Database ⌄

Type CD_Product ⌄

Zone com.apple.coredata.cloudkit.zone ⌄

Fields 3 ⌄

CD_entityName String

Product

CD_name String

Stapler

CD_quantity String

2

Cancel Save

Figure 53-16

53.9 Summary

The first step in adding CloudKit support to an Xcode SwiftUI project is to add the iCloud capability, enabling both the CloudKit service and remote notifications, and configuring a container to store the databases associated with the app. The migration from Core Data to CloudKit is simply a matter of changing the code to use NSPersistentCloudKitContainer instead of NSPersistentContainer and re-building the project.

CloudKit databases can be queried, modified, managed, and monitored from within the CloudKit Console.

Chapter 54

54. An Introduction to SwiftData

The preceding chapters covered database storage using Core Data. While Core Data is a powerful and flexible solution to data storage, it was created long before the introduction of SwiftUI and lacks the simplicity of SwiftUI's approach to app development. Introduced in iOS 17, SwiftData addresses this shortcoming by providing a declarative approach to persistent data storage that is tightly integrated with SwiftUI.

This chapter introduces SwiftData and provides a broad overview of the key elements required to store and manage persistent data within iOS apps.

54.1 Introducing SwiftData

The SwiftData framework integrates seamlessly with SwiftUI code and offers a declarative way to store persistent data within apps. Implemented as a layer on top of Core Data, SwiftData provides access to many of its features without the need to write complex code.

The rest of this chapter will introduce the SwiftData framework classes and outline how to integrate SwiftData into your iOS app projects. In the next chapter, titled *"A SwiftData Tutorial"*, we will create a project that demonstrates persistent data storage using SwiftData.

54.2 Model Classes

The SwiftData model classes represent the schema for the data to be stored and are declared as Swift classes. Consider the following class representing the data structure of an address book app:

```
class Contact {
    var firstname: String
    var lastname: String
    var address: String

    init(firstname: String, lastname: String, address: String) {
        self.firstname = firstname
        self.lastname = lastname
        self.address = address
    }
}
```

To store the contact information using SwiftData, we need to designate this class as a SwiftData model. To make this declaration, all that is required is to import the SwiftData framework and add the @Model macro to the class:

import SwiftData

@Model
```
class Contact {
    var firstname: String
    var lastname: String
    var address: String
```

455

```
init(firstname: String, lastname: String, address: String) {
    self.firstname = firstname
    self.lastname = lastname
    self.address = address

}
}
```

54.3 Model Container

The purpose of the Model Container class is to collect the model schema and generate a database in which to store instances of the data model objects. Essentially, the model container provides an interface between the model schema and the underlying database storage.

Model containers may be created directly or by applying the *modelContainer(for:)* modifier to a Scene or WindowGroup. In both cases, the container must be passed a list of the models to be managed. The following code, for example, creates a model container for our Contact model:

```
let modelContainer = try? ModelContainer(for: Contact.self)
```

In the following example, the model container is initialized using three models:

```
let modelContainer = try? ModelContainer(for: Contact.self, Message.self,
CallLog.self)
```

The following code, on the other hand, uses the *modelContainer(for:)* modifier to create a model container for a WindowGroup:

```
var body: some Scene {
    WindowGroup {
        ContentView()
    }
    .modelContainer(for: Contact.self)

}
```

54.4 Model Configuration

Model configurations can be applied to model containers to configure how the persistent data is stored and accessed. A model container might, for example, be configured to store the data in memory, in a specific file, or to access data in read-only mode. The following code creates a model configuration for in-memory data storage and applies it to a new model container:

```
let modelConfig = ModelConfiguration(isStoredInMemoryOnly: true)
let modelContainer = try? ModelContainer(
                            for: Contact.self,
                 configurations: modelConfig)
```

54.5 Model Context

When a model container is created, SwiftUI creates a binding to the container's model context. The model context tracks changes to the underlying data and provides the programming interface through which the app code performs operations on the stored data, such as adding, updating, fetching, and deleting model objects.

When a model container is created, a binding to the model context is placed into the app's environment, where it can be accessed from within scenes and views as follows:

```
@Environment(\.modelContext) var modelContext
```

The model context provides several methods for accessing the database, for example:

```
// Insert a model object
modelContext.insert(contact)

// Delete a model object
modelContext.delete(contact)

// Save all changes
modelContext.save()
```

54.6 Predicates and FetchDescriptors

Predicates define the criteria for fetching matching data from a database and take the form of logical expressions that evaluate to true or false. The following code creates a predicate to filter the contacts whose last name is "Smith":

```
let namePredicate = #Predicate<Contact> { $0.lastname.contains("Smith") }
```

Once the predicate has been declared, it is used to create a FetchDescriptor as follows:

```
let descriptor = FetchDescriptor<Visitor>(predicate: namePredicate)
```

Finally, the fetch descriptor is passed to the model context's *fetch()* method to obtain a list of matching objects:

```
let theSmiths = try? modelContext.fetch(descriptor)
```

In addition to filtering fetch results, the fetch descriptor can also be used to sort the returned matches. The following descriptor, for example, sorts the fetch results by contact last name:

```
let descriptor = FetchDescriptor<Visitor>(predicate: namePredicate,
                        sortBy: [SortDescriptor(\Contact.lastname)])
```

The SortDescriptor may also be used to specify the sorting order of the fetch results. The following SortDescriptor example will reverse the sorting order when used in a *fetch()* call:

```
let descriptor = FetchDescriptor<Visitor>(predicate: namePredicate,
        sortBy: [SortDescriptor(\Contact.lastname, order: .reverse)])
```

54.7 The @Query Macro

The @Query macro provides a convenient way to fetch objects from storage and uses the observability features of SwiftUI to ensure that the results are always up to date. In the simplest form, the @Query macro can be used to fetch all of the stored contact objects from the database:

```
@Query var contacts: [Contact]
```

Once declared, the contacts array will automatically update to contain the latest contacts without the need to call the *fetch()* method on the model context.

The @Query macro can also be used to filter results using predicates and sort descriptors, for example:

```
@Query(filter: #Predicate<Contact> { $0.lastname.contains("Smith") }, sort:
[SortDescriptor(\Contact.lastname, order: .reverse)]) var theSmiths: [Visitor]
```

54.8 Model Relationships

Relationships between SwiftData models are declared using the @Relationship macro. Suppose, for example, that our address book app keeps a phone call log for each of our contacts. This will require a model class containing the date and time of the call:

```
@Model
```

```
class CallDate {

    var date: Date

    init(date: Date) {
        self.date = date
    }
}
```

To associate a contact with the list of calls, we need to establish a relationship between the Contact and CallDate models. This is achieved using the @Relationship macro in the Contact model as follows:

```
@Model
class Contact {
    var firstname: String
    var lastname: String
    var address: String

    @Relationship var calls = [CallDate]()

    init(firstname: String, lastname: String, address: String) {
        self.firstname = firstname
        self.lastname = lastname
        self.address = address
    }
}
```

With the relationship established, we can access the *calls* array property of contact model objects to access the list of associated calls. In the following code, for example, a new call entry is added to a contact's call log:

```
contact.calls.append(CallDate(date: Date.now))
```

When a model object is deleted, the default behavior is for any related objects to remain in the database. This means that if we deleted a contact, all of their calls would remain in the database. While this may be the desired behavior in other situations, it does not make sense to keep the log entries in our address book example. To delete all of the call data when a contact is removed, we can specify a deletion rule. In this case, the *cascade* option is used to remove all related data down through the entire chain of relationships:

```
@Relationship(deleteRule: .cascade) var calls = [CallDate]()
```

The full list of deletion rules is as follows:

- **cascade** - Removes all related objects.

- **deny** - Prevents the removal of objects containing relationships with other objects.

- **noAction** - Leaves the related objects unchanged, leaving in place references to the deleted objects.

- **nullify** - Does not remove the related objects but nullifies references to the deleted objects.

54.9 Model Attributes

The @Attributes macro applies behavior to individual properties in a model class. A common use is to specify unique properties. For example, to prevent duplicate last names, the @Attribute macro would be used as follows:

```
@Model
class Contact {
    var firstname: String
    @Attribute(.unique) var lastname: String
    var address: String

    @Relationship var calls = [CallDate]()

    init(firstname: String, lastname: String, address: String) {
        self.firstname = firstname
        self.lastname = lastname
        self.address = address
    }
}
```

Finally, a property within a model class may be excluded from being stored in the database using the @Transient macro:

```
@Model
class Contact {
    var firstname: String
    var lastname: String
    var address: String
    @Transient var tempAddr: String
```

54.10 Take the Knowledge Test

Click the link below or scan the QR code to test your knowledge and understanding of SwiftData:

https://www.answertopia.com/a7fx

54.11 Summary

SwiftData combines many of the features of Core Data with the convenience of SwiftUI to provide a simple way to store persistent data in iOS apps. The database schema are declared as Swift classes and adapted into SwiftData models using the @Model macro. The model container collects the model classes and uses them to create and manage the underlying database system. The model context tracks changes to the data and provides a programming interface for adding, searching, and modifying the stored data objects. Data is fetched using predicates, fetch descriptors, and the @Query macro. Relationships between models are established using the @Relationship macro, while the @Attributes macro allows rules to be applied to individual model class properties.

Chapter 55

55. A SwiftData Tutorial

This chapter will demonstrate how to use SwiftData by creating an example app project. The project will demonstrate how to declare models, create a model container, access the model context, add and delete data entries, establish relationships, and perform database searches.

55.1 About the SwiftData Project

The project will consist of a rudimentary visitor logging app containing a list of customers and the dates and times of their visits. Once the basics of the app are working, we will extend the project to allow the visitor list to be searched.

55.2 Creating the SwiftDataDemo Project

Launch Xcode and create a new Multiplatform App project named *SwiftDataDemo*.

55.3 Adding the Data Models

The first requirement for our app is the model that will store visitors' first and last names. Press Cmd-N and use the Swift file template to create a file named *Visitor.swift*. Open the file and add the model declaration:

```swift
import Foundation
import SwiftData

@Model
class Visitor {
    var firstname: String
    var lastname: String

    init(firstname: String, lastname: String) {
        self.firstname = firstname
        self.lastname = lastname
    }
}
```

Note the use of the @Model macro to declare the class as a SwiftData model. Repeat the above steps to add a second Swift file named *LogEntry.swift* that reads as follows:

```swift
import Foundation
import SwiftData

@Model
class LogEntry {

    var date: Date

    init(date: Date) {
        self.date = date
```

```
    }
}
```

55.4 Setting up the Model Container

With the models declared, the next step is to add the model container to the app's main scene. To do so, edit the *SwiftDataDemoApp.swift* file, import the SwiftData framework, and apply the *modelContainer(for:)* modifier to the WindowGroup, passing it a reference to the Visitor model:

```
import SwiftUI
import SwiftData

@main
struct SwiftDataDemoApp: App {
    var body: some Scene {
        WindowGroup {
            ContentView()
        }
        .modelContainer(for: Visitor.self)
    }
}
```

55.5 Accessing the Model Context

The model container will create an environment object containing the model context. We will need access to this context to insert, fetch, and delete data entries, starting with the *ContentView.swift* file:

```
import SwiftUI
import SwiftData

struct ContentView: View {

    @Environment(\.modelContext) var modelContext
.
.
```

55.6 Designing the Visitor List View

The app's home screen will display a list of visitor names. To simplify the code, we will declare this list in a separate view and call it from the content view. Add a new SwiftUI View file to the project named *VisitorListView.swift* and make the following changes:

```
import SwiftUI
import SwiftData

struct VisitorListView: View {

    @Environment(\.modelContext) var modelContext
    @Query var visitors: [Visitor]

    var body: some View {
        List {
```

```
                ForEach (visitors) { visitor in
                    NavigationLink(value: visitor) {
                        if (visitor.lastname.isEmpty) {
                            Text("Edit new visitor")
                                    .foregroundColor(Color.gray)
                        } else {
                            Text("\(visitor.lastname), \(visitor.firstname)")
                        }
                    }
                }
                .onDelete(perform: deleteVisitors)
            }
        }

    func deleteVisitors(_ indexSet: IndexSet) {
        for index in indexSet {
            let visitor = visitors[index]
            modelContext.delete(visitor)
        }
    }
}

/*
#Preview {
    VisitorListView()
}
*/
```

The above changes begin by obtaining access to the model context. The SwiftData @Query macro is then used to extract all the stored Visitor entries and place them in an array named *visitors*. A ForEach loop iterates through the visitors array, displaying each visitor as a list item. Finally, the *.onDelete()* modifier is applied to the ForEach loop and configured to call the *deleteVisitors()* function, which calls the model context's *delete()* method to remove the selected visitor.

55.7 Establishing the Relationship

The next view to be added is the visitor detail view, which will be displayed when a new visitor is added and to add log entries for existing visitors. Since each visitor will have their own log entries, we need to establish a relationship between the Visitor and LogEntry models. This will allow us to list and add log entries belonging to individual visitors. To establish the relationship, add the following @Relationship declaration to the *Visitor.swift* model:

```
import Foundation
import SwiftData

@Model
class Visitor {
    var firstname: String
    var lastname: String
```

```
@Relationship(deleteRule: .cascade) var visits = [LogEntry]()

init(firstname: String, lastname: String) {
    self.firstname = firstname
    self.lastname = lastname
}
}
```

Note that we have set the deleteRule parameter to *cascade*. This ensures that all related log entries are removed when a visitor is deleted.

55.8 Creating the Visitor Detail View

The visitor detail view will be used when adding new visitors and entries to a visitor's log. This will require an additional SwiftUI View file named *VisitorDetailView.swift*. Create this file and edit it as follows:

```
import SwiftUI

struct VisitorDetailView: View {

    @Bindable var visitor: Visitor

    var body: some View {
        Form {

            Section("Visitor") {
                TextField("First name", text: $visitor.firstname)
                TextField("Last name", text: $visitor.lastname)
            }

            Section("Visit History") {

                Button("Add Visit", action: addVisit)

                ForEach(visitor.visits) { visit in
                    Text(visit.date.formatted(date: .abbreviated,
                                              time: .shortened))
                }
            }
        }
        .navigationTitle("Visitor Detail")
        .navigationBarTitleDisplayMode(.inline)
    }

    func addVisit() {
        visitor.visits.append(LogEntry(date: Date.now))
    }
```

```
}

/*
#Preview {
    AddVisitorView()
}
*/
```

When called, the visitor detail view will be passed a Visitor object. This is declared as @Bindable because the TextFields need to bind to the *firstname* and *lastname* properties of the Visitor object. A ForEach loop then iterates through the log entries for the current visitor using the *visits* relationship declared in the Visitor model:

```
ForEach(visitor.visits) { visit in
    Text(visit.date.formatted(date: .abbreviated, time: .shortened))
}
```

Similarly, the relationship is used to append new entries to the visitor's log when the Add Visit button is clicked:

```
func addVisit() {
    visitor.visits.append(LogEntry(date: Date.now))
}
```

55.9 Modifying the Content View

The final task before testing the app is to design the main screen. Load the *ContentView.swift* file and make the following modifications:

```
import SwiftUI

struct ContentView: View {

    @Environment(\.modelContext) var modelContext

    var body: some View {
        NavigationStack {
            VisitorListView()
                .navigationTitle("Visitors")
                .navigationDestination(for: Visitor.self,
                            destination: VisitorDetailView.init)
                .toolbar {
                    Button("New Visitor", systemImage: "plus",
                                        action: addVisitor)
                }
        }
    }

    func addVisitor() {
        let visitor = Visitor(firstname: "", lastname: "")
        modelContext.insert(visitor)
    }
}
```

.

.

The layout consists of the VisitorListView embedded in a NavigationStack. The Navigation destination for the visitor list items is set to the VisitorDetailView, which is passed the selected Visitor object. A button is also placed in the toolbar, which uses the model context to insert a new visitor into the database.

55.10 Testing the SwiftData Demo App

Run the app on a device or simulator and tap the + button in the toolbar to add a new visitor, as shown below:

Figure 55-1

Select the new visitor list entry to display the detail view and enter a first and last name, then click the Add Visit button to add an entry to the log:

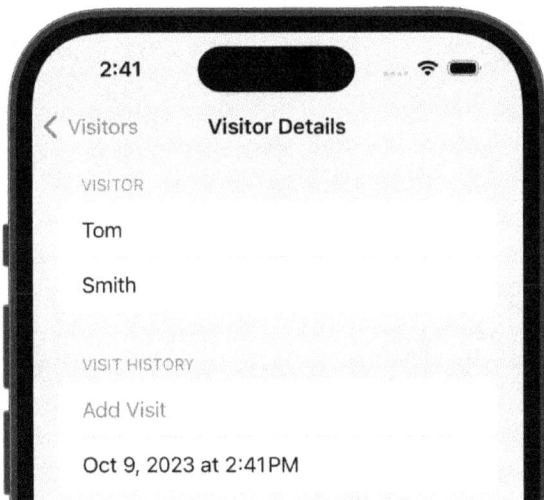

Figure 55-2

Return to the main screen and repeat the above steps to add more visitors, adding multiple log entries for each visitor. Stop and restart the app and verify that the visitors and log entries are restored.

55.11 Adding the Search Predicate

The last task in this tutorial is to make the visitor list searchable. Begin by editing the *ContentView.swift* file to add a search text state and to apply the *searchable()* modifier to the VisitorListView, passing it a binding to the search text state:

```
struct ContentView: View {
```

```
@Environment(\.modelContext) var modelContext
@State private var searchText = ""

var body: some View {
    NavigationStack {
        VisitorListView(searchText: searchText)
            .navigationTitle("Visitors")
            .searchable(text: $searchText)
            .navigationDestination(for: Visitor.self,
                        destination: VisitorDetailView.init)
            .toolbar {
                Button("New Visitor", systemImage: "plus",
                                        action: addVisitor)

            }
    }
}
.
.
```

Next, we need to alter VisitorListView so that it can be passed the search text. To do this, we will need to add an initializer to the class as follows:

```
struct VisitorListView: View {

    @Query var visitors: [Visitor]
    @Environment(\.modelContext) var modelContext

    var body: some View {
.
.

            .onDelete(perform: deleteVisitor)
        }
    }

    init(searchText: String) {

    }
.
.
```

As currently implemented, the @Query macro is configured to find all the stored Visitor entries as follows:

```
@Query var visitors: [Visitor]
```

Within the new initializer, we now need to assign a different query to the *visitors* variable when a search string has been entered. Queries are created by calling the SwiftData *Query()* method and passing it a filter predicate. From inside the initializer, this new query must be assigned to the *visitors* variable. When accessing a variable from an initializer, the variable name must be prefixed with an underscore (_). We can, therefore, modify our code as follows:

A SwiftData Tutorial

```
init(searchText: String) {
    _visitors = Query(filter: #Predicate {

    } )
}
```

The next step is to define the predicate, which needs to return a true or false value. If no search text has been entered, the predicate needs to return a true value so that all of the visitors are listed:

```
init(searchText: String) {
    _visitors = Query(filter: #Predicate {
        if searchText.isEmpty {
            return true
        }
    } )
}
```

If the user has entered a search string, the predicate needs to compare it to the last name of the current Visitor object and return the Boolean result. Within the predicate, the current Visitor object is referenced by *$0*, giving us access to the *lastname* property for comparison against the search text. To ensure the comparison is case-insensitive, we will use the *localizedStandardContains()* method for the comparison, as follows:

```
init(searchText: String) {
    _visitors = Query(filter: #Predicate {
        if searchText.isEmpty {
            return true
        } else {
            return $0.lastname.localizedStandardContains(searchText)
        }
    } )
}
```

Rerun the app and enter some visitors with the same last name. Start typing a last name in the search box at the bottom of the screen and check that the list updates with matching visitors, as illustrated in Figure 55-3:

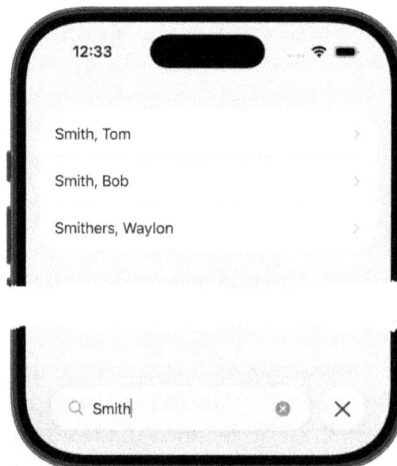

Figure 55-3

55.12 Summary

This chapter provided a tutorial demonstrating using SwiftData to provide persistent storage for an iOS app. Topics covered included declaring models and a model container and then accessing and using the model context to store and retrieve data. The app was then extended to add a search feature.

56. Building Widgets with SwiftUI and WidgetKit

Widgets allow small amounts of app content to be displayed alongside the app icons that appear on the device home screen pages, the Today view, and the macOS Notification Center. Widgets are built using SwiftUI in conjunction with the WidgetKit Framework.

The focus of this chapter is to provide a high-level outline of the various components that make up a widget before exploring widget creation in practical terms in the chapters that follow.

56.1 An Overview of Widgets

Widgets are intended to provide users with "at a glance" views of important, time-sensitive information relating to your app. When the user taps a widget, the corresponding app is launched, taking the user to a specific screen where more detailed information may be presented. Widgets are intended to display information that updates based on a timeline, ensuring that only the latest information is displayed to the user. A single app can have multiple widgets displaying different information.

Widgets are available in three *size families* (small, medium, and large), of which the widget must support at least one size. They can be implemented such that the information displayed is customizable by the user.

Widgets are selected from the widget gallery and positioned by the user on the device's home screen. To conserve screen space, iOS allows widgets to be stacked, allowing users to flip through each widget in the stack with a swiping gesture. A widget can increase the probability of moving automatically to the top of the stack by assigning a relevancy score to specific timeline entries. For example, the widget for a weather app might assign high relevancy to a severe weather warning in the hope that WidgetKit will move it to the top of the stack, thereby increasing the likelihood that the user will see the information.

56.2 The Widget Extension

A widget is created by adding a *widget extension* to an existing app. A widget extension consists of a Swift file, an *app configuration intent* class (required if the widget is to be user configurable), an asset catalog, and an *Info.plist* file.

The widget itself is declared as a structure conforming to the Widget protocol, and it is within this declaration that the basic configuration of the widget is declared. The body of a typical widget declaration will include the following items:

- **Widget kind** – Identifies the widget within the project. This can be any String value that uniquely identifies the widget within the project.

- **Widget Configuration** – A declaration that conforms to the appropriate intent protocol. This includes a reference to the *timeline provider* containing the information to be displayed, the widget display name and description, and the size families supported by the widget. WidgetKit supports two types of widget configuration: *static configuration* and *app intent configuration*.

- **Entry View** – A reference to the SwiftUI View containing the layout that is to be presented to the user when the widget is displayed. This layout is populated with content from individual *timeline entries* at specific points in the *widget timeline*.

In addition to the widget declaration, the extension must also include a placeholder View defining the layout to be displayed to the user while the widget is loading and gathering data. This may be declared manually or configured to be automatically generated by WidgetKit based on the entry view included in the Widget view declaration outlined above.

56.3 Widget Configuration Types

When creating a widget, the choice must be made regarding whether it should be created using the static or intent configuration model. These two options can be summarized as follows:

- **App Intent Configuration** – Used when the widget needs to provide a configuration option to the user, for example, allowing the user to select the news publications from which headlines are to be displayed within the widget.

- **Static Configuration** – Used when the widget has no user-configurable properties.

When the configuration app intent option is used, the configuration options presented to the user are declared within a WidgetConfigurationIntent instance.

The following is an example widget entry containing a static configuration designed to support both small and medium size families:

```
struct DemoWidget: Widget {
    let kind: String = "DemoWidget2"

    var body: some WidgetConfiguration {
        StaticConfiguration(kind: kind, provider: Provider()) { entry in
            DemoWidgetEntryView(entry: entry)
                    .containerBackground(.fill.tertiary, for: .widget)
        }
        .configurationDisplayName("My Widget")
        .description("This is an example widget.")
        .supportedFamilies([.systemSmall, .systemMedium])
    }
}
```

The following listing, on the other hand, declares a widget using an app intent configuration:

```
struct DemoWidget: Widget {
    let kind: String = "DemoWidget"

    var body: some WidgetConfiguration {
        AppIntentConfiguration(kind: kind, intent: ConfigurationAppIntent.self,
                               provider: Provider()) { entry in
            DemoWidgetEntryView(entry: entry)
                .containerBackground(.fill.tertiary, for: .widget)
        }
        .configurationDisplayName("A Simple Widget")
        .description("This is an example widget.")
```

```
        .supportedFamilies([.systemSmall, .systemMedium])
    }
}
```

56.4 Widget Entry View

The widget entry view is simply a SwiftUI View declaration containing the layout to be displayed by the widget. Conditional logic (for example, *if* or *switch* statements based on the *widgetFamily* environment property) can present different layouts subject to the prevailing size family.

Except for tapping to open the corresponding app, widgets are non-interactive. As such, the entry view will typically consist of display-only views (in other words, no buttons, sliders, or toggles).

When WidgetKit creates an instance of the entry view, it passes it a *widget timeline entry* containing the data to be displayed on the views that make up the layout. The following view declaration is designed to display city name and temperature values:

```
struct DemoWidgetEntryView : View {
    var entry: Provider.Entry

    var body: some View {
        ZStack {
            Color("demoBackgroundColor")
            DemoSubView(entry: entry)
        }
    }
}
```

56.5 Widget Timeline Entries

The purpose of a widget is to display different information at specific points in time. For example, the widget for a calendar app might change throughout the day to display the user's next appointment. The content displayed at each point in the timeline is contained within *widget entry* objects conforming to the TimelineEntry protocol. Each entry must, at a minimum, include a Date object defining the point in the timeline at which the data in the entry is to be displayed, together with any data needed to populate the widget entry view at the specified time. The following is an example of a timeline entry declaration designed for use with the above entry view:

```
struct WeatherEntry: TimelineEntry {
    var date: Date
    let city: String
    let temperature: Int
}
```

If necessary, the Date object can be a placeholder to be updated with the actual time and date when the entry is added to a timeline.

56.6 Widget Timeline

The widget timeline is simply an array of widget entries that defines the points in time that the widget is to be updated, together with the content to be displayed at each time point. Timelines are constructed and returned to WidgetKit by a *widget provider*.

56.7 Widget Provider

The widget provider is responsible for providing the content displayed on the widget. The provider must conform to either the TimelineProvider or AppIntentTimelineProvider protocols, depending on whether the widget supports static or app intent configuration. At a minimum, it must implement the following methods:

- **snapshot()** – The *snapshot()* method (*getSnapshot()* for static configuration) of the provider will be called by WidgetKit when a single, populated widget timeline entry is required. This snapshot is used within the widget gallery to show how the widget would appear if the user added it to the device. Since real data may not be available at the point that the user is browsing the widget gallery, the entry returned should typically be populated with sample data.

- **timeline()** - This method is responsible for assembling and returning a Timeline instance containing the array of widget timeline entries that define how and when the widget content is to be updated, together with an optional *reload policy* value. For static configuration, the method is called *getTimeline()*.

- **placeholder()** - The *placeholder()* method returns a widget view to be displayed while the app initializes. For static configuration, the method is called *getPlaceholder()*

The following code excerpt declares an example app intent configuration timeline provider:

```
struct Provider: AppIntentTimelineProvider {

    func placeholder(in context: Context) -> SimpleEntry {
        SimpleEntry(date: Date(), configuration: ConfigurationAppIntent())
    }

    func snapshot(for configuration: ConfigurationAppIntent,
                  in context: Context) async -> SimpleEntry {
        SimpleEntry(date: Date(), configuration: configuration)
    }

    func timeline(for configuration: ConfigurationAppIntent,
                  in context: Context) async -> Timeline<SimpleEntry> {
        var entries: [SimpleEntry] = []

        // Construct timeline array here

        return Timeline(entries: entries, policy: .atEnd)
    }
}
```

56.8 Reload Policy

When a widget is displaying entries from a timeline, WidgetKit needs to know what action to take when it reaches the end of the timeline. The following predefined reload policy options are available for use when the provider returns a timeline:

- **atEnd** – At the end of the current timeline, WidgetKit will request a new timeline from the provider. This is the default behavior if no reload policy is specified.

- **after(Date)** – WidgetKit will request a new timeline after the specified date and time.

- **never** – The timeline is not reloaded at the end of the timeline.

56.9 Relevance

As previously mentioned, iOS allows widgets to be placed in a stack in which only the uppermost widget is visible. While the user can scroll through the stacked widgets to decide which is to occupy the topmost position, this presents the risk that the user may not see an essential update in time to act on the information.

To address this issue, WidgetKit is allowed to move a widget to the top of the stack if the information it contains is relevant to the user. This decision is based on various factors, such as the user's previous behavior (for example, checking a bus schedule widget at the same time every day), together with a relevance score assigned by the widget to a particular timeline entry.

Relevance is declared using a TimelineEntryRelevance structure. This contains a relevancy score and a time duration for which the entry is relevant. The score can be any floating point value and is measured relative to all other timeline entries generated by the widget. For example, if most relevancy scores in the timeline entries range between 0.0 and 10.0, a relevancy score of 20.0 assigned to an entry may cause the widget to move to the top of the stack. The following code declares two relevancy entries:

```
let lowScore = TimelineEntryRelevance(score: 0.0, duration: 0)
let highScore = TimelineEntryRelevance(score: 10.0, duration: 0)
```

If relevancy is to be included in an entry, it must appear after the date entry, for example:

```
struct WeatherEntry: TimelineEntry {
    var date: Date
    var relevance: TimelineEntryRelevance?
    let city: String
    let temperature: Int
}
.
.
let entry1 = WeatherEntry(date: Date(), relevance: lowScore, city: "London",
temperature: 87)

let entry2 = WeatherEntry(date: Date(), relevance: highScore, city: "London",
temperature: 87)
```

56.10 Forcing a Timeline Reload

WidgetKit requests a timeline containing the time points and content to display to the user when a widget is launched. Under normal conditions, WidgetKit will not request another timeline update until the end of the timeline is reached, and then only if required by the reload policy.

Situations commonly arise, however, where the information in a timeline needs to be updated. A user might, for example, add a new appointment to a calendar app that requires a timeline update. Fortunately, the widget can be forced to request an updated timeline by making a call to the *reloadTimelines()* method of the WidgetKit WidgetCenter instance, passing through the widget's *kind* string value (defined in the widget configuration as outlined earlier in the chapter). For example:

```
WidgetCenter.shared.reloadTimelines(ofKind: "My Kind")
```

Alternatively, it is also possible to trigger a timeline reload for all the active widgets associated with an app as follows:

```
WidgetCenter.shared.reloadAllTimelines()
```

56.11 Widget Sizes

As previously discussed, widgets can be displayed in small, medium, and large sizes. The widget declares which sizes it supports by applying the *supportedFamilies()* modifier to the widget configuration as follows:

```
struct SimpleWidget: Widget {
    private let kind: String = "SimpleWidget"

    var body: some WidgetConfiguration {
        AppIntentConfiguration(kind: kind, intent: ConfigurationAppIntent.self,
                                  provider: Provider()) { entry in
            SimpleWidgetEntryView(entry: entry)
        }
        .configurationDisplayName("Weather Fun")
        .description("Learning about weather in real-time.")
        .supportedFamilies([.systemSmall, .systemMedium])
    }
}
```

The following figure shows the built-in iOS Calendar widget in small, medium, and large formats:

Figure 56-1

56.12 Widget Placeholder

As previously mentioned, the widget extension must provide a placeholder. This view is displayed to the user while the widget is initializing and takes the form of the widget entry view without any data or information. Consider the following example widget:

Figure 56-2

The above example, of course, shows the widget running after it has received the timeline data to be displayed.

During initialization, however, the placeholder view resembling Figure 56-3 would be expected to be displayed:

Figure 56-3

Fortunately, SwiftUI includes the *redacted(reason:)* modifier, which may be applied to an instance of the widget entry view to act as a placeholder. The following is an example of a placeholder view declaration for a widget extension using the *redacted()* modifier (note that the reason is set to *placeholder*):

```
struct PlaceholderView : View {
    var body: some View {
        SimpleWidgetEntryView()
            .redacted(reason: .placeholder)
    }
}
```

56.13 Take the Knowledge Test

Click the link below or scan the QR code to test your knowledge and understanding of WidgetKit:

https://www.answertopia.com/apcs

56.14 Summary

Widgets allow apps to present important information to the user directly on the device's home screen without launching the app. Widgets are implemented using the WidgetKit Framework and take the form of extensions added to the main app. Widgets are driven by timelines, which control the information displayed to the user and when it appears. Widgets can support small, medium, and large formats and may be designed to be configurable by the user. Users can place widgets into a stack when adding them to the home screen. By adjusting the relevance of a timeline entry, a widget can increase the chances of being moved to the top of the stack.

57. A SwiftUI WidgetKit Tutorial

From the previous chapter, we now understand the elements that make up a widget and the steps involved in creating one. In this, the first of a series of tutorial chapters dedicated to WidgetKit, we will begin creating an app that includes a widget extension. After completing these tutorials, a functioning widget will have been created, including widget design and timelines, support for different size families, deep links, and configuration using intents.

57.1 About the WidgetDemo Project

The project created in this tutorial is the early prototype of a weather app designed to teach children about weather storms. The objective is to provide the user with a list of severe weather systems (tropical storms, thunderstorms, etc.) and display a second screen describing the weather system when a storm type is selected.

A second part of the app is intended to provide real-time updates on severe weather occurring in different locations around the world. When a storm is reported, a widget will be updated with information about the type and location of the storm, together with the prevailing temperature. When the user taps the widget, the app will open the screen containing information about that storm category.

Since this app is an early prototype, however, it will only provide weather updates from two cities, and that data will be simulated rather than obtained from a genuine weather service. However, the app will be functional enough to demonstrate how to implement the key features of WidgetKit.

57.2 Creating the WidgetDemo Project

Launch Xcode and select the option to create a new Multiplatform App project named *WidgetDemo*.

57.3 Building the App

Before adding the widget extension to the project, the first step is to build the basic structure of the app, consisting of a List view populated with some storm categories, which, when selected, will appear in a detail screen.

The first requirement is a structure to store the current weather type. Within the project navigator panel, right-click on the WidgetDemo folder and select the *New File from Template...* menu option, followed by the Swift File template. Click the Next button, name the file *WeatherType.swift*, and click the Create button. Load the new file into the editor and modify it so that it reads as follows:

```
struct WeatherType: Hashable {
    var name: String
    var icon: String
}
```

The detail screen will be declared in a new SwiftUI View file named *WeatherDetailView.swift*. Within the project navigator panel, right-click on the WidgetDemo folder and select the *New File from Template...* menu option. Select the SwiftUI View template option in the resulting dialog and click the Next button. Name the file *WeatherDetailView.swift* before creating the file.

With the *WeatherDetailView.swift* file selected, modify the view declaration so that it reads as follows:

```
import SwiftUI
```

```
struct WeatherDetailView: View {

    var weather: WeatherType

    var body: some View {
        VStack {
            Image(systemName: weather.icon)
                .resizable()
                    .scaledToFit()
                    .frame(width: 150.0, height: 150.0)
            Text(weather.name)
                .padding()
                .font(.title)
            Text("If this were a real weather app, a description of \(weather.
name) would appear here.")
                .padding()
            Spacer()
        }
    }
}


#Preview {
    WeatherDetailView(weather: WeatherType(
            name: "Thunder Storms", icon: "cloud.bolt"))
}
```

When rendered, the above view should appear in the preview canvas, as shown in Figure 57-1 below:

Figure 57-1

Next, select the *ContentView.swift* file and modify it to add a List view embedded in a NavigationStack as follows:

```
import SwiftUI

struct ContentView: View {
```

```
var body: some View {

    NavigationStack {
        List {
            NavigationLink(value: WeatherType(name: "Hail Storm",
                                              icon: "cloud.hail")) {
                Label("Hail Storm", systemImage: "cloud.hail")
            }

            NavigationLink(value: WeatherType(name: "Thunder Storm",
                                              icon: "cloud.bolt.rain")) {
                Label("Thunder Storm", systemImage: "cloud.bolt.rain")
            }

            NavigationLink(value: WeatherType(name: "Tropical Storm",
                                              icon: "tropicalstorm")) {
                Label("Tropical Storm", systemImage: "tropicalstorm")
            }
        }
        .navigationDestination(for: WeatherType.self) { weather in
            WeatherDetailView(weather: weather)
        }
        .navigationTitle("Severe Weather")
    }
}
}
```

Once the changes are complete, make sure that the layout matches that shown in Figure 57-2:

Figure 57-2

Using Live Preview, make sure that selecting a weather type displays the detail screen populated with the correct storm name and image.

57.4 Adding the Widget Extension

The next step in the project is to add the widget extension by selecting the *File -> New -> Target...* menu option. From within the target template panel, select the Widget Extension option, as shown in Figure 57-3, before clicking on the Next button:

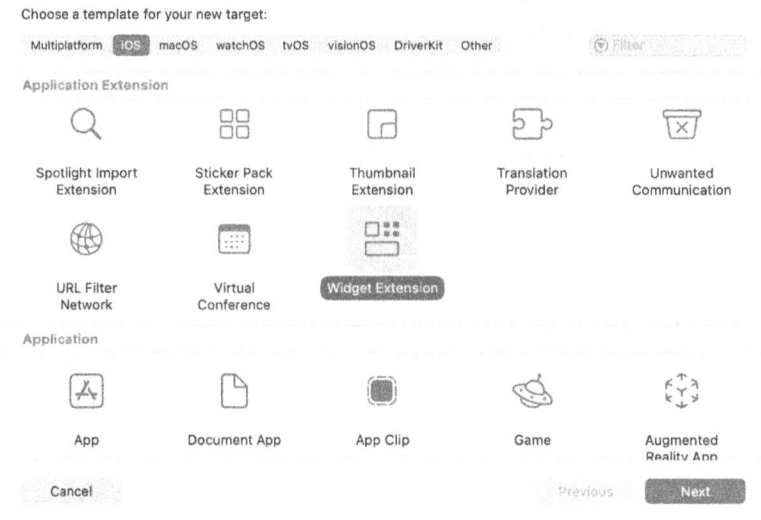

Figure 57-3

On the subsequent screen, enter WeatherWidget into the product name field. When the widget is completed, the user will be able to select the geographical location for which weather updates are to be displayed. To make this possible, the widget must use the intent configuration type. Before clicking on the Finish button, therefore, make sure that the *Include Configuration App Intent* option is enabled and the *Include Live Activity* and Include Control optiona are turned off, as shown in Figure 57-4:

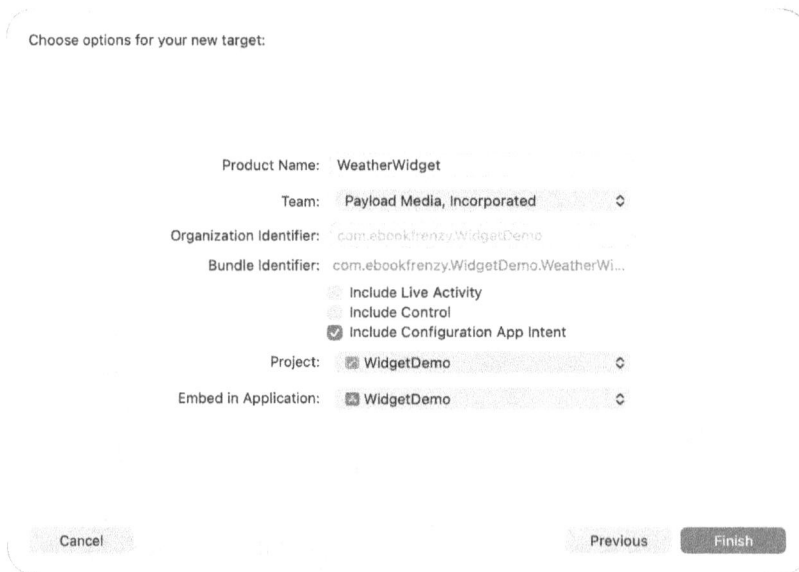

Figure 57-4

When prompted, click on the Activate button to activate the extension within the project scheme. This will ensure that the widget is included in the project build process:

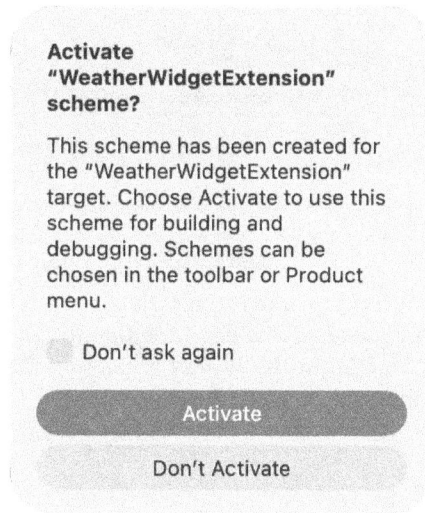

Activate "WeatherWidgetExtension" scheme?

This scheme has been created for the "WeatherWidgetExtension" target. Choose Activate to use this scheme for building and debugging. Schemes can be chosen in the toolbar or Product menu.

Don't ask again

Activate

Don't Activate

Figure 57-5

Once the extension has been added, refer to the project navigator panel, where a new folder containing the widget extension will have been added, as shown in Figure 57-6:

∨ 📁 WeatherWidget
  🦅 AppIntent
  🖼 Assets
  ⊞ Info
  🦅 WeatherWidget
  🦅 WeatherWidgetBundle

Figure 57-6

57.5 Adding the Widget Data

Now that the widget extension has been added to the project, the next step is adding some data and data structures to provide the basis for the widget timeline. Begin by right-clicking on the WidgetDemo folder in the project navigator and selecting the *New File from Template...* menu option.

From the template selection panel, select the *Swift File* entry, click on the Next button, and name the file *WeatherData.swift*. Before clicking on the Create button, make sure that the WeatherWidgetExtension entry is enabled in the Targets section of the panel, as shown in Figure 57-7, so that the file will be accessible to the extension:

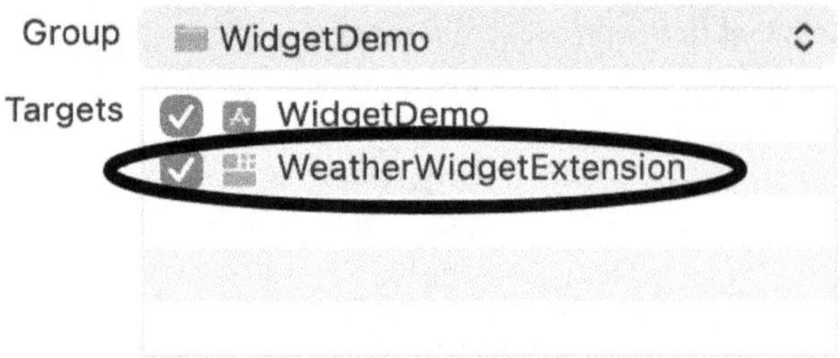

Figure 57-7

As outlined in the previous chapter, each point in the widget timeline is represented by a widget timeline entry instance. Instances of this structure contain the date and time that the entry is to be presented by the widget, together with the data to be displayed. Within the *WeatherData.swift* file, add a TimelineEntry structure as follows (noting that the WidgetKit framework also needs to be imported):

```
import Foundation
import WidgetKit


struct WeatherEntry: TimelineEntry {
    var date: Date
    let city: String
    let temperature: Int
    let description: String
    let icon: String
    let image: String
}
```

57.6 Creating Sample Timelines

Since this prototype app does not have access to live weather data, the timelines used to drive the widget content will contain sample weather entries for two cities. Remaining within the *WeatherData.swift* file, add these timeline declarations as follows:

```
    .
    .
let londonTimeline = [
    WeatherEntry(date: Date(), city: "London", temperature: 87,
            description: "Hail Storm", icon: "cloud.hail",
                    image: "hail"),
    WeatherEntry(date: Date(), city: "London", temperature: 92,
            description: "Thunder Storm", icon: "cloud.bolt.rain",
                    image: "thunder"),
    WeatherEntry(date: Date(), city: "London", temperature: 95,
            description: "Hail Storm", icon: "cloud.hail",
                    image: "hail")
]


let miamiTimeline = [
```

```
WeatherEntry(date: Date(), city: "Miami", temperature: 81,
      description: "Thunder Storm", icon: "cloud.bolt.rain",
            image: "thunder"),
WeatherEntry(date: Date(), city: "Miami", temperature: 74,
      description: "Tropical Storm", icon: "tropicalstorm",
            image: "tropical"),
WeatherEntry(date: Date(), city: "Miami", temperature: 72,
      description: "Thunder Storm", icon: "cloud.bolt.rain",
            image: "thunder")
]
```

Note that the timeline entries are populated with the current date and time via a call to the Swift *Date()* method. The provider will replace these values with more appropriate ones when WidgetKit requests the timeline.

57.7 Adding Image and Color Assets

Before moving to the next step of the tutorial, some image and color assets need to be added to the asset catalog of the widget extension.

Begin by selecting the *Assets* item located in the WeatherWidget folder in the project navigator panel, as highlighted in Figure 57-8:

Figure 57-8

Add a new entry to the catalog by clicking on the button indicated by the arrow in Figure 57-8 above. In the resulting menu, select the *Color Set* option. Click on the new Color entry and change the name to weatherBackgroundColor. With this new entry selected, click on the *Any Appearance* block in the main panel, as shown in Figure 57-9:

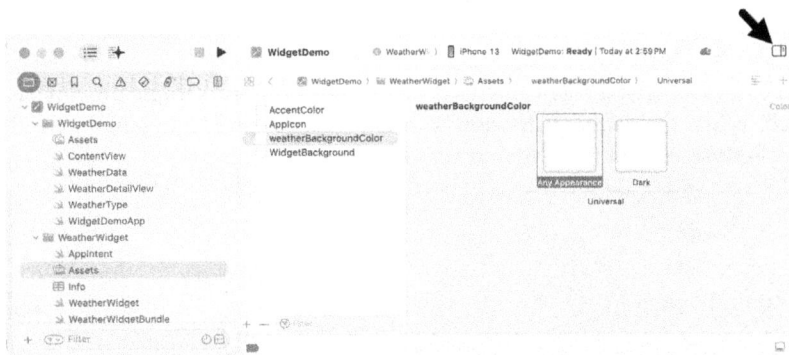

Figure 57-9

Use the button indicated by the arrow above to display the attributes inspector and locate the Color settings. Set

485

Content to *Display P3*, Input Method to *8-bit Hexadecimal*, and the Hex field to *#4C5057*:

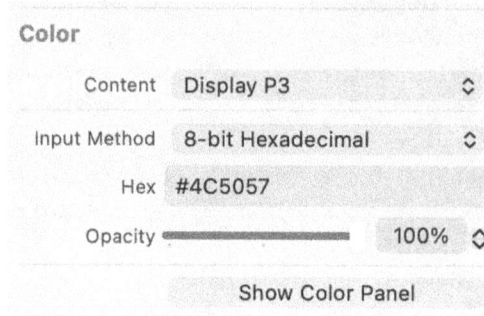

Figure 57-10

Select the Dark Appearance and make the same attribute changes, this time setting the Hex value to *#3A4150*.

Next, add a second Color Set asset, name it weatherInsetColor, and use #4E7194 for the Any Appearance color value and #7E848F for the Dark Appearance.

The images used by this project can be found in the *weather_images* folder of the sample code download available from the following URL:

https://www.payloadbooks.com/product/ios26code/

Once the source archive has been downloaded and unpacked, open a Finder window, navigate to the *weather_images* folder, and select, drag and drop the images onto the left-hand panel of the Xcode asset catalog screen, as shown in Figure 57-11:

Figure 57-11

57.8 Designing the Widget View

Now that the widget entry has been created and used as the basis for some sample timeline data, the widget view needs to be designed. When the widget extension was added to the project, a template widget entry view was included in the *WeatherWidget.swift* file, which reads as follows:

```
struct WeatherWidgetEntryView : View {
    var entry: Provider.Entry

    var body: some View {
        VStack {
            Text("Time:")
            Text(entry.date, style: .time)
```

```
            Text("Favorite Emoji:")
            Text(entry.configuration.favoriteEmoji)
        }
    }
}
```

As currently implemented, the view is passed a widget entry from which a date value and emoji are extracted and displayed on Text views.

Modify the view structure so that it reads as follows, keeping in mind that it will result in syntax errors appearing in the editor. These will be resolved later in the tutorial:

```
struct WeatherWidgetEntryView: View {
    var entry: Provider.Entry

    var body: some View {
        ZStack {
            Color("weatherBackgroundColor")
            WeatherSubView(entry: entry)
        }
    }
}


struct WeatherSubView: View {

    var entry: WeatherEntry

    var body: some View {

        VStack {
            VStack {
                Text("\(entry.city)")
                    .font(.title)
                Image(systemName: entry.icon)
                    .font(.largeTitle)
                Text("\(entry.description)")
                    .frame(minWidth: 125, minHeight: nil)
            }
            .padding(.bottom, 2)
            .background(ContainerRelativeShape()
                    .fill(Color("weatherInsetColor")))
            Label("\(entry.temperature)°F", systemImage: "thermometer")
        }
        .foregroundColor(.white)
        .padding()
    }
```

```
}
```

We also need to set the container background color of the WeatherWidgetEntryView when it is called in the body of the WeatherWidget declaration:

```
struct WeatherWidget: Widget {
    let kind: String = "WeatherWidget"

    var body: some WidgetConfiguration {
        AppIntentConfiguration(kind: kind,
          intent: ConfigurationAppIntent.self, provider: Provider()) { entry in
            WeatherWidgetEntryView(entry: entry)
                .containerBackground(Color("weatherBackgroundColor"),
                               for: .widget)
        }
    }
}
```

Since we have changed the view, the preview provider declaration will also need to be changed as follows:

```
#Preview(as: .systemSmall) {
    WeatherWidget()
} timeline: {
    WeatherEntry(date: Date(),
                      city: "London", temperature: 89,
               description: "Thunder Storm",
                     icon: "cloud.bolt.rain", image: "thunder")
    WeatherEntry(date: Date(),
                      city: "London", temperature: 89,
               description: "Hail",
                     icon: "cloud.hail", image: "hail")
}
```

57.9 Modifying the Widget Provider

When the widget extension was added to the project, Xcode added a widget provider to the *WeatherWidget. swift* file. This declaration now needs to be modified to make use of the WeatherEntry structure declared in the *WeatherData.swift* file. The first step is to modify the *snapshot()* method to use WeatherEntry and to return an instance populated with sample data:

```
.

.

struct Provider: AppIntentTimelineProvider {

.

.

    func snapshot(for configuration: ConfigurationAppIntent, in context: Context)
                                        async -> WeatherEntry {
        WeatherEntry(date: Date(), city: "London",
                        temperature: 89, description: "Thunder Storm",
                          icon: "cloud.bolt.rain", image: "thunder")
    }
```

Next, the *timeline()* method needs to be modified to return an array of timeline entry objects together with a reload policy value. Since user configuration has not yet been added to the widget, the *timeline()* method will be configured initially to return the timeline for London:

```
func timeline(for configuration: ConfigurationAppIntent, in context: Context)
                                          async -> Timeline<WeatherEntry> {

    var entries: [WeatherEntry] = []
    var eventDate = Date()
    let halfMinute: TimeInterval = 30

    for var entry in londonTimeline {
        entry.date = eventDate
        eventDate += halfMinute
        entries.append(entry)
    }

    return Timeline(entries: entries, policy: .atEnd)
}
```

The above code begins by declaring an array to contain the WeatherEntry instances before creating variables designed to represent the current event time and a 30-second time interval, respectively.

A loop then iterates through the London timeline declared in the *WeatherData.swift* file, setting the eventDate value as the date and time at which the event is to be displayed by the widget. A 30-second interval is then added to the eventDate ready for the next event. Finally, the modified event is appended to the entries array. Once all of the events have been added to the array, it is used to create a Timeline instance with a reload policy of *never* (in other words, WidgetKit will not ask for a new timeline when the first timeline ends). The timeline is then returned to WidgetKit via the completion handler.

This implementation of the *timeline()* method will result in the widget changing content every 30 seconds until the final entry in the London timeline array is reached.

57.10 Configuring the Placeholder View

The Final task before previewing the widget is to make sure that the placeholder view has been implemented. Xcode will have already created a *placeholder()* method for this purpose within the *WeatherWidget.swift* file, which reads as follows:

```
func placeholder(in context: Context) -> SimpleEntry {
    SimpleEntry(date: Date(), configuration: ConfigurationAppIntent())
}
```

This method now needs to be modified so that it returns a WeatherWidget instance populated with some sample data as follows:

```
func placeholder(in context: Context) -> WeatherEntry {
    WeatherEntry(date: Date(), city: "London",
                     temperature: 89, description: "Thunder Storm",
                         icon: "cloud.bolt.rain", image: "thunder")
}
```

57.11 Previewing the Widget

Using the preview canvas, verify that the widget appears, as shown in Figure 57-12 below:

Figure 57-12

The preview also includes a panel for stepping through the timeline entries, as shown in Figure 57-13 below:

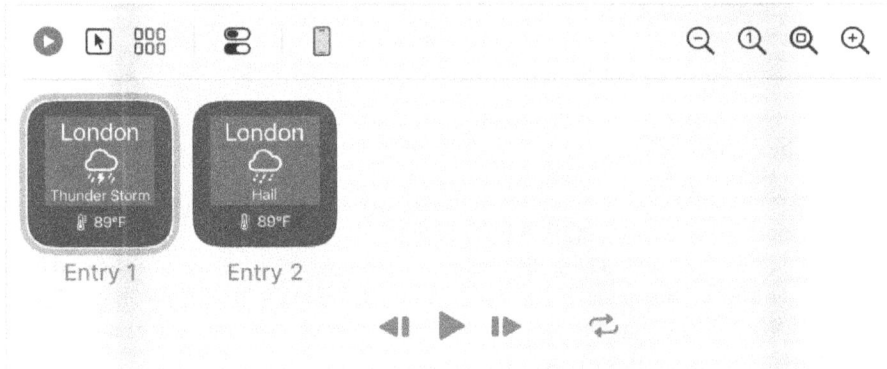

Figure 57-13

Before we can test the widget on a device or simulator, we must install the WidgetDemo app. In the Xcode toolbar, select WidgetDemo from the scheme menu:

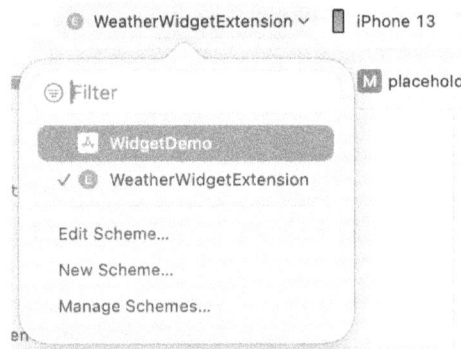

Figure 57-14

If the WidgetDemo target is not listed in the menu, select the *Manage Schemes...* option to display the dialog shown in Figure 57-15:

Figure 57-15

Click on the + button highlighted above and select WidgetDemo from the resulting dialog before clicking OK and closing the Manage Schemes dialog:

Figure 57-16

Next, test the widget on a device or simulator by changing the active scheme in the Xcode toolbar to the WeatherWidgetExtension scheme before clicking on the run button:

Figure 57-17

After a short delay, the widget will appear on the home screen and cycle through the different weather events at 30-second intervals:

Figure 57-18

57.12 Summary

The example project created in this chapter has demonstrated how to use WidgetKit to create a widget extension for an iOS app. This included the addition of the extension to the project, the design of the widget view and entry together with the implementation of a sample timeline. The widget created in this chapter, however, has yet to make use of the different widget size families supported by WidgetKit, a topic that will be covered in the next chapter.

58. Supporting WidgetKit Size Families

In the chapter titled *"Building Widgets with SwiftUI and WidgetKit"*, we learned that a widget can appear in small, medium, and large sizes. The project created in the previous chapter included a widget view designed to fit within the small-size format. Since the widget did not specify the supported sizes, it would still be possible to select a large or medium-sized widget from the gallery and place it on the home screen. In those larger formats, however, the widget content would have filled only a fraction of the available widget space. If larger widget sizes are to be supported, the widget should be designed to make full use of the available space.

In this chapter, the WidgetDemo project created in the previous chapter will be modified to add support for the medium widget size.

58.1 Supporting Multiple Size Families

Begin by launching Xcode and loading the WidgetDemo project from the previous chapter. As outlined above, this phase of the project will add support for the medium widget size (though these steps apply equally to adding support for the large widget size).

In the absence of specific size configurations, widgets are, by default, configured to support all three size families. To restrict a widget to specific sizes, the *supportedFamilies()* modifier must be applied to the widget configuration.

To restrict the widget to only small and medium sizes for the WidgetDemo project, edit the *WeatherWidget.swift* file and modify the WeatherWidget declaration to add the modifier. Also, take this opportunity to modify the widget display name and description:

```
struct WeatherWidget: Widget {
    let kind: String = "WeatherWidget"

    var body: some WidgetConfiguration {
        AppIntentConfiguration(kind: kind, intent: ConfigurationAppIntent.self,
                provider: Provider()) { entry in
            WeatherWidgetEntryView(entry: entry)
                .containerBackground(Color("weatherBackgroundColor"),
                        for: .widget)
        }
        .configurationDisplayName("My Weather Widget")
        .description("A demo weather widget.")
        .supportedFamilies([.systemSmall, .systemMedium])
    }
}
```

To preview the widget in medium format, edit the preview macro as follows:

```
#Preview(as: .systemMedium) {
```

```
    WeatherWidget()
} timeline: {
    WeatherEntry(date: Date(),
.

.
```

When the preview canvas updates, it will now include the widget rendered in medium size, as shown in Figure 58-1:

Figure 58-1

Clearly, the widget needs to take advantage of the additional space the medium size offers. To address this shortcoming, some changes to the widget view must be made.

58.2 Adding Size Support to the Widget View

The changes made to the widget configuration mean that the widget can be displayed in either small or medium size. To make the widget adaptive, the widget view needs to identify the size in which it is currently being displayed. This can be achieved by accessing the widgetFamily property of the SwiftUI environment. Remaining in the *WeatherWidget.swift* file, locate and edit the WeatherWidgetEntryView declaration to obtain the widget family setting from the environment:

```
struct WeatherWidgetEntryView: View {
    var entry: Provider.Entry

    @Environment(\.widgetFamily) var widgetFamily
.

.
```

Next, embed the subview in a horizontal stack and conditionally display the image for the entry if the size is medium:

```
struct WeatherWidgetEntryView : View {
    var entry: Provider.Entry

    @Environment(\.widgetFamily) var widgetFamily

    var body: some View {

        ZStack {
```

494

```
        Color("weatherBackgroundColor")

        HStack {
            WeatherSubView(entry: entry)
            if widgetFamily == .systemMedium {
                Image(entry.image)
                    .resizable()
            }
        }
    }
  }
}
```

When previewed, the medium-sized version of the widget should appear, as shown in Figure 58-2:

Figure 58-2

To test the widget on a device or simulator, run the extension as before, and once the widget is installed and running, perform a long press on the home screen background. After a few seconds have elapsed, the screen will change, as shown in Figure 58-3:

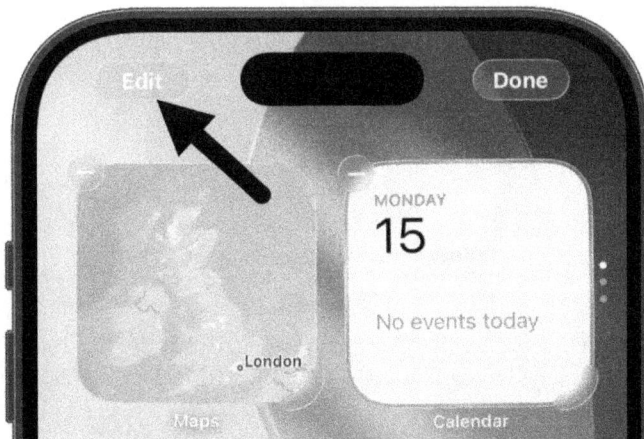

Figure 58-3

Supporting WidgetKit Size Families

To display the widget gallery, click on the Edit button indicated by the arrow in the above figure, followed by the Add Widget menu option, and enter WidgetDemo into the search field:

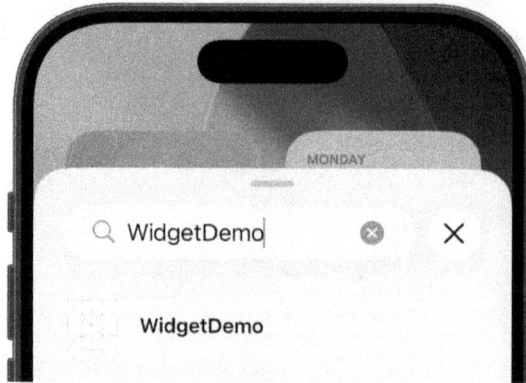

Figure 58-4

Select the WidgetDemo entry to display the widget size options. Swipe to the left to display the medium widget size, as shown in Figure 58-5, before tapping on the Add Widget button:

Figure 58-5

On returning to the home screen, click on the Done button located in the top right-hand corner of the home screen to commit the change. The widget will appear, as illustrated in Figure 58-6, and update as the timeline progresses:

Figure 58-6

Alternatively, perform a long press on the widget and make a selection from the size options in the resulting menu:

Figure 58-7

58.3 Take the Knowledge Test

Click the link below or scan the QR code to test your knowledge and understanding of WidgetKit size families:

https://www.answertopia.com/510q

58.4 Summary

WidgetKit supports small, medium, and large widget size families, and, by default, a widget is assumed to support all three formats. WidgetKit needs to be notified using a widget configuration modifier if a widget only supports specific sizes.

To fully support a size format, a widget should take steps to detect the current size and provide a widget entry layout that makes use of the available space allocated to the widget on the device screen. This involves accessing the SwiftUI environment widgetFamily property and using it as the basis for conditional layout declarations within the widget view.

Now that widget-size family support has been added to the project, the next chapter will add some interactive support to the widget in the form of deep linking into the companion app and widget configuration.

59. A SwiftUI WidgetKit Deep Link Tutorial

WidgetKit deep links allow the individual views that make up the widget entry view to open different screens within the companion app when tapped. In addition to the main home screen, the WidgetDemo app created in the preceding chapters contains a detail screen to provide the user with information about different weather systems. As currently implemented, however, tapping the widget always launches the home screen of the companion app, regardless of the current weather conditions.

The purpose of this chapter is to implement deep linking on the widget so that tapping the widget opens the appropriate weather detail screen within the app. This will involve some changes to both the app and widget extension.

59.1 Adding Deep Link Support to the Widget

Deep links allow specific areas of an app to be presented to the user based on the opening of a URL. The WidgetDemo app used in the previous chapters consists of a list of severe storm types. When a list item is selected, the app navigates to a details screen where additional information about the selected storm is displayed. In this tutorial, changes will be made to both the app and widget to add deep link support. This means, for example, that when the widget indicates that a thunderstorm is in effect, tapping the widget will launch the app and navigate to the thunderstorm detail screen.

The first step in adding deep link support is to modify the WeatherEntry structure to include a URL for each timeline entry. Edit the *WeatherData.swift* file and modify the structure so that it reads as follows:

```
.
.
struct WeatherEntry: TimelineEntry {
    var date: Date
    let city: String
    let temperature: Int
    let description: String
    let icon: String
    let image: String
    let url: URL?
}
.
.
```

Next, add some constants containing the URLs that will be used to identify the storm types that the app knows about:

```
.
.
let hailUrl = URL(string: "weatherwidget://hail")
```

```
let thunderUrl = URL(string: "weatherwidget://thunder")
let tropicalUrl = URL(string: "weatherwidget://tropical")
.
.
```

The last remaining change to the weather data is to include the URL within the sample timeline entries:

```
.
.
let londonTimeline = [
    WeatherEntry(date: Date(), city: "London", temperature: 87,
        description: "Hail Storm", icon: "cloud.hail",
            image: "hail", url: hailUrl),
    WeatherEntry(date: Date(), city: "London", temperature: 92,
        description: "Thunder Storm", icon: "cloud.bolt.rain",
            image: "thunder", url: thunderUrl),
    WeatherEntry(date: Date(), city: "London", temperature: 95,
        description: "Hail Storm", icon: "cloud.hail",
            image: "hail", url: hailUrl)
]

let miamiTimeline = [
    WeatherEntry(date: Date(), city: "Miami", temperature: 81,
        description: "Thunder Storm", icon: "cloud.bolt.rain",
            image: "thunder", url: thunderUrl),
    WeatherEntry(date: Date(), city: "Miami", temperature: 74,
        description: "Tropical Storm", icon: "tropicalstorm",
            image: "tropical", url: tropicalUrl),
    WeatherEntry(date: Date(), city: "Miami", temperature: 72,
        description: "Thunder Storm", icon: "cloud.bolt.rain",
            image: "thunder", url: thunderUrl)
]
.
.
```

With the data modified to include deep link URLs, the widget declaration now needs to be modified to match the widget entry structure. First, the *placeholder()* and *snapshot()* methods of the provider will need to return an entry that includes the URL. Edit the *WeatherWidget.swift* file, locate these methods within the IntentTimelineProvider structure, and modify them as follows:

```
struct Provider: AppIntentTimelineProvider {
    func placeholder(in context: Context) -> WeatherEntry {
        WeatherEntry(date: Date(), city: "London",
                                temperature: 89, description: "Thunder Storm",
                                    icon: "cloud.bolt.rain", image: "thunder",
                                        url: thunderUrl)
    }

    func snapshot(for configuration: ConfigurationAppIntent, in context: Context)
```

```
async -> WeatherEntry {
        WeatherEntry(date: Date(), city: "London",
                            temperature: 89, description: "Thunder Storm",
                                icon: "cloud.bolt.rain", image: "thunder",
                                        url: thunderUrl)
    }
.
.
```

Repeat this step for both declarations in the preview provider:

```
#Preview(as: .systemMedium) {
    WeatherWidget()
} timeline: {
    WeatherEntry(date: Date(),
                        city: "London", temperature: 89,
                description: "Thunder Storm",
                        icon: "cloud.bolt.rain", image: "thunder",
                        url: thunderUrl )
    WeatherEntry(date: Date(),
                        city: "London", temperature: 89,
                description: "Hail",
                        icon: "cloud.hail", image: "hail", url: thunderUrl)
}
```

The final task within the widget code is to assign a URL action to the widget entry view. This is achieved using the *widgetUrl()* modifier, passing through the URL from the widget entry. Remaining in the *WeatherWidget.swift* file, locate the WeatherWidgetEntryView declaration and add the modifier to the top-level ZStack as follows:

```
struct WeatherWidgetEntryView : View {
    var entry: Provider.Entry

    @Environment(\.widgetFamily) var widgetFamily

    var body: some View {
        HStack {
            WeatherSubView(entry: entry)
            if widgetFamily == .systemMedium {
                Image(entry.image)
                    .resizable()
            }
        }
        .widgetURL(entry.url)
    }
}
```

With deep link support added to the widget, the next step is to add support to the app.

59.2 Adding Deep Link Support to the App

When an app is launched via a deep link, it is passed a URL object, which may be accessed via the top-level view in the main content view. This URL can then be used to present different content to the user than would usually be displayed.

The first step in adding deep link support to the WidgetDemo app is to modify the *ContentView.swift* file to a navigation path to the NavigationStack, as outlined below. This will allow us to navigate to the detail view when a selection is made within the widget:

```
import SwiftUI
.
.
struct ContentView: View {

    @State var path = NavigationPath()

    var body: some View {
        NavigationStack(path: $path) {
            List {
.
.
```

When a view is displayed as the result of a deep link, the URL used to launch the app can be identified using the *onOpenUrl()* modifier on the parent view. Modify the ContentView declaration to add the *onOpenUrl()* modifier as follows:

```
.
.
var body: some View {
    NavigationStack(path: $path) {
        List {
.
.
        }
        .navigationDestination(for: WeatherType.self) { weather in
            WeatherDetailView(weather: weather)
        }
        .navigationTitle("Severe Weather")
        .onOpenURL(perform: { (url) in

            if (!path.isEmpty) {
                path.removeLast(path.count)
            }

            if (url == hailUrl) {
                path.append(WeatherType(name: "Hail Storm",
                                        icon: "cloud.hail"))
            } else if (url == thunderUrl) {
```

```
            path.append(WeatherType(name: "Thunder Storm",
                                    icon: "cloud.bolt.rain"))
        } else if (url == tropicalUrl) {
            path.append(WeatherType(name: "Tropical Storm",
                                    icon: "tropicalstorm"))
        }
    })
}
}
```

The code performs a comparison of the URL used to launch the app with each of the custom URLs supported by the widget. If a matching URL is found, a WeatherType instance is configured and appended to the navigation path. This, in turn, triggers the *navigationDestination()* modifier causing the WeatherDetailView to be displayed.

We have also added code that checks whether the navigation path is empty and, if necessary, removes any existing destinations. We are doing this because the app may already be displaying a detail view from a previous session when it is launched from the widget. If we append destinations to the non-empty path, the user will have to navigate back through any previous views if they decide to return to the home screen.

59.3 Testing the Widget

After making the changes, run the app and then the widget extension on a device or simulator and make sure that tapping the widget opens the app and displays the detail screen correctly configured for the current weather:

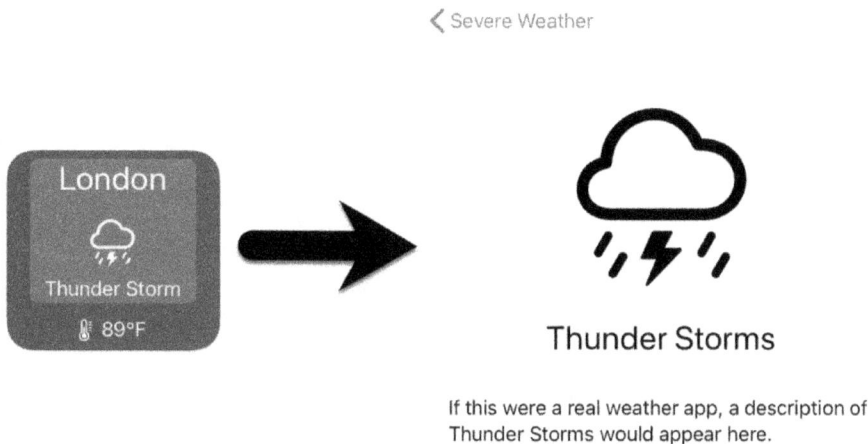

Figure 59-1

59.4 Summary

By default, a widget will launch the main view of the companion app when tapped by the user. This behavior can be enhanced by establishing deep links that take the user to specific areas of the app. This involves using the *widgetUrl()* modifier to assign destination URLs to the views in a widget entry layout. Within the app, the *onOpenUrl()* modifier is then used to identify the URL used to launch the app and initiate navigation to the corresponding view.

Chapter 60

60. Adding Configuration Options to a WidgetKit Widget

The WidgetDemo app created in the preceding chapters can only display weather information for a single geographical location. It is possible to make aspects of the widget user configurable using an app intent. In this chapter, we will enhance the widget extension so that the user can choose to view the weather for different cities. This will involve implementing a widget configuration intent and modifications to the widget provider declaration.

60.1 Reviewing the Project Code

When the widget extension was added to the WidgetDemo project in *"A SwiftUI WidgetKit Tutorial"*, we enabled the *Include Configuration App Intent* option. This selection caused Xcode to structure the template widget so that we can add configuration options without making significant changes to the existing code. For example, Xcode generated the *AppIntent.swift* file containing the following WidgetConfigurationIntent example class:

```
import WidgetKit
import AppIntents

struct ConfigurationAppIntent: WidgetConfigurationIntent {
    static var title: LocalizedStringResource = "Configuration"
    static var description = IntentDescription("This is an example widget.")

    // An example configurable parameter.
    @Parameter(title: "Favorite Emoji", default: "")
    var favoriteEmoji: String
}
```

We will modify this rudimentary example later to allow users to select weather information for different cities.

Xcode also based our widget provider (declared in the *WeatherWidget.swift* file) on the AppIntentTimelineProvider protocol, a prerequisite for supporting widget configuration. Conforming to the protocol requires that the *timeline()* and *snapshot()* functions are passed a reference to the app intent configuration as follows:

```
struct Provider: AppIntentTimelineProvider {
.

.

    func snapshot(for configuration: ConfigurationAppIntent, in context: Context)
async -> WeatherEntry {
.

.

    func timeline(for configuration: ConfigurationAppIntent, in context: Context)
async -> Timeline<WeatherEntry> {
.

.
```

With access to the configuration intent, we can change the widget to reflect the user's preferences.

Finally, Xcode added code to the WeatherWidget structure to create an AppIntentConfiguration instance, initialized with the ConfigurationAppIntent class declared in the *AppIntent.swift* file:

```
struct WeatherWidget: Widget {
    let kind: String = "WeatherWidget"

    var body: some WidgetConfiguration {
        AppIntentConfiguration(kind: kind, intent: ConfigurationAppIntent.self,
                        provider: Provider()) { entry in
            WeatherWidgetEntryView(entry: entry)
                .containerBackground(Color("weatherBackgroundColor"),
                        for: .widget)
        }
        .configurationDisplayName("My Weather Widget")
        .description("A demo weather widget.")
        .supportedFamilies([.systemSmall, .systemMedium])
    }
}
```

60.2 Adding an App Entity

The first requirement for our project is a structure that conforms to the AppEntity protocol that will be used to provide a list of the cities. Edit the *AppIntent.swift* file and add the following WidgetCity declaration:

```
struct WidgetCity: AppEntity {

    var id: String

    static let typeDisplayRepresentation:
            TypeDisplayRepresentation = "Change location"
    static let defaultQuery = WidgetCityQuery()

    var displayRepresentation: DisplayRepresentation {
        DisplayRepresentation(title: "\(id)")
    }
}
```

The above struct contains all mandatory properties for conforming to the AppEntity protocol. With these requirements met, we can now add properties to a list of city names and corresponding timelines:

```
struct WidgetCity: AppEntity {

    var id: String
    var timeline: [WeatherEntry]

    static let typeDisplayRepresentation:
            TypeDisplayRepresentation = "Change location"
    static let defaultQuery = WidgetCityQuery()
```

506

```
    var displayRepresentation: DisplayRepresentation {
        DisplayRepresentation(title: "\(id)")
    }


    static let cities: [WidgetCity] = [
        WidgetCity(id: "London", timeline: londonTimeline),
        WidgetCity(id: "Miami", timeline: miamiTimeline)
    ]
}
```

60.3 Adding Entity Query

The next step is adding the WidgetCityQuery structure referenced in the WidgetCity declaration above. The declaration must conform to the EntityQuery protocol by implementing the following functions:

- **entities(for:)** - Returns an array of app entities that match a specified id.

- **suggestedEntities()** - Returns an array containing the app entities available for selection in the widget configuration.

- **defaultResults()** - Returns the entity to be used as the widget's default configuration setting.

Remaining in the *AppIntent.swift* file, add the WidgetCityQuery struct as follows:

```
struct WidgetCityQuery: EntityQuery {
    func entities(for identifiers: [WidgetCity.ID]) async throws -> [WidgetCity] {
        WidgetCity.cities.filter {
            identifiers.contains($0.id)
        }
    }

    func suggestedEntities() async throws -> [WidgetCity] {
        WidgetCity.cities
    }

    func defaultResult() async -> WidgetCity? {
        WidgetCity.cities.first
    }
}
```

60.4 Modifying the App Intent

The configuration app intent needs to be updated to allow the user to select an option from the list of cities. Configuration options are declared using the @Parameter macro, including the option title and a variable to contain the current selection. To meet the requirements for the weather widget, modify ConfigurationAppIntent so that it reads as follows:

```
struct ConfigurationAppIntent: WidgetConfigurationIntent {
    static var title: LocalizedStringResource { "City Selection" }
    static var description: IntentDescription { "Select a city." }

    @Parameter(title: "Select a city")
```

```
    var currentCity: WidgetCity?
}
```

60.5 Modifying the Timeline Code

Before testing the configuration intent, the final step is to modify the provider *timeline()* method in the *WeatherWidget.swift* the file. Currently, the method is designed to display only the London timeline and reads as follows:

```
func timeline(for configuration: ConfigurationAppIntent,
              in context: Context) async -> Timeline<WeatherEntry> {
    var entries: [WeatherEntry] = []
    var eventDate = Date()
    let halfMinute: TimeInterval = 30

    for var entry in londonTimeline {
        entry.date = eventDate
        eventDate += halfMinute
        entries.append(entry)
    }

    return Timeline(entries: entries, policy: .atEnd)
}
```

The only change needed is to use the configuration intent parameter to access the timeline for the currently selected city:

```
func timeline(for configuration: ConfigurationAppIntent, in context: Context) async
-> Timeline<WeatherEntry> {
    var entries: [WeatherEntry] = []
    var eventDate = Date()
    let halfMinute: TimeInterval = 30

    if let timeline = configuration.currentCity?.timeline {
        for var entry in timeline {
            entry.date = eventDate
            eventDate += halfMinute
            entries.append(entry)
        }
    }

    return Timeline(entries: entries, policy: .atEnd)
}
```

Finally, the example ConfigurationAppIntent extension is no longer needed and must be deleted:

```
extension ConfigurationAppIntent {
    fileprivate static var smiley: ConfigurationAppIntent {
        let intent = ConfigurationAppIntent()
        intent.favoriteEmoji = "☐"
        return intent
```

```
        }

    fileprivate static var starEyes: ConfigurationAppIntent {
        let intent = ConfigurationAppIntent()
        intent.favoriteEmoji = "□"
        return intent
    }
}
```

60.6 Testing Widget Configuration

Run the widget extension on a device or simulator and wait for it to load. Once it is running, perform a long press on the widget to display the menu shown in Figure 60-1 below:

Figure 60-1

Select the *Edit Widget* menu option to display the configuration intent dialog, as shown in Figure 60-2:

Figure 60-2

Select the current location (or the Choose button if no city is displayed) to display the list of locations, then select Miami before tapping any screen area outside the dialog. On returning to the home screen, the widget should display entries from the Miami timeline.

60.7 Customizing the Configuration Intent UI

The final task in this tutorial is to change the accent colors of the intent UI to match those used by the widget. Since we already have the widget background color declared in the widget extension's *Assets* file from the steps in an earlier chapter, this can be used for the background of the intent UI.

The color settings for the intent UI are located in the build settings screen for the widget extension. To find these settings, select the WidgetDemo entry located at the top of the project navigator panel (marked A in Figure 60-3 below), followed by the WeatherWidgetExtension entry (B) in the Targets list:

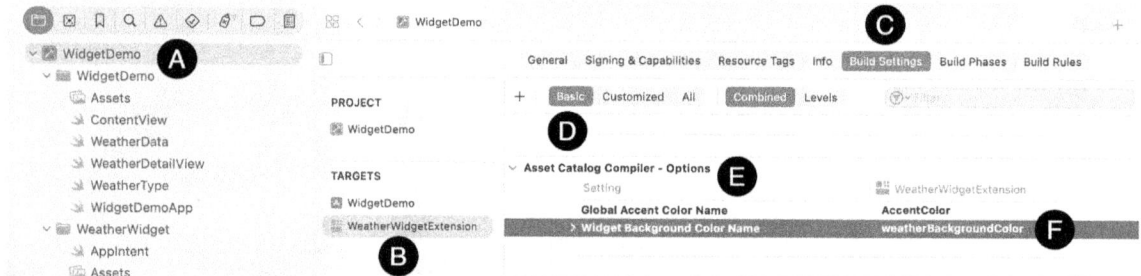

Figure 60-3

In the toolbar, select *Build Settings* (C), then the Basic filter option (D) before scrolling down to the *Asset Catalog Compiler – Options* section (E).

Click on the WidgetBackground value (F) and change it to *weatherBackgroundColor*. If required, the foreground color used within the intent UI is defined by the Global Accent Color Name value. Note that these values must be named colors declared within the *Assets* file.

Test the widget to verify that the intent UI now uses the widget background color:

Figure 60-4

60.8 Take the Knowledge Test

Click the link below or scan the QR code to test your knowledge and understanding of configurable WidgetKit widgets:

https://www.answertopia.com/in42

60.9 Summary

Widget extensions use configuration app intents to provide users with configuration options that change the widget's behavior or appearance. Once the configuration intent is implemented, each time the provider *timeline()* method is called, WidgetKit passes it a copy of the configuration object, the properties of which can be accessed to tailor the resulting timeline to match the user's preferences.

61. An Overview of Live Activities in SwiftUI

The previous chapters introduced WidgetKit and demonstrated how it can be used to display widgets that provide information to the user on the home screen, lock screen, and Today view. Widgets of this type present information based on a timeline you create and pass to WidgetKit. In this chapter, we will introduce ActivityKit and Live Activities and explore how these can be used to present dynamic information to the user via widgets on the lock screen and Dynamic Island.

61.1 Introducing Live Activities

Live Activities are created using the ActivityKit and WidgetKit frameworks and present dynamic information in glanceable form without restricting updates to a predefined timeline.

A single app can have multiple Live Activities, and the information presented can be sourced locally within the app or delivered from a remote server via push notifications. One important caveat is that updates to the Live Activity will not necessarily occur in real-time. Both the local and remote push notification options use background modes of execution, the timing and frequency of which are dictated by the operating system based on various factors, including battery status, the resource-intensive nature of the update task, and user behavior patterns. We will cover this in more detail in the next chapter.

In addition to displaying information, Live Activities may contain Button and Toggle views to add interactive behavior.

61.2 Creating a Live Activity

Once a Widget Extension has been added to an Xcode app project, the process of creating a Live Activity can be separated into the following steps, each of which will be covered in this chapter and put to practical use in the next chapter:

- Declare static and dynamic Activity Attributes.

- Design the Live Activity presentations for the lock screen and Dynamic Island.

- Configure and start the Live Activity.

- Update the Live Activity with the latest information.

- End the Live Activity when updates are no longer required.

61.3 Live Activity Attributes

The purpose of Live Activities is to present information to the user when the corresponding app has been placed in the background. The Live Activity attributes declare the data structure to be presented and are created using ActivityKit's ActivityAttributes class. Two types of attributes can be included. The first type declares the data that will change over the lifecycle of the Live Activity, such as the latest scores of a live sporting event or an estimated flight arrival time. The second attribute type declares values that will remain static while the Live Activity executes, such as the name of the sports teams or the airline and flight number of a tracked flight.

Within the ActivityAttributes declaration, the dynamic attributes are embedded in a ContentState structure using the following syntax:

```
struct DemoWidgetAttributes: ActivityAttributes {
    public struct ContentState: Codable, Hashable {
        // dynamic attributes here
        var arrivalTime: Date
    }

    // static attributes here
    var airlineName: String = "Pending"
    var flightNumber: String = "Pending"
}
```

61.4 Designing the Live Activity Presentations

Live Activities present data to the user via lock screen, Dynamic Island, and banner widgets, each of which must be designed to complete the Live Activity. These presentations are created using SwiftUI views. While the lock screen presentation (also used for the banner widget) consists of a single layout, the Dynamic Island presentations are separated into regions.

The layouts for the Live Activity widgets are defined in a configuration structure subclassed from the WidgetKit framework's Widget class and must conform to the following syntax:

```
struct DemoWidgetLiveActivity: Widget {
    var body: some WidgetConfiguration {
        ActivityConfiguration(for: DemoWidgetAttributes.self) { context in

        } dynamicIsland: { context in

            DynamicIsland {

                DynamicIslandExpandedRegion(.leading) {

                }
                DynamicIslandExpandedRegion(.trailing) {

                }
                DynamicIslandExpandedRegion(.bottom) {

                }
                DynamicIslandExpandedRegion(.center) {

                }
            } compactLeading: {

            } compactTrailing: {

            } minimal: {
```

```
            }
        }
    }
}
```

Each element is passed a context object from which static and current dynamic data values can be accessed for inclusion in the presentation views. For example, the arrival time and flight number from the previous activity attributes declaration could be displayed by the widget as follows:

```
Text("Arrival: \(context.state.arrivalTime)")
Text("Flight: \(context.attributes.flightNumber)")
```

61.4.1 Lock Screen/Banner

Starting at the top of the Widget declaration, the layout for the lock screen and banner presentation consists of an area the size of a typical lock screen notification. The following example will display two Text views in a VStack layout:

```
struct DemoWidgetLiveActivity: Widget {
    var body: some WidgetConfiguration {
        ActivityConfiguration(for: DemoWidgetAttributes.self) { context in
            VStack {
                Text("Arrival: \(context.state.arrivalTime)")
                Text("Flight: \(context.attributes.flightNumber)")


            }
        } dynamicIsland: { context in

.

.
```

61.4.2 Dynamic Island Expanded Regions

The Live Activity will display data using compact layouts on devices with a Dynamic Island. However, a long press performed on the island will display the expanded widget. Unlike the lock screen widget, the expanded Dynamic Island presentation is divided into four regions, as illustrated in Figure 61-1:

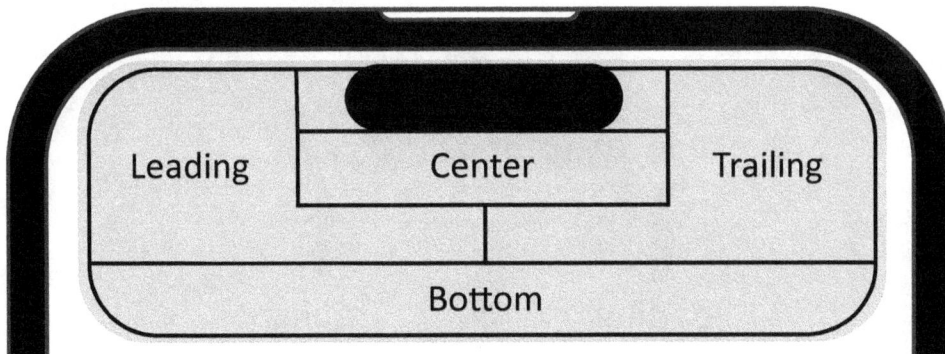

Figure 61-1

The following example highlights the code locations for each Dynamic Island region:

.

.

```
} dynamicIsland: { context in

    DynamicIsland {

        DynamicIslandExpandedRegion(.leading) {
            Text("Leading")
        }
        DynamicIslandExpandedRegion(.trailing) {
            Text("Trailing")
        }
        DynamicIslandExpandedRegion(.bottom) {
            Text("Bottom")
        }
        DynamicIslandExpandedRegion(.center) {
            Text("Center")
        }
    } compactLeading: {
.
.
```

The default sizing behavior of each region can be changed using priorities. In the following code, for example, the leading and trailing region sizes are set to 25% and 75% of the available presentation width, respectively:

```
DynamicIslandExpandedRegion(.leading, priority: 0.25) {
    Text("Leading")
}
DynamicIslandExpandedRegion(.trailing, priority: 0.75) {
    Text("Trailing")
}
```

61.4.3 Dynamic Island Compact Regions

The compact presentation is divided into regions located on either side of the camera, as illustrated in Figure 61-2:

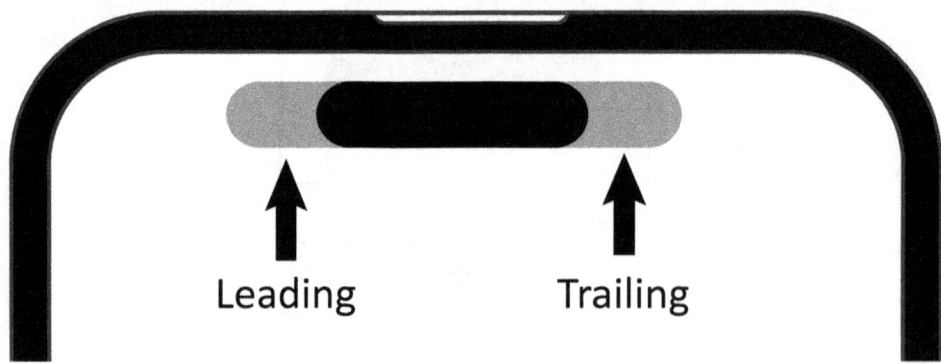

Figure 61-2

An example compact declaration might read as follows:

.

```
.
} compactLeading: {
    Text("L")
} compactTrailing: {
    Text("T")
} minimal: {
.
.
```

61.4.4 Dynamic Island Minimal

The Live Activity uses minimal presentations when multiple Live Activities are running concurrently. In this situation, the minimal presentation for one Live Activity will appear in the compact leading region (referred to as the *attached minimal*), while another appears as a d*etached minimal* positioned to the right of the camera:

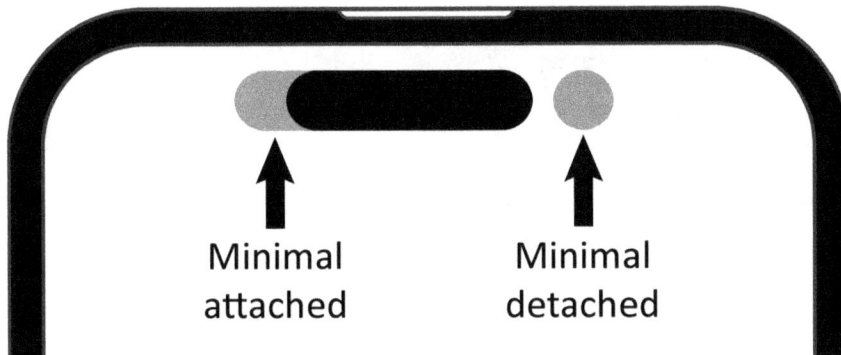

Figure 61-3

For example:

```
.
.
} minimal: {
    Text("M")
}
.
.
```

61.5 Starting a Live Activity

Once the data model has been defined and the presentations designed, the next step is to request and start the Live Activity. This is achieved by a call to the *Activity.request()* method. When the request method is called, an activity attributes instance, an initialized ContentState, and a push type must be provided. The push type should be set to *token* if the data updates will be received via push notifications or *nil* if updates are coming from the app.

An optional *stale date* may also be included. When the stale date is reached, the state of the Live Activity context will update to reflect that the information is out of date, allowing you to notify the user within the widget presentation. To check if the Live Activity is out of date, access the context's *isStale* property. The following code, for example, displays a message in the Dynamic Island expanded presentation when the data needs to be refreshed:

```
DynamicIslandExpandedRegion(.leading) {
```

```
VStack {
    Text("Arrival: \(context.state.arrivalTime)")
    Text("Flight: \(context.attributes.flightNumber)")

    if (context.isStale) {
        Text("Out of date")
    }
}
}
```

Set the *staleDate* parameter to *nil* if you do not plan to check the Live Activity status for this property.

Based on the above requirements, the first step is to create an activity attributes object and initialize any static properties, for example:

```
var attributes = DemoWidgetAttributes()
attributes.flightNumber = "Loading..."
```

The second requirement is a ContentState instance configured with initial dynamic values:

```
let contentState = DemoWidgetAttributes.ContentState(arrivalTime: Date.now + 60)
```

With the requirements met, the *Activity.request()* method can be called as follows:

```
private var activity: Activity<DemoWidgetAttributes>?
.
.
do {
    activity = try Activity.request(
        attributes: attributes,
        content: .init(state: contentState, staleDate: nil),
        pushType: nil
    )
} catch (let error) {
    print("Error requesting live activity: \(error.localizedDescription).")
}
}
```

If the request is successful, the Live Activity will launch and be ready to receive updates. In the above example, the push type has been set to nil to indicate the data is generated within the app. This would need to be changed to *token* to support updates using push notifications.

61.6 Updating a Live Activity

To refresh a Live Activity with updated data, a call is made to the *update()* method of the activity instance returned by the earlier call to the *Activity.request()* method. The update call must be passed an ActivityContent instance containing a ContentState initialized with the updated dynamic data values and an optional stale date value. For example:

```
let flightState = DemoWidgetAttributes.ContentState(arrivalTime: newTime)

Task {

    await activity?.update(
```

518

```
ActivityContent<DemoWidgetAttributes.ContentState>(
    state: flightState,
    staleDate: Date.now + 120,
    relevanceScore: 0
),
alertConfiguration: nil
)
}
```

If your app starts multiple concurrent Live Activities, the system will display the one with the highest relevanceScore. When working with push notifications, the content state is updated automatically, and the update call is unnecessary.

61.7 Activity Alert Configurations

Alert configurations are passed to the *update()* method to notify the user of significant events in the Live Activity data. When an alert is triggered, a banner (based on the lock screen presentation layout) appears on the device screen, accompanied by an optional alert sound. The following code example creates an alert configuration when a tracked flight has been significantly delayed:

```
var alertConfig: AlertConfiguration? = nil

if (arrvialTime > Date.now + 84000) {
    alertConfig = AlertConfiguration(
        title: "Flight Delay",
        body: "Flight now arriving tomorrow",
        sound: .default
    )
}
```

Note that the title and body text will only appear on Apple Watch devices.

Once an alert configuration has been created, it can be passed to the *update()* method:

```
await activity?.update(
    ActivityContent<DemoWidgetAttributes.ContentState>(
        state: flightState,
        staleDate: Date.now + 120,
        relevanceScore: 0
    ),
    alertConfiguration: alertConfig
)
```

61.8 Stopping a Live Activity

Live Activities are stopped by calling the *end()* method of the activity instance. The call is passed a ContentState instance initialized with the final data values and a dismissal policy setting. For example:

```
let finalState = DemoWidgetAttributes.ContentState(arrivalTime: Date.now)

await activity?.end(
    .init(state: finalState, staleDate: nil),
    dismissalPolicy: .default
```

)

When the dismissalPolicy is set to *default*, the Live Activity widget will remain on the lock screen for four hours unless the user removes it. Use *immediate* to instantly remove the Live Activity from the lock screen or *after()* to dismiss the Live Activity at a specific time within the four-hour window.

61.9 Take the Knowledge Test

Click the link below or scan the QR code to test your knowledge and understanding of SwiftUI Live Activities:

https://www.answertopia.com/oh2m

61.10 Summary

Live Activities provide users with timely updates via widgets on the device lock screen and Dynamic Island. Updated information can be generated locally within the app or sent from a remote server using push notifications. A Live Activity consists of a set of attributes that define the data to be presented and SwiftUI-based layouts for each of the widget presentations. Live Activity instances are started, stopped, and updated using calls to the corresponding Activity object. When working with push notifications, the activity will update automatically on receipt of a notification. Updates may also include an optional alert to attract the user's attention.

62. A SwiftUI Live Activity Tutorial

In this chapter, we will create a project demonstrating how to add a Live Activity to a SwiftUI-based iOS app using WidgetKit and ActivityKit. The project will include support for lock screen, Dynamic Island, and alert activity views, providing a practical example of activity widget attributes and creating, updating, and managing Live Activity instances.

62.1 About the LiveActivityDemo Project

The project created in this chapter will consist of a simple stock tracking app designed to track the fictitious price of Apple, Inc. shares (Ticker: APPL). In the initial steps, we will create a content view displaying updating price data values and buttons to start and stop the tracking. Once these steps are complete, the app will be extended to include a Live Activity widget.

62.2 Creating the Project

Launch Xcode and select the option to create a new Multiplatform App project named *LiveActivityDemo*. We will add push notification support in a later chapter, so enter an Organization identifier that uniquely identifies your app.

62.3 Building the View Model

The pricing data for the project will be provided by a view model class that uses a timer to generate random pricing information. Press Cmd-N and use the Swift File template to create a class file named *PricingViewModel. swift*. Once you have created the file, make the following changes to create the view model:

```
import Foundation


@MainActor
@Observable
class PricingViewModel {

    private var oldPrice: Float = 100
    var currentPrice: Float = 100
    var changePercent: Float = 0
    private var timerTask: Task<Void, Never>?

    func startTracking(ticker: String) async {
        await startUpdates()
    }


    func startUpdates() async {
        timerTask = Task {
            if let task = timerTask {
                while !task.isCancelled {
                    try? await Task.sleep(for: .milliseconds(10000))
                    update()
```

```
                }
            }
        }
    }

    func stopTracking() async {
        timerTask?.cancel()
    }

    private func update() {
        refreshPricing()
    }

    func refreshPricing() {
        oldPrice = currentPrice
        currentPrice = Float.random(in: 100...200)
        changePercent = (currentPrice - oldPrice) / oldPrice * 100
    }
}
```

The above changes declare the class as observable and add properties to contain the pricing data. Functions are also added to start and stop a timer, which, in turn, updates the pricing data at regular intervals, essentially simulating a live data feed. Now that we have a view model, the next step is to design the main content view.

62.4 Designing the Content View

The main content view will include the ticker, current price, and change percentage information. In addition, buttons labeled "Track" and "Stop" will be configured to call the view model *startTracking()* and *stopTracking()* functions, respectively.

Since the view model was declared as observable, the UI will update automatically as the pricing values change. Within Xcode, select the *ContentView.swift* file and modify it as follows:

```
import SwiftUI

struct ContentView: View {

    private var viewModel = PricingViewModel()
    let ticker = "APPL"

    var body: some View {

        let color = viewModel.changePercent < 0 ? Color.red : Color.green
        let arrow = viewModel.changePercent < 0 ?
                            "arrowshape.down.fill" : "arrowshape.up.fill"

        VStack(spacing: 20) {
            Text(ticker)
                .font(.system(size: 56))
```

```
    HStack {
        VStack {
            Text("Price: \(viewModel.currentPrice, specifier: "%.2f")")
                .foregroundColor(color)

            HStack {
                Image(systemName: arrow)
                Text(
        "Change: \(viewModel.changePercent, specifier: "%.0f")%")
            }
        }
        .foregroundColor(color)
        .font(.largeTitle)
    }

    HStack(spacing:20) {

        Spacer()

        Button(action: {
            Task {
                await viewModel.startTracking(ticker: ticker)
            }
        }, label: {
            Text("Track")
        })

        Spacer()

        Button(action: {
            Task {
                await viewModel.stopTracking()
            }
        }, label: {
            Text("Stop")
        })

        Spacer()
    }
    .font(.largeTitle)
}
.padding()

Spacer()
```

```
        }
}


#Preview {
    ContentView()
}
```

Note that the above code checks the view model's *changePercent* property to select the arrow direction and the color of the pricing text to reflect whether the price is increasing or decreasing.

Verify that the view appears in the Preview panel, as shown in Figure 62-1 and that the data updates after the Track button is clicked:

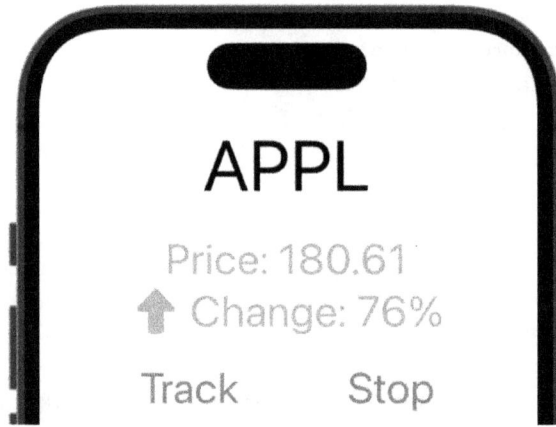

Figure 62-1

62.5 Adding the Live Activity Extension

The next step is to add the Live Activity widget extension by selecting the *File -> New -> Target...* menu option. From within the target template panel, select the Widget Extension option, as shown in Figure 62-2 before clicking the Next button:

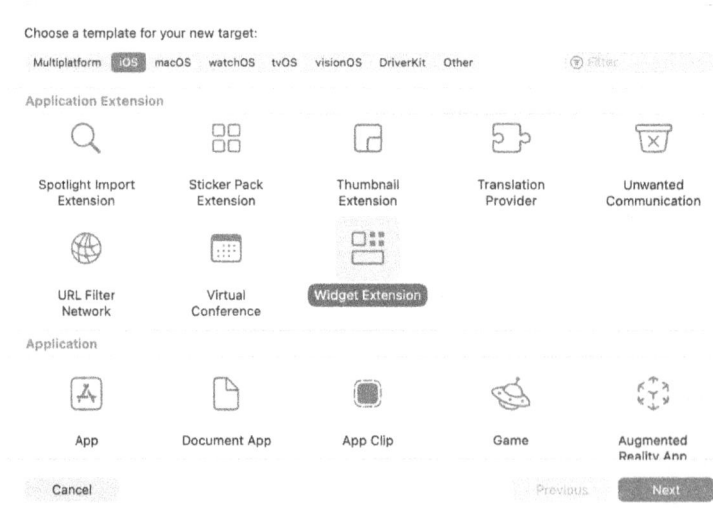

Figure 62-2

On the subsequent screen, enter DemoWidget into the product name field. Before clicking the Finish button, ensure the *Include Live Activity* option is enabled and that the *Include Configuration App Intent* and Include Control options are turned off, as shown in Figure 62-3:

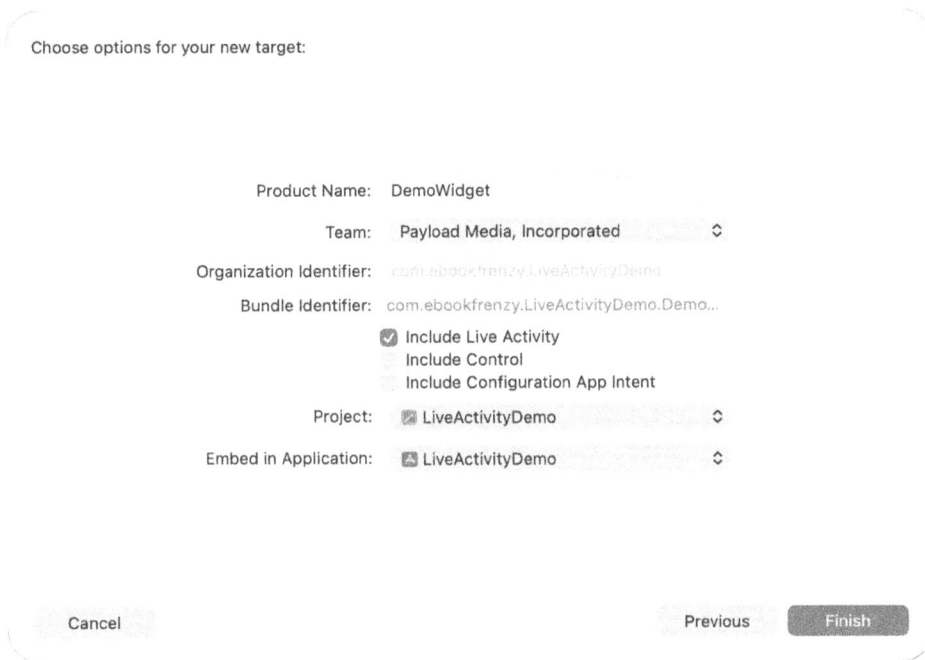

Choose options for your new target:

Product Name:	DemoWidget
Team:	Payload Media, Incorporated
Organization Identifier:	com.ebookfrenzy.LiveActivityDemo
Bundle Identifier:	com.ebookfrenzy.LiveActivityDemo.Demo...
	☑ Include Live Activity
	Include Control
	Include Configuration App Intent
Project:	LiveActivityDemo
Embed in Application:	LiveActivityDemo

Cancel   Previous   Finish

Figure 62-3

When prompted, click the Activate button to ensure the widget extension is included in the project build configuration.

Once the extension has been added, refer to the project navigator panel, where a new folder containing the widget extension will have been added, as shown in Figure 62-4:

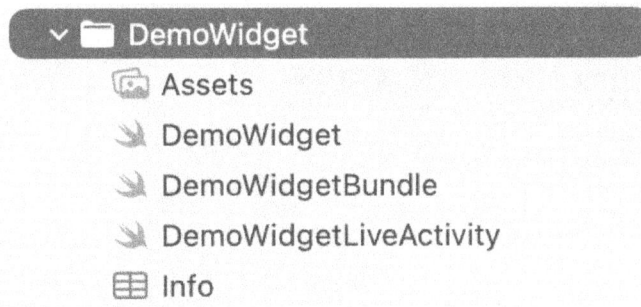

∨ 📁 DemoWidget
  🖼 Assets
  ⊿ DemoWidget
  ⊿ DemoWidgetBundle
  ⊿ DemoWidgetLiveActivity
  ⊞ Info

Figure 62-4

As we only need the Live Activity in our app, edit the *DemoWidgetBundle.swift* file and remove the *DemoWidget()* call:

```
import WidgetKit
import SwiftUI


@main
```

A SwiftUI Live Activity Tutorial

```
struct DemoWidgetBundle: WidgetBundle {
    var body: some Widget {
        DemoWidget()
        DemoWidgetLiveActivity()
    }
}
```

62.6 Enabling Live Activities Support

Live Activity support must be enabled once the main project has been created. Select the *LiveActivityDemo* target at the top of the Project Navigator panel (marked A in Figure 62-5) so that the main panel displays the project settings. From within this panel, select the LiveActivityDemo target entry (B), followed by the Info tab (C):

Figure 62-5

On the Info screen, locate the bottom entry in the list of properties and hover the mouse pointer over the item. When the plus button appears, click it to add a new entry to the list. From within the drop-down list of available keys, locate and select the *Supports Live Activities* option, as shown in Figure 62-6:

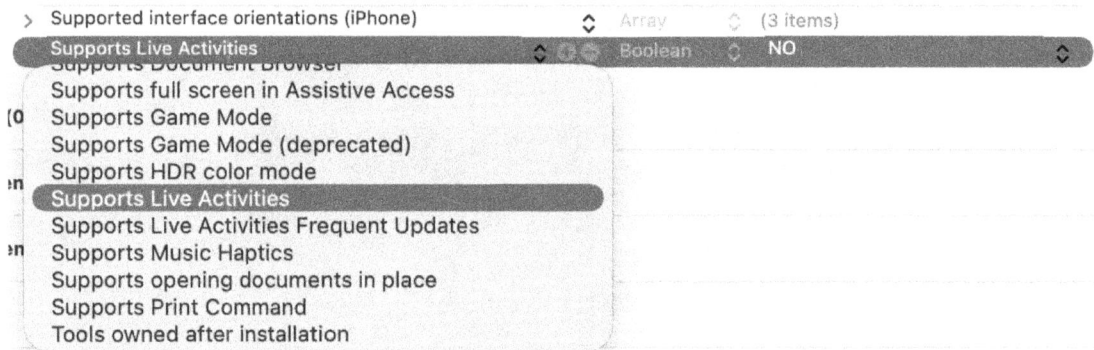

Figure 62-6

Within the value field for the property, change the setting to YES.

62.7 Enabling the Background Fetch Capability

The Live Activity widget will need to receive updates while the LiveActivityDemo app is in the background. To enable background support, select the Signing & Capabilities tab (marked A in Figure 62-7), followed by the + *Capability* button (B):

Figure 62-7

In the resulting dialog, enter *Background* into the filter bar, select the result, and press the keyboard enter key to add the capability to the project:

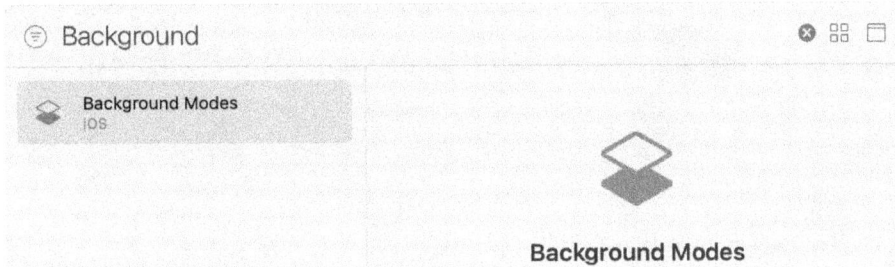

Figure 62-8

Once you have added the Background Modes capability, locate it in the Signing & Capabilities screen and enable Background Fetch mode:

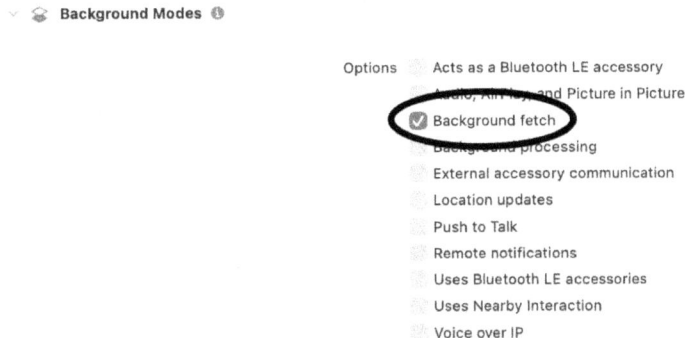

Figure 62-9

62.8 Defining the Activity Widget Attributes

When the widget intent was added to the project, Xcode added a file named DemoWidgetLiveActivity, which declares both the activity attributes and the various widget layout configurations. Before designing the layouts, we must specify the widget attributes for our project. Begin by editing the *DemoWidgetLiveActivity.swift* file and locating and deleting the template DemoWidgetAttributes structure:

```
struct DemoWidgetAttributes: ActivityAttributes {
    public struct ContentState: Codable, Hashable {
        // Dynamic stateful properties about your activity go here!
        var emoji: String
    }
}
```

```
—
        // Fixed non-changing properties about your activity go here!
        var name: String
}
```

Next, right-click on the DemoWidget folder in the Project Navigator panel, select the *New File from Template...* menu option, and create a new Swift file named *DemoWidgetAttributes.swift*. Before clicking the Create button, make sure that the widget extension is enabled in the Targets section, as highlighted in Figure 62-10:

Figure 62-10

Once you have created the file, modify it as follows:

```
import Foundation
import ActivityKit


struct DemoWidgetAttributes: ActivityAttributes {
    public struct ContentState: Codable, Hashable {
        var currentPrice: Float
        var changePercent: Float
    }


    var ticker = ""
}
```

For this project, we have declared two dynamic properties for the price and change percentage and one static variable for the ticker.

62.9 Adding the Percentage and Lock Screen Views

Before designing the widget layouts, we will add some views that we can call in the widget configuration code. The first of these views will display the widget on the lock screen and alert banner. Right-click on the DemoWidget folder in the Project Navigator panel, select the *New File from Template...* menu option, and create a new SwiftUI View file named *PercentView.swift*. Enable the widget extension target option, as shown in Figure 62-10 above, before clicking Create. Edit the new file and modify it as follows:

```
import SwiftUI
import WidgetKit


struct PercentView: View {


    var context: ActivityViewContext<DemoWidgetAttributes>
```

```
    var body: some View {


        let color = context.state.changePercent < 0 ? Color.red : Color.green

        ProgressView(value: abs(context.state.changePercent), total: 100) {
            context.state.changePercent < 0 ?
                        Image(systemName: "arrowshape.down.fill") :
                                    Image(systemName: "arrowshape.up.fill")
        }
        .progressViewStyle(.circular)
        .tint(color)
        .foregroundColor(color)
    }
}
```
```
#Preview {
    PercentView()
}
```

Repeat the above steps to create a SwiftUI View file named *LockScreenView.swift* and make the following changes:

```
import SwiftUI
import WidgetKit

struct LockScreenView: View {

    var context: ActivityViewContext<DemoWidgetAttributes>

    var body: some View {

        let color = context.state.changePercent < 0 ? Color.red : Color.green

        HStack {

            VStack(alignment: .leading, spacing: 8) {
              Text(context.attributes.ticker)
                .bold()
                .font(.title2)
                .foregroundColor(.white)

              Text("\(context.state.currentPrice, specifier: "%.2f")")
                  .font(.title3)
                  .foregroundColor(color)
            }

            Spacer()
```

```
              Text("\(context.state.changePercent, specifier: "%.0f")%")
                    .font(.largeTitle)
                    .foregroundColor(color)


              Spacer()

              PercentView(context: context)
                    .padding()
         }
         .padding()
         .activityBackgroundTint(Color.black)
         .activitySystemActionForegroundColor(Color.white)
      }
}


#Preview {
      LockScreenView()
}
```

62.10 Designing the Widget Layouts

The next task is to design the various widget layout components, beginning with the lock screen layout. Edit the
DemoWidgetLiveActivity.swift file and add a call to LockScreenView, passing it the activity context:

```
.
.
struct DemoWidgetLiveActivity: Widget {
    var body: some WidgetConfiguration {

        ActivityConfiguration(for: DemoWidgetAttributes.self) { context in
            LockScreenView(context: context)
        } dynamicIsland: { context in
.
.
```

Next, implement the leading, trailing, and bottom regions of the Dynamic Island expanded layout, including a
ternary statement to select the appropriate color:

```
.
.
} dynamicIsland: { context in

    DynamicIsland {

        let color = context.state.changePercent < 0 ? Color.red : Color.green

        DynamicIslandExpandedRegion(.leading) {
            Text(context.attributes.ticker)
                .font(.title3)
```

```
                .bold()
        }
        DynamicIslandExpandedRegion(.trailing) {
            Text("\(context.state.currentPrice, specifier: "%.2f")")
                .foregroundColor(color)
                .font(.title3)
                .bold()
        }
        DynamicIslandExpandedRegion(.bottom) {
            HStack {
                Text("Price change: ")
                Text("\(context.state.changePercent, specifier: "%.2f")%")
                    .foregroundColor(color)
                Spacer()
                PercentView(context: context)
            }
            .font(.title3)
            .bold()
        }
    } compactLeading: {
.
.
```

The compact and minimal regions will be used when the Live Activity is displayed in the Dynamic Island and can be implemented as follows:

```
.
.

    } compactLeading: {
        Text(context.attributes.ticker)
            .font(.title2)
            .bold()
            .foregroundColor(
                context.state.changePercent < 0 ? Color.red : Color.green)
    } compactTrailing: {
        Text("\(context.state.currentPrice, specifier: "%.2f")")
            .font(.title2)
            .bold()
            .foregroundColor(
                context.state.changePercent < 0 ? Color.red : Color.green)
    } minimal: {
        PercentView(context: context)
    }
    .widgetURL(URL(string: "http://www.apple.com"))
    .keylineTint(Color.red)
.
.
```

Finally, remove the following template preview code from the *DemoWidgetLiveActivity.swift* file:

```
extension DemoWidgetAttributes {
    fileprivate static var preview: DemoWidgetAttributes {
        DemoWidgetAttributes(name: "World")
    }
}

extension DemoWidgetAttributes.ContentState {
    fileprivate static var smiley: DemoWidgetAttributes.ContentState {
        DemoWidgetAttributes.ContentState(emoji: "□")
    }

    fileprivate static var starEyes: DemoWidgetAttributes.ContentState {
        DemoWidgetAttributes.ContentState(emoji: "□")
    }
}

#Preview("Notification", as: .content, using: DemoWidgetAttributes.preview) {
   DemoWidgetLiveActivity()
} contentStates: {
    DemoWidgetAttributes.ContentState.smiley
    DemoWidgetAttributes.ContentState.starEyes
}
```

62.11 Launching the Live Activity

The final step before testing the app is to add code to the view model to start, update, and stop the Live Activity. Open the *PriceViewModel.swift* file in the editor and make the following changes to the *startTracking()* function:

```
import Foundation
import ActivityKit
import WidgetKit


@MainActor
@Observable
class PricingViewModel {

    private var activity: Activity<DemoWidgetAttributes>?
    private var oldPrice: Float = 100
    var currentPrice: Float = 100
    var changePercent: Float = 0
    private var timerTask: Task<Void, Never>?

    func startTracking(ticker: String) async {
        let contentState = DemoWidgetAttributes.ContentState(
            currentPrice: currentPrice, changePercent: changePercent)
        var attributes = DemoWidgetAttributes()
```

```
    attributes.ticker = ticker

    do {
        activity = try Activity.request(
            attributes: attributes,
            content: .init(state: contentState, staleDate: nil),
            pushType: nil
        )
        await startUpdates()
    } catch (let error) {
        print("Error starting Live Activity: \(error.localizedDescription).")
    }
}
```
.
.

The above changes configure the content state using the DemoWidgetAttributes class populated with the pricing data and ticker symbol. Next, the Live Activity *request()* function is called to start the Live Activity. Since we use local data instead of push notifications, the pushType parameter is set to nil.

62.12 Updating the Live Activity

Next, edit the *update()* function to update the Live Activity with the latest pricing data:

```
private func update() {
    refreshPricing()

    let priceStatus = DemoWidgetAttributes.ContentState(
        currentPrice: currentPrice, changePercent: changePercent)

    Task {
        await activity?.update(
            ActivityContent<DemoWidgetAttributes.ContentState>(
                state: priceStatus,
                staleDate: nil,
                relevanceScore: 0
            ),
            alertConfiguration: nil
        )
    }
}
```

Once again, a content state is created using the refreshed pricing data and passed to the Live Activity *update()* function. We will add an alert configuration later in the chapter, so we have set this parameter to nil for now.

62.13 Stopping the Live Activity

In addition to stopping the timer, the *stopTracking()* function must end the Live Activity. This requires the following changes:

```
func stopTracking() async {
```

```
let finalState = DemoWidgetAttributes.ContentState(
        currentPrice: currentPrice, changePercent: changePercent)
timerTask?.cancel()
await activity?.end(.init(state: finalState, staleDate: nil),
        dismissalPolicy: .default)
}
```

62.14 Testing the App

Because the iOS simulator does not support the execution of background tasks, the best way to test the Live Activity is to run it on a physical device. With a device connected, launch the LiveActivityDemo app, start price tracking, and place the app in the background. Lock the device and then display the lock screen where the Live Activity widget should appear, as shown below:

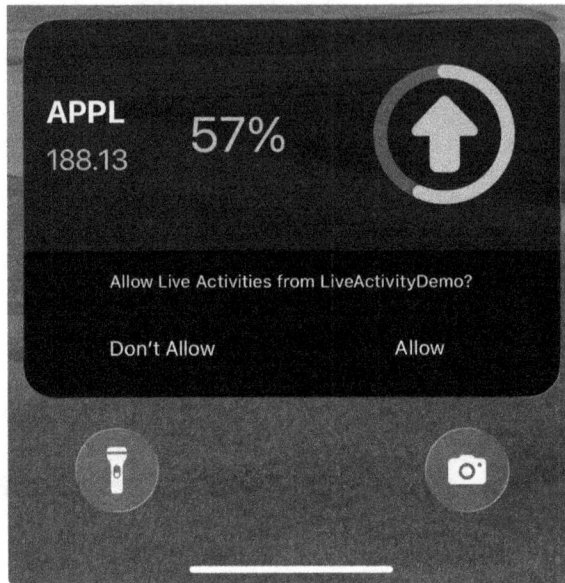

Figure 62-11

Tap the Allow button to enable the Live Activity and watch as the pricing data updates regularly. If your device has a Dynamic Island, unlock it and check that the pricing data appears as Figure 62-12. If your device does not have a Dynamic Island, run the app on a suitable simulator, start the price tracking, and place the app in the background. The Live Activity will still appear in the Dynamic Island, but the data will not update:

Figure 62-12

Next, perform a long press on the island to display the expanded view:

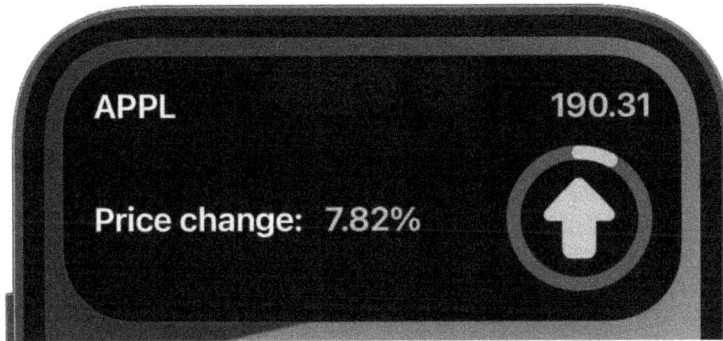

Figure 62-13

If you have access to another app containing a Live Activity, run it and start its Live Activity. Next, reinstall the LiveActivityDemo app, start the price tracking, and place the app in the background. The minimal widget layout should appear, as shown in Figure 62-14:

Figure 62-14

If the device on which you are testing is using the same Apple ID as the Mac on which Xcode is running, the live widget will also appear in the desktop status bar as shown in Figure 62-15:

Figure 62-15

62.15 Adding an Alert Notification

The final step in this example is to add an alert to notify the user when the stock price drops significantly. To do this, we will create an AlertConfiguration instance and pass it to the activity's *update()* function in the *PricingViewModel.swift* file:

```
private func update() {
    refreshPricing()

    let priceStatus = DemoWidgetAttributes.ContentState(
```

```
                        currentPrice: currentPrice,
                        changePercent: changePercent)

    Task {

        var alertConfig: AlertConfiguration? = nil

        if (changePercent < -25) {
            alertConfig = AlertConfiguration(
                title: "Price Drop Alert",
                body: "Stock price has decreased by more than 25%",
                sound: .default
            )
        }

        await activity?.update(
            ActivityContent<DemoWidgetAttributes.ContentState>(
                state: priceStatus,
                staleDate: nil,
                relevanceScore: 0
            ),
            alertConfiguration: alertConfig
        )
    }
}
```

Rerun the app on a physical device, start the price tracking, and place the app in the background. When the price change drops below 25%, the alert will sound, and the widget will appear on the screen, as shown in Figure 62-16:

Figure 62-16

If the widget is visible on your macOS desktop, alerts will also appear there.

62.16 Understanding Background Updates

The LiveActivityDemo app is designed to update the pricing data once every 10 seconds, and while you have been testing, this is the behavior you should be seeing. Since we are launching the app from within Xcode, it is essential to note that it is running while connected to the debugger. When the app is launched without the debugger (in other words, launched from the device screen), you will notice that the updates no longer occur as expected. In fact, it may take minutes or even hours for the widgets to update. This is because iOS does not guarantee that a background task will run when scheduled. Instead, iOS uses a predictive engine to decide which background tasks to run and when to run them based on various factors. These factors include the battery level, the time of day and frequency with which the user interacts with the app, and the time and resources required to complete each background refresh.

These limitations, intended to prevent background tasks from draining the battery or degrading the device's performance, do not apply when the app runs while connected to the debugger.

There are several options for mitigating the unpredictable nature of background tasks.

To increase the likelihood that your background tasks will run, ensure that the update tasks are brief and do not make excessive resource demands. Also, it may take a while for the predictive algorithms to begin scheduling updates for your app after the Live Activity starts, so wait a few hours before making any assumptions.

Another way to improve the user experience is to include an "out of date" notification on the widget presentations and a button to wake up the app and refresh the data. This approach will be covered in the *"Adding a Refresh Button to a Live Activity"* chapter.

Alternatively, switching from local updates to push notifications may improve performance, particularly when using a high priority. In the *"A Live Activity Push Notifications Tutorial"* chapter, we will convert the LiveActivityDemo project to use remote notifications.

62.17 Summary

This chapter created an example app project containing a Live Activity to present data on the device lock screen and Dynamic Island of iOS devices. The initial steps involved adding a widget extension to an Xcode project and enabling support for Live Activity updates. We then declared the Activity's widget attributes before designing the various UI layout regions. Next, we added code to start, update, and stop the Live Activity. Finally, an alert notification was added to the Activity.

Background updates are executed at the discretion of the operating system based on predictive algorithms. While it is possible to increase the chances that an update may be performed more frequently, there is no guaranteed way to predict when a Live Activity will be updated.

Chapter 63

63. Adding a Refresh Button to a Live Activity

The previous chapters introduced Live Activities and created an example project demonstrating Live Activities in action. While testing the example app, it became evident that, regardless of configuration settings, Live Activity updates can be infrequent when the app is in background mode. While we have limited control over when an update will be processed, this chapter will demonstrate how to compensate for this unpredictability by informing the user that information may be outdated and providing a convenient way to refresh the data from within the Live Activity widget.

63.1 Adding Interactivity to Live Activities

In addition to displaying information, Live Activity widgets may contain buttons and toggle views using the App Intents framework. This involves adding a class to the Live Activity widget extension that conforms to the LiveActivityIntent protocol and implementing a *perform()* method to be called when the user interacts with the button or toggle. For example:

```
struct UpdateScoreIntent: LiveActivityIntent {

    static var title: LocalizedStringResource = "Check for Updates"
    static var description = IntentDescription("Update latest match scores.")

    public init() { }

    func perform() async throws -> some IntentResult {
        // Code to perform the update goes here
        return .result()
    }
}
```

Once the intent has been declared, we can call it from within the Live Activity widget. The following code excerpt, for example, shows a Button view configured to call the UpdateScoreIntent intent:

```
Button(intent: UpdateScoreIntent(), label: {
    Text("Update")
})
```

In the rest of this chapter, we will modify the LiveActivityDemo project to provide a notice and a refresh button when the widget is displaying outdated information. When the button is tapped, it will launch an intent to update the Live Activity with the latest data.

63.2 Adding the App Intent

Load the LiveActivityDemo project into Xcode, right-click on the DemoWidget folder in the Project navigator panel, and select the *New File from Template...* option. Create a new Swift file named *RefreshIntent.swift*, making sure to enable the LiveActivityDemo and DemoWidgetExtension targets, as shown in Figure 63-1:

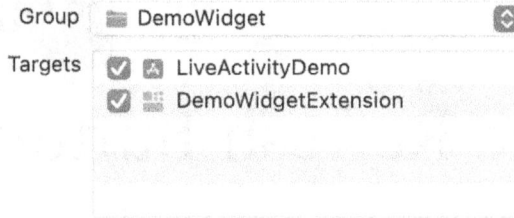

Figure 63-1

After creating the file, modify it so it reads as follows:

```
import Intents
import AppIntents

struct RefreshIntent: LiveActivityIntent {

    static let title: LocalizedStringResource = "Refresh Pricing"
    static let description = IntentDescription("Present the latest pricing.")

    public init() { }

    func perform() async throws -> some IntentResult {
        return .result()
    }
}
```

For this example, we only need to bring the app out of background mode so that the view model timer will update the stock price data. Though more complex apps will need the method to perform some tasks, calling the *perform()* method, even if all it does is immediately return, is enough to wake up the app and update the data.

63.3 Setting a Stale Date

We only need the refresh button to appear when the displayed data is outdated. We can do this by specifying a *stale date* when the Live Activity starts and each time it is updated. Edit the *PricingViewModel.swift* file and modify the activity *request()* and *update()* code to set a stale date:

```
func startTracking(ticker: String) async {
.
.
    do {
        activity = try Activity.request(
            attributes: attributes,
            content: .init(state: contentState, staleDate: Date.now + 15),
            pushType: nil
        )
        await startUpdates()
    } catch (let error) {
.
.
```

```
private func update() {
     .
     .

        await activity?.update(
            ActivityContent<DemoWidgetAttributes.ContentState>(
                state: priceStatus,
                staleDate: Date.now + 15,
                relevanceScore: 0
            ),
            alertConfiguration: alertConfig
        )
    }
     .
     .
```

63.4 Detecting Stale Data

The next step is to display a notice and a refresh button in the lock screen widget presentation layouts (the same steps may be followed for the Dynamic Island expanded presentation) when the Live Activity context's *isStale* property is set to true. Modify the *LockScreenView.swift* file as follows to add this behavior:

```
     .
     .
import AppIntents
     .
     .

    var body: some View {
        let color = context.state.changePercent < 0 ? Color.red : Color.green

        VStack(alignment: .leading) {
            HStack {

                VStack(alignment: .leading, spacing: 8) {
                    Text(context.attributes.ticker).bold()
                        .font(.title2)
                        .foregroundColor(.white)

                    Text("\(context.state.currentPrice, specifier: "%.2f")")
                        .font(.title3)
                        .foregroundColor(color)
                }

                Spacer()

                Text("\(context.state.changePercent, specifier: "%.0f")%")
                    .font(.largeTitle)
                    .foregroundColor(color)
                Spacer()
```

```
            PercentView(context: context)
                .padding()
        }

        if (context.isStale) {
            HStack {
                Text("Update required ")
                Button(intent: RefreshIntent(), label: {
                    Image(systemName: "arrow.clockwise.circle.fill")
                })
                Spacer()
            }
        }
    }
    .padding()
    .activityBackgroundTint(Color.black)
    .activitySystemActionForegroundColor(Color.white)
    }
}
```

63.5 Testing the Live Activity Intent

Run the app on a device or emulator, then stop the app from within Xcode to detach from the debugger. Relaunch the app from the device or emulator screen and start tracking. Place the app in the background and lock the device. Wait until the lock screen widget displays the update required message and the refresh button, as shown in Figure 63-2:

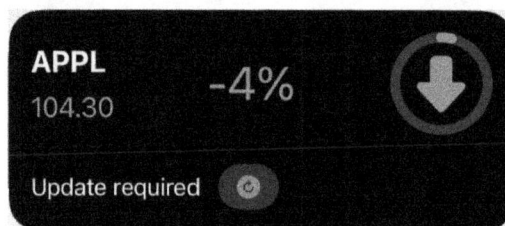

Figure 63-2

Tap the refresh button to update the pricing data. If you are testing on a physical device, iOS must may verify your identity before the refresh can be performed. The camera will need to see your face on devices with Face ID before the widget updates.

63.6 Take the Knowledge Test

Click the link below or scan the QR code to test your knowledge and understanding of how to add refresh support to a Live Activity:

https://www.answertopia.com/29pb

63.7 Summary

In addition to displaying information, Live Activity widgets may contain interactive buttons and toggle views. These views can be configured to trigger actions within the Live Activity extension via an App Intent. When combined with the Live Activity stale date property, this is a helpful way to notify the user of outdated data and provide a button to perform a refresh from within the widget.

64. A Live Activity Push Notifications Tutorial

Although we have demonstrated that Live Activities can be updated from within an app, a more likely scenario is that the updates will be generated by a remote server and sent to the device. This can be achieved using push notifications. This chapter will introduce push notifications and convert the LiveActivityDemo project from local updates to push notifications. The next chapter will demonstrate how to send test push notifications.

64.1 An Overview of Push Notifications

Push notifications have been available to iOS app developers for a while. They are how News apps notify you of breaking news stories, or a banking app might alert you to a suspicious credit card transaction. The push notification system has been upgraded to include a notification type specifically for Live Activity updates.

A typical push notification configuration will consist of your server-side application, the Apple Push Notification service (APNs), and the Live Activity on a device.

Simply put, the Live Activity on the device creates a *push token* uniquely identifying the device and activity. The server application creates a push notification containing the push token, several configuration values, and a JSON structure containing the latest data (called the *payload*) and sends it to the APNs. The APNs then delivers the payload to the device matching the push token. Upon receiving the push notification, the Live Activity content state updates automatically with the payload data, causing the widgets to refresh. The diagram in Figure 64-1 illustrates the push notification process:

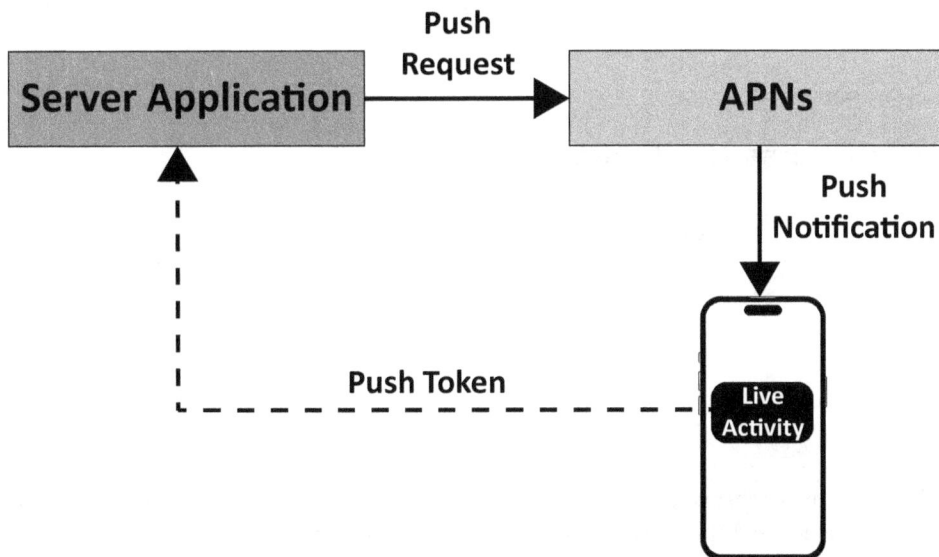

Figure 64-1

64.2 Registering an APNs Key

The first step in setting up push notification support is registering and downloading a key within the Apple Developer portal. This will require an Apple Developer Program membership. If you are not a member, follow the steps in the *"Joining the Apple Developer Program"* chapter to enroll.

Once you have membership, open a browser window, navigate to *https://developer.apple.com*, and log in to your account. From the portal home screen, locate and select the Keys link in the Certificates, IDs & Profiles section, as highlighted in Figure 64-2:

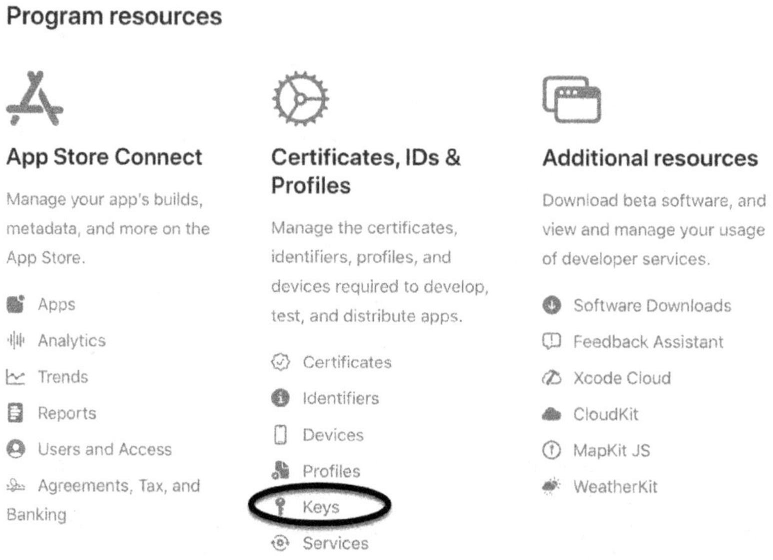

Figure 64-2

On the next screen, select Keys in the side panel (marked A in Figure 64-3), then click the + button (B) to register a new key:

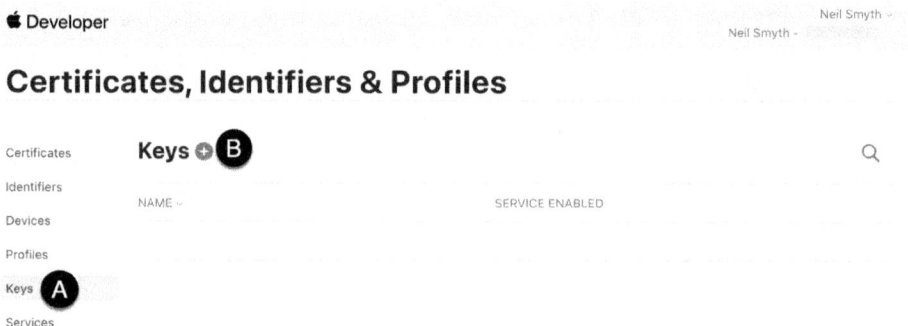

Figure 64-3

When the following screen appears, enter a Key name (for example, LiveActivityDemo) in the field marked A in Figure 64-4, and enable the Apple Push Notifications service option (B) before clicking the Configure button (C):

Figure 64-4

On the Configure Key screen, select *Sandbox* from the Environment and set the Key Restriction menu to *Team Scoped (All Topics)*:

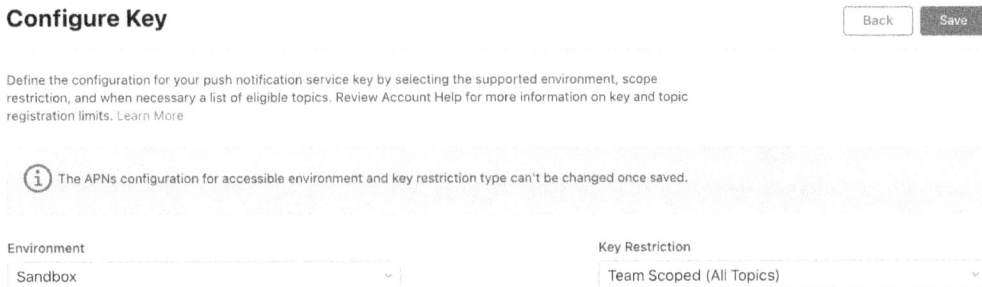

Figure 64-5

Click the Save button to return to Registration screen followed by the Continue button.

On the next screen, review the information before clicking on the Register button:

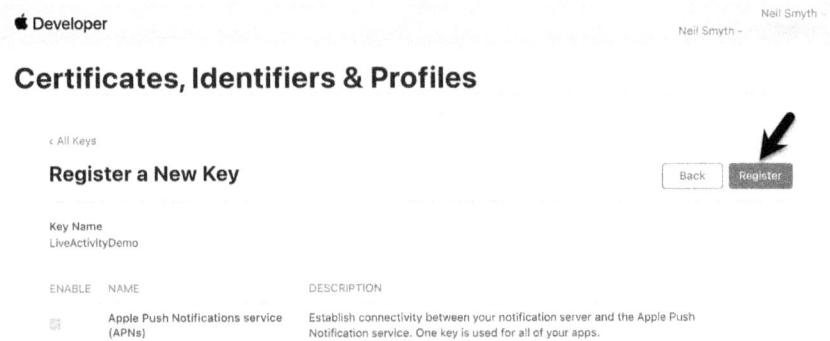

Figure 64-6

Once the key is registered, download the key file to a safe location (once it has been downloaded, it will not be possible to do so again) and note the Key ID. Both will be required in the next chapter when we start sending notifications.

64.3 Enabling Push Notifications for the App

The next step is to add Push Notification support to the LiveActivityDemo project. Load the project into Xcode and select the *LiveActivityDemo* target at the top of the Project Navigator panel (marked A in Figure 64-7) so that the main panel displays the project settings. From within this panel, select the *Signing & Capabilities* tab (B) followed by the LiveActivityDemo target entry (C):

Figure 64-7

Click on the "+ Capability" button (D) to display the dialog shown in Figure 64-8. Enter *Push Notifications* into the filter bar, select the result, and press the keyboard enter key to add the capability to the project:

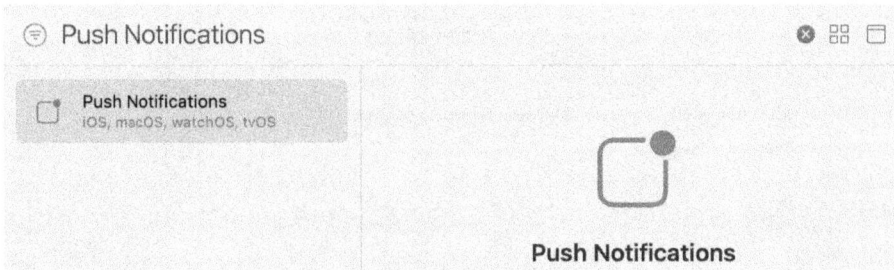

Figure 64-8

64.4 Enabling Frequent Updates

Like the background fetch operations outlined in the previous chapter, the system imposes a budget that limits the frequency of push notifications. If your Live Activity requires frequent updates, you can request an increased notification budget by enabling the *Supports Live Activity Frequent Updates* entitlement.

With the LiveActivityDemo target still selected in the project navigator panel, select the *Info* tab within the main panel, as shown in Figure 64-9:

Figure 64-9

Once selected, locate the bottom entry in the list of properties and hover the mouse pointer over the item. When the + button appears, click it to add a new entry to the list. From within the drop-down list of available keys, locate and select the *Supports Live Activity Frequent Updates* key, as shown in Figure 64-10:

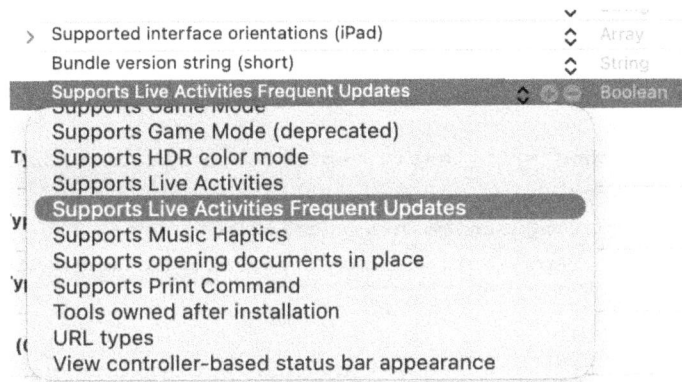

Figure 64-10

After you have added the key, change its value to YES.

64.5 Requesting User Permission

Apps that use push notifications must seek the users' permission when first launched. This ensures that the user is aware that push notifications are being used and allows them to decline. This requires the addition of an *app delegate* to our project. App delegates are used to perform tasks during the early stages of the app launch process. SwiftUI apps are based on the App protocol, which does not provide app delegate support directly. Instead, we will have to add the delegate manually in the *LiveActivityDemoApp.swift* file, as follows:

```
import SwiftUI

@main
struct LiveActivityDemoApp: App {

    @UIApplicationDelegateAdaptor private var appDelegate: AppDelegate

    var body: some Scene {
        WindowGroup {
            ContentView()
        }
    }
}


class AppDelegate: UIResponder, UIApplicationDelegate {
    func application(_ application: UIApplication, didFinishLaunchingWithOptions
                    launchOptions: [UIApplication.LaunchOptionsKey : Any]? =
                                                        nil) -> Bool {

    }
}
```

The *didFinishLaunchingWithOptions* method will be called once the app has started and provides us access to low-level classes and objects that SwiftUI usually shields us from. One such object is the UINotificationCenter instance, which we will use to request remote notifications permission from the user as follows:

```
class AppDelegate: UIResponder, UIApplicationDelegate {
    func application(_ application: UIApplication, didFinishLaunchingWithOptions
```

```
                    launchOptions: [UIApplication.LaunchOptionsKey : Any]? =
                                                        nil) -> Bool {
        Task {
            do {
                let allowed = try await requestAuthorizationForNotifications()
                if allowed {
                    DispatchQueue.main.async {
                        UIApplication.shared.registerForRemoteNotifications()
                    }
                } else {
                    print("Error requesting push notification permission.")
                }
            } catch {
                print(error.localizedDescription)
            }
        }
        return true
    }


    func requestAuthorizationForNotifications() async throws -> Bool {

        let notificationCenter = UNUserNotificationCenter.current()

        do {
            let allowed = try await notificationCenter.requestAuthorization(
                                                    options: [.alert, .sound])
            return allowed
        } catch {
            throw error
        }
    }
}
```

Run the app on a physical device and tap the Allow button when the dialog shown in Figure 64-11 appears:

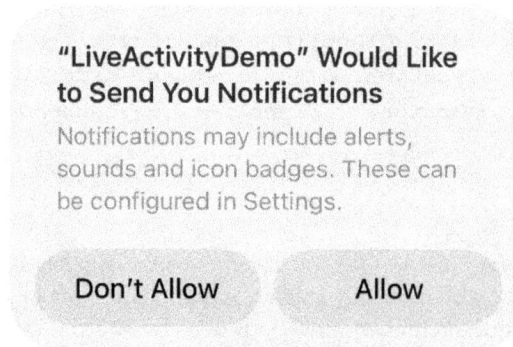

Figure 64-11

64.6 Changing the Push Type

Now that we have enabled push notification support for our project and received permission from the user, the Live Activity *request()* method call must be updated to use push notifications. Edit the *PricingViewModel.swift* file, locate the *startTracking()* method, and modify the *request()* call as follows:

```
func startTracking(ticker: String) async {

.

.

    do {
        activity = try Activity.request(
            attributes: attributes,
            content: .init(state: contentState, staleDate: nil),
            pushType: .token
        )
        await startUpdates()
    } catch (let error) {

.

.
```

When a push notification arrives, the pricing data will be updated automatically. Since we no longer need to update the widgets, the call to *startUpdates()* has been removed. Take this opportunity to delete the following redundant method declarations from the PricingViewModel class:

- startUpdates()

- update()

- refreshPricing()

The *timer* and *oldPrice* variables and references can also be removed as follows:

```
@Observable
class PricingViewModel {

    private var activity: Activity<DemoWidgetAttributes>?
    private var timerTask: Task<Void, Never>?
    private var oldPrice: Float = 100
    var currentPrice: Float = 100
    var changePercent: Float = 0

.

.

    func stopTracking() async {
        let finalState = DemoWidgetAttributes.ContentState(
                currentPrice: currentPrice, changePercent: changePercent)
        timerTask?.cancel()

        await activity?.end(.init(state: finalState, staleDate: nil),
                dismissalPolicy: .default)
    }

.
```

64.7 Obtaining a Push Token

The push server will need a copy of the app's push token to deliver updates to the Live Activity on a specific device. When using push notifications in your own projects, you need to obtain this token and pass it to your server so that it can communicate with the user's device. For this example, however, we will output the push token to the console and then copy and paste it into our server-side testing environment.

When the activity push request is made, the system will issue a push token that uniquely identifies the activity and device. This action occurs asynchronously, so we must wait for the token to become available before using it. It is also possible for the token to change during the lifespan of the activity, and each new token will need to be forwarded to the server. For this purpose, we can use the activity's *pushTokenUpdates()* method both to wait for the token and receive notification of token changes. Remaining in the *startTracking()* method, add the following code to obtain and display the push tokens as they are issued:

```
func startTracking(ticker: String) {
        .
        .

    do {
        activity = try Activity.request(
            attributes: attributes,
            content: .init(state: contentState, staleDate: nil),
            pushType: .token
        )
    } catch (let error) {
        print("Error starting Live Activity: \(error.localizedDescription).")
    }

    Task {
        for await pushToken in activity!.pushTokenUpdates {
            let pushTokenString = pushToken.reduce("") {
                $0 + String(format: "%02x", $1)
            }

            print("New Push Token: \(pushTokenString)")
        }
    }
}
```

Once you have made the above changes, run the app on a physical device, tap the Track button, and refer to the console where the push token should be visible. In the next chapter, we will learn how to use this token to send push notifications to the Live Activity.

64.8 Removing the Refresh Button

Since the modified Live Activity no longer controls how and when pricing updates will be available, the refresh button added in the previous chapter is unnecessary. To remove the button, delete the following code from the *LockScreenView.swift* file:

```
if (context.isStale) {
    HStack {
```

```
                        ~~Text("Update required ")~~

                        ~~Button(intent: RefreshIntent(), label: {~~
                            ~~Image(systemName: "arrow.clockwise.circle.fill")~~
                        ~~})~~
                        ~~Spacer()~~
                    ~~}~~
                ~~}~~
            }
        .padding()
    .
    .
    .
```

Finally, locate *RefreshIntent.swift* file in the Project navigator panel, and delete it from the project. The modifications are complete and the Live Activity is ready to receive push notifications.

64.9 Take the Knowledge Test

Click the link below or scan the QR code to test your knowledge and understanding of Live Activity push notifications:

https://www.answertopia.com/1xqu

64.10 Summary

Push notifications use the Apple Push Notification service to deliver content to apps remotely and have been extended to support remote Live Activity updates. Preparing a Live Activity to work with push notifications is a multi-step process involving registering an APNs key, creating a push token, requesting user permission, and making minor changes to the Live Activity code. With these steps completed in the LiveActivityDemo project, the next chapter will explain how to send push notifications to the Live Activity.

65. Testing Live Activity Push Notifications

The previous chapter explained how to add support for push notifications to a Live Activity. Once enabled for push notifications, the Live Activity is ready for testing.

Test push notifications can be sent from the CloudKit console or the command line using the curl tool. This chapter will demonstrate both options, including generating the authentication key required for sending notifications from the command line and declaring a notification payload.

In the next chapter, *"Troubleshooting Live Activity Push Notifications"*, we will outline techniques for identifying and resolving push notification problems.

65.1 Using the Push Notifications Console

The best way to begin push notification testing is using the CloudKit console. The console provides an easy way to send push notifications and, more importantly, identify why the Live Activity may not have received a notification on the user's device.

To access the CloudKit console, open a browser window, navigate to *https://icloud.developer.apple.com/*, and sign in using your Apple Developer credentials. Once you have signed in, select the Push Notifications option in the dashboard, as highlighted in Figure 65-1:

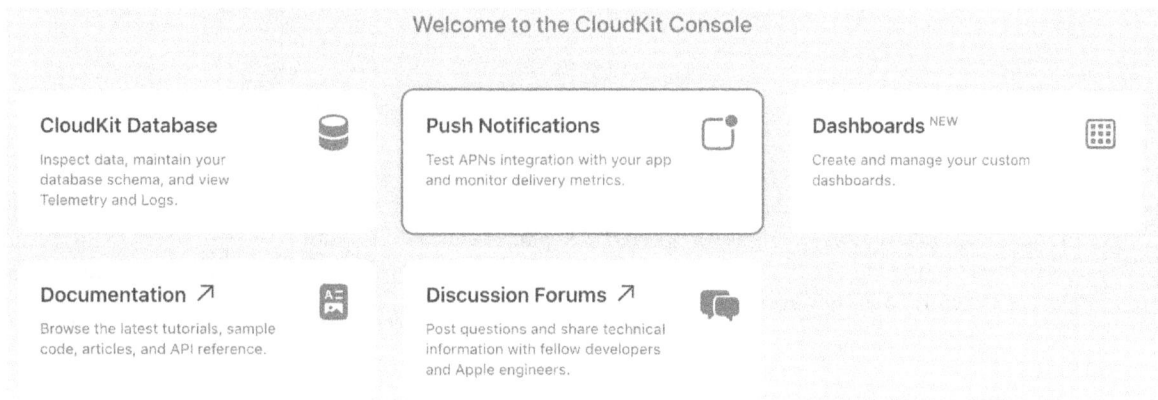

Welcome to the CloudKit Console

CloudKit Database
Inspect data, maintain your database schema, and view Telemetry and Logs.

Push Notifications
Test APNs integration with your app and monitor delivery metrics.

Dashboards NEW
Create and manage your custom dashboards.

Documentation ↗
Browse the latest tutorials, sample code, articles, and API reference.

Discussion Forums ↗
Post questions and share technical information with fellow developers and Apple engineers.

Figure 65-1

Use the drop-down menu (marked A in Figure 65-2) to select the LiveActivityDemo project, then click the *Enable Push Notifications* button (B):

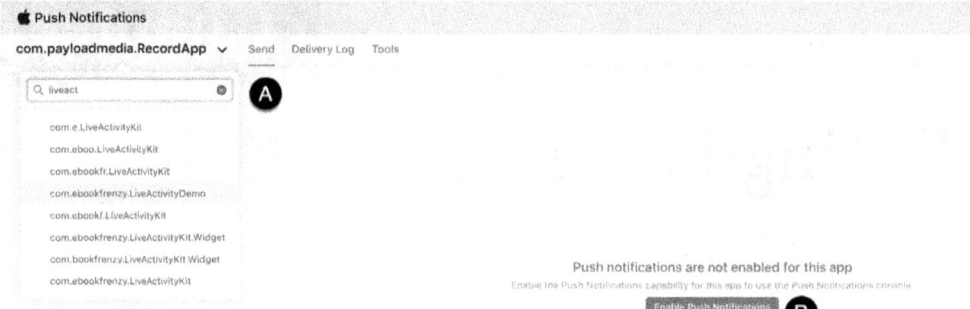

Figure 65-2

Once notifications have been enabled, select the Send tab and click on the *Create New Notification* button:

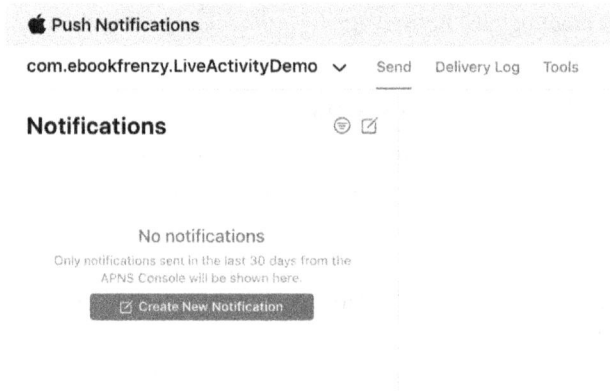

Figure 65-3

The New Notification screen will appear ready for the notification details to be entered.

65.2 Configuring the Notification

In the General section of the New Notification screen, enter a name for the test and set the Environment menu to Development (the Production setting is for when the app has been published on the App Store). Next, return to Xcode, run the app on a device and start tracking, copy the push token from the Xcode console and paste it into the Device Token field in the CloudKit console:

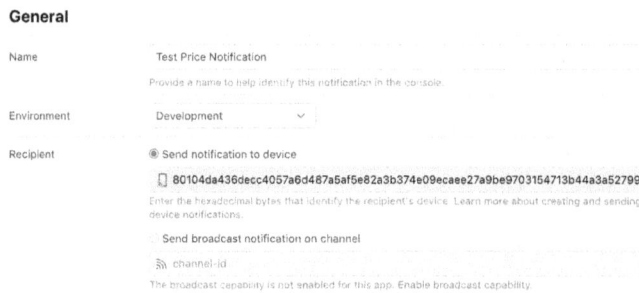

Figure 65-4

In the Request Headers section, the *apns-topic* field is read-only and will already contain your app Bundle Identifier. Select the *apns-push-type* menu and change the selection to *liveactivity*. The *apns-expiration* setting can specify a date and time when the APNs service should stop trying to send the notification. The default setting will only make one push attempt. The single delivery attempt option is actually more robust than the name suggests, and this setting is adequate for most requirements.

The *apns-priority* value can be set to 1 (low), 5 (medium), or 10 (high). Use low priority for non-time-sensitive updates and high priority for critical alerts. For most uses, however, medium is the recommended priority:

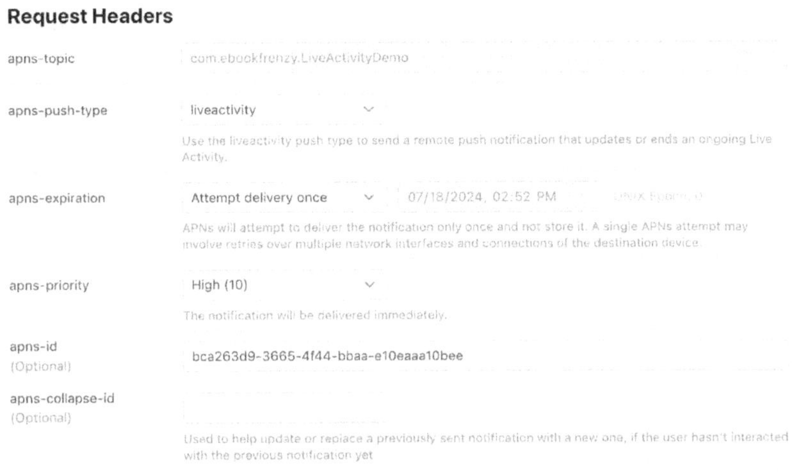

Request Headers

apns-topic	com.ebookfrenzy.LiveActivityDemo
apns-push-type	liveactivity
	Use the liveactivity push type to send a remote push notification that updates or ends an ongoing Live Activity.
apns-expiration	Attempt delivery once 07/18/2024, 02:52 PM
	APNs will attempt to deliver the notification only once and not store it. A single APNs attempt may involve retries over multiple network interfaces and connections of the destination device.
apns-priority	High (10)
	The notification will be delivered immediately.
apns-id (Optional)	bca263d9-3665-4f44-bbaa-e10eaaa10bee
apns-collapse-id (Optional)	Used to help update or replace a previously sent notification with a new one, if the user hasn't interacted with the previous notification yet

Figure 65-5

The final section will contain the notification payload, which requires additional explanation.

65.3 Defining the Payload

The notification payload is declared using JSON and must contain the following information:

- **timestamp** - The timestamp ensures that the Live Activity is updated only with the most up-to-date push notification. Notifications containing a timestamp identical to or earlier than the previous notification are discarded. For this reason, you must provide a new timestamp each time you send a push notification. The timestamp is calculated as the number of elapsed seconds since January 1, 1970, and can be obtained using the following online Epoch calculator:

https://www.epochconverter.com/

Alternatively, open a Terminal window on your Mac and run the following command:

```
date +%s
```

- **event** - This value specifies the action associated with the push notification and should be set to "update".

- **content-state** - The content state defines the updated data to be displayed by the Live Activity. It must match exactly the dynamic variable names and data types declared in the Live Activity widget attributes structure.

Return to the CloudKit console, enable the JSON View switch (highlighted in Figure 65-6 below), and enter the following JSON declaration into the text box, where *<recent timestamp>* is replaced with the current value:

```
{
    "aps": {
```

```
    "event": "update",
    "content-state": {
        "currentPrice": 310,
        "changePercent": 37
    },
    "timestamp": <recent timestamp>
    }
}
```

Once the payload has been entered, the console will report that the JSON is valid and the notification is ready to send:

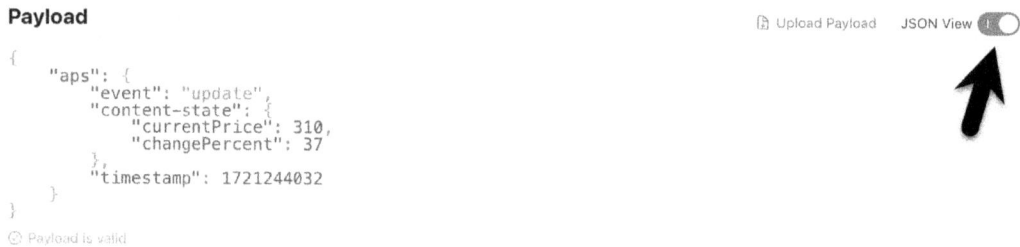

Payload   Upload Payload   JSON View

```
{
    "aps": {
        "event": "update",
        "content-state": {
            "currentPrice": 310,
            "changePercent": 37
        },
        "timestamp": 1721244032
    }
}
```
Payload is valid

Figure 65-6

65.4 Sending the Notification

Before sending the notification, ensure the app is still running on your device and check the Xcode console to confirm that the push token is unchanged from when it was pasted into the notification form. Place the app into the background, return to the CloudKit console, and click the Send button. After a short delay, the console will report a problem with the entered information or attempt to send the notification. Check the Live Activity widget on the lock screen of your device to see if the price information has updated to the values contained in the payload. If nothing happens, it is time to troubleshoot the notification using the steps outlined in the next chapter.

65.5 Sending Push Notifications from the Command Line

Another way to test push notifications is from the command line of a Terminal window on your Mac using the *curl* command. This technique has the advantage that it can be used to automate sending multiple notifications without having to create each one in the CloudKit console manually. It also allows us to generate the timestamp dynamically.

Behind the scenes, the CloudKit console automatically generated an authentication token for us that is required to send push notifications. To generate this for the command line, you will need the Key ID and the key file saved in the *"A Live Activity Push Notifications Tutorial"* chapter. You will also need your Apple Developer Team ID, which can be found by selecting the Membership details option in the Apple Developer console. You will also need to specify the Bundle ID of your app (known as the *topic* in this context).

Once this information has been gathered, open a Terminal window, change directory to a suitable location, create a new file named *push.sh,* and edit it as follows:

```
#!/bin/bash
TEAM_ID="<Your Team ID here>"
TOKEN_KEY_FILE_NAME="<Path to your P8 key file here>"
AUTH_KEY_ID="<Your Key ID here>"
```

```
TOPIC="<Your app Bundle ID here>"
APNS_HOST_NAME=api.sandbox.push.apple.com


JWT_ISSUE_TIME=$(date +%s)
JWT_HEADER=$(printf '{ "alg": "ES256", "kid": "%s" }' "${AUTH_KEY_ID}" | openssl
base64 -e -A | tr -- '+/' '-_' | tr -d =)
JWT_CLAIMS=$(printf '{ "iss": "%s", "iat": %d }' "${TEAM_ID}" "${JWT_ISSUE_TIME}"
| openssl base64 -e -A | tr -- '+/' '-_' | tr -d =)
JWT_HEADER_CLAIMS="${JWT_HEADER}.${JWT_CLAIMS}"
JWT_SIGNED_HEADER_CLAIMS=$(printf "${JWT_HEADER_CLAIMS}" | openssl dgst -binary
-sha256 -sign "${TOKEN_KEY_FILE_NAME}" | openssl base64 -e -A | tr -- '+/' '-_' |
tr -d =)
AUTHENTICATION_TOKEN="${JWT_HEADER}.${JWT_CLAIMS}.${JWT_SIGNED_HEADER_CLAIMS}"
echo $AUTHENTICATION_TOKEN
```

Save the file and run it using the following command:

```
sh ./push.sh
```

On successful execution, the script should print the authentication token.

Use Xcode to launch the LiveActivityDemo app on a device and copy the latest push token from the console. Edit the *push.sh* script file and add the token as follows:

```
#!/bin/bash
ACTIVITY_PUSH_TOKEN="<Your push token here>"
.
.
```

Finally, the *curl* command can be added to the script. This consists of the authentication and push tokens and the push type, topic, priority, and expiration settings. The command must also include the notification payload with a current timestamp using the same JSON syntax used in the CloudKit console. With these requirements in mind, add the following lines to the end of the *push.sh* file:

```
curl -v \
  --header "authorization: bearer ${AUTHENTICATION_TOKEN}" \
  --header "apns-topic: <your bundle id here>.push-type.liveactivity" \
  --header "apns-push-type: liveactivity" \
  --header "apns-priority: 10" \
  --header "apns-expiration: 0" \
  --data '{"aps":{"timestamp":'$(date +%s)',"event":"update","content-state":{"cu
rrentPrice":500,"changePercent":50}}}' \
  --http2  https://api.development.push.apple.com:443/3/device/$ACTIVITY_PUSH_
TOKEN
```

Note that the topic header consists of your bundle ID followed by *.push-type.liveactivity* and that we are using the *date +%s* command to create the timestamp.

Check the push token is still valid, execute the push script, and check the output for errors. If the APNs accepted the notification, the output will end as follows:

```
> apns-expiration: 0
> Content-Length: 105
> Content-Type: application/x-www-form-urlencoded
```

```
>
* We are completely uploaded and fine
< HTTP/2 200
< apns-id: 92F32B4C-9527-0CAD-32FA-AC0B4A9200B1
< apns-unique-id: 4090d3d1-b615-250a-79e5-d39e3801b542
<
* Connection #0 to host api.development.push.apple.com left intact
```

If the notification does not update the Live Activity widgets, record the *apns-unique-id* in the curl output and use it to diagnose the problem using the steps in the *"Troubleshooting Live Activity Push Notifications"* chapter.

65.6 Summary

Test push notifications can be sent to a Live Activity using either the CloudKit console or from the command line using the *curl* command. For both options, the notification must include the push token from the device and a JSON payload containing the updated Live Activity content state. An additional authentication token is required when testing is performed using the command line. The token is generated using the Key ID and file created in the previous chapter.

66. Troubleshooting Live Activity Push Notifications

It can be frustrating when a Live Activity fails to update in response to a push notification, and identifying the cause can initially seem challenging. Part of the problem is that push notifications and Live Activities use systems over which we have little control, such as the APNs, the predictive engine that decides when the device is ready to accept a push notification, and the background process on the device that automatically updates the Live Activity's content state when the notification is received.

As we will explain in this chapter, while diagnosing a push notification problem may seem daunting, some steps can be taken to identify and correct potential problems.

66.1 Push Notification Problems

A push notification will typically fail either because the APNs did not send the notification, the device did not receive the notification, or the Live Activity could not process the notification. In the rest of this chapter, we will explore some of these areas and provide tips to identify and correct the issue.

66.2 Push Notification Delivery

A common issue with push notifications is that the device may ask the APNs to store the notification and retry sending it later. Much like background updates, this can be for various reasons, including battery status, low power mode being active, or because the Live Activity has exceeded the notification frequency budget. When a Live Activity does not update, the first step is to check the log for the notification.

After the notification has been sent using the CloudKit console, it will appear in the left side panel. Select the notification and look for the Delivery Log section of the detail page, as shown in Figure 66-1. If the notification was delivered, the final log entry will read "successfully delivered to the target device":

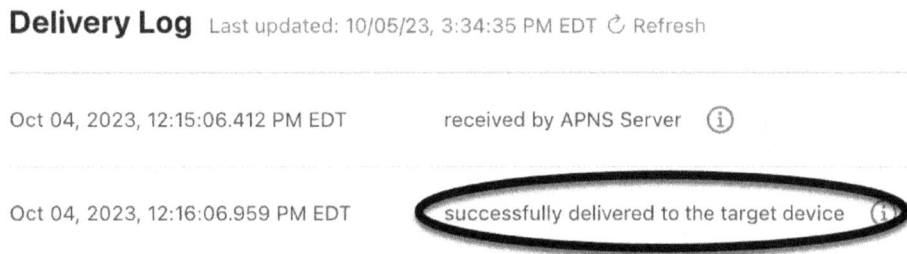

Figure 66-1

If the notification has been delayed, the log will state the reason. In Figure 66-2, for example, the device has requested that the notification be stored and retried later to conserve battery life:

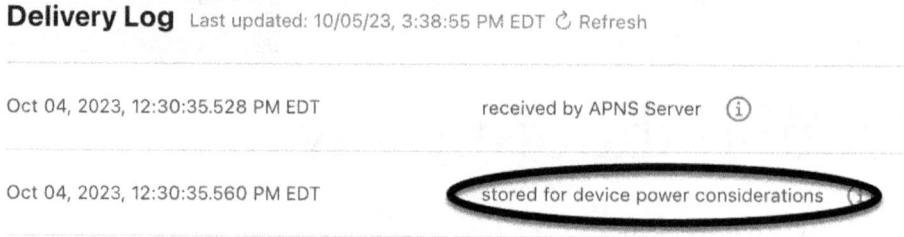

Delivery Log Last updated: 10/05/23, 3:38:55 PM EDT ↻ Refresh

Oct 04, 2023, 12:30:35.528 PM EDT   received by APNS Server ⓘ

Oct 04, 2023, 12:30:35.560 PM EDT   stored for device power considerations ⓘ

Figure 66-2

Hover the mouse pointer over the information icon next to the log entry for a description of the status. Refresh the log until it reports a successful delivery. If there is no change to the status, try sending another notification (remembering to provide an updated timestamp in the payload).

If you send notifications from the command line, copy the unique id from the *curl* output, select the Delivery Log tab in the Cloudkit console Push Notifications screen, and paste the id into the search field. Select the id in the search results to display the log history and check the most recent status.

If the device continues to defer the notification delivery, sending another notification with the priority set to 10 (High) will typically result in a successful delivery.

66.3 Check the Payload Structure

A successful push notification delivery does not guarantee that the Live Activity will update. A common cause for this is a mismatch between the payload and the Live Activity content state model. Before moving on to the next steps, verify that the variable names and data types in the payload precisely match the dynamic variables declared in the Live Activity's widget attributes declaration.

66.4 Validating the Push and Authentication Tokens

Although the CloudKit console will typically report an invalid push token, it is worth checking that the one you are using is still valid. To do so, click on the Tools tab (marked A in Figure 66-3) in the console, select Device Token Validator (B), and paste your push token into the text box (C):

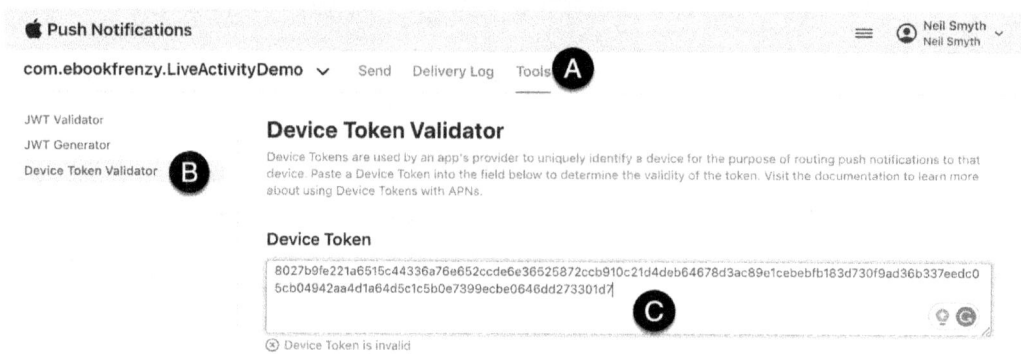

 Push Notifications   Neil Smyth
                                                                                             Neil Smyth

com.ebookfrenzy.LiveActivityDemo ⌄   Send   Delivery Log   Tools **A**

JWT Validator   **Device Token Validator**

JWT Generator   Device Tokens are used by an app's provider to uniquely identify a device for the purpose of routing push notifications to that
                                     device. Paste a Device Token into the field below to determine the validity of the token. Visit the documentation to learn more
Device Token Validator **B**   about using Device Tokens with APNs.

                                     Device Token

                                     8027b9fe221a6515c44336a76e652ccde6e36625872ccb910c21d4deb64678d3ac89e1cebebfb183d730f9ad36b337eedc0
                                     5cb04942aa4d1a64d5c1c5b0e7399ecbe0646dd273301d7| **C**

                                     ⊗ Device Token is invalid

Figure 66-3

Note that just because a token passes the validation test, it does not necessarily mean that it is still the token that your app is using. Check the Xcode console to verify that you are still using the correct token to send the notification.

66.5 Checking the Device Log

If the notification was delivered and the push token is correct, the next step is to check the device log for error messages. This can often highlight problems such as a bundle identifier mismatch or the payload structure not matching the widget attributes. Within Xcode, select the *Window -> Devices and Simulators* menu option and, in the resulting dialog, select your device before clicking the *Open Console* button as indicated in the figure below:

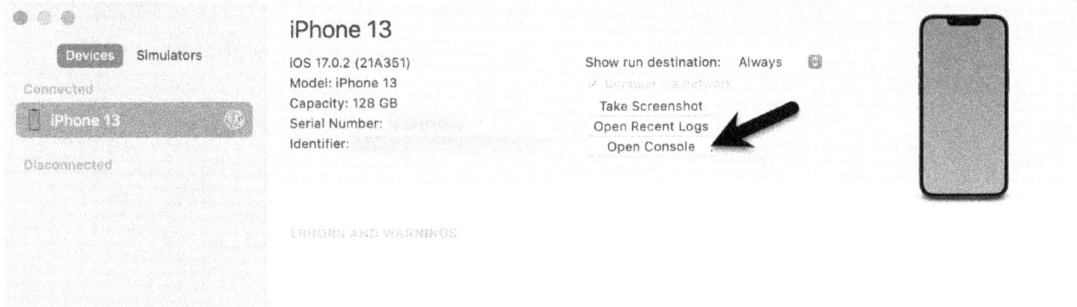

Figure 66-4

Within the Console window, click the button to start streaming and select the Errors and Faults tab. In the search bar at the top of the window, insert liveactivity after the "fault" message type:

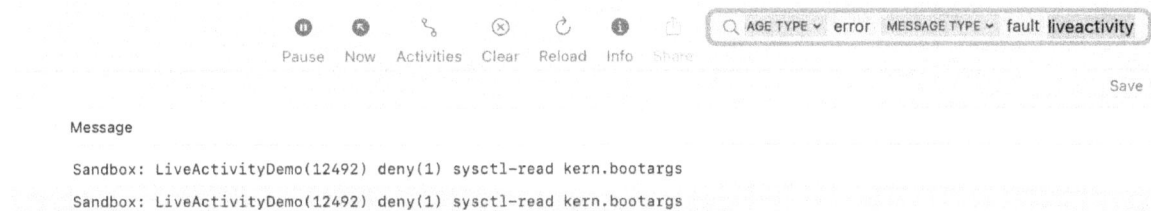

Figure 66-5

Keep the device console open while sending another notification and check for any warnings and errors that might provide insight into the problem.

66.6 Take the Knowledge Test

Click the link below or scan the QR code to test your knowledge and understanding of Live Activity push notification troubleshooting:

https://www.answertopia.com/olhw

66.7 Summary

While the system may seem opaque, there are only a few possible reasons why Live Activity may not update in response to a push notification. Either the APNs identified a problem with the notification (such as an expired token), the device requested a deferred delivery, or the Bundle ID or payload data did not match the Live Activity. As outlined in this chapter, there are several ways to investigate push notification problems, including using the CloudKit and Device consoles.

Index

Index

Index

Index

Index

Index

U

V

W

Index